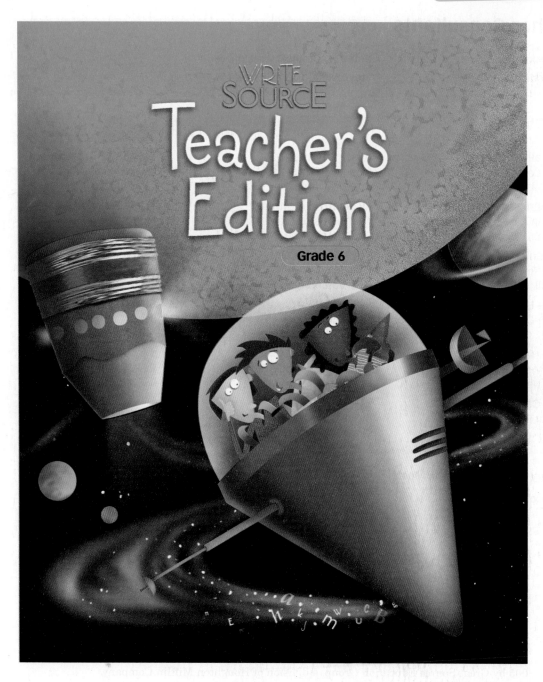

Write Source
Teacher's Edition
Grade 6

Patrick Sebranek, Dave Kemper,
and Verne Meyer

WRITE SOURCE®

GREAT SOURCE EDUCATION GROUP
a division of Houghton Mifflin Company
Wilmington, Massachusetts

Teacher Consultants

Patty Beckstead, St. George, Utah

Amy Goodman, Anchorage, Alaska

Debra McConnell, Williston, Vermont

Steve Mellen, Temple Hills, Maryland

Reviewers

Dawn Calhoun Bray
Houston County School System
Warner Robins, Georgia

Vallie J. Ericson
Sheboygan Area School District
Sheboygan, Wisconsin

Paula Denise Findley
Arkansas River Educational Cooperative
White Hall, Arkansas

Michelle Harden-Brown
Savannah-Chatham Southwest Middle
Savannah, Georgia

Kevin F. Harrington
Baldwin Middle School
Baldwin, New York

Beverly Canzater Jacobs
Solon City Schools
Solon, Ohio

Alissa Lowman
Hillside Middle School
Northville, Michigan

Elizabeth F. Manning
A.E. Phillips Laboratory School
Ruston, Louisiana

Rhea Mayerchak
Omin Middle School
Boca Raton, Florida

Steve Mellen
Prince George's County Public Schools
Temple Hills, Maryland

Diana L. Mooney
Lake Denoon Middle School
Muskego, Wisconsin

Ellen Nielsen
Clovis Unified School District
Clovis, California

Geraldine Ortego
Lafayette Parish District Office
Lafayette, Louisiana

Addie Rae Tobey
Shaker Heights Middle School
Shaker Heights, Ohio

Bridget Wetton
Alpine Union School District
San Diego, California

Susan Wilson
South Orange/Maplewood
    School District
South Orange, New Jersey

Peggy Zehnder
Bellingham School District
Bellingham, Washington

Editorial: **Mary Anne Hoff, Patricia Moore**

Production: **Compset**

Technology Connection for *Write Source*

Visit our Web site for additional student models, writing prompts, updates for citing sources, multimedia reports, information about submitting your writing, and more.

The Write Source Web site . . . . www.thewritesource.com

Printed in China

International Standard Book Number: 0-669-50707-5

2 3 4 5 6 7 8 9 10 - RRDS - 11 10 09 08 07 06 05

contents

The Forms of Writing

RESEARCH WRITING

Speaking and Writing to Learn

SPEAKING TO LEARN

WRITING TO LEARN

The Basic Elements of Writing

WORKING WITH WORDS

A Writer's Resource

Selecting Ideas

Improving Organization

Proofreader's Guide

Teacher Resources

An Overview

With the help and feedback of teachers from all over the country, we've taken some of the things you and your students have always loved about *Write Source* and made them even better. We've included a variety of new features to help students improve writing and learning skills across the curriculum and on state writing assessments, plus we've added materials to help teachers help all their students become better writers, thinkers, and learners.

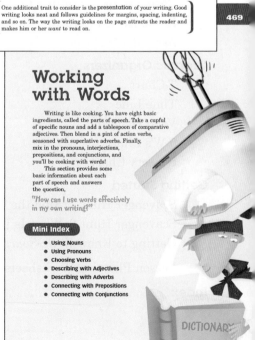

Comprehensive

The new *Write Source* provides even more information on the writing process and forms of writing, including

- **integrated six-traits instruction in every writing unit;**
- detailed **coverage of all the key forms of writing,** complete with student notes;
- a wide variety of activities in the pupil edition that **support active instruction and immediate application of writing forms** and related grammar skills;
- guidelines in the Teacher's Edition for **differentiated instruction** to help teachers **meet the needs of English language learners, struggling, and advanced students**.

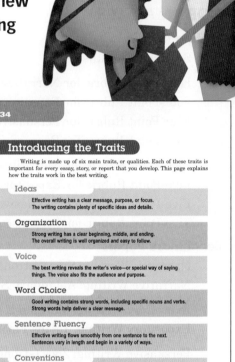

34

Introducing the Traits

Writing is made up of six main traits, or qualities. Each of these traits is important for every essay, story, or report that you develop. This page explains how the traits work in the best writing.

Ideas

Effective writing has a clear message, purpose, or focus. The writing contains plenty of specific ideas and details.

Organization

Strong writing has a clear beginning, middle, and ending. The overall writing is well organized and easy to follow.

Voice

The best writing reveals the writer's voice—or special way of saying things. The voice also fits the audience and purpose.

Word Choice

Good writing contains strong words, including specific nouns and verbs. Strong words help deliver a clear message.

Sentence Fluency

Effective writing flows smoothly from one sentence to the next. Sentences vary in length and begin in a variety of ways.

Conventions

Good writing is carefully edited to make sure it is easy to understand. The writing follows the rules for punctuation, grammar, and spelling.

One additional trait to consider is the presentation of your writing. Good writing looks neat and follows guidelines for margins, spacing, indenting, and so on. The way the writing looks on the page attracts the reader and makes him or her *want* to read on.

469

Student-friendly

The new pupil editions maintain the same personal, reassuring, voice unique to all the *Write Source* materials, plus new features that will truly make it students' favorite writing resource.

- The **friendly voice, colorful artwork,** and **humorous illustrations** capture student interest.
- **Student models** help students understand what is expected in each lesson while color coding and graphic organizers help students understand and remember key points.
- **Integrated writing activities and prompts** help students apply to their writing what they have learned in the lesson.
- **Six-trait checklists in every unit** serve as handy references.

Working with Words

Writing is like cooking. You have eight basic ingredients, called the parts of speech. Take a cupful of specific nouns and add a tablespoon of comparative adjectives. Then blend in a pint of action verbs, seasoned with superlative adverbs. Finally, mix in the pronouns, interjections, prepositions, and conjunctions, and you'll be cooking with words!

This section provides some basic information about each part of speech and answers the question,

"How can I use words effectively in my own writing?"

Mini Index

- Using Nouns
- Using Pronouns
- Choosing Verbs
- Describing with Adjectives
- Describing with Adverbs
- Connecting with Prepositions
- Connecting with Conjunctions

DICTIONARY

Easy to Implement

Flexible enough to serve as the foundation for a writing-based language arts program or as a supplement to any literature program, *Write Source* offers

- a **clear, logical sequence for instruction,** beginning with the writing process and the six traits and then applying this information to specific genres;
- a **grade-specific pupil edition for every grade—6, 7, and 8**;
- a **wraparound Teacher's Edition** with pupil edition facsimiles, step-by-step lesson plans, assessment information, and support for six-trait instruction.

Strategies for Writing Across the Curriculum

Write Source helps students improve their writing and learning skills in all subject areas with

- **guidelines for cross-curricular writing forms** to build students' writing skills for social studies, science, and math classes;
- information on **important classroom skills including listening, giving oral presentations, taking notes, completing assignments, and taking tests.**

336

Writing for Assessment

On some state and school tests, you may be asked to read a story and write a response to it. The next two pages give you an example of such a test. Read the directions, the story, and notice the student's underlining and comments (in blue). Then read the student's response on pages 338–339.

Response to Literature Prompt

DIRECTIONS:
- Read the following story.
- As you read, make notes. (Your notes will not be graded.)
- After reading the story, write an essay. You have 40 minutes to read, plan, write, and proofread your work.

When you write, focus on the main characters in the story. Show your insight into how the characters change as they interact with each other. Use clear organization, and support your focus with examples from the text.

Acquiring the Taste

When Maria and Janelle became seventh graders, they thought they were pretty grown-up. They had graduated from Franklin Elementary and now attended Westmore Junior High. The old posters of cats and koalas had come down from their bedroom walls, and new posters of rock stars had gone up. Maria and Janelle decided they even needed to learn how to drink coffee. One Saturday morning, they met at Chiara's Coffee Shop and ordered cappuccinos.

"Bleck!" Maria said, letting the coffee dribble out of her mouth and back into the cup. "How can adults drink this stuff?"

Janelle laughed. "Cappuccino is an acquired taste." She took a sip and winced.

"If *acquired* means *awful,* I have to agree," Maria said. She took another taste. The stuff was bitter and burning. She gasped and started to choke.

Janelle leaned toward her and patted her back. "Maria, pull yourself together. Somebody's staring at us."

Integrated Grammar Instruction

A variety of **activities for building mechanics, usage, and grammar skills** are included in every unit in the pupil edition as well as in the **Proofreader's Guide, Working with Words,** and **Writing Effective Sentences sections** of the pupil editions. Additional grammar activities are also available in the *SkillsBook, Interactive Writing Skills CD-ROM,* and *Daily Language Workouts.*

Six-Trait Instruction and Test Preparation

Write Source integrates the six traits of effective writing into each lesson and provides benchmark papers and guidelines for helping students perform well on writing assessments. See next page for details.

Six Traits, Assessment, and Test Preparation in *Write Source*

The new *Write Source* program provides detailed guidelines to help students become better writers and revisers using the six traits of effective writing along with a variety of lessons, activities, and guidelines to prepare students for high stakes writing assessments.

Connections to the Six Traits of Effective Writing

Write Source now incorporates the six traits of writing into the writing process. Each core writing unit integrates six-trait rubrics into the lesson so students have a reference for

- **reviewing the expectations,**
- **assessing their work throughout the writing process,**
- **revising and editing their work.**

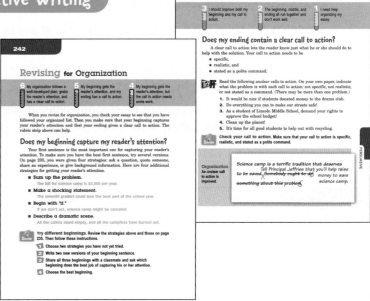

Assessment and Test Preparation

Ideal to prepare students for state assessments, the *Write Source* program

- offers **writing and mechanics, usage, and grammar pretests, posttests,** and **quarterly tests** modeled after state assessments;
- focuses on the **core forms of writing most commonly included on writing assessments;**
- includes **writing for tests guidelines** and prompts in each unit;
- provides **genre-specific writing prompts, rubrics, and benchmark papers** for every core form of writing.

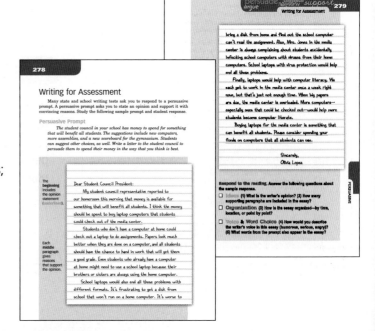

Write Source Research Base

Feature from *Write Source*	Research Base/Citation
Students need frequent writing opportunities to become strong writers. *Write Source* provides daily scaffolded writing activities in every lesson that help students learn to apply writing strategies, write to learn, and prepare for writing assessments.	National Reading Panel (2000). *Teaching children to read: An evidence-based assessment of the scientific research literature on reading and its implications for reading instruction.* Washington, D.C.: National Institute of Child Health and Human Development. U.S. Department of Education Office of the Secretary (2001). *Back to school, moving forward: What No Child Left Behind means for America's communities.* Washington, D.C.
Teaching writing as a process enables students to gain control over the complex task of writing. Furthermore, research suggests that when writing is taught as a process, student achievement increases (e.g., Hillocks, 1986; Holdzkom, Reed, Porter, & Rubin, 1982; Keech & Thomas, 1979).	Hillocks, G., Jr. (1986). Research on written composition: New directions for teaching, Urbana, IL. *ERIC Clearinghouse on Reading and Communication Skills.* Holdzkom, D., Reed, L., Porter, H.J, & Rubin, D.L. (1982). *Research within reach: Oral and written communication.* St. Louis: Cemrel, Inc. Keech, C., & Thomas, S (1979). *Compendium of promising practices in composition instruction. Evaluation of the Bay Area Writing Project.* Berkeley, CA: California University School of Education.
Mastery of the mechanics of writing— punctuation, spelling, and correct usage—is important to becoming an effective writer whose writing is understood and taken seriously (Graves, 1994; Spandel, 2001). In *Write Source,* skills lessons are introduced when they are meaningful in the context of students' writing. Opportunities for extensive skills practice are found in the pupil edition, *SkillsBook, Interactive Writing Skills CD-ROM,* and *Daily Language Workouts.*	Graves, D. H. (1994). *A fresh look at writing.* Portsmouth, NH: Heinemann. Spandel, V. (2001). *Creating writers through 6-trait writing assessment and instruction.* (3rd ed.) Boston: Addison Wesley Longman.
Writing across the curriculum lessons for every form of writing help students connect writing in the same mode to different content areas and helps them use writing as a tool for thinking and learning (Perkins, 1992; Vacca & Vacca, 2002).	Perkins, D. (1992). *Smart schools: Better thinking and learning for every child.* New York: The Free Press. Vacca, R. T., & Vacca, J. L. (2002). Content area reading: Literacy and learning across the curriculum (7th ed.). Boston: Allyn & Bacon.
Understanding the six traits of effective writing and how to revise effectively is essential to becoming a skillful, independent writer (Spandel, 2001). Six-trait writing instruction has also been shown to improve student writing test scores (Jarner, Kozol, Nelson, & Salsberry, 2000).	Jarner, D., Kozol, M., Nelson, S., & Salsberry, T. (Fall/Winter 2000). Six-trait writing model improves scores at Jennie Wilson Elementary. *Journal of School Improvement.* www.ncacasi.org/jsi/2000vli2/six_trait_model.adp. Spandel, V. (2001). *Creating writers through 6-trait writing assessment and instruction.* (3rd ed.) Boston: Addison Wesley Longman.

Program Resources

Pupil Edition

The *Write Source* pupil editions for grades 6, 7, and 8 reflect the latest and best research on writing and learning and provide everything a student needs to become a better writer, thinker, and learner, including

- **clear coverage of the writing process and the six traits of writing within every unit** to help students become focused writers and revisers;

- **a friendly, reassuring voice, colorful artwork,** and **humorous illustrations** that talk to students;

- **integrated mechanics, usage, and grammar activities** so students improve key skills through every writing unit;

- **student models for every form of writing** to motivate students and help them understand what is expected of them in each lesson;

- **guidelines for cross-curricular writing forms** to build writing skills in other content areas, including social studies, science, and math;

- **strategies for developing other useful classroom skills** including listening, making oral presentations, note taking, and taking tests.

Grade 6 Pupil Edition shown.

Teacher's Edition

The *Write Source Teacher's Edition* makes implementing the new program a breeze for all teachers—including new teachers and those not specifically trained in writing instruction. Clear and easy-to-follow, this resource includes

- **a wraparound format** with reduced pupil edition pages and step-by-step **teacher notes correlated to national standards;**

- additional **information on the writing process and six traits** (as well as alternative 4- and 5-point rubrics) for teachers new to these topics;

- **differentiated instruction** for English language learners, struggling, and advanced students as well as **support for cross-curricular writing instruction** in science, social studies, and math;

- **an emphasis on core forms of writing commonly included on state writing assessments**, genre-specific writing prompts, benchmark papers, and tests to assess students' understanding of mechanics, usage, and grammar skills.

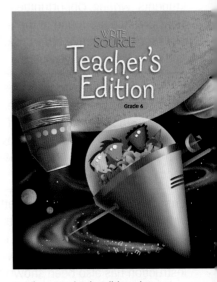

Grade 6 Teacher's Edition shown.

Teacher's Resource Pack

The **Teacher's Resource Pack** provides a variety of additional resources to help teachers get the most out of the *Write Source* program—

SkillsBook

Designed to help students practice and improve their essential grammar, mechanics, and usage skills, each *SkillsBook* for grades 6, 7, and 8 addresses the basic writing and language skills covered in the pupil edition "Proofreader's Guide" with

- **more than 90 editing and proofreading activities,**
- **clear and easy-to-follow activities,**
- additional "Next Step" **follow-up or enrichment activities.**

SkillsBook Teacher's Edition is also included.

Assessment Book

This convenient teacher resource provides **copy masters for a pretest, interim tests,** and a **posttest** to help teachers monitor students' progress.

Overhead Transparencies

Convenient overhead transparencies feature graphic organizers and benchmark papers for whole-class instruction.

Write Source Interactive Writing Skills CD-ROM

Packed with interactive activities that support six language skill areas, including punctuation, mechanics, spelling, usage, understanding sentences, and parts of speech, this student-friendly CD-ROM provides

- **animated lessons that explain a key grammar concept,**
- **engaging, interactive activities,**
- **printable and e-mailable reports** for students' scores on each activity.

Daily Language Workouts

This flexible teacher's resource builds students' editing and proofreading skills through **5-to-10 minute language activities.**

Grade 6 Teacher's Resource Pack components shown.

A Closer Look at the Teacher's Edition

Teacher's Edition lessons provide explicit instruction presented in a wraparound format that shows reduced pupil edition pages accompanied by background notes, lesson plans, guidelines for differentiating instruction, assessment guidelines, and copy masters for a variety of writing tools and strategies.

Writing Standards addressed within each unit are listed at the beginning of each unit overview. The writing standards covered within the program are based on a blend of selected state and NCTE standards.

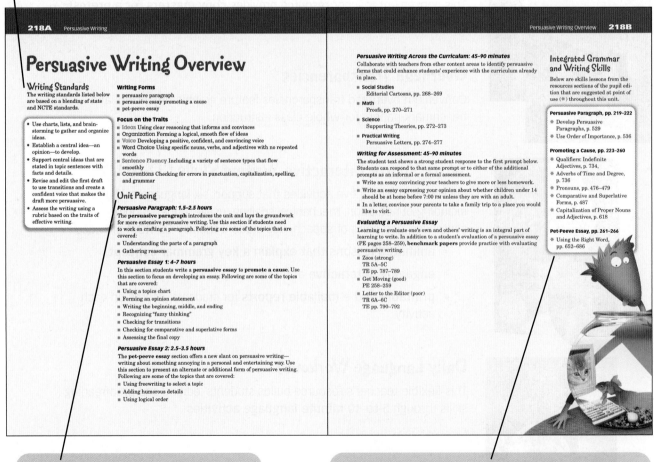

Persuasive Writing Overview

Writing Standards

The writing standards listed below are based on a blending of state and NCTE standards.

- Use charts, lists, and brain-storming to gather and organize ideas.
- Establish a central idea—an opinion—to develop.
- Support central ideas that are stated in topic sentences with facts and details.
- Revise and edit the first draft to use transitions and create a confident voice that makes the draft more persuasive.
- Assess the writing using a rubric based on the traits of effective writing.

Writing Forms
- persuasive paragraph
- persuasive essay promoting a cause
- pet-peeve essay

Focus on the Traits
- **Ideas** Using clear reasoning that informs and convinces
- **Organization** Forming a logical, smooth flow of ideas
- **Voice** Developing a positive, confident, and convincing voice
- **Word Choice** Using specific nouns, verbs, and adjectives with no repeated words
- **Sentence Fluency** Including a variety of sentence types that flow smoothly
- **Conventions** Checking for errors in punctuation, capitalization, spelling, and grammar

Unit Pacing

Persuasive Paragraph: 1.5–2.5 hours
The **persuasive paragraph** introduces the unit and lays the groundwork for more extensive persuasive writing. Use this section if students need to work on crafting a paragraph. Following are some of the topics that are covered:
- Understanding the parts of a paragraph
- Gathering reasons

Persuasive Essay 1: 4–7 hours
In this section students write a **persuasive essay** to **promote a cause**. Use this section to focus on developing an essay. Following are some of the topics that are covered:
- Using a topics chart
- Forming an opinion statement
- Writing the beginning, middle, and ending
- Recognizing "fuzzy thinking"
- Checking for transitions
- Checking for comparative and superlative forms
- Assessing the final copy

Persuasive Essay 2: 2.5–3.5 hours
The **pet-peeve essay** section offers a new slant on persuasive writing—writing about something annoying in a personal and entertaining way. Use this section to present an alternate or additional form of persuasive writing. Following are some of the topics that are covered:
- Using freewriting to select a topic
- Adding humorous details
- Using logical order

Persuasive Writing Across the Curriculum: 45–90 minutes
Collaborate with teachers from other content areas to identify persuasive forms that could enhance students' experience with the curriculum already in place.
- **Social Studies**
  Editorial Cartoons, pp. 268–269
- **Math**
  Proofs, pp. 270–271
- **Science**
  Supporting Theories, pp. 272–273
- **Practical Writing**
  Persuasive Letters, pp. 274–277

Writing for Assessment: 45–90 minutes
The student text shows a strong student response to the first prompt below. Students can respond to that same prompt or to either of the additional prompts as an informal or a formal assessment.
- Write an essay convincing your teachers to give more or less homework.
- Write an essay expressing your opinion about whether children under 14 should be at home before 7:00 PM unless they are with an adult.
- In a letter, convince your parents to take a family trip to a place you would like to visit.

Evaluating a Persuasive Essay
Learning to evaluate one's own and others' writing is an integral part of learning to write. In addition to a student's evaluation of a persuasive essay (PE pages 258–259), **benchmark papers** provide practice with evaluating persuasive writing.
- Zoos (strong)
  TR 5A–5C
  TE pp. 787–789
- Get Moving (good)
  PE 258–259
- Letter to the Editor (poor)
  TR 6A–6C
  TE pp. 790–792

Integrated Grammar and Writing Skills

Below are skills lessons from the resources sections of the pupil edition that are suggested at point of use (✳) throughout this unit.

Persuasive Paragraph, pp. 219–222
- ✳ Develop Persuasive Paragraphs, p. 529
- ✳ Use Order of Importance, p. 536

Promoting a Cause, pp. 223–260
- ✳ Qualifiers: Indefinite Adjectives, p. 734,
- ✳ Adverbs of Time and Degree, p. 736
- ✳ Pronouns, pp. 476–479
- ✳ Comparative and Superlative Forms, p. 487
- ✳ Capitalization of Proper Nouns and Adjectives, p. 618

Pet-Peeve Essay, pp. 261–266
- ✳ Using the Right Word, pp. 652–686

Unit Pacing details the key topics and approximate length of each lesson.

Integrated Grammar and Writing Skills lists pupil edition skills lessons that are suggested for the unit. These lessons are indicated with the (✳) symbol at point of use within each lesson.

The **Additional Grammar Skills** section of the unit overview suggests additional relevant skills lessons found in other program components including the *SkillsBook, Interactive Writing Skills CD-ROM,* and *Daily Language Workouts.*

Objectives for the lesson are listed at the beginning of each lesson.

Scaffolded lessons provide teachers with a variety of choices for teaching each form of writing: a paragraph, a fully developed essay, an alternative essay, writing across the curriculum, and writing for assessment.

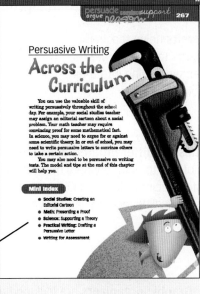

Across the curriculum activities in the writing units provide opportunities for students to apply specific writing forms to different content areas including
- social studies,
- math,
- science,
- assessment.

A Closer Look at the Teacher's Edition, continued

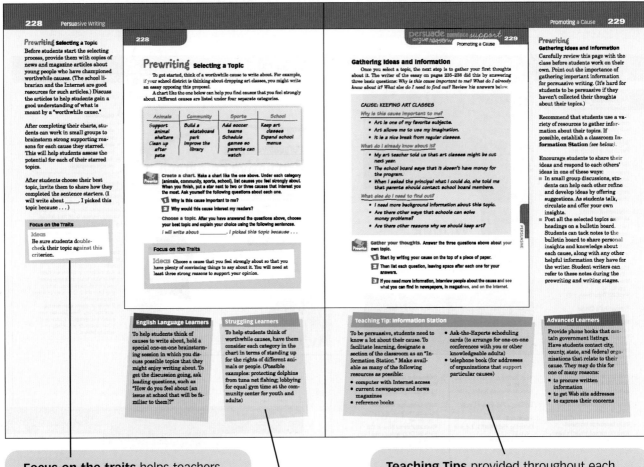

Focus on the traits helps teachers work with students to incorporate the six traits of effective writing into their own writing process.

Teaching Tips provided throughout each lesson offer useful ideas for helping students with specific aspects of the lessons.

Guidelines for differentiated instruction are provided at point of use to help teachers meet the individual needs of all their students including English language learners, struggling learners, and advanced students.

Graphic organizers are included as copy masters at the back of the Teacher's Edition. References to these additional resources are provided throughout the lessons at point of use.

TR 13 **803**

5 W's Chart

Subject:

Who?	What?	When?	Where?	Why?

Student Self-Assessments in each core unit provide opportunities for students to evaluate and score their own work based on the six traits of effective writing.

Evaluating a Persuasive Essay

As you read through the persuasive essay below, focus on the writer's strengths and weaknesses. Then read the student self-assessment on the next page. (The student essay below contains some errors.)

Get Moving

Many students have televisions, stereos, and computers in their homes. They have cable channels to watch, stacks of CD's to listen to, and games to play. These things entertain them, but can cause problems if they do them to much. Friends, schoolwork, and health are things that can suffer because of to much home entertainment.

For one thing, to much time alone can hurt friendships. Not being in sports or other activities gets people in the habit of being by themselves. They sometimes become to shy. Because they spend to much time alone. Then they wonder why they don't have any friends.

In addition, coming home from school and turning on the TV or computer puts off getting started on schoolwork. Instead of doing assignments right after school, students might wait until there to tired to do a good job. Even worse, they might not do there homework at all. That is a big problem!

Even health can be a problem for those who sit around to much. Doctors say that young people are out of shape and overwieght. Bad habits that start early can cause problems later on. Almost everyone needs to be more active.

There probably are good shows to watch on TV and computer games that teach things. Sitting around the house to much is not good. Everyone needs to be careful about letting toys take to much of their time. If kids want to have more friends, think better, and feel better, they need to get moving!

persuade support
argue
Promoting a Cause 259

Student Self-Assessment

The assessment that follows includes the student's comments about his essay on page 258. In the first comment, the student mentions something positive from the essay. In the second comment, the student points out an area for possible improvement. (The writer used the rubric and number scale on pages 256–257 to complete this assessment.)

5 Ideas
1. My opinion about my cause is clear.
2. My paragraph on health effects could have more information.

5 Organization
1. I talk about one problem in each paragraph.
2. I could have used better transitions between paragraphs.

4 Voice
1. My call to action is strong.
2. I could have been more convincing overall.

3 Word Choice
1. My audience will understand my words.
2. I overused the words "problem" and "problems."

4 Sentence Fluency
1. I used some complex sentences.
2. I could have made my sentences flow more smoothly.

3 Conventions
1. I used commas correctly in a series.
2. I still get confused using "to" and "there."

Use the rubric. Assess your essay using the rubric on pages 256–257.
1. On your own paper, list the six traits. Leave room after each trait to write one strength and one weakness.
2. Then choose a number (from 1 to 6) that shows how well you used each trait.

Student Self-Assessment

After students use the rubric to assess their own essays, you may wish to have them share their essays and self-assessments with partners or in small groups for peer evaluation.
■ Do they think the assessment is accurate, too lenient, or too critical?
■ What concrete examples support their evaluations?

Remind students to show respect toward each other and to focus on the writing and not the writer when making comments.

To give students additional practice with evaluating a persuasive essay, use a reproducible assessment sheet (TE page 799) and one or both of the benchmark papers listed in the Benchmark Papers box below. You can use an overhead transparency while students refer to their own copies made from the copy masters. For your benefit a completed assessment sheet is provided for each benchmark paper.

English Language Learners

To help students learn about providing feedback, have them read the following pairs of sentences and tell which sentence is more appropriate as feedback and why they made the choice.
• You don't spell very well.
• The essay has some words that are hard to spell. You could check the list of spelling words on pages 645–651.

• It would be helpful if you organised your ideas in paragraphs.
• You jump all over the place. The inappropriate feedback focuses on the person not the writing and does not give concrete help to improve the writing.

Benchmark Papers

Zoos (strong)
TR 5A–5C
TE pp. 787–789

Letter to the Editor (poor)
TR 6A–6C
TE pp. 790–792

TR 5A **787**

Persuasive Writing

Zoos

1 "Look, Mom," the little girl says, tugging on her mothers hand.
2 Its a baby elephant!" I watch her eyes light up as she stares at the live
3 Elephant.cam. Like her, I enjoy watching the mother elephant care
4 for her baby. It had been born several months ago. The hidden camera
5 makes it possible to view them, yet no crowds upset them. Zoos, one of
part of American society
als from aardvarks to
e outside of China, 10 of
s born at the San Diego
orilla born in captivity
ould probably have
ere not in zoos.
ecies. In zoos
s so that they can be
ndangered list. This has
e, and Przhevalski's
The Manatee Rescue
how zoos help protect
jured, sick, or orphaned

790 TR 6A

Persuasive Writing

1 San Diego Union-Tribune
2 Letter to the Editor

3 Dear Editor:
4 I am a sixth grader. Some things that the government do bother
5 me. The thing that bothers me is the port of entry at San Ysidro
6 California. People have to open these gates. They should open with a
7 pulley or open electrically.
8 Someone I know was seriously hurt opening one of those big
9 heavy gates. Each lane has a heavy gate at the port of entry. She has
10 been out of work a long time. Worse than that, she is in alot of pain.
11 People should not get hurt on the job.
12 There are alot of different agencys at the Port of Entry. One of
13 them could look at this problem. There is the INS (Immigration and
14 Naturalization Service). There is Customs. There is the Border Patrol.
15 There is the GSA (General Services Administration). All these agencys
16 are busy spending money on computer systems. They forgot about
17 some of the simple things like gates. I'm going to tell you that one
18 more time. All these agencys are busy spending money on computer
19 systems. They forget about simple things like gates. Then, they pay
20 alot of money to the people who is hurt and can't work.
21 The solution is simple. All the agencys could band together and

Benchmark papers for core units offer practice in evaluating essays. An essay rated "good" appears in the Pupil Edition. Essays rated "poor" and "strong" are provided as copy masters in the Teacher's Edition and as transparencies.

Yearlong Timetable

The suggested Yearlong Timetable is just that—suggested. It presents a sequence of writing units based on a five-day-per-week writing class. Your teaching week may offer fewer hours for teaching writing. That's why the Teacher's Edition provides guidelines to help you customize the timetable and the sequence of units to meet your particular needs.

First Quarter

Wk	Writing Lesson	Pupil Edition
1	Getting Started	
2	Understanding the Writing Process	5–10
	One Writer's Process	11–19
3	One Writer's Process (cont.)	20–28
	Keeping Journals and Learning Logs	431–440
4	Understanding the Traits of Writing	33–44
	Writing a Descriptive Paragraph	71–73
5	Writing a Descriptive Paragraph (cont.)	74
	Using a Rubric	45–56
	Peer Responding	29–32
6	Listening and Speaking	417–422
	Publishing Your Writing	57–64
	Creating a Portfolio	65–69
7	Describing an Event	75–80
8	Describing an Event (cont.)	80–82
	Taking Classroom Tests	459–467
9	Writing a Narrative Paragraph	93–96

Second Quarter

Wk	Writing Lesson	Pupil Edition
1	Sharing an Experience	97–106
2	Sharing an Experience (cont.)	107–134
3	Writing a Biographical Narrative	135–140
4	Writing a Biographical Narrative (cont.)	140–142
	Writing for Assessment	152–155
5	Writing an Expository Paragraph	157–160
6	Explaining a Process	161–168
7	Explaining a Process (cont.)	169–198
8	Writing a Classification Essay	199–204
9	Writing a Classification Essay (cont.)	204
	Writing for Assessment	214–217
	Portfolio Review	

Third Quarter

Wk	Writing Lesson	Pupil Edition
1	Writing Stories	343–347
2	Writing Stories (cont.)	348–352
3	Writing Poems	353–356
4	Writing Poems (cont.)	357–361
	Completing Writing Assignments	449–458
5	Writing a Persuasive Paragraph	219–222
	Promoting a Cause	223–228
6	Promoting a Cause (cont.)	229–260
7	Writing a Pet-Peeve Essay	261–265
8	Writing a Pet-Peeve Essay (cont.)	265–266
	Writing for Assessment	278–281
9	Making Oral Presentations	423–430
	Portfolio Review	

Fourth Quarter

Wk	Writing Lesson	Pupil Edition
1	Writing a Response Paragraph	283–286
	Writing a Book Review	287–294
2	Writing a Book Review (cont.)	295–322
3	Writing a Fictionalized Journal Entry	323–328
4	Writing for Assessment	336–341
	Portfolio Review	
	Taking Notes	441–448
5	Building Research Skills	363–376
6	Writing a Summary Paragraph	377–380
7	Writing a Research Report	381–391
8	Writing a Research Report (cont.)	392–400
9	Writing a Research Report (cont.)	401–410
	Developing Multimedia Presentations	411–415

Lesson Planning Guidelines

The authors of the *Write Source* program understand that teachers of writing need a wealth of resources that can be used flexibly. The guidelines here will assist you in using the *Write Source* program to best advantage for you and your students.

Determining Priorities

The first step in planning is to determine the priorities for the year. What must you accomplish with your students by the end of the year? To establish your priorities, you will need to

- become familiar with state and local curriculum requirements for the grade you teach;
- understand the content of any state or standardized tests that your students will take; and
- evaluate the writing experience and ability of your students by examining their records and portfolios from previous years, administering a classroom writing test (including the Pretest in the *Write Source* Assessment Book, available in the Teacher's Resource Pack), and/or observing samples of students' writing early in the year.

Once you have determined the major focus of instruction for the year, you will need to consider other factors, such as how much time you have to spend on writing instruction and practice, in what order you will address the priorities, and other topics you want to include to round out your writing plan.

Time Allotment

The time allotted for writing instruction will vary according to school and classroom schedules. To help you make the most of the time you have, each Unit Overview provides the following information about the upcoming unit:

- the objectives and content of the unit,
- a range of times that could be spent on the unit subsections, and
- related *Write Source* materials that can be used to supplement instruction.

With this information, you can begin to sketch out your schedule, balancing instruction with time available for writing.

Yearly Planning

The priorities you have established form the basis for your yearly plan. Once you know what students must accomplish, then you can begin to determine what you need to teach, when to teach it, and how long you will spend teaching it. To plan a year-long writing curriculum,

- list the priorities for the year,
- determine the *Write Source* units that support your priorities,
- lay out a sequence of units, and
- determine how long to devote to particular units according to student need.

Re-evaluate your overall plan several times during the year to make adjustments.

Sequencing the Units

The *Write Source* pupil edition is divided into six sections: The Writing Process, The Forms of Writing, Speaking and Writing to Learn, The Basic Elements of Writing, A Writer's Resource, and Proofreader's Guide. Familiarity with these sections will help you in your planning (see below and the table of contents).

The authors of the *Write Source* program recommend that before you begin formal writing instruction you spend some class time helping students become familiar with the book so that they can get the most out of it. Getting Started activities (see TE pages xlv–xlvi and 805–807) will help you ensure that your students know the extent of the resources available to them and can use them to become better writers, thinkers, and learners in all their classes. The next step is to move to the first section of the book, The Writing Process. These chapters will provide a common foundation of writing knowledge for your students about the writing process and the traits of effective writing.

There is no specific order for teaching the forms of writing. Plans for teaching the major writing units will depend on state, district, or school curriculum; the state test; and specific classroom assignments. Address the following considerations to make your planning decisions:

- Take into account the timing of state or standardized writing tests.

- Coordinate with schoolwide or content-area assignments. (For example, if the whole grade studies biography, then you will want to address that form in a timely way. If the social studies teacher assigns a research report, then support your colleague and students by providing instruction in how to do a research report.)

- Use Descriptive Writing as a way to observe students' writing abilities. It is a shorter unit than the full-blown core writing units (Narrative Writing, Expository Writing, Persuasive Writing, and Response to Literature) and description is a feature of all genres.

The final sections of *Write Source*—The Basic Elements of Writing, A Writer's Resource, and Proofreader's Guide—can be used as resource sections for your student writers when they have questions about writing skills and strategies. They are integrated into the Forms of Writing chapters so that each form is well supported by appropriate writing skills and strategies (see Unit Planning below). However, students can access these sections at any time to answer their questions about sentences, paragraphs, parts of speech, punctuation, and so forth.

Unit Planning

As you plan each writing unit, there are a number of choices that you will make to best meet the needs of your students and the curriculum. The units purposely have an abundance of information to accommodate the writing needs of many students, so you will want to choose the parts of each unit that help you achieve your priorities. Use the information below and in each Unit Overview in conjunction with the Unit Planning Worksheet (TE pages 808–809) to begin to make appropriate choices for your students.

How much of the unit should I cover?

Each of the four core writing units (Narrative Writing, Expository Writing, Persuasive Writing, and Response to Literature) and Research Writing have multiple sections. Students have the opportunity to write a paragraph, a full-blown essay, a second essay, across-the-curriculum forms, and a response to a writing prompt. You may decide to use all or most of the writing opportunities for a form of writing that is very important in your curriculum. On the other hand, you may decide that your students can already write well-constructed paragraphs and only need to work on the full-blown essay or the second essay.

How do I select the best supporting skills and resources?

Each Unit Overview offers a list of skills and strategies available in other parts of the pupil edition and in other program components that support the writing form. Use your knowledge of your students, based on assessments and observation, to help you decide which integrated skills and strategies to use. Multiple opportunities exist for some skills, and you will want to decide how much is enough for your students.

What sections should I focus on within the writing process?

The pupil edition takes students through the writing process for each form of writing. Consider your students' familiarity with the steps of the writing process and how much time you should devote to each. The section on revising offers you the opportunity to teach each of the six traits; however, as you probably know, it is best to focus on only one or two traits at a time. At the beginning of the year, concentrate on ideas or organization. Later in the year, work on voice, word choice, and sentence fluency. Conventions will be present throughout the year in the section on editing.

Do I need to cover all the activities in Writing Across the Curriculum?

The Writing Across the Curriculum activities are included to illustrate how the various writing forms can be woven throughout the whole curriculum. An effective use of these activities is to share them with the content-area teachers, who may decide to integrate them into their classes. Students can study the sample passages as examples of the genres, and they can write their own if they need further practice in a genre.

Scope and Sequence

FORMS OF WRITING	Grade 6	Grade 7	Grade 8
Narrative Writing			
biographical narrative	✔		✔
learning experience		✔	
narrative prompts	✔	✔	✔
paragraph	✔	✔	✔
personal experience	✔		
phase autobiography		✔	✔
Expository Writing			
cause-and-effect essay		✔	
classification essay	✔		✔
comparison-contrast essay		✔	✔
expository prompts	✔	✔	✔
how-to essay	✔		
paragraph	✔	✔	✔
Persuasive Writing			
editorial		✔	
paragraph	✔	✔	✔
personal commentary			✔
persuasive essay	✔		
persuasive prompts	✔	✔	✔
pet-peeve essay	✔		
position essay			✔
problem-solution essay		✔	
Response to Literature			
book review	✔		
fictionalized journal entry	✔		
letter to an author			✔
literary interpretation		✔	
paragraph	✔	✔	✔
poetry review		✔	
response prompts	✔	✔	✔
response to literature	✔	✔	✔
theme analysis			✔

	Grade 6	Grade 7	Grade 8
Descriptive Writing			
event	✔		
familiar place		✔	
paragraph	✔	✔	✔
person			✔
Creative Writing			
animal poems	✔		
decision story		✔	
future event story	✔		
photograph poems			✔
quest story			✔
weather poems		✔	
Research Writing			
famous person report		✔	
important place report			✔
multimedia presentation	✔	✔	✔
natural event report	✔		
summary paragraph	✔	✔	✔
Writing to Learn			
completing writing assignments	✔	✔	✔
journal writing	✔	✔	✔
note taking	✔	✔	✔
taking classroom tests	✔	✔	✔

THE WRITING PROCESS

	Grade 6	Grade 7	Grade 8
Prewriting			
Selecting a Topic			
brainstorm	✔	✔	✔
character chart		✔	✔
cluster	✔	✔	✔
focus statement	✔	✔	✔
freewrite	✔	✔	✔
grid	✔	✔	
life map		✔	
life list			✔
list	✔	✔	✔
sentence starters	✔	✔	✔
table diagram		✔	✔

	Grade 6	Grade 7	Grade 8
topic chart	✔	✔	✔
topic sentence	✔		
Gathering Details			
analyze topic	✔		
answer questions	✔	✔	✔
avoid plagiarism	✔	✔	✔
before-after chart			✔
cause-effect chart		✔	
cluster	✔	✔	
collection sheet		✔	
counter an objection			✔
details chart			✔
five W's and H	✔	✔	✔
freewrite	✔	✔	
gathering grid		✔	✔
gathering objections			✔
gathering reasons			✔
list details	✔	✔	✔
media grid	✔	✔	✔
opinion statement	✔	✔	
personality web	✔		
problem-solution chart		✔	
sensory chart	✔	✔	✔
sentence starters			✔
sorting chart			✔
table diagram		✔	✔
theme chart			✔
time line	✔	✔	✔
tracking sources	✔	✔	✔
underline details	✔		
understanding opinions and facts	✔		
"what if?" chart			✔
Organizing Details			
developing viewpoint			✔
figures of speech	✔		
gathering grid	✔		
list	✔	✔	✔
note cards	✔	✔	✔
opinion statement		✔	

	Grade 6	Grade 7	Grade 8
order of importance	✔		✔
order of location	✔	✔	✔
outline ideas	✔	✔	✔
plot chart	✔		
simile and metaphor		✔	
thesis statement	✔	✔	✔
time line	✔		✔
time order	✔	✔	✔
topic sentence	✔	✔	✔
Venn diagram			✔

Sizing Up Your Topic

	Grade 6	Grade 7	Grade 8
list background information		✔	
write questions	✔		✔

Writing

Beginning Paragraph

	Grade 6	Grade 7	Grade 8
ask a question		✔	✔
background information		✔	✔
connect with reader			✔
dramatic scene		✔	
engaging voice	✔		✔
focus statement	✔	✔	✔
interesting details		✔	✔
interesting fact	✔	✔	✔
middle of action	✔	✔	
opening sentence	✔		
opinion statement	✔		
quotation	✔	✔	✔
share an experience		✔	
storyboard		✔	
time and place			✔
topic sentence	✔	✔	✔
words with feeling		✔	

Middle Paragraphs

	Grade 6	Grade 7	Grade 8
action words		✔	✔
build to high point	✔	✔	
comparisons	✔		
details	✔		✔
dialogue	✔	✔	✔

	Grade 6	Grade 7	Grade 8
explain terms			✔
facts			✔
focus on one scene	✔		
key event		✔	
make comparison			✔
personal feelings	✔		✔
propose a solution		✔	
sensory details		✔	✔
summarize problem		✔	
topic sentence		✔	✔
transitions	✔	✔	✔
Ending Paragraph			
answer an objection		✔	
call to action		✔	
closing sentences	✔	✔	
explain theme		✔	
final action	✔		
final comment	✔		✔
final scene			✔
interesting fact		✔	
key idea		✔	✔
new insight		✔	
quotation			✔ ₂
refer back to beginning		✔	
reflect on experience		✔	
restate opinion	✔		
restate thesis		✔	✔
summarize	✔	✔	✔

Revising

Ideas			
answer the 5 W's	✔		
answer objections		✔	
clear message	✔	✔	✔
comparisons			✔
definitions			✔
dialogue	✔	✔	✔
explanations			✔
focus statement	✔	✔	✔

	Grade 6	Grade 7	Grade 8
fuzzy thinking	✔		✔
key events		✔	
main points		✔	
memory details	✔		✔
qualifiers	✔		
quotations			✔
reflective details	✔		✔
response to objection			✔
sensory details	✔	✔	✔
"show, don't tell"	✔	✔	✔
sources			✔
surprising details			✔
unnecessary details	✔		
well-chosen topic		✔	

Organization

	Grade 6	Grade 7	Grade 8
arrangement of reasons			✔
call to action		✔	
clear beginning	✔	✔	✔
clearly connected details			✔
direct dialogue			✔
ending summarizes theme		✔	✔
logical order	✔		✔
main supporting points	✔	✔	
order of location		✔	
paragraph unity		✔	
point-by-point		✔	
precise pattern			✔
summarized dialogue			✔
thesis statement			✔
time order	✔	✔	✔
topic sentences	✔	✔	✔
transition words	✔	✔	✔
two-part focus statement			✔

Voice

	Grade 6	Grade 7	Grade 8
active			✔
balance of facts and feelings			✔
confident	✔	✔	✔
consistent point of view			✔
dialogue	✔	✔	✔

	Grade 6	Grade 7	Grade 8
enthusiastic		✔	✔
fits audience	✔	✔	✔
formal	✔	✔	✔
informal	✔	✔	✔
interested		✔	✔
knowledgeable	✔	✔	
mood			✔
natural	✔	✔	✔
original		✔	
passive			✔
persuasive		✔	
positive	✔	✔	
sincere		✔	
tone			✔

Word Choice

	Grade 6	Grade 7	Grade 8
adjectives and adverbs	✔	✔	✔
alliteration	✔		
appropriate		✔	✔
connotation		✔	✔
descriptive words	✔	✔	✔
figures of speech	✔		
inflammatory words		✔	
literary words		✔	✔
modifiers	✔		✔
onomatopoeia	✔	✔	
participles		✔	
personification		✔	
precise terms		✔	✔
qualifiers			✔
quotations			✔
repeated words	✔		
specific nouns	✔	✔	✔
synonyms	✔		
technical terms			✔
tone			✔
unfair words			✔
unnecessary modifiers	✔		✔
vivid verbs	✔	✔	✔

	Grade 6	Grade 7	Grade 8
Sentence Fluency			
balanced sentence			✔
choppy sentences	✔	✔	✔
complete sentences	✔		✔
complex sentences	✔	✔	
compound sentences	✔	✔	
conjunctions		✔	✔
expanded sentences			✔
fragments	✔		
modeling			✔
prepositional phrases		✔	
rambling sentences	✔	✔	✔
run-on sentences	✔	✔	
sentence combining	✔		✔
series of words	✔		
short sentences		✔	
simple sentence	✔		
smooth flow	✔	✔	✔
variety of beginnings		✔	✔
variety of lengths	✔	✔	✔
wordy sentences			✔
Editing			
Capitalization			
beginning of sentences	✔	✔	✔
proper adjectives	✔	✔	✔
proper nouns	✔	✔	✔
Grammar			
comparatives and superlatives	✔	✔	
compound subjects joined by "and"		✔	
compound subjects joined by "or"		✔	
correct forms of verbs	✔	✔	✔
double subjects			✔
homophones	✔	✔	✔
pronoun agreement			✔
shifts in verb tense	✔	✔	
subject-verb agreement	✔	✔	✔
Punctuation			
apostrophes to show possession	✔	✔	✔
commas after introductory word groups	✔		✔

	Grade 6	Grade 7	Grade 8
commas after items in a series	✔	✔	✔
commas in compound sentences	✔	✔	✔
commas to set off explanations		✔	
commas with parenthetical expressions			✔
end punctuation	✔	✔	✔
punctuating appositives		✔	
punctuating complex sentences		✔	✔
punctuating dependent clauses			✔
punctuating dialogue	✔	✔	✔
punctuating equal adjectives		✔	
punctuating titles	✔		
punctuating works-cited page	✔		✔
quotation marks around direct quotations		✔	✔
Spelling			
commonly misused words	✔	✔	✔
double-checking words	✔	✔	✔

WRITING ACROSS THE CURRICULUM

Narrative Writing

	Grade 6	Grade 7	Grade 8
anecdote (science)	✔		
autobiography (math)			✔
class minutes (practical)	✔		
classroom journal (social studies)	✔		
cultural experience (social studies)		✔	
e-mail message (practical)			✔
historical moment (social studies)			✔
incident report (practical)		✔	
learning-log entry (math)		✔	
natural formation (science)			✔
story problems (math)	✔		
TV script (science)		✔	

Expository Writing

	Grade 6	Grade 7	Grade 8
concept (math)	✔		
directions (practical)	✔		
e-mail request (practical)		✔	
explanation (science/math)	✔	✔	
extended definition (science)		✔	
friendly letter (social studies)		✔	
lab report (science)			✔

	Grade 6	Grade 7	Grade 8
memo (practical)			✔
news report (social studies)			✔
process (math)			✔
survey (social studies)	✔		
Persuasive Writing			
business letter (practical)		✔	✔
campaign speech (social studies)		✔	
editorial (social studies)			✔
editorial cartoon (social studies)	✔		
graph (math/science)		✔	✔
letter (practical)	✔		
proof (math)	✔		
proposal (science)		✔	
statistical argument (math)			✔
theory (science)	✔		
Response to Literature			
article summary (science)	✔	✔	✔
biography (social studies)	✔		
evaluation form (practical)	✔	✔	✔
historical photo (social studies)			✔
interview (social studies)		✔	
Descriptive Writing			
classified ad (practical)		✔	
different time (social studies)	✔		
eyewitness report (social studies)			✔
famous place (social studies)		✔	
field trip (science)			✔
lab report (science)		✔	
natural event (science)	✔		
object (math)			✔
project proposal (practical)			✔
riddle (math)		✔	
term (math)	✔		
thank-you note (practical)	✔		

GRAMMAR	Grade 6	Grade 7	Grade 8
Understanding Sentences			
complete predicates	✔	✔	✔
complete subjects	✔	✔	✔
compound predicates	✔	✔	✔
compound subjects	✔	✔	✔
delayed subjects	✔	✔	✔
dependent clauses	✔	✔	✔
direct objects	✔	✔	✔
independent clauses	✔	✔	✔
indirect objects	✔	✔	✔
modifiers	✔	✔	✔
simple predicates	✔	✔	✔
simple subjects	✔	✔	✔
types of phrases	✔	✔	✔
understood subjects and predicates	✔	✔	✔
Using the Parts of Speech			
Adjectives			
articles	✔	✔	✔
common adjectives	✔	✔	✔
comparative adjectives	✔	✔	✔
compound adjectives	✔	✔	✔
demonstrative adjectives	✔	✔	✔
indefinite adjectives	✔	✔	✔
irregular forms	✔	✔	✔
positive adjectives	✔	✔	✔
predicate adjectives	✔	✔	✔
proper adjectives	✔	✔	✔
superlative adjectives	✔	✔	✔
Adverbs			
adverbs of degree	✔	✔	✔
adverbs of manner	✔	✔	✔
adverbs of place	✔	✔	✔
adverbs of time	✔	✔	✔
comparative adverbs	✔	✔	✔
conjunctive adverbs	✔	✔	✔
irregular forms	✔	✔	✔
positive adverbs	✔	✔	✔
superlative adverbs	✔	✔	✔

	Grade 6	Grade 7	Grade 8
Conjunctions			
coordinating conjunctions	✔	✔	✔
correlative conjunctions	✔	✔	✔
subordinating conjunctions	✔	✔	✔
Interjections	✔	✔	✔
Nouns			
abstract nouns	✔	✔	✔
collective nouns	✔	✔	✔
common nouns	✔	✔	✔
compound nouns	✔	✔	✔
concrete nouns	✔	✔	✔
object nouns	✔	✔	✔
plural nouns	✔	✔	✔
possessive nouns	✔	✔	✔
predicate nouns	✔	✔	✔
proper nouns	✔	✔	✔
singular nouns	✔	✔	✔
subject nouns	✔	✔	✔
Prepositions			
prepositional phrases	✔	✔	✔
Pronouns			
antecedents	✔	✔	✔
demonstrative pronouns	✔	✔	✔
indefinite pronouns	✔	✔	✔
intensive pronouns	✔	✔	✔
interrogative pronouns	✔	✔	✔
object pronouns	✔	✔	✔
personal pronouns	✔	✔	✔
possessive pronouns	✔	✔	✔
reflexive pronouns	✔	✔	✔
relative pronouns	✔	✔	✔
singular and plural pronouns	✔	✔	✔
subject pronouns	✔	✔	✔
Verbs			
action verbs	✔	✔	✔
active or passive voice	✔	✔	✔
future continuous tense verbs	✔	✔	✔
future perfect tense verbs	✔	✔	✔
future tense verbs	✔	✔	✔

	Grade 6	Grade 7	Grade 8
gerunds	✔	✔	✔
helping verbs	✔	✔	✔
infinitives	✔	✔	✔
intransitive verbs	✔	✔	✔
linking verbs	✔	✔	✔
participles	✔	✔	✔
past continuous tense verbs	✔	✔	✔
past perfect tense verbs	✔	✔	✔
past tense verbs	✔	✔	✔
present continuous tense verbs	✔	✔	✔
present perfect tense verbs	✔	✔	✔
present tense verbs	✔	✔	✔
singular and plural verbs	✔	✔	✔
transitive verbs	✔	✔	✔
transitive or intransitive verbs	✔	✔	✔

Mechanics

Abbreviations

	Grade 6	Grade 7	Grade 8
acronyms	✔	✔	✔
address abbreviations	✔	✔	✔
common abbreviations	✔	✔	✔
initialisms	✔	✔	✔

Capitalization

	Grade 6	Grade 7	Grade 8
abbreviations	✔	✔	✔
days, months, holidays	✔	✔	✔
first words	✔	✔	✔
geographic names	✔	✔	✔
historical events	✔	✔	✔
letters	✔	✔	✔
names of people	✔	✔	✔
official names	✔	✔	✔
organizations	✔	✔	✔
particular sections of the country	✔	✔	✔
proper nouns and adjectives	✔	✔	✔
races, languages, nationalities, religions	✔	✔	✔
school subjects	✔	✔	✔
titles	✔	✔	✔
titles used with names	✔	✔	✔
words used as names	✔	✔	✔

	Grade 6	Grade 7	Grade 8
Numbers			
comparing numbers	✔	✔	✔
numbers in compound modifiers	✔	✔	✔
numbers under 10	✔	✔	✔
numerals only	✔	✔	✔
sentence beginnings	✔	✔	✔
time and money	✔	✔	✔
very large numbers	✔	✔	✔
Plurals			
adding an 's	✔	✔	✔
compound nouns	✔	✔	✔
irregular spelling	✔	✔	✔
nouns ending in *ch*, *sh*, *s*, *x*, and *z*	✔	✔	✔
nouns ending in *f* or *fe*	✔	✔	✔
nouns ending in *ful*	✔	✔	✔
nouns ending in *o*	✔	✔	✔
nouns ending in *y*	✔	✔	✔
plurals that do not change	✔	✔	✔
Punctuation			
Apostrophes			
in contractions	✔	✔	✔
in place of omitted letters or numbers	✔	✔	✔
to express time or amount	✔	✔	✔
to form plural possessives	✔	✔	✔
to form possessives with compound nouns	✔	✔	✔
to form possessives with indefinite pronouns	✔	✔	✔
to form singular possessives	✔	✔	✔
to form some plurals	✔	✔	✔
to show shared possession	✔	✔	✔
Colons			
after salutations	✔	✔	✔
between numbers in time	✔	✔	✔
to introduce lists	✔	✔	✔
to introduce sentences	✔	✔	✔
Commas			
between items in a series	✔	✔	✔
in compound sentences	✔	✔	✔
in dates and addresses	✔	✔	✔
in direct address	✔	✔	✔

	Grade 6	Grade 7	Grade 8
to keep numbers clear	✔	✔	✔
to separate equal adjectives	✔	✔	✔
to separate introductory clauses and phrases	✔	✔	✔
to set off appositives	✔	✔	✔
to set off dialogue	✔	✔	✔
to set off explanatory phrases	✔	✔	✔
to set off interjections	✔	✔	✔
to set off interruptions	✔	✔	✔
to set off nonrestrictive phrases and clauses	✔	✔	✔
to set off titles or initials	✔	✔	✔
Dashes			
for emphasis	✔	✔	✔
to indicate interrupted speech	✔	✔	✔
to indicate a sudden break	✔	✔	✔
Ellipses			
to show omitted words	✔	✔	✔
to show pauses	✔	✔	✔
Exclamation Points			
to express strong feelings	✔	✔	✔
Hyphens			
between numbers in a fraction	✔	✔	✔
in compound words	✔	✔	✔
to avoid confusion	✔	✔	✔
to create new words	✔	✔	✔
to divide words	✔	✔	✔
to form adjectives	✔	✔	✔
to join letters to words	✔	✔	✔
Italics and Underlining			
for scientific and foreign words	✔	✔	✔
in handwritten material	✔	✔	✔
in printed material	✔	✔	✔
in titles	✔	✔	✔
Parentheses			
to add information	✔	✔	✔
Periods			
after abbreviations	✔	✔	✔
after initials	✔	✔	✔
as decimal points	✔	✔	✔
at end of sentences	✔	✔	✔

	Grade 6	Grade 7	Grade 8
Question Marks			
at end of direct questions	✔	✔	✔
at end of indirect questions	✔	✔	✔
to show doubt	✔	✔	✔
Quotation Marks			
for quotations within quotations	✔	✔	✔
for special words	✔	✔	✔
placement of punctuation	✔	✔	✔
to punctuate titles	✔	✔	✔
to set off long quoted material	✔	✔	✔
to set off quoted material	✔	✔	✔
to set off a speaker's exact words	✔	✔	✔
Semicolons			
to join two independent clauses	✔	✔	✔
to separate groups that contain commas	✔	✔	✔
with conjunctive adverbs	✔	✔	✔
Usage			
Spelling			
consonant endings	✔	✔	✔
i before *e*	✔	✔	✔
silent *e*	✔	✔	✔
words ending in *y*	✔	✔	✔
Using the right word	✔	✔	✔

Getting Started Activities

The *Write Source* pupil edition is full of helpful resources that students can access throughout the year while they are developing their writing skills. Getting Started activities are provided as copy masters on TE pages 805–807. They will

■ help students discover the kinds of information available in different sections of the book,

■ teach students how to access that information,

■ familiarize students with the layout of the book.

The more familiar students are with the text, the more proficient they will be in using its resources. (The answer key for the activities is on the next page.)

Scavenger Hunts

Students enjoy using scavenger hunts to become familiar with a book. The scavenger hunts we provide can be done in small groups or as a class. They are designed for oral answers, but you may want to photocopy the pages for students to write on. Also, you may want to vary the procedure, first having students take turns finding the items and then, on the next scavenger hunt, challenging students to "race" for the answers.

After your students have done each scavenger hunt, you can challenge them to create their own versions. For example, small groups can work together to create "Find the Fours" or "Search for Sixes" scavenger hunts and then exchange their "hunts" with other groups.

Special Challenge: Develop questions that teams of students try to answer using the book. Pattern this activity after a popular game show.

Other Activities

■ Give students the following assignment: Across the top of a sheet of paper, write down three things you find difficult about school (e.g., taking notes, taking tests, writing essays, spelling, using commas). Then explore your book to find chapters, sections, examples, and so on, that might help you with your problem area. Under each problem, write the titles or headings and the page numbers where you can find help. Keep this sheet to use throughout the year.

■ A variation on the above activity is to have students write down all the subject areas they study and list under each heading the parts of the book that might help them in that subject.

■ Have students write a thought-trap poem: After reviewing the book, close it. The first line of your poem will be the title of the book. Then list thoughts and feelings about the book, line by line. When you have listed everything you want to say, "trap" your thoughts by repeating the title.

■ Have pairs of students create poster-size advertisements for the book. Each ad should have a headline, list important features (what is in the book) and benefits (whom it can help and how), show an example of illustrations (made by tracing or copying), and urge readers of the ad to get their books now!

■ Have students imagine that they are each going to send a copy of *Write Source* to a pen pal in another state. Have each student write a letter to send along with it to tell the pen pal about the book.

Getting Started Activity Answers

Scavenger Hunt 1: Find the Threes

1. topic sentence, body, closing sentence
2. place yourself in the middle of the action, begin with a surprising statement or fact, start with someone speaking
3. Possible answers: likewise, like, as, also, in the same way, similarly
4. share the character's thoughts, actions, and dialogue; describe his or her appearance; reveal what others in the story think or say about this character
5. add sensory details, explain body language, use dialogue
6. Possible answers: tribe, congregation, family, class, team, flock, herd, gaggle, clutch, litter, batch, cluster, bunch
7. Possible answers: books, plays, book-length poems, magazines, movies, newspapers, radio and TV programs, videos, cassettes, CD's, aircraft, ships
8. Possible answers: WHO, FAQ, ROM, AIDS, CETA, MADD, NAFTA, NASA, NATO, OSHA, PAC, PIN, SADD, SWAT, VISTA, WAC, WAVES

Scavenger Hunt 2: What Is It?

1. chronological (time) order, order of location, order of importance comparison, and logical order (page 551)
2. categories or groups of things that people need in order to live a full life (page 545)
3. a writer's first chance to get everything down on paper (page 8)
4. a way to organize your research (page 388)
5. any type of portfolio available on a CD or Web site (page 66)
6. who, what, where, when, why (page 103)
7. an expository essay that explains a subject by dividing it into parts (page 199)
8. collecting ideas by thinking freely about all the possibilities (page 560)

Getting to Know *Write Source*

1. 636
2. 354–357
3. 352
4. 268–269
5. 448
6. 604
7. 548
8. 521–522
9. 350
10. 150–151

Why Write?

This story by a middle school student will help answer this question.

Mr. Gibson made Randy my lab partner. I thought, "Great! I have to work with one of the biggest goof-offs in school."

One day my "partner" was absent. Mr. Gibson said that Randy and his older brother were beekeepers, and they were getting in a new shipment of bees. Randy, a beekeeper? I couldn't believe it.

That night I wrote about Randy in my journal. The more that I wrote, the more I began to understand him. He may not have liked school very much, but he still was learning a lot. He just did some of it in his own way.

Writing will do that. It can help you understand the people and the experiences in your life. What could be more important than that?

Maybe that's why you should write!

Mini Index

- **Reasons to Write**
- **Starting Points for Writing**

Why Write?

Ask students to estimate how many answers they can come up with to the question "Why write?" Then have them complete a 5-minute **freewrite** (see below) using the prompt "Why write?" See if students meet their estimated goal.

Have students share their ideas in groups. Give each group chart paper on which they convert all their thoughts into a numbered list of reasons. Title each chart "Why Write?" Can they increase the number of reasons on this list by brainstorming?

Post the charts in the room and compare the lists. Have the class work together to compile the lists on one master chart. Discuss with the students how working in cooperative groups can be more productive than working alone.

Teaching Tip: Freewriting

During a freewrite, students write quickly and continuously for a 5- or 10-minute period about a specific topic or prompt. They should not stop or pause, plan what they will write, organize their thoughts, or correct their writing. This will help them develop the ability to put ideas in writing fluently. Emphasize that the purpose of freewriting is to record ideas, not to write perfectly. Freewriting is sometimes called fast writing.

Reasons to Write

Revisit the group charts from the previous page. Ask students to get back into their cooperative groups, divide their list of reasons into categories, and label each category using the categories in their text. Point out that there may be reasons that won't fit into any of the categories. Students can place these unique reasons under a new category of their making or under a *Miscellaneous* heading.

Reasons to Write

Good things will happen if you write for the four reasons listed below. You will learn a lot about yourself and become a better writer.

1. To Explore Your Life

Writing in a personal journal helps you learn about yourself. All you have to do is set aside 10 or 15 minutes every day and write about people, places, and events in your life. (See pages 432–433 for more information.)

 Writing in a personal journal is great practice. You might already set aside time to practice a musical instrument or an athletic skill. Do the same with your writing.

2. To Understand New Ideas

Writing in a learning log helps you become a better student. In a learning log, you write about new ideas presented in your classes and in your reading assignments. Think of a learning log as your all-purpose study helper. (See pages 435–438 for more information.)

3. To Show Learning

Your teachers assign paragraphs, essays, and reports to see how well you are learning. To do well on these assignments, you must (1) understand the subjects you are studying and (2) use your best writing skills.

4. To Share Ideas

Write personal narratives (true stories), made-up stories, and poems. These forms of writing are meant to be shared with your classmates.

 Write to explore. Write nonstop for 5 to 8 minutes about something that happened to you yesterday or today. Write for the entire time. If you get stuck, write "I'm stuck" until something comes to mind. When you finish, you will have written a lot and learned something about yourself. Congratulations!

English Language Learners

Point out that a learning log is a great way for students to keep track of new vocabulary, too. Encourage students to record new words they read or hear and then use a dictionary to add a definition for each one. Also have them write one or two sentences that show how to use each new word in context.

Starting Points for Writing

If you want to write, but you can't think of a good topic, review the ideas listed on this page. You're sure to find plenty of good starting points. (See pages **544–547** for more topics.)

Sample Topics

DESCRIBING (*telling what a topic looks like, sounds like, and so on*)

People: a neighbor, a friend, someone you wish you were like, a movie character

Places: an attic, an alley, the gym, a river, a church, a hideaway

Objects or things: a poster, a photograph, a stuffed animal, a hat

NARRATING (*telling about something that happened*)

having a great day, making a mistake, showing friendship, moving, learning to _____ , getting hurt, doing something funny, learning a lesson

EXPLAINING (*sharing information*)

How to . . . make your favorite food, make a friend, earn extra money, play a game, dress in style, fix something, clean a bedroom

The causes of . . . thunderstorms, earthquakes, erosion, the flu, baldness

Kinds of . . . music, friends, heroes, exercise, snack foods, diets, TV shows

Definition of . . . courage, faith, school, teamwork, love

PERSUADING (*expressing your opinion about a topic*)

dieting, dress codes, bicycle helmets, security officers in schools, curfews, recycling programs, movie or music reviews

 Find a topic. Write "Starting Points for Writing" at the top of a piece of paper. Then list these headings—Describing, Narrating, Explaining, and Persuading—down the left-hand margin. Leave space between each heading. Write two new writing ideas under each heading. Add other ideas throughout the school year.

Starting Points for Writing

Divide the class into four groups to develop charts of writing topics for each mode of writing. Assign one mode to each group: Describing, Narrating, Explaining, and Persuading. Have students in each group brainstorm ideas for topics for their mode that are not already listed in the book. Each group should record their ideas on chart paper. Afterward, the charts can be posted for discussion.

✸ For more information about finding a writing topic or a starting point, see PE pages 544–547.

Struggling Learners

Some students have a difficult time finding topics that interest them. Spend some extra time with such students to encourage them to talk about the things that interest them. They may not realize that an interest in dirt bikes or a particular kind of music could be turned into a good writing topic. After identifying topics that students really care about, be sure to provide opportunities for students to write about them rather than always prompting them with a specific focus.

The Writing Process Overview

Writing Standards

The writing standards listed below are based on a blending of state and NCTE standards.

- Learn about the writing process.
- Understand how to use the six traits of effective writing when drafting, revising, and editing.
- Learn how to use rubrics and the six traits of effective writing to assess writing.
- Learn about ways to use technology to publish writing.

Writing Process

- **Prewriting** Explore topics, gather details, and plan the organization.
- **Writing** Using the prewriting plan, complete a first draft.
- **Revising** Based on the six traits of effective writing, revise drafts by adding, deleting, and rearranging text.
- **Editing** Check revised writing for correctness, prepare a final copy, and proofread the final copy for errors.
- **Publishing** Share work with others.

Focus on the Traits

- **Ideas** Establishing a clear focus and collecting specific details
- **Organization** Forming a clear beginning, middle, and ending
- **Voice** Developing a special way of saying things that fits the audience
- **Word Choice** Using specific nouns and verbs to deliver a clear message
- **Sentence Fluency** Writing sentences that create a smooth flow
- **Conventions** Checking for errors in punctuation, capitalization, spelling, and grammar

Unit Pacing

Understanding the Writing Process: 90 minutes

This section introduces the five steps of the **writing process**. Use this section if students are not familiar with the process or if you want to provide a refresher. Following are some of the topics that are covered.

- Developing good writing habits
- Seeing the writing process in action

One Writer's Process: 2.25–3 hours

In this section, students follow one writer's process from prewriting through publishing. Use this section to demonstrate each step of the writing process in action. Following are some of the topics that are covered.

- Setting writing goals
- Using a cluster to select a topic
- Revising a first draft
- Editing for conventions
- Assessing a final copy
- Reflecting on the writing process

Peer Responding: 45–90 minutes

In this section, students learn how to engage in peer-responding sessions. Use this section to teach students how to give specific, constructive feedback to peers. Following are some of the topics that are covered.

- Learning how to respond to writing
- Completing a response sheet

Understanding the Traits of Writing: 3–3.75 hours

In this section students learn how the six traits of effective writing guide the writing process. Use this section to lay the groundwork for all future writing assignments. Following is one of the topics that is covered.

- Understanding the six traits of effective writing.

Using a Rubric: 1.5–2.25 hours

This section focuses on using a rubric to guide the students' writing and to assess finished work. Use this section to teach students how to use a rubric to establish goals for writing, how to revise and edit with a rubric, and how to assess with a rubric. Following are some of the topics that are covered.

- Using a rubric as a writing guide
- Using a rubric as a revising tool
- Assessing with a rubric

Publishing Your Writing: 1.5–2.25 hours

This section offers basic design guidelines and discusses how to create a Web site and publish online. Use this section to explore different ways students can share their writing and prepare it for publication. Following are some of the topics that are covered.

- Ways to publish
- Designing a piece of writing
- Designing a Web site

Creating a Portfolio: 90 minutes

In this section, students learn about the different types of portfolios and the parts of a portfolio. Use this section to teach students how to create a portfolio and how to select work to include in it. Following are some of the topics that are covered.

- Kinds of portfolios
- Parts of a portfolio
- How to plan a portfolio
- Portfolio reflections

Integrated Grammar and Writing Skills

Below are skills lessons from the resources sections of the pupil edition that are suggested at point of use (✱) throughout this unit.

Understanding the Writing Process, pp. 5–10

✱ Forms of Writing, pp. 554–555

One Writer's Process, pp. 11–28

✱ Graphic Organizers, pp. 548–549
✱ Writing Techniques, pp. 558–559

Understanding the Traits of Writing, pp. 33–44

✱ Vocabulary-Building Techniques, pp. 562–563
✱ More Effective Sentences, pp. 570–571

Publishing Your Writing, pp. 57–64

✱ Format and Guidelines, pp. 576–577
✱ Graphics, pp. 574–575

Additional Grammar Skills

Below are skills lessons from the *Daily Language Workout* that you can weave into your unit instruction.

Understanding the Writing Process

One Writer's Process

Understanding the Traits

Using the Writing Process

5

Understanding the Writing Process

You may already know about the writing process from experience. Just think of your best stories, reports, and essays. You probably worked very hard on each one, making many changes from one draft to the next. To do your best work, you must take your writing through a series of steps before sharing it. That is why writing is called a *process*.

The writing process is the key to unlocking your true writing potential. By taking a little time at each step along the way, you can become a stronger writer. You'll be amazed at the doors that writing can open for you.

This chapter will help you understand the writing process and build good writing habits along the way.

Mini Index

- Developing Good Writing Habits
- The Writing Process
- The Process in Action
- Getting the Big Picture

Understanding the Writing Process

Understanding the Writing Process

Objectives

- learn to develop good writing habits through frequent reading and writing
- learn the descriptions of the five steps of the writing process: prewriting, writing, revising, editing, and publishing

To help develop the concept of "process," ask students to think of something they like to do, such as skateboarding, making jewelry, or playing an instrument. Then have them list the steps involved in that process.

Then have a volunteer read this page aloud to review why the writing process is important.

Developing Good Writing Habits

Ask students to fold a sheet of paper into three columns and label them *Reading*, *Writing*, and *Interests*.

Make reading part of your life.

In the first column, have students list what they read each week. The list may include some of the following: reading for school—schoolwork and homework; entertainment—books, comic books, newspapers, and magazines; sales materials—advertisements and mailings; and communications from family and friends—e-mails and letters.

Make writing part of your life.

In the second column, students should list what they write. This list might include some of these forms: school—essays, reports, stories, and tests; home—homework, a diary or journal, letters, e-mail, and cards; trips—postcards, letters, and travel journals.

Write about topics that are important to you.

Have students list specific things that interest them. Ideas may include types of hobbies, school subjects, pets, places they like, relatives they enjoy, or things they would like to learn more about.

6

Developing Good Writing Habits

To become a good writer, you must act like one. Following the tips listed on this page will help you do that.

Make reading part of your life.

Read lots of books, magazines, and newspapers. This will help you acquire an ear for good writing.

> Reading is to the mind what exercise is to the body.
>
> —Sir Richard Steele

Make writing part of your life.

Write as often as you can. Write early in the morning, late at night, or anytime in between. Just keep writing!

> Writing is not apart from living. Writing is a kind of double living.
>
> —Catherine Drinker Bowen

Write about topics that are important to you.

It's important for you to write about things you're interested in. Otherwise, it's like going out for softball when your favorite sport is track.

> When I speak to students about writing, I tell them to write about what they know.
>
> —Robert Cormier

 Write about a quotation. Write nonstop for 3 to 5 minutes about one of the quotations on this page. Consider what it means to you.

English Language Learners

Students may have a difficult time interpreting the quotes.

- The quote by Sir Richard Steele compares reading to exercise. If exercise helps the body stay healthy and grow stronger, then reading helps the mind stay healthy and grow stronger.
- The second quote explains that writing can be considered a way of living, rather than as an activity that is separate from living. Discuss with students how this can be so.
- The quote by Robert Cormier can be explained as a method for choosing a topic. If students write about what they know, then they will find writing a more meaningful process.

Advanced Learners

Have students make a three-column chart with the headings *Profession, Reading,* and *Writing.* Ask them to list at least five careers and specific reading and writing requirements for each. (Possible responses: actor—script, rehearsal schedule; tour guide—map, background information about the attractions)

PREWRITE write *revise* edit *publish* **7**
Understanding the Writing Process

The Writing Process

Experienced writers use the writing process to help them do their best work. The steps in the process are described below.

The Steps in the Writing Process

Prewriting At the start of an assignment, a writer explores possible topics before selecting one to write about. Then the writer collects details about the topic and plans how to use them when writing.

Writing During this step, a writer completes a first draft using the plan as a guide. This draft is a writer's *first* chance to get everything down on paper.

Revising After reviewing the first draft, a writer changes any ideas that are not clear or complete. A wise writer will ask at least one other person to review the draft, as well.

Editing A writer then checks his or her revised writing for correctness before preparing a neat final copy. The writer proofreads the final copy for errors before sharing or publishing it.

Publishing This is the final step in the writing process. Publishing is to a writer what an exhibit is to an artist— an opportunity to share his or her work with others.

Assess your process. On your own paper, explain the process you used to complete your best piece of writing—what you did first, second, third, and so on. How similar was your process to the one described above?

PROCESS

The Writing Process

The Steps in the Writing Process

Before students open their books, try this activity to familiarize students with the writing process.

- Print one step of the writing process on each of five large sheets of paper (Prewriting, Writing, Revising, Editing, Publishing).

- Hand out the sheets to five volunteers. Have these students line up in random order in front of the class holding the papers so that everyone can read the steps.

- Ask the class to arrange the students so that the steps are in the correct order.

- Then ask students to tell what they know about each step in the writing process.

- Then have students turn to this PE page 7 and compare their results with what is in the book. Point out any pertinent differences.

The Process in Action

Explain that part of the writing process is determining a **form of writing** (*see below*) to develop. Oftentimes, the writing assignment will dictate the form. However, when the form of writing isn't assigned, the writer must consider the audience and the purpose in order to make a good decision about form.

✱ For an extensive list of writing forms and their definitions, see PE pages 554–555.

Prewriting Selecting a Topic

Suggest that students keep a topic list in a notebook. Every time they think of a topic that interests them, they can jot it down on that one list. Throughout the year, when lively discussions crop up, remind students to note the topic of the discussion on their list.

Prewriting Gathering Details

Ask each student to begin gathering information for possible writing ideas and keeping it in a folder. Encourage them to collect things that may be useful for a piece of writing, such as magazine or newspaper articles, Web pages, e-mails, flyers, or anything that informs them about something of interest.

8

The Process in Action

The next two pages show you the writing process in action. Use this information as a general guide for each of your writing assignments. This graphic reminds you that you can move back and forth between the steps in the writing process during an assignment.

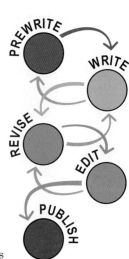

Prewriting Selecting a Topic

■ Search for possible writing topics that meet the requirements of the assignment.
■ Select a specific topic that really interests you.

Gathering Details

■ Learn as much as you can about the topic before you start writing.
■ Consider what to emphasize in the writing—either an interesting part of the topic or your personal feelings about it. This will be the focus, or thesis, of your writing.
■ Decide which details you want to include in your writing. Also decide on the best way to organize the details.

Writing Developing the First Draft

■ When you write your first draft, concentrate on getting your ideas on paper. Don't try to produce a perfect piece of writing.
■ Use the details you collected and your prewriting plan as a general guide but feel free to add new ideas as you go along.
■ Make sure your writing has a beginning, a middle, and an ending.

 Write on every other line and on only one side of the paper when using pen and paper. Double-space on a computer. This will give you room for revising, the next step in the process.

Teaching Tip: Forms of Writing

Determining the appropriate form of writing requires the writer to know who will read the piece (audience) and why the piece is being written (purpose). You can give students practice with identifying audience and purpose with this activity.

● Bring in written materials (newspapers, brochures, directions, manuals, magazine stories, and so on).

● Ask students to identify the audience and the purpose.
● Then ask students to brainstorm some topics and figure out an appropriate audience and purpose for each. They should decide on a form of writing after identifying the audience and purpose.

For example:
Topic: baseball game summary

Audience: fans
Purpose: to provide information and create a sense of being there
Forms of writing: news story
Format: headings, photos

PREWRITE
write *revise* **edit** publish

9

Understanding the Writing Process

Revising Improving Your Writing

- Review your first draft, but only after setting it aside for a while.
- Use these questions as a general revising guide:
  - **Do I sound interested in my topic?**
  - **Do I say enough about it?**
  - **Are the ideas clear and in the right order?**
  - **Does the beginning draw the reader into the writing?**
  - **Does the closing remind the reader about the importance of the topic?**
  - **Are the nouns and verbs specific?**
  - **Are the modifiers (adjectives and adverbs) colorful?**
  - **Are the sentences varied? Do they read smoothly?**
- Try to have at least one other person review your work.

Editing Checking for Conventions

- Edit for correctness by checking for punctuation, capitalization, spelling, and grammar errors. Also ask someone else to check your writing for errors.
- Then prepare a neat final copy of your writing. (See pages 24–26 for ideas.) Proofread this copy for errors before sharing it.

Publishing Sharing Your Writing

- Share your finished work with your classmates, teacher, friends, and family members.
- Decide whether you will include the writing in your portfolio.
- Consider submitting your writing to your school newspaper or some other publication.

 Consider the steps. On your own paper, list one new thing that you learned on pages 8–9 about each step in the writing process.

PROCESS

Revising Improving Your Writing

Point out that *revising* means "re-seeing" a piece of writing. Tell students that it is important to think critically about their writing and be willing to look at it from new perspectives. Sometimes they may need to consider making big changes to improve a piece of writing.

Editing
Checking for Conventions

There is a danger of introducing new errors when students prepare a neat final copy. Therefore, it is important that they **proofread** *(see below)* carefully.

Publishing Sharing Your Writing

Ask students if they have ever "judged a book by its cover." What makes a book appealing to read? Discuss ways to make a reader want to pick something up and read it.

Teaching Tip: Proofreading

Students may think that the best way to proofread a paper is to read it over again, looking for errors. Proofreading actually works best when you compare the final copy to the copy containing the editing changes. Demonstrate correct proofreading form by placing the edited copy beside the final version. Place one hand on each version and compare papers, using your fingertips to mark your progress. Work with one small portion of text at a time, checking for mistakes.

Getting the Big Picture

Before students read PE page 10, help them think about the characteristics of good writing:

- What makes a piece of writing interesting?
- What makes a piece of writing easy to understand?

Discuss the traits of effective writing on PE page 10. Use a three-legged stool as a graphic organizer:

- Which three traits are the foundation of the writing? (ideas, organization, voice)

List these traits on the seat of the stool.

Then ask:

- Which three traits does a writer use to refine a piece of writing? (word choice, sentence fluency, conventions)

Label each leg of the stool with one of these traits.

Ask:

- How can the three-legged stool help you understand the traits? (The three legs support the seat; the seat represents the main characteristics of good writing.)

 Focus on the Process

1. D
2. A
3. C
4. E
5. B

Getting the Big Picture

At this point, you may be wondering why writing has to be this involved. "Why can't I just sit down, write, and be done?" Well, you can, but your work won't be as good as it would have been if you had used the writing process.

Writers can't think of everything at once. They begin with the "big picture"—ideas, organization, and voice—and slowly sharpen their focus to look at individual sentences, words, and conventions (punctuation, spelling, capitalization, and grammar). These six qualities of writing are often called the six traits.

☐ **Ideas**

  ☐ **Organization**

    ☐ **Voice**

      ☐ **Word Choice**

        ☐ Sentence Fluency

          ☐ Conventions

 Focus on the process. Imagine that you will be writing an essay describing a spring day. On your own paper, match each activity on the left to its proper place in the writing process on the right.

___ 1. Check my writing for grammar, spelling, and punctuation.

___ 2. Gather details about what I would see, hear, feel, smell, and taste on a spring day.

___ 3. Move paragraphs so that they make more sense.

___ 4. Illustrate my description and post it on the fridge.

___ 5. Write a strong beginning, middle, and ending.

A. Prewriting
B. Writing
C. Revising
D. Editing
E. Publishing

English Language Learners

Some students may have difficulty understanding the idiom *getting the big picture*. Point out that this term means "understanding the overall structure and content of a piece of writing." Then review the first three traits of writing. Provide specific examples of these three traits from simple pieces of writing that they have recently read.

prewrite EDIT *revise* write *publish* 11

One Writer's Process

Whether you want to tell a funny story, describe a roaring waterfall, or complain about something unfair, you have many things to write about. The challenge is writing down exactly what you want to say. The best way to express yourself is to use the writing process.

This chapter shows you how sixth-grader Reece King used the writing process to tell the story of meeting his closest friend. From the start, it was obvious how meaningful this event was to him. As he moved through the stages of the writing process, his story got better and better.

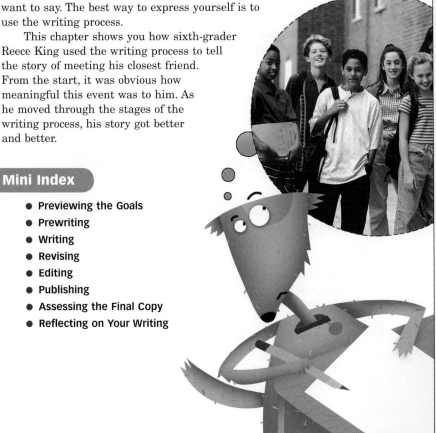

Mini Index

- Previewing the Goals
- Prewriting
- Writing
- Revising
- Editing
- Publishing
- Assessing the Final Copy
- Reflecting on Your Writing

One Writer's Process

Objectives

- examine the goals and rubric for narrative writing
- learn how one writer used graphic organizers, such as clusters and time charts, to select a writing topic and organize details
- learn how one writer completed the revising and editing steps
- study ideas for creating a final copy suitable for publishing

Before they read this page, have students recall their approach to writing assignments in the past:
- What piece of writing do you best remember working on?
- Where did you get your idea?
- Did you write a draft and then revise or edit? How did that go?

Explain that they will follow one writer, Reece, as he uses the writing process.

English Language Learners

Throughout this unit, when assigning partners or groups, be aware that it may be difficult for these students to share their ideas in extended oral discussions or in written work. Group these students with language-proficient students who are cooperative and positive, and monitor their participation.

Previewing the Goals

The goals of narrative writing are set up according to the traits of effective writing. Ask:

- How will these goals help Reece get started with his writing?
- How can Reece use the goals as he continues writing?

✳ For a better understanding of the goals, examine the rubric for narrative writing on PE pages 130–131.

 Answers

1. He should use ideas that include important details and relevant dialogue about the specific event.
2. He should write an opening that catches the reader's attention, followed by details in the order in which they occurred, and, finally, a strong ending.
3. His narrative should sound natural, as though Reece were speaking.

12

Previewing the Goals

Before Reece began writing, he looked at the goals for his narrative assignment, which are shown below. These goals helped him get started. He also previewed the rubric for narrative writing on pages 130–131.

GOALS OF NARRATIVE WRITING

Ideas
Use details and dialogue to tell about a specific experience or event. Make the reader want to know what happens next.

Organization
Open with a clear beginning that pulls the reader into the narrative. Then present ideas in the order in which they happened.

Voice
Write the narrative in a way that sounds natural—like the real you. Give the people in your narrative voice, too.

Word Choice
Use specific nouns, vivid verbs, and well-chosen modifiers.

Sentence Fluency
Use a variety of sentence styles that flow smoothly from one idea to the next.

Conventions
Be sure that your punctuation, capitalization, spelling, and grammar are correct.

To understand the important goals for Reece's assignment, answer the following questions:

1. What types of ideas should he use to tell his story?
2. How should he organize his ideas?
3. How should his narrative sound?

prewrite EDIT *write* *publish*
revise
One Writer's Process **13**

PROCESS

Prewriting Selecting a Topic

Reece was asked to write a personal narrative about meeting a special friend for the first time. Since he has many friends, he used a cluster (also called a web) to decide which one to write about.

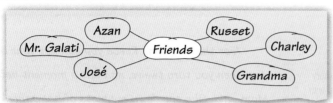

Mr. Galati — Azan — Friends — Russet — Charley
José — Grandma

 Have you ever used a cluster? Try one now by clustering the names of your own friends. Could you write a story about a first meeting with one of the friends that you identified?

Gathering and Organizing Details

The time chart below helped Reece gather and organize details about meeting his dog, Russet. Reece focused on the five senses, personal feelings, and things that people said.

First ➔	Next ➔	Last
At first, Mom said, "No pets. Not until you're 12 years old." Breakfast—she put her foot down. Waiting outside Humane Society. Excited. Knew just what my dog would be like.	Looked for a golden retriever. Saw little white terrier. Mean. Snarled. Shepherd with droopy look. Big old basset. Lots of mutts. Lots of barking.	Mom asks, "Have you decided?" Headache from all the barking. I tell her "HE'S NOT HERE!" I can see Russet in my mind. Then I saw him! His eyes were right!

Try It Have you ever used a time chart to gather details? What about a time line? (See page **548**.) Use a graphic organizer to gather details about a first meeting with one of your friends. Were you able to collect a lot of details?

Prewriting Selecting a Topic

Try It Answers

Answers will vary.

Prewriting
Gathering and Organizing Details

Review the time chart. Note that the sample includes words, phrases, and sentences.

Explain that a **time line** *(see below)* can also be used to collect and arrange details.

✱ Find examples of graphic organizers that can help in gathering and organizing details for writing on PE pages 548–549 and TE pages 800–804.

Have students find notes in Reece's time chart that focus on the five senses. Next, ask them to identify notes that reflect personal feelings. Finally, have them find dialogue.

Try It Answers

Answers will vary.

Writing
Developing Your First Draft

As students read or listen to Reece's draft, have them note particular strengths or weaknesses. Have students keep these questions in mind:

- How well is Reece following his goals for writing?
- What are the strong and weak points in Reece's draft?

Have students begin a list of the events from the first page of Reece's draft in the order in which they happened. Working from the draft to a list of events will help students see the relationship between a planning chart or list and a draft. A sample list follows:

1. Reece's mom said he had to turn twelve before he could get a pet.
2. Reece and his mom went to the Humane Society.
3. A woman let Reece and his mom in.

Writing Developing Your First Draft

Reece sat down to write his story. He used the ideas he had gathered and organized in his chart. His head was full of thoughts, and he wanted to get them all down on paper. (There are errors in Reece's first draft.)

> The story starts with the problem and dialogue.

"For the last time Reece you can get your own dog when you turn twelve, and not a moment before" Mom said. She set down my plate of hot pancakes.

That was disappointing to me.

A week later, my moment arrived. In exactly thirty seconds, the humane society would open. Mom stood beside me.

> Details help create a clear picture.

"I hope they have the one I want," I said. I even knew his name: Russet. I had imagined the perfect dog. He'd be a retreiver puppy with a tale that wouldn't quit wagging. He'd be standing up at the gate of his cage, yipping. We'd know we were meant for each other. "Come on its a minute past!"

> Dialogue moves the action along.

"Reece!"

The door was unlocked by a nice lady who came up to the other side of the door. I waited, and then I opened the door. I said "Good morning mam. We need a dog."

She said, "Why don't you go have a look."

English Language Learners

If students aren't familiar with the Humane Society, explain that it is an organization that rescues unwanted animals, takes care of them, and tries to find them a new home.

prewrite EDIT *write publish*
revise
One Writer's Process

15

PROCESS

> "Thanks!" I moved around the lady. I went to the door. The room beyond had cages. The moment my foot hit the cement, barking filled the air. There must have been thirty dogs in there. But which one was Russet?
>
> The first dog was little. He growled at me. "I don't want you, either," I said and moved on. Next was a cute mutt. I kept going. Another dog and another, but where was my retriever?
>
> I wandered the whole place twice. There wasn't a single retriever. I couldn't believe it. Maybe I missed it. After all, a puppy would be pretty small. While the dogs yapped, I searched their eyes. None of them was right.
>
> "Have you decided?" Mom asked.
>
> "He's not here, Mom!" I said. "I can't believe it. After all this waiting." Then I saw him! His outside was wrong, but his eyes were right. . . .

Details appear in time order.

Tension builds: What will happen?

 On page 13, Reece used a time chart to decide what he would say first, next, and last. Does his first draft follow this chart? Does he add any new details or leave any out? Explain.

Help students note strengths and weaknesses in Reece's first draft by asking these questions:

- What do you like about Reece's draft?
- What don't you like about Reece's draft?
- How well do the features pointed out in the side notes work?

Tell students to continue their chronological list of events while reading the second page of Reece's draft. A sample list of events follows:

1. Reece entered the Humane Society and saw at least 30 dogs.
2. Reece looked over all the dogs, but none looked right to Reece.
3. Finally, Reece spotted Russet.

 Answers

The first draft generally follows the notes in the time chart.

Reece added some details: more dialogue, description of Reece's actions, *pancakes, a week later,* dog's name, description of what dog would look like and how he would behave, details about the kennel, details about Reece's feelings.

Reece left out some details: did not give breeds and descriptions of dogs—*little, white terrier; shepherd with droopy look; big old basset.*

English Language Learners

Be sure to explain the meanings of the American idioms appearing in the draft.

Idioms on pages 14 and 15 include the following:

- go have a look (go inside and look around to see what you can find)
- the moment my foot hit the cement (as soon as I entered the room)
- moved on (continued to walk)
- pretty small (very small)

Revising

Focusing on the Big Picture

Point out that Reece began revising by focusing on only three traits, the three that relate most closely to his ideas and how to get them across effectively. Explain that trying to revise for everything at once is too hard to do. Students will have an easier time revising if they break up the task.

 Answers

Answers will vary.

Encourage students to be specific in their suggestions for improvements. As a special challenge, ask students to implement the changes they think will improve Reece's draft. For example, if students think there should be a clearer description of the dogs or more dialogue in Reece's draft, have partners rewrite the paragraph and include details that they imagine.

Revising   Focusing on the Big Picture

After Reece finished his first draft, he looked again at the goals on page 12 and used them as a revising guide. His thoughts tell you what changes he plans to make.

Ideas

Use details and dialogue to tell about a specific experience or event. Make the reader want to know what happens next.

> "My overall idea is good, but I left out some important details from my time chart. I'll add some of those details."

Organization

Open with a clear beginning that pulls the reader into the story. Then present ideas in the order in which they happened.

> "I shouldn't tell Russet's name before I describe him. I'll move that part."

Voice

Write the story in a way that sounds natural—like the real you. Give the people in your narrative voice, too.

> "I could reword a few of my sentences so they sound more like me."

 Team up with a partner to review Reece's first draft. Write down at least two things that you like about the draft and one or two things that could be improved.

English Language Learners

Use a picture to help illustrate the idiom *the big picture*. Draw a simple scene and explain what the whole picture is about. Point to one element of the picture and explain that this is one detail of the picture, but it is not the whole picture. Relate the picture to a piece of writing: the whole piece of writing gives a main or overall idea. The parts of the writing, for example, individual words or punctuation, are not the whole piece of writing.

To focus on the big picture, Reece is planning to make changes that help readers understand his main idea: that he has enough details, that the information is organized in a sensible way, and that the writing sounds natural. Later, he will focus on some of the smaller parts.

Struggling Learners

If any students have difficulty evaluating Reece's draft, provide them with the following questions to structure their review:

- Is the order of events clear?
- Is it clear who is speaking throughout the dialogue portions of the essay?
- Does the writer make his feelings known?

Reviewing Reece's First Revision

After Reece reviewed his first draft, he made the following revisions, or changes.

Reece adds dialogue to make his essay more interesting.

"For the last time Reece you can get your own

dog when you turn twelve, and not a moment before"
    She repeated, "Not a moment before!"
Mom said. She set down my plate of hot pancakes. ∧
    "And not a moment after."
~~That was disappointing to me.~~
                At last I was twelve years old.
A week later, my moment arrived. ∧ In exactly

thirty seconds, the humane society would open.
        "Just hold on."
Mom stood beside me. ∧

To improve the essay, details are added, moved, and cut.

    "I hope they have the one I want," I said. I even

knew his name: Russet. I had imagined the perfect

dog. He'd be a retreiver puppy with a tale that

wouldn't quit wagging. He'd be standing up at the

gate of his cage, yipping. We'd know we were meant

for each other. "Come on its a minute past!" ∧

    "Reece!"
            Finally,
~~The door was unlocked by~~ a nice lady ~~who came~~
        unlocked ∧
~~up to the other side of~~ the door. I waited . . . ∧

The voice is improved by rewriting a boring sentence.

 Review Reece's changes. Find an idea or a detail that he added, one that he cut, one that he moved, and one that he rewrote.

Reviewing Reece's First Revision

In the first part of the draft, Reece made a number of changes. He moved some sentences around, added some details, and pruned some unnecessary thoughts. Teach students the acronym *MAP*:

<u>m</u>ove
<u>a</u>dd
<u>p</u>rune

This will come in handy when they revise. Remind them to ask themselves, "Have I *MAP*'d my first draft?"

TryIT **Answers**

Possible answers:

Added: his mother's dialogue in the first paragraph; *At last I was twelve years old;* Mom's dialogue, *"Just hold on."*

Cut (or pruned): *That was disappointing to me.*

Moved: reference to his dog's name

Rewrote: the first sentence in the last paragraph on this page

---

Revising

Using a Peer Response Sheet

Have students work in pairs or as a class to fill out a peer response sheet on Reece's revised story. Tell them to focus only on his ideas, the organization, and his voice.

Afterward, have the pairs or the class compare their work to the peer response sheet on this page. Point out that Chiara did not just say, "It was good." She pointed out effective techniques and requested specific details. Suggest to students that, when possible, they should pose their suggested changes as questions so that their comments sound less critical. Offer specific questions that students can ask to help their classmates revise:

- What else happened at the beginning?
- Can you tell more about that?
- What was the speaker doing?
- How do these two events relate?

 Answers

Answers will vary.

Revising Using a Peer Response Sheet

One of Reece's classmates read his story. She used a rubric like the one on pages 130–131 and spotted more places that could use improvements. Reece's classmate wrote her comments on a "Peer Response Sheet."

> ### Peer Response Sheet
>
> Writer: _Reece King_   Responder: _Chiara Davidson_
>
> Title: _"Looking at the Inside"_
>
> What I liked about your writing:
>
> * _You start right in the middle of the action._
>
> * _I like your voice. You sure wanted a dog._
>
> * _You use real-sounding dialogue._
>
> Changes I would suggest:
>
> * _Add a few details in the beginning._
>
> * _I'd like to know what kind of retriever you want._
>
> * _Sometimes, tell what the speakers are doing when_
>
>   _they say something._

 Review the classmate's suggestions for improvements listed above. Which one do you think is the most important? Explain. Also add one suggestion of your own. Focus on the ideas, organization, and voice in the writing.

prewrite **EDIT** *write* *publish*
revise

19

One Writer's Process

PROCESS

Revising with a Peer Response

Using the comments made by his classmate, Reece revised his story again. The new details and quotations he used filled out his narrative.

> *Give more details in the beginning.*
>
> "For the last time Reece you can get your own
>
> dog when you turn twelve, and not a moment before"
>
> Mom said. She set down my plate of hot pancakes.
>
> She repeated, "Not a moment before!"
> *I started to spread the butter.*
> ∧"And not a moment after."
> *It was Saturday, April 24 2004.*
> A week later, my moment arrived.∧At last I
>
> was twelve years old. In exactly thirty seconds, the
> *her hand on my shoulder.*
> humane society would open. Mom stood beside me, ∧
>
> "Just hold on."
>
> "I hope they have the one I want," I said. I had
> *golden*
> imagined the perfect dog. He'd be a∧retreiver puppy
>
> with a tale that wouldn't quit wagging. He'd be
>
> standing up at the gate of his cage, yipping. We'd
>
> know we were meant for each other. I even knew his
> *I said, knocking on the door.*
> name: Russet. "Come on its a minute past!"∧
> *Mom pulled me back.*
> "Reece!"∧. . .

> *Tell what kind of retriever.*

> *Tell what Mom was doing.*

 Have you ever used peer responding during a writing assignment? Discuss the experience with your classmates. Consider why peer responding is (or could be) helpful.

Advanced Learners

Point out that newspaper columnists frequently include their e-mail addresses for reader feedback. Bring newspapers in and have students work in pairs to compose a note to one such columnist explaining that they are studying the writing process. Have them ask whether or not the columnist seeks peer review before submitting an article for publication.

Revising with a Peer Response

Try It **Answers**

Answers will vary.

Students may note that their peers make unkind comments or do not offer specific ideas for making improvements. Validate their frustrations and discuss how giving an effective response is also a skill that must be learned, and remind them that students will improve with more practice. Students will learn more about peer responding later in the unit (PE pages 29–32).

 **Revising**
Focusing on Words and Sentences

To help students focus on word choice and sentence fluency, have them turn to the rubric on PE pages 130–131. Read through the two relevant rows with students so that they will better understand what to look for as they read Reece's draft.

 Answers

Answers will vary.

Revising Focusing on Words and Sentences

Once Reece had finished revising his ideas, organization, and voice, he began checking the style of his writing. He thought about what he had written and considered what he should change to make everything sound more effective.

Word Choice

Use specific nouns, vivid verbs, and well-chosen modifiers.

"Some of my words are kind of dull. I'll choose stronger nouns and verbs."

Sentence Fluency

Use a variety of sentence styles that flow smoothly from one idea to the next.

"Some parts are choppy. I'll put some sentences together and use transitions."

Try It Team up with a partner to review Reece's revised writing on page 19 for style. Identify two nouns, verbs, or adjectives that could be more specific, vivid, or colorful. Then find one or two sentences that could be improved.

English Language Learners

Students' vocabulary may be too limited to come up with many replacement words. Pair them with a helpful peer for this activity. Suggest that they make clusters to find new words, putting the dull word in the center and using a dictionary or thesaurus to add more lively words around it.

Struggling Learners

Break down the **Try It** activity for struggling learners. Have them search for one set of words at a time. Then have them consider which of these words could be replaced by more specific, vivid, or colorful synonyms.

PROCESS

Checking Reece's Improvements in Style

Reece's next step was to concentrate on the style or sound of his ideas. He paid special attention to the effectiveness of the words and the sentences.

> The word choice is improved, and choppy sentences are combined.

"For the last time Reece you can get your

own dog when you turn twelve, and not a moment

before" Mom ~~said~~. *snapped* She set down my plate of hot

pancakes, ~~She~~ repeated, "Not a moment before!" *and*

I started to spread the butter. "And not

a moment after."

A week later, my moment arrived. It was

Saturday, April 24 2004 *and* At last I was twelve years

old. In exactly thirty seconds, the humane society

would open *its doors* Mom stood beside me, her hand on my

shoulder, "Just hold on."

"I hope they have the one I want," I said. *Over the last five months,* I had

imagined the perfect dog. He'd be a golden retriever

puppy with a tale that wouldn't quit wagging. He'd

be standing up at the gate of his cage, yipping.

The moment our eyes would meet,

We'd know we were meant for each other. . . .

> Words are added at the beginning of sentences to vary the sentence style.

 Compare your comments about the style of Reece's writing (page 20) with the changes he actually made. How are they alike or different?

Checking Reece's Improvements in Style

Before students read this page, tell them that Reece decided to come up with a stronger verb than *said* in the speaker tag, *Mom said. . .* in the third line. Ask them to look at PE page 19 and predict what word Reece might have used instead.

Ask students to generate a list of verbs that can replace *said*. Compile the list on chart paper and post it in the classroom where students can refer to it as they write. Encourage students to add to it throughout the year. Words that could replace *said* include *whispered, confided, screamed, snickered, mumbled, muttered, called,* and *scolded.*

Point out that Reece added **transitions** (*see below*) to make his writing smoother. He connected the date to his birthday with *and* and he added a signal for time (*over the last five months*).

 **Answers**

Answers will vary.

Teaching Tip: Transitions

Transitions show how ideas are related. Use transitions to show location, time, comparison, contrast, and more. A writer may use transitions to connect and combine sentences for clarity, variety, and fluency. Refer to the lists on PE pages 572–573 for examples of transitions. Ask students to write pairs of related sentences and use a transition to combine each pair. Begin with this example: *Johanna finished her homework. Johanna went to basketball practice.* Point out that the sentences are short and choppy, and, without a transition, it is unclear in what order the events take place. Students may combine the two sentences using a transition word that shows a time relationship: *After Johanna finished her homework, she went to basketball practice.*

Editing **Checking for Conventions**

Before reading the Editing checklist, ask students to work together in groups to think of common convention errors. List ideas on the board or chart paper. Title the list *Common Convention Errors*.

Have them group and categorize the convention errors they have listed. Lead them to discover the following categories: punctuation, capitalization, spelling, and grammar.

Post the charts in the room and compare the lists. Have the class work together to compile the lists on one master chart.

 Answers

Possible answers:
- commas around *Reece* in first sentence
- end punctuation in first sentence
- delete period after *pancakes*
- comma in date, April 24,
- numbers 12 and 30
- capitalization in Humane Society
- spelling of *retriever* and *tail*

22

Editing **Checking for Conventions**

Once Reece was pleased with the way his story sounded, he checked his work for conventions. (Conventions deal with the rules for correct punctuation, capitalization, spelling, and grammar.)

Conventions

Be sure that your punctuation, capitalization, spelling, and grammar are correct.

> *"Spelling and punctuation are tough. I'll ask a classmate to help me catch everything."*

For help with writing rules, Reece turned to the "Proofreader's Guide" in the back of his *Write Source* book. He also used a checklist to help him look for errors.

Editing Checklist

PUNCTUATION
- _____ **1.** Do I use end punctuation after all my sentences?
- _____ **2.** Do I use commas correctly?
- _____ **3.** Do I use apostrophes to show possession (*boy's bike*)?

CAPITALIZATION
- _____ **4.** Do I start all my sentences with capital letters?
- _____ **5.** Do I capitalize all proper nouns?

SPELLING
- _____ **6.** Have I spelled all my words correctly?
- _____ **7.** Have I double-checked words my spell checker might miss?

GRAMMAR
- _____ **8.** Do I use correct forms of verbs (*had gone*, not *had went*)?
- _____ **9.** Do my subjects and verbs agree in number?
- _____ **10.** Do I use the right word (*to, too, two*)?

 Team up with a partner. Using the checklist above, find two or three errors in Reece's revised draft on page 21.

Checking Reece's Editing for Conventions

Before writing a final copy, Reece checked his narrative for spelling, punctuation, capitalization, and grammar errors. (See the inside back cover of this book for a list of the common editing and proofreading marks.)

Punctuation mistakes are fixed.

"For the last time, Reece, you can get your

own dog when you turn ~~twelve~~ 12, and not a moment

before," Mom snapped. She set down my plate of

hot pancakes and repeated, "Not a moment before!"

I started to spread the butter. "And not a

moment after."

Use of numbers is corrected.

A week later, my moment arrived. It was

Saturday, April 24, 2004, and at last I was ~~twelve~~ 12

years old. In exactly ~~thirty~~ 30 seconds, the humane

Capitalization errors are corrected.

society would open its doors. Mom stood beside

me, her hand on my shoulder, "Just hold on."

"I hope they have the one I want," I said. Over

the last five months, I had imagined the perfect

Spelling and usage errors are corrected.

dog. He'd be a golden (retriever) retriever puppy with a ~~tale~~ tail

that wouldn't quit wagging. He'd be standing . . .

 Review Reece's editing for conventions in the paragraphs above. Did you find some of the same errors when you reviewed page 21?

PROCESS

Checking Reece's Editing for Conventions

Before students look at Reece's work on this page, review the editing and proofreading marks on the inside back cover of the pupil edition. If editing marks are new to students, provide some practice for them by writing the following sentences on the board. Ask volunteers to mark them with the proper editing marks:

- At one time, dogs were the most popular kind of pet.
- Cats are now the most popular.
- Do you like cats or dogs better?
- I (usualy) *usually* have liked cats better.

Then check students' recognition of the marks as they are used in Reece's paper on pages 21 and 23.

 **Answers**

Answers will vary.

Advanced Learners

Point out that there is one type of punctuation used in Reece's narrative that is not mentioned in the Editing checklist. Challenge advanced learners to identify this type of punctuation and compose one more checklist question to address it. (Possible response: Do I use quotation marks to set apart dialogue?)

Publishing Sharing Your Writing

Whether students are writing or keyboarding their final copy, it is important that they know how to format their work for effective presentation. Explain to them your own formatting requirements at this time as well.

As a fun way to get students to focus on the specifics involved in making a final copy, have them work in groups to create a presentation of the tips provided on this page. They should also include any of your formatting preferences.

Some creative ideas include: a talk show, a talk radio program, a TV commercial, a rap song, or a video.

Publishing Sharing Your Writing

Reece used the tips below to help him write the final copy of his story. (See pages **25–26**.)

Focus on Presentation

Tips for Handwritten Copies

- Use blue or black ink and write neatly.
- Write your name following your teacher's instructions.
- Skip a line and center your title; skip another line and start your writing.
- Indent every paragraph and leave a one-inch margin on all four sides.
- Write your last name and page number on every page after page 1.

Reece King

King 2

Looking at the Inside

"For the last time, Reece, you can get your own dog when you turn 12, and not a moment before," Mom snapped. She set down my plate of hot pancakes and repeated, "Not a moment before!"

I started to spread the butter. "And not a moment after."

A week later, my moment arrived. It was Saturday, April 24, 2004, and at last I was 12 years old. In exactly 30 seconds, the Humane Society would open its doors. Mom stood beside me, her hand on my shoulder. "Just hold on."

"I hope they have the one I want," I said. Over the last five months, I'd imagined the perfect dog. He'd be a golden retriever puppy with a tail that wouldn't quit wagging. He'd be standing up at the gate of his cage, yipping. The moment our eyes would meet, we'd know we were meant for each other. I even knew his name: Russet. "Come on! It's a minute past!" I said, knocking on the door.

"Reece!" Mom pulled me back.

Finally, a nice lady unlocked the door and opened it.

I said, "Good morning, ma'am. We need a dog."

She replied, "Why don't you go have a look?"

"Thanks!" I dodged around the lady and rushed to the door marked "Kennel." The room beyond was lined with cages. The moment my foot hit the cement, barking filled the air. There must have been 30 dogs in there, and all of them were shouting, "Me! Me! Pick me!" But which one was Russet?

Tips for Computer Copies

- Use an easy-to-read font and a 10- or 12-point type size.
- Double-space and leave a one-inch margin around each page.

Reece's Final Copy

Reece felt great about his final story. It really captured the exciting day when he met his closest "friend."

Reece King

Looking at the Inside

"For the last time, Reece, you can get your own dog when you turn 12, and not a moment before," Mom snapped. She set down my plate of hot pancakes and repeated, "Not a moment before!"

I started to spread the butter. "And not a moment after."

A week later, my moment arrived. It was Saturday, April 24, 2004, and at last I was 12 years old. In exactly 30 seconds, the Humane Society would open its doors. Mom stood beside me, her hand on my shoulder. "Just hold on."

"I hope they have the one I want," I said. Over the last five months, I'd imagined the perfect dog. He'd be a golden retriever puppy with a tail that wouldn't quit wagging. He'd be standing up at the gate of his cage, yipping. The moment our eyes would meet, we'd know we were meant for each other. I even knew his name: Russet. "Come on! It's a minute past!" I said, knocking on the door.

"Reece!" Mom pulled me back.

Finally, a nice lady unlocked the door and opened it.

I said, "Good morning, Ma'am. We need a dog."

She replied, "Why don't you go have a look?"

"Thanks!" I dodged around the lady and rushed to the door marked "Kennel." The room beyond was lined with cages. The moment my foot

---

Reece's Final Copy

Students who have used a rubric before can use the rubric on PE pages 130–131 to assess Reece's final copy on PE pages 25–26 before looking at the teacher scores on PE page 27. Students should justify each score they give with an accompanying comment.

If students have not used a rubric to assess a piece of writing, have them read Reece's final copy with his writing goals in mind (PE page 12). Students should work with a partner to discuss how successfully they think Reece achieved those goals.

Advanced Learners

Explain that writers frequently use titles with a "twist" to capture their reader's attention. Ask students to locate text in the essay that refers to the "looking at the inside" twist. Then have them find newspaper and magazine articles that include twists in their titles.

(Example: Firefighter Team Gets Extinguished in Charity Finals)

Have students tell which part of the narrative they like best and why. Ask them to point out two strong verbs, two specific nouns, and two details that add to the enjoyment of the story.

Invite students to comment on the ending. Use the prompt: *What lesson does Reece learn from this experience?* (Sometimes you have to look at what is inside someone rather than what is on the outside.)

King 2

hit the cement, barking filled the air. There must have been 30 dogs in there, and all of them were shouting, "Me! Me! Pick me!" But which one was Russet?

The first dog was a little terrier that growled at me. "I don't want you, either," I said and moved on. Next was a cute mutt. I kept going. A shepherd, a bulldog, a hound—but where was my golden retriever?

I wandered the whole place twice. There wasn't a single retriever. I couldn't believe it. Maybe I missed it. After all, a puppy would be pretty small. While the dogs leaped at their gates and yapped, I searched their eyes. None of them was right.

"Have you decided?" Mom asked, coming up behind me.

"He's not here, Mom!" I said. "I can't believe it. After all this waiting." Suddenly, I saw him. His outside was wrong, but his eyes were right. "Here! This is the one. This is Russet!"

Mom blinked at the puppy. "He's a beagle."

"You're looking at the outside," I said. I stuck my fingers in the cage. Russet bounced up to lick my hand. "You've got to look at his inside. He's the one."

That was the day I met my best friend. On that day, I learned that sometimes you need to look at the inside and not the outside. That beagle mutt sure turned out to be my Russet. I wouldn't trade him for any other dog in the world. And I doubt Russet would trade me for any other kid, either.

Assessing the Final Copy

Reece's teacher used a rubric like the one that appears on pages 130–131 to assess his final copy. A 6 is the very best score that a writer can receive for each trait. The teacher also included comments under each trait.

6 Ideas

What a creative twist, to write about a dog as your best friend! Your use of sensory details and dialogue makes the story so real. Well done.

5 Organization

Your story follows a clear time organization.

6 Voice

I can hear you speaking to me in every line!

5 Word Choice

Your use of strong verbs and specific nouns is good throughout.

4 Sentence Fluency

Though the first page is very smooth, the second page feels a little choppy. A few more transitions could help next time.

6 Conventions

Your story is error free. Great work!

Review the assessment. Do you agree with the comments and scores made by Reece's teacher? Why or why not? Explain your feelings in a brief paragraph.

Assessing the Final Copy

Have students compare their assessment of the final draft from PE page 25 with the teacher's assessment on this page. Encourage students to also compare their assessments with those of their peers.

- Is your assessment similar to the teacher's assessment?
- On what traits does your assessment differ?
- Where do your scores differ from those of your classmates?

As a class, review and discuss the rubric on PE pages 130–131 for any trait on which there is disagreement. Is it possible to make the scores consistent with each other?

Reflecting on Your Writing

Emphasize that writers need to think about their work even after they complete a final copy. Reflecting on their writing is a good way for students to focus on how to improve in the future.

Reflecting on Your Writing

After the whole process was finished, Reece filled out a reflection sheet. This helped him think about the assignment and plan for future narrative writing.

Reece King

My Personal Narrative

1. **The best part of my narrative is . . .**
   the voice. Even Mrs. Wilson says so. She said she can hear my voice in every line. That's great. Mrs. Wilson says that the voice is the personality in the writing.

2. **The part that still needs work is . . .**
   sentence fluency. I should have combined a few choppy sentences on the second page.

3. **The main thing I learned about writing a personal narrative is . . .**
   it's a process. If I'd quit after the first draft, my story never would've been what I wanted.

4. **In my next narrative, I would like to . . .**
   write about people instead of dogs.

5. **Here is one question I still have about writing a narrative:**
   What's the difference between a personal narrative and a story?

English Language Learners

Students may be confused by this usage of *reflection*. Point out that this word has more than one meaning. They will probably know the more common meaning of *reflection*—an image of oneself, as in a mirror. Point out that the intended meaning of *reflection* in this context is "a way of looking back and thinking about something."

Peer Responding

Dancers practice in front of mirrors to see how well they are dancing. Writers don't have mirrors to tell them how well they are writing. To see their work from another angle, writers need the opinions of readers.

How do readers know what to look for in writing? One way is to use a rubric. A rubric can help them focus on the right traits at the right time. And how can readers share their reactions and suggestions? They can use a response sheet to organize comments, or simply talk about the writing in a group.

In this chapter, you will learn how to share your writing—and how to respond to the work of others. You'll do your reacting on paper and in small groups. Either way, a careful peer response can be just what a writer needs to improve a piece of writing.

Mini Index

- **Basic Rules of Peer Responding**
- **Writing-Group Guidelines**

Peer Responding

Objectives
- learn the basic rules of peer responding
- study guidelines for the author and the responder in peer-responding sessions

Ask students to consider how sports or hobbies are judged or rated in games, tournaments, or shows. Prompt students by asking:
- Do you think the way your favorite sport or hobby is judged or refereed is fair?
- What would you change?

The judging system used in figure skating is one set of criteria that might be used as an example. Instant replay in football is another possible topic that you could raise. Follow the discussion by asking students to read the unit introduction on this page.

Basic Rules of Peer Responding

Address the class as if they were writers to show good and bad peer response. First, give positive feedback in very general terms: *This was so good! You are a great writer!* Then criticize weaknesses and offer no helpful suggestions: *This was boring! I don't get it.*

Ask:
- How did the positive (negative) feedback make you feel?
- How helpful is this feedback?

Next, cite specific strengths: *You used lots of dialogue and strong action verbs to make the story exciting. I was caught right away by your opening paragraph.* Cite weaknesses and offer suggestions: *Could you use transitions to combine some sentences to make them flow more smoothly? What were you feeling at the end of the story?*

Encourage students to respond to each other specifically and respectfully when they review each others' writing.

Using a Response Sheet

 Answers

No answers are required.

Basic Rules of Peer Responding

Learning how to respond well to other people's writing takes planning and practice. Whether you're working with a small group or with one other person, follow the basic rules below.

- **Make a plan.** Decide what steps you will follow for reading and responding to the piece of writing. (Find out about the assignment, review the rubric, read the piece once through, and so on.)
- **Listen and cooperate.** Encourage the writer by listening carefully and making positive suggestions.
- **Respond with respect.** Focus on the writing, not the writer, and think before you respond.

Using a Response Sheet

One of the best ways to react to someone else's writing is to complete a response sheet.

 As you read the following paragraphs about a special childhood object, focus on the writer's strengths and weaknesses. Then read the sample response sheet shown on the next page.

My Best Friend

Elmo is not a fancy guy, but he would definitely stand out in a crowd. His whole body is red, except for an orange, bulb-shaped nose and a pair of golf-ball-shaped eyes with black pupils. His hands have a few gigantic fingers, his feet have no toes, and his mouth spreads across his face in a huge smile. Staying in fashion has never been a problem for Elmo, because he doesn't wear clothes.

His voice sounds something like mine, but it's higher. It really gets shrill when I tickle him and he laughs. He can even sing, and his favorite tune is the "A, B, C" song. These days, he talks and sings less than he used to. Elmo doesn't have ears.

respect cooperate SHARE react **31**
comment
Peer Responding

Peer Responding

Point out to students that the responder should complete the Peer Response Sheet in writing so that the writer will have a record of the suggestions and comments as he or she revises the draft.

PROCESS

Peer Response Sheet

A classmate responded to the writing on the previous page using the following plan.

1 First he read the writing to get the overall picture.

2 Next he read the piece again, focusing on its strengths and weaknesses.

3 Then he filled out a response sheet.

Peer Response Sheet

Writer: _Lien_   Responder: _Dean_

Title: _"My Best Friend"_

What I liked about your writing:

* You were brave to write about Elmo. Lots of us liked him when we were little, but we don't admit it now.

* You have lots of details telling how Elmo looks, sounds, and feels. Nice job!

* Your voice is friendly and funny. It fits the subject.

Changes I would suggest:

* At the end of the second paragraph, the fact that Elmo doesn't have ears seems out of place.

* The assignment asked you to tell why the object was important to you. Add why you care about Elmo.

Practice. Exchange a recent piece of writing with a classmate.

1 Read the writing once to get an overall feel for it.

2 Then read it again, focusing on what you like and what you might improve.

3 Fill out a response sheet like the one above.

Writing-Group Guidelines

The Author's Role

Encourage the author to read the piece aloud to the peer responder(s) so that handwriting and existing editing do not interfere with the responder's understanding of the writing. When students read aloud their own writing, they may discover problems they had not noticed while reading the work silently.

The Responder's Role

Remind students that they must be sensitive to the feelings and efforts of the author. Point out that the responder will also take the author's role and should offer the kind of help he or she wants to receive. Emphasize the importance of giving positive and specific feedback.

Students should use two response processes if time permits: an oral review with a partner or group as outlined on this page, and a written revision (using a *Peer Response Sheet*) with a different partner.

Writing-Group Guidelines

You can read your writing out loud to a partner or a group and get immediate feedback. If you've never been in a writing group before, it might be helpful to work with a classmate first. You can take turns practicing the author's and the responder's roles.

The Author's Role

As the author, you need to choose a piece of writing that you want someone to review. The writing can be at any stage in the process. If possible, make a copy for each member of the group. Then follow these guidelines.

- **Provide your readers** with a copy of the rubric you used for your writing.
- **Introduce your writing** but don't say too much.
- **Read your writing out loud** or have people read it silently.
- **Ask others for comments** and listen to what they say.
- **Take notes** to help you remember what was said.
- **Be open and polite** when you explain your writing.
- **Ask your group for help** with any writing problems.

The Responder's Role

As the responder, you need to show interest and respect. Follow these guidelines.

- **Review the rubric** for the form of writing you are responding to so that you will know what to listen for.
- **Listen carefully and take notes** to help you remember what you want to say.
- **Ask questions** if you are confused about something or want to know more.
- **Tell what works well** in the writing.
- **Tell what needs to be improved** by politely making specific suggestions.

Remember, don't just say, "Everything is great."

Understanding the

Traits of Writing

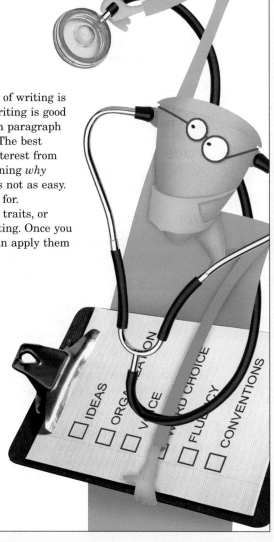

conventions ideas *sentence fluency* **VOICE** *organization* *word choice* 33

How can you tell if a piece of writing is good? One way is very easy: Writing is good when it keeps you reading from paragraph to paragraph. It's that simple. The best stories and essays hold your interest from start to finish. However, explaining *why* something keeps you reading is not as easy. You need to know what to look for.

This chapter identifies the traits, or qualities, found in all good writing. Once you understand these traits, you can apply them to everything you write.

Mini Index

Understanding the Traits of Writing

Objectives

- understand the six traits of writing: ideas, organization, voice, word choice, sentence fluency, conventions
- choose a good topic, use details to hold interest, create a strong beginning and ending, organize the middle part, and write with a natural voice
- choose specific nouns and verbs, improve sentence fluency and style, and use correct conventions

Before students read PE page 33, have them discuss this question:
- What makes a story good?

Introducing the Traits

Have students make a review sheet to help them learn the traits.

1. Fold a piece of paper into thirds horizontally like a business letter. Then fold the thirds in half in the same direction. You will end up with a folded piece of paper $8\frac{1}{2}$" $\times$ $1\frac{3}{4}$."

2. Now unfold the paper and fold it in half lengthwise. When you unfold the paper, you will have two columns of six boxes each.

3. Cut along the left column horizontal creases as far as the vertical fold to make flaps. *(See the diagram below.)*

4. Glue the back of the uncut right column to a piece of construction paper to make it sturdier.

5. Place the organizer on the desk, close the flaps, and label the front of each flap from top to bottom as follows: *Ideas, Organization, Voice, Word Choice, Fluency,* and *Conventions*. Use one color for the first three traits, and use a second color for the last three traits.

As students study each trait on PE pages 34–44, they can lift the trait flap and take brief notes in the blank spaces to create a handy review sheet.

Introducing the Traits

There are six main traits, or qualities, found in writing. You will do your best work if you keep these traits in mind when you write. This page introduces the traits. The next 10 pages provide a closer look at each one.

Ideas

Excellent writing has a clear message, purpose, or focus. The writing contains plenty of specific ideas and details.

Organization

Effective writing has a clear beginning, middle, and ending. The overall writing is well organized and easy to follow.

Voice

The best writing reveals the writer's voice—his or her special way of saying things.

Word Choice

Good writing contains strong words, including specific nouns and verbs. The words fit the audience and deliver a clear message.

Sentence Fluency

Effective writing flows smoothly from one sentence to the next. Sentences vary in length and begin in a variety of ways.

Conventions

Good writing is carefully edited to make sure it is easy to understand. The writing follows the rules for punctuation, grammar, and spelling.

One additional trait to consider is the **presentation** of your writing. Good writing looks neat and follows guidelines for margins, spacing, indenting, and so on. The way the writing looks on the page attracts the reader and makes him or her *want* to read on.

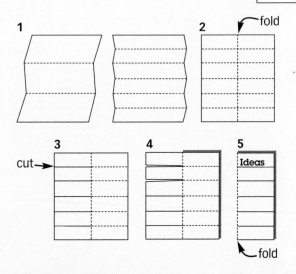

Advanced Learners

Have students choose a favorite author and freewrite for five or ten minutes about why they like that author's writing. Ask them to concentrate on what the author does to make them want to keep reading.

conventions ideas *sentence fluency*
VOICE *organization* *word choice* **35**
Traits of Writing

PROCESS

Understanding Ideas

Nothing is more important than having great ideas in your writing. Just as a chef needs the best ingredients to make a delicious meal, a writer needs quality ideas to create a strong story or essay.

What is the key to good writing?

Good writing starts with a well-chosen topic or main idea—one that interests you and works well for your assignment. You must really care about a writing topic and know your audience.

What makes a writing topic good?

Effective writing topics provide the right amount of information for your assignments.

Sample Assignment: Recall an experience in which you learned something.

Possible Topics

- **Too Broad**   Things I've learned from Great-grandma
- **Too Narrow**   Last night's e-mail message from Great-grandma
- **Just Right**   A memorable afternoon with Great-grandma

How should I write about a topic?

Good writing has a clear focus. It identifies a certain part of a topic or a feeling you have about it. Notice how the following statement brings a clear focus to the topic.

> **Focus statement:** *A memorable afternoon with Great-grandma* (topic) *taught me about her experiences in school* (a certain part).

 Practice choosing a good topic and a clear focus by following these directions: *Recall the hardest thing you have ever done. Then write a focus statement about this topic.* (Use the information on this page as a guide for your work.)

Understanding Ideas

Students open up the flap labeled *Ideas* and take bulleted notes on the inside left-hand side after reading these pages. Model this on an overhead projector by doing a **think aloud** *(see below)* with the first shaded paragraph (example: *chef needs good ingredients, writer needs quality ideas*). Remind students to use phrases instead of full sentences.

Students should continue their note-taking on the right-hand inside flap as needed.

Encourage students to design an icon to help them remember ideas. One idea might be a light bulb. They might add it to the labeled flap if space permits.

Try It Answers

Answers will vary.

Teaching Tip: Think Alouds

A think aloud is a way to model a thought process. By verbalizing what you are thinking, you can help students learn how to think through a problem for themselves.

English Language Learners

A hands-on activity may help students to understand the term *focus* as it applies to writing. Use a pair of binoculars or a camera to demonstrate. Have each student adjust the lens so that the view is clear, or "in focus." Then relate the concept to writing. A writer must think of a topic and then put it "into focus" by expressing it in one clear statement. Provide a simple example by working with students to repeat the exercise in the pupil edition, narrowing a topic and then creating a clear focus statement.

Ask students to suggest details (facts, statistics, examples, thoughts, and feelings) about this prompt: *What is it like to be a student at this school?* List their ideas on the board.

Then ask each student to write a paragraph in response to the prompt and to use some of these details and/or ideas of their own. Ask volunteers to read their paragraphs aloud. Discuss which details make the paragraph enjoyable and/or informative.

 **Answers**

Answers will vary.

36

How can I use details to hold the reader's interest?

Details are what make writing worth reading. Writing that does not have enough details can be boring, like this idea: "Great-grandma told me what things were like when she was growing up." Including details such as facts, statistics, examples, and personal thoughts or feelings would make the idea more interesting. (See the following chart.)

Fact A fact is a detail that can be proved.

> Great-grandma went to school in England.

Statistic A statistic is a fact that uses numbers.

> In Great-grandma's day, nine out of ten boys wore shorts and knee-high socks to school.

Example An example is a detail that supports a fact.

> Great-grandma said her teachers were very strict. (*fact*)
> Students had to recite their lessons at the beginning of each class. If they couldn't, they had to stay after school. (*supporting example*)

Thoughts/Feelings Thoughts and feelings are the writer's own ideas and attitude about the topic.

> Each morning, Great-grandma had to walk two and a half miles to school. (*fact*)
> It must have been a long walk, especially in bad weather. (*personal thought*)

 Choose one of your own narratives or essays or find a news story to review for details. Label any facts, statistics, examples, thoughts, or feelings that you find. (If the writing is long, label just the first few paragraphs.)

conventions ideas *sentence fluency*
VOICE *organization* *word choice* **37**
Traits of Writing

Understanding Organization

Effective writing is built on a strong foundation, with a clearly developed beginning, middle, and ending. In addition, the details in a well-written essay or report follow a specific method of organization.

How can I write a strong beginning?

In the best essays, the beginning paragraph does two things. It (1) gets the reader's attention and (2) identifies the topic and focus of the paper. Here are several ways to get the reader's attention and introduce a topic.

Present interesting information about your topic.

When I perform a front wheelie on my stunt bike, people always say it looks easy.

Make a surprising statement.

I practiced the fox hop on my stunt bike hundreds of times before I got it right.

Ask a question.

Have you ever wished you could fly?

Share a brief story about the topic.

The very first time I rode a stunt bike, I hit a rut and broke my arm in two places.

Sample Beginning

The beginning paragraph below starts with a surprising statement. It then gives background information and states the topic.

I couldn't stand my front teeth! The rest of my face was fine—long brown hair, green eyes, freckled cheeks, and a dimpled chin. Unfortunately, when I smiled, all people saw were my crooked teeth. A week later, all they saw were my shiny new braces.

 Share a strong beginning from something you have written or read. Explain how the beginning gets the reader's interest.

Understanding Organization

Tell students to open the flap on their review sheet labeled *Organization* and take bulleted notes on the inside left-hand side after reading PE pages 37–39. Do a think aloud to model the process for bulleted notes using the pink-shaded paragraph. Remind students to use phrases instead of full sentences.

Example:
- effective writing—strong foundation
- clear beginning, middle, ending
- well-organized details

Encourage students to design an icon to illustrate organization. Have students share their designs and add their own icon to the labeled flap if space permits. Common icons for organization are: a brick wall, a jigsaw puzzle, an outline, and a hamburger (top bun = beginning, meat = the middle, and bottom bun = the ending).

 **Answers**

Answers will vary.

Discuss with the class which method of organization would work best for a few sample topics.

Begin with these ideas for topics:
- a history of trains (chronological order)
- a description of the Eiffel Tower (location)
- what you want to spend your allowance on (order of importance)
- how a pet can improve your life (logical order or categories).

Have students suggest their own topics and brainstorm how they could best organize details when writing about them.

 **Answers**

Answers will vary.

38

How can I organize details in the middle part?

The way the details are organized depends on the form of the writing. (Also see pages 534–537 and 550–551.)

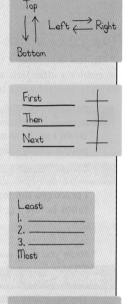

DESCRIPTIVE

Organize details by *location*.

At the top of my closet, **you will find boxes of shoes and sweaters lining the shelf.** Below the shelf **is the clothes bar. Clothes are crammed together in this space.** On the floor, **there are piles of shoes and games that I just toss in.**

NARRATIVE

Organize details *chronologically* (in time order).

First **the orthodontist jammed metal bands around my molars.** Then **he glued sharp little squares of steel to all of my front teeth.** Next **he attached little wires to the squares.**

PERSUASIVE

Organize details by *order of importance*.

First of all, **letting students wear regular clothes saves money.** Second, **it sends the proper message.** Third, **and most importantly, it helps students become more responsible.**

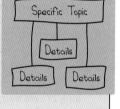

EXPOSITORY

Organize details by *logical order* or *categories*.

What can we do to save our environment? First of all, **we must stop littering.** In addition, **we must promote recycling.** Equally important, **we must reuse materials whenever possible.**

 Complete a graphic organizer and write a short passage following one of the methods of organization above. Your writing should include at least three or four sentences.

For additional practice, ask students to think of appropriate methods of organization for essays or narratives about these topics:
- giving reasons for wearing seat belts (persuasive)
- recalling a weekend trip (narrative)
- detailing the layout of an amusement park (descriptive)
- giving information about after-school programs (expository)

conventions ideas sentence fluency
VOICE organization *word choice* **39**
Traits of Writing

PROCESS

How can I write a strong ending?

You can write a strong ending paragraph by doing one or more of the following things.

Remind the reader about the paper's focus.

The school board may think study hall is a waste of time, but most students don't. Many of us struggle with our homework load. Without study hall, we'll be that much further behind. Ask your parents to call school board members and tell them to keep study hall.

Review the main points.

There are many things to consider before you make a dog part of your family. To choose the right dog, remember to find out the dog's age and notice its personality. Also remember that choosing to have a pet carries many responsibilities.

Emphasize the importance of one of the main points.

The East Bluff at Devils Lake really is a great stone castle. Climbing the bluff is like attacking a fortress. With a lot of hard work, hikers reach the top. There they are treated to a view fit for a king or a queen.

Say something to keep the reader thinking about the topic.

The next time you see me landing a flip at the bike park, remember that I've carefully assembled my own bike. I know every inch of it. That gives me the confidence to try difficult stunts.

Sample Ending

The paragraph below reminds the reader about the topic and says something to keep the reader thinking.

Now when I look in the mirror, I'm glad I had braces. I use my new smile every day. Unfortunately, after the braces came off, I started to break out. Oh well! Maybe I'll look great by the time I'm 16.

Try IT Share a strong ending from something you have written or read. Explain what types of information are included in this part.

Bringing a piece of writing to a satisfying close is a skill that requires some work. Often, immature writers will simply stop writing or write "the end" when they run out of ideas. To help students appreciate strong endings, try one of these activities:

- Tell a familiar fairy tale ("Little Red Riding Hood" or "The Three Little Pigs") without the ending.
- Read aloud a short book (a picture book will work well), stopping several pages before the end.

Ask students to talk about how effective a story is without its ending. After some discussion, add the ending and have students compare their opinion of the story with and without the ending. Explain that a good ending causes the reader to have a sense of completion and satisfaction with the whole piece of writing.

 **Answers**

Answers will vary.

Understanding Voice

Ask students to open the flap on their review sheet labeled *Voice*. Have them take notes on the information on this page. Move around the room and check to see that students are using phrases and bullets as they record the important points.

Remind students to create an icon for voice. Possible icons are a fingerprint (everyone's voice is unique, as are their fingerprints) or a microphone.

 **Answers**

Answers will vary.

Understanding Voice

> Author Ralph Fletcher says, "Writing that has voice is writing that breathes." Voice gives writing energy and life. It is that special something that makes you say, "Hey, I like how that essay sounds."

How can I write with voice?

If you are truly interested in your topic, your writing will have voice. As writer Donald Graves says, "When a writer makes a good choice of a topic, voice booms through."

> **The writer isn't very interested in the topic, so this writing lacks voice.**
>
> One of my ancestors was born in Rhode Island. She was kidnapped when she was little. That's about all I know.

> **The writer is clearly interested, so this writing has voice.**
>
> I wonder if my great-great-grandma knew what was happening when she was kidnapped. She must have been scared. How did the kidnappers treat her? How was she able to pick up their language so fast?

How can my writing voice sound more natural?

The three tips below will help you write more naturally.

- Keep a personal journal.
- "Talk" to friends and relatives in friendly letters and e-mail messages.
- Begin writing assignments by freely recording your thoughts about your topic.

> **This writing sounds natural.**
>
> When we were walking, I looked up and saw the moon was out. It made the fog seem to glow. Off in the distance, I heard a dog bark and then a chorus of barks. I felt a shiver crawl up my spine. It was probably just the cold.

 Write freely for 5 to 10 minutes about your day so far: *What has happened? How do you feel about what's happened?* Check your writing for voice by underlining words and phrases that sound like the real you.

English Language Learners

Students may have difficulty with the concept of voice. Point out that the language they use in their written work should sound like the language they use when they speak. To practice, invite students to speak on a topic that interests them. Compliment all friendly, animated tones and expressions, saying that you could *hear* in their *voices* the interest they have in their topic. Then have them write one or two sentences using the same "voice."

conventions ideas sentence fluency
VOICE organization *word choice* **41**
Traits of Writing

PROCESS

Understanding Word Choice

Author Cynthia Rylant pays careful attention to word choice. "When I write," Rylant says, "I seek words; I chase after them." She knows that her writing will be only as good as the words that she uses.

What are the most important words?

When you write, every word is important—but your nouns and verbs are the most important. Study the passages below.

GENERAL NOUNS AND VERBS

The boy cried after the accident.
He went to the woman in the room.

SPECIFIC NOUNS AND VERBS

The toddler sobbed after he pinched his finger.
He ran to his mother in the kitchen.

Using Specific Nouns

In the chart below, the first words under each category are general nouns. The second set of words is *more* specific. The third set of words is *very* specific. These very specific nouns are the best ones to use.

PERSON	PLACE	THING	IDEA
woman	monument	food	system
writer	national monument	fruit	government
J. K. Rowling	Statue of Liberty	blueberry	democracy

Using Specific Action Verbs

Specific action verbs can make your writing more vivid. Action verbs like *glared* and *observed* say more than the overused, ordinary verb *looked*.

General verb: **Ms. Lang looked at the noisy students.**
Vivid verb: **Ms. Lang glared at the noisy students.**

 Make a chart like the one above and fill it in with your own nouns (a person, a place, a thing, and an idea). The nouns at the bottom of your chart should be very specific.

Understanding Word Choice

Tell students to open the flap on their review sheets labeled *Word Choice*. Have them take notes as they read this page. Remind students to use bullets and phrases as they record the notes.

Next, have students design an icon to remind them of the importance of word choice and place it on the labeled flap. Possible icons might be: a can of alphabet soup; a dictionary; or a superhero with *Verb/Noun* on his/her shirt, lifting dumbbells to show the idea of using strong words.

One way students can work on word choice is to **improve vocabulary skills** *(see below)*.

 Answers

Answers will vary. If students find it difficult to come up with their own nouns for the *Idea* column, you can make that column optional.

Teaching Tip: Improving Vocabulary Skills

Students can improve their vocabulary by using a variety of techniques: understanding roots and their prefixes and suffixes, using context to determine the meaning of unfamiliar words, recording new words in a vocabulary journal, and using new words in their writing and speaking. An increased vocabulary will give students a wider word choice as they write.

✳ For more information on how students can build their vocabulary skills, see PE pages 562–563.

English Language Learners

English learners may need more practice with specific nouns. Offer a general noun, such as *animal, food,* or *music.* Have students work in pairs to list as many specific nouns as they can.

Understanding
Sentence Fluency

Ask students to open the flap on their review sheet labeled *Sentence Fluency*. Have them take notes on the information on this page. Be sure that students use phrases and bullets as they record the important points.

Remind students to create an icon to represent sentence fluency. Possible icons are a variety pack of cereal or a train with alternating short and long cars of different colors to indicate a variety of sentence lengths and styles.

The more students understand about **sentence structure** *(see below),* the more they will be able to manipulate sentences and affect the flow of their writing.

42

Understanding Sentence Fluency

Good writing is something that you can read without breaking a sweat. The sentences flow naturally, making the writing enjoyable from start to finish.

What does it mean to write fluent sentences?

Sentences are fluent when they flow smoothly from one to the next and follow these guidelines.

- Every sentence is important.
- A reader can easily follow the ideas.
- Short, choppy sentences have been combined to read smoothly.
- Transition words connect the ideas.

How can I improve my sentence style?

You can improve your sentence style by combining choppy sentences into longer, smoother ones. (See pages 512–514.)

SHORT, CHOPPY SENTENCES

Chinwe plans to go hiking. She will go hiking tomorrow.

COMBINING USING A KEY WORD

Chinwe plans to go hiking **tomorrow**.

SHORT, CHOPPY SENTENCES

My lazy cat takes long naps. It naps on top of the TV.

COMBINING USING A PREPOSITIONAL PHRASE

My lazy cat takes long naps **on top of the TV**.

SHORT, CHOPPY SENTENCES

Parnell picked up the flat stone. He examined its strange markings.

COMBINING USING A COMPOUND VERB

Parnell **picked up** the flat stone and **examined** its strange markings.

Teaching Tip: Sentence Structure

Understanding sentence structure will help students improve the variety and fluency of sentences in their writing. Review basic sentence patterns, and have students practice sentence diagramming to help them understand how the parts of a sentence fit together.

＊ For more information about sentence patterns and sen-

tence diagramming, see PE pages 570–571.

conventions ideas *sentence fluency*
VOICE *organization word choice* **43**
Traits of Writing

PROCESS

What else can improve sentence style?

You can improve your sentences by using a variety of beginnings. If too many of your sentences begin in the same way, your writing will sound boring. (Also see page **522**.)

> **TOO MANY SENTENCES BEGINNING IN THE SAME WAY**
>
> William looked at his science project. He picked it up and glued one more piece in place. He set it down. He thought, "Now, I am ready for the science fair."
>
> **VARIED BEGINNINGS**
>
> William looked at his science report. Then he picked it up and glued one more piece in place. After setting it down, he thought, "Now, I am ready for the science fair."

Another way to improve your style is to change the length of your sentences. If too many of your sentences have the same number of words, your writing will sound monotonous.

> **TOO MANY SENTENCES OF THE SAME LENGTH**
>
> Soccer is becoming more popular in the United States. Many schools have started soccer programs. Students are now able to play on organized teams. Soccer is a sport in which both boys and girls can play. They can easily play together on the same teams.
>
> **VARIED LENGTHS**
>
> Soccer is becoming more popular in the United States. Since many schools have started soccer programs, more students are now able to play on organized teams. Both boys and girls can easily play together on the same teams.

 Choose one of your own narratives or essays or find a news story to review for sentence fluency. Do all of the sentences read smoothly? Do they have varied beginnings and lengths? (If the writing is long, review just the first few paragraphs.)

Try It Answers

Answers will vary. Have students note any transitions that are used to combine sentences, resulting in a variety of lengths and structures.

Understanding Conventions

Have students complete their review sheets by jotting notes about the information on PE page 44 under the flap labeled *Conventions*. Be sure that students use phrases and bullets as they record the important points.

Students should design a final icon to represent conventions (punctuation, capitalization, grammar, and spelling). Possible icons are a red pen or a police officer (representing the need to police your work for punctuation, capitalization, grammar, and spelling).

Many students will be overwhelmed by the length of the Editing checklist. Explain that when the time comes to edit a piece of writing, they may read for only two or three conventions at a time. As they progress with their writing, you can point out which conventions they typically have trouble with so they can focus specifically on those areas.

44

Understanding Conventions

Conventions are simply the rules of language. Punctuation, capitalization, grammar, and spelling all have special rules. When you follow these rules, the reader can focus on your ideas instead of being distracted by mistakes.

How can I make sure my writing follows the rules?

A conventions checklist like the one below can guide you as you edit and proofread your writing. When you are not sure about a certain rule, refer to the "Proofreader's Guide." (See pages 579–749.)

Conventions

PUNCTUATION
_____ 1. Do I use end punctuation after all my sentences?
_____ 2. Do I use commas correctly?
_____ 3. Do I use apostrophes to show possession (*boy's bike*)?

CAPITALIZATION
_____ 4. Do I start every sentence with a capital letter?
_____ 5. Do I capitalize the proper names of people and places?

SPELLING
_____ 6. Have I checked my spelling?

GRAMMAR
_____ 7. Do I use correct forms of verbs (*had gone*, not *had went*)?
_____ 8. Do my subjects and verbs agree in number?
_____ 9. Do I use the right words (*to, too, two*)?

English Language Learners

Be aware that students may have additional language issues to address, such as the use of articles, irregular verbs, and pronouns. As they begin to write, help each student identify the specific areas they may need to target.

Struggling Learners

As students learn more about the errors they make, they can customize their Conventions checklist to address those trouble areas each time they edit a piece of writing.

Advanced Learners

Before discussing the Conventions checklist, challenge students to compose a list of punctuation, capitalization, spelling, and grammar rules. Then have them compare their list to the checklist in the pupil edition.

Using a Rubric

How do you become a good athlete? You learn the necessary skills, practice and compete as much as you can, and evaluate each performance. In many ways, that's how you become a good writer, too. You learn the important skills, practice different types of writing, and evaluate each finished product.

This chapter explains a basic skill—using a rubric. **Rubrics** are charts that help you measure or evaluate your writing. This book includes rubrics for four important types of writing. Each rubric is organized according to the traits of writing.

Mini Index

Using a Rubric

Objectives
- understand and read rubrics
- revise, edit, and assess writing using a rubric

Most students are probably familiar with reviewers who rate movies with stars or other objects ("two thumbs up!"). Ask:

- What do movie reviewers consider when deciding on their opinion of a movie? (sample answers: quality of the script, the acting, the pacing of the action)
- How do movie reviewers decide how many stars to give a movie? (They might compare the movie against some standards that they apply to all movies, or they might rate the movie according to how they liked it personally.)

Just as movies have elements, or traits, that the reviewers consider, so does writing. And, just as movie reviewers rate a movie, students can rate a piece of writing. In this chapter, students will learn how to rate a piece of writing by using a rubric, standards against which the class will compare pieces of writing. Ask:

- Have you used a rubric before?
- How would you explain a writing rubric to someone who has never used one?

Understanding Rubrics

Point out that the thermometers are part of the rating guide used in this book. Ask:

- Why is a graphic device helpful in evaluating writing? (It is easier to grasp the meaning of a symbol than it is to read a lengthy description.)

Have students brainstorm things that they can rate or score, such as restaurants, movies, video games, books, or music. Select one idea for which the class will develop a rating guide.

Rating Guide

Work with the class to create a rubric that explains each score in the rating system.

Example: Rate a restaurant with 1 to 4 forks.

- Four forks means exceptional service, delicious food, lovely décor, and great value.
- Three forks means good service, tasty food, nice décor, and reasonable value.
- Two forks means fair service, okay décor, and less-than-average value.
- One fork means poor service, dingy décor, and poor value.

46

Understanding Rubrics

You already rate things in everyday life: "I give this song a 10!" "That movie gets four stars!" You can also rate writing using a rubric. The rubrics in this book rate writing using the following scale.

| 6 Amazing | 5 Strong | 4 Good | 3 Okay | 2 Poor | 1 Incomplete |

Your essays and stories can be rated for each of the main traits of writing—*ideas, organization, voice, word choice, sentence fluency,* and *conventions.* For example, in one of your essays, the ideas may be "strong" and the organization may be "good." That would give you a 5 for ideas and a 4 for organization.

Rating Guide

This guide will help you understand the rating scale.

A **6** means that the writing is truly **amazing**.
It goes way beyond the requirements for a certain trait.

A **5** means that the writing is very **strong**.
It clearly meets the main requirements for a trait.

A **4** means that the writing is **good**.
It meets most of the requirements for a trait.

A **3** means that the writing is **okay**.
It needs work to meet the main requirements for a trait.

A **2** means that the writing is **poor**.
It needs a lot of work to meet the requirements for a trait.

A **1** means that the writing is **incomplete**.
It is not yet ready to assess for a trait.

Reading a Rubric

For the rubrics in this book, each trait has its own color bar (green for *ideas*, pink for *organization*, and so on). There is a description for each rating to help you evaluate for a particular trait.

Rubric for Expository Writing

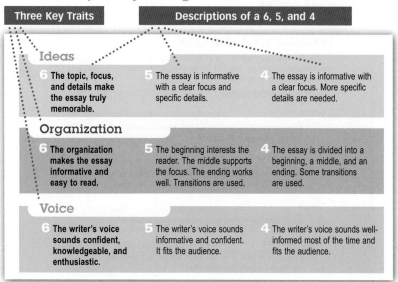

Three Key Traits	Descriptions of a 6, 5, and 4	
Ideas		
6 The topic, focus, and details make the essay truly memorable.	**5** The essay is informative with a clear focus and specific details.	**4** The essay is informative with a clear focus. More specific details are needed.
Organization		
6 The organization makes the essay informative and easy to read.	**5** The beginning interests the reader. The middle supports the focus. The ending works well. Transitions are used.	**4** The essay is divided into a beginning, a middle, and an ending. Some transitions are used.
Voice		
6 The writer's voice sounds confident, knowledgeable, and enthusiastic.	**5** The writer's voice sounds informative and confident. It fits the audience.	**4** The writer's voice sounds well-informed most of the time and fits the audience.

Guiding Your Writing

Learning how to use a rubric helps you . . .

- think like a writer—understanding your goal,
- make meaningful changes in your writing—using the traits of writing, and
- assess your final copies—rating their strengths and weaknesses.

Review the complete expository rubric. Review the rubric on pages 194–195 and list one thing that you learned from reviewing it and one question that you have about it. Share this information with your class.

Reading a Rubric

To get students focused on the rubric structure, ask:

- What happens to the score as you move to the right on the rubric?

Be sure that students understand that the rating decreases and the need for changes or improvement increases.

Guiding Your Writing

Emphasize that by looking over the rubric first, the writer can better understand the goals for a particular type of writing. Keeping these goals in mind should help the writer do his or her best work.

Getting Started with a Rubric

Point out that page 48 does not show a rubric; the rubric, with numbers, appears on pages 194–195. Students should use pages like this one, which will appear at the beginning of each core writing unit, as a guideline to help them create a piece of writing that will eventually measure up well against the rubric. Be sure that students understand each goal, the relationship between the goals and the traits, and how each goal can improve their writing.

Getting Started with a Rubric

At the beginning of each main writing unit, you will see a page like the one below. This page, which is arranged according to the traits of writing, explains the main requirements for developing the writing in the unit.

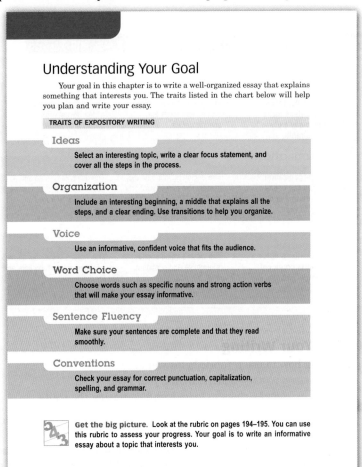

Understanding Your Goal

Your goal in this chapter is to write a well-organized essay that explains something that interests you. The traits listed in the chart below will help you plan and write your essay.

TRAITS OF EXPOSITORY WRITING

Ideas
Select an interesting topic, write a clear focus statement, and cover all the steps in the process.

Organization
Include an interesting beginning, a middle that explains all the steps, and a clear ending. Use transitions to help you organize.

Voice
Use an informative, confident voice that fits the audience.

Word Choice
Choose words such as specific nouns and strong action verbs that will make your essay informative.

Sentence Fluency
Make sure your sentences are complete and that they read smoothly.

Conventions
Check your essay for correct punctuation, capitalization, spelling, and grammar.

Get the big picture. Look at the rubric on pages 194–195. You can use this rubric to assess your progress. Your goal is to write an informative essay about a topic that interests you.

PROCESS

A Closer Look at Understanding Your Goal

To use the "Understanding Your Goal" rubric at the beginning of each writing unit, follow these steps.

1 **Review the entire chart** to get the big picture about the form of writing.

2 **Focus your attention** on *ideas, organization,* and *voice* because these traits are so important at the beginning of a writing project. (See below.)

3 **Read the requirements** under each of these three traits. When you consider *ideas,* for example, try to do these things:
- Select an interesting topic.
- Write a clear focus statement.
- Include a lot of details.

4 **Make sure to talk to your teacher** if you have any questions about the requirements for the assignment.

A Special Note About the Traits

At each step in the writing process, certain traits are more important than others. Keep this point in mind as you use a rubric.

During **Prewriting** and **Writing,** focus on the *ideas, organization,* and *voice* in your writing.

During **Revising,** focus on *ideas, organization, voice, word choice,* and *sentence fluency.* (For some assignments, your teacher may ask you to concentrate most of your attention on one or two of these traits.)

During **Editing** and proofreading, focus on *conventions.*

When **Assessing** a final copy, use all six traits. (For some assignments, your teacher may ask you to assess a piece of writing for just a few of the traits.)

 Write a paragraph. Review the rubric chart on page 48. Then write a short paragraph about a household pet that you find interesting.

A Closer Look at Understanding Your Goal

Ask students why they should focus on ideas, organization, and voice in the rubric at the beginning of each writing unit. (These three traits are most important during the prewriting and writing stages.)

A Special Note About the Traits

The purpose of writing a paragraph about an interesting animal or a household pet (*see **Write a paragraph** at the bottom of the pupil's edition page*) is for students to practice using the traits when they write. For this exercise, students do not need to go through an elaborate planning phase.

English Language Learners

Prior to the writing assignment, use stuffed animals or pictures of parrots, turtles, and so on, to help students think of specific words to describe how a favorite animal or pet looks, sounds, and feels to the touch. Ask questions as prompts. (*Is your dog's coat soft and fluffy, like this dog's, or is it shiny and smooth? What sounds does your pet bird make? What color are your turtle's eyes?*) After each response, have the student add all suggested words to his or her cluster diagram.

Revising and Editing with a Rubric

Another approach students may use is to think of the six-point rubric scale as two halves. Ask students:

■ Do you think the first half (4–6) of the scale describes your writing, or does the second half (1–3) describe it?

This may help students narrow their focus. Once they determine which half of the rubric describes their writing, they can focus on the three appropriate ratings.

 **Answers**

Answer will vary. Many students may rate the paragraph as a 2 or a 3; it needs more details and a clearer focus. But accept any rating that a student can reasonably justify.

Revising and Editing with a Rubric

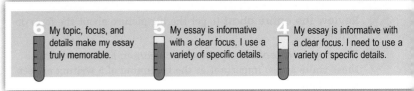

6 My topic, focus, and details make my essay truly memorable.

5 My essay is informative with a clear focus. I use a variety of specific details.

4 My essay is informative with a clear focus. I need to use a variety of specific details.

In each main writing unit, you will find a strip at the top of the pages dealing with revising and editing. Each strip covers one of the traits of writing and will help you improve your first drafts. The strip at the top of these two pages focuses on *ideas* for expository writing.

How can I use each strip to evaluate my first draft?

To use the strip, start by reading the number 5 description. Number 5 in the strip above says that your first draft should be informative, have a clear focus, and use a variety of specific details. Decide if your writing should get a 5 for ideas. If not, check the description for 6 or 4 and so on. Remember that a 5 means that the writing is *strong* for that trait.

(Sometimes it's hard to know for sure if a first draft deserves a 6, 5, or another number for a trait. Just come as close as you can and revise your writing as needed.)

 Review the sample paragraph below. Then rate the paragraph for ideas and explain your rating. (See pages 46–47 for help with rating a paper.)

My family has a guinea pig, and he is an interesting pet. Our pet, Gromit, is small, with red fur. Every time we bring him pellets and timothy hay, he greets us. All these things are interesting about my pet Gromit.

PROCESS

| 3 | My focus needs to be clearer. I need more specific details. | 2 | I need to narrow or expand my topic, and I need many more specific details. | 1 | I need to select a new topic and gather a variety of specific details. |

How can the strip help me revise my first draft?

After you find the proper rating on the strip for your paper, you will know what changes you should make. Here's what the writer of the paragraph on page 50 thought about ideas in her first draft.

- **Interesting topic:** I need to mention something about guinea pigs in general.
- **Clear focus:** Using Gromit to talk about all guinea pigs will work well.
- **Specific details:** I don't have enough details.

Making Changes

After deciding how to improve the ideas in her paragraph, the writer made the following changes.

The topic is made clearer.

A detail is added.

> *a short-earred animal that is really a type of rodent.*
> My family has a guinea pig, ~~and he is an~~
>
> ~~interesting pet.~~ Our pet, Gromit, is small, with red
> *He's a good singer, too.*
> fur. Every time we bring him pellets and timothy hay,
>
> he greets us. All these things are interesting . . .

 Revise your paragraph. Review and revise the paragraph you wrote on page 49. Use the strip on these two pages as a guide.

Be sure students understand that a specific or narrow topic is almost always a good choice. The writer must think about what he or she wishes to communicate and how long the written work will be.

Ask:
- Do you agree with the writer's revision ideas?

Making Changes

Point out that a good reason to write on every other line when drafting a piece of writing is so that the writer can make changes more easily. Note how the writer used the extra space to insert her revisions.

Struggling Learners

If students need a review of basic editing and proofreading marks, see the inside back cover of the pupil edition.

Assessing with a Rubric

A copy master for a blank assessment sheet is available on TE page 799. Students can use it now and throughout the year when they evaluate their own or other writers' work.

Now that students have been introduced to rubrics, you can return to Reece's essay and his teacher's assessment. First, have students read the rubric on PE pages 130–131. Then have them reread Reece's essay (PE pages 25–26). Then work through an assessment of Reece's essay as a class.

Compare your class assessment with the teacher's assessment on PE page 27.

52

Assessing with a Rubric

Follow the three steps below when you use a rubric—like the one on page 53—to assess a piece of writing.

1 **Create an assessment sheet.** On your own paper, list the key traits from the rubric (*ideas, organization,* and so on). Draw a line before each trait for your score and skip two or three lines between each trait for comments.

2 **Read the final copy.** Get an overall feeling for the writing to help you evaluate it.

3 **Assess the writing using the rubric.** To get started, read the descriptions for *ideas,* starting with the 5 rating. Decide which rating best fits the writing and put that number on your assessment sheet. Make comments as needed. Then go on to the other traits.

> ASSESSMENT SHEET   Title: _____
> ____ IDEAS
> ____ ORGANIZATION
> ____ VOICE
> ____ WORD CHOICE
> ____ SENTENCE FLUENCY
> ____ CONVENTIONS
> Evaluator: _____

Assess your pet paragraph. Create an assessment sheet like the one above. Then evaluate your paragraph using the expository rubric on pages 194–195. Try to write something you did well and something you'd like to improve for each trait. (See the sample on page 55.)

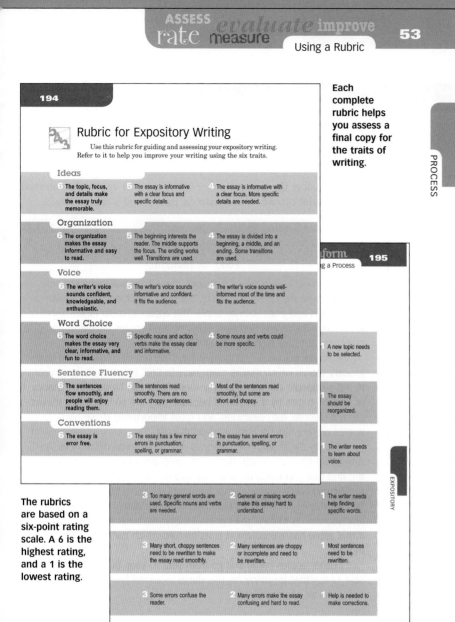

194

Rubric for Expository Writing

Use this rubric for guiding and assessing your expository writing.
Refer to it to help you improve your writing using the six traits.

Ideas

6 The topic, focus, and details make the essay truly memorable.

5 The essay is informative with a clear focus and specific details.

4 The essay is informative with a clear focus. More specific details are needed.

Organization

6 The organization makes the essay informative and easy to read.

5 The beginning interests the reader. The middle supports the focus. The ending works well. Transitions are used.

4 The essay is divided into a beginning, a middle, and an ending. Some transitions are used.

Voice

6 The writer's voice sounds confident, knowledgeable, and enthusiastic.

5 The writer's voice sounds informative and confident. It fits the audience.

4 The writer's voice sounds well-informed most of the time and fits the audience.

Word Choice

6 The word choice makes the essay very clear, informative, and fun to read.

5 Specific nouns and action verbs make the essay clear and informative.

4 Some nouns and verbs could be more specific.

Sentence Fluency

6 The sentences flow smoothly, and people will enjoy reading them.

5 The sentences read smoothly. There are no short, choppy sentences.

4 Most of the sentences read smoothly, but some are short and choppy.

Conventions

6 The essay is error free.

5 The essay has a few minor errors in punctuation, spelling, or grammar.

4 The essay has several errors in punctuation, spelling, or grammar.

...form **195**
...g a Process

1 A new topic needs to be selected.

1 The essay should be reorganized.

1 The writer needs to learn about voice.

3 Too many general words are used. Specific nouns and verbs are needed.

2 General or missing words make this essay hard to understand.

1 The writer needs help finding specific words.

3 Many short, choppy sentences need to be rewritten to make the essay read smoothly.

2 Many sentences are choppy or incomplete and need to be rewritten.

1 Most sentences need to be rewritten.

3 Some errors confuse the reader.

2 Many errors make the essay confusing and hard to read.

1 Help is needed to make corrections.

PROCESS

EXPOSITORY

Each complete rubric helps you assess a final copy for the traits of writing.

The rubrics are based on a six-point rating scale. A 6 is the highest rating, and a 1 is the lowest rating.

Review the following information about rubrics, the ones in this book in particular:

- When using a rubric, review each trait individually. Trying to evaluate writing for all six traits at one time is too hard.

- Decide whether the first half of the scale (4–6) describes a piece of writing or whether the second half of the scale (1–3) describes it. Then focus on the three appropriate ratings to see which one best describes the writing.

- Although rubrics are used to evaluate a piece of writing, they can also help guide the creation of the writing, especially when the writer sets up writing goals.

- Note that the colors of the bands match the colors of the writing goals at the beginning of each writing unit (see PE page 48).

Repeat with the rubric strips for the other writing traits.

❋ The complete six-point rubric for expository writing is found on PE pages 194–195. Four- and five-point rubrics are available on TE pages 769 and 773.

Doing a Peer Assessment

Use these or similar questions to prompt discussion as needed:

Ideas
- Does the writer have a clear main idea?
- Are the details all related to the author's main point?

Organization
- Are the details organized in a way that is clear to the reader?
- Does the beginning catch your attention?

Voice
- Does the writing make you want to read it aloud?
- Do you get the feeling that the author knows a lot about the subject?

Word Choice
- Can you visualize what the author is saying?
- Is there a word that is an especially good one for this piece of writing?

Sentence Fluency
- Is this piece of writing easy to listen to?
- Is there variety in sentence beginnings and length?

Conventions
- Is the author in command of the conventions?
- Are there errors that interfere with the author's message?

Doing a Peer Assessment

Just as you can use a rubric to assess your own writing, you can also use a rubric to assess your classmate's writing.

Expository Essay

In the essay below, the writer compares two types of apples. As you read the essay, pay special attention to its strong points and weak points.

Food for Thought

Bag lunches are populer at our school, especially when noodle surprise is on the hot-lunch menu. The basic bag lunch begins with a sandwich and ends with an apple. The apples in most lunch bags are Granny Smith and Red Delicious. These to apples have a lot in common, but they also have their differences.

Both apples are big in many ways. They are desplayed in all large grocery stores which makes them easy to find. They are stocked year round so people can always enjoy them. They can be eaten as snacks or as mini meals by themselves because they are so large. This makes them a favorite with everyone. And most importently these two apples are big hits because they taste great.

Granny Smith and Red Delicious also have some differences. A Granny Smith is green and has a tart taste. Because of the tartness the first bite can catch the eater by suprise. One of the things that makes this apple special is that it always seems to be crisp and fresh. The Red Delicious is a red apple with a sweet taste. This apple almost always lives up to its name because it delivers such a delicious taste. If this apple has a problem, it is its texture which can turn soft and mushey.

Other apples come and go from year to year. But it would be safe to say that for many people, these to apples have become as American as apple pie itself.

English Language Learners

Have students take turns reading the essay "Food for Thought" out loud. Discuss words, phrases, and idioms that may be unfamiliar:

- bag lunch (a lunch packed in a paper bag)
- noodle surprise (a meal made of noodles and other unidentifiable ingredients)
- Granny Smith, Red Delicious (kinds of apples)
- mini meal (a small meal)
- big hits (popular items)
- lives up to (is true to)
- mushy (soft and not firm)
- as American as apple pie (very American; apple pie is considered a standard American food)

PROCESS

Peer Assessment

To complete the assessment of "Food for Thought," the evaluator used the rubric for expository writing on pages 194–195. Beneath each trait, he identified one strength (1.) and one weakness (2.) in the writing.

ASSESSMENT SHEET   Title: *"Food for Thought"*

5   IDEAS
1. *The focus of the essay is clear.*
2. *A few of the details don't seem important (like where the apples are displayed).*

5   ORGANIZATION
1. *The essay has a beginning, a middle, and an ending.*
2. *More transitions could connect ideas.*

4   VOICE
1. *The writer sounds interested most of the time.*
2. *A personal comment or story would help.*

4   WORD CHOICE
1. *Most of the words are clear and easy to follow.*
2. *Some of the words are too general ("great," "big").*

4   SENTENCE FLUENCY
1. *Most of the sentences read smoothly.*
2. *Some sentence beginnings could be changed.*

3   CONVENTIONS
1. *The words are capitalized correctly.*
2. *There are some spelling and comma mistakes.*

Evaluator: *Tim Smith*

Review the assessment. On your own paper, explain why you agree with the assessment above (or why you don't). Consider each trait carefully.

Ask volunteers to read aloud the description on the rubric on PE pages 194–195 for each score on the assessment sheet on this page. (Example: *Ideas* rubric strip, score 5: *The essay is informative with a clear focus and specific details.*)

Have students form groups to discuss whether they agree or disagree with the score and with the comments on the strength and the weakness. Ask:
- Do you agree with Tim Smith's evaluation? Why?
- What would you rate differently?
- What other comments did you make as you read the essay?

Have the groups continue to read through the rubric for each trait and discuss the score and comments on the assessment sheet.

Ask groups to share their opinions and additional comments on the essay's strengths and weaknesses with the whole class.

Assessing a Sample Narrative

As an alternative to the individual activity suggested at the bottom of the page, have students assess the personal narrative in teams of two. The partners each independently score the essay for ideas, and then they compare and calibrate. If they are one point apart, they can move on to the next trait. If they are more than one point apart, they use the rubric to orally defend their score. When the assessment team finally agrees on new scores that are no more than one point apart, they can move on to the next trait.

Have teams share the scores (or a score range) with the class.

NOTE: In each core unit—narrative, expository, persuasive, and response to literature—there are two additional writing samples that teachers can use with students for further assessment practice (TE pages 776–798). The writing samples are provided in transparency form so that you can work together as a group. (A copy master version is available for students.) A reproducible assessment sheet, based on the traits of writing, allows you and students to rate the writing samples. Finally, a completed assessment sheet is provided to guide teachers through the assessment.

Assessing a Sample Narrative

As you read through the personal narrative below, pay attention to the strengths and weaknesses in the writing. Then follow the directions at the bottom of the page.

Squealer

I was so excited when I got first-chair trumpet in our middle school band. I even beat out Chuck, an eighth grader. That made him jealous, since I'd be playing all the trumpet solos.

For the spring concert, Mr. Moore handed out sheet music for "Summertime." It had a great trumpet solo, but it was really high. Chuck loaned me a "squealer" mouthpiece—extra small for playing really high notes. I learned the solo, and it worked great.

At dress rehearsal, the band played "Summertime," and I blew everyone away. Even Chuck said I rocked. I was so excited, I forgot to switch from the squealer to my regular mouthpiece for the next song, "I Love You, Porgy." It started with a real low solo. I tried to play it, but the squealer made every note blat and wobble. It was torture. Mr. Moore stared at me, pleading for just one good note, but I couldn't give it to him. Afterward, Chuck said I sounded like a bike tire losing air!

Well, I was embarrassed, but some good came of it. I asked Mr. Moore if Chuck could play the second solo. He said yes, and at the concert, we both sounded great.

 Use a narrative rubric. Assess the narrative you have just read using the rubric on pages 130–131 as a guide. Before you get started, create an assessment sheet like the one on page 55 in this chapter. Remember to leave room after each trait for comments.

Struggling Learners

Some students may have trouble learning to use rubrics. Doing so may be easier if the sample's subject area is one of personal interest. Provide a few alternative personal narratives from which these learners may choose (in addition to "Squealer").

perform display
POST print present **57**

Publishing Your Writing

To publish or share your writing, you need an audience. This is true whether you are handing in a writing assignment in language arts class or sending an e-mail message to a relative. Before you share your writing with anyone else, you should be happy with it yourself.

Your writing is ready for publication when it says exactly what you want it to say and is as close to error free as you can make it. In other words, you've given it your best effort.

In this chapter, you will find information on a variety of ways to publish your work.

Mini Index

- **Sharing Your Writing**
- **Preparing to Publish**
- **Designing Your Writing**
- **Making Your Own Web Site**
- **Publishing Online**

Publishing Your Writing

Objectives

- understand different ways to share writing
- learn how to format and design writing for publication
- plan and create a Web site
- publish writing online

Before students read this page, ask if anyone in the class has had a piece of writing published outside of school. There may be students who have published online or have participated in writing contests.

Then contrast these experiences to more informal, everyday kinds of publishing, such as sending an e-mail or reading written work to a family member.

Advanced Learners

Ask a group of students to publish their writing in a small class newspaper or magazine. They may use paragraphs and essays they have already written as well as new articles. They may also accept material from the rest of the class.

First, the group (or staff) should brainstorm and assign topics for new writing. Then, working individually, they should each collect details and write a first draft. They can exchange their drafts with a partner for revising and editing.

Next, the group should discuss the format and design of their publication. Each writer should do a final copy according to the style and format agreed upon. You can then duplicate the final copies.

Finally, the staff can collate, staple, and distribute the newspapers or magazines to the class.

Sharing Your Writing

Provide samples of a selection of the following forms of published writing: local newspapers, the school paper, magazines, books, flyers, greeting cards, and student writing portfolios. For a greater variety, ask students to bring some of these materials from home.

Use these or similar questions to help students understand how each publishing format suits the purpose of the writing:

- Would a greeting card be effective if it were set up as a memo?
- Does a newspaper lend itself to performing?

Explain that some common forms of writing used in business, school, and home settings have specific accepted formats. These include letters and envelopes, memos, and proposals.

* For formatting guidelines for certain forms of practical writing (memos, proposals, letters, and envelope addresses), see PE pages 576–577.

58

Sharing Your Writing

Some publishing ideas are easy to carry out, like sharing your writing with your classmates. Others take more time and effort, like entering a writing contest. Try a number of these publishing ideas during the school year. All of them will help you grow as a writer.

Performing
- Sharing with Classmates
- Reading to Various Audiences
- Preparing a Multimedia Presentation
- Videotaping for Special Audiences
- Performing Onstage

In School
- School Newspapers
- Classroom Collections
- School Handbooks
- Writing Portfolios

Self-Publishing
- Family Newsletters
- Greeting Cards
- Bound Writings
- Online Publications

Posting
- Classroom Bulletin Boards
- School or Public Libraries
- Hallway Display Cases
- Business Windows
- Clinic Waiting Rooms

Sending It Out
- Local Newspapers
- Young Writers' Conferences
- Magazines and Contests
- Various Web Sites

 Chart your publishing history. List the headings above on a piece of paper: *Performing, Posting, In School, Self-Publishing, Sending It Out.* Leave two or three lines between each heading. Under each heading, identify the publishing ideas that you have already tried. Then list and highlight those you would like to try.

Advanced Learners

Have students detail specific kinds of writing that could be shared in the ways listed above.

- What forms lend themselves to performing?
- What forms lend themselves to posting?
- What forms are appropriate for self-publishing?
- What forms are appropriate to send out?

PROCESS

Preparing to Publish

Your writing is ready to publish when it is clear, complete, and correct. Getting your writing to this point requires careful revising and editing. Follow the tips below to help you prepare your writing for publication.

Publishing Tips

- **Work with your writing.**
  Continue working until you feel good about your writing from beginning to end.

- **Ask for advice during the writing process.**
  Be sure your writing answers any questions your readers may have about your topic.

- **Revise the ideas, organization, and voice.**
  Every part of your writing should be clear and complete.

- **Check words, sentences, and conventions.**
  In addition, ask at least one classmate to check your work for these traits.

- **Prepare a neat finished piece.**
  Use a pen (blue or black ink) and one side of the paper if you are writing by hand. If you are writing with a computer, use a font that is easy to read. Double-space your writing.

- **Know your options.**
  Explore the many different ways to publish your writing.

- **Follow all publication guidelines.**
  Just as your teacher wants assignments presented in a certain way, so do the newspapers, magazines, or Web sites that review the writing you submit.

  Save all drafts for each writing project. This will help you keep track of the changes you have made. If you are preparing a portfolio, you may be required to include early drafts as well as finished pieces.

Preparing to Publish

Publishing Tips

Explain that if students follow the steps in the writing process introduced on PE pages 13–24 (prewriting, writing, revising, editing, and publishing), their writing should be ready for publication.

Designing Your Writing

After reviewing PE pages 60–62 with students, ask them to search for three examples of **effective design** *(see below)* in the samples of publications that were gathered for the lesson on sharing writing (PE page 58).

As an alternative to the activity at the bottom of PE page 60, assign one or more pairs of students to evaluate the effectiveness of the design in the three examples. Have each pair follow these steps:

- Prepare comments that pertain to the three categories on PE page 60—Typography, Spacing and Margins, and Graphic Devices.
- Join with the other pairs who evaluated the same sample and share comments with each other.
- Select one or two people to present general comments to the rest of the class.

Conclude with a general summary of what students found to be features of effective design, and discuss possibilities for using these features in their own work (for example, in social studies papers and science reports).

60

Designing Your Writing

Whenever you write, always focus on content *first*. Then think about how you want your paper to look. You can follow the guidelines below.

Typography

- Use an easy-to-read font for both the body and headings.
- Use an appropriate title and headings. A title sets the tone for your writing, and headings break the writing into smaller pieces.

Spacing and Margins

- Double-space your writing and leave one-inch margins on all four sides of your paper.
- Indent the first line of every paragraph.
- Use one space after every period.
- Avoid awkward breaks between pages. For example, don't leave a heading or the first line of a paragraph at the bottom of a page.

Graphic Devices

- Create bulleted or numbered lists.
- Include a table, a chart, or an illustration if it can help make a point clearer. (See pages **574–575** for examples.)
- Keep each graphic small enough so that it doesn't dominate the page. A larger graphic can be put by itself on a separate page.

 Share effective design. Find an article in a magazine, newspaper, or book that is well designed. Share the article with the class and identify the design features.

Teaching Tip: Effective Design

Point out that graphics may add information as well as interest to published writing. Brainstorm with students about the kinds of graphics they might use to improve the presentation of their writing. Ideas might include: drawings, photographs, diagrams, different kinds of graphs, tables, and maps. Discuss which graphics might fit with different topics and forms of writing.

＊ For more information on graphics that might be useful in essays and reports, see PE pages 574–575.

Advanced Learners

Provide circulars from newspapers. Have students find two advertisements—one well-designed and one poorly-designed—for the same type of product. Have students give three reasons why the well-designed one is more effective. (Possible responses: more colorful, more details shown, more realistic.)

Computer Design in Action

The following two pages show a well-designed student essay. The side notes explain all of the design features.

perform *display*
POST *print* *present*
Publishing Your Writing **61**

PROCESS

The title is 18-point and boldfaced.

The main text is 12-point type.

Headings are 14-point.

Margins are at least one inch all around.

Will Lee

Wake Up the Wild Side!

"In each of you, there is a wild creature screaming to get out," Ms. Hillary tells the drama club at the start of each meeting. "It's the part of you that can be a star on this stage." Then she begins our warm-ups, which really get our bodies and minds in gear. They also help the group start working together. Some warm-ups are for individuals, and some are for partners. Ms. Hillary uses both types at every meeting.

Individual Warm-Ups

Every meeting begins with warm-ups to help individuals find their "centers." One is "Shake It Out," and the other is "Greet the Sun."

- **Shake It Out:** In this warm-up, people stand on tiptoes with their hands stretched over their heads and shake out all the tension from their bodies. Everyone ends up completely loose and relaxed.
- **Greet the Sun:** Then everyone lies on the floor and rises like a plant, growing toward the sun. Everyone ends up with faces lifted and hands out like leaves.

Computer Design in Action

It may be necessary to review with students how to use the various formatting features of the word processing program, such as setting margins, changing font sizes, using bullets, and so on.

For fun, have students work from a published piece of writing and design a poor example. Students love to exaggerate and will enjoy creating the poor example. Display the poor designs side-by-side with the good ones to show the contrast.

The activity at the bottom of PE page 62 suggests that students create an effective design for an essay that they have written. Suggest that students make notes using the three headings listed on PE page 60 so that they plan their design before implementing it. Remind students to consider their audience, the purpose of the piece, and how they will produce the final copy (handwritten or on a computer) when planning their design.

Lee 2

Partner Warm-Ups

After "Shake It Out" and "Greet the Sun," everyone gets a partner. Ms. Hillary then leads one of the following warm-ups:

A bulleted list helps organize the essay.

- **Setting:** She shouts out a setting—optometrist's office, Niagara Falls, detention room, whatever—and the pairs must act out a scene in that location.
- **Character:** She names two characters—a pizza cook and a superhero, a dog and a salesperson, a genius and a child—and each partner must play one role and create a scene between the characters.
- **Conflict:** She calls out a conflict—an argument over a goat, a staring contest, two couch potatoes with two TV remotes—and partners have to act out a scene that shows that conflict.

Ready to Act

Once the individual and partner warm-ups are completed, the whole group is ready to act together. With everyone's wild side fully awake, it's time to hit the stage.

Design a page. Using the guidelines on page 60, create an effective design for an essay you've already written. Share your design with a classmate to get some feedback: Does your design help make your writing clear and easy to follow? Will any of it distract the reader?

Making Your Own Web Site

You can make your own Web site if your family has an Internet account. Ask your provider how to get started. If you are using a school account, ask your teacher for help. Then start designing your site. Use the questions and answers below as a starting point.

How do I plan my site?

Think about how many pages you want on your Web site. Should you put everything on one page, or would you like to have several pages? Check out other sites for ideas. Then plan your pages by sketching them out.

How do I make the pages?

Start each page as a text file using your computer. Many new word-processing programs let you save a file as a Web page. If yours doesn't, you will have to use Web page editing software or add HTML (Hypertext Markup Language) codes to format the text and make links to graphics and other pages. You can find instructions about HTML on the Net or at the library.

How do I know whether my pages work?

You should always test your pages. Using your browser, open your first page. Then follow the links to make sure they work correctly and that all the pages look right.

How do I get my pages on the Net?

You must upload your finished pages to the Internet. (Ask your Internet provider how to do this.) After the upload, visit your site to make sure it still works. Also check it on other computers if possible.

How do I let people know about my site?

Once your site is up, e-mail your friends and tell them to visit it!

 Keep a journal of Web pages that impress you. Answer these questions about each one: What is especially good about this page? What could be better? When designing your own pages, check your journal for ideas to use.

Making Your Own Web Site

Ask students to work in teams to find well-designed and appropriate Web sites. Have each team present their site to the class using a projector or by printing out out the material. Each team should address the two questions in the **Try It** activity in their presentation.

To keep the audience engaged, have students fold a sheet of paper into three columns. In the first column, they record the URL, the Web site's name, and a description. In the second column, they rate the design of the Web site on a scale of 1 to 6 (to reinforce the six-point scale). In the last column, they note the best design feature of the Web site. Have the class vote on the site with the best design.

NOTE: Warn students that because anyone can access a Web site, they should *never* publish any identifying information, such as phone numbers, addresses, or private information, online.

 **Answers**

Answers will vary.

PROCESS

Publishing Online

Emphasize the importance of checking with parents and teachers before students send writing and contact information to a Web site.

Encourage students to work through the Write Source Web site.

Publishing Online

The Internet offers many publishing opportunities, including online magazines and writing contests. The information below will help you submit your writing on the Net. (Always get a parent's approval first.)

How should I get started?

Check with your teacher to see if your school has its own Internet site where you can post your work. Also ask your teacher about other Web sites. There are a number of online magazines that accept student writing.

How do I search for possible sites?

Use a search engine to find places to publish. Some search engines also offer their own student links.

How do I submit my work?

Before you do anything, make sure that you understand the publishing guidelines for each site. Be sure to share this information with your teacher and your parents. Then follow these steps:

- **Send your writing in the correct form.**
  Some sites have online forms. Others will ask you to send it by mail or e-mail. Always explain why you are sending your writing.
- **Give the publisher information for contacting you.**
  However, don't give your home address or other personal information unless your parents approve.
- **Be patient.**
  A site should contact you within a week, but it may be several weeks before you hear whether your writing will be used or not.

Does Write Source have a Web site?

Yes. You can visit our Web site at www.thewritesource.com. The "Publish It" link lists Web sites that accept student submissions.

Visit the Write Source Web site. Use the "Publish It" link. Find out what forms of writing the Write Source would like to see you submit. (Check for your grade level.) Also visit at least two of the other publishing sites that are listed. Find out their requirements for submitting work.

Creating a Portfolio

How can you judge your progress as a writer? One of the best ways is to put together a writing portfolio. A portfolio is a collection of your best writing completed during a semester or a grading period. With a portfolio, you can compare different pieces of writing to see how you have improved over time.

Think of a portfolio as a form of publishing your writing. Instead of sharing just one piece, a portfolio lets you share an entire "writing album." A portfolio presents a clear picture of you as a writer. It says, "This is who I am; this is what I can do."

Creating a Portfolio

Objectives

- learn about different types of portfolios
- understand the parts of a portfolio
- choose writing for a portfolio, reflect on your writing samples, and plan future writing goals

Ask students to talk about any experiences they have had with portfolios:

- Have you ever kept a portfolio of your writing?
- If so, what did you include and how did you choose it?
- Why can you learn from keeping a portfolio?
- What can teachers learn from your portfolio?

Types of Portfolios

Discuss the different types of portfolios with students.

■ What kind of portfolio have you kept in the past?

■ What kind of portfolio do you like best? Why?

■ What kind of portfolio do you think would be most helpful to you as a writer?

Unless your school, district, or state has specific requirements for the kinds of portfolios students must keep, encourage students to keep a different kind of portfolio from what they may have kept in the past.

Types of Portfolios

There are four types of portfolios you should know about: a showcase portfolio, a growth portfolio, a personal portfolio, and an electronic portfolio.

Showcase Portfolio

A showcase portfolio presents the best writing you have done in school. A showcase is the most common type of portfolio and is usually put together for evaluation at the end of a grading period.

Growth Portfolio

A growth portfolio shows your progress as a writer. It contains writing assignments that show how your writing skills are developing:

● writing beginnings and endings,

● writing with voice, and

● using specific details.

Personal Portfolio

In a personal portfolio, you save writing that you want to keep and share with others. Many professional people—including writers, artists, and musicians—keep personal portfolios. You can arrange this type of portfolio according to different types of writing, different themes, and so on.

Electronic Portfolio

An electronic portfolio is any type of portfolio (showcase, growth, or personal) available on a CD or a Web site. Besides your writing, you can include graphics, video, and sound with this type of portfolio. Now your writing can be available to friends and family members no matter where they are!

Select your best writing. Let's say you were going to create a showcase portfolio for your last two or three years in school. On your own paper, list four pieces of writing that you would include in this portfolio. Explain your choices.

English Language Learners

Throughout the year help students select pieces of writing for their portfolios. Use the activity to emphasize how their language and writing skills have improved and to focus on specific strong points in the examples of "best" writing in their showcase portfolios.

PROCESS

Parts of a Portfolio

A showcase portfolio is one of the most common types of portfolios used in schools. It may contain the parts listed below, but always check with your teacher to be sure.

- A **table of contents** lists the writing samples you have included in your portfolio.
- A **brief essay** or **letter** introduces your portfolio—telling how you put it together, how you feel about it, and what it means to you.
- A **collection of writing samples** presents your best work. Your teacher may require that you include all of your planning, drafting, and revising for one or more of your writings.
- A **cover sheet for each sample** explains why you selected it.
- **Evaluations**, **reflections**, or **checklists** identify the basic skills you have mastered and those skills that you still need to work on.

Gathering Tips

- **Keep track of all your work,** including prewriting notes, first drafts, and revisions for each writing assignment. Then, when you put together a portfolio, you will have everything that you need.
- **Store all of your writing in a pocket folder.** This will help you avoid dog-eared or ripped pages.
- **Set a schedule for working on your portfolio.** You can't put together a good portfolio by waiting until the last minute.
- **Take pride in your work.** Make sure your portfolio shows you at your best.

 Reflect on your writing progress. Imagine that your teacher wants you to put together a portfolio, including a paragraph about your writing progress. Write such a paragraph, telling what is easy or hard for you about writing. Also tell what types of writing you like to do best, what your favorite piece of writing is, and so on.

Parts of a Portfolio

Gathering Tips

If possible, invite a former student to share his or her showcase portfolio. Have the student discuss what was learned from building the portfolio.

You can also invite someone from private business, such as an architect, an interior designer, or an artist, to share a "showcase" portfolio. These real-world applications will help students understand how useful a portfolio can be outside the school setting.

Planning Ideas

As students go through the process of choosing pieces of writing for their portfolios, they may wish to have one or two classmates read several selections and offer suggestions and opinions. Remind students that the final decision must be made by the author because it is his or her portfolio.

Planning Ideas

The following tips will help you choose your best pieces of writing to include in your portfolio.

1 Be patient.

Don't make quick decisions about which pieces of writing to include in your portfolio. Just keep gathering everything—including all your drafts—until you are ready to review all of your writing assignments.

2 Make good decisions.

When it's time to choose writing for your portfolio, review each piece. Remember the feelings you had during each assignment. Which one makes you feel the best? Which one did your readers like the best? Which one taught you the most?

3 Reflect on your choices.

Read the sample reflections on page 69. Then answer these questions about your writing:

- Why did I choose this piece?
- Why did I write this piece? (What was my purpose?)
- How did I write it? (What was my process?)
- What does it show about my writing abilities?
- What would I do differently next time?
- What have I learned that will make me a better writer?

4 Set future writing goals.

After putting together your portfolio, set some goals for the future. Here are some of the goals that other students have set:

I will write about topics that really interest me.

I will spend more time on my beginnings and endings.

I will make sure that my sentences read smoothly.

 Plan a portfolio cover. On a piece of plain paper, design a creative cover for a portfolio folder. Include your name and an interesting title. Add sketches or photos related to your writing, your classes, your favorite pastime, and so on.

PROCESS

Sample Portfolio Reflections

When you take time to reflect on your writing assignments, think about the process that you used to develop each one. Also think about what you might do differently next time. The following samples will help you with your own reflections.

Student Reflections

> The story about my ancestor in New York is my most interesting piece of writing, ever. I couldn't believe how much I learned about this person. All of my research was actually fun. Ms. Peña always tells us to write about topics that really interest us. Now I know just what she means.
>
> —DeAndra Barker

> One of our first assignments this year was to write about a life-changing experience. My narrative about playing in a basketball tournament turned out to be the best thing that I wrote all year. Instead of telling everything about the tournament, I focused on one important part. I wrote about my friend becoming ill and how his illness changed me. I like just about everything about this story, except that it could use more dialogue.
>
> —Todd Ryan

Professional Reflections

> I wrote *Mad Merlin* by combining legends of Camelot with histories and myths. As I look back at the novel, though, I see it is mostly about my own life. Good fiction is that way—creative in the details but otherwise full of truth.
>
> —J. Robert King

> With each book I write, I become more and more convinced that the books have a life of their own, quite apart from me.
>
> —Madeleine L'Engle

Sample Portfolio Reflections

Tell students that they may share their reflections or keep them private.

Student Reflections

Have students choose a piece of work and write a brief reflection about it.

Professional Reflections

For an enrichment activity, ask students to look up Web sites for some of their favorite living authors to see if they contain reflections on their writing. Have students share any information they find.

English Language Learners

Students may benefit from oral, rather than written, reflections on their work. Ask them to select one piece of writing from their showcase portfolios and tell you why it is among their best pieces of work. Ask them such questions as *How did following the writing process help you?* Urge them to remember and build on this success.

Advanced Learners

Ask students to do some research about the people quoted in the "Professional Reflections" section, J. Robert King and Madeleine L'Engle. Have students write a paragraph about one of the authors and present it to the class. How many books did they write? What kinds of books did they write? At what age did they begin their writing career?

Descriptive Writing Overview

Writing Standards

The writing standards listed below are based on a blending of state and NCTE standards.

- Use lists to explore possible topics.
- Create a description with details that show rather than tell.
- Draft an essay that has a clear beginning, middle, and end and that is organized by time order or order of location.
- Revise drafts to make ideas clearer and details more colorful.
- Edit drafts to ensure correct conventions.

Writing Forms

- descriptive paragraph
- descriptive essay about an event

Focus on the Traits

- **Ideas** Gathering specific, sensory details
- **Organization** Using order of location or time order
- **Voice** Developing an engaging voice that is natural and sincere
- **Word Choice** Using descriptive words and figures of speech
- **Sentence Fluency** Varying sentence beginnings to improve sentence flow
- **Conventions** Checking for errors in punctuation, capitalization, spelling, and grammar

Unit Pacing

Descriptive Paragraph: 2.25–3 hours

Students write a **descriptive paragraph** about a favorite place. The paragraph lays the groundwork for more extensive descriptive writing. Use this section if students need to work on crafting a paragraph. Following are some of the topics that are covered:

- Using a list to explore different topics
- Gathering details that show, not tell
- Using order of location

Descriptive Essay: 3.75–5.25 hours

The **descriptive essay** can take many forms. This section asks students to describe a **place** they know. Use this section to focus on developing an essay. Following are some of the topics that are covered:

- Using a topics chart
- Organizing details using time order or order of location
- Using figures of speech
- Writing an effective beginning, middle, and ending
- Using an engaging voice

Across the Curriculum: 2.25–3 hours

Collaborate with teachers from other content areas to identify descriptive forms that could enhance students' experience with the curriculum already in place. Some forms could be used easily in more than one curriculum area.

■ **Social Studies**
Describing a Scene in a Different Time, pp. 84–85

■ **Math**
Describing Geometric Terms, pp. 86–87

■ **Science**
Describing a Natural Event, pp. 88–89

■ **Practical Writing**
Creating a Thank-You Note, pp. 90–91

Integrated Grammar and Writing Skills

Below are skills lessons from the resources sections of the pupil edition that are suggested at point of use (✳) throughout this unit.

Descriptive Paragraph. pp. 71–74

✳ Create Descriptive Paragraphs, p. 527
✳ Show, Don't Tell, p. 557

Describing an Event, pp. 75–82

✳ Show Powerful Action, p. 482
✳ Find Interesting Details, p. 531
✳ Use Chronological Order, p. 534
✳ Use Order of Location, p. 535

Additional Grammar Skills

Below are skills lessons from other components that you can weave into your unit instruction.

Writing a Descriptive Paragraph

SkillsBook

Interactive Writing Skills CD-ROM

Parts of Speech:
Verbs 1—Linking and Helping

Daily Language Workout

Describing an Event

SkillsBook

Interactive Writing Skills CD-ROM

Parts of Speech: Verbs 1—Action

Daily Language Workout

70

Descriptive Writing

Descriptive Writing
Descriptive Paragraph

What animal has two points on top of its head, big bright eyes, sharp claws, and an appetite for rodents? You might have said, "a cat, of course!" but what about an owl—or even the double-crested dinosaur called a Dilophosaurus? All three of these animals could easily fit the description.

When you write a description, you want to make sure your reader knows exactly what you are talking about. In this chapter, you will write a paragraph describing an interesting animal. Your goal is to tell about the creature's shape, size, and color, as well as the sounds it makes and the way it moves. With words alone, you can capture a wild animal!

Writing Guidelines

Subject:	An animal you have seen
Form:	Descriptive paragraph
Purpose:	To describe an animal
Audience:	Classmates

Descriptive Paragraph

Objectives
- understand the content and structure of a descriptive paragraph
- choose an animal to describe
- plan, draft, revise, and edit a descriptive paragraph

A **descriptive paragraph** gives a detailed picture of a person, place, thing, or event. Effective descriptive paragraphs use many sensory details.

✳ Additional information about descriptive paragraphs is on PE page 527.

Use either or both of these suggestions to introduce the genre:
- Ask students where they have read or heard descriptions (books, newspapers, magazines, TV shows, everyday conversation). Encourage them to discuss what makes a good description.
- Ask students to draw what they visualize as you read aloud the description in the opening sentence of the first paragraph. Then have students compare their drawings.

Descriptive Paragraph

After reading "Night Visitor," have students go back and list the descriptive details that helped them visualize what they were reading.

 Respond to the reading.

Review the questions orally with students so that you can explore why they chose particular details.

Answers

Ideas **1.** by identifying the topic (animal) in its natural setting

Organization **2.** order of location (the viewer sees the whole owl and then, starting with the head, sees each body part until the wings are mentioned)

Voice & Word Choice **3.** Possible choices:

- head swiveled slowly
- round, lemon-colored eyes
- deep, sad voice
- wide, powerful wings
- glided away into the darkness

72

Descriptive Paragraph

   A **descriptive paragraph** gives a detailed picture of a person, a place, a thing, or an event. It begins with a **topic sentence** that tells what the paragraph is about. The sentences in the **body** give all of the descriptive details about the topic. The **closing sentence** wraps up the paragraph. The paragraph below uses colorful details to describe a special bird of prey.

Night Visitor

Topic sentence
....

   In the glowing sunset, the great horned owl sat straight and still on top of the fence post. With pointed ears and a thick, long body, its shadow looked like a cat. The owl's head swiveled slowly from side to side like a security camera. Its ears listened for the softest

Body

sound. Its round, lemon-colored eyes looked for even the slightest movement. The owl's deep, sad voice haunted the darkness with *who-who-whoooooooo*. Then the owl was

Closing sentence
....

ready to move on. It spread its wide, powerful wings, lifted from its perch, and glided away into the darkness.

 Respond to the reading. On your own paper, answer the following questions.

☐ Ideas **(1) How is the topic introduced?**

☐ Organization **(2) What method of organization (time order, order of location, order of importance) did the writer use? Explain.**

☐ Voice & Word Choice **(3) What words or ideas make the animal seem real to the reader?**

English Language Learners

These students can benefit from having a visual to go with "Night Visitor." Show a picture of an owl. Have students point to the relevant parts of the picture as you read the sentences that describe parts of the animal's body.

Struggling Learners

Highlight descriptive details by making two lists—one labeled Sights and the other labeled Sounds. Help students use the lists to categorize related phrases from "Night Visitor," such as *glowing sunset* and *ears listened*.

Advanced Learners

Have students identify comparisons used in "Night Visitor." Discuss how these pairings, such as *shadow/cat* and *eyes/lemons*, help create effective images. Encourage students to think of other comparisons the writer could use, such as *darkness/ink*.

DESCRIPTIVE

Prewriting Selecting a Topic

To get started, you need to choose an animal that you've seen either in real life or in pictures. The animal should interest you. The writer of the paragraph on page 72 made the following list of possible topics using sentence starters.

> ### Animals I Have Seen
>
> The most beautiful animal is . . . a toucan.
> The most mysterious is . . . a great horned owl.
> The ugliest animal is . . . an armadillo.
> The smallest animal is . . . a mouse.
> The scariest animal is . . . a black bear.
> The funniest animal is . . . a flying squirrel.

 Select a topic. Create your own list of animals by completing the sentence starters above. Then choose one that really interests you to describe in a paragraph.

Gathering Details—Show, Don't Tell

In a descriptive paragraph, the goal is to *show* readers something instead of *telling* them about it. Details that show are specific and colorful.

 Collect your details. Answer the following questions to gather specific details about your animal.

- What does your animal's head look like?
- What does its body look like?
- What color and texture are its fur, feathers, or skin?
- What does it sound like?
- Where do you usually find it?
- What unusual or interesting things does it do?
- What can you compare this animal to?

Prewriting Selecting a Topic

Provide students with pictures from magazines of animals in natural settings. Distribute the pictures randomly, and let students use them as inspiration for their paragraphs.

Prewriting
Gathering Details—Show, Don't Tell

To give students practice in gathering details, have them brainstorm a list of words and phrases that describe a favorite stuffed animal or pet. Tell students not to identify the animal. Have them exchange their lists with a partner and guess what kind of animal is being described.

Emphasize the difference between showing and telling by using these two examples:
- My stuffed bear is cute.
- My bear is about 12 inches tall. It has curly mohair fur that is shocking pink. Its nose is long, and the end is black. My bear has a squarish face with brownish black eyes. It looks kind of thoughtful, but friendly.

* Additional information about show, don't tell is on PE page 557.

Writing Creating Your First Draft

As students begin to think about a topic sentence, tell them to reread the topic sentence for "Night Visitor" on PE page 72. Suggest that they use that topic sentence as a model for their own writing.

Revising

Improving Your Paragraph

Remind students that order of location is just one way to organize ideas for a descriptive paragraph. They may also choose time order or order of importance.

Editing Checking for Conventions

Remind students to use a dictionary to check the spelling of any words of which they are uncertain. After students edit their own paragraphs, have them trade papers with a partner and check each other's work for errors.

74

Writing Creating Your First Draft

The goal of a first draft is to get all of your ideas and details down on paper. Follow the guidelines below.

- Start with a topic sentence that catches your reader's interest.
- Arrange the descriptive sentences in the body according to location. Include the details that you gathered on page 73.
- End with a sentence that keeps the reader thinking about the topic.

 Write your first draft. Get your best ideas and details down on paper. Describe the animal from top to bottom or from left to right. Then give your paragraph a title.

Revising Improving Your Paragraph

When you revise, consider how well you've used ideas, organization, voice, word choice, and sentence fluency in your first draft.

 Review your paragraph. Use the following questions as a guide when you revise your paragraph.

1 Is my topic sentence clear?

2 Have I organized the details in my paragraph using order of location?

3 Do I sound interested in the topic?

4 Do I use specific nouns, verbs, and adjectives?

5 Do I use complete sentences that read smoothly?

Editing Checking for Conventions

Carefully edit your revised paragraph for punctuation, capitalization, spelling, and grammar. Then write a neat final copy.

 Edit and proofread your work. Use the following questions to check your paragraph for errors. Then write a neat final copy.

1 Do I use correct punctuation, capitalization, and spelling?

2 Do I use correct words (*to, two, too*) and grammar?

English Language Learners

During the revising stage, students may need assistance in coming up with more specific nouns, verbs, and adjectives. Ask questions that give students a choice of words. For example, a student may write, "My cat makes a sound when she is happy." Ask, "Is it a loud or soft sound? Is it a purr or a growl?" Encourage students to incorporate the answers to your questions into their writing.

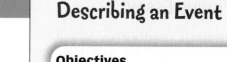

Descriptive Writing

Describing an Event

"This is Maylie Wilson reporting for the Safari Channel. I'm standing above a big old bullfrog in its natural habitat. Notice the tremendous strength of those hind legs. How about those bulging eyes? I think this bullfrog is ready to defend its territory against anyone, and I'm going to move out of range now!"

Describing an event is sort of like filming a documentary. Your job is to capture the moment so people anywhere in the world can experience it for themselves. In this chapter, you will write about an event— an animal in action—and take your readers on an animal safari!

Writing Guidelines

Subject:	**An event**
Form:	**Descriptive essay**
Purpose:	**To clearly describe an animal in action**
Audience:	**Classmates**

Describing an Event

Objectives
- understand the content and form of a descriptive essay
- plan, draft, revise, edit, and publish a descriptive essay

One kind of **descriptive essay** describes an event by focusing on the important actions or on one particularly exciting part.

Tell students that when they write a descriptive essay, these questions can help them:
- Observations: What did you see, hear, and smell?
- Impact: What details will stay with you long after the event is over?
- The 5 *W*s: Answer the *who? what? when? where?* and *why?* questions.

English Language Learners

Students may have difficulty with the idioms on PE page 75. Help them identify the meaning of the following:
- how about (used to point out something)
- out of range (out of reach)
- capture the moment (show what it was like to be there)

Struggling Learners

To help students analyze Maylie Wilson's report, have them answer the following questions:
- <u>Who</u> was the reporter?
- <u>What</u> was she observing?
- <u>Where</u> was the animal?
- <u>Why</u> did the reporter decide to leave?

Advanced Learners

Have students reread Maylie Wilson's news report and then write a paragraph that describes the moment from the frog's point of view. Remind them to use vivid descriptive words and phrases.

Descriptive Essay

Do a **dramatic reading** *(see below)* of the model for students, and then discuss the model.

- How does the beginning get the reader right into the action? (with the sound of the bullfrog's song)
- What are some of the action verbs that are used in the middle part? (shrieked, glared, leapfrogged, gripped, pinned)
- How does the ending show us the writer's feelings about what he saw? (I hadn't moved an inch during this amazing battle. I was still standing on the sticky riverbank.)

✱ Additional information on using powerful action verbs is on PE page 482.

Descriptive Essay

In this sample essay, the writer describes a very natural event—two bullfrogs fighting. As you read the description, review the notes in the left margin. They explain the important parts of the writing.

The Face-Off

BEGINNING
The beginning puts the reader right into the middle of the action.

"Rom-rom-rom!" The booming song echoed across the murky river. I hurried to find its source. My toes squished through the sticky riverbank mud as I followed the song. I stopped. There it was, an olive green bullfrog at the edge of the river.

MIDDLE
The middle uses action verbs and vivid details to describe the bullfrogs in battle.

The bullfrog was a stone, sitting completely still. It had fixed its bulging eyes on a pile of branches in the water. "Hick!" it shrieked. From the middle of the branches came another "Hick," as the answering bullfrog disappeared into the dirty water. In a single motion, the first bullfrog used its long, powerful legs to leap into the river. It surfaced a few feet from the other bullfrog. For a split second, the two glared at each other. Then, in a flash, one leapfrogged the other with a huge splash.

All of a sudden, sounds of fighting filled the air. One frog chased the other until it was pushed against twigs and stones at the river's edge. It

Teaching Tip: Dramatic Reading

Doing a dramatic reading will help students understand the impact vivid action verbs and sensory details can have in descriptive writing. As you read, use your voice (stressing syllables, changing the loudness, altering the tone and pace) to add to the suspense of the description.

English Language Learners

Before reading "The Face-Off," show students a picture of a bullfrog. Be sure they have a concrete image of this animal. Invite students to share anything they know about bullfrogs.

express **SPECIFY** portray
picture describe
Describing an Event **77**

DESCRIPTIVE

gripped the first bullfrog with its thumbs. If these bullfrogs were wolves, I'm sure I would have heard them snarling and growling at each other.

After wrestling near the surface, the frogs disappeared underwater. When they reappeared, they looked like a four-legged, two-headed monster. Then one frog pinned the other underwater. When the victim broke free, it escaped into the river. The other frog floated lazily in the now-calm water.

I hadn't moved an inch during this amazing battle. I was still standing on the sticky riverbank. I never would have thought that funny-looking creatures like bullfrogs were really more like gladiators in disguise.

ENDING

The ending shares the writer's feelings about what he has seen.

Respond to the reading. Answer the following questions about the essay.

☐ Ideas **(1)** How is the topic introduced? **(2)** What two or three details do you especially like?

☐ Organization **(3)** How is the essay organized—by time, by location, or by both time and location?

☐ Voice & Word Choice **(4)** What words show that the writer is interested in the subject?

Respond to the reading.

Answers

Ideas **1.** with the sound of the bull-frog
2. Possible choices:
■ one leapfrogged the other with a huge splash
■ a four-legged, two-headed monster
■ gladiators in disguise

Organization **3.** The event is described by both time and location. The writer tells, step by step, how the bullfrog fight develops. By describing where the bullfrogs are in relation to the river, the writer also uses location to describe the event.

Voice & Word Choice **4.** Possible choices:
■ I hurried
■ I stopped
■ I hadn't moved an inch
■ I was still standing

English Language Learners

As students discuss the writer's word choices for "The Face-Off," be sure they understand that the following words are not meant to be taken literally:

- song
- stone
- four-legged, two-headed monster
- gladiators

Point out that the writer compares the frogs to stone and gladi- ators. Help students understand that it is the qualities of stone (solid, unmoving) and gladiators (fierce fighters) that the writer is calling forth. If the term *gladiator* is unfamiliar to students, explain that this is a kind of soldier from long ago.

Advanced Learners

Point out that the writer starts the essay with a sound word. Explain that this is called *onomatopoeia* and that it is a writing tool often used to capture a reader's atten- tion. Have students identify the other example of ono- matopoeia in "The Face-Off" (Hick!). Invite them to use this device in their own essays.

Prewriting Selecting a Topic

Suggest that students think about animals with which they are familiar, such as dogs, cats, squirrels, and birds. Remind them that it is easier to describe something that they have observed in everyday life than something that they have only read about.

Prewriting Gathering Details

✱ Additional information on finding interesting details is on PE page 531.

When students finish gathering details, have them share the details with a partner. Have partners guess what animal they are hearing about.

78

Prewriting Selecting a Topic

The general topic for your essay is an animal. However, your specific assignment is to write about an animal in action. To get started, you need to think about different animals and what they do. A chart like the one below is a good way to brainstorm for ideas.

Topic Chart

Animal	Action
tiger	stalks prey
salmon	swims upstream to spawn
penguin	waddles clumsily onshore
blue jay	watches over a bird feeder
hunting dog	retrieves a duck
house cat	curls up to sleep

Create a topic chart. In the first column, list different animals that you would like to write about. In the second column, list an action or event related to each animal. When you complete your chart, select one animal for your essay. Pick one whose actions you can describe effectively.

Gathering Details

One way to gather details about a topic is to analyze it. (*Analyze* means to "think carefully about something.") Analyzing helps you consider a topic in several different ways.

Gather details. Answer the following questions to analyze your topic.

1. What does the animal look like? (Describe it from top to bottom or from front to back.)
2. What do I see, hear, smell, or feel when I see or think about this animal in action?
3. What is the animal similar to and different from?
4. What are its strengths and weaknesses?

English Language Learners

To assist students in searching for topics, show pictures of animals in action. Encourage students to name the animals and suggest words for their actions. Use students' responses to make a group chart of topics and details.

Advanced Learners

After students complete their topic charts, have them identify the verbs they used and try to replace them with more vivid examples. For example:

- snake ~~crawls~~ slithers through the woods
- frog ~~jumps~~ plops onto a lily pad
- horse ~~eats grass~~ grazes in the pasture

express SPECIFY describe portray
picture
79
Describing an Event

Organizing Your Details

When writing about an animal in action, you may use two different methods of organization in your essay—time order and order of location.

- **Time order** (*first, second, third*): You will use this method of organization to describe an animal in action or any other event. For example, the writer of the essay on pages 76–77 uses time order.

- **Order of location** (*top to bottom, front to back*): You may also use this method if part of your essay describes the animal in detail.

Organize your details. Imagine you are a filmmaker creating a movie that shows an animal in action. List in order the scenes or details you will share with your audience. Here is part of the writer's organizing list for the essay on the fighting frogs.

1 Follow the sound of a bullfrog
2 Discover the first bullfrog
3 Second bullfrog appears
4 Fight starts
5 Frogs disappear underwater
6 One escapes, fight ends

Using Figures of Speech

You can use figures of speech to make your descriptive writing clearer and more creative. Two common figures of speech are similes and metaphors. They both create special word pictures.

- A **simile** compares two different things using *like* or *as*.
  The owl swiveled its head from side to side like a security camera.

- A **metaphor** compares two different things without using *like* or *as*.
  The bullfrog was a stone, sitting completely still.

Write a descriptive simile and metaphor about your animal in action. If you like how either one turns out, include it in your essay.

Prewriting
Organizing Your Details

Tell students that time order is also called chronological order. Point out that writers often use transition words or phrases like *first* and *next* or *last week* and *next month* to show the order of events.

* Additional information about chronological order is on PE page 534.

If students choose order of location to describe an event, they might use words or phrases like *next to, before, above,* or *below*.

* Additional information about order of location is on PE page 535.

Prewriting
Using Figures of Speech

Have students practice turning **similes into metaphors** (*see below*) by removing *like* or *as*.

Remind students that there are many common similes involving animals that they should avoid (e.g., quick as a rabbit, sly as a fox, slow as a turtle).

Answers will vary.

Teaching Tip: Similes into Metaphors

Demonstrate the difference between similes and metaphors by turning a simile into a metaphor.
- Simile: The squirrel flies from branch to branch *like* a trapeze artist.
- Metaphor: The squirrel *is* a trapeze artist, flying from branch to branch.

English Language Learners

Students may find it easier to focus on creating similes instead of metaphors. For guided practice, use the chart on PE page 78 to help students create similes for some of the actions they listed. (Example: The cat looked *like a baby* curled up to sleep.)

Struggling Learners

If students have difficulty incorporating comparisons into their descriptions, suggest specific categories of actions and sensory details that might help.
- Does the animal sound like a musical instrument?
- Do its movements make you think of a particular vehicle?
- Is its tail similar to a plant you have seen?

Writing
Starting Your Descriptive Essay

Explain that whether students start an essay by placing themselves in the scene or by observing the scene, they should use vivid details that bring the scene to life.

Discuss what the subject is in the first sentence of each beginning (the narrator, the peacock), and discuss what this change in **point of view** *(see below)* does to the beginnings.

Writing Using an Engaging Voice

If students are unsure about their voice, tell them to read their writing out loud. By hearing their writing, they will be able to judge whether they come across as natural, sincere, and enthusiastic. Students may even find that they can edit their writing more easily after hearing someone read it aloud.

Writing Starting Your Descriptive Essay

The beginning paragraph should introduce the event—your animal in action—in an exciting way. Here are two approaches.

Beginning Paragraph

■ **Put yourself in the description.** Tell where you were, what you were doing, or how you felt.

> The writer makes a personal connection.
>
> *When I was in preschool, we visited the zoo on Sunday afternoons. An enormous, mean peacock always roamed around near the main entrance. I imagined that it was a multicolored, screaming monster waiting to attack. It terrified me.*

■ **Observe the scene.** Focus your description on the animal, and not on your personal connection with it.

> The writer focuses on the animal.
>
> *The peacock at the local zoo was enormous and mean. It always roamed around near the main entrance. To some of the younger kids, it wasn't just a bird, it was a multicolored, screaming monster.*

Using an Engaging Voice

Voice is the special way that a writer expresses his or her ideas. It shows that the writer really cares about the subject and the audience. Keep the following tips about your voice in mind as you write.

- Use a natural, sincere voice.
- Write as if you were sharing the description in a conversation.
- Show enthusiasm throughout your essay.

 Write your beginning paragraph. Choose one of the approaches above to get started. If you don't like how your first attempt turns out, try another one.

Teaching Tip: Point of View

Students may not be conscious of the effects that using different points of view can have on writing. Bring in examples of magazine articles and books that have descriptions that use both the first- and third-person points of view. Read aloud samples, and discuss with students the different feelings the points of view convey. Often first-person accounts feel more immediate and personal.

Third-person accounts can feel more objective and reasoned. Discuss different times you would want to use one voice or the other.

Struggling Learners

Point out that the two example beginnings are similar because they use the same adjectives *(enormous, mean peacock; multicolored, screaming monster)*. Then discuss specific ways the paragraphs differ; for example, the first one uses the words *I* and *me*, the second one uses *it*.

Developing the Middle Part

In the middle paragraphs of your essay, you should describe your animal in action. Your goal is to show the reader what happened in a clear and creative way. Use your organizing list from page 79 as a guide.

Middle Paragraphs

Here are two sample middle paragraphs. Each paragraph focuses on one specific scene or action. (The writer puts himself in the description.)

> The paragraph describes one scene.

One day without warning, the peacock jumped onto the sidewalk in front of me. It skipped from side to side almost as if it were trying to block my path. Then it spread its huge blue, green, and gold tail feathers. Suddenly, that bird was twice as big as I was! The peacock stretched its long neck and let out a high-pitched scream. I screamed right back and ran to my dad.

> The paragraph describes a second scene that focuses on the two peacocks.

Another time when our class visited the zoo, I saw the peacock attack another peacock. It put its head down and ran as fast as it could toward the other peacock. Its long tail was dragging across the grass. The second peacock did not know it was going to be attacked. It had a strange look on its face and jumped a foot or two off the ground. Then they both stretched their necks and danced around each other making screeching noises. Looking at those two screaming beasts made me want to get back on the bus.

DESCRIPTIVE

 Write your middle paragraphs. Create a clear, interesting, well-organized picture for your reader. Try to focus on one main scene in each paragraph.

Writing

Developing the Middle Part

If students have difficulty writing the middle paragraphs, suggest that they sketch two or three different scenes in which their animal might be found. They can use the sketches to help them gather details for each paragraph.

English Language Learners

Consider requiring only one middle paragraph for English language learners. As a prewriting activity, have students orally tell about an event related to an animal in action before writing about it.

Struggling Learners

If students have difficulty thinking of scenes for their middle paragraphs, prompt them with questions like the following:
- Has your animal ever made you laugh?
- Did your animal ever hide from you?
- How does your animal react when other animals are nearby?

Writing Ending Your Essay

Tell students that a good ending should explain why the writer found the topic interesting enough to write about. The ending should do more than just repeat what has already been said. It should add something new to keep the reader's interest.

Revising and Editing

Consider having students give each other **peer reviews** (*see below*). This will help each writer find out where descriptive details are lacking or are ineffective.

82

Ending Your Essay

Your ending paragraph should wrap things up and say something to keep the reader thinking about your animal.

Ending Paragraph

> The writer makes a final personal connection.
>
> *Most people think that peacocks are beautiful, gentle birds. Not me. I think they are scary. Each feather on a peacock's tail has a design that looks like a weird, spooky eye. And all those eyes always seem to be watching me. That's why I avoid peacocks whenever I can.*

 Write your ending paragraph. When you write your ending, make a final comment about the animal or event to help the reader remember it.

Revising and Editing

A first draft can always be improved. You may need to make an idea clearer or a detail more colorful. Consider these questions when you revise.

- ☐ **Ideas** Do I include enough descriptive details about the animal and its actions?
- ☐ **Organization** Do I use time order to organize the details?
- ☐ **Voice** Do I sound interested in my topic? Do I put myself in the essay as the narrator, or do I observe and report the action?
- ☐ **Word Choice** Do I use descriptive words and figures of speech? Do I use specific nouns and strong action verbs?
- ☐ **Sentence Fluency** Do my sentences flow smoothly when I read them out loud? Do I vary my sentence beginnings?

 Revise your first draft. Revise your essay, using the questions above as a guide.

 Edit your description. Use the checklist on page 128 when you edit. The checklist will help you look at punctuation, capitalization, spelling, and grammar. Then write and proofread your final copy.

Teaching Tip: Peer Review

Having peers read each other's essays can be very helpful during the revising process. Stress that readers should focus on content, not conventions, at this point. They are like movie reviewers, who say when a scene does or doesn't work. If anything confuses readers, or if they would like to know more about something, they should ask the writer for more details. Peer reviews help writers discover where they need to add descriptive details or where the order of their descriptions may be confusing.

English Language Learners

Help students look for transition words (*first, next, then, at last*) in their writing that make time order clear. If transitions are missing, help students add them in appropriate places to make their writing clearer.

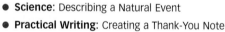

83

Descriptive Writing
Across the Curriculum

Descriptive writing is often assigned in other classes. For example, in social studies, you may be asked to describe life in a different time. In math, you may be asked to describe a geometric shape. In science class, you may be asked to describe a common—or not so common—natural event.

To write strong descriptions, you need to know lots about your topic: what it looks like, how it works, where it occurs, what makes it special, and so on. If your description is a success, a reader will be able to picture the topic in his or her mind.

Mini Index

- **Social Studies:** Describing a Scene in a Different Time
- **Math:** Describing Geometric Terms
- **Science:** Describing a Natural Event
- **Practical Writing:** Creating a Thank-You Note

Across the Curriculum

Objective
- To apply descriptive writing skills to other subject areas

The lessons on the following pages provide samples of descriptive writing students might do in different content areas. Assigning these forms of writing will depend on
- the skill level of your students,
- the subject matter they are studying at any particular time,
- and the writing goals of your school, district, or state.

Coordinate writing-across-the-curriculum activities with teachers in other subject areas.

Struggling Learners

Ask students to recall a time they have described something in another class. Have them orally repeat the details that they remember.

Advanced Learners

Discuss how descriptive writing can be used in adults' careers. Brainstorm ideas for the following:
- astronaut
- police officer
- architect
- journalist
- chef

Social Studies:
Describing a Scene in a Different Time

Point out some of the vivid details that effectively capture the scene. You might mention the following:

- dusty stagecoaches
- towering, snowcapped mountains
- muddy stagecoach trail
- wood-plank sidewalks

Tell students that these colorful details create a distinct picture of a particular place and time. Without these details, readers would have difficulty visualizing the scene.

84

Social Studies:
Describing a Scene in a Different Time

Descriptive writing is one way to share information about a different time and place. The student writer of the following essay puts herself back in time to bring to life a Colorado town during the gold rush.

Gold Rush Days

The **beginning** sets the scene.

It's 1891. The town of Cripple Creek, Colorado, has appeared almost overnight since gold was discovered nearby. Hundreds of people arrive by crowded trains and by dusty stagecoaches. Others also come on foot or by horseback to make their fortunes.

The **middle** describes the topic from a distance as well as up close.

Towering, snowcapped mountains surround the town. Pikes Peak, one of the highest points in the Rocky Mountains, can be seen to the east. A muddy stagecoach trail follows the shoulders of the big peak and winds down toward the wild new town. The land all around Cripple Creek is full of tree stumps. The wood from these trees was used to build houses and mining tunnels. Hills above the town are dotted with piles of dirt from all the new mines.

Hotels, cafes, churches, and saloons line the dirt streets of Cripple Creek. People hurry along wood-plank sidewalks. Because of the gold, there's a lot of money here, but prices are very high. The people who sell the tools, food, and supplies that miners need are trying to get rich just like the miners.

The **ending** offers a final thought.

Cripple Creek is growing by leaps and bounds, but its future depends on the miners. If they strike it rich, who knows how big the town will get!

Struggling Learners

Point out the place names the writer uses (Cripple Creek, Colorado; Pikes Peak; Rocky Mountains). Discuss how these specific details make the author sound knowledgeable and the essay seem more authentic.

express describe portray
picture

DESCRIPTIVE

Writing Tips

Before you write . . .

- **Choose a different time and place that interests you.**
  Select a topic related to the subjects you are studying.
- **Do your research.**
  Learn as much as you can about your topic. Make sure to study any pictures that you can find.
- **Take notes.**
  Write down important details that will help you with your description.

During your writing . . .

- **Write a clear beginning, middle, and ending.**
  In the beginning, set the scene. In the middle part, describe the time and place. End with a final thought about it.
- **Organize your thoughts.**
  When you describe a place, you may describe it from top to bottom, from left to right, or from far to near.
- **Use an engaging voice.**
  Your voice should sound as though you know a lot about your topic and are really interested in it.

After you've written a first draft . . .

- **Check for completeness.**
  Make sure that you have included enough information so that the reader can see your topic in his or her mind.
- **Check for correctness.**
  Proofread your essay to make sure there are no mistakes in punctuation, capitalization, spelling, or grammar.

 Choose a time and place that interests you. Then write a creative and complete description about it to share with your classmates.

Writing Tips

Suggest that students imagine they are walking around in the place they are describing. Have them describe everything they see. Students might also make a map of their place. This will help them place the landmarks and historic sites that they will be writing about.

As a follow-up activity, have student work in pairs to read aloud their descriptions to each other. Listeners make a sketch of what they visualize from the description.

Answers will vary.

English Language Learners

To reduce the burden of research for students not yet proficient in English, encourage them to write about an interesting place they have actually seen. This may be a setting in their homeland, a place they have visited on vacation, or a location in the neighborhood.

Struggling Learners

If students struggle with going back in history, encourage them to leap into the future. Science fiction is motivational to many students, since they need rely only on their imaginations.

Math: Describing Geometric Terms

Tell students that describing math concepts requires clear and precise language. The reader should be able to visualize the geometric object, even without an illustration.

Math: Describing Geometric Terms

Descriptive writing can be used when writing about geometric terms. In each paragraph below, notice how the student describes a geometric term.

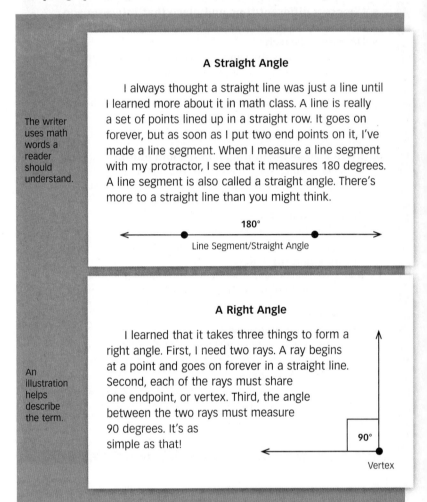

A Straight Angle

I always thought a straight line was just a line until I learned more about it in math class. A line is really a set of points lined up in a straight row. It goes on forever, but as soon as I put two end points on it, I've made a line segment. When I measure a line segment with my protractor, I see that it measures 180 degrees. A line segment is also called a straight angle. There's more to a straight line than you might think.

The writer uses math words a reader should understand.

180°

Line Segment/Straight Angle

A Right Angle

I learned that it takes three things to form a right angle. First, I need two rays. A ray begins at a point and goes on forever in a straight line. Second, each of the rays must share one endpoint, or vertex. Third, the angle between the two rays must measure 90 degrees. It's as simple as that!

An illustration helps describe the term.

90°

Vertex

express SPECIFY portray
picture describe
Writing in Math

87

Writing Tips

Before you write . . .

- **Review the geometric term** you plan to describe.
- **Be sure you understand all of the vocabulary** that is needed to describe the term.
- **Make a plan,** starting with the simplest part of your description.
- **Jot down details** that will help you write a clear and interesting description.

During your writing . . .

- **Study your basic plan.**
- **Describe everything very carefully** and be sure each sentence is clear.
- **Use math words your reader will understand** and explain any words that may be confusing.
- **Add details** in a logical order.
- **Include an illustration** if it helps describe the term.

After you've written a first draft . . .

- **Check for completeness.**
  Be sure that you used the correct vocabulary to describe your term.
- **Check for order.**
  Read through your description to make sure it is organized in a logical way.
- **Check for correctness.**
  Are all the words spelled correctly? Are the sentences capitalized and punctuated correctly?

DESCRIPTIVE

 Write your own description of a geometric term—possibly one of the polygons or triangles. Use the tips listed above. Share your description with your classmates.

Writing Tips

As students work on a description of a geometric shape, tell them to read it aloud to a partner, to see if the partner can visualize the shape. Encourage partners to give each other tips on ways to clarify their descriptions.

Answers will vary.

English Language Learners

Prepare students to use the specialized vocabulary that will be needed for this task. Before they begin writing, engage students in brainstorming terms they might need. If they do not know a particular word, help them draw the concept so you can identify and supply the vocabulary they need.

Struggling Learners

If students have difficulty beginning their paragraphs, have them use the following sentence stem: *When I draw a ____, I ____.* This allows them to start with a complex sentence. It also establishes a personal connection, which for many students is the easiest method of writing descriptions.

Advanced Learners

Suggest that students write their descriptions of geometric shapes in riddle form. They should try to write six sentences about the shape so that they provide enough details to help their classmates correctly identify the shape.

Science: Describing a Natural Event

Tell students to list the action verbs and vivid details that make "Fog" an effective description. Discuss how the writer's choice of words creates a picture that comes across clearly.

88

Science: Describing a Natural Event

The world is filled with fascinating subjects to describe. Plants, landforms, animals, and weather all offer many excellent topics. In the following essay, a student describes what it is like to experience the arrival of fog.

Fog

The **beginning** gets the reader's attention.

Yesterday morning, I was standing by myself on the side of the road waiting for the school bus. A strange mist silently crept toward me just as daylight broke in our valley.

The **middle** describes the topic using specific details.

I first noticed the mist swallowing the mountains on the horizon. After that, it covered the woods behind our house. I saw the tall, white steeple vanish on the North Park Freedom Church, and then the church itself disappeared into the white vapor. My heart started beating faster as the thick, soupy cloud gulped my house and all the houses around it. It continued to float toward me! Then the sidewalk across the street slowly disappeared. Inch by inch, the street in front of me seemed to evaporate. All at once, I was inside a huge, wet cloud. Within seconds, I heard the roar of an engine and the high-pitched squeal of brakes. The school bus had come to my rescue.

The **ending** offers a final thought.

My imagination got the best of me that morning. Maybe I was still a little sleepy, or maybe the quiet affected me. Whatever the reason, I had almost forgotten that fog is really just warm, moist air traveling over the cold surface of the earth.

English Language Learners

After reading "Fog," work with students to identify action verbs that are not intended to be taken literally (*crept, swallowing, covered, vanish, gulped, come to my rescue*). Be sure students understand that these are words the writer used to make the writing interesting, even though fog does not actually do these actions.

Advanced Learners

This description uses personification effectively to describe the action of fog. This is an unusual literary device for most scientific writing. Have students find other examples of writing that use literary devices in a scientific context (the most common is science fiction writing).

express SPECIFY portray
picture describe
89

Writing in Science

DESCRIPTIVE

Writing Tips

Before you write . . .

- **Choose a topic that interests you.**
  If possible, select a natural event that you have seen or experienced yourself.
- **Research your topic.**
  Think about your experience with the topic and read about it. Take notes during your research.

During your writing . . .

- **Write a clear beginning, middle, and ending.**
  Grab your reader's attention in the beginning part. In the middle, describe your topic in the most interesting way you can. Close with a final thought about it.
- **Organize your thoughts.**
  Think about the organization of your description. The one on page 88 is organized from far away to very close. If there is a lot of action, you should probably organize your description according to time.
- **Use specific words.**
  A strong description contains specific nouns, vivid verbs, and effective modifiers (adjectives and adverbs).

After you've written a first draft . . .

- **Check for completeness.**
  Make sure that you have included all the details that the reader needs to understand your description.
- **Check for correctness.**
  Proofread your description for punctuation, capitalization, spelling, and grammar.

 Select a natural event to describe. Gather plenty of details about your topic. Then describe it in an essay using the tips above.

Writing Tips

If students choose to describe something familiar, like a thunderstorm, be sure they don't assume they know everything about it and, therefore, don't need to do research. The more thorough their understanding of their topic is, the more effective their description of the event's impact will be.

Have students read their descriptions aloud. Remind them to read with expression and enthusiasm.

Answers will vary.

English Language Learners

In preparing for this assignment, have students create a sensory web with one branch for each sense. Help them use the web to describe what they saw, heard, felt, and smelled during the natural event they have chosen as a topic. Tell students to use some of the ideas from the web in their writing.

Struggling Learners

Encourage students to draw two sketches as they prewrite. One should depict the natural event in action, and the other should illustrate some of its after-effects. Have students refer to their drawings as they work through their description.

Practical Writing: Creating a Thank-You Note

Tell students that a well-written thank-you note can make a strong impression on its recipient. The immediacy of e-mail and instant messaging may be tempting, but a handwritten thank-you note shows that you care enough to take extra time to express your gratitude.

90

Practical Writing:
Creating a Thank-You Note

Descriptive writing appears in almost any form. Descriptions add life to letters, e-mail messages, notes, and greeting cards. The writer of this thank-you note describes a snowboard to his aunt.

❖ ❖ ❖ ❖ ❖ ❖ *Thank You* ❖ ❖ ❖ ❖ ❖ ❖

Dear Aunt Gloria,

The **beginning** identifies the reason for the note.

Thanks for the gift certificate you sent me for my birthday. I used it to buy what every kid here in Duluth wants, a freestyle snowboard!

The **middle** describes the topic.

The board I bought is called the Atomic Storm. If you stood it up next to me, you would see that it is almost as tall as I am. It is about 10 inches wide, which makes it a lot wider than an old-fashioned ski. The front is called the nose, and it is rounded, like the end of a paper clip. The design on it is awesome. Bright orange rows of flames spill all the way down the shiny black center. When you get to the back, or the tail, of the board, you find out that the fire is coming from a slick red race car. The tail of the board is rounded, just like the nose.

The **ending** gives some final thoughts.

I love my new board. It's perfect for getting big air at the snowboard park and doing spins and tricks like a pro. I'll send you some pictures of me using it.

Love,

Ty

Struggling Learners

Discuss how the thank-you note would sound without the middle paragraph. Ask:
- Would Aunt Gloria still know how much Ty likes his gift?
- Would she be able to picture the snowboard with her mind's eye?

Advanced Learners

Have students draw pictures of the snowboard based on the detailed description in Ty's letter. Then have them compare the drawings.

express SPECIFY portray
picture describe
91
Practical Writing

Writing Tips

Before you write . . .

- **Select a topic.**
  Choose a topic for your thank-you note: a special gift that you received from a family member or friend.
- **List main ideas you want to include.**
  Since you are thanking someone for a gift, consider what it looks like, why you like it, and how you are using it.
- **Gather specific details.**
  List details to describe the gift.
- **Consider your feelings.**
  Ask yourself how you feel about the gift.

During your writing . . .

- **Organize your thoughts.**
  State the reason for the note in the beginning. Give the descriptive details in the middle part. Offer a final thought in the ending part.
- **Use colorful words.**
  Use specific nouns, strong action verbs, and colorful adjectives to describe the gift.

After you've written a first draft . . .

- **Check for completeness.**
  Keep your paragraphs fairly short. Are there enough details to make your description clear and fun to read? Do your sentences flow smoothly?
- **Check for correctness.**
  Proofread your note to make sure there are no mistakes in punctuation, capitalization, spelling, or grammar.

 Create a thank-you note for a family member or friend. Describe a special gift in your note. Use the tips above and the sample note on page 90.

DESCRIPTIVE

Writing Tips

✳ If students are interested in sending their thank-you notes, model correct envelope format for students or refer them to PE page 577.

As an alternative, tell students they can write about something other than a gift. For example, they might write a thank-you note for a special outing with an aunt or uncle, such as a visit to the local ballpark, zoo, or museum. Or they might write a thank-you for spending a weekend with a family member or friend.

Answers will vary.

Advanced Learners

Suggest that students write a thank-you note to a company that makes a product they especially like or to a local business they often frequent. Businesses are often charmed by such letters and will usually send a reply, which makes this a very reinforcing activity. Set up a bulletin board where you can showcase the kinds of responses that are received.

Narrative Writing Overview

Writing Standards

The writing standards listed below are based on a blending of state and NCTE standards.

- Use charts and clusters to gather and organize ideas.
- Support central ideas with sensory details and the use of dialogue.
- Revise drafts to use transitions and strong modifiers.
- Assess writing using a rubric based on the traits of effective writing.

Writing Forms

- narrative paragraph
- narrative essay about sharing an experience
- biographical narrative

Focus on the Traits

- **Ideas** Including sensory details
- **Organization** Forming a clear beginning, middle, and end
- **Voice** Using a natural voice that includes the use of dialogue
- **Word Choice** Choosing specific adjectives and adverbs
- **Sentence Fluency** Combining sentences to vary sentence length and form, and thus improve the flow and smoothness of the narratives
- **Conventions** Checking for errors in punctuation, capitalization, spelling, and grammar

Unit Pacing

Narrative Paragraph: 1.5–2.25 hours

The **narrative paragraph** introduces the unit and lays the groundwork for more extensive narrative writing. Use this section if students need to work on crafting a paragraph. Following are some of the topics that are covered.

- Using a cluster to write down surprising experiences
- Creating a chart to gather details
- Writing a surprising story

Narrative Essay 1: 4.5–6.75 hours

This section asks student to **share an experience.** Use this section to focus on developing an essay. Following are some of the topics that are covered.

- Creating a topics chart
- Using a personality web and a sensory chart to gather details
- Writing a beginning, a middle, and an ending
- Using dialogue to show, not tell
- Combining sentences to vary sentence lengths

Narrative Essay 2: 2: 2.5–3.5 hours

The **biographical narrative** section offers a new slant on narratives—writing about an event in another person's life. Use this section to present an alternate or additional form of narrative writing. Following are some of the topics covered.

- Creating a line diagram to choose a topic
- Using the 5 W's and H questions to gather details
- Organizing details on a time line
- Writing a narrative that follows a story line pattern (beginning, rising action, high point, ending)

Narrative Writing Across the Curriculum: *1.5–2.25 hours*

Collaborate with teachers from other content areas to identify narrative forms that could enhance students' experience with the curriculum already in place.

- **Social Studies**
Classroom Journals, pp. 144–145

- **Math**
Story Problems, pp. 146–147

- **Science**
Anecdotes, pp. 148–149

- **Practical Writing**
Class Minutes, pp. 150–151

Writing for Assessment: *45–90 minutes*

The student text shows a strong student response to the first prompt below. Students can respond to that same prompt or to either of the additional prompts as an informal or a formal assessment.

- Write a story about a day in your life that you would like to live over again.
- Write a story about a package that is left on your doorstep.
- Write a story about the nicest thing you've ever done for someone else.

Evaluating a Narrative Essay

Learning to evaluate one's own and others' writing is an integral part of learning to write. In addition to a student's evaluation of a narrative essay (PE pages 132–133), **benchmark papers** provide practice with evaluating narrative writing.

- Suzie (strong)
TR 1A–1C
TE pp. 776–778
- A Knotty Problem (good)
PE pp. 132–133
- A January Surprise (poor)
TR 2A–2C
TE pp. 779–781

Integrated Grammar and Writing Skills

Below are skills lessons from the resources sections of the pupil edition that are suggested at point of use (✳) throughout this unit.

Writing a Narrative Paragraph

- ✳ Parts of a Paragraph, pp. 524–525
- ✳ Clustering, p. 544

Sharing an Experience

- ✳ Writing Prompts, pp. 546–547
- ✳ Adjectives, pp. 486, 488–489
- ✳ Adverbs, pp. 490, 492
- ✳ Dialogue, pp. 588–589, 598–601, 624

Writing a Biographical Narrative

- ✳ Sentence Variety, pp. 511–514

Additional Grammar Skills

Below are skills lessons from other components that you can weave into your unit instruction.

Writing a Narrative Paragraph

Sharing an Experience

Writing a Biographical Narrative

Narrative Writing

Narrative Paragraph

The next time you're with a friend, pay attention to what you say to each other. Maybe you talk about what happened on your walk to school, about a movie you saw last night, about the time Grandpa won the karate championship. . . . You and your friends tell all kinds of stories!

You can capture your storytelling talents on paper by writing a narrative. The following pages will help you write a narrative paragraph about a pleasant surprise.

Writing Guidelines

Subject:	A pleasant surprise that you experienced
Form:	Narrative paragraph
Purpose:	To entertain
Audience:	Classmates

Objectives

- understand the content and structure of a narrative paragraph
- choose a topic (a surprise) to write about
- plan, draft, revise, and edit a narrative paragraph

A **narrative paragraph** tells a brief story. The assignment in this section asks students to tell about a pleasant surprise in their life. A paragraph is a form of writing that usually includes a topic sentence, middle sentences in the body, and a closing sentence.

✱ Additional information about the basic parts of paragraphs is on PE pages 524–525.

Point out to students that narratives are all around them—in what they read, in what they watch and see, and in what they hear.

Note that conversations with friends and family members almost always focus on personal stories. Have students think about any personal stories that they shared or heard during the day.

Narrative Paragraph

After you read through the sample with students, discuss the qualities that make it a narrative. (It tells about an experience, it is entertaining, and it is told in the first person.)

 Respond to the reading.

Review the questions orally with students so that you can explore why they chose particular details.

Answers

Ideas **1.** Possible choices:
- thing that went "bump"
- drifting off to sleep
- hcard footstep
- somebody in the room
- window open
- something crashed
- leaping up
- took a swing
- a yowl

Organization 2. in the order in which they happened from beginning to end (chronological)

Voice & Word Choice **3.** Possible choices:
- Sure, I had only 10 bucks . . . , but it was my 10 bucks!
- I began to laugh. Some cat burglar that was . . . !

Narrative Paragraph

Some of the most entertaining stories contain surprises. Perhaps your hamster escaped from his cage, but at school you opened up your backpack and discovered him chewing on your math assignment. Maybe you spiked your hair, thinking it was "Crazy Hair Day," when it was actually "Picture Day." These kinds of surprises make entertaining narrative paragraphs. The following narrative paragraph tells about a nighttime surprise.

Topic sentence · · · · · · · · · ·

Body

Closing sentence · · · · · · · · · · · ·

Things That Go Bump

One night last week, I was surprised by a thing that went "bump!" I was just drifting off to sleep when I heard a footstep in my dark bedroom. I gasped and sat up. Somebody was in the room with me. My door was shut, but the window was open. That's how the intruder must have gotten in. Something crashed, and coins went rolling all over the floor. My bank! Sure, I had only 10 bucks and some change, but it was my 10 bucks! Leaping up, I flipped on the light and took a swing at the burglar. With a yowl, Whiskers jumped over my fist and shot back out the window. Even as I was shaking, I began to laugh. Some cat burglar that was—my own cat!

 Respond to the reading. Answer the following questions on your own paper.

☐ Ideas **(1)** What ideas or details build suspense for the ending?

☐ Organization **(2)** How does the writer organize the events in the paragraph?

☐ Voice & Word Choice **(3)** What words or phrases show you that the writer enjoys this topic?

English Language Learners

Students may have difficulty understanding the idioms in this sample. Provide extra help as needed to "translate" such expressions.

Idioms on page 94 include the following:
- things that go bump [in the night] (unexpected, often scary noises heard at night)
- bucks (dollars)
- flipped on the light (turned on the light)
- took a swing (made a gesture to punch or hit)
- cat burglar (a thief who enters a building by climbing through a window).

Struggling Learners

To help students process the events in the sample, ask them to retell the story about the cat burglar by designing it as a comic strip that uses no words. Have students compare the number of frames each of them used to represent the story.

Prewriting **Selecting a Topic**

Surprising things happen every day. The writer of "Things That Go Bump" used a cluster to write down some of his surprising experiences.

Cluster

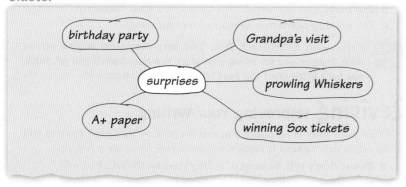

Create a cluster. In the middle of your paper, write the word "surprises" and circle it. Then create a cluster of four or five of your own surprising experiences. Choose one of these experiences to write about.

Gathering Details

To gather details, the writer of the sample paragraph on page 94 listed what happened first, what he expected to happen next, and what surprise actually happened.

Chart

What Happened First	What I Expected to Happen Next	What Surprise Actually Happened
heard a sound in my room at night	to see a burglar	saw my cat Whiskers

Chart your surprise. Make a chart like the one above. Write what happened first, what you expected to happen next, and what surprise happened.

Prewriting **Selecting a Topic**

After reading the section, ask: What makes something a surprise? (It is unexpected. It is not what you think will happen.)

Have students work in groups or individually to choose a topic. Circulate among students who are working on their own and hold **writing conferences** *(see below)* to provide guidance and answer questions.

✳ Additional information about clustering can be found on PE page 544.

Prewriting **Gathering Details**

To provide practice, suggest this topic: *Recall a time when there was an unexpected substitute teacher in class.*

Have students gather details about this topic by completing a chart like the one shown.

Teaching Tip: Writing Conferences

Not all conferences have to be lengthy or formal. Students can benefit from short, focused conversations at their desks with the teacher. Because the conversation addresses their own particular need at just the right time, students are more likely to absorb the information.

What follows are two ways to help students find a topic:

- Think about the last few telephone calls you've had. What did you talk about? Did you tell any stories about what had happened recently? Did anything surprise you?
- Think about any e-mails or letters you sent recently. What did you write about? What was happening in your life at the time? Did anything surprise you?

Writing
Developing the First Draft

As students read about the parts of a paragraph, ask them to read the corresponding parts in the sample paragraph on PE page 94.

Remind students that their narrative paragraph should
- be suspenseful and
- tell the events in the order in which they happened.

The first draft can be completed as an in-class or at-home assignment.

Revising **Improving Your Writing**

Students may be overwhelmed by the number of items to check for during revision. Suggest that they focus on only one item at a time.

Editing **Checking for Conventions**

Consider having students **peer-edit** *(see below)* a partner's paper. It is sometimes easier to see errors in someone else's writing.

96

Writing Developing the First Draft

A narrative paragraph has a topic sentence, a body, and a closing sentence. Each part serves a different purpose.

- The **topic sentence** introduces your story in an interesting way.
- The **body** uses sensory details to describe what happened.
- The **closing sentence** wraps up your paragraph.

 Write your first draft. Write your surprising story in your natural voice. Imagine you are telling your story to a classmate. If you get stuck, look back at the chart you used to gather details on page 95.

Revising Improving Your Writing

Once your story is on paper, you can revise it so that your readers will feel like they experienced it right along with you. Here are a few tips.

- **Show, don't tell.** Instead of telling readers "Nakita had a fit," show them by writing "Nakita waved her hands and hollered."
- **Check the order.** Tell the events in the order they happened.
- **Build up to a high point.** Increase the excitement as you lead up to the conclusion.
- **Check words and sentences.** Use strong nouns and verbs and make sure your sentences flow smoothly.

 Revise your paragraph. Check your ideas, organization, voice, word choice, and sentence fluency as you revise your narrative paragraph. Look for ways to improve your topic sentence, body, and closing sentence.

Editing Checking for Conventions

After completing your revised draft, check your story for correct use of punctuation, grammar, spelling, and so on.

Edit your work. Use the following questions to make sure your narrative paragraph is free of errors.

1 Have I checked for errors in capitalization and grammar?

2 Have I checked my punctuation and spelling?

Proofread your story. Give your copy a final look.

Teaching Tip: Peer Editing

Students can become so familiar with their own papers that they have difficulty seeing errors. As first-time readers, peers are more likely to stumble over poor word choice and grammatical errors. Pair students to edit each other's papers. Partners can underline or mark places that need to be corrected.

English Language Learners

When assigning partners for peer editing, have these students work with cooperative, considerate students who are proficient in English. It may be most effective if such partnerships are ongoing throughout the unit, so that students feel comfortable and confident while sharing their work.

tell **share** remember
relate narrate 97

Narrative Writing

Sharing an Experience

Like everyone else, you have stories to tell. Think about how many times you have said, "Guess what happened to me!" or "Do you know what I did?" Your life is full of stories. You took a trip, broke your arm, or finally got your own pet. Writing a personal narrative is a way to share one of your important stories. It's also a way for you to learn about yourself and your special place in the world.

Think about personal experiences that you could share with your classmates. You could write about something that happened to you, something you did, or someone you have a special relationship with. Here are some guidelines to help you get started.

Writing Guidelines

Subject:	A personal experience
Form:	Personal narrative
Purpose:	To share a true experience
Audience:	Classmates

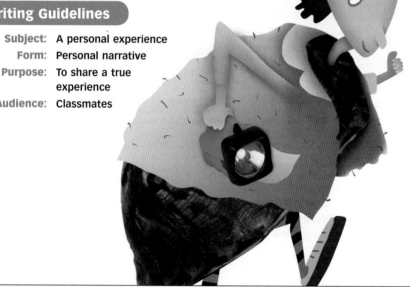

Sharing an Experience

Objectives

- understand what a personal narrative is
- understand the content and form of a personal narrative
- plan, draft, revise, edit, and publish a personal narrative

A **personal narrative** is a story that tells about your own personal experiences. It might describe

- what you did,
- what happened to you, or
- who you have a special relationship with.

Talk about different personal narratives students may have written recently. Examples may include the following:

- a diary or a journal entry about their day
- a letter or an e-mail to a friend or relative telling about what's happening in their lives

To get students thinking about their lives and experiences, ask them to create a time line that lists important, interesting, or entertaining events for each year they include on the time line.

Understanding Your Goal

Traits of Narrative Writing

Three traits relate to the development of the content and the form. They provide a focus during prewriting, drafting, and revising.

- Ideas
- **Organization**
- Voice

The other three traits relate more to form. Checking them is part of the revising and editing process.

- **Word Choice**
- **Sentence Fluency**
- **Conventions**

✳ The six-point rubric on PE pages 130–131 is based on these traits. Four- and five-point rubrics are available on TE pages 768 and 772.

To help students internalize the traits, use this activity:

- List the traits on a piece of paper. Make enough copies for each student to have one trait.
- Cut the traits into individual strips and randomly give a strip to each student.
- Have students create a simple drawing to illustrate the trait they've been given.
- Have students form groups that contain all six traits. Students should share their illustrations depicting their traits with other group members.

98

Understanding Your Goal

Your goal in this chapter is to write an essay about an interesting personal experience. The traits listed in the chart below will help you plan and write your personal narrative.

TRAITS OF NARRATIVE WRITING

Ideas
Use details and dialogue to tell about a specific experience or event. Make the reader want to know what happens next.

Organization
Open with a clear beginning that pulls the reader into the story. Then present ideas in the order in which they happened.

Voice
Write the story in a way that sounds natural. Use dialogue to give the people in your story voice.

Word Choice
Use specific nouns, vivid verbs, and well-chosen modifiers.

Sentence Fluency
Use a variety of sentence styles that flow smoothly from one idea to the next.

Conventions
Be sure that your punctuation, capitalization, spelling, and grammar are correct.

 Get the big picture. Look at the rubric on pages 130–131. You can use this rubric to assess your progress. Your goal is to write an engaging essay about a personal experience.

Personal Narrative

In this personal narrative, the student author writes about a special person who taught her about turtles. The side notes point out the main parts of the narrative.

Turtle Lady

BEGINNING

The beginning catches the reader's attention and gives an idea of what the story is about.

When we first moved to Florida, Dad and I went to the ocean every week and enjoyed just taking walks on the beach. The beach was usually deserted, except for some seagulls and a few sand crabs. However, one night, we spotted a campfire way down the beach. We went to check it out. As we got closer, we saw someone sitting in the sand near the dying flames. The glow of the fire revealed an old woman wearing a long orange coat and a red bandanna.

"Stop right there! Don't move," the woman whispered loudly. Not far from where I stood, I made out the shape of a huge turtle digging in the sand. "That turtle needs her space right now."

"Why, what's wrong?" I whispered back.

MIDDLE

The middle includes details and dialogue that introduce an important person in the story.

"She's digging out a nest, and she'll lay her eggs there tonight. When she's done, she'll go back to the sea."

"Who are you?" I whispered.

She came closer, and I smelled the campfire on her tattered clothing. "My name is Dolly Cripps, but you can call me Turtle Lady because I rescue turtles. Now if you two promise to be quiet, I'll tell you more about loggerheads." Then she began talking about the turtles.

Every week we hiked up the beach to visit Dolly, and every time she taught us more about the loggerheads. We'd sit in the sand near her fire, and Dolly would tell us about the turtles that she had helped. She must have been very

NARRATIVE

Personal Narrative

Work through this sample story with the class, pointing out the elements that make it a good personal narrative.

Ideas

- The author tells about a personal experience.

Organization

- The beginning of the story grabs the reader's attention and puts the reader right in the story.
- The story is told in clear time order and flows smoothly.

Voice

- The author uses natural dialogue and specific details.

Respond to the reading.

Answers

Ideas **1.** meeting a woman who rescues loggerhead turtles

Organization **2.** in the order in which the events happen

Voice & Word Choice **3.** Possible choices:

- Every week we hiked up . . . to visit Dolly
- an amazing thing happened
- if we hadn't been there
- neatest thing I've ever done

MIDDLE
The middle includes details that tell what happened first, second, third, and so on.

old because she knew turtles that were more than 100 years old!

After a couple of months, an amazing thing happened. The sand near the nest began to ripple and shake. A couple days later, dozens of little turtles tunneled their way out from under the sand and scrambled toward the sea. The waves tossed some of them back onto the shore. That's when Dolly, Dad, and I grabbed any baby turtles that landed upside down and couldn't get up. We quickly rescued them and gently placed them back in the ocean. If we had not been there, the hatchlings would have died, or they might have become some seagull's supper.

Rescuing those turtles was the coolest thing I've ever done. As quickly as the turtle rescue had begun, it was over. The turtles no longer needed us.

ENDING
The ending tells how the writer felt after her experience.

As the last turtle disappeared into the ocean, I turned to the turtle lady and asked, "Will we see you again next year?"

"Maybe," she answered. "Wherever my turtles are, that's where I will be."

Respond to the reading. Why is "Turtle Lady" such a good personal narrative? To find out, answer the following questions.

☐ Ideas **(1)** What specific experience does the writer share?

☐ Organization **(2)** How does the writer organize the events in the story?

☐ Voice & Word Choice **(3)** What words and phrases show that the writer is interested in her topic?

English Language Learners

Point out that the personal narratives that inexperienced students write do not have to be as long as the sample. What is important is that the narratives have a clear beginning, middle, and end.

Idioms appearing in this narrative include:

- hanging out (sitting leisurely)
- check it out (get information)
- scrambled (moved quickly)
- neatest thing (best or most rewarding event).

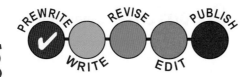

Prewriting

Before you are ready to write your narrative, you need to choose a personal experience to write about. After selecting a topic, you will continue prewriting by gathering and organizing details.

Keys to Effective Prewriting

1. Select an experience that you know well and would like to share.

2. Make sure you can answer the 5 W questions about the experience.

3. Think about and describe the people in your narrative.

4. Put the events in order by using a quick list or a time line.

5. Gather details about sights, sounds, and other senses related to your narrative.

NARRATIVE

Prewriting
Keys to Effective Prewriting

Remind students of the purpose of the prewriting stage in the writing process. (It's when the writer gets ready to write.)

The Keys to Effective Prewriting lays out the process students will be guided through on PE pages 102–106.

- Suggest that students look at the time lines about their lives that they created (see TE page 97) as they think about a writing topic.
- Ask students to name the 5 W questions. (Who? What? When? Where? Why?)
- Tell students they will read about a quick list (mentioned in item 4) later in the lesson when they are organizing their ideas.

Prewriting Selecting a Topic

Focus on the Traits

Ideas
- Be sure students read this before they select a topic.
- After brainstorming ideas, have pairs of students narrow their topic choices.

✱ See more about choosing a topic on PE pages 546–547.

Read aloud these sports accounts. Focusing on the narrative traits (PE page 98), discuss which story starter is more effective and why.

A. *Last night, the Eagles played the Rockets. Eagles player Diego Jones was hurt at the start. The team then trailed for most of the game. The Rockets played well. Then the Eagles made several baskets and won the game.*

B. *Last night our Eagles played with amazing courage and skill. The team trailed by at least three points for most of the game. Then a devastating injury took out star player Diego Jones. All seemed lost, until freshman Don Chang stole the ball and made a three-pointer to tie the game. Fouled by the opposition, he was called to the foul line, where he sank both free throws to win in the final seconds of the game. The crowd's cheers rocked the gym.*

102

Prewriting Selecting a Topic

The key to a good personal narrative is finding an interesting topic—one that both you and the reader will enjoy. The chart below shows how one writer gathered story ideas by remembering different people, places, animals, and experiences.

People I Know	Places I've Been	Animals I Remember	Things I've Done
My brother Sam	The Liberty Bell	B. J., the dog	Marched in a parade
My friend Kenny	Cuba	Big raccoon	Met Tom Jones
Tyisha, the dancer	My uncle's wedding	Snake at the campground	Explored a cave

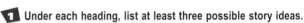

Prewrite **Brainstorm for topics.** On your own paper, draw a chart like the one above. Use the same four headings for your categories. Then fill in the chart using the directions below.

1 Under each heading, list at least three possible story ideas.

2 Now go over your ideas and circle the topic that you think would make the best story. (You will use this topic in the next exercise.)

Focus on the Traits

Ideas Your topic does not have to be a complicated one. In fact, a short trip or a simple event can often make a great story. Think about important experiences that took place within a short period of time—a day, an hour, or even just a few minutes.

Struggling Learners

For students who have difficulty choosing a personal experience to write about, suggest that they identify an experience that parallels the "Turtle Lady" model. Have them think about a time when they just happened to be in "the right place at the right time" in order to experience an event.

tell **share** *remember*
relate
Sharing an Experience

103

Sizing Up Your Idea

Now that you have a story idea, you must decide if it will make a good personal narrative. Your narrative should tell about an experience you had at a specific time and place. You can use the 5 W's to find out if your story idea has all of these details.

1. **Who** are the people in my story?
2. **What** main experience will I write about?
3. **When** and **where** did the experience take place?
4. **Why** did the experience change me?

Size up your story idea. Write your answers to the 5 W questions above. Review your answers. Do you have enough details to write a good story? If not, choose another idea from your chart (page 102).

Gathering Details About People

A personal narrative tells about your own experience, so you will be one person in your story. Other people and animals may appear as well. A personality web can help you gather details about the people in your story.

Personality Web

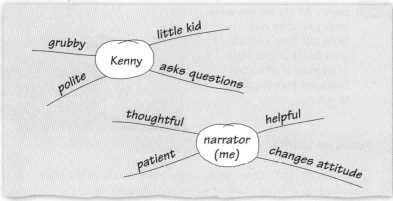

Make personality webs. Create a personality web for each important person in your story. Write each person's name in a circle and include details about the person on the lines.

NARRATIVE

Prewriting
Putting Events in Order

After students have jotted down their quick list, have them share the list with a partner to be sure that the order is chronological.

Focus on the Traits

Organization
Phrases such as "one night" or "as we got closer" can work well as transitions.

The main concern at the drafting stage is to get all the ideas down in chronological order. Transitions can be added during the revising stage.

104

Prewriting Putting Events in Order

Once you've completed your personality webs, it's time to list the events in your story. Most narratives are organized in chronological (time) order. That means events appear in the order in which they happened. A quick list like the one below is one way to organize events.

Quick List

> *My Friend Kenny*
>
> – I thought little kids were a pain.
> – Uncle Eddie asked me to volunteer at bike camp.
> – There were tons of little kids at the camp.
> – I thought bike camp would be a drag.
> – I made friends with a neat little kid named Kenny.
> – I learned to like little kids.

 Create your quick list. On your own paper, make a list like the one above. Write your story idea at the top. Then write the main details of your story in the order in which they happened, from beginning to end.

Focus on the Traits

Organization Once you have the main details of the story in chronological order, think of some transition words and phrases that could help tie your ideas together. (See pages 572–573.) You could add these words to your quick list.

tell **share** remember
relate
Sharing an Experience **105**

Gathering Sensory Details

A good story has lots of colorful, specific details. Some of these details should relate to the senses. Then the reader is able to imagine not only what things look like but also how things sound, smell, taste, and feel.

Making a sensory chart, like the one below, is one way you can gather sensory details about your experience.

Sensory Chart

SENSORY DETAILS

I saw...	– little kids riding trikes – squirmy kids
I heard...	– Uncle Eddie – trike bells and bike horns
I smelled...	– chocolate on Kenny's clothes
I felt...	– Kenny's sticky little fingers – pain in my foot
I tasted...	– (could almost taste) the chocolate bar smeared on Kenny's face

Prewrite **Create a sensory chart.** List the five senses with space after each one. Then recall your experience and fill in the chart as completely as you can. (It's all right to have lots of details for some senses and only a few or none for others.) You will use some of these details in your narrative.

Focus on the Traits

Voice The details and feelings you use in your writing are part of your natural voice. The words you choose to describe what you saw, heard, smelled, tasted, or touched are also part of your voice.

NARRATIVE

Prewriting
Gathering Sensory Details

- Specific sensory details help readers feel that they are right in the middle of the action.
- Adding too many details or details that are not related to the story can distract readers and make the narrative less effective. For example, if the narrator of "Turtle Lady" had written a lot about the family's new house, the details would have been unrelated to the story.

Focus on the Traits

Voice

After reviewing the boxed material, go over the sample sensory chart.
- How do students think the writer feels about little kids in general and Kenny in particular?
- What details make them think so?

The writer seems to think little kids are annoying. Details that indicate this include the following:
- squirmy kids
- Kenny's sticky little fingers
- pain in my foot
- chocolate bar smeared on Kenny's face

English Language Learners

Students may need help thinking of sensory details.
- Model the exercise by naming sensory details related to a familiar object in the classroom.
- Guide students as they practice describing something else.
- Help them describe all aspects of their topic. (However, point out that all five senses may not be relevant.)

Prewriting
Reviewing Your Details

Work as a class to complete the **Try It** exercise orally.

 **Answers**

1. **Who:** mom, narrator, cat
   What: whining sound in the dryer scared mom
   When: one evening
   Where: laundry room
   Why: the cat was caught in the dryer when it was turned on.

2. **Transition words:**
   one evening, all of a sudden, as I raced downstairs, after that

3. **Sensory details:**
   wet clothes, tossed, slammed door, ran upstairs, whining sound, yelled, raced, louder and louder, flung open, eyes bugged out, hair looked like a cartoon character, darted

Point out that "A Hair-Raising Experience" is a narrative paragraph, not a full essay. Ask:

- What details could you add to turn this paragraph into a narrative essay?
- Which parts of the paragraph could be expanded and how?

Have students brainstorm dialogue that they would use to help make this paragraph into an essay.

106

Prewriting Reviewing Your Details

Before you begin writing your story, look over your prewriting quick list, personality web, and sensory chart. Be sure you've collected enough details to write a good personal narrative.

 Read the paragraph below. Then answer these questions about the details used in "A Hair-Raising Experience."

1. Have the 5 W's (*who, what, when, where,* and *why*) been answered?
2. What transitions show the time order of the paragraph?
3. What sensory details help create a clear picture?

A Hair-Raising Experience

1 One evening, my mom was downstairs doing the laundry.
2 As usual, she was trying to do 10 jobs at once when she grabbed
3 the wet clothes from the washer and tossed them into the dryer.
4 She slammed the dryer door, turned the timer, and started to
5 run upstairs. All of a sudden, a whining sound stopped her in her
6 tracks. The sound was coming from the dryer. She yelled for me.
7 As I raced downstairs, the sound grew louder and louder. I flung
8 open the dryer door. There to our surprise was Mica, our cat. He
9 looked like someone who had just gotten off a Tilt-A-Whirl ride.
10 His eyes bugged out, and his hair looked like a cartoon character
11 with a finger in an electric outlet. Mica darted out of the dryer
12 and up the stairs. After that, Mom always checked out the dryer
13 before slamming the door, and Mica stayed clear of the laundry
14 room for a long, long time.

 Examine your details. Review your prewriting activities before you begin to write your first draft. Use the following guidelines.

1 Be sure you can answer the 5 W's (*who, what, when, where,* and *why*) about your story.

2 Check your quick list to make sure the events are listed in the order that they happened.

3 Review the details in your sensory chart.

Advanced Learners

Explain that similes are often used to convey sensory details. Have students identify the two similes included in "A Hair-Raising Experience." Discuss how these similes create a detailed visual picture. For example, stating that the cat's hair *looked like a cartoon character with a finger in an electric outlet* is an effective way of describing the effect of sta- tic electricity on the cat's hair. The other simile is [*the cat*] *looked like someone who had just gotten off a Tilt-A-Whirl ride*. Encourage students to include at least one simile in their own narrative.

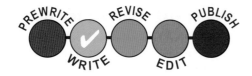

Writing

PREWRITE · WRITE ✓ · REVISE · EDIT · PUBLISH

Now that you have gathered and organized your ideas, you are ready to write the first draft of your narrative. Focus on putting your ideas on paper in the best order. Use your own unique storytelling voice.

Keys to Effective Writing

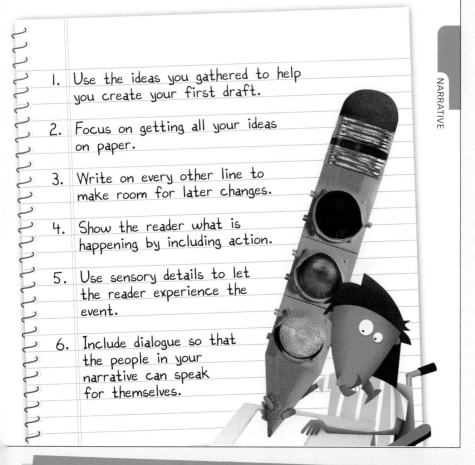

1. Use the ideas you gathered to help you create your first draft.

2. Focus on getting all your ideas on paper.

3. Write on every other line to make room for later changes.

4. Show the reader what is happening by including action.

5. Use sensory details to let the reader experience the event.

6. Include dialogue so that the people in your narrative can speak for themselves.

NARRATIVE

Writing

Keys to Effective Writing

Remind students that the writing stage is when they get to write, or draft, their ideas on paper.

The Keys to Effective Writing lays out the process students will be guided through on PE pages 107–112.

Remind students they can refer back to these strategies as they are writing their **draft** *(see below)*.

Teaching Tip: Drafting

Here are some tips that will help students manage their drafts.

- Put your name and the date on your paper.
- Leave space to add a title later.
- Number each page in the upper right corner.
- Write on every other line.

- Clip draft pages with prewriting materials, and store them in your writing folder or portfolio.

Writing Getting the Big Picture

Focus on the parts of a narrative to make sure that students understand the overall structure of this form of writing. Point out that the specific example for each part relates to the model narrative that is shown on PE pages 109–112.

Writing Getting the Big Picture

The chart below shows how the parts of a personal narrative fit together. (The examples are from the narrative on pages 109–112.) You're ready to write your narrative once you . . .

- collect plenty of details about the experience.
- organize the details according to time.

BEGINNING

The **beginning** paragraph introduces the experience and makes the reader want to know what happens next.

Opening Sentences
Little kids are a pain—or so I thought. Then Uncle Eddie asked me to volunteer at bike camp. . . .

MIDDLE

The **middle** part gives details about what happened first, second, third, and so on. It also answers the *who, what, when,* and *where* questions.

When I arrived at bike camp . . .

My first job was to teach . . .

Kenny and I saw a lot . . .

By the end of camp, I wished . . .

ENDING

The **ending** tells *why* or *how* you were changed because of this experience.

Closing Sentences
Little kids just don't know much yet. They need a big kid, like me, to give them some attention and answer their questions. . . .

Starting Your Personal Narrative

Once you have a plan for your story, you are ready to write your first draft. Write as though you were telling a friend your story. The first paragraph should catch your friend's interest and introduce your story. Here are several ways to begin your narrative.

> **Beginning**
>
> Middle
>
> Ending

- **Place yourself in the middle of the action.**
  When Uncle Eddie asked me to volunteer at bike camp, I said, "Sure." Secretly, I didn't want to because I thought little kids were a pain.
- **Begin with a surprising statement or fact.**
  Little kids can be a real pain!
- **Start with someone speaking (dialogue).**
  "Get off the field!" my friends and I yelled.

Beginning Paragraph

> The writer catches the reader's interest with dialogue.
>
> The writer introduces the story.

"Get off the field!" That's what my friends and I are always yelling at the little kids who get in the way when we are trying to have a game of softball. Little kids are a pain—or so I thought. Then Uncle Eddie asked me to volunteer at bike camp. The camp is a special Saturday when kids learn safety rules for riding their trikes and bikes. I didn't want to, but my family always helps run the camp, so I politely told Uncle Eddie, "Sure."

 Write your beginning. On your own paper, write the beginning of your story. Try using one of the three ways suggested on this page.

NARRATIVE

Writing

Starting Your Personal Narrative

Emphasize that each one of the **story beginnings** *(see below)* offered for the sample paragraph could work.

Use one or more of these strategies to start the writing stage:

- Have students fold a piece of paper horizontally into thirds and create a different lead for each method described (place yourself in the action, start with a surprising statement or fact, and begin with dialogue). Students see which lead best grabs a writing partner's attention.
- If students have trouble coming up with an "interesting" beginning, explain that they can work to improve the beginning during the revising stage.
- If students are writing a draft as an in-class activity, offer help to individuals as needed. If you assign the writing for homework or free time, be sure students show you their first draft. You may also want to check the writing steps on PE pages 110–112 to see if there is anything you want to review with students before they begin writing independently.

Writing
Developing the Middle Part

Though students may focus on dialogue during the writing phase, they will have an opportunity to check the form of their written dialogue during the editing phase.

Point out that the narrator of the sample shares his feelings in two ways:

- through direct statement (little kids are a pain, I didn't want to, I wasn't looking forward to it, I wished I had a little brother)
- through word choice and sensory details (constant beep, sea of little kids, bunch of ants, mumbled, squirmy, grubby, smeared, sharp pain, and so forth)

The second way is an example of **show, don't tell** *(see below)*.

Emphasize that it is possible to have too many details. Students need to stay focused on the essential details related to their surprising event.

110

Writing   Developing the Middle Part

Once you have your reader's attention, you want to keep it by adding interesting details. Don't tell everything, though. Tell just enough to capture the main event. Here are some things to remember as you write.

- Include lots of sensory details.
- Let the people in the narrative tell the story using their own words (dialogue).
- Share your feelings throughout the story.

Middle Paragraphs

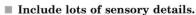

> **Strong sensory details (blue) let the reader "see and feel" the experience.**
>
> **Dialogue makes the people seem real.**
>
> When I arrived at bike camp, I heard the ringing ting-a-ling of trike bells and the constant beep, beep, beeping of bike horns. The parking lot was a sea of little kids pedaling around and around and back and forth. They looked like a bunch of ants rushing around but going nowhere.
>
> "Kyle," Uncle Eddie said, "it looks like we have our work cut out for us today."
>
> "Yeah," I mumbled. I wasn't looking forward to this at all.
>
> My first job was to teach the squirmy little kids on trikes to watch out for hazards. One grubby little five-year-old rode over my foot. "What's a haz—zard?" he asked. A chocolate bar was smeared in a brown mustache under his nose. Suddenly he put his trike in reverse and rolled back over my foot. A sharp pain shot up my leg.

Teaching Tip: Show, Don't Tell

Teachers often tell students that good writers *show* the reader what they mean or feel rather than tell them outright. Use the sample to help students understand the difference between the two ways of conveying ideas. Read the paragraph once without the blue text and a second time with everything included. Ask students how the blue details change the middle paragraphs.

tell **share** remember
relate narrate

"It is something dangerous," I said. I was talking very slowly so he couldn't tell how much my foot hurt. "A hazard is something that can hurt you or someone else," I answered. I was thinking to myself, "You are a hazard!"

"Boy, you sure are smart," said the little boy, whose name was Kenny.

Kenny and I saw a lot of each other all day. He was full of questions, and he looked up to me as if I had all the answers. He became my talking shadow.

By the end of camp, I wished that I had a little brother just like Kenny. When he reached out to shake my hand, he said, "Thanks for helping me." I didn't even notice the chocolate on my hand until he was pedaling away to meet his dad.

Personal feelings show how Kenny is changing the writer.

NARRATIVE

Write your middle paragraphs. Before you start writing, read through the details you collected on your quick list (page 104) and on your sensory chart (page 105). Keep the following tips in mind.

Drafting Tips

- **Remember that your purpose** is to share a true personal experience with your classmates.
- **Relax and write freely.** Don't try to get everything perfect at this time.
- **Add any new ideas** that occur to you as you write.

Ask students to read parts of the model that show how the narrator's feelings are changing toward Kenny:

- He looked up to me as if I had all the answers.
- became my talking shadow
- wished I had a little brother like Kenny
- didn't even notice the chocolate on my hand

Writing Drafting Tips

Remind students that they are drafting, not writing the final product. Assure them they can refer to their earlier prewriting work, but they shouldn't worry about including everything. As they write, they may leave out some ideas and add in new details.

After students write their middle paragraphs, have them use a blue colored pencil or pen to underline sensory details. They should be able to identify the dialogue and the personal feelings they used to develop this part of their personal narrative.

Writing

Ending Your Personal Narrative

Story endings (*see below*) are particularly difficult for writers. Emphasize that each one of the possible endings for the sample narrative is a good one.

If the writing is an in-class activity, circulate and ask students how they are doing. If students are writing at home, be sure to check with them about their ending during the revising stage.

112

Writing Ending Your Personal Narrative

After you share the most important moment, bring your story to a close in the final paragraph. Here are three ways for you to end your narrative.

> Beginning
>
> Middle
>
> ▶ **Ending**

- **Tell how the experience changed you.**

  By the end of bike camp, I decided that I was wrong about little kids. Kenny taught me that I should give them a break—and maybe some answers, too. The kids at camp learned a lot, but so did I. Now I can't wait for next year's camp.

- **Relate the experience to the audience.**

  I guess we all need to realize that we shouldn't make decisions about others until we get to know them. If we do, we could miss out on some neat experiences. Kids are people, too—just littler—and they can be a lot of fun.

- **Tell why the experience was important.**

Ending Paragraph

> **The writer tells why the experience was important.**
>
> *Did I say that little kids are a real pain? Well, I was wrong. Little kids just don't know much yet. They need a big kid, like me, to give them some attention and answer their questions. And maybe someday, when they're bigger, they'll remember and be nice to little kids, too.*

Write your ending. Try one of the three ways listed above. Remember to keep it short and simple. It shouldn't go on too long.

Form a complete first draft. Put together a complete copy of your first draft. Then you will be ready to revise your writing.

Provide students with a variety of short articles and narratives. Have them select and read aloud their favorite endings from those pieces. Discuss each of the choices as a class, and determine why each ending works so well. Encourage students to use these endings as models for their own writing.

Ask students who find it difficult to end their narrative to think about their purpose for writing:

- Was their purpose to share an experience that changed them?
- Was it to educate their readers about something?
- Was it to highlight the importance of the experience?

Emphasize that the ending of their narrative writing should address their specific purpose for writing.

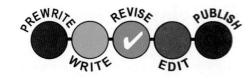

Sharing an Experience
113

Revising

When you revise, you improve your first draft in many ways. You might spice up descriptions, add dialogue, or experiment with different beginnings and endings. Revision can make even a ho-hum draft into something special.

Keys to Effective Revising

1. Set your narrative aside for a while so you can revise with a fresh perspective.

2. Read through your entire narrative to see how it works as a whole.

3. Check your beginning, middle, and ending to make sure each part works well.

4. Make sure your own unique storytelling voice comes through.

5. Check your words and sentences.

6. Use the editing and proofreading marks inside the back cover of this book.

NARRATIVE

Revising

Keys to Effective Revising

The Keys to Effective Revising lays out the process students will be guided through on PE pages 113–124.

- If time allows, wait until the next day to begin revising so that students will look at their writing with fresh eyes.
- After reviewing PE page 113, discuss the importance of the first two keys. Writers are too close to their work and often become overly concerned with certain details and lose sight of the piece as a whole.

Revising for Ideas

The rubric strips that run across all the revising pages (PE pages 114–123) are provided to help students focus their revising and are related to the full rubric on PE pages 130–131.

After reading the basic instruction, have students review the rubric strip on PE pages 114–115. Students will look in their drafts for

- answers to the 5 W questions (Who? What? When? Where? Why?);
- sensory details (sight, sound, smell, touch, taste).

Have them make a separate pass through their writing to look for each element.

 **Answers**

Who: narrator, Mom, cousin Buster
What: visit cousin Buster
When: every other weekend
Where: family farm
Why: Buster teaches the narrator things and they have a great time

---

114

Revising for Ideas

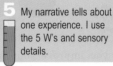

6 My narrative tells about one experience. The details make the reader want to read the whole story.

5 My narrative tells about one experience. I use the 5 W's and sensory details.

4 My narrative tells about one experience. More details would make it better.

When you revise for *ideas*, be sure you have focused on one experience. Check to see if you have answered the 5 W's and included sensory details. The rubric above will guide you as you work to improve your ideas.

Will readers understand my narrative?

To make sure your readers understand your narrative, include details that answer the 5 W's.

1. **Who** are the people in my narrative?
2. **What** events are included in this experience?
3. **When** do the events happen?
4. **Where** does my narrative take place?
5. **Why** is this experience important?

 Read the following paragraph and answer the *who, what, when, where,* and *why* questions.

1   Every other weekend, Mom drives me out to the family farm
2 where my older cousin, Buster, teaches me all kinds of new things.
3 He has taught me how to shoot arrows, fix an engine, and bale hay.
4 Usually, we spend the evenings in his workshop. The last time we
5 got together, Buster taught me how to carve a piece of wood into a
6 simple whistle. I really enjoyed carving and can hardly wait to start
7 my next project. I'd like to carve a figure of a wolf, but that may be
8 too hard for now. No matter what Buster teaches me, we have a
9 great time together.

Check your ideas. Read through your first draft. Be sure your narrative includes details that answer the 5 W's.

tell **share** remember
relate narrate   **115**
Sharing an Experience

3 I need to focus on one experience. Some of my details don't relate to the topic.

2 I need to focus on one experience and answer the 5 W's.

1 I need to choose a different experience to write about.

Have I included enough sensory details?

You have included enough sensory details if they help your readers use their imaginations—and their five senses—to connect with your experience.

 In the following paragraph, find and list at least five sensory details.

1   During the summer of 2001, my family lived on a busy street
2 in Cincinnati. During the daytime, buses rumbled and screeched
3 right in front of our second-floor apartment. The noise and oily
4 exhaust from these vehicles is something I will always remember.
5 In the heat of that summer, we passed the time playing hearts
6 or rummy. My little sister often sat in an old rocking chair and
7 watched us. Mom always made sure that there was a pitcher of
8 sweet lemonade in the fridge. Once in a while, she'd even surprise
9 us with some chocolate ice cream. It may have been hot and
10 noisy, but that summer was one of the best ones ever.

 Review your details. Have you included a variety of sensory details in your narrative. Do your details bring your narrative to life for your readers?

NARRATIVE

Ideas
A sensory detail and a detail that tells "where" are added.

> When I arrived at bike camp, I heard the ringing
> *and the constant beep, beep, beeping of bike horns*
> ting-a-ling of trike bells. The parking lot was a sea
>   *around and around and back and forth*
> of little kids pedaling. They looked like a bunch of
>
> ants rushing around but going nowhere.

Ask the class to score the model narrative paragraphs on PE pages 114–115, using the rubric strip. Guide students to score the paragraphs as a 4 or a 5 and to support their opinions.

For additional practice, supply students with a basic paragraph to revise. Ask them to rewrite the paragraph by adding 3–5 sensory details.

Try IT **Answers**

Possible sensory details:
sight: busy street
sound: buses rumbled and screeched, noise, noisy
smell: oily exhaust
touch: heat, ice cream, hot
taste: sweet lemonade, chocolate ice cream

Revising for Organization

After reading the basic instruction with students, discuss the rubric strip. Students will review their writing to look for
- a beginning, middle, and end;
- chronological order;
- transitions.

Students may work with a partner to evaluate how well their beginnings grab a reader's attention.

116

Revising for Organization

6 My organization makes my narrative enjoyable and easy to read.

5 My events are in time order, and I use transitions well. I have a clear beginning, middle, and ending.

4 My events are in time order. Most of my transitions are helpful. I have a beginning, middle, and ending.

When you revise for *organization*, use the rubric strip above to guide you. Check your narrative for a strong beginning, middle, and ending.

How do I check the beginning?

You check the beginning of your narrative by asking yourself the three questions below.

1. How does my beginning get the reader's attention?
2. What does my reader need to know to understand my experience?
3. What other way could I begin my narrative? (See page 109.)

Reread your opening. Then answer each of the questions listed above. Make the changes that would improve your beginning.

How do I check the middle?

You check the middle by making sure you have arranged events in the order in which they happened. This is called chronological order, or time order. Transition words can help you move the reader through your story. Here are some transition words that **show time**. (See page 572.)

first	while	meanwhile	soon	then
second	then	today	later	next
third	when	tomorrow	afterward	as soon as

Review for time order. Check the middle paragraphs of your narrative to make sure your events are in chronological order. Also make sure that you used transitions to move your reader easily through your story.

3 Some of my events are out of order. I need more transitions. My beginning or ending is weak.

2 I need to use time order and transitions in order to create a clear beginning, middle, and ending.

1 My narrative is confusing. I need to learn about time order.

How do I check the ending?

You check your ending by asking the following questions.

1. Does my narrative end soon after the most important event?

2. How will my reader know the experience was important to me?

3. What other way could I end my narrative?

 Check your ending. Use the questions listed above to see if you have written an effective ending.

NARRATIVE

Organization
In the middle paragraph, a sentence is moved, and a transition word is added.

> Kenny and I saw a lot of each other all day.
>
> He was full of questions, and he looked up to me
>
> as if I had all the answers. He became my talking
>   When
> shadow. He reached out to shake my hand, ~~and~~ *he*
>
> said, "Thanks for helping me." I didn't even notice
>
> the chocolate on my hand until he was pedaling
>
> away to meet his dad. By the end of camp, I
>
> wished that I had a little brother just like Kenny.

Help students work on the ending of their narratives by asking them:

- Why was this experience important to you?

To ensure that students practice revising their beginning, middle, and end, have them schedule **peer conferences** *(see below)*.

- Each student makes conference appointments with three different students.
- Students should read the beginning of their essays during their first appointment, get feedback, and make changes.
- They repeat the process, reading the middle part during the second conference.
- Finally, they read and revise the ending with input from the third conference.

This will give each writer feedback from three different peer conferences.

Teaching Tip: Peer Conferences

Remind students that during a peer conference they want to tell a partner something that they like about the writing and some possible improvement the writer could make to the piece.

Revising for Voice

After reading the instruction, have volunteers read aloud the two writers' descriptions. Help students to compare and contrast the voices of writers 1 and 2.

- Writer 1 sounds very energetic and upbeat (flipped, jabbed, whoa).
- Writer 2 sounds weary and is expecting the worst (sighed, what a day, what could go wrong, screamed).

For the **Try It** exercise, have students work with a partner to compare the voices in their writing.

 **Answers**

Students' writings will vary.

Review the rubric strip before students start revising for voice.

118

Revising for Voice

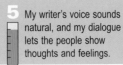

6 My writer's voice creates an unforgettable experience for the reader.

5 My writer's voice sounds natural, and my dialogue lets the people show thoughts and feelings.

4 My writer's voice sounds natural, but I need to use more dialogue.

When you revise for *voice*, check to see if your writing sounds natural, as if you were talking to someone. Also make sure you have used dialogue. The rubric above can guide you as you revise for voice.

Have I used a natural-sounding voice?

Your voice sounds natural if your reader can "hear" your personality in your narrative. You can check your voice by paying special attention to the way you use words. In each paragraph below, a different writer describes the same event. Notice how the personality and voice of each writer comes through in the writing.

> **Writer 1:**
> I flipped open my locker and jabbed my hand in. I got a fistful of fuzz. "Whoa. What's this critter doing in my locker!"

> **Writer 2:**
> I pulled open my locker and sighed. What a day! What could go wrong now? I reached in and felt something furry and alive. "Yikes! A rat!" I screamed.

 Write for about 3 to 5 minutes about the experience below. Use your imagination to add lots of details. Your writing should sound like you're telling a story to a friend. When you finish, underline words and phrases that show your unique personality, or voice.

> While cleaning up after a parade, I found a $50 bill on a littered street.

 Check your voice. Read through your personal narrative. Underline two sentences that show your unique voice. Then check the rest of your narrative for places where the voice can be improved. Revise as needed.

English Language Learners

Students may have difficulty improving voice in their writing. Point out that the language in their narratives should sound like the language they use when they speak to a classmate. As each student reads aloud his or her narrative, point out parts that don't sound as natural as they could. If necessary, help the student reword problem areas.

Advanced Learners

For the **Try It** activity, encourage students to incorporate an additional person into their experience—a person from a different generation or from a foreign country. Have them include dialogue that reflects not only their own unique personality but also that of their imaginary character.

tell **share** *remember narrate relate*

Sharing an Experience

119

 3 Sometimes my writer's voice sounds natural, but I need to improve my dialogue.

2 My writer's voice does not sound natural. I need to use dialogue.

1 I need to understand what a natural-sounding voice is.

How can dialogue improve my narrative?

Using dialogue in your writing helps you "show" instead of just "tell." Dialogue can make your narrative feel as if it is happening right now. As you write dialogue, remember that a five-year-old child would not speak like your English teacher. Here are some tips for writing dialogue. (See page 556.)

- Think about the people in your story and choose words that each of them would use.
- Make the words sound like everyday conversation.
- Indent each time a different person speaks.

 Write an exchange of dialogue between one of the pairs of people listed below. (See page 556.)

- A coach and a player
- A clerk and a customer
- Two friends
- A brother and sister

 Read your narrative carefully. Make changes if your voice or the dialogue doesn't sound right.

Voice
Dialogue is changed to fit the little boy's age.

"A hazard is something that can hurt you or someone else," I answered. I was thinking to myself, "You are a hazard!"

"Boy, ~~I think~~ you sure are ~~intelligent~~ smart," said the little boy, whose name was Kenny.

NARRATIVE

Good **dialogue** *(see below)* sounds believable. Read aloud and discuss whether the dialogue below sounds realistic.

- "Give me $10.95," demanded the store clerk.
- "If you please, I would prefer that you not enter my bedroom," said 13-year-old Kyle to his baby sister.

As an alternative to the main **Try It** activity, ask student partners to choose roles for the exercise. The partners should pass a paper back and forth silently, writing dialogue for their roles. Explain that guidelines for punctuating dialogue are provided on PE pages 126–127.

 **Answers**

Dialogue will vary.

Teaching Tip: Dialogue

A speaker tag is the collection of words that identify the speaker.

- Read aloud a passage of ongoing dialogue that has a variety of speaker tags.
- Read it again, replacing each tag with *said*.
- Give students the following sample sentence: "I saw you last night," said Mark. Have them brainstorm possible replacement speaker tags and try

them out in the sentence. Examples include: . . . whispered my arch enemy, . . . laughed my sister, . . . snarled the detective.

- Ask them how each tag changes the meaning of the sentence.
- Have students look through their own writing for examples of effective speaker tags and for ones that could be revised.

Revising for Word Choice

Use the following activity to explore adjectives:

- Write the following adjectives on the board: velvet, four, red, round, huge, tiny, wooden, square, pink, twelve.
- Then list the following categories: size, shape, color, number, and material.
- Have students sort the adjectives into the appropriate categories.
- Then ask them to add three new adjectives to each category.

✱ Find additional information about using adjectives and adverbs on PE pages 486, 488–489, 490, 492.

 **Answers**

Possible answers: endlessly, oldest, early, torrential, quietly, worried

---

120

Revising for Word Choice

6 My exceptional word choice captures the experience.

5 I use adjectives and adverbs that add meaning. I replace overused words with synonyms.

4 Most of my adjectives and adverbs add meaning. I need to replace a few overused words with synonyms.

When you revise for *word choice*, check to see if you used adjectives and adverbs to capture your experience. Also check to see if you have replaced overused words with synonyms. The rubric above can help you.

Have I used adjectives and adverbs well?

You have used adjectives and adverbs well if they help create a clear and interesting picture. Adjectives describe nouns or pronouns. Adverbs add meaning to verbs, adjectives, and other adverbs. The example below shows how a writer improved a basic sentence by adding adjectives and adverbs. (See pages 486–493.)

> **BASIC SENTENCE**
> The cafeteria served sandwiches.
>
> **IMPROVED SENTENCE**
>   adj.   adj. adj.   adv.
> The school cafeteria served spicy sub sandwiches yesterday.

 Copy this paragraph and fill in the missing adjectives and adverbs. Compare your paragraph with a classmate's.

> Our soccer team had practiced ___*(adverb)*___ to get ready
> for the championship game with our ___*(adjective)*___ rival. I arrived
> ___*(adverb)*___ on Saturday to find a flooded field, ruined by the
> ___*(adjective)*___ rain the night before. After running to the gym, I found
> our coach talking ___*(adverb)*___ to some other ___*(adjective)*___ players
> about postponing the game.

 Revise for adjectives and adverbs. In your narrative, use adjectives and adverbs to help create a clear picture.

English Language Learners

English learners may need practice selecting vivid, meaningful adjectives. Display pictures of pairs of familiar objects such as a giraffe and an elephant. Point out that both could be described as *big,* but other words would give a more distinct feeling. Provide examples, such as *a towering giraffe* and *a gigantic elephant.* Ask students to suggest other replacements. Repeat with other pairs of pictures.

tell **share** remember narrate relate

121

Sharing an Experience

3 I need to add more adjectives and adverbs. I need to replace overused words with synonyms.

2 I don't use adjectives and adverbs. I keep using the same words again and again.

1 I need help choosing adjectives, adverbs, and synonyms.

NARRATIVE

Have I checked for overused words?

Writers often use synonyms—other words that mean almost the same thing—to replace overused or dull words. You can use a dictionary or a thesaurus to find just the right words for your writing.

 Write a synonym for each of the frequently overused words below. Then write a sentence using each synonym. The first one has been done for you.

1. mad

    angry: I was angry after missing the bus.

2. went   **4.** cold   **6.** good

3. bad   **5.** big   **7.** happy

 Revise to replace overused words. Look at each sentence in your narrative. Make a list of words that you feel are dull or overused. Replace them with synonyms.

Word Choice

A synonym replaces the word "help."

Two adjectives and an adverb are added.

Then Uncle Eddie asked me to ~~help~~ *volunteer* at bike camp.

The camp is a *special* Saturday when kids learn *safety* rules for

riding their trikes and bikes. I didn't want to, but my

family always helps run the camp, so I *politely* told Uncle

Eddie, "Sure."

If necessary, review how to use a **thesaurus** *(see below)*.

 Answers

Possible answers:

2. *tore:* Kaneesha tore across the park to grab the escaping dog.

3. *disastrous*: The burnt vegetables made this a really disastrous meal.

4. *frigid:* I'd describe sleeping in a tent in the middle of the winter as a frigid experience.

5. *huge:* Trent's family had a huge party for his parents' anniversary.

6. *superb:* The play we saw last night was superb.

7. *thrilled:* Betty was thrilled to be home after spending hours picking up litter with the Girl Scouts.

Ask students to suggest other overused words, such as *nice*. Post a list of boring, overused words in the classroom.

Teaching Tip: Thesaurus

Students may need a refresher in using a thesaurus. There are generally two types, dictionary style or indexed style. In the former, words are organized alphabetically. You look up the word for which you are searching synonyms, and the entry provides the synonyms right there.

In the indexed style, the book is divided into two sections. At the back is an alphabetical index. At the front are groups of words organized by number and grouped by theme and meaning. You look up the word for which you want synonyms in the alphabetical index at the back of the thesaurus.

Point out that the thesaurus option on a personal computer or a hand-held spell checker with a thesaurus option will not be as thorough as a print version.

Revising for Sentence Fluency

Have students read the instruction and complete the **Try It** exercise before they revise their drafts.

Make sure students understand that using sentences of similar length creates a choppy rhythm and a boring paragraph.

 Answers

1. 7	8. 7
2. 7	9. 6
3. 6	10. 5
4. 6	11. 5
5. 5	12. 6
6. 6	13. 7
7. 7	

All the sentences are about the same length. This makes a choppy, repetitive rhythm. The paragraph is boring and not easy to read.

Discuss how many words create a short, medium, and long sentence. Model this with the children's book *Alexander and the Terrible, Horrible, No-Good, Very Bad Day* by Judith Viorst.

- Read the first sentence aloud and ask students to guess the number of words it contains (62 words).
- Then read the second sentence (14 words) through the fifth sentence (6 words).
- Discuss the effect of the different sentence lengths.

122

Revising for Sentence Fluency

6 My sentences are skillfully written and keep the reader's interest throughout.

5 My sentences flow smoothly, and I have a variety of sentence lengths.

4 I vary my sentence lengths, but I need to combine a few to make them flow more smoothly.

When you revise for *sentence fluency*, you need to check your writing for a variety of sentence lengths. You may need to combine some sentences to have a smoother flow. The above rubric will help guide you.

Are too many sentences of the same length?

You check your sentence lengths by counting the number of words in each sentence. When you speak, you automatically use sentences of many different lengths. This gives a natural flow to your sentences. When you write, you want to do the same.

 Read the following paragraph. Write down the number of words in each sentence. What did you discover about the sentence fluency of this paragraph?

(1) I see the shoe-shine man each morning. (2) He is always in the same spot. (3) He looks older than my grandpa. (4) Each day he wears green pants. (5) He has a red cap. (6) He has a long leather vest. (7) In its pockets are brushes and polish. (8) His stand is near the train stop. (9) He smiles at me every morning. (10) "Hello," he says, and nods. (11) We talk about my homework. (12) While we talk, he shines shoes. (13) He waves as I leave for school.

Revise **Revise your paper for sentence lengths.** Read through your narrative and check your sentences.

1 Write down the number of words in each of your first 10 to 15 sentences.

2 Do you have a variety of sentence lengths?

3 What did you discover about sentence fluency in your narrative?

English Language Learners

Read the sample paragraph aloud to students, emphasizing the choppy, staccato rhythm. Then use various ways to change the rhythm. For example, change the first two sentences to *Each morning, I see the shoe-shine man in the same spot.*

3 I need to combine more sentences to have a better variety of lengths and a smoother flow.

2 My sentences are all the same length. I need to combine some of them.

1 Most of my sentences need to be combined or rewritten.

How do I combine sentences?

Two easy ways to combine short sentences are (1) creating compound sentences and (2) using a series of words. (Also see pages 513–516.)

CREATE COMPOUND SENTENCES

I see the shoe-shine man each morning. He is always in the same spot.
I see the shoe-shine man each morning, and he is always in the same spot.
(Two sentences are combined using a comma and the conjunction *and*.)

USE A SERIES OF WORDS

Each day he wears green pants. He has a red cap. He has a long leather vest.
Each day he wears green pants, a red cap, and a long leather vest.
(Three short sentences are combined into one using a series of words.)

 Below are two sets of sentences. Combine each of the sets, using the method given in parentheses.

1. I've always enjoyed reading about dinosaurs.
   I didn't realize that they had once lived in my neighborhood.
   (Create a compound sentence using a conjunction.)

2. My grandmother has taught me how to sew.
   She also showed me how to crochet and quilt.
   (Combine sentences using a series of words.)

 Combine sentences. Look at your word count (page 122). Combine some short sentences using the methods given above.

Sentence Fluency
Two sentences are combined.

> *and*
> He was full of questions, He looked up to me as if I
> had all the answers. He became my talking shadow.

NARRATIVE

Review how you can create a compound sentence or a series of words using the word *and*.

Try It Answers

Possible answers:
1. I've always enjoyed reading about dinosaurs, but I didn't realize that they had once lived in my neighborhood.
2. My grandmother has taught me how to sew, crochet, and quilt.

In addition to using compound sentences, students may be able to use **compound subjects and predicates** *(see below)* as a way to combine sentences.

When students are ready to practice the use of all seven coordinating conjunctions, use the following mnemonic device:

ON San Francisco BAY
(ON SF BAY)

O=or	**N**=nor	
S=so	**F**=for	
B=but	**A**=and	**Y**=yet

Teaching Tip: Compound Subjects and Predicates

A compound subject includes two or more nouns that share the same verb (or verbs). A compound predicate includes two or more verbs that share the same subject (or subjects). The coordinating conjunctions *and* and *or* are almost always used when forming compound subjects and predicates.

❋ See PE pages 497, 503, 514, and 744–745 for more information.

The use of *and* creates a plural subject that requires a plural verb. However, a compound subject connected by the word *or* needs a verb that agrees in number with the subject closest to it:

> The students or the coach is the first to get off the bus.

❋ See PE page 509 for more practice.

Revising Using a Checklist

If students are unclear about the meaning or purpose of any question in the checklist, they can return to the related section for a more thorough explanation.

You may want students to make a clean copy of their narrative as a homework assignment.

124

Revising Using a Checklist

 Check your revising. On a piece of paper, write the numbers 1 to 12. If you can answer "yes" to a question, put a check mark after that number. If not, continue to work with that part of your essay.

Ideas

_____ **1.** Do I tell about one important event?

_____ **2.** Do I answer all the 5 W's in my narrative?

_____ **3.** Do I include sensory details?

Organization

_____ **4.** Are my beginning, middle, and ending effective?

_____ **5.** Have I cut unnecessary details?

_____ **6.** Have I reorganized parts that were out of place?

Voice

_____ **7.** Does my voice sound natural?

_____ **8.** Have I used dialogue?

Word Choice

_____ **9.** Do my adjectives and adverbs make my narrative clearer?

_____ **10.** Have I replaced overused words?

Sentence Fluency

_____ **11.** Have I checked my sentence lengths?

_____ **12.** Have I used combining to vary my sentences?

 Make a clean copy. When you've finished revising your essay, make a clean copy before you begin to edit.

Struggling Learners

Help students personalize the checklist process to address their individual needs. For example, if students have particular difficulty with word choice, have them first circle the adjectives and underline the nouns they modify in red. Then have them circle the adverbs and underline the words they modify in blue.

For students who struggle with remembering the 5 W's, have them refer to the list on PE page 103 and label each corresponding narrative detail as it occurs.

Sharing an Experience

125

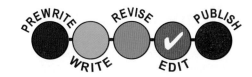

Editing

After you've finished revising your narrative, it's time to edit it for your use of conventions: punctuation, capitalization, spelling, and grammar.

Keys to Effective Editing

1. Use a dictionary, a thesaurus, and the "Proofreader's Guide" in the back of this book.

2. Check for any words or phrases that may be confusing to the reader.

3. Check your writing for correctness of punctuation, capitalization, spelling, and grammar.

4. Edit on a printed computer copy. Then enter your changes on the computer.

5. Use the editing and proofreading marks inside the back cover of this book.

NARRATIVE

Editing Keys to Effective Editing

Remind students that **editing** (*see below*) is the stage at which they correct errors in their writing to make it easy for their audience to read.

The Keys to Effective Editing lays out the process students will be guided through on pages 126–128.

- Suggest that students make several passes through their papers, looking for only one type of error (punctuation, capitalization, spelling, grammar) at a time.
- To check for spelling, have students read their drafts in reverse. As students read the words in isolation, without context, they can focus on the spelling.
- After students edit their writing, encourage them to have a trusted classmate check for errors as well. It is often easier to spot errors in someone else's writing than in one's own.

Point out the editing checklist on PE page 128, which can guide students through the editing process.

Teaching Tip: Revising vs. Editing

Revising is like redecorating a room, while editing is like making sure everything in the room is in the proper place. One deals with the entire structure; the other deals with clarity and neatness. Ask students to name the step—revising or editing—during which the following would occur:

- checking end punctuation (editing)

- rewriting the last paragraph (revising)
- fixing the character's dialogue to sound natural (revising)
- correcting a misspelled word (editing)

Editing for Conventions

Students will need to pay special attention to punctuating dialogue.

✳ For additional information on punctuating dialogue, see PE pages 588–589, 598–601, 624.

Consider doing item 7 in the **Try It** with the class. The speaker tag divides the sentence into two parts. Point out that the second part, after the speaker tag, completes the sentence that begins before the speaker tag. Therefore, *because* does not begin with a capital letter.

 Answers

1. Mom asked, "What time does the party start?"
2. Ben said, "Right after supper."
3. "You have to finish your homework first," she reminded him.
4. He answered, "I'll start right now."
5. Later, his mom called up the stairs, "Thuan is here."
6. "Great!" Ben shouted.
7. "I'll be right down," he added, "because I just finished."

126

Editing for Conventions

6 My essay is error free from start to finish.

5 I have a few minor errors in punctuation, spelling, or grammar.

4 I need to correct some errors in punctuation, spelling, or grammar.

When you are editing for *conventions*, you need to check for spelling, grammar, capitalization, and punctuation errors. The rubric above and the information below can help you edit for dialogue.

Have I punctuated dialogue correctly?

To be sure you know how to correctly punctuate dialogue, review the following rules. (Also see page **556**.)

● Commas are used to set off the words of the speaker from the rest of the sentence.

  "A raccoon crawled down the chimney," Laura announced, "and I think it's still in there."

● Sometimes an exclamation point or a question mark separates the speaker's words from the rest of the sentence.

  "Are you sure it went down the chimney?" Regina asked.

● The speaker's exact words are placed within the quotation marks.

  "I'm positive!" Laura replied.

 Copy and punctuate the following lines of dialogue.

1. Mom asked What time does the party start?
2. Ben said Right after supper.
3. You have to finish your homework first she reminded him.
4. He answered I'll start right now.
5. Later, his mom called up the stairs Tomas is here.
6. Great! Ben shouted.
7. I'll be right down he added because I just finished.

Edit dialogue. Use the rules and examples above to make sure you have punctuated your dialogue correctly.

English Language Learners

Students may need extra help with punctuation rules. Prior to the **Try It** activity, help students add the necessary punctuation marks to the following two sentences, explaining why each one is needed:

● I'm late for soccer practice Beth said.
● That's all right Tim replied. The coach is setting up the goals.

You might also have students come to the board with partners to work together to punctuate the sentences.

tell **share** *remember* *narrate* *relate* **127**
Sharing an Experience

3	2	1
Some of my errors confuse the reader. I need to fix punctuation of my dialogue.	I need to correct many errors that make my narrative and dialogue hard to read.	I need help making corrections, especially with my dialogue.

How do I know when to indent dialogue?

As you write your narrative, remember that you need to indent and begin a new paragraph each time a different person speaks.

In the following paragraph, the dialogue runs together.

> "It's snowing!" cried my sister. "I hope it snows all night," I added. "Maybe we'll have a snow day, and we won't have to go to school tomorrow," she replied. "I hope so," I yelled. "Let's do a snow dance!"

To be correct, dialogue should be indented each time a new person speaks.

> "It's snowing!" cried my sister.
> "I hope it snows all night," I added.
> "Maybe we'll have a snow day, and we won't have to go to school tomorrow," she replied.
> "I hope so," I yelled. "Let's do a snow dance!"

Check the dialogue in your narrative. Have you started a new paragraph each time there's a new speaker? Mark each sentence that should begin a new paragraph with the paragraph symbol (¶). Indent these sentences when you copy over your narrative.

Conventions
Quotation marks are added.
Dialogue is indented for a change in speaker.

> "Kyle," Uncle Eddie said, "it looks like we have our work cut out for us today."
>
> ¶ "Yeah," I mumbled. I wasn't looking forward to this at all.

NARRATIVE

To practice punctuating dialogue:

- Put each word in the sentence below on a word card. Have ten students line up and hold the cards facing the class so that the sentence reads: That dog chased my cat up the tree shouted Harry.
- Give a card with the open quote and one with the closed quote to two students. Have them punctuate the human sentence correctly. Do the same with the exclamation mark.

* If students have a speaker say more than one paragraph, refer them to PE page 598 for the rules about using quotation marks.

Editing Using a Checklist

Give students a few moments to look over the Proofreader's Guide in the back of their book. Throughout the year they can refer to the instruction, rules, and examples to clarify any checklist items or to resolve questions about their own writing.

Adding a Title

Students may find it helpful to work in pairs to get feedback on possible titles. Partners may come up with some creative ideas.

128

Editing Using a Checklist

 Check your editing. On a piece of paper, write the numbers 1 to 12. If you can answer "yes" to a question, put a check mark after that number. If not, continue to edit for that convention of writing.

Conventions

PUNCTUATION

_____ **1.** Do I use end punctuation after all my sentences?

_____ **2.** Do I use commas after introductory word groups?

_____ **3.** Do I use commas after items in a series?

_____ **4.** Do I use commas in all my compound sentences?

_____ **5.** Do I use apostrophes to show possession (*boy's bike*)?

CAPITALIZATION

_____ **6.** Do I start all my sentences with capital letters?

_____ **7.** Do I capitalize all proper nouns?

SPELLING

_____ **8.** Have I spelled all my words correctly?

_____ **9.** Have I double-checked the words my spell checker may have missed?

GRAMMAR

_____ **10.** Do I use correct forms of verbs (*had gone*, not *had went*)?

_____ **11.** Do my subjects and verbs agree in number? (She and I *were* going, not She and I *was* going.)

_____ **12.** Do I use the right words (*to, too,* and *two*)?

Adding a Title

- Use strong, colorful words: **A Weird and Wonderful Artist**
- Give the words rhythm: **My Little Buddy Kenny**
- Be imaginative: **Turtle Lady**

English Language Learners

Students will benefit from working with you or a partner to use the checklist. To build students' confidence, it may be helpful to focus on only one convention per session. Once students understand and make the corrections necessary for that convention, move on to the next one.

Publishing Sharing Your Narrative

After you have worked so hard to improve your story, make a neat final copy to share. You may also decide to present your story in the form of an illustration, a skit, or a recording. (See the suggestions below.)

Make a final copy. Follow your teacher's instructions or use the guidelines below to format your story. (If you are using a computer, see page 60.) Create a clean copy of your narrative and carefully proofread it.

Focus on Presentation

- Use blue or black ink and write neatly.
- Write your name in the upper left-hand corner of page 1.
- Skip a line and center your title; skip another line and start your writing.
- Indent every paragraph and leave a one-inch margin on all four sides.
- Write your last name and the page number in the upper right-hand corner of every page after the first one.

NARRATIVE

Record Your Storytelling

Record yourself telling your narrative. Play the recording back and think of ways to improve your storytelling. Keep trying until you are satisfied. Share the final recording with friends or family.

Create a Skit

Read your narrative to a group of classmates. Decide who will play which parts. Then practice and perform the story for your class.

Illustrate Your Narrative

Pick an important part of your narrative and draw a picture of it. Post the picture and the story in your classroom.

Publishing Sharing Your Narrative

Have groups of five students sit around a table. Have each student pass his or her narrative to the student sitting in the chair to the right. Students then read the narrative they now hold. When everyone is done, students pass the writing to the right again. Repeat these steps until each student has read five different stories.

Some students may be reluctant to share their narratives with the class. If so, allow these students to work in smaller groups, or change the format and ask for volunteers to share their writing with the class.

Rubric for Narrative Writing

A rubric is a chart that helps you evaluate your writing. The rubrics in this book are based on a 6-point scale, in which a score of 6 indicates an amazing piece of writing and a score of 1 means the writing is incomplete and not ready to be assessed. The rubric covers each of the basic traits of writing—ideas, organization, voice, word choice, sentence fluency, and conventions.

Rubrics can guide you as you write because they tell what elements to include in your writing and how to present them.

✱ Four- and five-point rubrics for narrative writing can be found on TE pages 768 and 772.

130

Rubric for Narrative Writing

Use this rubric for guiding and assessing your narrative writing. Refer to it whenever you want to improve your writing.

Ideas

6 **The narrative tells about an unforgettable experience. The details make the story truly memorable.**

5 The writer tells about an interesting experience. Details help create the interest.

4 The writer tells about an interesting experience. More details are needed.

Organization

6 **The organization makes the narrative enjoyable and easy to read.**

5 The narrative is well organized, with a clear beginning, middle, and ending. Transitions are used well.

4 The narrative is well organized. Most of the transitions are helpful.

Voice

6 **The writer's voice creates an unforgettable experience for the reader.**

5 The writer's voice sounds natural and creates interest in the story. Dialogue is used.

4 The writer's voice creates interest in the story. More dialogue is needed.

Word Choice

6 **The writer's exceptional word choice captures the experience.**

5 Strong nouns and verbs and well-chosen modifiers create vivid, clear pictures.

4 Modifiers are used. Strong nouns and active verbs would improve sensory images.

Sentence Fluency

6 **The sentences are skillfully written and original. They keep the reader's interest.**

5 The sentences show variety and are easy to read and understand.

4 The sentences are varied, but some should flow more smoothly.

Conventions

6 **The narrative is error free.**

5 The narrative has a few minor errors in punctuation, spelling, or grammar.

4 The narrative has several errors in punctuation, spelling, or grammar.

tell **share** remember
relate

Sharing an Experience **131**

3 The writer needs to focus on one experience. Some details do not relate to the story.

2 The writer needs to focus on one experience. Details are needed.

1 The writer needs to tell about an experience and use details.

3 The order of events needs to be corrected. More transitions need to be used. One part of the narrative is weak.

2 The beginning, middle, and ending all run together. The order is unclear.

1 The narrative needs to be organized.

3 A voice can usually be heard. More dialogue is needed.

2 The voice is weak. Dialogue is needed.

1 The writer has not gotten involved in the story. Dialogue is needed.

3 Strong nouns, verbs, and modifiers are needed to create sensory images.

2 General and overused words do not create sensory images.

1 The writer has not yet considered word choice.

3 A better variety of sentences is needed. Sentences do not read smoothly.

2 Incomplete and/or short sentences make the writing choppy.

1 Few sentences are written well. Help is needed.

3 Some errors confuse the reader.

2 Many errors make the narrative confusing and hard to read.

1 Help is needed to make corrections.

NARRATIVE

Evaluating a Narrative

Ask students if they agree with the sample self-assessment on PE page 133. If they agree with the criticisms, ask them to suggest improvements based on the comments in the self-assessment. If they disagree with any comment, ask them to explain why.

Ideas **add sensory details**—shiny, red, metal knitting needles; lovely, soft, green yarn; filthy and shredded; cover my eyes and bawl

Organization **ending**—If I keep on trying, I'll finally be able to give Grandma the gift she deserves.

Voice **add dialogue**—"I'll teach you how," my Aunt Elena offered. "Don't worry, Jessie," Aunt Elena said calmly. "We can try again."

Word Choice **change overused words**—*show, pretty, dirty, surprised, scarf*

Sentence Fluency **combine sentences**—She gave me some . . . knitting needles and demonstrated how to cast on the stitches; Then she showed me some knitting patterns that looked really hard; When we went to the hospital, Nana was . . .

Conventions **spelling**—stitches, patient, scarf

Evaluating a Narrative

As you read the narrative below, focus on the writer's strengths and weaknesses. (The essay contains some errors.) Then read the student self-evaluation on page 133.

A Knotty Problem

"I'm sorry, Jessie, but I don't have time to show you how to knit right now," my mother was saying. "Why don't you just use your allowance money to buy Nana a scarf?"

"I think she should get a special, home-made scarf," I said.

My mother just sighed. So my Aunt Elena said she would show me how. She gave me some knitting needles. She showed me how to cast on the stiches. Then she was showing me some of the knitting patterns. They looked really hard. Then Aunt Elena took me to the craft store. We picked out some pretty yarn. It was Nana's favorite color.

I only had a couple of week's. Every day after I finished my homework I would try to knit the scarf. It did not go well. I got the yarn all knotted. Aunt Elena was really pateint. She would unravel the work and show me where I went wrong. After a few more days, the yarn was all dirty. We had pulled it out over and over again. I wanted to cry.

In the end Aunt Elena told me not to get upset and that we would try again. We put the yarn and a picture of the scraf in a box for Nana. When we went to the hospital. Nana was surprised when she opened the box. My mom was surprised too when she saw what was inside.

I told them that Aunt Elena promised to help me with a scarf. So until I finish the scarf, Aunt Elena and I will get together for Sunday afternoon knitting.

 **133**

Sharing an Experience

Student Self-Assessment

The assessment below shows how the writer of "A Knotty Problem" rated her own essay. First she used the rubric and number scale on pages 130–131 to rank each trait. Then she made two comments under each trait. The first tells about something she did well in the narrative. The second comment points out something that she feels she could have done better.

 4 Ideas

1. My narrative answers the 5 W's.
2. I could have used more sensory details.

 5 Organization

1. My story has a clear beginning, middle, and ending.
2. In the ending, I could have told why the experience was important to me.

 4 Voice

1. My voice sounds like me most of the time.
2. More dialogue could have helped me "show" instead of just "tell" my story.

_____ **Word Choice**

1. I like my title.
2. I should have replaced overused words with synonyms.

 3 Sentence Fluency

1. I combined a couple of sentences.
2. I could have combined more of the short, choppy sentences.

 4 Conventions

1. The dialogue is punctuated correctly.
2. I forgot to check my spelling.

 Use the rubric. Assess your narrative using the rubric shown on pages 130–131.

1 On your own paper, list the six traits. Leave room after each trait to write one strength and one weakness.

2 Then choose a number (from 1 to 6) that shows how well each trait was used.

NARRATIVE

Student Self-Assessment

To give students additional practice with evaluating a narrative essay, use a reproducible assessment sheet (TE page 799) and one or both of the **benchmark papers** listed in the Benchmark Papers box below. You can use an overhead transparency while students refer to their own copies made from the copy masters. For your benefit a completed assessment sheet is provided.

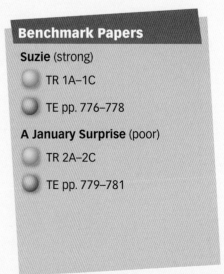

Benchmark Papers

Suzie (strong)

TR 1A–1C

TE pp. 776–778

A January Surprise (poor)

TR 2A–2C

TE pp. 779–781

Reflecting on Your Writing

Have students date and save their reflections throughout the school year. Each time they add one, have them reread earlier reflections to see how they have changed or grown as writers. Students may notice how much more comfortable they have become as writers over the course of the term.

Reflecting on Your Writing

You've worked hard to write a narrative that your classmates will enjoy. Now take some time to think about your writing. Finish each sentence starter below on your own paper. Thinking about your writing will help you see how you are growing as a writer.

My Narrative

1. The best part of my narrative is . . .

2. The part that still needs work is . . .

3. The main thing I learned about writing a personal narrative is . . .

4. In my next narrative, I would like to . . .

5. Here is one question I still have about writing a narrative:

English Language Learners

To build students' confidence, offer positive remarks about specific ways in which they have improved their writing and language skills. Then ask:

- What skills could you work on for the next writing assignment?
- What writing goals do you have?

This activity will help them improve their skills in a manageable way.

Narrative Writing

Biographical Narrative

"What happened when your friend got her new bike?" "What happened when your mother went to Puerto Rico?" "What happened when your older brother joined the soccer team?" If you sat down with a friend or family member and asked, "What happened when . . . ?" you would probably hear some great stories.

Writing about an important event in another person's life can help you and others understand that person. This type of writing is called a *biographical narrative*, and the next few pages will help you write one.

Writing Guidelines

Subject:	An event from someone else's life
Form:	Biographical narrative
Purpose:	To understand another person
Audience:	Classmates

Biographical Narrative

Objectives
- know what a biographical narrative is
- use what was learned about personal narrative to create a biographical narrative
- plan, draft, revise, edit, and share a biographical narrative

A **biographical narrative** tells a story about an event in another person's life.

Discuss the meaning of *biography*:
- *bio–* means "life"
- *–graphy* means "a writing about a specific subject."

Biography is the written account of a person's life.

Students are likely to be familiar with biographies. Show examples of biographies of historical and present-day people. Explain that friends and relatives may also be the subjects of biographies. Ask:

Where else can you find biographical narratives? (political campaigns, newspaper articles, personal journals).

Biographical Narrative

A biographical narrative focuses on a single event. Use one or more of the ideas below to familiarize students with the genre.

- Have students complete a 5- to 10-minute freewrite using the stem *I remember when _____* . . . They should fill in the blank with the name of a friend or relative and retell a story.
- Before students read "The Last Reckless Ride," ask them to think about a close encounter they have had with wildlife, or an encounter they have heard about. Ask for volunteers to share their stories.
- Review what students know about the content and form of a narrative. You may wish to direct them to reread the rubric on PE pages 130–131.

136

Biographical Narrative

A biographical narrative tells the story of a single event in a person's life. The event should reveal something interesting about the person. Sharese, the writer of the biographical narrative below, tells a story about her father.

The Last Reckless Ride

BEGINNING

The beginning introduces the event.

My dad used to be a thrill seeker. He enjoyed extreme sports like bungee jumping and rock climbing, and he took lots of careless risks. But one day, when he was riding his mountain bike, things got too extreme—even for him.

It was a perfect day for riding. The sun was shining, the air was brisk, and people weren't yet crowding the high trails. My dad pumped the pedals of his mountain bike and climbed the gravel path. Once he reached the high point of the trail, he shot downhill. The rear tire of his bike sprayed gravel, and the front tire bounced down the path. He picked up speed and whooped as he tore around a corner.

MIDDLE

Specific details move the story along.

Suddenly, something jumped up in the path ahead of him. It was a black bear!

Dad jammed on the brakes. He left a long skid on the path behind him and slid to within 10 feet of the bear.

It stared right at him and growled.

RISING ACTION

Dialogue adds to the rising action.

"Easy . . . easy," Dad said. There would be no way to ride past the bear. Dad glanced back over his shoulder. If he tried to turn around, the bear would just chase him down.

The bear stepped toward my dad.

That's when Dad got off the bike and lifted it like a shield. "Take it easy. We're both scared." He took a step back. "I'll go this way, and you go that way."

tell share remember
relate narrate
Biographical Narrative 137

The bear took another step forward.

Dad's heart pounded. He should have had a noisemaker on his bike to scare off bears. His life was on the line because of his own carelessness.

Lifting his bike overhead, Dad said in a deep voice, "Back, you! Back, bear!"

The bear stopped in its tracks and sniffed. Then it turned and ambled off into the woods.

My dad trembled as he lowered the mountain bike. His legs felt like jelly. He turned and walked his bike back up the trail. Just to make sure he scared off any other bears, he sang at the top of his lungs.

That close call got Dad's attention. From then on, he was less reckless in his extreme sports.

HIGH POINT

At the high point, the reader is most concerned about what will happen.

ENDING

The ending tells how the person changed.

NARRATIVE

Respond to the reading. Answer the following questions about the biographical narrative.

☐ **Ideas** (1) What details make the story come alive?

☐ **Organization** (2) How does the writer begin the story?
(3) How does she organize the middle?
(4) How does she end her narrative?

☐ **Voice & Word Choice** (5) What words or phrases show that the writer enjoys this story?

Respond to the reading.

Ask students why they made the choices they did.

Answers

Ideas **1.** Possible choices:

- sun shining
- air brisk
- pumped the pedals
- shot downhill
- sprayed gravel
- tire bounced
- whooped
- jammed on the brakes
- long skid on the path
- growled
- lifted bike like a shield
- heart pounded
- life was on the line
- sniffed
- ambled
- trembled
- legs felt like jelly
- sang at the top of his lungs

Organization **2.** she begins at the end, talking about a change that took place

3. she tells about the experience in chronological order

4. she returns to the beginning, explaining why the change took place

Voice & Word Choice **5.** in addition to all the details that make the story come alive, the writer uses humorous phrases and amusing dialogue: things got too extreme—even for him, got Dad's attention.

Prewriting Selecting a Topic

As students create their line diagram, direct them to include at least one family member and one close friend.

Prewriting Gathering Details

Students will probably need time to interview the subject of their narrative. Remind students to write out their questions before they speak to the person.

Point out that *how* has been added to the 5 W questions.

Prewriting Selecting a Topic

Think about your favorite people: family members, friends, teachers, or even famous people. What stories do you know about them?

Sharese, the writer of the sample biographical narrative, used a line diagram to list her favorite people and stories about their lives.

Line Diagram

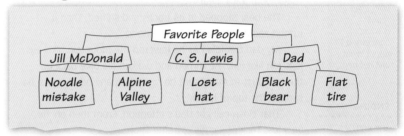

 Choose your topic. Create your own line diagram. List favorite people and story ideas about their lives. Then choose the best story.

Gathering Details

To write a biographical narrative, you must learn as much as you can about the person's experience. Sharese used questions based on the 5 W's and H to interview her father.

5 W's and H List

1. Who was with you when you ran into the bear? no one
2. What did you do when you saw it? skidded to a stop and held up my bike like a shield
3. Where did this happen? on a bike trail in the mountains
4. When did it happen? on a cool spring morning five years ago
5. Why did it happen? because I didn't carry a noisemaker
6. How did the event change you? was less reckless after that

 Use the 5 W's and H questions. If possible, interview the person you are writing about. Base your interview questions on the 5 W's and H.

tell share remember
relate narrate
Biographical Narrative **139**

Organizing Details

Narratives are usually organized by time. First one thing happens, and then another, and another, and so on. To organize her details, Sharese used a time line. Above the time line, she identified the most important actions. Below, she wrote details related to each action.

Time Line

Rode down trail	Met the bear	Used bike as shield	Shouted at bear
spraying gravel	skidded to a stop	heart pounded	turned back

 Create a time line. Using the model above, organize the details of your biographical narrative in a time line.

Focus on the Traits

Organization The best narratives follow a pattern called a story line. The **beginning** grabs the reader's interest and starts the story. Next, **rising action** increases the excitement. The **high point** shares the story's most exciting part. Last of all, the **ending** wraps up the story.

Story Line

HIGH POINT
Shouted at bear

RISING ACTION
Used bike as shield

Met bear

BEGINNING
Rode down trail

ENDING
Decided to be more careful

Prewriting Organizing Details

A time line is a way to organize events into chronological or time order. The expanded time line on PE page 139 includes the events plus related descriptive details.

Focus on the Traits

Organization
A story line contains the beginning, middle, and end of a narrative. The middle includes the rising action and high point. The ending gives the resolution. The story line helps reveal the "emotional" level of the narrative.

NARRATIVE

English Language Learners

Provide more hands-on practice with recognizing the main story elements—beginning, rising action, high point, and resolution—by drawing on the board a diagram similar to the one on PE page 139. Fill in the diagram using events from a familiar or recently read biographical story.

Writing Creating Your First Draft

Consider having students write three different story beginnings.

- Ask each student to fold a paper into thirds and label each column with a suggested way to start a story.
- After they write three beginnings, they should read them to a partner. Based on the partner's reactions, each student can choose the most effective starting sentence.

Remind students that as they work on the middle of the story, they can remove or add details.

If students have conducted interviews, before they begin writing have them think about the most memorable things that their subject said. Point out that this is the dialogue they should be sure to include. Have them add the dialogue to their time lines in the appropriate place so they will remember to include it as they write.

Writing Creating Your First Draft

Follow your time line as you write your first draft. Use the tips below to guide your writing.

BEGINNING Grab the reader's attention and start the story.

- **Begin with an interesting fact.** *My dad used to be a thrill seeker.*
- **Use a quotation.** *"I was careless the day I met a bear."*
- **Start in the middle of the action.** *My dad pumped the pedals of his mountain bike and climbed the gravel path.*

MIDDLE Build the excitement in the narrative.

- **Be selective.** Tell only the important parts. Leave out anything that doesn't move the story along.
- **Use action and dialogue.** Show what happened and use dialogue.
- **Use sensory details.** Include sights, sounds, smells, textures, and tastes so that the reader can experience the story.
- **Build to a high point.** Use the action, dialogue, and sensory details to build to the most exciting part of the story.

ENDING Bring your story to a close.

- **Describe the final action.** Write what happens after the high point.
- **Tell why the event was important.**
- **Focus on how it changed the person.**

 Write the first draft. Use your time line from page 139 as a general writing guide but feel free to add new details as they come to mind. If you enjoy telling the story, your writing voice will be natural and interesting.

Advanced Learners

Encourage students to use the device of suspense to build to a high point. Demonstrate by rereading the third paragraph of "The Last Reckless Ride" (PE page 136), replacing *a black bear* with *the largest animal he had ever seen!* Ask students how the next paragraph could be modified to accommodate the fact that the reader doesn't know yet that what "jumped up in the path ahead of him" was a bear. For example, the second sentence could be reworded to end "...slid to within 10 feet of a gigantic black bear!" Encourage students to include suspense in their own writing.

Revising **Improving Your Writing**

After you finish writing, set your narrative aside for a little while. When you are ready to revise, keep the following traits in mind.

☐ **Ideas** Add sensory details (*sights, sounds, smells, tastes, textures*) to parts that seem dull or unclear.

> The rear tire of his bike sprayed gravel, and the front tire bounced down the path.

☐ **Organization** Check the time order of the action. Your story should flow from one action to the next.

> Dad jammed on the brakes. He left a long skid on the path behind him and slid to within 10 feet of the bear.

☐ **Voice** Make sure the reader can "hear" your storytelling voice. Does it match how you feel at different parts in the story— excited, frightened, relieved, proud?

> My dad trembled as he lowered the mountain bike. His legs felt like jelly.

☐ **Word Choice** Look for overused words that could be replaced by synonyms.

OVERUSED	LIVELY
looked	glanced
pushed	jammed
walked very slowly	ambled

☐ **Sentence Fluency** Combine short, choppy sentences into longer sentences that flow smoothly.

SHORT, CHOPPY SENTENCES	COMBINED SENTENCE
The sun was shining. The air was brisk. People weren't yet crowding the high trails.	The sun was shining, the air was brisk, and people weren't yet crowding the high trails.

 Revise your narrative. Add sights, sounds, smells, tastes, and textures. Rearrange any events that are out of order. Make sure your voice matches your feelings.

NARRATIVE

Revising **Improving Your Writing**

To help students with their revising, have them consider the following strategies:

- Have students make several passes through their narratives, reviewing for a single trait at a time.
- Remind students to count the words in their sentences to decide whether they need to shorten or lengthen some. Students may want to use **inserts** or **flaps** (*see below*).

✳ Find additional information about sentence variety on PE pages 511–514.

Teaching Tip: Inserts and Flaps

The need for revising may be so extensive that there is not enough room for students to make the changes on their draft. Here are a few ways to solve this problem.

- ***Inserts*** Students can write the new material on a separate piece of paper and label it as Insert A, B, C, and so on. They should also indicate on the original draft where Insert A belongs with the circled words *Insert A*. They should number the insert with the same page number as the draft, followed by *A*.

- ***Flaps*** Students can write replacement material on a separate piece of paper and tape it directly on top of their draft to cover up the material they want to replace. If the replacement material is longer than what is being replaced, they tape at the top only.

- ***Spider legs*** Students can write the new material on a separate piece of paper and then cut away the excess blank paper. This flap can then be taped to the side of the draft with an arrow indicating where the material should be inserted.

Editing Checking for Conventions

- Form editing groups of four students. Each student should choose to be responsible for one of the editing categories: punctuation, capitalization, spelling, or grammar. Each student should read and edit the papers of the other members of the group.
- Have them underline any errors they see and then pass the paper to the next "expert." When each paper has been corrected by all members of the group, it should be returned to the writer for correction.

Publishing Sharing Your Writing

If time permits, have students form new groups and share their biographical narratives. They may read them aloud or pass them around.

If any students are extremely reluctant to share their work, help them identify why they are uncomfortable and, if possible, help them find a way to work around the concern.

Editing Checking for Conventions

Once you have completed your revising, it's time to focus on editing your narrative. Keep the following trait in mind.

Conventions

Once your story sounds the way you want it to, check your punctuation, capitalization, spelling, and grammar. The following checklist can help you.

PUNCTUATION

_____ 1. Do I use end punctuation after all my sentences?

_____ 2. Do I use commas correctly?

_____ 3. Do I use apostrophes to show possession (*boy's bike*)?

CAPITALIZATION

_____ 4. Do I start all my sentences with capital letters?

_____ 5. Do I capitalize all proper nouns?

SPELLING

_____ 6. Have I spelled all my words correctly?

GRAMMAR

_____ 7. Do I use correct forms of verbs (*had gone,* not *had went*)?

_____ 8. Do my subjects and verbs agree in number?
(She and I *were* going, not She and I *was* going.)

_____ 9. Do I use the right words (*to, too,* and *two*)?

Edit your biographical narrative. Make sure your words are lively and your sentences flow smoothly. Also proofread your narrative after writing a final copy.

Publishing Sharing Your Writing

Narratives are meant for sharing. They help us connect with people around us—friends, family members, and classmates.

Share your biographical narrative. Read your narrative to as many audiences as possible. You'll see how narratives bring people together.

tell **share** remember
relate narrate **143**

Narrative Writing
Across the Curriculum

Writing narratives is a common activity in every one of your classes. For example, in social studies you may be asked to write journal entries or keep class minutes. In math, you may be asked to write story problems. In science class, you may be asked to connect a personal experience to a scientific concept.

To write strong narratives, no matter what the class, you must learn as much as you can about your topic and share the key details about it. If everything works out, your writing will help your readers understand as much as you do about your topic.

Mini Index

- **Social Studies:**
  Writing Classroom Journals
- **Math:** Writing Story Problems
- **Science:** Writing an Anecdote
- **Practical Writing:**
  Recording Class Minutes
- **Writing for Assessment**

Across the Curriculum

Objectives
- apply what students have learned about narrative writing to other curriculum areas
- practice writing for assessment

The lessons on the following pages provide samples of narrative writing students might do in different content areas. The particular form used in each content area may also be used in a different content area (for example, students can write a classroom journal for a science lesson just as well as for a social studies lesson).

Assigning these forms of writing will depend on

- the skill level of your students,
- the subject matter they are studying in different content areas,
- and the writing goals of your school, district, or state.

Social Studies: Writing Classroom Journals

Have students share any experience they have had writing journal entries (students may keep writing journals or personal diaries).

Have students explain why this journal entry can be considered a narrative form of writing:

- It tells about what happens to someone.
- It is organized in chronological or time order.
- It includes details.
- It includes what the writer thinks about what happens.

Discuss how it differs from the narrative writing students have done so far

- It has a particular format.
- A sketch is included.
- It doesn't have dialogue.

144

Social Studies: Writing Classroom Journals

Writing in a classroom journal can help you learn. When you write about what happens in class, you remember details better and gain a deeper understanding of the subject. The following journal entries are from a social studies class.

The date is given first.

The student reflects on events in class.

The student records details learned in class.

Monday, October 18: Today Mr. Henry showed us a video about Mexico City. It's huge! I thought New York City was big, but Mexico City has millions more people. It's the biggest city in the world.

The coolest part of the video showed the Plaza of the Three Cultures. It has ruins of an Aztec temple. Those ruins are 600 years old!

After the video, Mr. Henry told us what happened at the plaza. He said that on one day in 1521, the Aztecs and Cortez had a battle, and 40,000 Aztecs died. What a horrible day! Still, that was the beginning of Mexico.

Tuesday, October 19: Today Mr. Henry passed around postcards from his trip to Mexico. There sure are lots of beautiful places.

The most amazing pictures were from Chichen Itza. It's an ancient Mayan city. It has a gigantic pyramid called the Great Pyramid. The Mayans lived near it 1,300 years ago.

Struggling Learners

If students have difficulty using complete sentences to record facts as they are presented in class, instruct them to jot down events and details in outline form or on a cause/effect chart. They can then reorganize the information in journal entry paragraph format later on.

Writing Tips

Before you write . . .

- **Set up your journal.**
  Designate part of a notebook for your journal and also make sure to follow your teacher's guidelines.

During your writing . . .

- **Record the date.**
  Write the date of each journal entry.
- **React to what you are learning.**
  Record the most important facts. Also write your thoughts and any experiences that relate to the information you are studying.
- **Include sketches.**
  Make a sketch in your journal if your teacher shows you a picture of something interesting. Also copy and label any important diagrams. Pictures can help you remember as you look back at your journal.

The Great Pyramid

After you've written a first draft . . .

- **Reread your work.**
  Read the journal to help you remember what you're learning in class.
- **Review your journal for essay ideas.**
  Look through your journal whenever you need writing ideas.

 Write a journal entry about something you learned in social studies class. Remember to record the facts but also include your thoughts and feelings about them.

NARRATIVE

Writing Tips

Use the following activity as an introduction to writing a journal entry.

- ■ Have students freewrite a journal entry for the most recent writing or language lesson.
- ■ Remind them to begin with the date of the class and to include what they learned and how they felt about the lesson.
- ■ Ask volunteers to share their journal entries and discuss how they are similar and different. Students may remember different details and have different reactions to them.

Try It Answers

Answers will vary.

Math: Writing Story Problems

This activity gives students insight into the structure and development of word problems. The activity is also a good way to connect literature and math.

Review the instruction and the model with students. Point out that the math variables are not a part of the story itself. The variables are added in order to create a math problem. For the activities in this lesson, the math variables are provided for students.

146

Math: Writing Story Problems

One way to create a story problem is to base it on a familiar fable, fairy tale, or nursery rhyme. In his math class, Alex wrote a story problem based on one of Aesop's fables.

The **beginning** summarizes the story.

The **middle** gives the variables, the problem to solve, and the story problem.

The **ending** shows the solution.

The Ant and the Grasshopper

One fine winter day, an ant was drying grain that he had collected in the summer. A hungry grasshopper came begging for food. The ant asked, "Why didn't you store food during the summer?" He replied, "I spent the summer singing." The ant said, "If you sing all summer, you go hungry in the winter."

Math Variables: Each day an ant

- gathers 6 grams of food, and
- eats 2 grams of food.

Problem to Solve: How many days must an ant work to gather enough food for a year?

Story Problem: An ant eats 2 grams of food every day of the year. He can gather 6 grams each day. How many days must he work to gather a year's supply of food?

1. First, find out how many grams of food the ant eats in a year. (365 x 2 = 730 grams of food eaten in one year)
2. Then find out how many days it will take to gather 730 grams of food. (730 ÷ 6 = 121.6 days needed to collect the food)

Solution: The ant needs to work 121.6 days to gather enough food for a year.

tell **share** remember narrate relate   **147**
Writing in Math

Writing Tips

Before you write . . .
- **Find a short fable, fairy tale, or nursery rhyme.**
- **Read the story and think of how you can include math variables.** For example, the rates of speed could be one variable in the fable of the tortoise and the hare.

During your writing . . .
- **Prepare a summary of the story.**
- **List the math variables.**
- **State the problem to be solved.**
- **Write the story problem.**
- **Explain each step that is used to solve the problem.**

After you've written a first draft . . .
- **Make sure your story summary and story problem are clear.**
- **Check your answer.**
- **Get a classmate to try to solve your problem.**
- **Check your writing for conventions.**

NARRATIVE

 Write a story problem and solution using the following fable, math variables, and problem to solve. Revise and edit carefully.

Summary of story:

The Crow and the Pitcher

A thirsty crow saw a pitcher and flew to it. The pitcher contained so little water that the crow could not reach it. He flew off, brought back a stone, and dropped it in. One by one, the stones raised the water until the crow could finally take a drink.

Math variables:
- The pitcher contains 3 inches of water.
- Each stone will raise the water 5/8 of an inch.

Problem to solve: How many stones must the crow drop to raise the water level up to 8 inches?

Answers

Possible answer:

Story Problem: A pitcher has 3 inches of water in it. A thirsty crow cannot reach the water unless it is 8 inches high. The crow keeps adding stones to the pitcher to raise the water level. Each stone raises the water level 5/8 of an inch. How many stones must the crow drop into the pitcher in order to raise the water level up to 8 inches?

1. First, find out how many inches the water must rise. (8 − 3 = 5 inches)
2. Then find out how many stones it will take to raise the water 5 inches. (5 ÷ 5/8 = 8)

Solution: The crow must drop 8 stones into the pitcher to raise the water level high enough so that he can drink.

English Language Learners

Students may not be familiar with many nursery rhymes or folk tales. Bring in some children's books for them to read for ideas, or allow them to use stories from their native country.

Advanced Learners

Have students estimate how altering the value of the variables would affect the answer:
- What if the number of inches contained in the pitcher is doubled?
- What if the size of the stone is halved?

Have them solve each modified story problem.

Science:
Writing an Anecdote

Before reading the page, ask students the following question: What kind of writing are you most familiar with in science classes? (Students may have experience doing science problems, writing research reports, writing up experiments.)

Ask students to explain how writing about science experiments is similar to narrative writing.

- It tells about an experience in the order in which the events happened.
- It draws a conclusion.
- A science report about a scientist could also be structured like a biographical narrative.

In this lesson students are introduced to an anecdote, a brief story that helps make an idea clearer. An anecdote is usually drawn from personal experience. When students connect a concept to their personal lives, they are more likely to understand and remember it. Here a student explains the concept of buoyancy by sharing an experience he or she had.

148

Science: Writing an Anecdote

When you write an anecdote, you tell a brief story to help make an idea clearer. This type of writing is helpful for learning scientific ideas. In the sample below, a student used a personal experience to help explain the concept of buoyancy. (Also see page 558.)

The **beginning** paragraph sets up the story.

The **middle** explains the scientific concept and illustrates it.

The **ending** reflects on the story.

Oh, Buoyancy!

When Ms. Allard started teaching us about buoyancy, everybody said, "Huh?" Well, I understood right away because of my adventure in a canoe.

My sister Sarah took me canoeing, and I accidentally tipped over the boat. We flipped into the water, but our life jackets popped us up. Unfortunately, the metal canoe sank.

"Oh no! The canoe!" I shouted.

Sarah just laughed. "It'll come back up."

Sure enough, even though it was full of water, that metal canoe rose to the surface. "How did it do that?"

"It has buoyancy material in each end," Sarah said. "It's foam, like our life jackets."

We dumped out as much water as we could. Then we started bailing.

"Each time we throw a gallon of water out of the boat, the boat rises by a gallon."

"I get it. As the canoe weighs less, it sits higher."

"Right. That's buoyancy."

After that day, I'll always understand buoyancy. It's just too bad we had to get all wet in the process.

English Language Learners

To help students think of principles of science, discuss common activities like the following:

- falling out of bed (gravity);
- stumbling forward when a train suddenly stops (inertia).

Then discuss how students might develop an anecdote to explain a particular scientific concept.

Idioms appearing in the student model include the following:

- Huh? (I don't understand)
- tipped over (caused something to go upside down)
- flipped into (fell into)
- popped us up (helped us to float)
- sure enough (it was true)
- dumped out (got rid of)
- get it (understand)

tell **share** remember
relate
Writing in Science **149**

Writing Tips

Before you write . . .

- **Select a story that illustrates an idea or a concept.**
  Think about how the things you are learning in science relate to your everyday experiences. For example, when you're outside, have you ever noticed that frost sometimes remains in a shaded spot but has evaporated in the sunlit areas? That experience tells you something about freezing and evaporation.

- **Get your science facts correct.**
  Check into the scientific facts behind your story.

During your writing . . .

- **Let the story tell itself.**
  Have fun writing your story so the reader will have fun reading it.

- **Be clear and direct.**
  Make your explanation of the idea or concept as simple and clear as possible.

After you've written a first draft . . .

- **Revise your first draft.**
  Make sure that your story is complete, easy to follow, and interesting.

- **Check for accuracy.**
  Double-check your facts and details.

- **Edit for correctness.**
  Check for punctuation, spelling, capitalization, and grammar errors.

NARRATIVE

Try It Think of an experience you have had that illustrates a principle of science. Use that experience and write an anecdote to help your classmates understand the concept.

Writing Tips

If students are completing this writing in language arts, work with science teachers to come up with some basic concepts that students are familiar with and that they can turn into an anecdote.

 **Answers**

Answers will vary.

Struggling Learners

For the **Try It** activity, help students select an anecdote by providing a chart with columns labeled *science principle, factors,* and *situation*. Chart the concept discussed in the "Writing Tips":

- The science principle is *frost*.
- The factors are *light, shade, heat,* and *evaporation*.
- The situation is *frost remaining in the shady spot*.

Suggest that a possible anecdote could involve playing soccer on a partially shaded field, resulting in a partially slippery playing surface.

Next, list science concepts from previously studied curriculum in the first column. Elicit from students the factors related to each of these concepts. Encourage students to think of a situation related to these factors and to then weave it into a personal story.

Practical Writing:
Recording Class Minutes

Writing up notes about what happened in a meeting is a common occurrence in many different settings (businesses, governments, charitable organizations, and so on).

- It is helpful to people who were absent.
- It allows people who attended the meeting to check their understanding of what happened.

Formats for writing up minutes for a meeting can vary, but they usually tell the following information:

- name of the group
- date the meeting took place
- who was absent (or present)
- topic(s) of the meeting
- what happened
- list of materials handed out
- indication of what will occur between this and the next meeting
- date for the next meeting is scheduled

Practical Writing: Recording Class Minutes

Class minutes tell the story of what happened in class. They can remind you about important information and help an absent classmate catch up. The following minutes were taken in a social studies class.

The **beginning** states the class information.

Social Studies, Third Period
Wednesday, November 17, 2004

Absent: Laura Parker and José Velasquez

Topic: Mississippi Mound Builders

Handout: Ms. Lindell handed out a fact sheet on mound builders (attached). She pointed out two things:
 1. Mississippi Mound Builders built large mounds as temples, burial sites, and bases for government.
 2. This culture lasted for 1,000 years, from 700 to 1700.

The **middle** identifies each activity in the order it happened.

Video: Ms. Lindell showed a video about Cahokia, IL.
 1. Monk's Mound is 100 feet tall.
 2. More than 100 other mounds are near Cahokia.
 3. This was once a society of 40,000 people.
 4. Builders hauled baskets of dirt on their backs.

Discussion: Ms. Lindell stressed two things:
 1. The cities had complex government and trade.
 2. Most mound builders died in the 1500s because of diseases from Europe.

The **ending** lists the assignment.

Assignment: Ms. Lindell had the class write journal entries about mound builders.

Writing Tips

Before you write . . .

- **Check the format.**
  Follow your teacher's guidelines for class minutes or use the model on page 150 as a guide.

During your writing . . .

- **Record the basic class information.**
  Make sure you note the day's topic and the students who are absent.
- **Be brief.**
  Write your minutes so that a reader can quickly tell what happened in class.
- **Write down the key points.**
  Consider what an absent person needs to know to keep up. Don't write down everything, but listen carefully to find out what the teacher considers most important.
- **Write neatly.**
  Make sure everyone can read your writing.

After you've written a first draft . . .

- **Double-check activities and assignments.**
  Make sure your information is complete. Ask a classmate to review the minutes to see if you missed anything.
- **Edit and proofread the minutes.**
  Correct any errors in your minutes. Other students may depend on them for makeup work, so it's important to be accurate.

 For class minutes in any subject area, follow the writing tips above. Record only the most important facts and examples.

NARRATIVE

Writing Tips

Point out that writing up minutes is a method of taking notes. Minutes should be brief and should focus on the key points. It is a good idea to have another person who was there check the minutes before making them final.

Have each student record minutes for the first half of this language arts lesson. It will be interesting to compare the many different versions of the minutes.

Ask for a few volunteers to share their minutes with the class. Ask:

- Did the writer focus on key points?
- Do the minutes include enough, or too much, information?

 **Answers**

Minutes will vary according to the class and subject chosen, but the format you assign should be followed.

English Language Learners

Some students may have difficulty finding the right words to summarize the key points in a classroom session. Work with them to write minutes for this lesson.

Advanced Learners

To extend this activity, encourage advanced students to add a section titled *Further Study*. Under this heading students may generate a list of related topics to explore outside of class in order to broaden their understanding of the information discussed in class.

Writing for Assessment

If your students must take school, district, or state assessments this year, focus on the writing form on which they will be tested.

Create a poster that reviews strategies that can be helpful in an on-demand test situation. The list may include the following:

- Have the proper supplies: paper, pens, or pencils.
- Read through the entire question before you start.
- Think about the traits, content, and structure of the required writing form.
- Take notes and plan before beginning to write.
- Pace your writing according to the amount of time allowed.
- Reread slowly when revising and editing.

Review the main traits of a narrative. Ask students to look for these as they read the model:

- Is an experience recreated through details?
- Does it have a beginning, middle, and end?
- Is it told in time order?
- Does it use natural language and dialogue?

Writing for Assessment

Many state and school writing tests ask you to write a response to a narrative prompt. A narrative prompt asks you to recall a personal experience or respond to a "what if" question. Study the following sample prompt and student response.

Narrative Prompt

Choose a day in your life that you would like to live over again. Would you like it to be the same or different? Write a story about what you would do on that day.

The **beginning** states the focus of the narrative (underlined).

> "Tony, this is the last time that I'm going to tell you to get up and get ready for school." I hardly heard those words before falling back to sleep. This was a big mistake. <u>If I could live yesterday over again, I would want it to be different, especially at the start.</u>
>
> Most importantly, I would get out of bed early enough to make it to school on time. Then I'd be there to hear my math teacher go over the assignment instead of sitting in the principal's office. And I need all the help I can get in math.
>
> The middle of the day would be different, too. I wouldn't have rushed out of the house without grabbing my lunch. Eating lunch would have kept me from getting grouchy. Then I

Each **middle** paragraph covers one main point.

tell share remember
relate
Writing for Assessment **153**

wouldn't have acted so stupid when I got home.

After school, I wouldn't have slammed our front door and blamed my mother for my bad day. I wouldn't have been sent to my room for being snotty. Instead, I would have relaxed and watched TV for a while before supper.

Yesterday could have easily been a better day, but I can't live my life over. I was surprised how much better it felt to get up right away this morning, have a good breakfast, and leave for school on time with a lunch in my hand. My mother felt much better about everything, too.

The **ending** paragraph reflects on the experience.

NARRATIVE

Respond to the reading. Answer the following questions about the sample response.

☐ **Ideas** (1) What is the focus of the writer's response? (2) How does the focus relate to the prompt? (3) What are some of the key details in the writing?

☐ **Organization** (4) How is the response organized?

☐ **Voice & Word Choice** (5) Do the writer's feelings come through in this writing? Give examples.

Respond to the reading.

Before students answer the specific questions, ask their opinions of the sample.

Ideas 1. If I could live yesterday over again, I would do things differently.
2. It relates directly to the prompt.
3. The narrator would change the following things:
- get out of bed early
- hear the math teacher go over the assignment
- would not be in the principal's office
- would have brought lunch
- would not be grouchy
- would not slam the door
- would not be rude to mother
- would relax before supper

Organization 4. in chronological or time order

Voice & Word Choice 5. Possible choices:
- This was a big mistake.
- If I could live yesterday over, I would . . .
- I need all the help I can get.
- I wouldn't have acted so stupid.
- I can't live my life over.
- I was surprised at how much better it felt . . .

Writing Tips

Point out that students must approach writing-on-demand assignments differently from open-ended writing assignments and that timed writing creates pressures for everyone.

Narrative Prompts

To teach students who must take timed assessments how to approach their writing, allow them the same amount of time to write their response essay as they will be allotted on school, district, or state assessments. Break down each part of the process into clear chunks of time. For example, you might give students

- 15 minutes for reading, note-taking, and planning,
- 20 minutes for writing,
- 10 minutes for editing and proofreading.

Tell students when time is up for each section. Start the assignment at the top of the hour or at the half-hour to make it easier for students to keep track of the time.

If your state, district, or school requires students to use and submit a graphic organizer as part of their assessment, provide a copy of one of the reproducible charts (TE pages 800–804) or refer students to PE pages 548–549.

154

Writing Tips

Use the following tips as a guide when responding to a narrative writing prompt.

Before you write . . .

- **Understand the prompt.**
  Remember that a narrative prompt asks you to tell a story.
- **Plan your time wisely.**
  Spend several minutes taking notes and planning before you start writing. Use the last few minutes to read over what you have written.

During your writing . . .

- **Decide on a focus for your narrative.**
  Use key words from the prompt in your focus statement.
- **Be selective.**
  Tell only the main events in your story.
- **End in a meaningful way.**
  Reflect on the experience or story.

After you've written a first draft . . .

- **Check for completeness and correctness.**
  Present the events of your story in order. Delete any unneeded details and correct any errors as neatly as possible.

Narrative Prompts

- One morning you open your front door, and there's a large package sitting outside. What's in it? Who put it there? What do you do with it? Write a story about the package.
- Tell the story about the nicest thing you've ever done for someone else.

 Plan and write a response. Respond to one of the prompts listed above. Complete your writing within the time limit your teacher sets. Afterward, list one part you like and one part you could improve.

Narrative Writing in Review

Purpose: In narrative writing, you *tell a story* about something that has happened.

Topics: An experience you have had
An event from someone else's life

Prewriting

Select a topic from your own life or interview other people about an episode in their lives. (See page 102.)

Size up your idea using the 5 W's to see if it will make a good personal narrative. (See page 103.)

Gather important details about the people involved and the order of events. List sensory details to use in the narrative. (See pages 103–106.)

Writing

In the beginning part, catch the reader's interest and introduce your story. (See page 109.)

In the middle part, tell the events of the story. Use sensory details and dialogue. Use your own words and show your feelings throughout the story. Bring the story to a high point. (See pages 110–111.)

In the ending, tell why the event was important, tell how it changed the people involved, or relate the experience to your audience. (See page 112.)

Revising

Review the ideas, organization, and voice first. Then check **word choice** and **sentence fluency.** (See pages 114–123.)

Editing

Check your writing for conventions. Review punctuation of dialogue. Ask a friend to edit the writing, too. (See pages 126–128.)

Make a final copy and proofread it for errors before sharing it with other people. (See page 129.)

Assessing

Use the narrative rubric to assess your finished writing. (See pages 130–131.)

NARRATIVE

Narrative Writing in Review

Refer students to this page whenever they write narrative paragraphs or essays. You may also allow them to refer to this review while they are doing a sample assessment. As they become more familiar with the writing form during the year, they will need to refer to the list less frequently.

Expository Writing Overview

Writing Standards

The writing standards listed below are based on a blending of state and NCTE standards.

- Make a cluster to gather ideas.
- Support a focus statement with three topic sentences and closing sentences.
- Revise drafts to add details and clarify information.
- Assess writing using a rubric based on the traits of effective writing.

Writing Forms

- expository paragraph
- expository essay about explaining a process
- classification essay

Focus on the Traits

- **Ideas** Writing a clear focus statement
- **Organization** Including an interesting beginning, a middle that explains all the steps in a process, and a clear ending
- **Voice** Using an informative, confident voice that fits the audience
- **Word Choice** Choosing specific nouns and action verbs
- **Sentence Fluency** Writing complete, smooth sentences
- **Conventions** Checking for errors in punctuation, capitalization, spelling, and grammar

Unit Pacing

Expository Paragraph: 1.5–2.25 hours

The **expository paragraph** introduces the unit and lays the groundwork for more extensive expository writing. Use this section if students need to work on crafting a paragraph. Following are some of the topics that are covered.

- Studying a sample paragraph
- Brainstorming to select a topic
- Using a formula to write a topic sentence
- Arranging how-to steps in the correct order
- Closing with a statement that wraps up the instructions

Expository Essay 1: 4.5–6.75 hours

This section asks students to write an essay explaining **how to do or make something**. Use this section to focus on developing an essay. Following are some of the topics that are covered.

- Using a cluster and a list to choose a topic
- Sizing up a topic
- Writing a focus statement
- Creating a chart to organize the steps in the process
- Writing topic sentences that cover different parts of the process
- Using transitions to lead the reader through the explanation
- Matching voice with audience
- Expanding choppy sentences and fixing fragments

Expository Essay 2: 2.25–3 hours

The **classification essay** section offers a new slant on expository writing—explaining a topic by dividing it into its parts. Use this section to present an alternate or additional form of expository writing. Following are some of the topics covered.

- Freewriting to gather details
- Organizing with a line diagram
- Researching the topic and taking notes
- Summarizing the topic and ending with an interesting thought

Expository Writing Across the Curriculum: 2.25–3 hours

Collaborate with teachers from other curriculum areas to identify expository forms that could enhance students' experience with the curriculum already in place. Following are the subject areas and forms that are taught in this unit.

- **Social Studies**
Creating a Survey, pp. 206–207
- **Math**
Explaining a Concept, pp. 208–209
- **Science**
Writing an Explanation, pp. 210–211
- **Practical Writing**
Drafting Directions, pp. 212–213

Writing for Assessment: 2.25–3 hours

The student text shows an example of a strong student response to the first prompt listed below. Students can respond to that same prompt or to either of the additional prompts as an informal or a formal assessment.

- Write an essay explaining why respecting others is important or why being disrespectful can be harmful.
- Write an essay explaining which three rules your school would have if it could only have three rules, and tell why these rules are so important.
- Write an essay explaining what makes a good friend.

Evaluating an Expository Essay

Learning to evaluate one's own and others' writing is an integral part of learning to write. In addition to a student's evaluation of an expository essay (PE pages 196–197), **benchmark papers** provide practice with evaluating narrative writing.

- Malcolm X and Eleanor Roosevelt (strong)
TR 3A–3C
TE pp. 782–784
- Making Amazing Maps (good)
PE pp. 196–197
- Yo-Yos Flood Del Mar Hills School (poor)
TR 4A–4B
TE pp. 785–786

Integrated Grammar and Writing Skills

Below are skills lessons from the resources sections of the pupil edition that are suggested at point of use (✱) throughout this unit.

Writing an Expository Paragraph, pp. 157–160

- ✱ Write Expository Paragraphs, p. 528
- ✱ Listing, p. 545
- ✱ Topic Sentences, pp. 552–553

Explaining a Process, pp. 161–198

- ✱ Organizing Details, pp. 550–551
- ✱ Connecting Sentences, pp. 572–573
- ✱ Complete Sentences, pp. 504–505
- ✱ Commas in a Series, p. 582
- ✱ Commas in Introductory Word Groups, p. 590

Writing a Classification Essay, pp. 199–204

- ✱ Unity of Details, p. 538

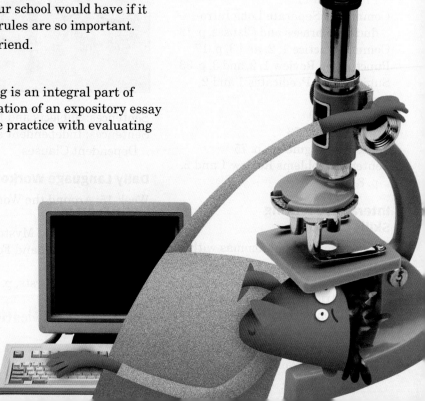

Additional Grammar Skills

Below are skills lessons from other components that you can weave into your unit instruction.

Writing an Expository Paragraph

SkillsBook

Interactive Writing Skills CD-ROM

Daily Language Workout

Explaining a Process

SkillsBook

Interactive Writing Skills CD-ROM

Expository Writing

Daily Language Workout

Writing a Classification Essay

SkillsBook

Interactive Writing Skills CD-ROM

Daily Language Workout

Expository Writing

Expository Paragraph

What can you do really well? Can you shoot a free throw or kick a soccer ball? Do you know how to wash a dog, make an omelet, or calculate the lowest common denominator? Think about what you know how to do and how you could explain it to someone else.

Writing that explains things is called *expository* writing. Most essays, reports, and newspaper articles are examples of expository writing. In each case, the writer knows something that he or she wants to explain to the reader.

In this chapter, you will write an expository paragraph about something you know how to do. You will become the teacher, sharing your knowledge with your classmates.

Writing Guidelines

Subject:	**Something you know how to do**
Form:	**Expository paragraph**
Purpose:	**To share knowledge**
Audience:	**Classmates**

Expository Paragraph

Objectives

- understand the content and structure of an expository paragraph
- choose a topic (something you know how to do) to write about
- plan, draft, revise, and edit an expository paragraph

Tell students that **expository writing**, or writing that explains things, is a part of their everyday lives. Ask them to name some things they've read recently that tell how to do something. Sample responses could include the following:

- instructions for a computer game
- directions to someone's house
- a recipe
- washing instructions for clothes
- guidelines for filling out a form

Expository Paragraph

To illustrate the parts of a paragraph, draw a hamburger on the board. Tell students that the top part of the bun is the topic sentence and the bottom part is the closing sentence. The burger itself is the body, or the middle sentences.

✱ Additional information about writing expository paragraphs is on PE page 528.

Respond to the reading.

Answers

Ideas 1. making a delicious omelet

Organization 2. The writer organized details in time order, because it is important to follow a recipe step by step. Words that indicate time order are *first, second, next, then,* and *finally.*

Voice & Word Choice 3. Possible word choices:

■ delicious
■ all you need
■ enjoy

Voice: The tone is encouraging.

158

Expository Paragraph

The expository paragraph is a basic form of writing. It almost always begins with a **topic sentence**, which tells the reader what the paragraph is about. The sentences in the **body** explain or support the topic sentence, and the **closing sentence** wraps up the paragraph. The paragraph below was written by a student who likes to cook her own breakfast.

Topic sentence

Body

Closing sentence

How to Make an Omelet

You can make a delicious omelet, even if you've never cooked before. For tools, all you need are a bowl, a hand beater, a frying pan, and a spatula. For ingredients, you need two eggs, two tablespoons of milk, a quarter cup of grated cheese, a little salt and pepper, and a pat of butter. First, break the eggs into a bowl and add the milk, salt, and pepper. Second, mix everything with the beater until it is foamy. Next, heat the frying pan and add the butter. Make sure the melted butter covers the whole bottom of the pan. When the butter begins to sizzle, pour the egg mixture into the pan and sprinkle the cheese over it. Let it cook until the eggs get firm around the edges. Then use the spatula to flip half of the omelet over the other half, like a taco. Give it another minute or so to melt the cheese and finish cooking the eggs. Finally, slide the omelet onto your plate and enjoy!

Respond to the reading. On your own paper, answer each of the following questions.

☐ **Ideas** (1) What is the topic of the paragraph?

☐ **Organization** (2) How did the writer organize details in the paragraph (time order or order of importance)? Explain.

☐ **Voice & Word Choice** (3) What words or ideas show you that the writer is really interested in the topic?

English Language Learners

Students may benefit from having visuals to go with the expository paragraph on page 158. Bring in a spatula, a hand beater, and a picture of an omelet. Discuss the following terms:

● foamy (full of bubbles and air)
● sizzle (make the hissing sound of frying fat)
● sprinkle (scatter in tiny pieces)
● firm (becoming solid, not soft)

● flip: turn over with a quick motion

Struggling Learners

To reinforce the concept of time order, invite students to explain orally how to prepare other favorite foods. Remind them that even a task as simple as making toast requires that the steps be done in a particular order.

Prewriting Selecting a Topic

When it comes to choosing a topic, think of things you know how to do. Can you bunt a baseball? Do you know how to draw cartoons or care for a pet? Have you ever set up a tent or built a fort?

The writer of the sample paragraph on page 158 brainstormed a list of "Things I Know How to Do."

Brainstorm List

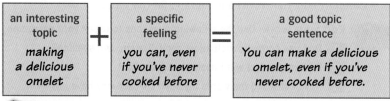

Things I Know How to Do

fix a flat tire	whistle	make balloon animals
make an omelet	knit	do a French braid
study for a test	juggle	play trombone

Brainstorm and select a topic. Using the list above as a guide, make your own list of things you know how to do. Then choose one that really interests you, one you could explain in a paragraph.

Writing a Topic Sentence

Write a sentence that tells the reader what your how-to paragraph will be about. A good topic sentence does two things: (1) It names the topic, and (2) it states your feelings about it. Here is a simple formula for writing good topic sentences:

an interesting topic	+	a specific feeling	=	a good topic sentence
making a delicious omelet		*you can, even if you've never cooked before*		*You can make a delicious omelet, even if you've never cooked before.*

Write your topic sentence. Write a topic sentence for your paragraph. Use the basic formula shown above. You may have to try a couple of times before your sentence says exactly what you want it to say.

Prewriting Selecting a Topic

If students are having difficulty listing possible topics, have them think about things they do after school, such as practicing an instrument or doing homework. Have them also consider simple activities, such as walking the dog or washing dishes.

✴ Additional information about listing is on PE page 545.

Prewriting
Writing a Topic Sentence

Tell students that they are connecting two ideas: their topic and how they feel about it. Suggest that they jot down all the feelings they have about the topic. Then they can decide which feeling about the topic makes the strongest sentence. For example:

Topic:
Making a friendship bracelet

Feelings:
fun, easy, rewarding, relaxing

Sentence:
Making a friendship bracelet is both easy and fun.

✴ Additional information about topic sentences is on PE pages 552–553.

Struggling Learners

Students who are stuck for topics can think back to activities they have explained to others in the past. Ask them questions such as the following:

• Have you taught a child to ride a bike or tie a shoe?
• Have you shown a friend how to play a new game?
• Have you demonstrated to an adult how to make a sharp turn on in-line skates?

Advanced Learners

Challenge students to create a topic sentence for each activity on their prewriting lists, and then have students decide, with the help of peers, which subject to develop fully.

Writing Creating Your First Draft

Have students list transition words that they could use in their paragraphs. After students finish their first drafts, tell them to highlight the transition words they actually use.

Revising
Improving Your Paragraph

Have students trade papers with a partner. Tell partners to read each other's paragraphs and make suggestions for revisions.

Editing Checking for Conventions

Invite students to read aloud their paragraphs to the rest of the class. Encourage students to listen carefully for the steps in the process and for the style of the writing.

Writing Creating Your First Draft

When you write a first draft, your goal is to get all your ideas and details down on paper. Follow the suggestions below.

- Start with your topic sentence.
- Arrange the how-to steps in the correct order.
- End with a closing sentence that wraps up the instructions and shows your enthusiasm for the topic.

 Write your first draft. Try to get all of the important information down on paper, including the materials needed and the steps to follow.

Revising Improving Your Paragraph

When you revise your first draft, consider the effectiveness of the *ideas, organization, voice, word choice,* and *sentence fluency* in your paragraph.

 Review and revise your paragraph. Use the following questions as a guide when you revise.

1. Is my topic sentence clear?
2. Have I clearly explained all the steps in the correct order?
3. Do I sound interested in the topic?
4. Do I use specific nouns and action verbs?
5. Do I write complete sentences that read smoothly?

Editing Checking for Conventions

Carefully edit your revised paragraph for *conventions.*

 Edit your work. Use the following questions to check your paragraph.

1. Do I use correct punctuation, capitalization, and spelling?
2. Do I use correct word usage and grammar?
3. Have I checked the words my spell checker may have missed?

Proofread your paragraph. After making a final copy of your how-to paragraph, check it one more time for errors.

Advanced Learners

Have students copy each sentence of their paragraphs onto separate index cards, shuffle them, and exchange them with a partner. If the partner's rearrangement matches the original paragraph, the student will know that the topic sentence and closing sentence are easily identifiable and effective and that the transition words clearly signal the order of steps.

describe solve.
define explain inform **161**

Expository Writing

Explaining a Process

How do you make spaghetti? How do you find the secret passage to the next level of your favorite video game? How do you skateboard or snowboard? The answers to questions like these may involve several steps. When you explain how to do or make something in an essay, you are doing expository writing.

In this chapter, you will write an expository essay. Your how-to essay should tell readers exactly what materials they will need and what steps they should follow. You will do your best writing if you choose a topic you care about—something you do well or enjoy doing.

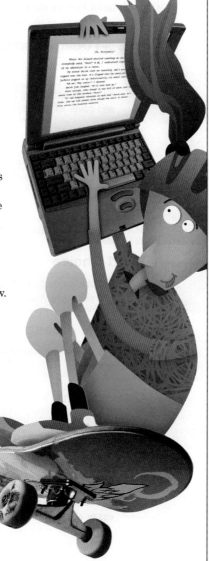

Writing Guidelines

Subject:	Something you know how to do or make
Form:	How-to essay
Purpose:	To explain how to do or make something
Audience:	Classmates

Explaining a Process

Objectives
- understand the goal of expository writing
- understand the content and form of expository writing
- plan, draft, revise, and publish a how-to essay

A **how-to essay** explains how to do or make something. It usually includes:
- the materials needed
- the specific steps in the process
- an explanation of the steps
- an interested, knowledgeable voice

To prepare students for the essay, have them discuss the kinds of things they like to do or make. Tell them to start a list of possible topics. Remind them that the topic they choose must involve a step-by-step process.

Understanding Your Goal

Traits of Expository Writing

Three traits relate to the development of the content and the form. They provide a focus during prewriting, drafting, and revising.

- Ideas
- Organization
- Voice

The other three traits relate more to form. Checking them is part of the revising and editing process.

- Word Choice
- Sentence Fluency
- Conventions

✳ The six-point rubric on PE pages 194–195 is based on these traits. Four- and five-point rubrics are available on TE pages 769 and 773.

162

Understanding Your Goal

Your goal in this chapter is to write a well-organized, interesting essay that explains how to do or make something. The traits listed in the chart below will help you plan and write your how-to essay.

TRAITS OF EXPOSITORY WRITING

Ideas
Select an interesting how-to topic, write a clear focus statement, and cover all the steps in the process.

Organization
Include an interesting beginning, a middle that explains all the steps, and a clear ending. Use transitions to help you organize.

Voice
Use an informative, confident voice that fits the audience.

Word Choice
Choose words such as specific nouns and specific action verbs that will make your essay informative.

Sentence Fluency
Make sure your sentences are complete and that they read smoothly.

Conventions
Check your essay for correct punctuation, capitalization, spelling, and grammar.

 Get the big picture. Look at the rubric on pages 194–195. You can use this rubric to assess your progress. Your goal is to write an informative essay about how to do or make something.

English Language Learners

Students may feel discouraged by the length and detail in this chart. Review the basic traits from PE page 34. Then point out that each step in the process will be explained separately in the pages to come.

Expository Essay

In the following expository essay, Lamarr explains how to give a dog a bath—step-by-step.

How to Give Your Dog a Bath

BEGINNING

The beginning introduces the topic and presents the focus statement (underlined).

If you or any of your friends have a dog, you know how much fun a pet can be. You also know that a dog can be a lot of work, especially if he is very active. It doesn't take long for a high-energy dog to look a mess and smell even worse. When that happens, it's time to gather up the dog shampoo and conditioner and freshen up your dog. If you follow these steps, bathing your dog can be easy and enjoyable.

MIDDLE

The middle paragraphs include materials needed and provide a step-by-step explanation.

To begin, get the bath ready and gather what you need. Use a nylon collar and leash (leather gets ruined by water) to control your dog during the bath. Your dog also needs something to stand on so he won't slip. A bath mat or towel will make him feel secure. Make sure the water is warm. Water that is too hot can burn a dog's skin. Cold water—especially from an outside hose—may scare your dog and send him running. Next, you'll need a way to get water all over your dog. A shower hose is the easiest method, but a plastic bucket can work well, too. You'll also need a special dog shampoo and conditioner because human shampoo is too strong for dogs. Of course, you'll need some big towels for the end of the bath.

To continue, begin bathing your dog. Get your dog nice and wet. Then use enough shampoo to make a foamy lather on his coat. Talk to your dog all the time to help him relax.

EXPOSITORY

Expository Essay

Work through this sample essay with the class, pointing out the elements that make it a good expository essay.

Ideas
- The writer chooses an interesting topic to which many people can relate.
- There is a clear focus statement about bathing a dog.
- The details are memorable.

Organization
- The process is described clearly from beginning to end.
- Clear transitions are used (to begin, to continue, to finish).

Voice
- The writer sounds knowledgeable and confident.

Respond to the reading.

Answers

Ideas 1. by saying that having a dog can be fun, but it can also be a lot of work

Organization 2. time order

Voice & Word Choice 3. Possible choices:

- Get the bath ready and gather what you need.
- A bath mat or towel will make him feel secure.
- Make sure the water is warm.
- Water that is too hot can burn a dog's skin.
- Human shampoo is too strong for dogs.
- Talk to your dog all the time to help him relax.
- Rinse your dog with fresh, warm water.
- Dogs love this part!
- Play tag with him or offer him a chew treat.

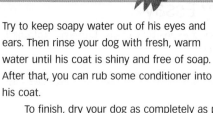

MIDDLE
The middle paragraphs also provide important supporting details.

Try to keep soapy water out of his eyes and ears. Then rinse your dog with fresh, warm water until his coat is shiny and free of soap. After that, you can rub some conditioner into his coat.

To finish, dry your dog as completely as possible. Use big towels and give your dog a complete rubdown. Dogs love this part! However, watch out because wet dogs like to shake. If you choose to use a hair dryer to dry your dog, keep it moving because holding it over one area too long could burn his skin. If you are outside, you'll discover that dogs like to roll when they're wet. After your dog shakes himself, play tag with him or offer him a chew treat— anything to keep him from rolling in the dirt!

ENDING
The ending offers some final thoughts.

If you treat your dog calmly and gently, giving him a bath should be fun. Dogs that get used to taking baths learn to enjoy them. Remember, whenever your dog starts smelling too doggy, it's time to gather your supplies and wash him until he's clean and huggable again.

Respond to the reading. After reading the sample essay, answer the following questions to discover how to use four important traits in your writing.

☐ **Ideas** (1) How does the writer get your attention?

☐ **Organization** (2) Is the essay organized by order of importance, time order, or order of location?

☐ **Voice & Word Choice** (3) List words and phrases that show the writer cares about the topic.

English Language Learners

Work with students in a group, having them take turns reading aloud portions of the sample essay. After each passage, pause and ask leading questions to assure comprehension.

- What things do you need to give a dog a bath?
- How do you begin bathing your dog?

After you have discussed the essay together, have students answer the response questions orally.

Advanced Learners

Invite students to brainstorm new titles for the essay that are creative yet still hint at the topic. To get them started, suggest two sound techniques to try:

- rhyme (*Dog Shower Power*)
- alliteration (*Dealing with Dirty Dogs*)

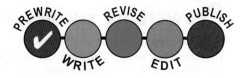

165
Explaining a Process

Prewriting

Prewriting is the first step in the writing process. It involves selecting a topic, gathering specific details, and organizing your ideas.

Keys to Effective Prewriting

1. Select a topic that you know well and want to write about.

2. Write a focus statement that clearly states the main idea of the essay.

3. Gather details that will make your explanation clear and interesting.

4. Organize your details using a cluster, chart, or gathering grid.

5. Use a list or an outline as a planning guide.

EXPOSITORY

Prewriting
Keys to Effective Prewriting

Remind students of the purpose of the prewriting stage in the writing process. (It's when the writer gets ready to write.)

The Keys to Effective Prewriting lays out the process students will be guided through on PE pages 166–170.

Remind students that the prewriting phase is just as important as the writing phase. If students thoroughly complete each part of the prewriting step, they should find that the actual writing will flow smoothly and easily. Once students select a topic, write a focus statement, and gather and organize details, they should feel confident that they have all the essential ingredients for their essay.

Prewriting Selecting a Topic

As an alternative to having students make a cluster, ask them to do a 5-minute personal brainstorming session to help choose a topic.

- Each student numbers a clean sheet of paper from 1 to 10 and titles it "Things I Know How to Do or Make."
- Once the session begins, students try to come up with ten different ideas.
- Tell students that they must remain quiet during the brainstorming activity.
- When the five minutes are up, tell students to review their lists and put a star next to their three favorite topics.

✱ See more about choosing a topic on PE pages 546–547.

Prewriting Selecting a Topic

The purpose of your essay is to explain how to do or make something. However, your essay should be more than just a list of directions. ("First, do this. Then, do this.") You also need to include details that will interest and inform the reader.

First, you need to think about things you know how to do or make. Making a cluster or web diagram like Soledad's below is one way to gather ideas for writing topics.

Cluster

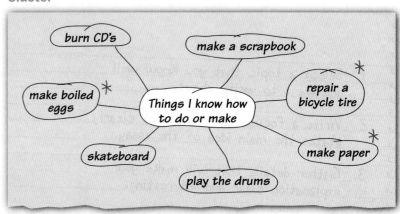

Create your own cluster. Start your cluster with "Things I know how to do or make." List as many ideas as you can. Then put a star (✱) next to two or three of your favorite topics.

Focus on the Traits

Ideas You need a topic that has enough steps and details to keep your audience interested. You also need to understand the activity well enough to explain it clearly. Consider a topic that is especially fun, challenging, or unusual.

**Teaching Tip:
Prewriting Conference**

Take a walk around the classroom while students are working on their clusters. Check in with every student to make sure he or she is coming up with enough ideas. Ask students to describe the steps involved in two of their favorite topics.

English Language Learners

Clusters and other graphic organizers may be particularly helpful to these students. Provide a warm-up exercise by working with them to create one or more simple cluster diagrams on the board. Use topics such as kinds of dogs, winter games, or geographic features.

Sizing Up Your Topic

You will want to select a how-to topic that is just the right size—not too narrow and not too broad. Making a list of the steps can help you choose the right topic.

If you look at Soledad's lists below, you'll see that "Repairing a bicycle tire" may be too broad or complicated, while "Making boiled eggs" may be too narrow. "Making paper," however, has about the right number of steps.

Making boiled eggs
- Put eggs in pot of water
- Bring to a boil
- Cover, shut off heat
- Let sit 15 minutes

Making paper
- Tear up newspaper
- Blend with water
- Pour pulp into a pan
- Strain pulp
- Tip onto felt
- Roll pulp between felt pieces
- Hang paper to dry

Repairing a bicycle tire
- Remove nails or glass
- Remove the wheel
- Push valve stem inside
- Pry tire edge over the rim
- Work the inner tube out
- Clean the puncture area
- Apply glue and let dry
- Press the patch over the puncture
- Pull the tube back into place
- Inflate the tube a little
- Work the tire into place

EXPOSITORY

Prewrite **Size up your topic.** On your own paper, write the two or three starred topics from your cluster (page 166). Beneath each topic, list each of the necessary steps. Then ask yourself these questions about each topic:

1 Did I include all the necessary steps?

2 Is this topic too narrow? Too broad? About right?

3 Does the topic include interesting steps?

Choose your topic. After evaluating your topics, choose the best one.

English Language Learners

To help students through the steps in their process, have them close their eyes and imagine themselves completing each step. Ask questions such as these:

- What materials do you have to use?
- What is the first thing you normally do?
- What do you do next? Write that down.

Students can use the notes they develop here for the prewriting activity on PE page 168.

Prewriting Sizing Up Your Topic

Inform students that for this writing assignment a process with four steps is too limited, but a process with eleven steps is too broad. Suggest that they aim for seven or eight steps.

Struggling Learners

For students who get bogged down writing the steps for multiple topics, have them orally describe the processes. A partner can count and record the number of steps mentioned, then help evaluate whether there are too few, too many, or just the right amount.

Prewriting
Writing a Focus Statement

Tell students that the specific feeling of the focus statement should be a positive one. No one wants to read about a process that is considered very complicated or unappealing.

Prewriting
Gathering and Sorting Details

Before students gather and sort details, have them do the following to help them organize the steps in a process:

- Fold a sheet of paper in thirds horizontally.
- Label the top third "To begin," the middle third "To continue," and the bottom third "To finish."
- Jot down notes about each step in the corresponding place.

✽ Additional information about organizing details is on PE pages 550–551.

Focus on the Traits

Organization
Suggest that students trade their graphic organizers with a partner. Tell partners to read the charts carefully to make sure the sequence of the steps makes sense. Have partners give each other tips to make the progression smoother.

Prewriting Writing a Focus Statement

Writing a focus (thesis) statement helps you explain the main idea of the essay and shows exactly what you will cover in your how-to essay.

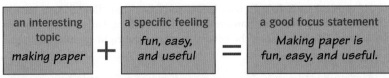

| an interesting topic *making paper* | + | a specific feeling *fun, easy, and useful* | = | a good focus statement *Making paper is fun, easy, and useful.* |

Write your focus statement. Use the formula above to write your focus statement. Make sure you include a specific feeling about the topic.

Gathering and Sorting Details

The following chart lists the materials and steps needed to make paper.

Chart

Topic	Materials Needed	Steps
How to make paper	– old newspapers – blender and water – pan – piece of wire screen – two pieces of felt – rolling pin	To begin – Tear up newspaper – Mix with water To continue – Pour pulp into a pan – Strain pulp To finish – Tip onto piece of felt

Gather and sort your details. Create a chart like the one above for your own topic. Organize the "steps" under three headings: "To begin," "To continue," and "To finish."

Focus on the Traits

Organization Graphic organizers like the one above can help you organize the steps in your process. Also see page 170.

Planning Your Paragraphs

When you listed the steps for your how-to essay, you organized them into three parts: how the activity begins, how it continues, and how it ends. Each part can become a middle paragraph in your essay. For each middle paragraph, you will need to write a topic sentence.

Writing Topic Sentences

Each of your topic sentences can start with one of the following phrases: *to begin, to continue, to finish.* Then complete the sentence by telling what steps or information the paragraph will cover. Here are the topic sentences for the middle paragraphs in the essay on pages 163–164. Each one covers a different part of the dog-washing process.

- ■ ***To begin,*** get the bath ready and gather what you need.
- ■ ***To continue,*** begin bathing your dog.
- ■ ***To finish,*** dry your dog as completely as possible.

Write your topic sentences. Use the steps you listed (page 168) and the points below to help you write these sentences.

1 What information is covered first?
Topic sentence: To begin,

2 What information is covered next?
Topic sentence: To continue,

3 What information is covered last?
Topic sentence: To finish,

EXPOSITORY

Focus on the Traits

Voice If you watch how-to shows on TV, you'll notice that the cooks or builders do more than just go through the steps one by one. They often talk about how they got involved in the project or why they enjoy it. This helps viewers stay interested. Sharing similar details in your writing will create a personal voice and keep the reader interested.

Prewriting
Planning Your Paragraphs

Emphasize that the steps students wrote on their charts will form the *middle* paragraphs of their essay. Have them turn to PE pages 163–164 and notice how the middle paragraphs are the actual instructions.

Prewriting
Writing Topic Sentences

Point out that the topic sentences *introduce* the information each paragraph will cover. They are not steps in the process, but instead they tell what part of the process is coming up.

Focus on the Traits

Voice

Have students jot down four or five ideas for details that reveal their feelings about the process. Encourage students to consider specific incidents or experiences that were funny or unusual.

English Language Learners

Provide helpful prompts for students as they focus on voice. For example, ask:

- Why is the process fun?
- How can you help your readers to feel that they would like the activity, too?

Have them express their answers orally and then jot down written notes.

Struggling Learners

To help students recall specific memories about their topics, ask:

- When and where did you observe the activity before you tried it?
- Did you have problems at first? What made you keep trying?
- What was your first big success? How did other people react to it?

170

Prewriting **Organizing Your Ideas**

Have students use color coding for their organized lists. For example, students might use a yellow highlighter to mark the focus statement, a green marker to underscore each topic sentence, and a red marker for the details.

Prewriting **Organizing Your Ideas**

You have already created a focus statement, listed the steps or details, and written the topic sentences. Now you need to put these pieces of your essay in the best order.

Below is an *organized list* for Soledad's essay. She used the directions to create her *organized list* of steps and topic sentences for her essay.

Directions	Organized List

Write your focus statement.

Making paper is fun, easy, and useful.

1. Write your first topic sentence.

List any steps.

1. *To begin, prepare the paper pulp.*
   - *Tear up paper*
   - *Put water in blender*
   - *Add shredded paper*
   - *Blend paper and water*

2. Write your second topic sentence.

List any steps.

2. *To continue, work with the pulp.*
   - *Pour into pan with clean water*
   - *Stir gently and cover screen*
   - *Lift screen to drain*

3. Write your third topic sentence.

List any steps.

3. *To finish, press the paper after it has drained.*
   - *Remove paper from screen*
   - *Squeeze out extra water*
   - *Hang to dry*

 Prewrite

Make an organized list. To create your list, follow the directions above. You will use this list when you write your essay.

171

Explaining a Process

Writing

Once you've finished your prewriting, it's time to write your first draft. You're ready to write a first draft when you know enough about your topic and have written a clear focus statement.

Keys to Effective Writing

1. Use your organized list as a planning guide.

2. Get all your ideas on paper in your first draft.

3. Write on every other line for later changes.

4. Use a clear topic sentence for each paragraph.

5. Add clear, step-by-step details.

6. Use transitions to tie everything together.

EXPOSITORY

Writing Keys to Effective Writing

Remind students that the writing stage is when they get to write, or draft, their ideas on paper.

The Keys to Effective Writing lays out the process students will be guided through on PE pages 172–176.

Writing Getting the Big Picture

Remind students that the focus statement should:

- tell something personal and positive,
- reveal the writer's enthusiasm for the topic in a way that immediately lets readers know they're about to read something interesting.

Tell students that the closing sentences should wrap up the essay in an upbeat way. The goal is to entice readers to try what they have just read about.

Writing Getting the Big Picture

The chart below shows how the parts of a how-to essay fit together. (The examples are from the sample essay on pages 173–176.) You're ready to write your essay once you . . .

- know enough about the steps in the process.
- state your topic in a clear focus statement.
- plan your paragraphs and write your topic sentences.

BEGINNING

The **beginning** introduces the topic and tells why the activity is important or interesting. It also gives the focus statement.

Focus Statement
After a few tries, I found that making paper is fun, easy, and useful.

MIDDLE

The **middle** gives all the how-to information, including any materials needed and a step-by-step explanation.

Three Topic Sentences
To begin, prepare the paper pulp.

To continue, work with the pulp.

To finish, press the paper after it has drained.

ENDING

The **ending** may summarize the process and offer some final thoughts.

Closing Sentences
So have some fun, be creative, and save a tree. Give papermaking a try!

Struggling Learners

Ask your school librarian for copies of several magazines that are grade-appropriate and then help students use the indexes to locate how-to articles. Together, find good models of focus statements, topic sentences, and closing sentences. Discuss particular words the authors use to make the articles engaging and easy to follow.

describe solve inform
define
173
Explaining a Process

Starting Your Essay

In the first part of your expository essay, you should introduce the topic, say something interesting or fun about it, and state your focus.

You can also add voice to your essay if you begin with a personal story.

- **Share how you became interested in this process.**
- **Tell how you first learned this process.**
- **Show why the reader may like the activity.**

Beginning Paragraph

In the paragraph below, Soledad uses a story to capture the reader's attention. The focus statement gives the main idea of the essay—making paper is fun, easy, and useful.

> | The writer's interest is explained. |
> | Materials are listed. |
> | The focus statement is given (underlined). |

> On a class trip to the Natural History Museum, I saw paper that had been made by ancient Egyptians. It was beautiful, and I wondered if I could make paper, too. I discovered that if you want to make paper, you need the following items: old newspapers, a piece of wire screen, a bucket or pan, two pieces of felt, a rolling pin, a blender, and some water. <u>After a few tries, I found that making paper is fun, easy, and useful.</u>

Write your beginning paragraph. When you write your beginning paragraph, do the following three things:

1 Introduce your topic in an interesting way.

2 Include a clear focus statement.

3 Lead into your first middle paragraph.

Writing **Starting Your Essay**

Tell students that they will put the focus statement at the end of the first paragraph.

- In order to engage readers right from the start, they need to open the beginning paragraph in an interesting way.
- Suggest that students begin by telling a story, using a quotation, providing a definition, or using imagery.
- Tell them to write two or three lead sentences and then decide which one they like the best.

EXPOSITORY

English Language Learners

During the drafting stage (PE pages 173–176), have students work with trusted partners who are strong writers. As you review how to get started, remind students that they have taken notes regarding why their readers might enjoy the activity. These ideas, as well as their focus statement, will form the opening paragraph of their essay.

Writing
Developing the Middle Part

As students write the middle part, have them use their color codes or symbols, as mentioned on TE page 170, to stay organized. Highlighting these key sentences will help students remember to use them.

Writing
Connecting Your Sentences

Tell students to read aloud their sentences to make sure they have used the correct transition word or phrase. Emphasize that connecting sentences helps to make writing smoother and more readable.

✳ Additional information about connecting sentences is on PE pages 572–573.

Writing Developing the Middle Part

In the middle paragraphs of your how-to essay, you must explain the process step-by-step. Each paragraph should cover one main part of the process (1, 2, and 3 in your organized list from page 170). Look at how the steps are handled in the middle paragraphs on these two pages.

Beginning
Middle
Ending

Connecting Your Sentences

The following transitions can be used to connect sentences and to show chronological or time order in a how-to essay.

First	One	First of all	One way	To begin
Second	Then	Next	Another way	To continue
Third	Another	Finally	A third way	To finish

Remember: The last sentence of each paragraph should get the reader ready to move on to the next part of the process.

Middle Paragraphs

In the three middle paragraphs that follow, the underlined transitions help connect the sentences. The transitions move the reader from one step to the next.

Topic sentence 1

Specific steps and details linked with transitions (underlined)

To begin, prepare the paper pulp. You can make pulp from newspapers, brown paper bags, magazine pages, or just about any other kind of paper. First, tear the paper into small strips. Then, pour two cups of water into the blender. Next, sprinkle in a few handfuls of the shredded paper. Finally, cover the blender, press the medium-speed button, and blend for a few seconds. When the mixture in the blender looks like thick potato soup, your paper pulp is ready.

Struggling Learners

✳ Make a handy reference list of transition terms and phrases for students to use by copying onto a sheet of chart paper the examples from *Connecting Your Sentences* on this page and *Words that can be used to show time* on PE page 572. Display the list in the classroom.

**Topic
sentence 2**

Transitions
(underlined)

**Topic
sentence 3**

To continue, work with the pulp. Pour it into a
flat pan with clean water and a piece of wire screen
in it. <u>Now</u> is the time to add fun things like grass,
flower petals, or glitter. <u>During this step,</u> keep the
pulp from settling on the bottom by stirring it
gently. <u>After that,</u> move the screen around so that
the paper pulp settles onto it. Cover the screen
as evenly as possible. <u>Then,</u> slowly lift it out of the
water and let the water drain.

To finish, press the paper after it has drained.
Turn your paper-covered screen over onto one of the
pieces of felt. The paper should fall off the screen
easily. If it doesn't, just tap the back of the screen.
<u>Next,</u> put the other piece of felt on top of the
paper. Roll the rolling pin over the top layer of felt
to squeeze out all the extra water. <u>Finally,</u> remove
the damp paper from between the pieces of felt and
hang it in a sunny place. In about three hours, you
will have a sheet of paper.

Write your middle paragraphs. Using your organized list from page
170, write your middle paragraphs. Follow the "Drafting Tips" below.

Drafting Tips

- **If you have trouble getting started,** try writing as if you
  were talking to a friend about your topic.
- **If you have trouble continuing with your writing**,
  write for 3- to 5-minute spans with breaks in between. See
  what happens.

EXPOSITORY

Writing **Drafting Tips**
Visual learners might benefit from
making a storyboard *(see below)*
showing the steps in the process. As
they write, they can refer to the pictures to remind them of the sequence of events.

Teaching Tip: Making a Storyboard

A storyboard serves as a visual
road map for students to follow as
they write. In a storyboard, students fill small boxes with
sketches and a few words depicting each step that they will write
about. The boxes are set up in
sequential order, sometimes with
arrows pointing from one box to
the next. Setting up a storyboard
helps students organize their
essay as they think through the
step-by-step process that they are
going to explain in words. Make
up a model storyboard for the
paragraphs on PE pages 174–175
and pass it around for students to
become more familiar with the
concept.

Writing Ending Your Essay

Encourage students to write three or four different endings. Have them read the endings to themselves to decide which one is the best.

 **Answers**

Answers may vary, but students' responses should show that they understand that the first choice is brief, snappy, and engages the reader by encouraging him or her to try making paper.

Writing Ending Your Essay

After you've explained all the steps, you may end your essay by summarizing the process and making some final comments about your topic. Your ending may also encourage the reader to try the activity.

Beginning

Middle

Ending

Ending Paragraph

End with an invitation to try the activity.

Papermaking is an easy, inexpensive hobby that is lots of fun. Your friends and family will love to get notes and cards on your homemade paper. You can also feel proud that you are helping to save trees by recycling paper. So have some fun, be creative, and save a tree. Give papermaking a try!

 Read the three sets of final sentences below. Which one of these three endings do you think works the best? Why?

1. So have some fun, be creative, and save a tree. Give papermaking a try!

2. This recycling of paper creates more ideas. Besides that, you'll enjoy wrapping gifts or covering school books with your paper.

3. I, like the ancient Egyptians, can now make beautiful paper.

Write your ending. Now write an ending for your essay that includes some final thoughts about the process. Encourage the reader to try it.

Form a complete first draft. Write a complete copy of your essay. Write on every other line to make room for your revising changes.

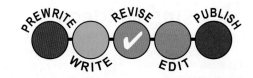

Revising

A first draft never turns out just right. One part may need more details. Another part may not be clear enough. To fix or improve these parts, you need to revise your first draft.

Keys to Effective Revising

1. Read through your entire draft to get a feeling of how well your essay works.

2. Make sure your focus statement states your topic clearly.

3. Check your paragraphs to make sure the steps and details are clear and in the right order.

4. Your essay should have a personal, yet confident voice.

5. Check your words and sentences.

6. Use the editing and proofreading marks inside the back cover of this book.

EXPOSITORY

Revising

Keys to Effective Revising

The Keys to Effective Revising lays out the process students will be guided through on PE pages 178–188.

Suggest that students number a sheet of paper from 1 to 6. Then have them check their essay for each item in the Keys to Effective Revising list, one by one. If they feel their draft needs more work for any item on the list, they should put a note next to that number. If they feel their draft is fine for an item, they can put a check mark next to the number.

Revising for Ideas

The rubric strips that run across all of the revising pages (PE pages 178–187) are provided to help students focus their revising and are related to the full rubric on PE pages 194–195.

Tell students that vivid details help readers visualize what they are reading. Memory details and reflective details engage readers by providing insights into the writer's feelings about the process.

178

Revising for Ideas

6 My topic, focus, and details make my essay truly memorable.

5 My essay is informative with a clear focus. I use a variety of specific details.

4 My essay is informative with a clear focus. I need to use a variety of specific details.

When you revise your essay for *ideas*, you check for these things: that your topic is the right size, your focus statement is clear, and your supporting details are specific. The rubric strip above will help guide you.

How can I add variety to my details?

You can improve your how-to essay by adding personal details. Here are three types of personal details and a chart prepared by the student who wrote the essay about making paper.

1. **Memory details** include personal memories about what happened as you learned to do or make something. The details might include how you became interested in the topic or the mistakes you made as you first learned the process.

2. **Reflective details** include personal thoughts about the process and why it is important to you.

3. **Sensory details** include descriptions of what the activity looks, feels, tastes, smells, or sounds like.

Memory details	Reflective details	Sensory details
I saw Egyptian paper in a museum. Once I added glitter.	I like recycling. People like notes on handmade paper.	Pulp looks like potato soup. It smells like a wet dog.

Check your details. Make a chart like the one above for your topic.

1 Write the three types of details across the top.

2 Then list several specific details under each type.

3 Checkmark any details that could make your essay more interesting.

English Language Learners

During the revision stage (PE pages 178–188), provide time to offer one-on-one assistance and suggestions to students, or pair them with considerate, cooperative students who are strong writers.

Struggling Learners

If students have difficulty coming up with details, invite them to close their eyes, picture themselves engaged in the activity, and orally describe what they feel, see, smell, hear, touch, or taste. Have a partner take notes, and then the two students can highlight words, phrases, or ideas that could be added to the essay to make it more engaging.

define *describe solve inform* **179**
Explaining a Process

3 My focus needs to be clearer. I need more specific details.

2 I need to narrow or expand my topic, and I need many more specific details.

1 I need to select a new topic and gather a variety of specific details.

Are my details specific enough?

If your details paint a clear, vivid picture for your reader, they are specific enough. If your details are general and not very interesting, you need to make them more colorful. Using specific details makes the process easier to understand.

> **GENERAL DETAIL**
> **Next, add some paper.** *(How do you add it? How much? What kind?)*

> **SPECIFIC DETAIL**
> **Next,** sprinkle in a few handfuls of the shredded **paper.**

 Read the sentences below about making a sandwich. Rewrite the sentences, adding details that will make the process clearer and more complete. (To think of specific details, ask questions such as *what kind? how much?* and *how?*)

> **Take some bread. Put peanut butter and jelly on it.**

 Review your writing. Look for places in your essay that need specific details. Have a partner read your essay and point out any parts that are unclear or incomplete. Add specific details wherever they are needed.

Ideas
Specific details are added.

> *To begin, prepare the paper pulp. You can*
> *newspapers, brown paper bags, magazine pages, or*
> *make pulp from just about any other kind of*
> ∧
> *paper. First, tear the paper into small strips. Then,*
> *pour two cups of water into the blender. Next, . . .*

EXPOSITORY

Answers will vary.

Answers should include details about the following:

- how much bread, peanut butter, and jelly to use
- where to put the peanut butter and jelly
- how and where to spread the peanut butter and jelly
- how to put the bread together to form the sandwich
- how to cut the sandwich, (squares, triangles, or some other shape)
- whether to cut the crust

English Language Learners

Once again, visualizing themselves doing the activity they have written about may help students. Have them picture themselves on television, showing their viewers how to do the task or activity while they provide a detailed voice-over. What details do they need to add to their essays to make that voice-over interesting and helpful?

Struggling Learners

While students review their own writing, have them apply what they learned in the **Try It** activity. Suggest that they brainstorm other *how* and *what* questions they might ask themselves as they look to add specific details. For example:

- How heavy? How far? How soft? How loud? How fast?
- What color? What size? What shape? What temperature? What price?

Revising for Organization

Before students number their topic sentences, point out that if they've written more than three, it will be their last one that finishes the explanation, not the third one (as stated on the chart).

Revising for Organization

6 My organization makes my essay informative and easy to read.

5 My beginning interests the reader. The middle supports the focus. The ending works well, and I use transitions.

4 My essay is divided into a beginning, a middle, and an ending. I use some transitions.

When you revise for *organization,* check to see if your thoughts are organized into three main parts: a beginning, a middle, and an ending. Also check your transitions. Use the rubric strip above as a guide.

How do I check my overall organization?

You can check the overall organization of your how-to essay by making sure the details in each paragraph are in the right place. Use the chart below.

| BEGINNING PARAGRAPH | The **focus statement** states your topic. It belongs somewhere in the opening paragraph. |

| MIDDLE PARAGRAPHS | The **first topic sentence** begins the explanation of the process. The **second topic sentence** continues the explanation. The **third topic sentence** finishes the explanation. |

| ENDING PARAGRAPH | The **closing sentences** summarize the process and encourage the reader to try it. |

Check your organization. Carefully check each part of your essay.

1 Underline the focus statement in your essay.

2 Place a **1** next to the first topic sentence, a **2** next to the second topic sentence, and a **3** next to the third topic sentence.

3 Then place a star (✱) at the beginning of the ending paragraph.

4 Compare your essay to the chart above. Fix any out-of-place parts.

3 My beginning or ending is weak. The middle needs a paragraph for each main point. More transitions are needed.

2 My beginning, middle, and ending all run together. I need paragraphs and transitions.

1 I need to learn how to organize my thoughts.

How can I use transitions?

In a how-to essay, the steps of the process must be clear and in the correct order. That's why transitions such as *first, second, next,* and *then* are so important. They help lead the reader step-by-step through your explanation.

You can also use prepositional phrases to show connections between the steps. The following prepositions can be used to help organize your essay. (Also see pages **494–495** and **742** for more information about using prepositions.)

PREPOSITIONS				
about	before	during	in	through
after	below	for	near	until
along	between	from	off	with

PREPOSITIONAL PHRASES

Cover the bowl and let the mixture rest for a while. After two hours, **add two teaspoons of salt and a little oil to the batter.** Along with the salt and oil, **add . . .**

 Review for transitions. Read your paper. Are the steps easy to follow? If not, add transition words and prepositional phrases that will make your directions clearer.

Organization
Two prepositional phrases are added.

During this step,
∧Keep the pulp from settling on the bottom by
        After that,
stirring it gently.∧Move the screen around so that

the paper pulp settles onto it. Cover the screen . . .

EXPOSITORY

To give students practice using prepositions, have them
- write a quick paragraph describing their morning routine on a typical school day,
- place the events in a step-by-step order,
- show the connections between the steps.

As students share their paragraphs with the class, have the other students jot down any prepositions they hear.

English Language Learners

Have students take turns creating and drawing their own prepositional phrases using the prepositions shown in the box. For example, for the word *in*, they might draw a dog in a doghouse.

Struggling Learners

If students need additional practice with prepositions, bring in some on-level how-to books from the school library. Ask students to choose one how-to lesson to read and have them note any prepositions that are used. Discuss how the authors use prepositions. For example, it could be to give specific directions or to make clear transitions.

Revising for Voice

One way for students to check for voice is by reading aloud their work. Suggest that students have a partner read their essay to them. The writer can then hear what works and what doesn't work in his or her own essay.

 Answers

1. classmates
2. teacher
3. friends

182

Revising for Voice

| **6** I sound knowledgeable, confident, and enthusiastic. | **5** I sound well-informed and confident. My voice fits my audience well. | **4** I sound well-informed, and my voice fits my audience. |

When revising your essay for *voice,* check to see if you sound confident and enthusiastic. The words you use should fit your audience, purpose, and topic. The rubric strip above can guide you.

Does my voice fit my audience?

You use a different voice each time you speak. It all depends on whether you are talking to teachers, parents, or friends. In writing, your voice should also change depending on your audience and your topic. To check your voice, answer three questions:

1. Who is my audience?
2. How should I speak to that audience?
3. How should I present my topic to that audience?

Audience	Teacher	Classmates	Friends
Voice	formal, polite	informal, but respectful	very informal

 Number your paper from 1 to 3. Write which of the audiences listed above in red would fit the voice in each of the following sentences.

1. Would you hand me that pencil?
2. May I please borrow a pencil?
3. Hey, got a pencil I could use?

Voice
A phrase is changed to fit the audience.

Press the medium-speed button and blend for

a few seconds. When the mixture in the blender

like thick potato soup
looks ~~really gross~~, your paper pulp is ready.
               ∧

describe solve inform
define
Explaining a Process **183**

3 Sometimes I sound unsure, and my voice needs to fit my audience better.

2 I sound unsure. My voice needs to fit my audience better.

1 I need to figure out what voice is.

Is my voice too informal?

Your voice in an expository essay is probably too informal if it sounds like you're talking to a friend. The two explanations below are similar in many ways, but the two voices are very different. The first is too casual or informal for this topic. The second is just right.

Voice 1: TOO INFORMAL

First, grab a couple of eggs and whack 'em against the side of the bowl. Dump them into the bowl. Next, throw in a little milk, a pinch of salt, and a drop of vanilla for extra oomph. Whip it all up with a fork and pour it into a hot pan. Keep pushing everything around until all the raw stuff is gone. Then, chow down!

Voice 2: JUST RIGHT

Select two large eggs. Crack them one at a time into a bowl. Add one tablespoon of milk for each egg, a quarter teaspoon of salt, and a drop of vanilla. Next, mix everything together with a fork. Then, empty the bowl into a sizzling, buttered pan. Stir the eggs until they firm up into a hot, golden heap. Then, eat and enjoy.

 Compare the two explanations shown above. List four words or phrases that make "Voice 1" too informal for an essay.

 Listen to your voice. Read your essay and listen to your voice. Is it "too informal" or "just right"?

1 Write down three words from your writing that fit your audience.

2 Then look for words from your writing that don't fit.

3 Replace the words that don't fit with ones that match the voice you want to create in your essay.

(right margin, vertical) EXPOSITORY

Have students imagine they will be reading aloud their essays to a group of peers who are strangers. This may help them achieve the right tone—not too informal and not too formal.

 **Answers**

Some of the words that make Voice 1 too informal include *grab, whack 'em, dump, throw, extra oomph, whip, keep pushing, raw stuff,* and *chow down.*

English Language Learners

Pair students with trusted partners for the **Try It** activity at the bottom of the page. Have both the student and the partner listen to evaluate whether the voice is "just right."

Limited knowledge of American idioms, slang, and colloquial language may prevent students from understanding what makes the first paragraph too informal. Show how the informal language in the first paragraph is changed in the more formal paragraph.

- grab (select)
- whack (crack)
- dump (add)
- throw in (add)
- extra oomph (extra flavor)
- whip (mix)
- keep pushing (stir)
- raw stuff (until they firm up)
- chow down (eat)

Advanced Learners

Have students record each of their prewriting topic ideas on separate sticky notes and then sort them into those that could be written in an informal voice and those that would require a formal voice. Remind students that there are no right or wrong answers as long as they can explain their choices.

Revising for Word Choice

Have students highlight the nouns in their essay. Then tell them to decide, one at a time, which could be replaced by a more specific noun.

 **Answers**

Answers will vary.

Students should show that they can think of more specific nouns and use them correctly in a sentence.

184

Revising for Word Choice

6 The words I use make my essay very clear, informative, and fun to read.	**5** Specific nouns and action verbs make my essay clear and informative.	**4** I use some specific nouns and verbs, but I could use more.

When you revise for *word choice*, check your nouns and verbs. Do you use specific nouns? Do you use action verbs? Do your words help the reader understand the steps in the process? The rubric strip above can guide you.

Do I use specific nouns?

If your nouns name a particular person, place, thing, or idea, they are most likely specific. (See the chart below.) In a how-to essay, specific nouns can make your directions much clearer. For example, the specific word "hammer" gives your reader a clearer picture than the general word "tool."

Specific nouns make your writing stronger and more interesting. In the chart below, the top row lists *general* nouns. The second row shows *specific* nouns, and the bottom row gives *very specific* nouns. (See pages **470–471**.)

PERSON	PLACE	THING	IDEA
worker	building	food	sickness
cook	restaurant	fish	cancer
baker	delicatessen	salmon	leukemia

 For each general noun listed below, write a specific noun. Then use that noun in a sentence.

1. cheese

1. cheese–mozzarella
Next, sprinkle the grated mozzarella on the pizza.

2. dog   **3.** tree   **4.** sport   **5.** fruit   **6.** feeling

 Check your nouns. Replace the general nouns with more specific nouns wherever it will help make your writing clearer. (Remember that not all general nouns need to be replaced.)

English Language Learners

Play a matching game with students.

- Pair each student with a cooperative partner.
- Provide a general noun to the pair and have them work together to find a specific one. For example, say *pet* and ask partners to name a specific noun *(dog)*.
- Once students have had a few successes, challenge them to be even more specific, as in *pet: dog: beagle.*
- Repeat this activity on PE page 185 with general and specific verbs.

describe *solve* inform
define explain **185**
Explaining a Process

3 I use too many general words. I need specific nouns and verbs.

2 I use general nouns and verbs and leave out words. My essay is hard to understand.

1 I need help finding the right words.

Do I use specific action verbs?

If your verbs tell precisely what is happening in a sentence, you are using specific action verbs. Specific verbs describe movement and action and make your explanation stronger. Use a thesaurus to find just the right word.

General Verb	Specific Verbs
put	place, slide, enter, press, draw, set, insert, include, add, pour

 Number your paper from 1 to 4. For each of the sentences below, choose a word from the above chart to replace the verb "put." (Each sentence contains clues for choosing a specific verb.)

1. Slice a potato in half and use a marker to *put* a design on it.
2. Next, *put* a knife alongside the outline and cut a shallow line around the design.
3. Then, *put* the knife in deeper and cut away the potato outside the line.
4. Finally, *put* your potato stamp on an ink pad and try it out.

 Examine your paper. Replace general or overused verbs in your essay with specific action verbs.

Word Choice
General and overused verbs are replaced.

> Then, ~~put~~ *pour* two cups of water into the blender. Next,
> *sprinkle* ~~add~~ in a few handfuls of the shredded paper. Finally,
> cover the blender, press the medium-speed . . .

EXPOSITORY

Remind students that, in addition to checking for specific action verbs, they should also check to make sure they don't repeat words. Sometimes when students work on a written assignment over the course of several days, they don't realize that they have used some of the same words over and over. When students do find repeated words, have them use a **thesaurus** *(see below)* to find replacements.

 Answers

1. draw
2. insert
3. slide
4. press

Teaching Tip: Thesaurus

Students may need a refresher in using a thesaurus. A thesaurus can be used to find synonyms for dull or overused words. Explain that there are generally two types:

- dictionary style—entries are organized alphabetically
- index style—the back of the book includes an index with words in alphabetical order

Using the sample sentence "I ran to school," show students how to find the verb *to run* in the thesaurus. Model choosing a word that fits the context and that is appropriate for the voice and audience. Emphasize that the goal of using a thesaurus is to make the writing more interesting and varied, not to throw in as many "hard words" as possible.

Struggling Learners

Discuss the difference between using a thesaurus and using a dictionary. Write the verbs *run, draw,* and *argue* on the board and have students look up those words in both resources in order to compare the results. Students can use the on-line versions of a dictionary and thesaurus that are part of word processing software.

Revising for Sentence Fluency

Tell students that sentence variety is the key to good writing. Short sentences are fine, but putting too many short sentences together makes an essay sound choppy. A short sentence followed by a long sentence makes for a more interesting, more readable piece of writing.

 **Answers**

Answers will vary.

Students should show an understanding of using specific details to enliven their writing.

186

Revising for Sentence Fluency

6 My sentences flow smoothly, and people will enjoy reading them.

5 My sentences read smoothly. I don't have any fragments or choppy sentences.

4 Most of my sentences read smoothly, but I need to expand a few choppy ones.

When you revise for *sentence fluency,* begin by reading your sentences out loud. They should read smoothly. If you have used a lot of short sentences or fragments, your sentences will sound choppy and not very interesting. The rubric strip above can guide you.

How can I fix my choppy sentences?

If too many sentences in your essay are short and choppy, you may want to expand them by adding details. You can do this by answering the 5 W's and H (*who? what? where? when? why?* and *how?*).

Sentence: **Wipe the paintbrush.**

Where? Wipe the paintbrush **against the palette**.

When? **After dipping the paintbrush into paint,** wipe it against the palette.

Why? After dipping the paintbrush into paint, wipe it against the palette **to avoid drips.**

How? After dipping the paintbrush into paint, **gently** wipe it against the palette to avoid drips.

 Add specific details to the following sentences using some or all of the 5 W's and H.

1. Plant the marigolds.
2. Dribble the ball.
3. Mix the plaster.
4. Cut the paper.

 Expand your sentences. Use the 5 W's and H to expand some of the short sentences in your essay. Be careful, though, not to overload your sentences with too many words and details. Just pick the best ones.

English Language Learners

Provide extra help by turning the **Try It** exercise into a group game. First, print the questions *Where?, When?, Why?,* and *How?* on index cards. Have a student read aloud a sentence from the exercise. Hold up each card in turn and let a student suggest a way to expand the sentence to answer the question.

Struggling Learners

After students compose a new sentence using one of the **Try It** prompts, have them color-code it, using different markers to underline details that tell *who, what, when, where, why,* and *how.*

3 Some of my sentences are choppy, and I need to fix some fragments.

2 I need to rewrite many of my sentences so they don't confuse my reader.

1 I need to rewrite most of my sentences.

How can I fix fragments?

A fragment is part of a sentence, but it doesn't express a complete thought. It can be fixed by adding a subject or verb or by combining the fragment with a sentence. (See pages 504–505.)

Fragment	Sentence
After we review the recipe,	**we gather the ingredients.**

Sentence	Fragment
Don't place a cake in the oven	**until the oven is hot enough.**

 Turn the fragment in each set below into a complete sentence by connecting it with the other sentence.

1. Add a handful of baking chips. If you like a sweeter cake.
2. Wear an oven mitt. While taking hot pans out of the oven.
3. When baking aromas fill the room. I feel hungry.

 Check for fragments. As you read your essay, make sure you used complete sentences. Correct any fragments.

Sentence Fluency
A fragment is fixed, and a sentence is expanded.

> Roll the rolling pin over the top layer of felt. To
>
> squeeze out all the extra water. Finally, remove the
> from between the pieces of felt and
> damp paper. Hang it in a sunny place.

EXPOSITORY

One way to help students identify a sentence fragment is by having them read their writing aloud. Tell students to listen for incomplete thoughts, which are sentence fragments. **Complete sentences** (*see below*) contain complete thoughts. Many students need help distinguishing complete sentences from sentence fragments

✳ Additional information about complete sentences is on PE pages 504–505.

Try It Answers

Possible answers:
1. If you like a sweeter cake, add a handful of baking chips.
2. While taking hot pans out of the oven, always wear an oven mitt.
3. Whenever baking aromas fill the room, I feel hungry.

Teaching Tip: Complete Sentences

Every complete sentence has a subject and a predicate. A subject is the part of the sentence that either does something or is being talked about. A predicate tells the action or says something about the subject.

✳ If students have trouble distinguishing fragments from complete sentences, refer them to PE pages 690–697 for additional practice.

Revising Using a Checklist

As students work their way through the checklist, walk around the classroom to see how they're doing. Offer to help students who may be struggling with any of the items on the checklist.

Revising Using a Checklist

 Check your revising. On a piece of paper, write the numbers 1 to 13. If you can answer "yes" to a question, put a check mark after that number. If not, continue to work with that part of your essay.

Ideas

_____ **1.** Do I focus on an interesting idea?
_____ **2.** Have I divided my idea into interesting topic sentences?
_____ **3.** Do I use enough specific details?

Organization

_____ **4.** Do I include a beginning, a middle, and an ending?
_____ **5.** Have I cut unnecessary details?
_____ **6.** Have I reorganized parts that were out of place?

Voice

_____ **7.** Do I show interest in—and knowledge of—my topic?
_____ **8.** Does my voice fit my audience? My purpose? My topic?

Word Choice

_____ **9.** Do I use specific nouns and active verbs?
_____ **10.** Do I use colorful adjectives and adverbs?

Sentence Fluency

_____ **11.** Have I written clear sentences and avoided fragments?
_____ **12.** Have I fixed any choppy sentences?
_____ **13.** Do I use a variety of sentence beginnings and lengths?

 Make a clean copy. When you've finished revising your essay, make a clean copy before you begin to edit.

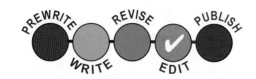

Editing

After you've finished revising your essay, it's time to edit your work for your use of conventions: punctuation, capitalization, spelling, and grammar.

Keys to Effective Editing

1. Use a dictionary, a thesaurus, and the "Proofreader's Guide" in the back of this book.

2. Check for any words or phrases that may be confusing to the reader.

3. Check your writing for correctness of punctuation, capitalization, spelling, and grammar.

4. Edit on a printed computer copy. Then enter your changes on the computer.

5. Use the editing and proofreading marks located on the inside back cover of this book.

EXPOSITORY

Editing **Keys to Effective Editing**

The Keys to Effective Editing lays out the process students will be guided through on PE pages 190–192.

While some students can edit their own work, others have difficulty seeing their mistakes. After each student edits his or her own work, have partners exchange essays and mark any errors that the writer may have missed. **Peer editing** *(see below)* is a useful tool that you should encourage students to use.

Teaching Tip: Peer Editing

When students edit each other's work, they give each other valuable feedback on their writing. Students who read a piece of writing for the first time will spot errors that the writer hasn't noticed because the writer has spent more time focusing on the ideas than the conventions. For guidelines, have peers refer to the editing checklist on PE page 192.

Advanced Learners

Put students in groups of three or four and have them conduct a "round-robin" edit of one another's work. Each student should have a different colored pen, and each should begin by editing his or her own essay. If a student has a question about a particular notation, the peer who used that color of pen can be consulted for further information.

Editing for Conventions

Review with students the difference between independent and subordinate clauses. Tell students that an independent clause can stand alone and could be written as a sentence. A subordinate, or dependent, clause cannot stand alone; it depends on the rest of the sentence. Give students an example of both kinds of clauses.

- Independent clause: *We always get to school on time* because we take the bus.
- Subordinate clause: *When I hear the birds chirp*, I realize that I'll have to get out of bed soon.

Tell students to look through a book for examples of introductory word groups that are set off by commas. Tell students that the comma helps readers follow the writer's train of thought.

✱ Additional information about commas with introductory word groups is on PE page 590.

Try It Answers

1. Because of their soft colors, sand paintings are unique.
2. For birthday or holiday gifts, I often make sand paintings.
3. After you glue the board, gently sprinkle on your first color.

190

Editing for Conventions

6 My essay is completely error free.	**5** I have a few minor errors in punctuation, spelling, or grammar.	**4** I need to correct some errors in punctuation, spelling, or grammar.

When you edit for *conventions*, you need to check for capitalization, grammar, spelling, and punctuation errors. On this page and the next, you will edit for conventions in two ways: using commas with introductory word groups and using commas in a series. The rubric strip above can guide you.

Do I use commas with introductory word groups?

When you begin a sentence with an introductory word group—a phrase or a clause—you need to set it off with a comma. One word group that is often used to begin a sentence is a *prepositional phrase*. (See page 742.) The phrase below starts with a preposition (For) and ends with the object of the preposition (results).

> **INTRODUCTORY PHRASE**
>
> For best results, **sprinkle the sand evenly across the section to be covered.**

In addition, when you begin a sentence with a clause that starts with a subordinating conjunction (After), you should set it off from the main sentence with a comma. (See page 744 for a list of subordinating conjunctions.)

> **INTRODUCTORY CLAUSE**
>
> After you add the dye, **stir the sand quickly to spread the color throughout.**

 On your own paper, rewrite the following sentences. First, move the italicized phrase or clause to the front of each sentence. Then, punctuate each one correctly.

1. Sand paintings are unique *because of their soft colors*.
2. I often make sand paintings *for birthday or holiday gifts*.
3. Gently sprinkle on your first color *after you glue the board*.

 Check your essay. Find any introductory phrases or clauses in your essay. Be sure you punctuated them correctly.

English Language Learners

Throughout the editing stage (PE pages 190–192), pair students with cooperative partners or place them in "editing groups" to provide support and suggestions regarding correct punctuation, capitalization, spelling, and grammar.

describe solve inform
define explain **191**
Explaining a Process

3 Some of my errors may confuse the reader. I need to fix them.

2 I need to correct many errors that make my essay confusing and hard to read.

1 I need help making corrections, especially with my commas.

Do I use commas correctly in a series?

If you use commas to separate a series of three or more words, phrases, or clauses, you are using them correctly. See the examples below.

COMMAS TO SEPARATE WORDS

Gather together your glue, scissors, and fabric.

COMMAS TO SEPARATE PHRASES

Fabric squares can be added to decorate wall hangings, to trim place mats, or to cover pillows.

COMMAS TO SEPARATE CLAUSES

Sue gives them as presents, Daniel displays them for decoration, and Ranell uses them as gift wrapping.

Try IT Practice using commas in a series. Copy the sentences below and place commas in the proper places.

1. Art allows you to have fun get involved and be creative.

2. In art, you can draw paint or sculpt.

3. You can work on your own with a partner or in a group.

 Edit for commas. Check your essay to see that you punctuated words, phrases, or clauses in a series. Make any necessary corrections.

EXPOSITORY

Conventions
Commas are used after an opening phrase and in a series.

After a few tries I found that making paper is fun
                 ∧,   ∧,
easy and useful.
     ∧,

Point out that commas are used to separate a series of words, a series of phrases, and a series of clauses. The purpose of the comma is for readers to understand each item as a separate thing or idea. Without commas, readers would be left puzzling over which items are separate and which belong together.

✳ Additional information about commas in a series is on PE page 582.

Try IT Answers

1. Art allows you to have fun, get involved, and be creative.
2. In art, you can draw, paint, or sculpt.
3. You can work on your own, with a partner, or in a group.

Editing Using a Checklist

Give students a few moments to look over the Proofreader's Guide in the back of their book. Throughout the year they can refer to the instruction, rules, and examples to clarify any checklist items or to resolve questions about their own writing.

Go around the room while students are working through the Editing Checklist. If you notice that several students seem to have difficulty with one particular area, devote fifteen minutes to a review session.

Editing Adding a Title

Many students have a hard time with titles. Take students to the library and tell them to scan the shelves for titles. Have them write down five or six titles that sound intriguing. Then discuss what makes these titles good. When you return to the classroom, tell students to write three titles for their essay. Then have students choose the title that they think works best. Discuss which of the three approaches was most effective—a word picture, repeating a sound, or using action words.

192

Editing Using a Checklist

 Check your editing. On a piece of paper, write the numbers 1 to 12. If you can answer "yes" to a question, put a check mark after that number. If not, continue to edit for that convention.

Conventions

PUNCTUATION

_____ 1. Do I use end punctuation after all my sentences?

_____ 2. Do I use commas after introductory word groups?

_____ 3. Do I use commas after items in a series?

_____ 4. Do I use commas in all my compound sentences?

_____ 5. Do I use apostrophes to show possession (*boy's bike*)?

CAPITALIZATION

_____ 6. Do I start all my sentences with capital letters?

_____ 7. Do I capitalize all proper nouns?

SPELLING

_____ 8. Have I spelled all my words correctly?

_____ 9. Have I double-checked the words my spell-checker may have missed?

GRAMMAR

_____ 10. Do I use correct forms of verbs (*had gone*, not *had went*)?

_____ 11. Do my subjects and verbs agree in number? (She and I *are* going, not She and I *is* going.)

_____ 12. Do I use the right words (*to, too, two*)?

Adding a Title

Write a title for your expository essay, using any one of the following suggestions.

- Create a word picture: **Making Amazing Maps**
- Repeat a sound: **From Pulp to Paper**
- Use action words: **Print with Potatoes**

Publishing   **Sharing Your Essay**

After you have worked so hard writing your essay, you'll want to proofread it and make a neat copy to share. You may also decide to present your essay as a demonstration, an online essay, or a poster. (See the suggestions below.)

Make a final copy. Follow your teacher's instructions or use the guidelines below to format your essay. (If you are using a computer, see page 60.) Create a clean final copy of your essay and carefully proofread it.

Focus on Presentation

- Use blue or black ink and write neatly.
- Write your name in the upper left corner of page 1.
- Skip a line and center your title; skip another line and start your writing.
- Indent every paragraph and leave a one-inch margin on all four sides.
- Write your last name and the page number in the upper right corner of every page after the first one.

Give a Demonstration

In class, demonstrate the process you covered in your essay. (See pages 426–430 for more information about giving demonstrations.)

Create a Poster

Make a poster based on your essay. List the steps in the process. Make sure the instructions are clear; then decorate your poster in an eye-catching way.

Post Your Essay Online

Search for an online bulletin board related to the subject of your essay. Post your work for others who have the same interest. (Get permission before posting your essay.)

EXPOSITORY

Publishing   **Sharing Your Essay**

Give each student a chance to shine. Whether students choose to demonstrate their process, create a poster, or post their essay online, they should all have a few moments to share their work with the rest of the class. For students who post their work online, you could all gather around the classroom computer. If you have several computers in your classroom, you can group students around them while the author reads aloud his or her essay.

✱ Four- and five-point rubrics for expository writing can be found on TE pages 769 and 773.

Rubric for Expository Writing

Use this rubric for guiding and assessing your expository writing. Refer to it to help you improve your writing using the six traits.

Ideas

6 **The topic, focus, and details make the essay truly memorable.**

5 The essay is informative with a clear focus and specific details.

4 The essay is informative with a clear focus. More specific details are needed.

Organization

6 **The organization makes the essay informative and easy to read.**

5 The beginning interests the reader. The middle supports the focus. The ending works well. Transitions are used.

4 The essay is divided into a beginning, a middle, and an ending. Some transitions are used.

Voice

6 **The writer's voice sounds confident, knowledgeable, and enthusiastic.**

5 The writer's voice sounds informative and confident. It fits the audience.

4 The writer's voice sounds well-informed most of the time and fits the audience.

Word Choice

6 **The word choice makes the essay very clear, informative, and fun to read.**

5 Specific nouns and action verbs make the essay clear and informative.

4 Some nouns and verbs could be more specific.

Sentence Fluency

6 **The sentences flow smoothly, and people will enjoy reading them.**

5 The sentences read smoothly. There are no short, choppy sentences.

4 Most of the sentences read smoothly, but some are short and choppy.

Conventions

6 **The essay is error free.**

5 The essay has a few minor errors in punctuation, spelling, or grammar.

4 The essay has several errors in punctuation, spelling, or grammar.

describe solve inform
define explain   **195**
Explaining a Process

3 The focus of the essay needs to be clearer, and more specific details are needed.

2 The topic needs to be narrowed or expanded. Many more specific details are needed.

1 A new topic needs to be selected.

3 The beginning or ending is weak. The middle needs a paragraph for each main point. More transitions are needed.

2 The beginning, middle, and ending all run together. Paragraphs and transitions are needed.

1 The essay should be reorganized.

3 The writer sometimes sounds unsure, and the voice needs to fit the audience better.

2 The writer sounds unsure. The voice needs to fit the audience.

1 The writer needs to learn about voice.

3 Too many general words are used. Specific nouns and verbs are needed.

2 General or missing words make this essay hard to understand.

1 The writer needs help finding specific words.

3 Many short, choppy sentences need to be rewritten to make the essay read smoothly.

2 Many sentences are choppy or incomplete and need to be rewritten.

1 Most sentences need to be rewritten.

3 Some errors confuse the reader.

2 Many errors make the essay confusing and hard to read.

1 Help is needed to make corrections.

EXPOSITORY

Evaluating an Expository Essay

Ask students if they agree with the sample self-assessment on PE page 197. If they agree with the criticisms, ask them to suggest improvements based on the comments. If they disagree with a comment, ask them to explain why.

Ideas incomplete supply list— add bowl, wooden stick, toothpick, and watercolors or food coloring.

Organization misplaced detail— move the tip about cleaning the bowl to be the third sentence in the fourth paragraph.

Voice add a story—though not necessary, adding a story about a map she has made might have made Anna's essay more personal.

Word Choice variety of words—in fourth paragraph, change the sixth sentence: Drag a toothpick through the wet plaster to make rivers.

Sentence Fluency sentence combining—in first paragraph, combine the last three sentences; in second paragraph, combine the last two sentences.

Conventions comma usage—in third paragraph, add a comma between *finished* and *mix;* in fourth paragraph, add a comma between *dries* and *use;* in fifth paragraph, no comma between *impressed* and *and.*

Evaluating an Expository Essay

As you read through Anna's expository essay below, focus on the strengths and weaknesses. (The essay contains several errors.)

Making Amazing Maps

For your next geography project, why not make a plaster map? All you need is a copy of a map, a bag of plaster, some water, vinegar, and a board for the map's base. It's fun. It's easy. It really gives you a better idea of geography.

The first thing you should do is copy the outline of the map onto your board. Make sure the board or piece of plywood is large enough to fit your map. Don't worry about mistakes. The drawing will be covered with plaster.

When your drawing is finished mix your plaster. Put about two cups of dry plaster into a bowl. Add a little water at a time until the mixture is like thick oatmeal. Use a few drops of vinegar to make the plaster dry slower. Rinse out the bowl as soon as you empty it so the plaster doesn't get hard.

Now it's time to shape your map. Pour some plaster onto your board. Check your map to see what the geography of the country is like. Shape the plaster—thinner along a coast and built up for mountains. Use your fingers or a wooden stick to create lakes. Use a toothpick to make rivers through the wet plaster. After your map dries use watercolors or food coloring to paint deserts, beaches, rivers, and grasslands.

Making plaster maps is great fun. You are creating something interesting and you are actually learning about an area's geography. You can feel the hills and rivers as well as see them. Your teacher will be impressed, and you will have a much clearer view of the world.

Student Self-Assessment

The assessment below includes comments by Anna, who evaluated her own essay (on page 196). Notice that she includes a positive comment first. Then she points out an area of her writing that could be improved. (The writer used the rubric and number scale on pages 194–195.)

 4 Ideas

1. *I'm pretty sure my topic will interest my classmates, and I've used some specific details about shaping the map.*
2. *My list of supplies isn't complete.*

5 Organization

1. *I wrote a clear topic sentence for each paragraph.*
2. *The tip about cleaning the bowl should be in the fourth paragraph.*

 4 Voice

1. *It is clear that I enjoy making plaster maps.*
2. *I could have added a story about maps I have made.*

3 Word Choice

1. *I use a few strong action verbs.*
2. *I should have used the word "use" less.*

4 Sentence Fluency

1. *I didn't have any fragments.*
2. *Some short sentences could have been expanded or combined, and I could have used more transitions.*

4 Conventions

1. *I couldn't find any errors in spelling or capitalization.*
2. *In the future, I need to use commas more carefully.*

 Use the rubric. Assess your essay using the rubric on pages 194–195.

1 On your own paper, list the six traits. Leave room after each trait to write one strength and one weakness.

2 Then choose a number (from 1 to 6) that shows how well you used each trait.

EXPOSITORY

To give students additional practice with evaluating an expository essay, use a reproducible assessment sheet (TE page 799) and one or both of the **benchmark papers** listed in the Benchmark Papers box below. You can use an overhead transparency while students refer to their own copies made from the copy masters. For your benefit, a completed assessment sheet is provided.

Benchmark Papers

Malcolm X and Eleanor Roosevelt (strong)

○ TR 3A–3C

○ TE pp. 782–784

Yo-Yos Flood Del Mar Hills School (poor)

○ TR 4A–4B

○ TE pp. 785–786

Reflecting on Your Writing

Tell students to save their reflections in a writing folder. Have them reread the reflections periodically to help them evaluate the progress they are making in their writing. If students notice a recurring problem, encourage them to spend a little more time on that aspect of the writing process.

198

Reflecting on Your Writing

Now that you've completed your expository essay, take a moment to reflect on it. Complete each starter sentence below on your own paper. These thoughts will help you prepare for your next writing assignment.

My Expository Essay

1. The best part of my essay is . . .

2. The part that still needs work is . . .

3. The main thing I learned about writing an expository essay is . . .

4. The prewriting activity that worked best for this essay was . . .

5. In my next piece of expository writing, I would like to . . .

6. Here is one question I still have about writing an expository essay:

describe solve
define inform **199**

Expository Writing
Classification Essay

One way to explain a topic is to divide it into its parts. That's true whether you're talking about a sandwich, a bicycle, or the United States government. Knowing the different parts of a subject helps people understand the whole.

An expository essay that explains a subject in this way is called a classification essay. Often, teachers assign this kind of writing as a way of checking students' understanding of a subject covered in class.

In this chapter, you will learn how to write your own classification essay. You may choose to explain a topic that you know a lot about, or you may tackle a subject that you want to understand better.

Writing Guidelines

Subject:	A topic with different parts
Form:	Classification essay
Purpose:	To explain
Audience:	Classmates

Classification Essay

Objectives
- understand the content and structure of a classification essay
- choose a topic to write about
- plan, draft, revise, and edit a classification essay

A **classification essay** explains a topic that is made up of several parts. This type of essay requires close attention to organization, since there must be a logical arrangement of the explanation of the parts.

Ask students whether they can think of books or essays they have read that explained topics that were made up of many parts. For example, they may have come across such writing in many of their textbooks. Make a list on the board of the topics students remember.

Classification Essay

As students read the classification essay on instruments, remind them of the skills that they learned in the first part of this unit. Point out that the focus statement has been underlined. Ask students to analyze it based on the formula they learned about earlier:

interesting topic + specific feeling = good focus statement

The focus statement itself does not reveal a specific feeling. Direct students to analyze the full introduction and to discuss specific ways in which the writer makes the topic sound interesting and fun. Also discuss how the writer's voice comes through clearly right from the start.

Classification Essay

In the following student essay, Jana explains the main types of band instruments and tells why each type is different. She learned about the types of instruments by attending a band information night.

BEGINNING
The topic is introduced, and the focus statement names the types (underlined).

MIDDLE
Each middle paragraph explains one type of instrument.

What Instrument Are You?

At the beginning of school this year, I went to the band information night. I never knew there were so many instruments! Saxophones come in four different sizes. Some instruments have wooden reeds, and others have mouthpieces. There are even four different kinds of drums. I was so confused. Then Mrs. Delgato explained it all to me. Our band program uses just three types of instruments: brass, woodwinds, and percussion.

Most brass instruments are made out of brass, of course, or some other kind of metal. They get their sound from blowing into the mouthpiece. The size of the mouthpiece and the length of tubing create different pitches. Cornets have small mouthpieces and short tubing, so they can play high notes. Trombones have medium mouthpieces and tubing, so they hit the middle range of notes. Tubas and sousaphones have huge mouthpieces and lots of tubing, which is why they sound so low.

Woodwinds get their name because they used to be made of wood and the sound comes

MIDDLE
Each middle paragraph provides examples.

from blowing into them. Some clarinets, oboes, and bassoons are still made of wood. Flutes and piccolos are metal. These two woodwinds make sound by having the player blow air over an opening. Other woodwinds create sound with a vibrating wooden reed.

Percussion instruments make noise when one thing hits another thing. A drumstick hits a drumhead or wood block, or a mallet hits a bar on a xylophone. Did you know a piano is actually a percussion instrument, too? It makes sounds when hammers hit metal strings! Most percussion instruments, like cymbals or bass drums, don't have an exact pitch. Others, like chimes and kettledrums, do.

ENDING
The ending reflects on the ideas in the essay.

Once Mrs. Delgato explained the different kinds of instruments to us, I didn't feel so overwhelmed. Instead of walking out the door, I checked out all the instruments and found the one that was just right for me: the trombone. Now that I've begun to learn to play, I bet there's a right instrument for everyone.

EXPOSITORY

Respond to the reading. On your own paper, answer the following questions about the sample essay.

☐ Ideas **(1)** Without looking, how many different instruments can you remember from the essay?
(2) What details helped you remember these instruments?

☐ Organization **(3)** How does the writer organize her description of band instruments?

☐ Voice **(4)** How does she show her interest in this topic?

Have students look for transition words in the essay. Discuss why transition words are not so important in this particular classification essay. (Transitions often help with time order, location, or order of importance. Those concepts aren't necessary to an explanation of the instruments.)

Respond to the reading.

Answers

Ideas 1. Students' answers will vary but should include at least four or five instruments.

2. Answers will vary but should reflect details from the essay.

Organization 3. The writer organizes her description by type of instrument: brass, woodwinds, and percussion.

Voice 4. Possible answers:
- I never knew there were so many instruments!
- Then Mrs. Delgato explained it all to me.
- Did you know a piano is actually a percussion instrument, too?
- Now that I've begun to learn to play, I bet there's a right instrument for everyone.

Prewriting Selecting a Topic

Have small groups work together to brainstorm topics. Tell students to add on to the six listed on this page. Then compile a class list from which students can choose a topic for their essays. If several students choose the same one, encourage them to gather research as a group.

Prewriting
Freewriting to Gather Details

Remind students that while freewriting, they should not be concerned with sentence fluency, organization, voice, or conventions. Their primary objective is to get their ideas down without worrying about the structure of their writing.

Tell students that once they begin to organize their details, they'll need to make sure they have gathered details that are related to the topic. By paying attention to the unity of details, students will write well-organized paragraphs.

✴ Additional information about the unity of details is on PE page 538.

202

Prewriting Selecting a Topic

To choose a topic for a classification essay, think of topics that can be divided into different types, or groups. Jana wrote a list of things she had learned about recently. Then she chose a topic from that list.

> types of clouds   types of band instruments
> branches of government   the food pyramid
> the respiratory system   planets in the solar system

 Choose your topic. Write a list of topics you find interesting. (Try to write at least five.) Underline the topic you would like for your own essay.

Freewriting to Gather Details

To gather her thoughts about her topic, Jana decided to spend a few minutes freewriting. She wrote down whatever came to mind from the band information night she had attended.

> I sure love learning trombone. A slide is way cooler than valves or keys. Besides, there is no way I could remember all the keys on a saxophone! There are so many instruments. The brass are the loudest, I think. Once we get all those cornets and trombones and tubas going, we'll blow the woodwinds away. Of course, the drummers can make a lot of noise, too. Kettledrums are super loud, and what about the cymbals! But the flutes and clarinets have the prettiest sound. Like Mrs. Delgato says, "Never louder than lovely."

 Gather details. Write freely for 5 minutes about your topic. Write whatever comes to mind. The idea is to get down on paper everything you already know about your topic.

English Language Learners

A timed freewriting activity may create unnecessary pressure for students not yet proficient in English. To avoid calling attention to any special needs, however, offer an alternative activity for everyone in the class.

✴ Suggest that students use a cluster (see PE page 544) to gather details for classifying. Allow each student to select the activity that seems most helpful to him or her individually.

Struggling Learners

To help students come up with topics, list the classes available at your school. Under each class title, students can brainstorm and record topics they have recently studied. Encourage them to add their extracurricular activities as well, including any teams or organizations they belong to in which they are learning new skills.

Organizing with a Line Diagram

To organize her thoughts, Jana made a line diagram. She began with her main topic—band instruments—and then listed its three divisions: brass, woodwinds, and percussion. Next, she listed instruments that belonged to each division.

Line Diagram

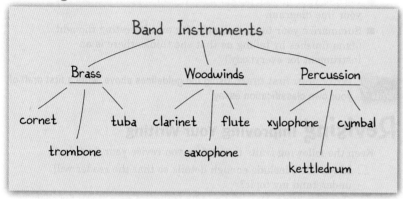

 Organize your thoughts. Make your own line diagram to organize the parts of your topic.

Researching the Topic

Looking at her line diagram, Jana decided to gather more examples of instruments for her essay. She also wanted to include a few details about each one. She visited the band room again and jotted down notes.

> Sousaphone – brass, low pitch
> Trombone – slide is three feet long!
> Clarinet, oboe, bassoon – woodwinds made of wood
> Flute, piccolo – woodwinds made of metal

 Do your research. Decide what details you still need to learn about your topic. Ask an expert or check the library. Take notes.

EXPOSITORY

Writing Creating Your First Draft

If time is limited, or students choose research-intensive topics, have groups of three students work together on one essay. Each student will be responsible for a middle paragraph and will become an expert in that one area. The group will work as a team to write the introduction and conclusion.

Revising Improving Your Writing

Because of their different writing styles, students working in a group will need to pay close attention to the revising steps in order to make sure the essay reads smoothly.

Editing Checking for Conventions

Have the group make three copies of the essay so that each student can edit and proofread it individually. When all three students have finished editing, have them come together and share their findings.

204

Writing Creating Your First Draft

Using your notes and freewriting as a guide, write your first draft. Concentrate on explaining your topic in the best possible order.

- In your first paragraph, introduce your topic. Give the reader a reason to be interested in it, too.
- Each of your middle paragraphs should explain one part of your line diagram.
- Summarize your topic and end with an interesting thought. (Jana finishes by telling us that she thinks there is an instrument for everybody.)

 Write your first draft. Using the guidelines above, write a first draft of your own classification essay.

Revising Improving Your Writing

Keep the following traits in mind as you revise your first draft.

- ☐ **Ideas** Do I include enough details so that the reader will understand my topic?
- ☐ **Organization** Does the middle include a paragraph for each part of my topic? Do my ideas appear in a logical order?
- ☐ **Voice** Do the words and details I use show that I am interested in my topic?
- ☐ **Word Choice** Do I use specific nouns and strong verbs?
- ☐ **Sentence Fluency** Do my sentences read smoothly?

 Revise your writing. Carefully consider the questions above. Then revise your writing as needed to make it clear and interesting.

Editing Checking for Conventions

When your revising is completed, edit your paper for conventions.

- ☐ **Conventions** Have I checked spelling, capitalization, and punctuation? Have I also checked for commonly misused words (*to, too, two*) and other grammar errors?

 Edit your work. Edit your essay using the two questions above. Have someone else check it over, too. Then make a final copy and proofread it.

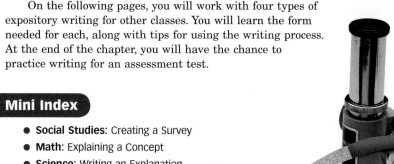

205

Expository Writing
Across the Curriculum

Expository writing is used to share information, so you will find it in every school subject. In social studies, you may be asked to take a survey and present the results. In science, you may write up an explanation of how something works. In math, you may have to explain a concept. In any class, you may be asked to write directions. All are forms of expository writing.

On the following pages, you will work with four types of expository writing for other classes. You will learn the form needed for each, along with tips for using the writing process. At the end of the chapter, you will have the chance to practice writing for an assessment test.

Mini Index

- **Social Studies:** Creating a Survey
- **Math:** Explaining a Concept
- **Science:** Writing an Explanation
- **Practical Writing:** Drafting Directions
- **Writing for Assessment**

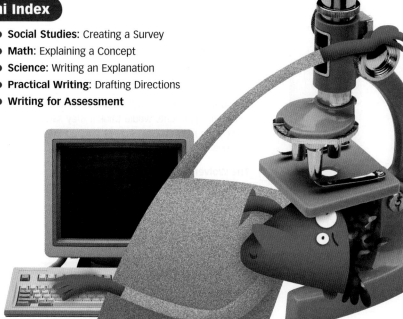

Across the Curriculum

Objectives
- to apply expository writing skills to other subject areas
- to practice writing for assessment

The lessons on the following pages provide samples of expository writing students might do in different content areas. The particular form used in each content area may also be used in a different content area (for example, students can write an explanation for social studies just as well as for science).

Assigning these forms of writing will depend on
- the skill level of your students,
- the subject matter they are studying in different content areas,
- and the writing goals of your school, district, or state.

Social Studies:
Creating a Survey

Emphasize the importance of the introduction. Tell students that survey readers need to understand the purpose of the survey. Therefore, the introduction should clearly explain what the survey is intended to find out.

Students will need to devise a tally chart to organize their survey results. Tell them to make a chart on lined paper using the following steps:

- Write all possible answers down the left side of the paper.
- Skip several lines between answers.
- Place a tally mark to the right of the answer each time a responder votes for that choice.
- Add up the votes for each answer and compare the totals.

206

Social Studies: Creating a Survey

A survey is a set of questions or choices given to a group of people. Their responses show what the group thinks about a certain subject or issue. LaToya created the following survey, which asks students to help choose a new school mascot.

The **beginning** introduces the topic.

A call to action is made.

The choices are listed.

Elwood Mascot Survey

The students and staff of Elwood Middle School will be choosing a new mascot. Each choice below is an animal that has special qualities that would make it a great mascot.

You can help make this decision! Make your opinion count by checking the box next to the mascot you would most like to represent Elwood Middle School:

☐ **The Roadrunners:** Roadrunners are quick. They would race all over the field or the court. Who could catch a roadrunner?

☐ **The Bears:** Bears are big and strong. They would power their way to victory. Would you want to tackle a bear?

☐ **The Cougars:** Mountain lions are very fierce. That's what our opponents would think if they saw this mascot on helmets and jerseys. Wouldn't you run from a cougar?

☐ **The Wolverines:** Wolverines are the toughest animals in the woods. They would be tough on fields, tracks, and courts. Who could beat a wolverine?

English Language Learners

Guide students to brainstorm possible topics for their surveys, or have them work with partners. Ask leading questions as prompts, such as the following:

- What would you like to learn?
- What topic could people have opinions about?
- What clear, simple questions should you ask in order to get the information you need?

Advanced Learners

Bring in several days' worth of newspapers and have students find examples of articles that are based on surveys of various topics, such as political preferences, exercise habits, or yearly income. Ask students whether they think people always give honest responses to surveys. Why or why not?

describe *solve.* *inform*
define explain   **207**

Writing in Social Studies

Writing Tips

Before you write . . .

- **Understand your purpose.**
  Be sure you understand why you are creating this survey.
- **List your choices.**
  Decide which questions or choices you will use on the survey.
- **Compare your choices.**
  Provide enough details to give the reader plenty of good information about each choice.

During your writing . . .

- **Organize your thoughts.**
  Introduce the survey, explain how to complete it, and then list the choices.
- **Keep it fair.**
  Write each question or choice in the same way. For example, if you write two details about the first choice, you should write two details for all the others. If you end one choice with a fun question, you should end all the choices with a fun or interesting question.

After you've written a first draft . . .

- **Check for completeness.**
  Make sure you have included all of the information needed to answer the questions (or make the choices) on your survey.
- **Check for correctness.**
  Proofread your survey several times for punctuation, spelling, capitalization, and other conventions.

 Write a survey asking your classmates about their favorite school lunch, TV show, restaurant, or musical group. Choose a topic your classmates will have opinions about.

EXPOSITORY

Writing Tips

Encourage students to write a brief summary describing their survey results. Have students read their survey summaries aloud to the rest of the class.

Try It Answers

Answers will vary.

Students will come up with a variety of topics. Check to see that they have provided at least four different choices for each question.

Math:
Explaining a Concept

Ask a volunteer to read aloud "Rates of Speed." Tell the student to read slowly and clearly. Then lead a discussion about how well the writer succeeded in putting a math concept into words.

- Ask students whether they followed the explanation. If students mention parts that were confusing, ask them to tell why they had difficulty following that part.
- Then have them identify what parts of this explanation are successful and why they think so.
- Work as a class to try to improve any parts of the explanation that several students found difficult.

Math: Explaining a Concept

One of the best ways to understand a topic is to explain it to someone else. In his math class, Josh was assigned to write an explanation of a math concept. He chose the concept of "rates of speed." He was surprised by how much more he knew about the concept after he finished his writing.

The **beginning** states the basic concept.

The **middle** part explains the concept.

The **ending** identifies ways to apply or use the concept.

Rates of Speed

In math, you use "rates of speed" to compare time to distance. For example, miles per hour (mph) is a very common way to describe the speed of cars, airplanes, and other machines.

Miles per hour is really just a ratio that tells how far something goes during a certain time. Other common rates of speed are feet per second (fps) and kilometers per hour (kph). A rate of speed used by scientists, especially astronomers, is the speed of light. It is 186,000 miles per second. It takes a ray of sunlight only about 8 minutes to travel the 93 million miles from the sun to the earth.

When figuring a rate of speed, ask these two questions: How far did it go? How long did it take? The first answer divided by the second is a rate of speed. So, if a train goes 120 miles in 2 hours, its rate of speed is $120 \div 2$, or 60 miles per hour.

Rates of speed are easy to use. To find out how far something traveled, multiply the time it traveled by its rate of speed. For example, if it took you 60 seconds to read this essay, the light you first used would be 11,160,000 miles away by now (60 seconds $\times$ 186,000 miles per second).

describe *solve.* *inform*
define

209

Writing in Math

Writing Tips

Before you write . . .

- **Select a topic.**
  If you have not been given a topic, use your math textbook or your notes to find a concept that you can write about.
- **Study your topic.**
  Pick a few examples that will help you make your writing clear. In the sample explanation, the speed of light provides a clear and interesting example.

During your writing . . .

- **Organize your thoughts.**
  Decide on an order for the information. You could start with a definition and offer some examples. Then explain the concept and how it relates to the real world.
- **Use examples and comparisons.**
  In the sample essay, the writer uses miles per hour as a common example of a rate of speed.
- **Think of some questions.**
  Include some questions in your essay. Choose questions that you can answer using the math concept.

After you've written a first draft . . .

- **Check your sources.**
  Make sure you have explained the concept correctly.
- **Keep it simple.**
  Look for places where your explanation may be unclear. Try to make your explanation as simple as possible.
- **Check for correctness.**
  Review facts and figures, as well as grammar, punctuation, spelling, and other conventions.

EXPOSITORY

 Write an explanation of a concept that you are learning in math class. Define the concept and include enough examples, details, and comparisons to make it clear to the reader.

Writing Tips

Tell students to imagine that they are writing their math explanation as if they were helping a friend. Most students have had the experience of explaining a concept to a classmate who needs help. Students may find that their explanation is friendly and clear when they take this approach.

Answers

Answers will vary, but students' explanations should show a clear understanding of the concept and enough examples, details, and comparisons to make the explanation clear.

Science:
Writing an Explanation

Ask students why they think the focus statement is placed at the beginning of the essay rather than at the end of the first paragraph (some readers may not know what geysers are, so it helps to define the topic). Point out the diagram and discuss its purpose (to help readers understand the explanation). Show students examples of field journals, such as bird guides, which often use diagrams to illustrate explanations.

Science: Writing an Explanation

Scientists often use expository writing to share their knowledge with readers. An essay that provides an explanation is a basic form of expository writing. Ravi's essay explains how and why a geyser erupts.

How a Geyser Erupts

The **beginning** introduces the focus statement (underlined).

Geysers are awesome eruptions of water or steam. Geysers can be found in many parts of the world and are often located near volcanoes. There are about 1,000 known geysers, and Yellowstone Park has more than half of them. In Iceland, people even use the steam that comes from geysers to generate electricity.

Geysers are created when water seeps down through the ground and touches hot molten rock called magma. The heat turns the water to steam. The trapped steam builds up pressure under more water.

The **middle** part provides supporting details.

Finally, the steam and hot water blast up through a crack and out of the ground. The blast reduces the pressure, and then the geyser stops. The process is repeated, and when the pressure builds up, the geyser erupts again.

The **ending** concludes the explanation.

Different geysers act in different ways. Old Faithful in Yellowstone Park erupts almost every hour. Other geysers may go months, or even years, between eruptions. Geysers are one of the true wonders of nature.

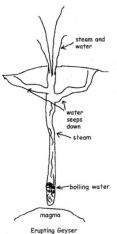

steam and water

water seeps down

steam

boiling water

magma

Erupting Geyser

describe solve inform
define explain

211

Writing in Science

Writing Tips

Before you write . . .

- **Do your research.**
  Make sure you understand the topic you plan to explain. Use different sources—textbooks, Internet sites, books in the library, and your own personal experiences.
- **Organize your thoughts.**
  Write a focus statement based on the details you have listed during your research.

During your writing . . .

- **Share specific details.**
  Choose details that will help explain the topic to the reader.
- **Use comparisons or illustrations.**
  Make comparisons to help the reader understand surprising or difficult facts about the topic. Also consider including drawings. In the sample essay, the writer uses a simple drawing to explain why geysers erupt.

After you've written a first draft . . .

- **Ask for another opinion.**
  Let several of your classmates read the essay. Do they understand it? Remember that the purpose of your essay is to write an explanation.
- **Check for organization.**
  Review each paragraph and sentence to make sure each thought leads naturally to the next thought.

EXPOSITORY

 Write an expository essay about a topic related to nature. Think of things like weather, landforms, and the oceans. Research your topic and write a short essay in which you share what you have learned with your classmates.

Writing Tips

Tell students that when they are deciding which aspect of their topic to illustrate, they should think about the part they are having the most difficulty writing about. That part would benefit from a diagram. Tell students that a diagram should clarify information that is confusing or hard to put into words.

Try It Answers

Answers will vary, but essays should contain a focus statement, a middle paragraph or two providing supporting details, and an ending that concludes the explanation.

English Language Learners

Have students work with trusted partners or within a supportive group to complete the research, organization, drafting, illustrating, and revising of their essays.

Advanced Learners

Encourage students to select more obscure nature topics, as in the example essay on *geysers*, where the terms will actually need to be defined in the first paragraph. Some examples are *vertebrates*, *botany*, and *pumice*.

Practical Writing:
Drafting Directions

Discuss the importance of giving clear directions. Ask students to talk about situations in which they were lost, either with friends or their family, because of poor or unclear directions. Encourage them to share what happened and to tell how getting clear directions helped them find their way.

Practical Writing: Drafting Directions

The key to writing directions is giving clear and complete information in the correct order. The following sample, written by the drum major of a middle school marching band, gives directions to a location where band members must meet.

The **beginning** identifies the directions.

The **middle** states the steps.

The **ending** gives the final information.

How to Reach the Memorial Day Parade Route

Memorial Day is Monday, May 31, and the band will march in the city parade. All band members must attend. We will walk together to the parade route, but keep a copy of these directions in case you arrive late.

Come to the Franklin Middle School band room by 8:00 on Monday morning. Put on your uniform and put together your instrument. By 8:15, Ms. Robertson will walk with the group to the parade's meeting place at the Lincoln statue on Jenkins Street. Here are the directions:

1. Leave from the front door of the school and turn left on Evans Street.
2. Walk to the railroad tracks. Look for trains and cross the tracks.
3. Continue on Evans Street until it meets Randolf Street.
4. Turn left on Randolf Street.
5. Follow Randolf around a sharp curve and over a bridge.
6. Turn right on Jenkins Street. The Lincoln statue is on the right.
7. Wait in the parking lot just beyond the statue.

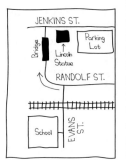

The total walk is one mile and should take about a half hour. See you there!

Writing Tips

Before you write . . .

- **Think about the start and finish of the route.**
  If your readers are coming from different directions, think of a common starting point for everyone.
- **Check a map.**
  Trace the route from start to finish. Make sure that you choose a path that is direct, easy to follow, and safe. You might even include a basic map in your directions.

During your writing . . .

- **Provide specific street names.**
  Give the name of each street, as well as details about the street. ("Follow Randolf around a sharp curve.")
- **List landmarks.**
  Mention spots along the way that will help readers know they are on the right course. ("Walk to the railroad tracks" or "the Lincoln statue is on the right.")
- **Provide times and distances.**
  Tell readers how long the trip is. ("The total walk is one mile and should take about a half hour.")
- **Use left/right, north/south, east/west.**
  Explain which way to turn. ("Turn right on Jenkins Street.")

After you've written a first draft . . .

- **Follow your own directions.**
  If possible, walk the route to test your directions.
- **Check the details.**
  Double-check all the turns, streets, and landmarks carefully.

 Write directions from your school to an important location in your city or town. Provide every detail that a stranger would need to make the trip. Then ask a classmate to read your work to see if the directions are clear.

 EXPOSITORY

Writing Tips

Emphasize the use of landmarks. Tell students that people using a set of directions for the first time will be reassured by finding landmarks as they go. For example, if you aren't supposed to turn right on Main Street but you should bear right, you might want to give a landmark. You could say, "Bear right, heading toward Tony's Hardware Store."

Another tool often used in directions is the face of a clock. For example, you might say, "When you get to the intersection of Green and Maple Streets, veer right at two o'clock." That indicates that the street you will turn onto appears in the position of the two on a clock.

Before they do the **Try It** activity, tell students that they may find it helpful to make a simple map to check the accuracy of their directions.

Try It Answers

Answers will vary.

Writing for Assessment

Think about your own state assessment as students review the essay. Some states have timed essays, while others do not. If your state assessment is timed, give students plenty of opportunities to write within specific time frames.

Writing for Assessment

Many state and school writing tests ask you to respond to an expository prompt. An expository prompt asks you to explain something or share information. Study the sample prompt and the student response below.

Expository Prompt

Learning to respect others is one of life's important lessons. Write an essay explaining why respecting others is important or why being disrespectful can be harmful.

The **beginning** introduces the focus of the writing (underlined).

    Learning to respect other people is very important. If you respect others, you will do better in school, get along with others well, and stay safe. Being disrespectful has the opposite effect—you can get in trouble, lose friends, and even get hurt.

The **middle** paragraphs each explain a different part of the focus.

    First, you can definitely get in trouble by ignoring your teachers' and parents' rules and guidelines. Talking while your teacher is giving a homework assignment, for example, shows disrespect. Then, if you do the assignment wrong and get a bad grade, your parents may ground you until you do better in school.

    Next, no one wants to lose friends. However, if you cheat when you play sports, just so you can win, your friends may not want to play with you anymore. Cheating is disrespectful to everyone who is playing the game.

Finally, being disrespectful can get you or someone else hurt. Suppose you go to a pool where lifeguards help keep you safe. They may tell you not to run or not to dive in the shallow end. If you don't listen, you or someone else could get hurt.

Learn to respect others. It is important. When you show respect to others, it makes life better for everyone, including yourself.

The **ending** reinforces the focus.

EXPOSITORY

Respond to the reading. Answer the questions to see how the following three traits were used in the sample response.

☐ Ideas (1) What is the focus of the writer's explanation? (2) What key words in the prompt also appear in the essay?

☐ Organization (3) How does the writer lead in to the topic, and how does she wrap it up?

☐ Voice (4) How would you describe the writer's voice in this essay (humorous, serious, angry)?

Respond to the reading.

Answers

Ideas 1. The writer's focus is on the effects of being disrespectful.
2. The phrase *learning to respect others* and *important* appear in the prompt and in the essay.

Organization 3. The writer leads in to the topic by stating that being disrespectful has three negative effects and then by elaborating on those three effects in three separate paragraphs. She wraps up the topic by saying that people should respect others.

Voice 4. The writer's tone is serious.

Advanced Learners

Have students brainstorm other examples the writer of the essay could have used to defend the statement *Learning to respect other people is very important.*

Writing Tips

Point out that students must approach writing-on-demand assignments differently from open-ended writing assignments and that timed writing creates pressures for everyone.

Expository Prompts

To teach students who must take timed assessments how to approach their writing, allow them the same amount of time to write their response essay as they will be allotted on school, district, or state assessments. Break down each part of the process into clear chunks of time. For example, you might give students

- 10 minutes for reading, note-taking, and planning,
- 25 minutes for writing,
- 10 minutes for editing and proofreading.

Tell students when time is up for each section. Start the assignment at the top of the hour or at the half-hour to make it easier for students to keep track of the time.

If your state, district, or school requires students to use and submit a graphic organizer as part of their assessment, provide a copy of one of the reproducible charts (TE pages 800–804) or refer students to PE pages 548–549.

216

Writing Tips

Before you write . . .

- **Understand the prompt.**
  Remember that an expository prompt asks you to explain.
- **Plan your time wisely.**
  Spend several minutes taking some notes and planning before you start writing. Use the last few minutes to read over what you have written.

During your writing . . .

- **Decide on a focus for your essay.**
  Keep your main idea or purpose in mind as you write.
- **Choose carefully.**
  Use clear examples and explanations.
- **End in a meaningful way.**
  Remind readers about the importance of the topic at the end of your explanation.

After you've written a first draft . . .

- **Check for completeness and correctness.**
  Write your supporting details in logical order and correct any errors in capitalization, punctuation, spelling, and grammar.

Expository Prompts

- If your school could have only three rules for students, what would they be? Explain why these three rules are so important.
- Making friends is an important part of life. Write an essay explaining what makes a good friend.

 Plan and write a response. Respond to one of the prompts listed above. Complete your writing within the period of time your teacher gives you. Afterward, list one part you like and one part you could improve.

describe *solve.* inform
define explain **217**
Expository Writing Checklist

Expository Writing in Review

Purpose: In expository writing, you *explain something* to readers.

Topics: How to do or make something
The causes of something
The kinds of something
The definition of something

Prewriting
Select a topic that you know a lot about or one that you want to learn about. (See pages 166–167.)

Write a focus (thesis) statement, telling exactly what idea you plan to cover. (See page 168.)

Gather the important steps or details and organize them according to time order or order of importance. (See pages 168–170.)

Writing
In the beginning part, introduce your topic, say something interesting about it, and state your focus. (See page 173.)

In the middle part, give the details or the steps that explain the focus. (See pages 174–175.)

In the ending, summarize your writing and make a final comment about the topic. (See page 176.)

Revising
Review the ideas, organization, and voice first. Then review for **word choice** and **sentence fluency**. Make sure that you have included the important details or steps. (See pages 178–187.)

Editing
Check your writing for conventions. Also have a trusted classmate edit your writing. (See pages 190–192.)

Make a final copy and proofread it for errors before sharing it. (See page 193.)

Assessing
Use the expository rubric to assess your finished writing. (See pages 194–195.)

EXPOSITORY

Expository Writing in Review

To make reviewing fun, write a collective class essay about writing an expository essay. Keep it light by having students offer ideas to help a bored sixth grader complete this assignment. For example:

■ First, brainstorm a list of topic ideas, and then tell your teacher that you have nothing to write about.

■ When you are ready to write the first draft, spend a lot of time looking for the perfect pencil. When you finally find the pencil, take it to the pencil sharpener and sharpen it again and again, until it's as sharp as possible.

Students will enjoy taking a light approach to the unit review.

Persuasive Writing Overview

Writing Standards

The writing standards listed below are based on a blending of state and NCTE standards.

- Use charts, lists, and brainstorming to gather and organize ideas.
- Establish a central idea—an opinion—to develop.
- Support central ideas that are stated in topic sentences with facts and details.
- Revise and edit the first draft to use transitions and create a confident voice that makes the draft more persuasive.
- Assess the writing using a rubric based on the traits of effective writing.

Writing Forms

- persuasive paragraph
- persuasive essay promoting a cause
- pet-peeve essay

Focus on the Traits

- **Ideas** Using clear reasoning that informs and convinces
- **Organization** Forming a logical, smooth flow of ideas
- **Voice** Developing a positive, confident, and convincing voice
- **Word Choice** Using specific nouns, verbs, and adjectives with no repeated words
- **Sentence Fluency** Including a variety of sentence types that flow smoothly
- **Conventions** Checking for errors in punctuation, capitalization, spelling, and grammar

Unit Pacing

Persuasive Paragraph: 1.5–2.5 hours

The **persuasive paragraph** introduces the unit and lays the groundwork for more extensive persuasive writing. Use this section if students need to work on crafting a paragraph. Following are some of the topics that are covered:

- Understanding the parts of a paragraph
- Gathering reasons

Persuasive Essay 1: 4–7 hours

In this section students write a **persuasive essay** to **promote a cause**. Use this section to focus on developing an essay. Following are some of the topics that are covered:

- Using a topics chart
- Forming an opinion statement
- Writing the beginning, middle, and ending
- Recognizing "fuzzy thinking"
- Checking for transitions
- Checking for comparative and superlative forms
- Assessing the final copy

Persuasive Essay 2: 2.5–3.5 hours

The **pet-peeve essay** section offers a new slant on persuasive writing—writing about something annoying in a personal and entertaining way. Use this section to present an alternate or additional form of persuasive writing. Following are some of the topics that are covered:

- Using freewriting to select a topic
- Adding humorous details
- Using logical order

Persuasive Writing Across the Curriculum: 45–90 minutes

Collaborate with teachers from other content areas to identify persuasive forms that could enhance students' experience with the curriculum already in place.

- **Social Studies**
  Editorial Cartoons, pp. 268–269
- **Math**
  Proofs, pp. 270–271
- **Science**
  Supporting Theories, pp. 272–273
- **Practical Writing**
  Persuasive Letters, pp. 274–277

Writing for Assessment: 45–90 minutes

The student text shows a strong student response to the first prompt below. Students can respond to that same prompt or to either of the additional prompts as an informal or a formal assessment.

- Write an essay convincing your teachers to give more or less homework.
- Write an essay expressing your opinion about whether children under 14 should be at home before 7:00 PM unless they are with an adult.
- In a letter, convince your parents to take a family trip to a place you would like to visit.

Evaluating a Persuasive Essay

Learning to evaluate one's own and others' writing is an integral part of learning to write. In addition to a student's evaluation of a persuasive essay (PE pages 258–259), **benchmark papers** provide practice with evaluating persuasive writing.

- Zoos (strong)
  TR 5A–5C
  TE pp. 787–789
- Get Moving (good)
  PE pp. 258–259
- Letter to the Editor (poor)
  TR 6A–6C
  TE pp. 790–792

Integrated Grammar and Writing Skills

Below are skills lessons from the resources sections of the pupil edition that are suggested at point of use (✱) throughout this unit.

Persuasive Paragraph, pp. 219–222

- ✱ Develop Persuasive Paragraphs, p. 529
- ✱ Use Order of Importance, p. 536

Promoting a Cause, pp. 223–260

- ✱ Qualifiers: Indefinite Adjectives, p. 734,
- ✱ Adverbs of Time and Degree, p. 736
- ✱ Pronouns, pp. 476–479
- ✱ Comparative and Superlative Forms, p. 487
- ✱ Capitalization of Proper Nouns and Adjectives, p. 618

Pet-Peeve Essay, pp. 261–266

- ✱ Using the Right Word, pp. 652–686

Additional Grammar Skills

Below are skills lessons from other components that you can weave into your unit instruction.

Writing a Persuasive Paragraph

● SkillsBook

Pronouns, p. 133
Antecedents, p. 134
Indefinite Pronouns, p. 135
Subject and Object Pronouns, p. 137
Possessive Pronouns, p. 139

● Interactive Writing Skills CD-ROM

Parts of Speech: Pronouns 1—
Antecedents, Number

● Daily Language Workout

Week 19: The Environment and
You, pp. 40–41
Week 19: Environmentally
Friendly, p. 96
Week 20: Pollution Control,
pp. 42–43
Week 20: Toxic Trash, p. 97

Promoting a Cause

● SkillsBook

Capitalization, 1 and 2 p. 41
Transitions, p. 73
Common and Proper Nouns, p. 125
Pronouns, p. 133
Special Kinds of Adjectives, p. 161
Types of Adverbs, p. 167

● Interactive Writing Skills CD-ROM

Mechanics: Capitalization 1—
Proper Nouns
Parts of Speech: Pronouns 2—
Types

● Daily Language Workout

Week 21: Air and Water Pollution,
pp. 44–45
Week 21: A Great Lake, Again, p. 98

Week 22: The American Colonies,
pp. 46–47
Week 22: Women's Rights, p. 99

Writing a Pet-Peeve Essay

● SkillsBook

Using the Right Word 1, 2, 3, and
4, p. 53
Using the Right Word Review 1
and 2, p. 58

● Interactive Writing Skills CD-ROM

Using the Right Word 1, 2, 3, and 4

● Daily Language Workout

Week 23: The Founding Fathers,
pp. 48–49
Week 23: Forever Free, p. 100
Week 24: Of Presidents and Daily
Life, pp. 50–51
Week 24: The Weekly Bath, p. 101

218

Persuasive Writing

Persuasive Writing
Persuasive Paragraph

If you could change one thing at school or at home, what would it be? How would you change it? Do you think you could convince other people to go along with the change?

Persuasive writing is your chance to get people to think the way you do about something. Advertisements, editorials, and even some letters are common kinds of persuasive writing.

In the next few pages, you'll write a persuasive paragraph about a change you'd like to make.

Writing Guidelines

Subject:	An important change
Form:	Persuasive paragraph
Purpose:	To convince readers to agree with you
Audience:	Classmates, parents, guardians, or school officials

Persuasive Paragraph

Objectives

- understand the content and structure of a persuasive paragraph
- choose a topic (an important change) to write about
- plan, draft, revise, and edit a persuasive paragraph

A **persuasive paragraph** tries to convince readers to agree with the writer. In most persuasive paragraphs, the writer states an opinion and supports the opinion with convincing reasons, facts, and details.

✱ Additional information about developing a persuasive paragraphs is on PE page 529.

Use one or both of these activities to familiarize students with the genre:

■ Ask students to describe a time when they tried to change someone's mind. Have them explain why they think they were or were not successful.

■ Provide students with newspapers and help them identify persuasive language in a variety of advertisements, editorials, and opinion letters.

Persuasive Paragraph

Discuss the writer's clever use of the word *ramp* in the title. Ask:

- Why is a good title important? (It immediately gets the reader's attention.)
- What is the author's opinion in this essay? (See the topic sentence.)

 Respond to the reading.

Review the questions orally with students to determine if they understand persuasion and can recognize persuasive language.

Answers

Ideas 1. Possible choices:

- state law requires equal access
- one student is in a wheelchair
- a ramp would open drama to more students

Organization 2. by order of importance

Voice & Word Choice 3. Possible choices:

- needs to add
- everyone has to have . . .
- most important reason
- would give more students the chance

220

Persuasive Paragraph

In a persuasive paragraph, the topic sentence states an opinion, the body sentences give reasons to support it, and the closing sentence restates the opinion. The following paragraph was written by a student concerned about access to the school stage.

Topic sentence

Body

Closing sentence

> ### Ramp It Up!
>
> Bryant Middle School needs to add a ramp to its auditorium stage. State law says that everyone has to have equal access to important parts of the school, and the stage is important. In this year's spring play, the student who is playing the Wizard of Oz is in a wheelchair. A ramp is needed so he can get up on the stage and also move down into the audience during performances. A ramp also would open drama to more students. That's the most important reason for it. Putting in a ramp isn't just about state laws or one student. The ramp would give more students the chance to perform.

 Respond to the reading. Write answers to the following questions.

- ☐ **Ideas** (1) What reasons does the writer give to support the opinion?
- ☐ **Organization** (2) How is the paragraph organized—by time, by location, or by order of importance?
- ☐ **Voice & Word Choice** (3) What specific words or phrases make this paragraph persuasive?

---

persuade convince *support* **221**
argue reason
Persuasive Paragraph

Prewriting **Selecting a Topic**

Think about the places where you spend the most time. What important changes would you like to make in each of those places? A chart like the one that follows can help you think about important changes.

Chart

Home	School	Martin Luther King, Jr., Park
Less dish duty Get cable	Make stage accessible Improve school food	Remove leash law Clean up graffiti

Think about important changes. Create a chart like the one above. Write down three places where you spend time. Under each one, list at least two changes you would like to make. Choose one change to write about in a persuasive paragraph.

Gathering Reasons

Everyone has opinions. To convince others to agree with your opinions, you need to provide strong support, or reasons. The writer of the sample paragraph on page 220 used listing to gather support for her opinion.

List

Bryant Middle School needs to build a ramp to the stage.

– State law says important spots need to be accessible.
– The actor playing the Wizard of Oz has a wheelchair.
– Anybody who wants to be in drama should be able to get onto our stage.

List your reasons. At the top of your paper, write the important change you chose to write about. Under it, write as many reasons as you can think of to support your opinion. Try to come up with at least three.

PERSUASIVE

Prewriting **Selecting a Topic**

Before students work on their own, brainstorm as a class topics to consider for their essays. List their answers to these questions on the board.

■ Where do you spend a lot of time?
■ How could those places be changed? (to make it safer, more fun, easier to use, cleaner, prettier).

Students may work in small groups or on their own to create their charts. Suggest that they refer to the list on the board for ideas. You may also wish to hold **writing conferences** *(see below)* to provide guidance and answer questions.

Prewriting **Gathering Reasons**

Have students gather reasons for their important change by creating a list of supporting reasons like the list shown. Encourage students to write as many reasons as possible. Then have them work with a partner to review their reasons and eliminate any that are weak or merely restatements of the same idea.

Teaching Tip: Writing Conferences

Not all conferences have to be lengthy or formal. As students work, stop by their desks to check on their progress. Brief, one-on-one discussions can help some students focus their thinking and gain confidence. Students are more likely to convey their thoughts and volunteer ideas when they are not concerned about comparing their ideas with those of their peers.

Questions like these can direct the conferences:
● Do you have a strong opinion about this topic?
● Is the change you're proposing important?
● How will the change affect others?
● What good reasons will you use to persuade others to support this change?

English Language Learners

Students with limited language skills may be uncomfortable when asked to share ideas in oral discussions. Have them work in smaller, supportive groups, or pair them with native or fluent English-speaking students who are cooperative and considerate.

Writing
Developing the First Draft

After students read the tips for writing their first draft, ask them to review the sample paragraph on PE page 220 to determine how the writer applied these tips.

Remind students to organize supporting reasons in order of importance.

✳ Additional information about using order of importance in persuasive paragraphs can be found on PE page 536.

The first draft can be completed as an in-class or at-home assignment.

Revising Improving Your Writing

To increase students' comfort level with the revising process, provide them with samples of first-draft paragraphs to **practice revising** (see below). Have students work with a partner or in small groups.

Editing Checking for Conventions

Before students come to you with questions, refer them to these resources for help:

- Proofreader's Guide (PE pages 578–749)
- classroom dictionary
- writing folder (in which they can check previous writing so as not to repeat errors)

222

Writing Developing the First Draft

Write the first draft of your paragraph. Use the following tips:

- Start with a sentence that clearly states your opinion.
- In the body, write sentences that give your supporting reasons.
- End with a sentence that restates your opinion.

 Write your first draft. When you write your first draft, include at least three good reasons to support your opinion.

Revising Improving Your Writing

After you complete the first draft of your paragraph, you are ready to revise it. Check your *ideas, organization, voice, word choice,* and *sentence fluency.*

 Revise your paragraph. Make the necessary changes to improve your first draft, using the questions below as a guide.

1 Does the topic sentence state a clear opinion?

2 What details should be added or removed?

3 Do I sound persuasive?

4 Have I used specific nouns and strong verbs?

5 Have I written complete sentences that flow smoothly?

Editing Checking for Conventions

Once you have revised your paragraph, check it for *conventions*.

 Edit your paragraph. Ask yourself the questions below.

1 Have I used correct spelling, punctuation, and capitalization?

2 Have I checked for errors in usage (*to, too, two; it's, its; there, their, they're*) and other grammar errors?

Proofread your paragraph. After making a neat final copy of your paragraph, check it one more time for errors.

Teaching Tip: Practice Revising

Many students are confused by the revising process. Write a first draft of a persuasive paragraph or use a benchmark paper (TE pages 787–792) and distribute copies. Discuss with students how to make the writing more persuasive.

- Is a stronger topic sentence needed?
- Do the reasons support the opinion?
- Are there enough reasons to convince the reader?
- Is more persuasive language needed?

Have students suggest specific words and phrases to use.

Struggling Learners

To help students state clear opinions, have them create opinion statements for each of these topics: outdated gym equipment, closed community center. (Possible responses: The school's outdated gym equipment needs to be replaced immediately. The community center should be reopened.)

persuade convince *support* **223**
argue *reason*

Persuasive Writing
Promoting a Cause

"Save the whales!" "Alba Moreno for class president!" "Reuse and recycle!" Each of these statements identifies a cause. Like most people, you probably have worthy causes that you support, too. If you feel strongly enough about them, you will want to persuade others to support them as well.

Persuasive writing is one way to get others to think the way that you do. To do this, you must express a thoughtful opinion and give strong reasons to support it. In this unit, you will be asked to write an essay that persuades others to support one of the causes that you believe in.

Writing Guidelines

Subject:	A cause that you believe in
Form:	Persuasive essay
Purpose:	To persuade others to agree with you
Audience:	Classmates

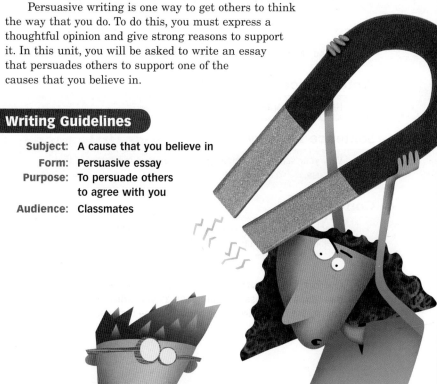

Advanced Learners

Stage a class debate about a school-related cause specific to your student population. (Possible causes: broadening extracurricular offerings; lengthening lunch period; requiring school uniforms)

Promoting a Cause

Objectives
- appreciate persuasive writing
- understand the purpose of a persuasive essay
- plan, draft, revise, edit, and publish a persuasive essay

A **persuasive essay** is a piece of writing that
- states an opinion,
- provides strong reasons to support that opinion,
- issues a call to action.

Prepare students to promote a cause by asking them to freewrite in response to these questions:
- What cause do you feel strongly about? For example, think about something you would like to see changed (school menu, weekend homework).
- Why is your cause important?
- Does your cause affect more than just a few people?

Invite students to share their freewrites, and have other students react to them. This will help students who select one of these causes as their essay topic to understand their audience and to prepare for opposing viewpoints.

224

Understanding Your Goal

Traits of Persuasive Writing

Three traits relate to the development of the content *and* the form. They provide a focus during prewriting, drafting, and revising.

- Ideas
- **Organization**
- Voice

The other three traits relate more to form. Checking them is more important during the revising and editing processes.

- **Word Choice**
- **Sentence Fluency**
- **Conventions**

✴ The six-point rubric on PE pages 256–257 is based on these traits. Four- and five-point rubrics are available on TE pages 770 and 774.

Have students copy the Traits of Persuasive Writing. Then have them cut apart the traits into strips and paste each trait across the top of a separate 5″ × 7″ blank note card. As students progress through their writing, they can jot down notes on each trait card to explain how they applied that trait to their essays. Later discuss the role each trait played in the development of their writing.

Understanding Your Goal

Your goal in this chapter is to write a well-organized persuasive essay about a cause you believe in. The traits listed in the chart below will help you plan and write your essay.

TRAITS OF PERSUASIVE WRITING

Ideas
Support your opinion about an important cause.

Organization
Create a smooth flow of ideas from the beginning through the middle to the ending.

Voice
Sound confident and sincere about your cause.

Word Choice
Use strong words and avoid repetition.

Sentence Fluency
Vary your sentence beginnings and the types of sentences that you use.

Conventions
Check your writing for errors in punctuation, capitalization, spelling, and grammar.

 Get the big picture. Look at the rubric on pages 256–257. You can use that rubric to assess your progress as you write. Your goal is to write a convincing persuasive essay about a cause that you believe in.

persuade convince *support*
argue *reason*

Promoting a Cause **225**

Persuasive Essay

The focus of the following persuasive essay is avoiding exotic pets, a cause that the writer feels strongly about. The writer begins by getting the reader's attention and stating an opinion. Then the writer supports the opinion with reasons and ends with a call to action.

BEGINNING

The beginning introduces the topic and states the opinion (underlined).

MIDDLE

The middle paragraphs give reasons that support the opinion.

Avoiding Exotic Pets

Last year, our neighbors got a dingo. As a puppy, this Australian wild dog was very friendly. By the time it was six months old, though, the dingo was big and mean. After it attacked our dog, Animal Control had to take the dingo away. What if our neighbors buy a baby crocodile next? Exotic pets might be interesting, but they can also cause a lot of trouble. People should think carefully before buying unusual pets.

One problem is that owners often don't think about what will happen when the animal grows. For example, potbellied pigs are cute when they're little, but they can be hard to handle later on. In fact, pigs may turn over furniture or dig up the backyard looking for something to eat. Owners may become frustrated with their pet's behavior.

Another problem is that owners who grow tired of their exotic pets have trouble finding new homes for them. Often, shelters can't take these pets, so owners turn them loose. Releasing exotic animals can be very harmful to native animals and dangerous for people. For example, foreign fish that have been released into lakes

PERSUASIVE

Persuasive Essay

Work through this sample essay with the class, pointing out the elements that make it good persuasive writing.

Ideas
- The author states a specific opinion introduced by a personal experience.
- The issue affects (could affect) a lot of people.

Organization
- The reasons are listed in order of importance, least to most important.
- The ending presents a specific call to action to take.

English Language Learners

This unit contains many models of student writing. Make sure students understand the meanings of American idioms used in these models.

Idioms in the persuasive essay on PE pages 225–226 include:

- hard to handle (hard to control or take care of)
- turn them loose (set them free; let them go)
- wiping out (killing; drastically reducing the number of)
- for the sake of (for the good of)

Respond to the reading.

Answers

Ideas **1.** People should avoid having unusual, exotic pets.

2. Owners aren't prepared for what happens when an animal gets bigger. They have trouble finding new homes for exotic animals. Exotic animals can carry dangerous diseases.

Organization 3. order of importance, from least to most important

Voice & Word Choice 4. yes

5. Possible choices:
- big and mean
- hard to handle
- frustrated
- harmful . . . and dangerous
- scarier yet
- deadly
- destructive

---

and rivers are wiping out native fish like bass and trout. Scarier yet, when a woman in Wisconsin reached into her flower garden, a large tropical snake attacked her.

The most serious problem is that exotic pets may carry dangerous diseases. For instance, monkey pox has become a problem in this country because infected animals brought it here from Africa. Even worse, some imported pets could also carry the deadly Ebola virus to the United States.

> The most important reason is saved for last.

ENDING
. . . .
> The ending summarizes the main points and makes a call to action.

Even though some owners are well prepared to keep exotic pets, most of these animals were never meant to be pets like dogs and cats. A big dog may cause some damage once in a while, but a pet wolf can chew through doors. Is it really worth it to keep an animal that can be destructive or even dangerous? <u>For the sake of these animals and the environment, people should avoid having unusual pets.</u>

Respond to the reading. Answer the following questions, which focus on important traits in writing.

☐ **Ideas** **(1)** What is the writer's opinion about the topic? **(2)** What are the three reasons that support the opinion?

☐ **Organization** **(3)** How are these reasons organized?

☐ **Voice & Word Choice** **(4)** Does the writer sound confident and sincere? **(5)** What words or phrases tell you so?

English Language Learners

Pair each student with a partner proficient in English, and direct partners to work together to answer the response questions at the bottom of the page.

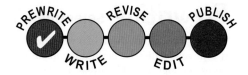

Prewriting

Prewriting is the first step in the writing process. It involves selecting a topic, gathering specific details, and organizing your ideas.

Keys to Effective Prewriting

1. Select a cause that you care about and that fits the assignment.

2. Gather details about the cause.

3. Write a clear opinion statement to guide you as you write.

4. Write topic sentences that support your opinion statement.

5. Create a list or an outline as a planning guide.

PERSUASIVE

Prewriting
Keys to Effective Prewriting

Remind students of the purpose of the prewriting stage in the writing process. (It's when the writer gets ready to write.)

The Keys to Effective Prewriting lays out the process students will be guided through on PE pages 228–232.

- Suggest that students look at what they wrote during the freewrite activity (see TE page 223) as they consider a cause for a topic (item 1).
- Students may be concerned about their ability to write an outline (item 5). Tell them that they will be guided through this process in the lesson.

Prewriting Selecting a Topic

Before students start the selecting process, provide them with copies of news and magazine articles about young people who have championed worthwhile causes. (The school librarian and the Internet are good resources for such articles.) Discuss the articles to help students gain a good understanding of what is meant by a "worthwhile cause."

After completing their charts, students can work in small groups to brainstorm strong supporting reasons for each cause they starred. This will help students assess the potential for each of their starred topics.

After students choose their best topic, invite them to share how they completed the sentence starters. (I will write about _____. I picked this topic because . . .)

Focus on the Traits

Ideas
Be sure students double-check their topic against this criterion.

228

Prewriting Selecting a Topic

To get started, think of a worthwhile cause to write about. For example, if your school district is thinking about dropping art classes, you might write an essay opposing this proposal.

A chart like the one below can help you find causes that you feel strongly about. Different causes are listed under four separate categories.

Animals	Community	Sports	School
Support animal shelters Clean up after pets	Build a skateboard park Improve the library	Add soccer teams Schedule games so parents can watch	Keep art classes Expand school menus

Create a chart. Make a chart like the one above. Under each category (animals, community, sports, school), list causes you feel strongly about. When you finish, put a star next to two or three causes that interest you the most. Ask yourself the following questions about each one.

1 Why is this cause important to me?

2 Why would this cause interest my readers?

Choose a topic. After you have answered the questions above, choose your best topic and explain your choice using the following sentences.

I will write about _____. I picked this topic because . . .

Focus on the Traits

Ideas Choose a cause that you feel strongly about so that you have plenty of convincing things to say about it. You will need at least three strong reasons to support your opinion.

English Language Learners

To help students think of causes to write about, hold a special one-on-one brainstorming session in which you discuss possible topics that they might enjoy writing about. To get the discussion going, ask leading questions, such as "How do you feel about [an issue at school that will be familiar to them]?"

Struggling Learners

To help students think of worthwhile causes, have them consider each category in the chart in terms of standing up for the rights of different animals or people. (Possible examples: protecting dolphins from tuna net fishing; lobbying for equal gym time at the community center for youth and adults)

Gathering Ideas and Information

Once you select a topic, the next step is to gather your first thoughts about it. The writer of the essay on pages 235–238 did this by answering three basic questions: *Why is this cause important to me? What do I already know about it? What else do I need to find out?* Review his answers below.

CAUSE: KEEPING ART CLASSES

Why is this cause important to me?

- Art is one of my favorite subjects.
- Art allows me to use my imagination.
- It is a nice break from regular classes.

What do I already know about it?

- My art teacher told us that art classes might be cut next year.
- The school board says that it doesn't have money for the program.
- When I asked the principal what I could do, she told me that parents should contact school board members.

What else do I need to find out?

- I need more background information about this topic.
- Are there other ways that schools can solve money problems?
- Are there other reasons why we should keep art?

Gather your thoughts. Answer the three questions above about your own topic.

1 Start by writing your cause on the top of a piece of paper.

2 Then list each question, leaving space after each one for your answers.

3 If you need more information, interview people about the cause and see what you can find in newspapers, in magazines, and on the Internet.

PERSUASIVE

Prewriting
Gathering Ideas and Information

Carefully review this page with the class before students work on their own. Point out the importance of gathering important information for persuasive writing. (It's hard for students to be persuasive if they haven't collected their thoughts about their topics.)

Recommend that students use a variety of resources to gather information about their topics. If possible, establish a classroom **Information Station** (*see below*).

Encourage students to share their ideas and respond to each others' ideas in one of these ways:

- In small group discussions, students can help each other refine and develop ideas by offering suggestions. As students talk, circulate and offer your own insights.
- Post all the selected topics as headings on a bulletin board. Students can tack notes to the bulletin board to share personal insights and knowledge about each cause, along with any other helpful information they have for the writer. Student writers can refer to these notes during the prewriting and writing stages.

Teaching Tip: Information Station

To be persuasive, students need to know a lot about their cause. To facilitate learning, designate a section of the classroom as an "Information Station." Make available as many of the following resources as possible:

- computer with Internet access
- current newspapers and news magazines
- reference books

- Ask-the-Experts scheduling cards (to arrange for one-on-one conferences with you or other knowledgeable adults)
- telephone book (for addresses of organizations that support particular causes)

Advanced Learners

Provide phone books that contain government listings. Have students contact city, county, state, and federal organizations that relate to their cause. They may do this for one of many reasons:

- to procure written information
- to get Web-site addresses
- to express their concerns

Prewriting
Understanding Opinions and Facts

Ask: Where can you go to check facts? (encyclopedias, newspapers, original sources, experts, reference books)

Remind students that when they use the Internet, they should be careful to use reliable, reputable sites, such as on-line encyclopedias.

✳ See PE page 366 for tips on using the Internet responsibly.

Consider completing the **Try It** exercise as an oral activity. Have students explain how they know which statements are facts and which are opinions.

 Answers

1. O	4. O
2. F	5. F
3. F	6. O

Prewriting
Writing an Opinion Statement

Have students write their opinion statement on a sentence strip. Tell them to place the strip across the top of their desk whenever they work on their essays. Point out that this statement should guide their thinking throughout the process of writing their persuasive essay.

230

Prewriting Understanding Opinions and Facts

After collecting enough information about the cause, you're ready to write your opinion statement. Before you do this, make sure that you are clear about the difference between facts and opinions. An opinion is a feeling or belief that you have about something. A fact is a detail that can be used to support an opinion. You can check a fact, but you can't check an opinion.

> **Opinion:** *School officials should keep art in our schools.*
> (This statement expresses a feeling and cannot be checked.)
>
> **Fact:** *The school administration has proposed to cut art classes.* (This statement can be checked.)

 Number a piece of paper from 1 to 6. Then decide if each statement below is a fact or an opinion. Write "O" for opinion and "F" for fact.

1. Carlos should run for class president.
2. Carlos has a 4.00 grade-point average.
3. Our band room is the size of a regular classroom.
4. Park Middle School needs a new band room.
5. Josie is the tallest player on our basketball team.
6. Josie is the best player on the team.

Writing an Opinion Statement

Your opinion statement must identify (1) your cause and (2) your feeling about it. Review the examples that follow.

> *People should think carefully* (feeling) *before buying exotic pets* (cause).
> *Art classes* (cause) *should be kept in our school* (feeling).

 Write an opinion statement. Remember that your opinion statement should express your true feelings about your cause. If your first statement doesn't work, write one or two more versions. Pick the best one.

Struggling Learners

First, select two students to model this activity for the class.

- Give the pair a topic (for example, school lunches).
- One partner is called FACT and can provide only true statements about the topic (for example, there are two choices for lunch).
- The second partner is called OPINION and can provide only personal feelings about the topic

(for example, pizza is the best item on the menu).

- Partners continue until they have exhausted the topic.

Then have the rest of the class work in pairs to write fact and opinion statements about a topic of their choice (for example, television, clothing, sports).

Making a Plan

Once you have written your opinion statement, the next step is to list the main supporting reasons. Each reason should help convince the reader to accept your opinion. See the reasons listed below.

> Opinion Statement: *Schools in our district should keep art classes.*
>
> First reason: *encourages creativity and trying new things*
>
> Second reason: *fun way to learn about other subjects*
>
> Third reason: *best place for many kids to make art*

Identify your supporting reasons. Write your opinion statement and then list at least three strong reasons that support your opinion.

Writing Topic Sentences

Each of your main reasons becomes a topic sentence for a supporting paragraph in your essay. Study the example that follows.

> Reason: *encourages creativity and trying new things*
> Topic sentence: *Art encourages people to be creative and try something new.*

Write your topic sentences. Turn each of your reasons into a strong topic sentence. Use the example above as a guide.

Focus on the Traits

Organization Think about the arrangement of your reasons. In persuasive essays, many writers either start with their most important reason or end with it.

PERSUASIVE

Prewriting Making a Plan

To help students think of reasons to support their opinion statements, have them ask themselves, *"Why should . . ."* followed by their opinion statement, and answer themselves, *". . . because . . ."*

Prewriting
Writing Topic Sentences

As a class, turn the other two reasons listed in the chart from Making a Plan into topic sentences.

Focus on the Traits

Organization
Suggest that students write each of their three topic sentences on one side of an index card. Tell them to record supporting facts and examples on the reverse. They can then move the cards around to experiment with the order and to decide which order will present the most convincing argument.

English Language Learners

Play the "Why?" game with students who have difficulty expressing reasons to support their opinions. First, have the student read his or her opinion aloud. Then ask, "Why? What is the most important reason that makes you feel this way?" Ask the student to respond orally and write the response on a sheet of paper. Then repeat the process. Have the student read aloud his or her opinion. Ask, "Why? What is another good reason that makes you feel this way?" Have the student add that sentence to the paper, leaving three or four lines between each response so that the list can be used as a skeleton for the organized list on PE page 232. Repeat this activity until the student has three strong reasons to support the opinion.

Prewriting Organizing Your Ideas

Explain to students that the facts and details that they choose to support each topic sentence are very important because this information shows how much they (the writers) know about the cause and how much they care about it.

Focus on the Traits

Voice

After reading the boxed material with students, review the directions for making an organized list that are part of the graphic, and discuss the sample organized list. Ask students to point out details that suggest that the writer knows a lot about school art classes.

Details include the following:
- freedom to imagine and experiment
- create Native American pouches
- special supplies not found in most homes
- peer support

232

Prewriting Organizing Your Ideas

Once you've written your topic sentences, identify the facts and details needed to support each topic sentence. The directions below can help.

Directions	Organized List
Write your opinion statement.	*Schools in our district should keep art classes.*
1. Write your first topic sentence.	*Art encourages people to be creative and try something new.*
List facts and details.	*– Have freedom to imagine* *– Able to experiment* *– Make ceramics, paintings, and drawings*
2. Write your second topic sentence.	*Art is a fun way to learn more about other subjects.*
List facts and details.	*– Study Native American culture in social studies* *– In art, create Native American pouches*
3. Write your third topic sentence.	*School is the best place for many kids to make art.*
List facts and details.	*– Need special supplies not found in most homes* *– Peers can offer support*

 Make an organized list. To create your list, follow the directions above. You will use this list as a guide when you write.

Focus on the Traits

Voice In a persuasive essay, it's important to sound convincing, and you will sound convincing if you know a lot about your cause.

Advanced Learners

Challenge advanced learners to provide more details for the sample's second topic sentence. Suggest science and music as other subject areas. (Possible responses: science—sculpting endangered animals native to a threatened habitat such as the rain forest; music—making and painting percussion instruments such as drums or maracas.)

Writing

A first draft lets you get all your ideas down on paper. You're ready to write a first draft when you have written a clear opinion statement and gathered supporting details.

Keys to Effective Writing

1. Use your organized list or outline as a planning guide.

2. Get all your ideas on paper in your first draft.

3. Write on every other line to make room for later changes.

4. Write a clear opinion statement; use topic sentences in the middle paragraphs that support your opinion.

5. Add specific details to support your topic sentences and interest the reader.

6. Use transitions to tie everything together.

PERSUASIVE

Writing Keys to Effective Writing

Remind students that the writing stage is when they get to write, or draft, their ideas on paper.

The Keys to Effective Writing lays out the process students will be guided through on PE pages 234–238.

- Point out to students that they have all their prewriting materials to help them write a successful first draft. Stress, however, that they shouldn't worry if this draft is not perfect. They will have several opportunities to improve their writing and to correct mistakes.

- Students will have a chance to learn more about effective transitions during the revising stage (PE pages 242–243). However, it may be helpful to review **transitions** (see below) now.

Teaching Tip: Transitions

Remind students that transitions are words and phrases that link, or connect, ideas. Explain that transitions can be used to

- link an idea in one sentence to an idea in another sentence,
- show how an idea in one paragraph is connected to ideas in other paragraphs,
- show the organization of ideas within a paragraph,

Work with students to create a list of transitions and signal words they might use as they write their persuasive essay. Examples are

- first of all,
- another important fact is,
- most importantly.

These particular transitions are used in persuasive essays because persuasive essays are usually organized by order of importance.

English Language Learners

* Provide examples for each of the four listed ways in which transitions can be used (see PE pages 572–573). Have students list these on paper so that they can refer to them when drafting or revising.

234

Writing Getting the Big Picture

Review the form of the persuasive essay, using the graphic on this page as a guide.

Ask:

■ How would you define the term *call to action?*
■ What are examples of a call to action, for each of these situations?
  □ Neighborhoods have too much litter.
  □ Many elderly residents need help with daily chores.
  □ Medical research is important.

Ask students how they think their persuasive essay will compare to the persuasive paragraph they wrote earlier. If necessary, help them to determine that the essay will provide much greater detail, will allow them to elaborate on their opinions, and will provide more of an opportunity for them to incorporate their individual voice and writing style.

Writing Getting the Big Picture

Once you have finished your prewriting, you are ready to begin the first draft of your persuasive essay. Remember, you are trying to convince the reader to agree with your feeling about a cause—and perhaps also to do something as a result.

The graphic below shows how the different parts of a persuasive essay fit together. (The examples are from the student essay on pages 235–238.)

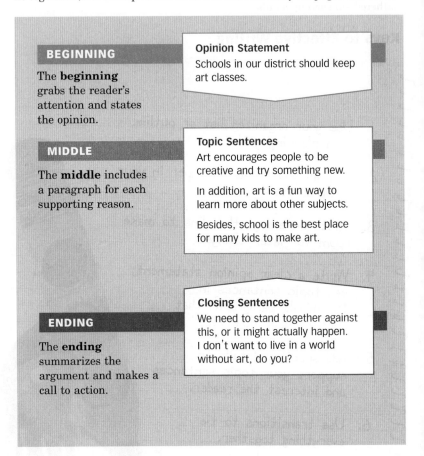

BEGINNING

The **beginning** grabs the reader's attention and states the opinion.

Opinion Statement
Schools in our district should keep art classes.

MIDDLE

The **middle** includes a paragraph for each supporting reason.

Topic Sentences
Art encourages people to be creative and try something new.

In addition, art is a fun way to learn more about other subjects.

Besides, school is the best place for many kids to make art.

ENDING

The **ending** summarizes the argument and makes a call to action.

Closing Sentences
We need to stand together against this, or it might actually happen. I don't want to live in a world without art, do you?

Starting Your Essay

Once you have written an opinion statement and organized your thinking, you're ready to start writing your essay. In the beginning paragraph of a persuasive essay, you should grab the reader's attention and state your opinion. Here are several good ways to begin:

- **Give some interesting information about your topic.**
- **Ask a question.**
- **Quote someone.**
- **Share an experience.**

Beginning
Middle
Ending

Beginning Paragraph

The writer of the following essay captures the reader's attention with a question and some interesting information and then shares an opinion statement (underlined).

> The topic is introduced.
>
> The paragraph ends with a clear opinion statement (underlined).

Can you imagine a world without art? Take away colorful paintings, metal sculptures, and beautiful photographs. Erase the artwork from book covers, magazine ads, and comic books. I don't want to live in a world without art, but I might have to. The school board is planning to cut art class. But this is wrong. Schools in our district should keep art classes.

 Write an opening. Write the beginning paragraph of your persuasive essay. Make sure that you grab the reader's attention and clearly state your opinion.

PERSUASIVE

Writing Starting Your Essay

Students have a tendency to begin all their writing in a way that is comfortable to them, but sometimes boring to readers. Familiarize students with different beginnings by reading aloud sample beginning paragraphs from several published works. Try to include an example of each beginning style listed at the top of the page. Have students identify the "hook" in each introduction.

Have students explore a different way to write a **beginning paragraph** *(see below)*.

Be sure that students have included a clear opinion statement in their opening paragraph. Suggest that they exchange papers with a partner. Have the partner identify the opinion statement.

Teaching Tip: Beginning Paragraphs

- Have students fold a piece of paper in half, and then in half again. Have them open the paper to reveal four squares.
- Direct students to write four different beginning sentences—one in each square—for each style described in the pupil edition (interesting information, a question, a quote, a personal experience).

- Have students share all their sentences in a group to get feedback on which ones work best.

Writing
Developing the Middle Part

Students may find it helpful to think of the middle part of the essay as a group of separate persuasive paragraphs. Since they've already had experience writing single persuasive paragraphs, they should be able to write a series of paragraphs.

Use the sample to illustrate this idea. For each paragraph, have students point out

- the opinion statement (or topic sentence),
- transition words,
- three supporting reasons (facts and examples that support the opinion),
- a closing sentence that restates the opinion.

236

Writing Developing the Middle Part

After writing your opening paragraph, you are ready to develop the middle part of your essay. Each middle paragraph must present a reason that supports the opinion statement. Specific details are used to support each reason. As you move from paragraph to paragraph, be sure to use transitions like *besides, in addition,* and so on, to help the reader follow your argument. (See pages 572–573.)

The following middle paragraphs are from the persuasive essay about keeping art classes in school. Each paragraph has three parts:

Beginning
Middle
Ending

1 The **topic sentence** (underlined) states a reason that supports the opinion statement. Transitions are often used in topic sentences to tie the paragraphs together.

2 The **body** provides details that support the reason, including **facts** and **examples**.

3 The **closing sentence** summarizes the information in the paragraph.

Middle Paragraphs

The topic sentence states a reason.

The body provides facts and examples.

The closing sentence gives a summary.

Topic sentence

Art encourages people to be creative and try something new. In art, students make ceramics, paintings, and drawings. Even though art teachers give directions, students have the freedom to follow their imaginations. Students experiment and make mistakes as they try to capture their dreams using clay, paint, and paper. There is no better place for creative thinking than in an art class.

In addition, art is a fun way to learn more about other subjects. For example, students in

Body

social studies class study Native American culture by reading books and surfing the Internet. In art class, they work with leather to make pouches like Native Americans do. Students feel a personal connection with the Native American tribes they are studying. Hands-on projects are an important

Closing sentence

way for students to learn more about other subjects.

Topic sentence

Besides, school is the best place for many kids to make art. Some kinds of art require lots of special supplies like clay, glazes, canvases, paints,

Body

and brushes. These expensive materials and tools are provided in art classes. Many students can't afford to have these things at home. It would

Closing sentence

be unfair to take away the students' chance to explore different kinds of art.

Write your middle paragraphs. Make sure that each paragraph includes one reason that is supported with facts and examples.

Drafting Tips

- **Follow your prewriting** plan as you begin to write.
- **Provide details** that support your opinion statement and topic sentences.
- **Use a voice** that sounds confident and positive.
- **Write freely** and focus on arranging your ideas in the best order.

PERSUASIVE

Ask students to describe in their own words how the sample writer uses the middle paragraphs to build a convincing argument (by providing three good reasons that show how art classes are valuable to a wide range of students; by providing lots of facts and examples to support these reasons).

Writing **Drafting Tips**

Remind students that they are writing a first draft. At this point, their main goal should be to develop their ideas in an organized form. Encourage them to use the plan that they created during prewriting but not to feel bound by it. As they write, they may move ideas around, add new details, or eliminate others.

Remind students to
- begin each paragraph with a topic sentence that supports the opinion (they can underline the sentence if it will help them stay focused),
- use transitions to connect ideas and paragraphs (refer them to the list of transitions from the activity on TE page 233).

Writing **Ending Your Essay**

Tell students to think of the end of their persuasive essay as just the beginning for their readers. The end should make their readers want to do something or believe something from now on.

Discuss the call-to-action examples and ask what each encourages readers to do or believe. Ask students to share any examples of calls to action they may have responded to in their own life (or refer to TE page 234), and discuss how all of these examples represent a beginning of sorts (for example, the call to action to clean up the neighborhood means the participants will begin their effort to organize and enlist volunteers. Evenutally they will begin the cleanup process).

Students should check to make sure that their call to action encourages readers to do or believe something.

238

Writing **Ending Your Essay**

The ending of your persuasive essay may be a good place to address a possible concern or objection to your opinion. It's also a good place to restate your opinion and make a call to action. A call to action encourages the reader to do something or to think a certain way.

Beginning

Middle

▶ **Ending**

Examples of a call to action

- Help save our energy resources by walking or riding a bike.
- Join us at the rally to save music in our schools.
- Don't let your pet run loose.

Ending Paragraph

| An objection is addressed (underlined), and the opinion is stated again.

The call to action encourages the reader to think about the problem. | *I know that some schools have money problems. But instead of cutting subjects, schools should think of ways to raise money to keep art classes. Art connects everything else we learn. It's hard to imagine a school dropping reading or math, but our school board plans to drop art class. We need to stand together against this, or it might actually happen. I don't want to live in a world without art, do you?* |

Write your ending. Write the last paragraph of your essay. Remember to state your opinion again and make a call to action. Also try to include a strong final sentence.

Form a complete first draft. Write a complete copy of your essay. Skip every other line if you write it by hand or double-space if you use a computer. This will give you room for revising.

English Language Learners

Students may have difficulty with the idiom *call to action*. Be sure they understand that it is a statement that urges the reader to say, "Yes! I agree!" and perhaps, "I want to do something to show my support!"

Struggling Learners

Have students answer the following three questions in order to determine whether or not a call to action is appropriate:

1) Who is your intended audience?
2) Is your call to action realistic for this audience?
3) What is the likelihood that your call to action will result in the desired outcome?

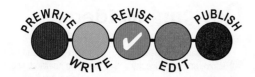

persuade convince support 239
argue reason
Promoting a Cause

Revising

A first draft can usually be improved in a number of ways. Paragraphs may need to be shifted around, and parts of the argument may need to be clearer. You revise your writing in order to fix problems like these.

Keys to Effective Revising

1. Read through your entire draft to get a feeling of how well your essay works.

2. Make sure your focus statement states your topic clearly.

3. Check your paragraphs to make sure your topic sentences support your focus statement and your details support your topic sentences.

4. Fine-tune your voice to sound confident and convincing.

5. Check your words and sentences.

6. Use the editing and proofreading marks inside the back cover of this book.

PERSUASIVE

Revising
Keys to Effective Revising

The Keys to Effective Revising lays out the process students will be guided through on PE pages 240–250.

- Invite volunteers to describe how they have applied one or more of these revision strategies to previous writing assignments and how these strategies have helped to improve their final product.

- Encourage students to share any personal revising tips that they think might be helpful here. Be sure to offer any tips of your own, too.

- Suggest that students use colored pencils to make revisions throughout the revising process. Tell them to make revisions for each trait in a different color. For example, when revising for ideas, they can use a green pencil. When revising for organization, they can use a pink pencil, and so on.

Depending on your students' familiarity with the traits and their level of expertise in writing, you may or may not want to have students revise their first drafts for all the traits. You may want to focus on just one or two traits for any particular form of writing.

Revising for Ideas

The rubric strips that run across all of the revising PE pages (240–250) are provided to help students focus their revising and are related to the full rubric on PE pages 256–257.

After reading the page, have students review the rubric strip on PE pages 240–241. Direct students to look in their drafts for

- a strong opinion supported by sensible, supportable reasons;
- qualifiers (terms such as *most* and *usually* that make ideas easy to support).

 Answers

1. **Take it or leave it.** Possible revision: Metal detectors will make this school feel like a prison.
2. **Jumping to conclusions.** Possible revision: Our pep band didn't raise much money this year, which might suggest that people don't appreciate us.
3. **Bandwagoning.** Possible revision: Some people believe that restaurant food is healthier than cafeteria food.

240

Revising for Ideas

6 The ideas in my essay inform and convince my reader.

5 I persuade my reader by using qualifiers and avoiding fuzzy thinking.

4 I use qualifiers, but I need to clear up some of my fuzzy thinking.

When you revise for *ideas*, you want to make sure your opinion and supporting reasons are sensible and can be supported. It's easier to support an opinion if you use *qualifiers*—terms such as *most* and *usually*. (See page 241 for more.) The rubric above can guide you.

How can I recognize "fuzzy thinking" in my writing?

You have used fuzzy thinking when an idea is misleading and cannot be fairly supported. Here are three types of fuzzy thinking to watch for.

Jumping to Conclusions

Avoid using one small fact to reach a big conclusion.

> **Last year, a kid got sick after lunch, so cafeteria food isn't healthy.**

Bandwagoning

Avoid using a group's opinion as if it were the truth.

> **None of my classmates think that metal detectors make schools safer.**

Take It, or Leave It

Avoid statements that don't leave room for discussion.

> **Either the pep band will sell 1,000 pizzas, or it will never play again.**

 Read the following examples. Then identify the type of fuzzy thinking each one contains. How could it be improved?

1. Either the principal will remove the metal detectors, or this school will be a prison.
2. Our pep band didn't raise much money this year, so nobody appreciates us.
3. Everybody knows that restaurant food is healthier than cafeteria food.

 Revise fuzzy thinking. Review your essay and look for places where you have used fuzzy thinking. Revise your writing to fix whatever "thinking" errors you find.

---

persuade convince *support*
argue reason **241**
Promoting a Cause

3 I need to use more qualifiers and improve my thinking.

2 I don't use qualifiers, and my thinking is not well supported.

1 I need to learn more about qualifiers and avoid fuzzy thinking.

How can qualifiers make my ideas easier to support?

Ideas that suggest "all" or "nothing" are difficult to support. That's why qualifiers are so important in persuasive writing. Read the two ideas below. Notice the qualifier in the second sentence.

Students in study hall can't work because of lunchroom noise.

Many **students in study hall can't work because of lunchroom noise.**

The qualifier "many" limits the idea, making it easier to support. Other helpful qualifiers include *most, often, usually, some,* and *in many cases.*

Try It Rewrite the following four statements. Add a different qualifier to each one.

1. Students think teachers assign too much homework.
2. Classrooms are crowded.
3. Students don't work hard.
4. Parents are too busy to help with homework.

Revise "all-or-nothing" ideas. Look for ideas that are difficult to support. Add qualifiers to limit these ideas.

Ideas
Fuzzy thinking is fixed, and a qualifier is added.

When the school board ~~cuts art class, every~~ *is planning to cut*

~~student artist will quit.~~ But this is wrong.

Schools should keep art classes. *in our district*

Art encourages people to be creative and . . .

PERSUASIVE

Qualifiers are important because they prevent writers and speakers from making generalizations that cannot be supported. Generalizations make a claim about a whole group that may be true for some but not for everyone.

Ask students which of these statements makes a more convincing argument for an adult. Why?

- Everyone in my class is allowed to stay up past 10:00 PM.
- I'm the only person who has to go to bed at 9:30 PM.
- Several of my friends are allowed to stay up past 10:00 PM.

Appropriate qualifiers make an argument more realistic, not so exaggerated.

✳ See more about qualifiers on PE pages 734 and 736.

Try It Answers

Possible answers:
1. Students usually think teachers assign too much homework.
2. Many classrooms are crowded.
3. Students often don't work hard enough.
4. Some parents are too busy to help with homework.

Review the use of editing and proofreading marks as shown at the bottom of PE page 241 and on the inside back cover.

English Language Learners

Pair students with partners who are proficient in English to orally complete the **Try It** activity. Then provide some simple all-or-nothing statements, such as *Eat spinach or you'll be weak; Be in bed by 8:30 or you'll fall asleep in class the next day.* Have students rewrite the sentences using qualifiers so that they are more sensible.

Struggling Learners

Guide struggling learners in using the rubric strips to self-score their own work. Have them practice by scoring an earlier piece of their writing or on a piece of writing by an anonymous writer.

Revising for Organization

After reading the basic instruction with students, discuss the rubric strip. Have students review their writing by looking for

- transitions within paragraphs,
- transitions between paragraphs.

As students revise, suggest that they circle transition words and phrases within and between paragraphs. This will help them identify where they may still need transitions to clarify ideas and to show how ideas are related.

To evaluate how well all their ideas flow, students can participate in **peer conferences** *(see below)*.

Have partners take turns reading aloud the **Try It** paragraphs to each other. After one partner reads the first paragraph, partners should discuss specifically where the lack of transitions makes ideas difficult to relate and understand. As the other reads aloud the paragraph with the transitions, partners should listen for and then discuss the difference in clarity.

242

Revising **for Organization**

6 My organization makes my essay logical and convincing.

5 My transitions connect my reasons well from beginning to end.

4 I use some transitions within each paragraph, but I need to link my paragraphs.

When you check your essay's *organization*, look for a smooth flow of ideas both within each paragraph and from one paragraph to the next.

How can I check the transitions in my paragraphs?

To check a paragraph for transitions, read it carefully, making certain that each sentence moves logically into the next.

 Read both paragraphs below. The first paragraph does not have transitions; the second one does. The transitions in the second one help the reader understand how the details relate to each other.

WITHOUT TRANSITION WORDS AND PHRASES

Kids who grow up in the city should go to a wilderness summer camp at least once. Kids will learn survival skills. They will learn how to purify water, to keep warm, and to stay calm during an emergency. Camping in the wilderness gives kids many new experiences and teaches them that not all wildlife is dangerous. Kids will come to enjoy and respect the world of nature.

WITH TRANSITION WORDS AND PHRASES

Kids who grow up in the city should go to a wilderness summer camp at least once. First of all, kids will learn survival skills. For example, they will learn how to purify water, to keep warm, and to stay calm during an emergency. Also, camping in the wilderness gives kids many new experiences and teaches them that not all wildlife is dangerous. As a result, kids will come to enjoy and respect the world of nature.

 Connect your sentences. Review each paragraph in your essay. Do you need to add a few transitions to show how your details relate to each other? Make any needed changes. See pages 572–573 for a list of transitions.

Peer conferences provide students with an opportunity to share their work with fellow students and receive immediate feedback. Since peers have been dealing with the same writing issues, they may have new insights to offer. Take time to review the guidelines (see PE pages 29–32) on how to offer helpful and appropriate feedback before pairs or small groups of students discuss their writing.

English Language Learners

Students may need help understanding *flow of ideas* and *logically*. To illustrate, have them think of a train. Each car follows another in a smooth sequence. Similarly, in a piece of writing that has a smooth flow of ideas, each sentence flows, or follows, in a pattern that is arranged logically, or, stated more simply, "in a way that makes sense."

persuade convince *support*
argue reason
Promoting a Cause **243**

| **3** I need to use transitions within my paragraphs and between my paragraphs. | **2** My beginning, middle, and ending run together. I need to create paragraphs. | **1** My organization is unclear, and I need to learn how to use transitions. |

How can transitions link my paragraphs?

Transitions can help show how the ideas in one paragraph are related to the ideas in others. Read the topic sentences below from a persuasive essay about improving a neighborhood playground. As you'll see, the transitions (in blue) show how the paragraphs' ideas are related.

> To begin with, **the playground at 6th Street and Rio Grande is a health hazard.**
>
> In addition, **the playground is an eyesore.**
>
> Finally, **fixing up the playground will send a positive message to neighborhood kids.**

Try It Read the following topic sentences from a persuasive essay about tutoring. Rewrite them, adding transitions that help show how the ideas are related. Choose from the following transitions: *First of all, Also, In addition, As a result,* and *Lastly.*

1. A tutoring program could help struggling students.
2. Tutoring would give teachers a break.
3. The program would let advanced students share what they know.

Organization
A transition is added between paragraphs.

> *Besides,*
> ∧*School is the best place for many kids to make art. Some kinds of art require lots of special supplies like clay, glazes, canvases, paints, and . . .*

PERSUASIVE

Encourage students to use the rubric strips to self-score their draft both before and after they make revisions.

After reading through the sample sentences, ask volunteers to offer other possible transition words and phrases to replace the ones shown in blue.

 Answers

Possible answers:
1. First of all, a tutoring program could help struggling students.
2. In addition, tutoring would give teachers a break.
3. Lastly, the program would let advanced students share what they know.

Advanced Learners

Pair advanced learners with students who need help with transitions. The advanced learners can check the essays for transition words/phrases and make suggestions where transitions would be helpful.

Revising for Voice

Remind students that voice is simply how the writer sounds to readers. The best way for students to figure out if their writing sounds confident is to read it aloud to a partner or a small group.

■ Listeners should be ready to point out any words and phrases that are uncertain or wishy-washy. (Make sure that students understand the difference between unsure language and qualifiers.)

■ Listeners should also be prepared to offer suggestions to help writers achieve a more confident voice.

Try It Answers

1. Possible; might be. possible revision: Another good reason for learning to swim is that swimming is an enjoyable activity.

2. Probably, might be, hopefully. possible revision: Public pools are often open to swimmers for a reasonable cost.

244

Revising for Voice

6 My voice is confident, positive, and convincing throughout the essay.

5 My voice is generally confident, positive, and convincing.

4 My voice is confident, but I need to use more positive words.

When you revise for *voice*, check to see how your essay sounds. You should try to sound confident and positive. The rubric above will guide you.

How can I make my voice sound confident?

You can make your writing voice sound confident by removing words that make you sound unsure about your ideas. Read the two examples below. The first one contains words (in blue) that make the writing sound unsure. The second example sounds much more confident.

> **UNSURE WRITING VOICE**
>
> Probably it would be a good idea if **students could learn to swim before they graduate from high school.** It seems like **there are many reasons for learning how to swim. Swimming is** supposed to be **a great all-around exercise**.

> **CONFIDENT WRITING VOICE**
>
> **Students should learn to swim before they graduate from high school. There are many reasons for learning how to swim. Swimming is a great all-around exercise.**

 Identify the words in the following sentences that make the writer sound unsure. Then rewrite each one to sound more confident.

1. Another possible reason for learning to swim would be that it can be an activity that might be enjoyable.

2. Probably you might be able to swim at a public pool for a cost that is hopefully reasonable.

 Check your voice. Review your essay for words that make you sound unsure of yourself. Sometimes it is necessary to qualify your ideas, but using too many qualifiers will make you sound unsure.

English Language Learners

Students may not understand why the highlighted phrases in the first model paragraph create an unsure writing voice. Emphasize the strengthening that takes place when the paragraph is revised. Then make the **Try It** activity an oral exercise in which students make suggested changes and then discuss why each one strengthens the original statement.

Promoting a Cause 245

3 At times my voice sounds confident, but I use some overly negative words.

2 I need to sound confident and avoid overly negative words.

1 I need to understand how to create a confident and positive voice.

How can I make my writing sound positive?

You can make persuasive writing sound positive by avoiding overly negative words. Always use strong, positive words to motivate your reader to agree with you.

 Find and replace overly negative words and phrases in each of the following sentences.

1. Our school doesn't give a rip about the marching band.
Our school doesn't care enough about the marching band.

2. Kids who don't exercise will turn into blobs.

3. You're a dummy if you don't pay attention in school.

4. The rule against hats in school is ridiculous.

 Revise for voice. Review your persuasive essay for overly negative words. Replace those words and phrases that are so negative they change the voice of the essay.

Voice
Negative words are replaced, and uncertain words are cut.

> can't afford
> Many students ~~are too broke~~ to have these things
> It would be ∧
> at home. ~~Maybe it might be a little bit~~ unfair to
> ∧
> take away the students' chance to explore different
>
> kinds of art.
>
>   I know that some schools have money . . .

PERSUASIVE

Point out to students that using overly negative or **colloquial language** *(see below)* in their essays may make readers think that they are not serious or knowledgeable about the cause. Stress that although students' writing should sound natural, their word choice should reflect a serious, knowledgeable tone.

Try It Answers

Possible answers:

1. Our school doesn't care enough about the marching band.
2. Children who don't exercise may become overweight.
3. You are the one who may lose out in the end if you don't pay attention in school.
4. Many of us think that the rule against hats in school is unreasonable.

Teaching Tip: Colloquial Language

Remind students that overly negative or colloquial language (familiar, localized language) may not be appropriate for their audience or purpose, even if such language does sound natural to them. Remind students to keep their audience in mind as they revise for voice. They should ask themselves:

- How might my audience react to this language?
- Will my audience be inspired by my voice?
- Will my audience disregard my ideas because of my voice?

English Language Learners

Comic books appeal because they offer visual support as students learn to read. However, because the text is predominantly dialogue, students can learn more colloquial and idiomatic language than is appropriate for formal writing. Have students bring in examples of comic books they might read, and work with them to create more formal language for some of the text.

Revising for Word Choice

Students may not see that they've repeated a word too often, but they'll be able to *hear* it.

- Have students record their essays into a tape recorder.
- Have them play back the essays and listen for repeated words.
- Suggest that students read their essay softly to themself or aloud to a partner. Usually, repeated words stand out right away after listening to the writing.

✱ Find out more about using pronouns to avoid repeating nouns on PE pages 476–479.

After students discuss the sample paragraph and read the instructions, have them complete the **Try It** exercise independently. Point out that if they cannot think of a synonym to replace a repeated word, they can use a thesaurus or synonym finder for help.

Try IT Answers

Answers may vary. Possible answers:
1. members of the council
2. lively, exhilarating
3. collect

246

Revising for Word Choice

6 The words I use in my essay are strong and help persuade the reader.	**5** No word is repeated too often, and I use specific adjectives.	**4** No word is repeated too often, but I could use a few more specific adjectives.

When you revise for *word choice*, you want to make sure your words keep the reader's attention and express your persuasive message. Use the rubric above to help you revise the words in your essay.

Do I repeat any words too often?

To find out if you have repeated some words too often, carefully read your essay. You can replace repeated words by using pronouns and synonyms. As you read the paragraph below, notice the effect of repeating one word over and over again.

> **People can use computers to connect with the outside world. For example, people (they) can meet new people (friends) in chat rooms. People can also play games, like chess, with people (other players) all over the world.**

Now read the paragraph again, substituting the words in parentheses. Did you notice a difference?

 Read the following examples. Then copy the sentences on your own paper, replacing the boldfaced words with pronouns or synonyms.

1. The student council is sponsoring a mock election. Earlier this week, **the student council** handed out information sheets.
2. Pep band is exciting! Not only do the students get to choose **exciting** music, but they have an **exciting** time jamming.
3. The sixth graders **gather** toys for a holiday drive. They **gather** video games, action figures, and board games.

 Check for repeated words. Read your essay and look for repeated words. Replace them with pronouns or synonyms.

Struggling Learners

Write the words *I, we, they, he, she,* and *people* on the board. Have students locate and circle these commonly repeated words in their writing. Next have them decide which to keep because it is clear who they refer to, and which to replace with nouns. Then have them check for repetition of other words.

persuade convince *support*
argue reason
Promoting a Cause **247**

3 I need to replace some words with synonyms and pronouns. I could use more specific adjectives.

2 I repeat many words and use general adjectives. I need to replace them.

1 I need to learn how to use synonyms, pronouns, and specific adjectives.

Do I use too many general adjectives?

Your adjectives should help send a specific message to the reader. Try to avoid weak words like *nice, good,* and *bad.*

 Study the pairs of sentences below. Which sentence in each pair sends a clear, specific message? Explain your choices.

1. a. The morning announcements contain good information.
  b. The morning announcements contain valuable information.

2. a. That new girl is nice.
  b. That new girl is friendly.

3. a. The pencil sharpener made a bad sound.
  b. The pencil sharpener made a clawing sound.

4. a. Tanya's little brother is interesting.
  b. Tanya's little brother is clever.

 Check your adjectives. Replace any general adjectives with adjectives that send clear, specific messages.

Word Choice
A general adjective and repeated words are replaced.

> Take away ~~good~~ colorful paintings, metal sculptures, and
> beautiful photographs. ~~Take away~~ Erase the artwork from
> book covers, magazine ads, and comic books. I don't
> want to live in a world without art, but I might . . .

PERSUASIVE

Create a "Word Wall for Overused Words."

- Write the words *nice, good, bad, happy, sad, glad,* and *mad* across the board.
- Challenge groups of students to list several clearer, more precise synonyms for each word.
- Ask volunteers to transfer the lists to a large piece of chart paper.
- Display the chart in the class-room so students can refer to it whenever they write.

Do the **Try It** activity together to be sure students understand why the correct responses are clearer and more specific.

Try It Answers

1. b. The word *valuable* suggests the information is important and useful. *Good* information could be any information that isn't bad.
2. b. The word *friendly* suggests the girl is warm and open. *Nice* just says she's not mean.
3. b. A *clawing* sound suggests a low, scratchy sound. A *bad* sound could be anything unpleasant.
4. b. The word *clever* suggests that a person is bright, imaginative, and inventive. A person could be *interesting* for any number of reasons, which makes it vague.

Revising for Sentence Fluency

Review the rubric strip for revising for sentence fluency and have students rate their first draft. Then discuss the example sentences. Make sure students understand the differences between the sentence types before having them do the **Try It** activity on their own.

 Answers

1. complex
2. simple
3. compound

To help students keep track of the sentence types they have used in their essays, suggest that they create a sentence variety profile:

- Have students write above each sentence in a paragraph: *S* for simple, *C* for compound, and *CX* for complex.
- Transfer the sentence labels to a separate sheet of paper, under the heads *Paragraph 1, Paragraph 2,* and so on.
- If they see too many *S*s together in any one paragraph, or if there are no *C*s or *CX*s in a paragraph, they will know that they have to revise for fluency.

248

Revising for Sentence Fluency

6 My sentences flow smoothly, and people will enjoy reading them.

5 I use a variety of sentences that flow smoothly.

4 I use simple and compound sentences, but I need some complex sentences.

When you revise for *sentence fluency*, you need to make sure you have used a variety of sentence types. If you use too many simple sentences, your writing may sound monotonous. The rubric above can help you.

Have I used a variety of sentence types?

You can check your writing for sentence variety by seeing how many simple, compound, and complex sentences you use. (See pages 515–517.)

- A **simple sentence** is a subject and predicate forming one complete thought.

  The school board is planning to cut art class.

- A **compound sentence** is two simple sentences joined by a comma and a coordinating conjunction such as *and, but, or, so, for,* or *yet.*

  I don't want to live in a world without art, but I might have to.

- A **complex sentence** is a simple sentence plus a clause beginning with a subordinating conjunction such as *when, after, because,* or *as.*

  Students experiment and make mistakes as they try to capture their dreams using clay, paint, and paper.

 Read the following sentences. For each one, identify whether it is simple, compound, or complex.

1. When people in the cafeteria are too noisy, students in study hall can't work.
2. Bellwood needs a different study hall.
3. It's hard to concentrate, and the smell of food is distracting.

Check your sentence variety. Read each paragraph of your essay. How many simple, compound, and complex sentences do you have in each one? If too many simple sentences appear together, rewrite some of them as compound or complex sentences. (See pages 515–517.)

English Language Learners

Provide extra help by writing simpler examples of the kinds of sentences on the board and then working with students to analyze the sentence parts (Possible sentences: Keesha spoke with the principal. The principal listened to her, but he couldn't change the schedule. After he attended the school board meeting, there was a change in the schedule.)

Struggling Learners

If students haven't used colored pencils on this draft, they can use a simplified method of tracking the sentence types in their essays. Have students underline sentences in three different colors to represent the three sentence types. This will make it obvious whenever one sentence type is used too often or too infrequently.

3 In some places, I use too many simple sentences. I need to combine some of them.

2 My writing has too many simple sentences. I need to combine many of them.

1 Most of my sentences need to be rewritten.

How can I improve my sentence variety?

You can improve your sentence variety by combining simple sentences in a number of ways. You can use a conjunction like *and, but, or, so, for,* or *yet* to form a compound sentence. You can also use a subordinating conjunction like *when, after, because,* or *as* to make a complex sentence.

> **TWO SIMPLE SENTENCES**
>
> The cafeteria is too loud. The sound fills the study hall.
>
> **ONE COMPOUND SENTENCE**
>
> The cafeteria is too loud, and the sound fills the study hall.
>
> **ONE COMPLEX SENTENCE**
>
> When the cafeteria is too loud, the sound fills the study hall.

 Combine each pair of simple sentences using the first word in parentheses. Then combine the pairs again using the second word.

1. People in the cafeteria are rude. Students in study hall struggle to work. (*so, when*)

2. The principal is looking for solutions. She knows this is a problem (*for, because*)

 Combine simple sentences. If you have too many simple sentences together, combine a few into compound or complex sentences.

Sentence Fluency
Sentences are joined.

> It's hard to imagine a school dropping reading or
> ~~but~~
> math, Øur school board plans to drop art . . .
> 𝒷,∖

Before having students complete the **Try It,** offer them some additional practice combining simple sentences. Write on the board the sentences shown below, and encourage students to suggest different combinations for compound or complex sentences.

- The gym equipment is old. Pieces of it are always falling off or breaking.
- The streets are filled with litter. It looks like no one cares about the neighborhood.
- Families want to be able to play outdoors. Parents don't want to have their children playing in dirty parks.

Some students may also want to share sets of simple sentences from their own drafts to get suggestions for ways to combine them.

Try It Answers

1. People in the cafeteria are rude, so students in study hall struggle to work./When people in the cafeteria are rude, students in study hall struggle to work.

2. The principal is looking for solutions, for she knows this is a problem./Because the principal knows this is a problem, she is looking for solutions.

PERSUASIVE

Struggling Learners

Students who have trouble evaluating the fluency of their sentences should read their essay into a tape recorder and then listen to the tape. Students may mean to say something other than what they've actually written, so unless they hear how it sounds, they often convince themselves that it sounds fine. (This is why, when someone else reads their work aloud, students tend to blame the reader for not reading it correctly.)

Revising Using a Checklist

Students will have a tendency to answer *yes* to all the questions in the checklist, so do not have them use the checklist until they have completed the revising steps on pages 240–250.

If students are writing the essay as an in-class assignment, provide time for them to make a clean draft. You may again want to re-mind them to double-space their drafts to make it easy to edit their work.

250

Revising Using a Checklist

 Check your revising. On a piece of paper, write the numbers 1 to 12. If you can answer "yes" to a question, put a check mark after that number. If not, continue to work with that part of your essay.

Ideas

_____ **1.** Do I focus on an interesting cause?

_____ **2.** Have I corrected any "fuzzy thinking" in my essay?

_____ **3.** Do I use qualifiers to make ideas easier to support?

Organization

_____ **4.** Do I include a beginning, a middle, and an ending?

_____ **5.** Do I use transitions within and between paragraphs?

_____ **6.** Have I reorganized parts that were out of place?

Voice

_____ **7.** Does my voice sound confident and positive?

_____ **8.** Does my voice fit my audience? My purpose? My topic?

Word Choice

_____ **9.** Have I replaced repeated words with synonyms and pronouns?

_____ **10.** Do I use strong adjectives and verbs?

Sentence Fluency

_____ **11.** Do I use different sentence types?

_____ **12.** Have I fixed short, choppy sentences by combining them?

 Make a clean copy. When you've finished revising, make a clean copy before you edit. This makes checking for conventions easier.

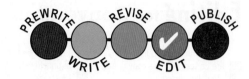

Promoting a Cause **251**

Editing

After you've finished revising your essay, it's time to edit it for your use of conventions: punctuation, capitalization, spelling, and grammar.

Keys to Effective Editing

1. Use a dictionary, a thesaurus, and the "Proofreader's Guide" in the back of this book.

2. Check for any words or phrases that may be confusing to the reader.

3. Check your writing for correctness of punctuation, capitalization, spelling, and grammar.

4. If you are using a computer, edit on a printed computer copy. Then enter your changes on the computer.

5. Use the editing and proofreading marks inside the back cover of this book.

PERSUASIVE

Editing **Keys to Effective Editing**

The Keys to Effective Editing lays out the process students will be guided through on pages 252–254.

- Be sure to have copies of dictionaries and thesauruses on hand as students edit.

- If necessary, review with students the page of Editing and Proofreading Marks on the inside back cover of the student edition.

- Caution those students who are using a computer not to rely solely on the word processor's spell checker to catch all their spelling mistakes. Point out that spell checkers do not catch words that are spelled correctly but used incorrectly. The computer will not catch the following types of errors:
  - ☐ if you use *too* instead of *to*
  - ☐ if you use *buy* instead of *by*
  - ☐ if you type *form* instead of *from*

Editing for Conventions

After reviewing the Editing for Conventions rubric strip and discussing the instruction for comparative and superlative forms, have students work independently or with a partner to complete the **Try It** activity.

✱ See PE page 487 for more instruction on comparative and superlative forms.

 **Answers**

Answers will vary but sentences should use the following forms of the words: wilder/wildest, more or less difficult/most or least difficult, quicker/quickest.

252

Editing for Conventions

6 My grammar and punctuation are correct, and the copy is free of spelling errors.

5 I have a few minor errors in punctuation, spelling, or grammar.

4 I need to correct some errors in punctuation, spelling, and grammar.

When you edit for *conventions*, you should focus on grammar, spelling, and punctuation. Use the rubric above to guide your editing.

How do I check comparative and superlative words?

The comparative form of an adjective compares two people, places, things, or ideas. (Also see pages **487** and **734.4**.)

■ One way to create the comparative form is to add the suffix *er* to a word.

  Toshi has a big **dog, but Lupe's dog is** bigger.

■ If the word has two or more syllables, add the word *more* to make it comparative.

  However, Lupe's dog is more annoying **than Toshi's.**

The superlative form of an adjective compares three or more people, places, things, or ideas. (See pages **487** and **734.5**.)

■ One way to make the superlative form is to add the suffix *est*.

  My sister has the biggest **gerbil I've ever seen.**

■ If the word has two or more syllables, use the word *most* to create the superlative form.

  Ravi is the most enthusiastic **pet owner I've ever seen.**

 Number your paper from 1 to 6. For each of the words below, write two sentences: one using its comparative form and one using its superlative form.

  wild   difficult   quick

 Check for comparatives and superlatives. Edit your paper to make sure you used the proper form for any comparatives or superlatives.

English Language Learners

Students learning English often have difficulty understanding when to use comparatives or superlatives. Provide groups of three pictures for extra practice. For example, display pictures of a large car, an elephant, and a building. Then work with students to create sentences such as *The elephant is bigger than the car* and *The building is the biggest thing of all*. Be sure to practice also with comparatives and superlatives requiring *more* and *most,* such as *This book was more exciting than that one,* but *this book was the most exciting book I ever read.*

persuade convince *support*
argue *reason*
Promoting a Cause 253

3 I need to correct errors that may confuse the reader.

2 I need to correct many errors that make my essay difficult to read.

1 I need help making corrections.

How do I know when to capitalize an adjective?

You need to capitalize proper adjectives, which are formed from proper nouns. The common noun it modifies is not capitalized. (See page **618.1**.)

PROPER NOUN	PROPER ADJECTIVE + COMMON NOUN
Shetland Islands	Shetland pony
Yorkshire, England	Yorkshire terrier
Canada	Canada goose

If the adjective is not proper, it is not capitalized.

potbellied **pig**   bald **eagle**

Try It Number your paper from 1 to 4. In each sentence, if an adjective needs a capital letter, write the correction on your paper.

1. Anthony's pet python came from the amazon jungle.

2. He could have had a plain old garden snake.

3. Kylee wanted a tasmanian devil.

4. I'd be happy with an arabian horse for a pet.

 Edit for conventions. Check your paper to make sure you have capitalized any proper adjectives.

Conventions
A proper adjective is capitalized.

Students feel a personal connection with the native american tribes they are studying. Hands-on projects are an important way for . . .

PERSUASIVE

The proper adjectives on the PE page are based on proper nouns that name places. Students may also be familiar with proper adjectives that are based on people's names, some of which have an adjective form and others of which are not changed:

- Shakespearean plays
- Monroe Doctrine

✱ For additional information about capitalizing proper nouns and adjectives see PE page 618.

After students complete the **Try It** activity, review their answers with them. Ask them to tell the proper noun from which the proper adjectives were formed in items 1 (Amazon), 3 (Tasmania), and 4 (Arabia).

Try It Answers

1. Amazon
2. Correct
3. Tasmanian
4. Arabian

English Language Learners

Students may require extra help with common and proper nouns. Pair them with cooperative, proficient partners and have them play a "Categories" game. Provide a worksheet that contains a 3-column chart. Label the columns *Category, Common Noun, Proper Noun*. Then, provide ideas for the category column, such as *foods, animals, games, kinds of dogs*. Have partners work together to provide examples to fill in the chart. Make sure that they use correct capitalization for proper nouns.

Struggling Learners

Point out that proper nouns name specific people, places, things, or ideas, and they, too, are capitalized. Have students capitalize the proper adjectives in these phrases:

- a cuban band (Cuban)
- his german shepherd (German)
- thanksgiving vacation (Thanksgiving)

Editing Using a Checklist

Give students a few moments to look over the Proofreader's Guide in the back of the pupil edition. Throughout the year, they can refer to the instruction, rules, and examples to clarify any checklist items or to resolve questions about their own writing.

Suggest that students make a separate pass for each stage of the editing process.

- First read through the essay to find punctuation mistakes.
- Then read to find mistakes in grammar. Pay special attention to make sure comparative and superlative forms are used correctly.
- Finally, look for mistakes in spelling.

Adding a Title

Students may think it's odd that they add the title near the end of the writing process even though it's the first thing readers see. Ask:

Why does adding the title at the end make more sense than writing it first? (At the end, students understand the entire piece more clearly. They may have gone in a new or different direction from what they planned.)

254

Editing Using a Checklist

 Check your editing. On a piece of paper, write the numbers 1 to 13. If you can answer "yes" to a question, put a check mark after that number. If not, continue to edit for that convention.

Conventions

PUNCTUATION

_____ **1.** Do I use end punctuation after all my sentences?
_____ **2.** Do I use commas after introductory phrases and transitions?
_____ **3.** Do I use commas between items in a series?
_____ **4.** Do I use commas in compound sentences?
_____ **5.** Do I use quotation marks around any direct quotations?

CAPITALIZATION

_____ **6.** Do I start all my sentences with capital letters?
_____ **7.** Do I capitalize all proper nouns and proper adjectives?

SPELLING

_____ **8.** Have I spelled all my words correctly?
_____ **9.** Have I double-checked the words my spell-checker may have missed?

GRAMMAR

_____ **10.** Do I form comparative and superlative forms correctly?
_____ **11.** Do I use correct forms of verbs (_had gone_, not _had went_)?
_____ **12.** Do my subjects and verbs agree in number? (She and I _are_ going, not She and I _is_ going)?
_____ **13.** Do I use the right words (_to, too, two_)?

Adding a Title

- Restate the call to action: **Shelter the Animals**
- Write a slogan: **Let's Band Together**
- Be creative: **Wherefore Art Thou, Art?**

Advanced Learners

Invite students to share any strategy they use to catch spelling errors. One strategy is to review the essay from finish to start. This forces the editor to focus on each word.

persuade convince *support*
argue reason
Promoting a Cause **255**

Publishing Sharing Your Essay

After you have worked so hard to write and improve your essay, make a neat final copy to share. You may also present your persuasive essay as an editorial, a speech, or a multimedia presentation.

Make a final copy. Follow your teacher's instructions or use the guidelines below to format your essay. (If you are using a computer, see page 60.) Create a clean final copy of your essay and carefully proofread it.

Focus on Presentation

- Use blue or black ink and write neatly.
- Write your name in the upper left corner of page 1.
- Skip a line and center your title; skip another line and start your writing.
- Indent every paragraph and leave a one-inch margin on all four sides.
- Write your last name and the page number in the upper right corner of every page after the first one.

Give a Speech

Present your persuasive essay to your classmates in the form of a speech. See pages 423–430 for more information about preparing a speech.

Submit to a Newspaper

Follow the paper's instructions for submitting an essay to your local or school newspaper.

Create a Multimedia Presentation

Turn your persuasive essay into a multimedia presentation. See pages 411–415 for more information.

PERSUASIVE

Publishing Sharing Your Essay

Students will work hard to turn in a neat, final copy of their essay, so it can be discouraging for them to have it returned covered with red correction marks. When reviewing a student's final essay, consider writing your comments on an attachment (such as the Assessment Sheet on TE page 799) or reserving critical comments for a conference. At that time you can address any problems in the essay using the Rubric for Persuasive Writing found on PE pages 256–257. This will help students retain pride in their work, while helping them grow as writers.

Encourage students to develop their own ideas for publishing. Remind them that visuals (e.g., illustrations, charts and graphs, dioramas, posters) can add impact and make their call to action more powerful and effective.

Provide space and time for students to present their essay.

Advanced Learners

Encourage students whose essays relate to community, environment, or school-related causes, to submit their essay to the local newspaper's "Letters to the Editor" page (see Submit to a Newspaper above). They also should receive parental permission prior to submission.

Rubric for
Persuasive Writing

A rubric is a chart that helps students evaluate their writing. The rubrics in this book are based on a 6-point scale, in which a score of 6 indicates an amazing piece of writing and a score of 1 means the writing is incomplete and not ready to be assessed. The rubric covers the basic traits of writing—ideas, organization, voice, word choice, sentence fluency, and conventions.

Rubrics can guide students as they write because the rubrics tell what elements to include in a piece of writing and how to present them.

✱ Four- and five-point rubrics for persuasive writing can be found on TE pages 770 and 774.

256

Rubric for Persuasive Writing

Use this rubric for guiding and assessing your persuasive writing. Refer to it whenever you want to improve your writing using the six traits.

Ideas

6 The clear reasoning informs and convinces the reader.

5 The essay has a clear opinion statement. Logical reasons support the writer's opinion.

4 The opinion statement is clear, and most reasons support the writer's opinion.

Organization

6 The organization logically presents a smooth flow of ideas from beginning to end.

5 The opening contains the opinion statement. The middle provides clear support. The transitions build strong connections.

4 The opening contains the opinion statement. The middle provides support. Some transitions do not work.

Voice

6 The writer's voice is confident, positive, and completely convincing.

5 The writer's voice is confident and helps persuade the reader.

4 The writer's voice is confident. It needs to persuade the reader.

Word Choice

6 Strong, engaging, positive words contribute to the main message. Every word counts.

5 Strong, positive words help make the message clear.

4 Strong, positive words are used, but some overused words need synonyms.

Sentence Fluency

6 The sentences flow smoothly, and people will enjoy reading the variety of sentences.

5 Variety is seen in both the types of sentences and their beginnings.

4 Varied sentence beginnings are used. Sentence variety would make the essay more interesting to read.

Conventions

6 The essay is free of errors.

5 Grammar and punctuation errors are few. The reader is not distracted by the errors.

4 Grammar and punctuation errors are seen in a few sentences. They distract the reader in those areas.

3 The opinion statement is clear. Reasons and details are not as complete as they need to be.

2 The opinion statement is unclear. Reasons and details are needed.

1 An opinion statement, reasons, and details are needed.

3 The beginning, middle, and ending exist. Transitions are needed.

2 The beginning, middle, and ending run together.

1 The organization is unclear. The reader is easily lost.

3 The writer's voice needs to be more confident and persuade the reader.

2 The writer's voice sounds bored.

1 The writer's voice can't be heard.

3 Many words need to be stronger and more positive.

2 The same weak words are used throughout the essay.

1 Word choice has not been considered.

3 Varied sentence beginnings are needed. Sentence variety would make the essay more interesting.

2 Most sentences begin the same way. Most of the sentences are simple. Compound and complex sentences are needed.

1 Sentence fluency has not been established. Ideas do not flow smoothly.

3 There are a number of errors that may confuse the reader.

2 Frequent errors make the essay difficult to read.

1 Nearly every sentence contains errors.

PERSUASIVE

Evaluating a Persuasive Essay

Ask students if they agree with the self-assessment on PE page 259. Then ask them to suggest specific changes for "Get Moving," based on the comments in the self-assessment.

Ideas **more information about health effects**—Regular exercise strengthens bones, builds muscle, and can reduce body fat.

Organization **better transitions between paragraphs**—Most importantly, young people who sit around too much may be putting their health at risk. I'm sure there are good shows to . . .

Voice **more convincing**—Friends, schoolwork, and health can suffer . . . ; some students wait until they're too tired.

Word Choice **Overused words**—Replace *problem* and *problems* in the paragraph about health with *issue* and *difficulties*.

Sentence Fluency **Combined sentences**—Young people may become shy because they . . . ; Even worse, they might not do their homework at all, which can be . . .

Conventions **Spelling**—too (. . . much, . . . shy, . . . tired); they're (. . . tired); their (. . . homework); overweight

258

Evaluating a Persuasive Essay

As you read through the persuasive essay below, focus on the writer's strengths and weaknesses. Then read the student self-assessment on the next page. (The student essay below contains some errors.)

Get Moving

Many students have televisions, stereos, and computers in their homes. They have cable channels to watch, stacks of CD's to listen to, and games to play. These things entertain them, but can cause problems if they do them to much. Friends, schoolwork, and health are things that can suffer because of to much home entertainment.

For one thing, to much time alone can hurt friendships. Not being in sports or other activities gets people in the habit of being by themselves. They sometimes become to shy. Because they spend to much time alone. Then they wonder why they don't have any friends.

In addition, coming home from school and turning on the TV or computer puts off getting started on schoolwork. Instead of doing assignments right after school, students might wait until there to tired to do a good job. Even worse, they might not do there homework at all. That is a big problem!

Even health can be a problem for those who sit around to much. Doctors say that young people are out of shape and overwieght. Bad habits that start early can cause problems later on. Almost everyone needs to be more active.

There probably are good shows to watch on TV and computer games that teach things. Sitting around the house to much is not good. Everyone needs to be careful about letting toys take to much of their time. If kids want to have more friends, think better, and feel better, they need to get moving!

Remind students that the beginning of a persuasive essay should grab the reader's attention. Propose that the beginning of "Get Moving" could be improved by including some interesting statistics about the effects of inactivity on children's health. Challenge students to incorporate reliable Internet research as well as information from print sources into a revised paragraph that would better capture the reader's attention.

persuade convince *support*
argue reason
Promoting a Cause **259**

Student Self-Assessment

The assessment that follows includes the student's comments about his essay on page 258. In the first comment, the student mentions something positive from the essay. In the second comment, the student points out an area for possible improvement. (The writer used the rubric and number scale on pages 256–257 to complete this assessment.)

5 Ideas
1. My opinion about my cause is clear.
2. My paragraph on health effects could have more information.

5 Organization
1. I talk about one problem in each paragraph.
2. I could have used better transitions between paragraphs.

4 Voice
1. My call to action is strong.
2. I could have been more convincing overall.

3 Word Choice
1. My audience will understand my words.
2. I overused the words "problem" and "problems."

4 Sentence Fluency
1. I used some complex sentences.
2. I could have made my sentences flow more smoothly.

3 Conventions
1. I used commas correctly in a series.
2. I still get confused using "to" and "there."

Use the rubric. Assess your essay using the rubric on pages 256–257.

1 On your own paper, list the six traits. Leave room after each trait to write one strength and one weakness.

2 Then choose a number (from 1 to 6) that shows how well you used each trait.

PERSUASIVE

Student Self-Assessment

After students use the rubric to assess their own essays, you may wish to have them share their essays and self-assessments with partners or in small groups for peer evaluation.

- Do they think the assessment is accurate, too lenient, or too critical?
- What concrete examples support their evaluations?

Remind students to show respect toward each other and to focus on the writing and not the writer when making comments.

To give students additional practice with evaluating a persuasive essay, use a reproducible assessment sheet (TE page 799) and one or both of the **benchmark papers** listed in the Benchmark Papers box below. You can use an overhead transparency while students refer to their own copies made from the copy masters. For your benefit a completed assessment sheet is provided for each benchmark paper.

English Language Learners

To help students learn about providing feedback, have them read the following pairs of sentences and tell which sentence is more appropriate as feedback and why they made the choice.

- You don't spell very well.
- The essay has some words that are hard to spell. You could check the list of spelling words on pages 645–651.

- It would be helpful if you organized your ideas in paragraphs.
- You jump all over the place.

The inappropriate feedback focuses on the person, not the writing, and does not give concrete help to improve the writing.

Benchmark Papers

Zoos (strong)

TR 5A–5C

TE pp. 787–789

Letter to the Editor (poor)

TR 6A–6C

TE pp. 790–792

Reflecting on Your Writing

In addition to completing the reflection sheet here, encourage students to reread any reflections they may have written earlier in the school year. This will remind them of their past successes as a writer and also help them recall those areas of their writing that need improvement. Students can then assess whether they have made progress in those areas, and if not, how they might deal with them in future writing assignments.

You may wish to have students complete items 5 and 6 after they have received feedback from you on the assignment. This may encourage them to be more forthright in their reflections.

Reflecting on Your Writing

Now that you've completed your persuasive essay, take a moment to reflect on it. Complete each starter sentence below on your own paper. Your thoughts will help you prepare for your next writing assignment.

My Persuasive Essay

1. The best part of my essay is . . .

2. The part that still needs work is . . .

3. The prewriting activity that worked best for me was . . .

4. The main thing I learned about writing a persuasive essay is . . .

5. In my next persuasive essay, I would like to . . .

6. Here is one question I still have about writing a persuasive essay:

Persuasive Writing
Pet-Peeve Essay

"I'm peeved" is an old-fashioned expression meaning "I'm irritated." A pet peeve may be something that bothers you a little bit more than it bothers others.

Writing about a pet peeve is another form of persuasive writing. In this form, a writer complains about something annoying but doesn't really expect to change it.

We all have pet peeves: people who chew gum with their mouths open, kids who always cut in line, parents who think they can rap. A pet-peeve essay gives you a chance to vent some frustration as you complain in a humorous way about something that irritates you.

Writing Guidelines

Subject:	Something that annoys you
Form:	A pet-peeve essay
Purpose:	To complain
Audience:	Classmates

Struggling Learners

To reinforce students' understanding of a pet peeve, have them ask one or two adults about things in everyday life that really annoy them. (Possible subjects: waiting in line at a store or bank, listening to other people's cell-phone conversations, rude drivers). Have students share their findings in class. Help students determine the appropriateness of these items as pet-peeve essay topics.

Pet-Peeve Essay

Objectives
- learn about a pet-peeve essay
- use what was learned about persuasive writing to create a pet-peeve essay
- plan, draft, revise, and edit a pet-peeve essay

A **pet-peeve essay** is a piece of persuasive writing that often uses humor to complain about something that annoys the writer.

Familiarize students with pet peeves by using one or more of the following ideas:

- Point out that although writers of pet peeves don't expect to change anything, they do want readers to be sympathetic and perhaps say to themselves, "Yes! I can see why you find that annoying!"

- Discuss the use of humor as a persuasive tool. Ask students why it might be more persuasive to complain using humor than to complain in a serious way. (People respond more positively to humor.)

- If possible, share samples of humorous essays by writers like Andy Rooney, who often write pet peeves.

Pet-Peeve Essay

Discuss the difference between a persuasive essay that promotes a cause and one that complains about an annoyance.

- The purpose of a persuasive essay is to convince readers to support a cause that the writer believes in.
- The main purpose of a pet-peeve essay is to complain.

Before students read "No More Mystery Meat," have them discuss pet peeves they have about school. (Steer students clear of any one person in particular, although they can talk about people in general, such as people who cut in line or speak out of turn.) Encourage students to see the humor in these annoying things.

Review the persuasive essay rubric on PE pages 256–257. Tell students to keep these traits and scores in mind as they read and respond to the sample essay.

262

Pet-Peeve Essay

The following pet-peeve essay was written by a student annoyed by the food served in the school cafeteria.

No More Mystery Meat

BEGINNING

The beginning introduces the pet peeve.

The cafeteria served "mystery meat" for lunch again today. At least, I think it was meat. It was chunky, brown, and coated with a yellow sauce. I've seen that stuff before. Sometimes the meat is served with noodles. Sometimes it's baked, and sometimes it's fried, but what it really is remains a mystery.

MIDDLE

Humor keeps the reader's attention.

Now, I don't like to complain. Still, it seems to me that after we spend a long morning of working math problems and studying science, the school could at least give us something good to eat. Imagine getting a slice of steaming, hot pizza, covered with lots of cheese! Picture some fried chicken or even a hot dog with all the fixings. We get these types of lunches at times, but not enough.

No, instead, we usually get something that doesn't even look like food. What is that

English Language Learners

Provide guidance regarding the idioms in the student model.

Idioms include the following:

- mystery meat (meat that you can't recognize)
- all the fixings (all the sauces, such as mustard and ketchup, that go with it)
- showing up (appearing)
- choke it down (eat it unhappily)

Advanced Learners

Remind students that voice and word choice are affected by one's audience. Have students identify choices of words in "No More Mystery Meat" that may be appropriate only for their classmates. (Possible responses: stuff, all I know, choke it down, a truckload of the stuff)

persuade convince reason support argue **263**
Pet-Peeve Essay

MIDDLE
Specific details make the complaint interesting.

tough brown stuff? All I know is that it certainly doesn't look like lunch to me! But it keeps showing up on our trays, and we can either choke it down or go hungry. That's not much of a choice.

It seems like we have mystery meat at least once a week, or maybe even more. Now that I think about it, maybe they get a truckload of the stuff and just keep on serving it week after week until it's all gone. Unfortunately, they never seem to run out of it! They also try to disguise this mystery meat, but we always recognize it.

ENDING
The last paragraph offers a humorous solution.

I have a better use for mystery meat. Next time it's served, I'll take it home to my dog, Jiggs. He likes chewing on old shoe leather like this.

Respond to the reading. On your own paper answer the following questions about the sample essay.

- ☐ Ideas **(1)** What complaint does the writer want to communicate?
- ☐ **Organization** **(2)** How did the writer organize the main ideas—by time, by location, or by logical order?
- ☐ Voice & Word Choice **(3)** What words and phrases show the writer's irritation?

PERSUASIVE

Respond to the reading.

Ask students to explain their responses.

Answers

Ideas **1.** tough, unappetizing meat served in the school cafeteria

Organization 2. logical order

Voice & Word Choice 3. Possible choices: mystery meat; chunky . . . a yellow sauce; I don't like to complain; school . . . good to eat; we usually get . . . look like food; tough brown stuff; choke it . . . not much of a choice; Unfortunately, they never run out; try to disguise; old shoe leather

Discuss the use of **humor** and **sarcasm** *(see below)* in "No More Mystery Meat."

- What words and phrases are meant to be funny? (Possible choices: mystery meat; I'll take it home . . . Jiggs.)
- Is the tone more comical or sarcastic? (sarcastic)
- What image did you find most amusing in the essay?

Teaching Tip: Humor and Sarcasm

Discuss the difference between humor and sarcasm with students.

- **Humor** draws on what is considered comical and absurd in life. Humor often creates funny images in readers' minds and causes outright laughter.
- **Sarcasm** is based on a contradiction between the literal meaning of words and the intended meaning. Sarcasm is frequently conveyed through tone of voice.

To demonstrate sarcasm as conveyed through tone of voice, read aloud the following sentence in a normal tone of voice and then with a sarcastic tone: *I love our school lunches.* Ask students how the writer of "No Mystery Meat" would say it. Then have them read aloud the following statements from "No More Mystery Meat."

- At least, I think it was meat.
- Now, I don't mean to complain.

English Language Learners

Students acquiring English may need extra help in understanding the humor in witty remarks, particularly puns. Be sure to provide simple examples, perhaps from age-appropriate joke books, and explain the humor when necessary.

Prewriting Selecting a Topic

Share your own personal pet peeves and interesting pet peeves you've heard about. (Newspaper fillers and syndicated columns often contain humorous stories related to people's reaction, or overreaction, to everyday annoyances.) Ask students to share the oddest pet peeves they've ever heard.

As students freewrite to find a topic, tell them to consider the humor in their ideas.

Prewriting
Adding Humorous Details

In a humorous essay, the subject matter becomes even funnier when writers use **figurative language** *(see below)* to create silly or absurd images in readers' minds. To spark ideas, suggest that students ask themselves

- Why does _____ annoy me?
- What does _____ (see, hear, touch, smell, taste) like that would make a funny comparison?
- What picture do I get in my mind whenever I think of _____?

264

Prewriting Selecting a Topic

To choose a topic for a pet-peeve essay, think of everyday annoyances—things that "bug" you. Does your brother or sister annoy you? Does riding the bus drive you crazy? Are the school lunches boring?

The writer of the sample pet-peeve essay used the freewriting below to discover a writing topic.

> *What bugs me? Let's see, I hate the way my sister follows me around. She always wants to meet my friends and talk to them. But I guess my friends kind of like her, and anyway, she's not that bad. The school bus! That's something I don't like. Well, except it's fun when José and Rick and I get the back seat and bounce over the railroad tracks. School isn't so bad, either. How about lunch—ack! What is that stuff? How come the cafeteria thinks we can eat fried shoe leather ? . . .*

 Choose your topic. Freewrite about your life. Go through your day and think about things that irritate you. Keep going until you settle on a topic that you can complain about in a pet-peeve essay. If you have trouble getting started, answer the question "What things bug me the most?"

Adding Humorous Details

Humor makes a pet-peeve essay fun to read. These techniques can help.

- **Make comparisons.** Comparing your pet peeve with something else can emphasize your feelings. In the sample essay, the writer compares mystery meat to an old piece of shoe leather.

- **Use exaggeration.** A writer can add humor to an essay by exaggerating. In the sample essay, the writer suggests that the mystery meat comes by the truckload.

 Create humorous details. Write at least one comparison and one exaggeration that you could use in your essay.

Teaching Tip: Figurative Language

Similes, metaphors, and hyperbole are kinds of figurative language often used in humorous writing. Discuss the definitions and share examples of each from published works.

- A **simile** is an indirect comparison that says one thing is like another, using *like* or *as*.

  The brownies were as hard as bricks.

- A **metaphor** is a direct comparison that implies one thing is like another without using *like* or *as*.

  The brownies were bricks.

- **Hyperbole** is an exaggeration that suggests something is bigger, smaller, funnier, worse, (and so on) than it actually is.

  You could build a fireplace with these brownies!

persuade convince reason support **265**
argue
Pet-Peeve Essay

Writing Organizing a Pet Peeve

When you write a basic persuasive essay, order of importance is an effective way to organize your ideas. With order of importance, you tell the most important reason first or last.

However, you can also arrange the reasons in a way that simply makes the best sense, called *logical order*. With this order, one reason is no more important than the one before or after it. This is the type of organization that is used in the pet peeve on pages 262–263.

Using logical order is like fitting the pieces in a jigsaw puzzle. The size and shape of one reason fits the size and shape of the next one. The graphic below shows how the three main reasons in the pet peeve fit together.

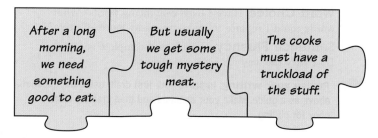

After a long morning, we need something good to eat.

But usually we get some tough mystery meat.

The cooks must have a truckload of the stuff.

Creating Your First Draft

Though an essay about a pet peeve is a lighter kind of persuasive essay, it still has a definite form. As you write your essay, follow these guidelines.

- **Introduce your pet peeve.** Maybe you could begin with a funny story about an annoying experience you had.

- **Discuss the pet peeve.** Help the reader understand why the topic annoys you. Remember to make comparisons and use exaggeration in your explanation. Organize your ideas in the best way. (See above.)

- **Close your essay by offering a solution.** Your solution might be reasonable: "It's time to start bringing my own lunch." It might be funny: "Next time I get mystery meat, I'll take it home to my dog, Jiggs. He likes chewing on just about anything."

 Write your first draft. Use the information above as a guide. Try to keep your writing voice light and humorous.

PERSUASIVE

Writing Organizing a Pet Peeve

To help students better understand the logical order of ideas shown in the graphic, have students experiment with reading the three reasons in a different order.

Writing Creating Your First Draft

Suggest that students use the three bulleted items on PE page 265 as a mini-outline or plan for their essay. Encourage students to try to arrange their main reasons in different orders to find the one that is most logical.

Students who have successfully completed the two previous persuasive writing assignments can work more independently on this essay.

Revising Improving Your Writing

Before students revise, consider having them assess their essay using the rubric on PE pages 256–257.

Because a pet-peeve essay is about something annoying, students may have overused the word *annoy (annoyed, annoying)*. Have them use a thesaurus to find synonyms for *annoy*.

Editing Checking for Conventions

Have students exchange papers with a partner for editing. Encourage students to check carefully for errors in usage.

✱ Find additional help with using the right word on PE pages 652–686.

Since students have a tendency to repeat the same errors from one assignment to the next, tell them to provide editing partners with suggestions for the kinds of errors to watch for.

Suggest that students look over the reflections they wrote for PE page 260.

■ How would they complete those sentences now after completing their pet-peeve essays?

■ Did they accomplish what they hoped to in response to item 5?

266

Revising Improving Your Writing

Read over your first draft. Revise it by asking yourself the following questions.

☐ **Ideas** Have I stated my complaint clearly? Have I included any comparisons or used any exaggerations? Do I need to cut any details that are off the subject?

☐ **Organization** Are my paragraphs easy to follow? Are the points in the paragraphs in the best order?

☐ **Voice** What would make my writing voice stronger? Does my essay sound like me?

☐ **Word Choice** Have I used convincing words? What words could I replace to make my essay more effective?

☐ **Sentence Fluency** Have I used complete sentences? Do I vary the way my sentences begin?

 Revise your writing. Improve your first draft, using the questions above as a guide. Make your changes and then create a clean copy for editing.

Editing Checking for Conventions

As you edit your essay, focus on the following questions.

☐ **Conventions** Have I carefully checked my work for punctuation, capitalization, and spelling errors? Have I also checked for errors in usage *(to, too, two; their, there, they're; its, it's)* and other grammar errors?

 Edit your work. Use the questions above to decide how to edit your essay. After making your changes, create a final copy and check it one more time for errors.

Struggling Learners

Under the Organization section of the Revising checklist, struggling learners may need additional questions that specifically focus on transitions. Use the following questions to begin a discussion about transitions:

● What transitions have I used within paragraphs?

● What transitions have I used between paragraphs?

Remind students to use PE pages 572–573 for a list of transitions.

persuade convince support
argue reason **267**

Persuasive Writing
Across the Curriculum

You can use the valuable skill of writing persuasively throughout the school day. For example, your social studies teacher may assign an editorial cartoon about a social problem. Your math teacher may require convincing proof for some mathematical fact. In science, you may need to argue for or against some scientific theory. In or out of school, you may need to write persuasive letters to convince others to take a certain action.

You may also need to be persuasive on writing tests. The model and tips at the end of this chapter will help you.

Mini Index

- **Social Studies:** Creating an Editorial Cartoon
- **Math:** Presenting a Proof
- **Science:** Supporting a Theory
- **Practical Writing:** Drafting a Persuasive Letter
- **Writing for Assessment**

Across the Curriculum

Objectives
- apply what students have learned about persuasive writing to other curriculum areas
- practice writing for assessment

The lessons on the following pages provide samples of persuasive writing students might do in different subject areas. Students may also have other kinds of persuasive writing (for example, a debate argument in social studies).

Assigning these forms of writing will depend on
- the skill level of your students,
- the subject matter they are studying in different content areas,
- and the writing goals of your school, district, or state.

Social Studies: Creating an Editorial Cartoon

After students have had time to study the cartoon, discuss how the writer conveyed the message.

- How does the cartoon illustrate the writer's opinion about drilling for oil in parks? (Oil showering the trees and the moose emphasizes how bad this idea is for the environment.)
- How does the cartoon use humor to be persuasive? (A moose holding an umbrella is funny, but it shows how vulnerable park animals are.)

Share and discuss additional examples of editorial cartoons from magazines and newspapers. (Avoid controversial topics that are intentionally or inadvertently insulting.) Point out that editorial cartoons may contain a caption but do not usually include an explanation. Readers have to be knowledgeable about the topic to "get the joke" and understand the cartoon's message. Help students recognize the opinion that is stated or implied in the caption or in the cartoon itself.

Social Studies:
Creating an Editorial Cartoon

A picture is worth a thousand words, especially when the picture is an editorial cartoon. An editorial cartoon is a drawing that pokes fun at a political or social problem.

The following editorial cartoon was created for a social studies class. While the paragraph explains the social problem, the cartoon does most of the persuading. What makes the cartoon persuasive? What makes it funny?

The paragraph explains the problem.

Social Problem: Some people think that oil companies should be allowed to drill for oil in some national parks and wildlife refuges. I think that this is a bad idea. If it really is a wildlife refuge, animals ought to be able to live there safely and naturally. This cartoon shows my opinion about this idea.

The drawing illustrates the problem.

persuade convince *reason support* **269**
argue
Writing in Social Studies

Writing Tips

Before you write . . .

- **Choose a problem you care about.**
  Think of things that worry you about your city, the country, or the world.
- **Do your research.**
  Read articles and gather information.
- **Think of symbols.**
  Consider symbols to use in your cartoon. In the example, the oil pump symbolizes the oil industry.
- **Use pictures as models.**
  Find a picture of an oil pump, for example, if you need to draw an oil pump.

During your writing . . .

- **Explain the problem.**
  Tell why the problem concerns you.
- **Draw your cartoon.**
  Concentrate on one or two images.
- **Write a caption below the cartoon, if necessary.**
  If your cartoon needs explaining, create a sentence or phrase that will get your point across. This sentence is called a caption.

After you've written a first draft . . .

- **Review your opening explanation.**
  Make sure that all of your ideas are clear.
- **Study your cartoon.**
  Redraw any parts that could be better.
- **Improve your caption.**
  Make sure each word has a purpose.

 Create an editorial cartoon about a social problem that concerns you. Use the tips above as a guide.

PERSUASIVE

Writing Tips

Have students work in small groups or as a class to generate a list of concerns about their city, country, or the world. If possible, make available several copies of local newspapers as well as magazines for young people (for example, *National Geographic Kids* and *Kids Discover Magazine*). Suggest that students skim the tables of contents and flip through the pages to get ideas for topics of interest to young people today.

Point out to students that unlike most published editorial cartoons, the cartoons they create for the **Try It** activity will include an explanation that clearly states their opinion about the topic.

As an alternative to a current event, students might create an editorial cartoon that relates to an issue or historical event they are studying in social studies.

 **Answers**

Cartoons will vary. Explanations should explain the social problem and state the writer's concerns.

Advanced Learners

Have students work with a partner and choose a social problem from a historical era that they have previously studied so that they have a clear understanding of different aspects of the issue. Challenge partners to create two editorial cartoons, each one representing a different perspective. (Possible issues: abolition, Revolutionary War)

Math: Presenting a Proof

Students may have a difficult time understanding how writing a proof relates to persuasive writing. Suggest that they think of it like this: If they can prove a math concept, they can convince others (and themselves) that the concept works.

Carefully review "Long Division Is Short Subtraction" with students. Point out that in the previous persuasive writing students have done, the opinion statement guided their writing. In a proof, the concept statement guides the writing.

270

Math: Presenting a Proof

The best way to show that a given math concept is correct is to prove it. This type of writing is called a "proof."

The **beginning** names the concept.

The **middle** shows two proofs.

The **ending** restates the concept.

Long Division Is Short Subtraction

Concept: Division is a quick form of subtraction.

Proof 1: Let's say we have a division problem: $42 \div 7 = ?$. One way to solve the problem would be to subtract 7 from 42 until we reach 0.

$$42 - 7 = 35$$
$$35 - 7 = 28$$
$$28 - 7 = 21$$
$$21 - 7 = 14$$
$$14 - 7 = 7$$
$$7 - 7 = 0$$

Then we just count how many 7's we subtracted to reach 0. The answer is 6. Of course, $42 \div 7 = 6$.

Proof 2: Let's try a harder problem: $209 \div 46 = ?$.

$$209 - 46 = 163$$
$$163 - 46 = 117$$
$$117 - 46 = 71$$
$$71 - 46 = 25$$
$$25 - 46 = ?$$

Our last subtraction would end with a negative number. That means 25 is our remainder. Then we count how many 46's we subtracted. The answer is 4, with a remainder of 25. Dividing it out brings the same answer ($209 \div 46 = 4$, remainder 25).

Conclusion: A division problem can be solved by using either division or subtraction.

271

Writing in Math

Writing Tips

Before you write . . .

- **Choose a math concept.**
  Think of math concepts you understand well. Make a list and choose one.
- **Study the concept.**
  Review the idea until you thoroughly understand it.
- **Experiment with ways to prove it.**
  Recall how your teacher first taught the idea to the class. Think of how you could prove the concept. Check books and Internet articles for other ways.
- **Plan your proof.**
  List the steps for proving the concept.

During your writing . . .

- **Introduce the math concept.**
  State what you will prove.
- **Give the proof or proofs.**
  Present the information in a step-by-step process.
- **Summarize your proof.**
  Restate your concept.

After you've written a first draft . . .

- **Check for completeness.**
  Include all of the information the reader will need.
- **Check for correctness.**
  Make sure there are no errors in your math, spelling, punctuation, and grammar.

 Choose a math concept to prove. (Here is an example: An even number plus or minus another even number will always equal an even number.) Then follow the tips above to present your proof.

PERSUASIVE

Writing Tips

Suggest that students look through math books and past math tests to identify concepts they have mastered. If possible, students should ask their math teacher(s) for ideas, based on the skill levels they have achieved.

Try It Answers

Answers will vary.

Science: Supporting a Theory

Read the introduction and "What Happened to the Dinosaurs?" with students. Have them identify the topic (extinction of dinosaurs) and the theory (a gigantic meteor or asteroid struck the earth and wiped out the dinosaurs). Then discuss the facts, examples, and details that the writer uses to support the theory.

Help students recognize how supporting a scientific theory can be considered persuasive writing:

- It encourages the acceptance of an idea or belief.
- It uses facts to support the topic.

272

Science: Supporting a Theory

A scientific theory is an idea or group of ideas that explains an event. When you support a theory, you back your ideas with facts and reasons. The following essay supports one theory about how the dinosaurs became extinct.

What Happened to the Dinosaurs?

The beginning introduces the topic and the theory.

There are many mysteries about dinosaurs. One of the most interesting is this question: "Why did they become extinct?" Scientists have been arguing about this since the first fossils were discovered. The most popular theory says that the earth was struck by a gigantic meteor or asteroid when dinosaurs lived all over the world.

The middle paragraphs describe the theory.

According to the theory, the huge meteor caused a shock wave of heat and strong winds that killed many dinosaurs. A big cloud of dust darkened the skies for years. That made the world grow colder because the sun couldn't shine through all the dust. There wasn't enough light for plants to grow. Without plant life, the dinosaurs couldn't survive.

Research backs up this theory. Scientists have found a crater in the Gulf of Mexico that was caused by a huge force at about the time the dinosaurs disappeared. They also have found in many places a layer of dirt that is made up of materials found in meteors. This layer was probably formed when the huge dust cloud settled to the ground.

The ending summarizes the writer's support for the theory.

Right now, no one knows for sure why the dinosaurs died, but every day scientists dig up new clues. Someday they may be able to prove the meteor theory. For now, it seems like a good explanation.

English Language Learners

Explain that a theory is an idea or a belief that can be proved or disproved.

- Many years ago, many people believed—had the theory—the earth was flat. However, this theory was proved false by Christopher Columbus and other explorers.

- Another example of a simple scientific theory is gravity— what goes up must come down (Sir Isaac Newton's apple).

persuade convince reason support 273
argue
Writing in Science

Writing Tips

> **Before you write . . .**
> - **Choose a topic.**
>   List scientific theories you are studying. Choose one to support.
> - **Research your topic.**
>   Read about the theory and make sure you understand it. Find strong reasons to support the theory.
> - **Take notes.**
>   Jot down facts, reasons, and examples.
>
> **During your writing . . .**
> - **Introduce the topic and the theory.**
>   Give the reader necessary background information.
> - **Develop the middle paragraphs.**
>   Explain how the theory works and support the explanation.
> - **End your essay.**
>   Summarize your support for the theory, adding any thoughts or final details.
>
> **After you've written a first draft . . .**
> - **Check for completeness.**
>   Make sure you have clearly explained the theory with reasons, facts, and examples.
> - **Check for conventions.**
>   Make sure there are no errors in spelling, punctuation, and grammar.

PERSUASIVE

 Select a scientific theory that you agree with—for example, the theory of global warming. Your teacher may suggest other topics. Do some research and then write a persuasive essay supporting the theory.

Writing Tips

Invite students to share ideas for science projects they are working on or have completed. Since many science projects are based on proving theories, these ideas can call to mind possible topics.

Stress how important it is not only for students to understand the theory they choose but also for them to be able to gather and present enough background information so that readers will understand it, too.

 Answers

Answers will vary.

Advanced Learners

To extend this activity, have students create a time line to illustrate the events and discoveries that led to the postulation of the theory they select. (Possible theory: The sun, rather than the earth, is the center of the universe.)

Practical Writing: Drafting a Persuasive Letter

Discuss the variety of reasons people have for writing persuasive letters. Some ideas you might share include the following:

- to complain to a company about the quality of a product
- to request a change in policy (for example, the operating hours of a skating rink, or park entrance fees)
- to request a refund or other compensation
- to convince a political leader to vote for something
- to invite a guest speaker to a special event

Some students may decide to write a persuasive letter that uses the opinions and reasons they developed for their persuasive paragraph (PE pages 219–222) or for their persuasive essay (PE pages 223–255). This is an excellent way to help students recognize the practical application of their writing efforts.

274

Practical Writing:
Drafting a Persuasive Letter

A polite persuasive letter can influence people and get things done. This sample letter talks about a dangerous intersection and what should be done about it.

The letter follows the correct format. (See pages 276-277.)

1414 Johnson Street
Walvan, WI 53000
April 20, 2004

Mayor Phillip Smith
Walvan City Hall
111 Main Street
Walvan, WI 53000

Dear Mayor Smith:

The beginning introduces the writer and the problem.

I am a student at Parker Lane Middle School. At a city council meeting last October, I asked the council to put up a stoplight at the intersection of 34th Avenue and Cottage Street. That is two blocks away from our school.

The body of the letter explains the problem.

Six months later, cars are still going too fast on 34th Avenue. That makes it dangerous for kids trying to cross the street on their way to and from school. I think that the city should put up a stoplight before someone gets hurt on that corner.

The closing calls for action.

I am not the only one who thinks this corner is dangerous. I have enclosed a petition asking for a stoplight, signed by more than 400 students, teachers, parents, and neighbors. Mayor Smith, please vote for putting a traffic light at 34th Avenue and Cottage Street.

Sincerely,

Ruby Keast

Ruby Keast

persuade convince support
argue reason **275**
Practical Writing

Writing Tips

Use the following tips as a guide when you are asked to write a persuasive letter. (Also see pages 276–277.)

Before you write . . .

- **Choose a topic you care about.**
  Think of problems that you would like to solve.
- **Form your opinion.**
  Write freely about the topic to understand it better.
- **Gather information as needed.**
  Collect details and facts that support your opinion.
- **Consider your reader.**
  Learn as much as you can about the organization or person you are writing to.

During your writing . . .

- **Keep it short.**
  Stick to important details. The letter should not be longer than one page. If you have extra information, such as the petition in the example letter, include it on separate pages.
- **Stay on the topic.**
  Make sure every sentence supports your argument.

After you've written a first draft . . .

- **Check for completeness.**
  Add any important reasons you forgot to include.
- **Check for correctness.**
  Read the letter several times. If possible, have someone else read it as well. Make sure that your letter is free of errors and that all names are capitalized and spelled correctly.

PERSUASIVE

 Think of a problem in your community. Find out who could help solve it. Write a persuasive letter to that person, making a strong but polite argument.

Parts of a Business Letter

Review the parts of a business letter, using the sample letter on PE page 274 as a model and guide.

If students have already written their letters, have them double-check to be sure they contain all the appropriate parts and that the parts follow the correct format.

Parts of a Business Letter

1 The heading includes your address and the date. Write the heading at least one inch from the top of the page at the left-hand margin.

2 The inside address includes the name, title, and address of the person or organization you are writing to.

■ If the person has a title, make sure to include it. (If the title is short, write it on the same line as the name. If the title is long, write it on the next line.)

■ If you are writing to an organization or a business but not to a specific person, begin the inside address with the name of the organization or business.

3 The salutation is the greeting. Always put a colon after the salutation.

■ If you know the person's name, use it in your greeting.

> **Dear Mr. Christopher:**

■ If you don't know the name of the person, use a salutation like one of these:

> **Dear Store Owner:**
> **Dear Sir or Madam:**
> **Dear Madison Soccer Club:**

4 The body is the main part of the letter. Do not indent your paragraphs; instead, skip a line between them.

5 The closing is placed after the body. Use **Yours truly** or **Sincerely** to close a business letter. Capitalize only the first word of the closing and put a comma after it.

6 The signature ends the letter. If you are using a computer, leave four spaces after the closing; then type your name. Write your signature between the closing and the typed name.

(Turn to page 577 for more about writing letters, as well as a set of guidelines for addressing envelopes properly.)

persuade convince support
argue reason **277**

Business-Letter Format

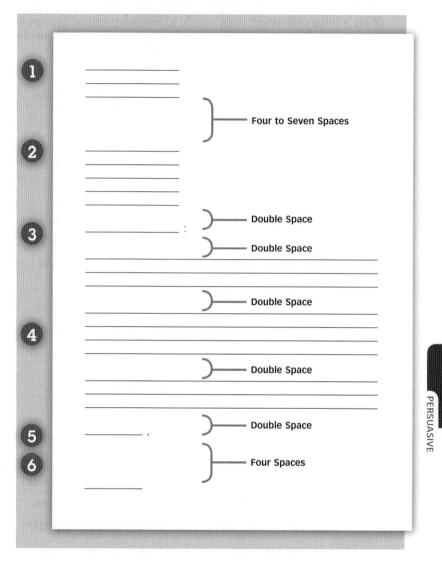

1

2

3

4

5

6

Four to Seven Spaces

Double Space

Double Space

Double Space

Double Space

Double Space

Four Spaces

PERSUASIVE

While printed letters have a more professional look, students may not have access to a computer or printer. When students are ready to write their final draft, have them put letter paper over a sheet of lined notebook paper that has one-inch margins at the sides, top, and bottom of the paper. (The lines may have to be darkened.) Students can use the margins and the lines as a guide to produce a neat, professional-looking letter.

Writing for Assessment

If your students must take school, district, or state assessments this year, focus on the writing form on which they will be tested.

Have students create bookmarks with test-taking tips for writing listed on each side. Tips may include

- underlining key words in the question,
- using outlines or story maps to plan and organize ideas,
- allowing enough time at the end for rereading and editing.

Encourage students to do a quick review of the tips each time they use their bookmark.

Review the main traits of persuasive writing. Ask students to look for the following as they read the model:

- a clearly stated opinion
- separate paragraphs each with a topic sentence that is a reason that supports the opinion
- facts and details to support each reason
- transitions that connect ideas in and between paragraphs
- use of convincing language

278

Writing for Assessment

Many writing assessment tests include a persuasive writing prompt. A persuasive prompt asks you to state an opinion and support it with strong reasons. Study the following sample prompt and student response.

Persuasive Prompt

Some students complain about having too much homework. Do you agree or disagree with them? Write an essay convincing your teachers to give more or less homework.

The **beginning** includes the opinion statement (underlined).

Students often complain about having too much homework. They say things like "It takes so long" or "I don't understand it." Some homework can help kids learn, but too much homework can make learning harder. Copeland Middle School students need less homework, not more.

Each **middle** paragraph gives a reason and details that support the opinion.

Students at Copeland are already busy. School goes from 8:00 in the morning to 3:00 in the afternoon. Kids who ride the bus may spend an extra hour just getting to school and back home. And some kids stay after school for an hour or two of sports. Add a couple of hours of homework, and that makes an 11-hour day!

Too much homework may cause students to do poor work. During a science video last week, two students fell asleep. They had always paid attention

persuade convince reason support 279
argue
Writing for Assessment

in class, but the night before, they stayed up late doing homework. Overloading kids with assignments can leave them too tired for school.

When there's too much homework, some kids feel like giving up. Teachers at Copeland might say that they give only 20 minutes of homework a day. Still, if six teachers each give just 20 minutes of homework, that's two hours of work. With all of that work, there's no time to relax.

Some homework is a good thing, but too much homework is not. It overloads kids who are already busy, makes it harder for some kids to learn, and can even make others want to give up. Teachers at Copeland Middle School should give less homework. Then maybe their students will learn even more.

The **ending** summarizes the essay and restates the opinion.

Respond to the reading. Answer the questions to learn about the student response.

☐ **Ideas** (1) What is the writer's opinion? (2) What key words in the prompt also appear in the essay? (3) What are two of the reasons that the writer has used to support the opinion?

☐ **Organization** (4) How is the essay organized— by time, location, or point by point?

☐ **Voice** (5) How would you describe the writer's voice in this essay (humorous, serious, angry)?

PERSUASIVE

Respond to the reading.

Answers

Ideas **1.** Copeland Middle School teachers should give less homework.
2. students . . . complain; too much homework; less homework
3. (Accept any two reasons) **Reason:** Students at Copeland are already busy. **Reason:** Too much homework may cause students to do poor work. **Reason:** When there's too much homework, some kids feel like giving up.

Organization 4. point by point

Voice 5. The writer's voice is serious and sincere.

Ask students if they think the writer of the model has presented a convincing argument. What could the writer have done to make the essay even more persuasive? (Possible answers: include more anecdotes about students; include a personal experience; offer a specific teacher's reason for giving homework as an opposing view; begin fourth paragraph with a transition, like, *Finally* or *More importantly*.)

English Language Learners

Students may not understand that the summary in the last paragraph is based on the arguments presented in the three middle paragraphs. Work with students to identify and write the three reasons stated in the summary paragraph. Then have them look for similar language in the three middle paragraphs. The relationship is clear for the first reason (already busy) and the third reason (want to give up), but the second reason may be harder to identify (it is harder for some kids to learn because they are tired).

Writing Tips

Point out that students must approach writing-on-demand assignments differently from open-ended writing assignments and that timed writing creates pressures for everyone.

Persuasive Prompts

To teach students who must take timed assessments how to approach their writing, allow them the same amount of time to write their response essay as they will be allotted on school, district, or state assessments. Break down each part of the process into clear chunks of time. For example, you might give students

- 15 minutes for reading, note-taking and planning,
- 20 minutes for writing,
- 10 minutes for editing and proofreading.

Tell students when time is up for each section. Start the assignment at the top of the hour or at the half-hour to make it easier for students to keep track of the time.

If your state, district, or school requires students to use and submit a graphic organizer as part of their assessment, provide a copy of one of the reproducible charts (TE pages 800–804) or refer students to PE pages 548–549.

280

Writing Tips

Before you write . . .
- **Understand the prompt.**
  Remember that a persuasive prompt asks you to state and support an opinion.
- **Use your time wisely.**
  Spend a few minutes taking some notes and planning before you start to write. When you finish, read over what you have written.

During your writing . . .
- **Form an opinion statement.**
  Think of an opinion that you can clearly support.
- **Build your argument.**
  Think of reasons to support your opinion.
- **End effectively.**
  Summarize your argument and restate your opinion.

After you've written a first draft . . .
- **Check for clear ideas.**
  Rewrite any ideas that sound confusing.
- **Check for conventions.**
  Correct errors in punctuation, spelling, and grammar.

Persuasive Prompts

- Some people say that children under 14 should be at home before 7:00 p.m. unless they are with an adult. Write an essay expressing your opinion about this idea.
- In a letter, convince your parents to take a family trip to a place you would like to visit.

 Write a response. Respond to one of the prompts above. Complete your writing within the period of time your teacher gives you. Afterward, list one part of your essay you like and one part you could improve.

---

persuade *convince*
argue *reason* *support* **281**
Persuasive Writing Checklist

Persuasive Writing in Review

Purpose: In persuasive writing, you work to *convince people* to think the way you do about something.

Topics: Your opinion about something
An action you feel is important
A worthy cause

Prewriting

Select a topic that you care about, one that you can present confidently and that is appropriate for your audience. (See page 228.)

Gather ideas about your topic. (See page 229.)

Write an opinion statement that identifies your "cause + feeling." (See page 230.)

Organize your ideas in a list or an outline with your opinion statement at the top, followed by topic sentences with supporting facts or details beneath each. (See pages 231–232.)

Writing

In the beginning part, grab the reader's attention and clearly state your opinion. (See page 235.)

In the middle part, devote a paragraph to each reason with supporting facts and examples. (See pages 236–237.)

In the ending, restate your opinion and make a call to action. (See page 238.)

Revising

Review the ideas, organization, and voice first. Then check for **word choice** and **sentence fluency.** Avoid repeated words and general adjectives. Use a variety of sentence structures. (See pages 240–249.)

Editing

Check your writing for conventions. Ask a friend to edit the writing, too. (See pages 252–254.)

Make a final copy and proofread it for errors before sharing it with your audience. (See page 255.)

Assessing

Use the persuasive rubric as a guide to assess your finished writing. (See pages 256–257.)

PERSUASIVE

Persuasive Writing in Review

Refer students to this page whenever they write a persuasive paragraph or essay. You may also allow them to refer to this review while they are doing a sample assessment. As they become more familiar with the writing form during the year, they will need to refer to the list less frequently.

Response to Literature Overview

Writing Standards

The writing standards listed below are based on a blending of state and NCTE standards.

- Use charts, clusters, and time lines to gather and organize ideas.
- Develop insights that show careful reading and understanding of theme, plot, and character development.
- Support insights through references to the text.
- Revise drafts to vary sentence structure and create a knowledgeable voice.
- Assess writing using a rubric based on the traits of effective writing.

Writing Forms

- response paragraph
- book review
- fictionalized journal entry

Focus on the Traits

- **Ideas** Developing a clear focus statement that shows a specific insight and understanding of a piece of literature
- **Organization** Forming a clear pattern of organization
- **Voice** Using a formal, knowledgeable voice supported by key details
- **Word Choice** Using the active voice and no unnecessary modifiers
- **Sentence Fluency** Varying sentence beginnings and avoiding rambling sentences
- **Conventions** Checking for errors in punctuation, capitalization, spelling, and grammar

Unit Pacing

Response Paragraph: 1.5–2.25 hours

The **response paragraph** introduces the unit and lays the groundwork for more extensive response writing. Use this section if students need to work on crafting a paragraph. Following are some of the topics that are covered.

- Listing novels and stories that have been read
- Using a cluster to identify main events
- Writing about an important event

Response Essay 1: 4.5 hours–6.75 hours

This section asks students to write a **response to literature** in the form of a **book review**. Use this section to focus on developing an essay. Following are some of the topics that are covered.

- Using a time line to list key events
- Writing a focus statement
- Checking for unnecessary details
- Using transitions to connect ideas
- Sounding knowledgeable and formal
- Using verbs correctly

Response Essay 2: 2.25 hours–3 hours

The **fictionalized journal entry** section offers a creative and new approach to responding to literature—writing a journal entry from the point of view of a book character. Use this section to present an alternate or additional form of responding to literature. Following are some of the topics covered.

- Selecting a character and an event from a novel
- Using a journal format

Response to Literature Across the Curriculum: *2.25 hours–3 hours*

Collaborate with teachers from other content areas to enhance your students' experience with the curriculum already in place.

- **Social Studies**
Reviewing a Biography, pp. 330–331

- **Science**
Summarizing an Article, pp. 332–333

- **Practical Writing**
Completing an Evaluation, pp. 334–335

Writing for Assessment: *45–90 minutes*

The student text shows a strong student response to a story presented in the text. Students can respond to that same story or to another story that is introduced in their text with this prompt:

- When you write, focus on the author's message in the story. Show your insight into the characters and ideas. Use clear organization and support your focus with examples from the text.

Evaluating a Book Review

Learning to evaluate one's own and others' writing is an integral part of learning to write. In addition to a student's evaluation of a book review (PE pages 320–321), **benchmark papers** provide practice with evaluating responses to literature.

- *Caddie Woodlawn* (strong)
TR 7A–7C
TE pp. 793–795
- Amazing (good)
PE pp. 338–339
- Gypsy and Woodrow
TR 8A–8C
TE pp. 796–798

Integrated Grammar and Writing Skills

Below are skills lessons from the resources sections of the pupil edition that are suggested at point of use (✱) throughout this unit.

Response Paragraph, pp. 283–286

✱ Punctuation of Titles, pp. 600, 602
✱ Writing About an Event, p. 533

Writing a Book Review, pp. 287–322

✱ Use Chronological Order, p. 534
✱ Present Tense, p. 483
✱ Action Verbs, p. 482
✱ Rambling Sentences, p. 507
✱ Develop Sentence Style, p. 522

Fictionalized Journal Entry, pp. 323–328

✱ Writing About a Person, p. 532

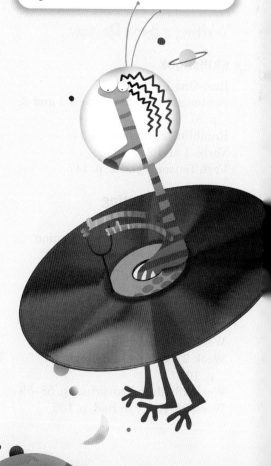

Additional Grammar Skills

Below are skills lessons from other components that you can weave into your unit instruction.

Writing a Response Paragraph

SkillsBook

Quotation Marks and Italics, p. 25
Punctuation Review 1, 2, and 3, p. 33

Interactive Writing Skills CD-ROM

Mechanics: Capitalization—Titles
Punctuation: Punctuating Titles

Daily Language Workout

Week 25: Facts from American History, pp. 52–53
Week 25: The Cost of War, p. 102
Week 26: Modern American History, pp. 54–55
Week 26: Peacemaker Assassinated, p. 103

Writing a Book Review

SkillsBook

Run-Ons 1 and 2, p. 77
Sentence Problems Review 1 and 2, p. 81
Rambling Sentences, p. 84
Verbs 1 and 2, p. 141
Verb Tenses 1 and 2, p. 147

Interactive Writing Skills CD-ROM

Parts of Speech: Verbs 1—Action
Parts of Speech: Verbs 2—Past, Present, and Future Perfect Tenses

Daily Language Workout

Week 27: Proverbs, pp. 56–57
Week 27: Seeing Is Believing? p. 104
Week 28: More Proverbs, pp. 58–59
Week 28: Early to Bed, p. 105

experience
answer

Response to Literature

evaluate
react

Writing a Fictionalized Journal Entry

SkillsBook

Apostrophes 1, 2, and 3, p. 27
Mixed Review, p. 39
Interjections, p. 173

Interactive Writing Skills CD-ROM

Punctuation: Using Apostrophes in Contractions

Punctuation: Using Apostrophes to Form Possessives

Daily Language Workout

Week 29: A Taste of World History, pp. 60–61
Week 29: The Islamic Religion, p. 106
Week 30: World-History Dates, pp. 62–63
Week 30: So Long, p. 107

Response to Literature
Response Paragraph

You're sitting in a movie theater, the lights dim, and the "Coming Attractions" begin. Each preview highlights a new movie. In a very short time, you know whether or not you want to see it.

A response to literature in the form of a paragraph is much like a movie preview. The writing must get right to the point and say something meaningful about the story. This type of response usually highlights an important event.

On the next page, you will read a sample paragraph that responds to a book. Then you will write a paragraph response of your own.

Writing Guidelines

Subject:	**An important event in a book or short story**
Form:	**A paragraph**
Purpose:	**To respond to a story**
Audience:	**Classmates**

Objectives
- understand the content and structure of a response paragraph
- choose a topic (an important event from a book) to write about
- plan, draft, revise, and edit a response paragraph

A **response paragraph** highlights or summarizes an important event in a book or a short story. A paragraph has a topic sentence, the body, and a closing sentence.

Use the following questions to conduct a brief discussion of movie previews:
- What are they?
- What is their purpose?
- What do you think of them?

Share a brief movie review with students. Point out that a paragraph response, like a movie review, focuses on a major event without giving away the whole story or the ending.

Response Paragraph

Point out how the writer of the response paragraph provides just enough background information about the characters for readers to understand why the event (building the fort) is important.

 Respond to the reading.

Review the questions to make sure students understand how to construct a response paragraph.

Answers

Ideas 1. The writer thinks building the fort is the most important part.
2. This is when Jess and Leslie begin their friendship.

Organization 3. Accept time order or logical order.

Voice & Word Choice 4. yes
5. Possible choices:
- shy boy . . . wants to be an artist
- new girl
- Terabithia, a secret meeting place
- cross a creek . . . old rope
- build a wooden fort . . . [that] takes them to a thousand places
- the day they begin . . . their friendship

284

Paragraph Response

When you write a paragraph about something you've read, it should focus on one event. The **topic sentence** identifies the story, the author, and the event. The details in the **body** of the paragraph describe the event, and the **closing sentence** tells why the event is important.

In the following response, Shandra writes about the book *Bridge to Terabithia.* She shares an event she thinks is very important.

Topic sentence · · · · · · · · · ·

A Friendship Fort

The most important event in Katherine Paterson's *Bridge to Terabithia* is when Jess and Leslie build their fort. Jess is a shy boy who wants to be an artist, and Leslie is the new girl in the neighborhood. They don't fit in with other kids, but they get along with each other. Together, Jess and Leslie create Terabithia, a secret meeting place in the woods. To get there, they must cross a creek by swinging on an old rope. Jess and Leslie build a wooden fort in Terabithia and spend a lot of time there. Their little wooden fort takes them to a thousand

Body

Closing sentence · · · · · · · · · · places. The day Jess and Leslie create Terabithia is the day they begin to build their friendship.

 Respond to the reading. On your own paper, answer the following questions.

☐ **Ideas** (1) What part of the story does the writer think is most important? (2) Why is it important?

☐ **Organization** (3) Is this paragraph organized by time, by order of importance, or by some other logical order?

☐ **Voice & Word Choice** (4) Does the writer sound knowledgeable about the story? (5) What words or phrases tell you so?

English Language Learners

Limited English vocabulary may make it difficult for students to see that certain words and phrases indicate that the writer is knowledgeable about the story.

- Discuss the possible responses to **Respond to the reading** question 5. Point out that these are specific story events and details that show the writer is familiar with and knowledgeable about the story.

- Read a brief version of a fairy tale, such as "The Three Little Pigs."
- Then call on volunteers to suggest important events and details from the story.
- Point out that remembering such details shows that they are very knowledgeable about the story. Explain that writing about events and details such as these gives writers a knowledgeable voice.

Prewriting Selecting a Topic

Your first step in writing a response to literature is choosing a book or short story to write about. Shandra began by listing novels and stories she had read. (See pages 600 and 602 for punctuation of titles.)

Books	Short Stories
Holes	"Gift of the Magi"
The Cay	"The Bell"
Bridge to Terabithia	"Legend of Sleepy Hollow"

 Choose a book or short story. On your own paper, list some of your favorite books or short stories. Circle the one that interests you the most.

Focusing on an Important Event

Think about things that happen in the story you've chosen. Focus on events that affect the whole story. A cluster like the one below can help you find the important events.

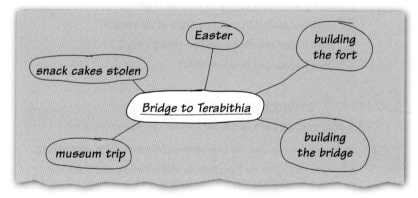

 Create a cluster. In the center of your cluster, write the title of the book or short story. Around it, write a number of important events. Then choose one event for your paragraph.

LITERATURE

Prewriting Selecting a Topic

Help students choose a book or short story as a topic for a response paragraph. Have them work together to create a list of titles from previous reading assignments and independent reading.

- Students can refer to their reading logs and reader-response journals for ideas.
- If time allows, have students browse classroom or library bookshelves and list titles.
- If students want to list books and short stories as shown, provide photocopies of the reproducible T-chart (TE page 800).
- Be sure they follow the conventions for capitalization and punctuation of titles.

* Instructions for capitalizing and punctuating titles can be found on PE pages 600 and 602.

Prewriting
Focusing on an Important Event

Discuss what makes a story event important. An important event usually

- involves the main character,
- changes the main character in some way,
- affects the outcome, and
- adds drama or suspense.

Struggling Learners

Monitor students as they work on making a cluster of important events in the story. To keep students focused, guide them with prompts related to the class discussion:

- Does the event involve the main character?
- Does it change the main character in some way?

- Does the event affect the outcome or how the story ends?
- Does the event add drama or suspense to make the story more interesting or exciting?

286

Writing Creating Your First Draft

Getting started is often the hardest part of writing, so help students over that first hurdle. Write on the board the following sentence pattern, which is based on the sample topic sentence on PE page 284.

- The most important event in _____'s [insert author's name] _____ [give title of book or story] is when _____ [name important event].

Students can use this sentence pattern to write their own topic sentences by filling in the blanks.

✳ Additional information about writing about an event is on PE page 533.

Revising
Improving Your Paragraph

Explain that opinions and feelings do not belong in a paragraph summarizing an important event. As students revise, tell them to look for words that signal opinions, such as *I think* or *I believe*.

Editing Checking for Conventions

Have students exchange papers to check for mistakes in grammar, punctuation, and spelling.

Writing Creating Your First Draft

Remember that a paragraph has three main parts: a topic sentence, the body, and a closing sentence. (See the sample on page 284.)

- **Topic sentence:** Write a sentence that names the book or short story, its author, and the main event you will focus on.
- **Body:** Write sentences that describe the event.
- **Closing sentence:** End with a sentence that tells why the event is important.

 Write the first draft of your paragraph. Use the information above as a guide.

Revising Improving Your Paragraph

After you've written your first draft, you need to revise your paragraph for *ideas, organization, voice, word choice,* and *sentence fluency.*

 Review your paragraph. Use the following questions as a guide when you revise.

1. Have I written about an important event?
2. Do my sentences appear in the best order?
3. Does my interest in the story show in my voice?
4. Have I used specific nouns and strong verbs?
5. Do my sentences flow smoothly?

Editing Checking for Conventions

Check your revised paragraph for correct use of conventions.

 Edit your work. Use the following questions to guide your editing.

1. Have I checked my punctuation, capitalization, and spelling? Have I underlined the title (or used quotation marks)?
2. Have I used the right words (*to, two, too; who's, whose*)?

Proofread your paragraph. After making a neat copy of your final paragraph, check it one more time for errors.

evaluate *PREVIEW* react answer *experience* 287

Response to Literature

Writing a Book Review

Have you ever been carried away by a book? You start to read but soon lose track of where you are and what time it is. For a while, nothing exists outside of the story, and you and the book soar together on a flight of fancy.

Writing a response to a book helps you relive those flights of fancy. In this assignment, you will write about an insight you have discovered in a book or story. As you recap the important events, you'll soar once more.

Writing Guidelines

Subject:	An insight about a story
Form:	An essay
Purpose:	To share an insight
Audience:	Classmates

Writing a Book Review

Objectives
- understand what a book review is
- understand the form and content of a book review
- plan, draft, revise, edit, and publish a book review

A **book review** is a brief essay in which you
- retell important events in the story, and
- relate an insight.

Explain that an insight is an important idea readers come to understand as they read and think about a book or story.

Talk about what it means to be "carried away" by a book. Ask students if they have ever been so involved in a book that they
- didn't hear their name called,
- relived parts of the story after putting the book down,
- dreamed of being a character in the book, or
- couldn't wait to get back to the book.

Struggling Learners

Students who are reluctant readers may not have experienced being carried away by a book they read on their own. However, they probably have had a memorable experience at some point with a book or story that was read to them by a teacher or parent.

- Encourage students to freewrite about that experience, using the stem *"I was so caught up in the story that I . . ."*

- Another possible approach is to have students freewrite about being carried away by a movie. The visual nature of film allows these students to learn about the elements of literature (such as plot, theme, and characters) without struggling to read a story.

Understanding Your Goals

Traits of a Response to Literature

Three traits relate to the development of the content and the form. They provide a focus during prewriting, drafting, and revising.

- Ideas
- **Organization**
- Voice

The other three traits relate more to form. Checking them is part of the revising and editing processes.

- **Word Choice**
- **Sentence Fluency**
- **Conventions**

✳ The six-point rubric on PE pages 318–319 is based on these traits. Four- and five-point rubrics are available on TE pages 771 and 775.

Explain to students that forming an insight means understanding (or *seeing*) how ideas or events are related to one another.

288

Understanding Your Goals

How do you know what to include in your response? For starters, your response must clearly and concisely retell the story and develop an insight. The chart that follows lists all the key traits of writing a response to literature.

TRAITS OF A RESPONSE TO LITERATURE

Ideas

Write a focus statement that tells what your insight is and support it with carefully selected details.

Organization

Organize your response using one of the organization patterns. (See page 551.)

Voice

Use a formal voice that fits the assignment and the audience.

Word Choice

Use active verbs instead of passive verbs and avoid too many modifiers.

Sentence Fluency

Vary sentence beginnings and avoid rambling sentences.

Conventions

Correct all errors in punctuation, capitalization, spelling, and grammar.

 Get the big picture. Look at the rubric on pages 318–319. You can use this rubric to assess your progress. Your goal is to write a book review that contains your personal insight about a book or short story.

Advanced Learners

Assign each student one of the six traits of an effective response to literature, if possible, according to their writing strengths. If there are more than six students, have pairs or small groups work together.

- Provide time for them to become "expert" in that trait by studying the appropriate revising or editing pages for that trait (PE pages 302–315).
- During the writing process, experts can support and advise classmates. For example, during prewriting the Ideas expert can help others develop a clear focus statement.

evaluate PREVIEW experience **289**
answer
react
Writing a Book Review

Writing a Book Review

Bud, Not Buddy is the winner of the 2000 Newbery Medal and the 2000 Coretta Scott King Award. The following essay by student writer Jiang Li tells how the events in the story lead to her understanding and insight.

BEGINNING

The beginning introduces the book and shows the writer's insight in the focus statement (underlined).

MIDDLE

The middle paragraphs summarize the main events that lead to the writer's insight.

Bud, Not Buddy

Bud, Not Buddy by Christopher Paul Curtis is a story about a young boy finding people who care about him. Like all of us, Bud knows that having people who care for you is a lucky thing. The "family" that Bud finds has some of the same qualities that a lot of families have today. This story shows that some members of a family may not be related, but they still care for each other.

When the story starts, 10-year-old Bud lives with his mother in Flint, Michigan. It is 1936, and the Great Depression is making life hard for most people. Times are very difficult, but they become more difficult for Bud after his mother dies. She never tells him who his father is. Bud thinks a man named Herman E. Calloway may be his father because of five posters his mother has kept through the years. The posters advertise a band named Herman E. Calloway and the Dusky Devastators of the Depression. Bud sets out to find Herman E. Calloway.

Many things happen to Bud as he searches. All of the situations that he comes across show readers what the Great Depression was like. For example, Bud spends time with other homeless people. He tries to leap into a boxcar of a moving train to get to another city. He also waits in food lines and eats at missions. We see how strangers help each other and become like the extended families we have today.

When Bud finally reaches Grand Rapids, he finds Calloway and tells him his story. Calloway says he is not Bud's father. However, he gives Bud jobs in exchange for room and board.

LITERATURE

Writing a Book Review

Work through this sample book review with students, pointing out the elements that make this essay a good response to literature.

Ideas

- The focus statement shows the writer's insight.
- Details support and develop the writer's insight.

Organization

- The beginning paragraph reveals the writer's insight and the ending paragraph restates the insight.
- The middle paragraphs summarize main events in chronological order.

Voice

- A formal voice is appropriate to the tone of the story.
- Description of characters and other specific details show the writer's knowledge.

Struggling Learners

Understanding the term *insight* is crucial to writing a response to literature. Applying the concept to well-known stories first, rather than to grade-level literature, may make it easier to understand.

Explain that having an *insight* means gaining an understanding of an important message or idea.

Do a think-aloud activity to model how you would develop insight into "Goldilocks and the Three Bears."

- Start by summarizing the story briefly, as you would in a book review. However, extend your modeling to show your thought process about what the storyteller might have wanted young listeners to understand.
- Elicit student ideas and guide them toward an appropriate

insight (for example, one insight might be that Goldilocks didn't have the right to enter a stranger's house and help herself.)
- If time allows, have students choose a movie that can be explored in a similar way. Have students focus on how the character changes and how the key events help them, as viewers, to understand the story.

Respond to the reading.

Answers

Ideas **1.** Some members of a family may not be related, but they still care for each other.

Organization **2.** The purpose of the four middle paragraphs is to summarize main events from the story. They also help show how the writer developed the insight expressed in the focus statement.

3. The last paragraph is like the first because

- it talks about the family that Bud has found;
- the last sentence of both paragraphs expresses the same insight, but in different words.

Voice **& Word Choice 4.** Possible choices:

- the Great Depression is making life hard . . .
- five posters . . . advertise a band named Herman E. Calloway and the Dusky Devastators . . .
- Bud [lives] . . . with homeless people. He tries to leap into a boxcar . . . [and] waits in food lines.
- Calloway . . . gives Bud jobs in exchange for room and board.
- five smooth rocks . . . turn out to be the key to Bud's identity.

MIDDLE
This paragraph shares details that continue to develop the writer's insight.

ENDING
· · · · · · · · · · · ·
The ending paragraph restates the writer's understanding of this story.

Bud doesn't unpack the few things he owns: an old blanket, five smooth rocks with letters and dots written on them, the five posters, and a picture of his mother. Because Calloway is a grumpy, rather mean person, Bud thinks about moving on, but the band members are good to Bud. For one thing, they buy him an old saxophone. This is one of the ways they show Bud that they care. The band members know each other's weaknesses and skills. They are a family in many ways, and Bud likes being a part of their lives.

The five smooth rocks, not the posters, turn out to be the key to Bud's identity. When Bud discovers that Calloway has a collection of smooth stones in the glove compartment of his car, he tells Calloway, "I've got some of these, Sir." Calloway turns out to be his mother's father, not Bud's father, but this makes Calloway his grandfather.

One of the best parts of the story is when Bud gets his old blanket out and remakes his bed. Now he knows this is the bed his mom slept in as a child. Readers know now that he isn't going to leave. Even though Bud never finds his father, he has found a "family" in the band members and a grouchy grandfather. Not all members of his family are related by blood, but they care for him as any family would.

Respond to the reading. Answer the following questions about the sample response.

☐ Ideas **(1)** What is the important insight stated in the first paragraph?

☐ Organization **(2)** What is the purpose of the four middle paragraphs? **(3)** How is the last paragraph like the first paragraph?

☐ Voice **& Word Choice (4)** Find some sentences and words that help to show the writer's voice.

Advanced Learners

Discuss forming an insight about literature as the process of seeing how events or actions are related and how they say something important about life.

- Remind students that Jiang Li's insight was that you don't need to be related to act like a family and care for each other.

- Have students reread Jiang Li's book review and look for specific actions that support her focus statement.

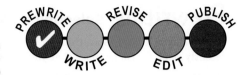

evaluate *PREVIEW* experience react answer
291
Writing a Book Review

Prewriting

Prewriting is the first step in the writing process. It involves selecting a book or story to write about, listing important events in the plot, writing a focus statement, and planning your paragraphs.

Keys to Effective Prewriting

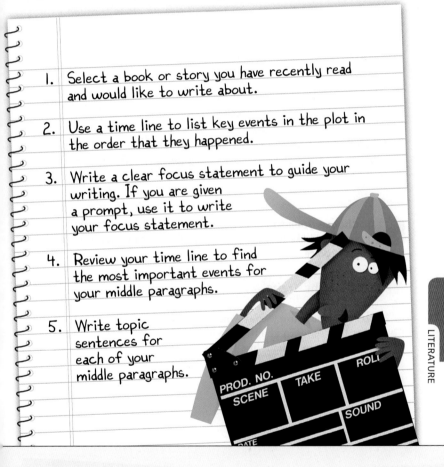

1. Select a book or story you have recently read and would like to write about.

2. Use a time line to list key events in the plot in the order that they happened.

3. Write a clear focus statement to guide your writing. If you are given a prompt, use it to write your focus statement.

4. Review your time line to find the most important events for your middle paragraphs.

5. Write topic sentences for each of your middle paragraphs.

LITERATURE

Prewriting
Keys to Effective Prewriting

Remind students that during the prewriting stage, they must select a topic, gather details, and decide how to organize those details.

The Keys to Effective Prewriting lays out the process students will be guided through on pages 292–294.

■ Suggest that students look at the list of titles they created earlier (see TE page 285) as they think about a book or story to write about.

■ Remind students that a focus statement (item 3) contains an insight or an understanding that they have formed about a book or a story. Tell students that they will learn more about writing a focus statement and developing an insight during prewriting.

Prewriting Selecting a Topic

To help students compose one-sentence summaries for their charts, model the following strategy, using a familiar tale.

- Answer these questions:
  1. Who is (are) the main character(s)?
  2. What does the main character want?
  3. What does the main character do?
- Use the answers to complete a "somebody-wants-so" summary sentence. For example, Hare (1) wants to prove he's faster than Tortoise (2), so he challenges Tortoise to a race (3).

Focus on the Traits

Ideas

As students explore the thoughts, feelings, and actions of the main character, tell them to also pay careful attention to what other story characters say and think about the main character.

292

Prewriting Selecting a Topic

To choose a good topic, think of novels, short stories, or plays you have recently read. Consider those that you know well and enjoyed reading.

 Chart your choices. Make a chart like the one shown below. In the first column, fill in three or four titles of stories you've read recently. In the second column, write a sentence that sums up the story.

Title	Story Summary
* The Talking Earth	Billie Wind travels alone through the Everglades.
"Zlateh the Goat"	Zlateh and Aaron save each others' lives.
The Miracle Worker	Annie Sullivan tries to teach Helen Keller to speak.

* I choose The Talking Earth because I really like the story. It's different, but I think other students will like it, too.

 Choose your topic. Review your chart and put a star next to the title you would like to write about. Beneath the chart, explain the reason for your choice.

Focus on the Traits

Ideas Each story that you read expresses important ideas about life. To learn about these ideas, pay careful attention to the main character's thoughts, feelings, and actions. In this way, you will develop an understanding or insight into the story.

Struggling Learners

Students may benefit from collaboration with other students when working on the **Chart your choices** activity. Therefore, pair students who have read some of the same texts.

- Have them each complete a chart, so they will have a copy to keep with their writing work.
- Encourage each student to choose at least one title to write about later.

If students have any trouble using the "somebody-wants-so" sentence strategy, model it yourself, using stories read in class. Then invite students to apply the technique.

Advanced Learners

Challenge students to determine whether each of the titles listed in the sample chart is a book or a short story. Ask how they can tell (by the punctuation in the title).

If students have read any of the works listed, have them discuss whether or not the summary is accurate. Encourage students to rewrite each summary, using the "somebody-wants-so" strategy.

evaluate PREVIEW experience **293**
answer
Writing a Book Review

Gathering Details

Once you select a story to review, the next step is to identify the important events in the plot. A time line like the one below allows you to list the events in the order in which they happened. After listing the events, you can use them to develop the insight you have about the story. An insight often centers around growing up or learning a lesson.

Time Line

Summary: *Billie Wind journeys alone through the Everglades.*

- *A fire reminds Billie of stories about serpents.*
- *An otter in a cave reminds her of a little man in a legend.*
- *The calls of birds and animals sound like human voices.*
- *The movement of animals shows that a hurricane is coming.*
- *Billie moves to higher ground with the animals and enters a cave.*
- *A panther saves Billie and a boy during the storm.*

Insight: *Billie learns that the animals are the source of many of her tribe's beliefs.*

 Make a time line. List the key events in the order in which they happened. (Try to list five or six events.) Study the events to help you discover how they lead up to your insight about the story you've read.

Focus on the Traits

Voice There's a good chance your writing will have a confident, knowledgeable voice if you know and understand the story well. So make sure you carefully review your story.

LITERATURE

Prewriting Gathering Details

If necessary, explain that the plot is what happens in a story.

Call attention to the sample time line.

- Remind students to list events in time order, which is the order in which they happened—not necessarily the order in which the events are introduced in the story.
- For example, a character may recall something that happened to her when she was much younger, or the narrator may describe an event that happened in the past. These events would be listed early in a time line.

* For more information about using chronological (or time) order, see PE page 534.

Focus on the Traits

Voice

To help students achieve a knowledgeable voice, have them fill in a **plot line** (*see below*) as they review their story. Students can use the completed plot line to retell the story to a partner. Encourage partners to point out any obvious gaps in the story line, any events that seem to be out of order, or anything else that is confusing.

Teaching Tip: Using a Plot Line

Draw a plot line on the board (see PE pages 139 and 351). Contrast a plot line, which shows the basic action of a story, with a time line, which shows many events. Explain that filling in a plot line helps you figure out if you know a story well enough to write about it. Have students help you fill in the plot line for a story they know.

English Language Learners

Suggest that students think of their chosen story as a movie and have them visualize scenes from the movie. For each scene, have students make notes on an index card. Then have them arrange the cards in the order in which the scenes happened. Tell students to use the cards to retell the story to a partner. If the order of events sounds right, students can use the cards to write a time line.

Advanced Learners

Challenge students to use their time line to fill in a plot line for their story. Then encourage students to use the plot line to help them develop an accurate insight. Invite them to explain their thinking to the class, so that others can hear and see how the process works.

Prewriting
Writing a Focus Statement

Use the following ideas as you discuss writing a focus statement.

- An insight often centers around growing up or learning a lesson.
- The word *teaches* in the sample insight suggests the character has had a learning experience.
- Invite the class to brainstorm a list of verbs that will help them express an insight in their focus statements. Provide a few words to help them get started, such as *teaches, learns, realizes, sees, accepts,* and *understands.*
- Caution students against beginning their focus statement with the phrase, "This book is about . . ."
- The sample focus statement on PE page 294 begins with a rewording of the summary in the sample chart on PE page 292.

Prewriting
Planning the Middle Part of Your Essay

Provide time for students to review their time lines. To help them figure out how many middle paragraphs they need, suggest that they limit the number of events in a paragraph to three or four.

294

Prewriting Writing a Focus Statement

In any story, the events will change the main character in some way. For example, the events in *The Talking Earth* teach Billie Wind to respect her tribe's beliefs.

In the time line you created on page 293, you listed the important events in the story. In your review, you will summarize these events and present your insight to the reader. Here is a formula that will help you write a two-part focus statement that will guide your book review.

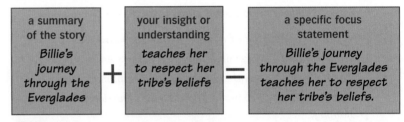

a summary of the story		your insight or understanding		a specific focus statement
Billie's journey through the Everglades	+	teaches her to respect her tribe's beliefs	=	Billie's journey through the Everglades teaches her to respect her tribe's beliefs.

Form a focus. Write a focus statement for your essay using the formula above. If you don't like how your first one turns out, write another.

Planning the Middle Part of Your Essay

Once you have written a focus statement, the next step is to plan the middle part of your essay. The first middle paragraph should cover events in your time line that happened early in the story. The second paragraph should cover the events that happened later on. (If you have a lot of events, you might need a third and even a fourth middle paragraph.)

Plan your middle paragraphs. Review your time line. Make sure you've listed all the important events.

1 Put one check next to the events that happen early in the story. (These events will be in your first middle paragraph.)

2 Put two checks next to the events that happen later on. (These events will be in your other middle paragraphs.)

3 Write topic sentences for your middle paragraphs. (See pages 552–553 for more information.)

Writing

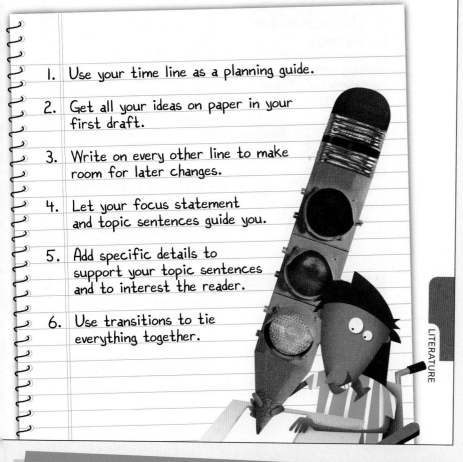

When you write your first draft, you turn your prewriting ideas into an essay. Your time line, focus statement, paragraph plan, and topic sentences will help you write your essay.

Keys to Effective Writing

1. Use your time line as a planning guide.

2. Get all your ideas on paper in your first draft.

3. Write on every other line to make room for later changes.

4. Let your focus statement and topic sentences guide you.

5. Add specific details to support your topic sentences and to interest the reader.

6. Use transitions to tie everything together.

LITERATURE

Writing Keys to Effective Writing

Remind students that the writing stage is when they get to write, or draft, their ideas on paper.

The Keys to Effective Writing lays out the process students will be guided through on pages 296–300.

Before students begin, suggest that they review their prewriting materials. They should have

- a clear focus statement that includes an insight or understanding to guide their writing,
- a plan for how many middle paragraphs to include, and
- topic sentences for each middle paragraph.

Remind students that their readers may not have read the book they are reviewing. They should keep this point in mind as they try to decide which details to include. They should choose **specific details** (*see below*) that are interesting, informative, and that support their insight.

Teaching Tip: Specific Details

Explain that specific details are exact and to the point. Good writers use specific details to help readers understand what they are reading.

Write the following sentence on the board:

A girl takes a trip that teaches her respect.

Have students compare the statement above to the sample focus statement on PE page 294. Ask:

- What is missing?
- What do you know from the specific details in the sample on PE page 294 that you could not tell from the shorter statement here?

Writing Getting the Big Picture

Although most professional book reviews devote a good deal of attention to an author's writing style and story sense, students can still benefit from hearing how a reviewer summarizes important story events. Share reviews for books students may have read. Consult with literature teachers for titles.

Suggest that students create a graphic organizer similar to this one to outline their book review.

■ Point out that for the middle, they should show one topic sentence for each middle paragraph.

■ Be sure students understand the difference in the way the insight is expressed in the beginning paragraph (it is stated) and in the ending paragraph (it is restated or explained). Students may not be able to fill in this part of their outline until after they've written the first two parts of their review.

■ Suggest that students use this outline to plan and organize each section of their review when they are ready to write it. It isn't necessary to complete the whole outline now.

296

Writing Getting the Big Picture

The chart below shows how the parts of a book review fit together. (The examples are from the essay about Billie Wind on pages 297–300.) You're ready to write your review once you . . .

● know enough about the story,
● state your topic in a clear, two-part focus statement, and
● plan your paragraphs.

BEGINNING

The **beginning** paragraph introduces the story and states the writer's insight in a focus statement.

Focus Statement
Billie's journey through the Everglades teaches her to respect her tribe's beliefs.

MIDDLE

The **first middle** paragraph covers early events in the story.

The **other middle** paragraphs cover events that occur later on.

Two Topic Sentences
During her travels, Billie sees and hears things that make her think of her tribe.

Billie has no way of knowing that a hurricane is coming soon.

ENDING

The **ending** explains the writer's insight into the story.

Closing Sentence
She finally understands exactly what her elders mean when they speak of "the talking earth," and now she can respect her tribe's beliefs.

Starting Your Review

The beginning paragraph should introduce the story and state your insight in a focus statement.

Beginning Paragraph

Read the beginning paragraph below. Notice how this paragraph begins with a general introduction and ends with a specific focus statement. Also review the first paragraph of the model on page 289.

▶ Beginning
Middle
Ending

The first part introduces the story.

The focus statement includes the writer's insight (underlined).

> _The Talking Earth_ by Jean Craighead George is about a Seminole Indian girl named Billie Wind. She doubts the beliefs held by her people. The elders speak of great serpents in the swamp, little people underground, and talking animals. Billie says she doesn't believe in anything she can't see, so she decides to take a trip alone through the swamps. <u>Billie's journey through the Everglades teaches her to respect her tribe's beliefs.</u>

Retelling in the Present Tense

A book review can be written in the past or present tense. The verbs in the sample paragraph above are all in the present tense (_is, doubts, speak, says, decides_). Because the events in a story happen again and again each time the story is read, it makes sense to discuss them in the present tense. In the essay you are about to write, you also should use the present tense.

Write your beginning. Write the first paragraph of your essay. Be sure to include information that introduces the story and state your insight in a focus statement.

LITERATURE

Writing Starting Your Review

Remind students that their beginning paragraph should do the following:

- Begin with a general introduction of the book.
- Provide some background about the main character and his or her problem or goal.
- End with a specific focus statement. Explain that although a focus sentence can appear anywhere in a paragraph, it is usually the first or last sentence.

Writing
Retelling in the Present Tense

Point out that students can write their review in either the past or present tense; they just need to keep all verbs in the same tense. Invite a volunteer to reread the sample paragraph with all the verbs in the past tense. Encourage the class to help with past-tense forms when necessary. Remind students that for regular verbs, the past tense is formed by adding _–d_ or _–ed_.

✱ For more about verb tenses, see PE page 483.

To give students a better idea of the shape that a beginning paragraph takes, draw an inverted triangle. (This graphic is often used to show how the lead of a newspaper article is written.)

- Inside the triangle, write the numerals 1 through 5 in a column, with 1 at the top and 5 at the point on the bottom.

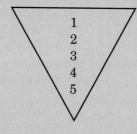

- Then, as you point to each number and say it aloud, have a volunteer read aloud the

corresponding sentence (first, second, and so on) in the sample paragraph.

- Explain how this inverted triangle shows that the sample writer began to write about the book in general terms and then ended up with a narrower, more specific focus statement at the close of the paragraph.

Writing
Developing the Middle Part

Use one or more of these ideas as students develop the middle of their essay.

- Point out that in the last sentence of the sample paragraph, the writer comes to a conclusion about the importance of the events in the first part of the story and makes a connection to the insight stated in the sample on PE page 297. Students can include a similar sentence at the end of a middle paragraph to link important events to their insight.
- Encourage students to use the transitions listed at the bottom of the page to show time order.
- Caution students against writing too much. Remind them to summarize events, not retell the whole book for their readers.
- Emphasize that their purpose is to summarize important events and to show how important events lead to the insight or understanding they gained as they read the book.

Ideally, their readers will be so interested that they will want to read the book themselves.

298

Writing Developing the Middle Part

The middle paragraphs should summarize the main events that lead to your insight. Start each middle paragraph with a topic sentence that introduces the events that follow. (Use your time line to help you with this part.)

Beginning
Middle
Ending

First Middle Paragraph

The first middle paragraph tells about the important events in the first part of the story.

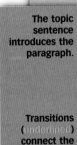

The topic sentence introduces the paragraph.

Transitions (underlined) connect the events.

During her travels, Billie sees and hears things that make her think of her tribe. First, a huge fire reminds her of a serpent because the flames are like the tongues of snakes. Then, in a cave, she mistakes a playful young otter for a little man like the one in her tribe's legends. Later, the calls of birds and animals begin to sound like human voices. She feels close to nature, but she still doesn't think that the beliefs of her elders are really true.

Transitions

The transitions below show time. These words can help make the ideas in your essay easier to follow. (Also see pages 572–573.)

about	before	later	soon	tomorrow
after	during	meanwhile	then	until
as soon as	finally	next	third	when
at	first	second	today	yesterday

English Language Learners

Use the transitions underlined in the sample paragraph to explain that some words show time and can be thought of as numbers.

- Equate *first* with 1, *then* with 2, and *later* with 3.
- Explain that a writer uses these transition words to make the order of events clear.
- Then discuss some of the easier transitions shown in the box, pointing out that many can

work together to show time order and can be thought of as numbers. For example, *before* and *after* can be thought of as 1 and 2; *yesterday, today,* and *tomorrow* can be thought of as 1, 2, 3.

- Encourage students to use transition words that show time in their writing, to make the order of events clear.

Second Middle Paragraph

The second middle paragraph tells about events that happen later in the story. You may write additional paragraphs as needed.

> The topic sentence introduces the paragraph.
>
> Details about each event help develop the writer's insight.

Billie has no way of knowing that a hurricane is coming soon. Then she notices the unusual movement of the animals and follows them to higher ground. Once again, she finds shelter in a cave with a boy and young panther. Later, the wind quiets down. Billie and the boy start to go outside, but they notice that the panther is not budging from the cave. Billie and the boy decide to stay in the cave because the panther does. The panther saves their lives.

 Write the middle of your review. Using the following tips, write the middle paragraphs of your essay. (Look again at the sample paragraphs.)

Drafting Tips

- **Talk about the story** with a classmate before you begin to write this part.
- **Review your time line** to make sure you've included all the significant events.
- **Include important details** that will help the reader understand your insight.
- **Write as freely as you can**, without being too concerned about neatness.

LITERATURE

To help students understand how to use details to develop an insight, ask:

What details in the sample help develop the writer's insight? (Possible responses: she notices the unusual movement of the animals; they notice that the panther is not budging; Billie and the boy stay in the cave because the panther does; the panther saves their lives)

Writing Drafting Tips

Discuss how to approach a first draft:

- When writing a first draft, students should get all of their ideas on paper.
- Students should follow their prewriting plan but be willing to include new ideas (or move in a new direction if an idea doesn't work or if they have a new idea altogether).
- A first draft doesn't need to be perfect. For now, students should concentrate on forming their ideas.

Have students work in pairs or small groups to review ideas for the middle paragraphs. They can take turns sharing their insights and the supporting details (events or actions) that will help readers understand the insights. Listeners should indicate whether an insight makes sense to them, based on those details.

Struggling Learners

Students may need some assistance making the connection between details and the insight. Ask a volunteer to share his or her insight and supporting details, so that you can do a think-aloud of the process.

As you do the think-aloud, have students listen for the kinds of questions you would ask yourself and a partner. Guide students toward questions that will help them work productively with their partners. Sample questions may include the following:

- Which details help support the connection to the insight?
- How do I know?

Writing Ending Your Book Review

By now, students should have recognized how the character in their book changed and how this change contributed to their own insight and understanding of the story. Nevertheless, some students may have to stop to figure this out before they can write an ending. Suggest that these students review their prewriting notes as they answer the following questions:

- What does the main character believe or feel at the beginning of the story?
- What happens to the main character during the story because of this belief or feeling?
- How does the main character believe or feel at the end of the story?

300

Writing Ending Your Book Review

Your focus statement introduced your insight into the story, and your closing paragraph should restate it. Ask yourself the following questions:

- What main events helped me gain an insight into the story?
- How does the change in the main character help my understanding of the story?
- How should I state my insight in the conclusion?

 Your insight is the message you want to leave with your readers. It often centers around *growing up* or *learning a lesson*.

Beginning
Middle
▶ **Ending**

Ending Paragraph

Read the ending paragraph below. The writer states that Billie learns an important lesson about nature and about her tribe.

The ending restates the writer's insight.

> After her journey, Billie understands that nature speaks to everyone. She sees that the animals really have been talking to her all along because they have been showing her how to live. She finally understands what her elders mean when they speak of "the talking earth," and now she can respect her tribe's beliefs.

 Write your ending. In your last paragraph, be sure to explain how the change in the main character helped you develop your insight.

Form a complete first draft. Make a complete copy of your essay. Double-space to leave room for revising.

English Language Learners

Students may need extra practice stating an insight in the first paragraph and then rephrasing it as an explanation in the last paragraph.

- Use the sample beginning (PE page 297) and ending on this page to show students that, after writing the focus statement, the reviewer could ask himself or herself, *What did the experience teach her?* Answering that question makes it easier to write the closing statement.
- Give a simple example of the opening and closing statements a writer might use in a review of a familiar story, fable, or folk tale. For example, the focus statement might be:

  In his race against the tortoise, the hare learned an important lesson.

The question might be:

  What did he learn?

And the closing statement might be:

  The hare learned that the fastest runners or workers are not always the most successful.

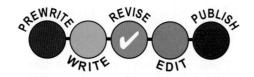

Revising

A first draft is never perfect. One of the paragraphs might be missing an important idea. Another might appear in the wrong place. Revising your essay can fix problems like these.

Keys to Effective Revising

1. Read through your entire draft to get a feeling of how well your essay works.

2. Make sure your focus statement clearly states your insight into the story.

3. Check your paragraphs to make sure the details support the topic sentences.

4. Work with your voice until it sounds personal and knowledgeable.

5. Check your words and sentences.

6. Use the editing and proofreading marks inside the back cover of this book.

LITERATURE

Revising

Keys to Effective Revising

The Keys to Effective Revising lays out the process students will be guided through on pages 302–316.

Encourage students to help each other overcome problems that frequently pop up in their writing. After reviewing the Keys to Effective Writing, divide students into small groups. Encourage group members to take turns sharing what they do during revising to fix these types of problems:

- a boring beginning
- a weak or missing topic sentence
- a lack of supporting details
- an abrupt and incomplete ending

Remind students to practice good listening and **group skills** *(see below)* as they share ideas.

Teaching Tip: Group Skills

It is important for students to develop good skills for working in pairs or groups. As you monitor group work, offer students advice on ways to correct any bad habits. Remind them to

- listen carefully to each other,
- be willing to share ideas,
- speak clearly and stay on topic,
- be polite and kind,
- respect the ideas and feelings of others,

- respect their own ideas and feelings.

* For more help with group skills, see the "Listening and Speaking" section on PE pages 417–422.

English Language Learners

Have students work in small groups of three or four. Group them with peers who have excellent listening and group skills. Students may benefit from having their drafts read aloud by a group member so that they can hear what works and what might need improvement.

Revising for Ideas

The rubric strips that run across PE pages 302–311 are provided to help students focus their revising. The ideas in these strips are related to the full rubric on PE pages 318–319.

Have students review the rubric on PE pages 302–303. Then ask students to look for the following features in their drafts:

- a focus statement that introduces the story and includes an insight
- key details that show a knowledge of the story

 Answers

1. b
2. a
3. a
4. b

After completing the **Try It** activity, have students use the formula on PE page 294 to show how the correct focus statements work. For example, point out the key parts of the first statement:

- As Jody cares for his pony, (summary)
- he learns about love and loss. (a specific insight)

302

Revising for Ideas

 6 My focus statement and details show knowledge and real insight into the reading.

5 My review has a two-part focus statement and all the necessary details.

4 My review has a two-part focus statement, but I need to cut a few unnecessary details.

When you revise for *ideas,* you're focusing on the thoughts and details in your essay. The rubric above will help you revise your essay for this trait.

Does my focus statement work?

Your focus statement works if it clearly introduces the story and includes your insight. Be sure you have used the formula below to write your focus statement. (Also see page **294**.)

EFFECTIVE FOCUS STATEMENT

Billie's journey through the Everglades (*summary of the story*) teaches her to respect her tribe's beliefs (*a specific insight*).

 Read each pair of focus statements below. For each pair, decide which statement works better. Be prepared to explain why.

1. a. As Jody cares for his pony, he works really hard.
   b. As Jody cares for his pony, he learns about love and loss.

2. a. Buck's trials and challenges increase his courage and leadership qualities.
   b. Buck tries hard, unlike his owners.

3. a. Meg's journey to save her father makes her more confident.
   b. Meg's journey to save her father is long.

4. a. The team's efforts to make the finals were valuable.
   b. The team's efforts to make the finals helped them realize that everyone has unique talents.

 Review your focus statement. Make sure that your focus statement introduces the story and contains a specific insight. If you're unsure the focus statement works, ask your teacher or a classmate for help.

Struggling Learners

Help students assess whether their own focus statement follows the formula shown here and on PE page 294.

- Provide photocopies of the reproducible T-chart (TE page 800).
- At the top of the left-hand column, have students write *summary of story*.
- At the top of the right-hand column, have students write *my insight*.

- Direct students to write each part of their focus statement under the appropriate heading.
- Then have students use the rubric to rate their focus statement and revise as needed.

evaluate   PREVIEW   experience
react   answer
303
Writing a Book Review

3 My focus statement has only one of the parts. I need to cut a few unnecessary details.

2 I need an effective focus statement and better details.

1 I need to learn how to write a focus statement and gather details.

Have I cut unnecessary details?

When summarizing a story, you should include only the key details. All other information should be cut. You should . . .

- delete anything that you repeated,
- cut unnecessary details, and
- drop unimportant personal thoughts and feelings.

 Write the paragraph below on your own paper. Using the list above as a guide, cut any details that are unnecessary. Afterward, share your work with a classmate.

1   "Dog's Eye View" is a pretty good story about a dog named
2   Moose. Lots of people give their pets funny names. One day,
3   Moose slips out of his owner's apartment and goes exploring.
4   The story follows Moose all around New York City. I love New
5   York City. Moose meets lots of interesting New Yorkers.

 Review your essay. Make sure your essay contains the main points and no unnecessary details. Revise your essay as needed.

Ideas
An unnecessary detail and personal comment are dropped.

> The Talking Earth by Jean Craighead George, ~~who also wrote My Side of the Mountain~~, is about a Seminole Indian girl named Billie Wind. ~~I liked it.~~

LITERATURE

Students may feel that any detail they include is important and necessary. Before asking them to do the **Try It** activity, stress that, in a book review, unnecessary details are details that

- say the same thing twice,
- have nothing at all to do with the focus statement,
- express their own thoughts and feelings.

If students need a refresher, review the use of proofreading marks as shown at the bottom of the page and on the inside back cover.

Try It Answers

[Revised Paragraph]

"Dog's Eye View" is a story about a dog named Moose. One day, Moose slips out of his owner's apartment and goes exploring. The story follows Moose all around New York City, where he meets lots of interesting New Yorkers.

Revising for Organization

Have students explain in their own words why the beginning paragraph for the sample works well to introduce the essay.

When revising for organization, students should make sure that
- their beginning paragraph is organized from general to specific, and
- they use transition words that show time.

Have students exchange drafts with a partner who can check to see that the beginning paragraph is organized properly.

 **Answer**

The novel *Tuck Everlasting* by Natalie Babbitt is the story of 10-year-old Winnie Foster. The story begins on a hot, dusty August day when Winnie wanders in the woods near her house. After a while, she discovers a natural spring. Just as Winnie is about to drink from the spring, her life changes, and she must make a big decision.

Revising for Organization

6 My opening, middle, and ending lead the reader smoothly through my essay.

5 My beginning is well organized. Transitions clearly connect sentences and paragraphs.

4 My beginning is organiz I use transitions to connect sentences.

When you revise for *organization*, focus on the way your writing is put together from beginning to end. Use the rubric above.

Is my beginning organized properly?

Your beginning paragraph for this essay should start with general information about your book and end with a specific insight or focus. Review the beginning paragraph below from the sample essay on page 289.

General ideas — *Bud, Not Buddy* by Christopher Paul Curtis is a story about a young boy finding people who care about him. Like all of us, Bud knows that having people who care for you is a lucky thing. The "family" that Bud finds has some of the same qualities that a lot of families have today. **Specific insight or focus** — This story shows that some members of a family may not be related, but they still care for each other.

 Write a beginning paragraph using the following sentences. Put the sentences in order from general information to a specific focus.
- The story begins on a hot, dusty August day when Winnie wanders in the woods near her house.
- Just as Winnie is about to drink from the spring, her life changes, and she must make a big decision.
- The novel *Tuck Everlasting* by Natalie Babbitt is the story of 10-year-old Winnie Foster.
- After a while, she discovers a natural spring.

 Check your beginning. Carefully review your beginning paragraph to make sure that it is organized from general to specific.

English Language Learners

Prior to the **Try It** activity, create this graphic organizer on the board, and use it to point out each element in the sample beginning paragraph.

Then have students complete the **Try It** activity by telling you aloud how to organize the paragraph, using the graphic organizer.

1. Name the story and give a brief statement about the main character.

2. Give two or three important details.

3. End with a specific insight or focus statement.

evaluate PREVIEW experience
react answer
305
Writing a Book Review

<table>
<tr><td>**3** My beginning should be better organized. I need to use transitions to connect sentences.</td><td>**2** I need to reorganize my beginning and use transitions.</td><td>**1** I need to learn how to organize my writing and connect my ideas.</td></tr>
</table>

What's the best way to connect my ideas?

One of the best ways to connect the sentences and paragraphs in your essay is to use transitions. Usually, you will use transition words that show time: *first, next, then, finally*. (See pages 572–573.)

 Read the paragraph below. On your own paper, write a revised version that adds a few more transition words or phrases. One transition word (*underlined*) has been added to get you started.

1 Gary Soto's story "The Drive-in Movies" is about a boy
2 who does chores for his mom so she will take him to a drive-
3 in movie. <u>First</u>, he makes his mother breakfast. He weeds
4 the garden and mows the lawn. He waxes their car with his
5 brother's help. The boy's mother takes the whole family to the
6 movies, but he is so tired from the chores that he falls asleep.

 Review your first draft. Check to make sure that you have included enough transition words and phrases in your essay. Be careful not to overuse them. Too many transition words can be a real distraction.

Organization
Transitions are added to make the ideas easier to follow.

> *First,*
> ∧A huge fire reminds her of a serpent because
>   *Then,*
> the flames are like the tongues of snakes.∧In a cave,
> she mistakes a playful young otter for a little man
>   *Later,*
> like the one in her tribe's legends.∧The calls of . . .

LITERATURE

---

* To do the **Try It** activity, challenge students to use a variety of time-order words, not just ordinary ones such as *first, then,* and *finally*. Suggest that they look at the list of time-related words on PE page 572 for ideas.

Try It Answers

[Possible response]

Gary Soto's story "The Drive-in Movies" is about a boy who does chores for his mom so she will take him to a drive-in move. <u>First</u>, he makes his mother breakfast. <u>A little later,</u> he weeds the garden and mows the lawn. <u>After that,</u> he waxes their car with his brother's help. <u>That evening,</u> the boy's mother takes the whole family to the movies, but he is so tired from the chores that he falls asleep.

A possible problem with encouraging student writers to use transition words is that they can then tend to overuse them. Ask students to try to decide if they have overused transitions as they take turns reading aloud their essay paragraphs during **peer conferences** (*see below*).

Teaching Tip: Peer Conferences

During peer conferences, students have a chance to share a work in progress with classmates. Writers benefit from feedback that is immediate and objective. Peers enjoy applying newly acquired writing skills as well as their own insights to help fellow students. Be sure to review guidelines for working in groups (PE pages 420 and 421) and how to present ideas during peer conferences. (For example, students should first compliment the writer on good use of transitions to show time order before pointing out places where transitions are needed or are overused.)

* For more information about peer responding, see PE pages 30–32.

Advanced Learners

Invite two students to model a peer conference. Remind them to be specific in their comments. For example, "That was great!" is not specific. A specific comment is "You used the transition words *first, later on, meanwhile,* and *finally,* so I could follow the order of the story easily." Discuss whether the comments and suggestions were helpful.

Revising for Voice

Have students compare the two paragraphs in order to understand why the first paragraph lacks a knowledgeable voice. They should note the following:

■ In the first sample, the writer uses the personal pronouns *I* and *me* to express opinions and feelings (for example, *I really loved, I was bored, I got a little interested, seemed real to me*) without providing any specific details or insight. (*Who cares about* is another phrase that focuses on the reviewer's opinions, not the story.)

■ In the second sample, the writer identifies the author, the main character, and the setting; the writer also explains what the fights show about Larry (an insight).

As students check their writing for a knowledgeable voice, tell them to look for places where they used the personal pronouns *I* or *me,* as these words may signal opinions or feelings.

Revising for Voice

6 I use a formal, knowledgeable voice to express a clear insight and understanding of the story.

5 I use a formal, knowledgeable voice to express my insight.

4 I use a formal voice, but it is not always knowledgeable.

When you revise for *voice*, you check your essay's language for understanding and interest. Is your voice knowledgeable? Is it formal enough? The rubric above and the information that follows will help you revise your review for voice.

How do I know if my voice is knowledgeable?

A *knowledgeable* voice uses facts to build a specific insight. The voice in the first paragraph below does not use facts. It results in a general feeling and not a specific insight.

GENERAL FEELING

> I really loved reading *Private Nobody.* At first, I was bored when the main character was joining the army. After all, who cares about the 1960s? Then I got a little interested because of all the fights. Those fights sure seemed real to me.

The voice in the next paragraph is knowledgeable because it focuses on facts that help the writer share a specific insight.

SPECIFIC INSIGHT

> *Private Nobody* by Greg Washington is about a young man named Larry who joins the United States Army in the late 1960s. He is sent to Vietnam and gets into lots of fights. However, the fights are with his fellow soldiers, not the enemy. The fights show that the young man was filled with anger even before he arrived in Vietnam.

Check for a knowledgeable voice. Review your essay, looking for places where you focus on your opinions or feelings instead of on facts and a specific insight. Revise to make your voice more knowledgeable.

3 I need to use a more formal voice and be more knowledgeable.

2 My voice is not formal or knowledgeable, so I need to fix it.

1 I need to understand how to create a formal, knowledgeable voice.

How do I know if my writing is formal enough?

When you speak to close friends, you say things like "Hey, what's up?" A book review, however, should be more formal. One way to make your writing more formal is to avoid street talk or slang.

 Read the following informal paragraph. On your own paper, list at least three words, phrases, or clauses that make the writing too informal. One phrase is underlined for you.

1   One night, Larry gets into a <u>giant smackdown</u>. He's on
2   guard duty when this one dude comes out of nowhere! Larry
3   tries to take off running, but he gets bashed. Larry wakes
4   up in an army hospital with this big humongous bandage on
5   his head and no memory at all. He can't even remember his
6   own name. He's like totally wacko. Letters from his mom and
7   girlfriend help him regain his memory, and eventually Larry gets
8   a Purple Heart medal.

 Check your level of language. As you revise your book review, pay special attention to words and phrases that sound too informal.

Voice
The language is made more knowledgeable and formal.

understands that nature speaks to everyone.
After her journey, Billie ~~gets a clue. I think~~
~~this part is the coolest.~~ She sees that the
animals really have been talking to her all along . . .

LITERATURE

Use one or more of the following ideas to discuss voice.

- Voice is how a piece of writing sounds to readers.
- A formal voice is one that sounds carefully worded. It does not sound casual or slangy.
- To explain the difference between formal and informal writing, you can draw an analogy to the difference between formal clothes (a suit or a fancy dress) and informal clothes (jeans and a T-shirt). You have to know when each is appropriate.
- To emphasize the sound of writing that is casual and slangy, read aloud the **Try It** paragraph before having students complete the activity on their own.

 Answers

Possible choices:
- line 1: giant smackdown
- line 2: one dude
- line 3: take off; bashed
- line 4: humongous
- line 6: like totally wacko

Revising for Word Choice

* Have students note the verb *is* and the past participle *attacked* in the passive-verb sample. Tell students that passive verbs always use a form of *to be* plus the past participle of the verb. (See PE pages 722 and 726–727.)

Do the **Try It** activity as a class. Ask volunteers to identify the passive verb in each sentence. Have the class work together to tell who is doing the action and who is receiving the action in each item. Then have volunteers offer suggestions for rewriting each sentence. Point out that they may have to add or change words when they rewrite some sentences.

Try It Answers

1. Billie Wind saves the panther cub.
2. She avoids the men in the swamp.
3. Billie enjoys her friendship with Petang the otter.
4. Billie's animal friends help her many times.

* See PE page 482 for more practice with active verbs.

308

Revising for Word Choice

6 My clear word choice creates a response that engages the reader.

5 I use active verbs and well-chosen modifiers to make the writing clear.

4 I use active verbs whenever possible. A few modifiers need to be cut.

When you revise your writing for *word choice*, you need to check your verbs to make sure most of them are active. Also, you should remove unnecessary modifiers. The rubric above will help you revise your word choice.

How can I make my verbs more active?

Sentences with active verbs are more exciting than those with passive verbs. A verb is active if the subject of the sentence is doing the action. A verb is passive if the subject is receiving the action. Below, the word *attack* is used as both a passive and an active verb. (See page 482.)

> **PASSIVE VERB**
>
> The panther is attacked by the alligator. (The panther receives the action.)
>
> **ACTIVE VERB**
>
> The alligator attacks the panther. (The alligator is doing the action.)

 Read the following sentences that contain passive verbs. In each sentence, ask yourself who or what is doing the action. Then rewrite the sentence, changing the passive verb to an active verb.

1. The panther cub is saved by Billie Wind.
   1. Billie Wind saves the panther cub.
2. The men in the swamp are avoided by her.
3. Her friendship with Petang the otter is enjoyed by Billie.
4. Billie is helped many times by her animal friends

 Check for passive verbs. Whenever necessary, change your passive verbs to active verbs.

For additional practice in recognizing passive versus active verbs, write on the board sentences that use the passive- and active-verb forms to describe the same situation. For example:

* A book is read by Devon.
* Devon reads a book.

Call on a volunteer to circle the verb and underline the subject in each sentence.

* Ask who is doing the action.

* Focus on the connection between the action that is taking place and the active verb form.
* Point out how the sentence is much stronger if the subject is doing, rather than receiving, the action.

evaluate PREVIEW experience
react answer **309**
Writing a Book Review

3 I need to change a few passive verbs to active verbs. Extra modifiers need to be cut.

2 I need to change many passive verbs to active verbs. Extra modifiers need to be cut.

1 I need help choosing both active verbs and modifiers.

Have I used too many modifiers?

Once Mark Twain wrote: "When you catch an adjective, kill it." He knew that too many adjectives and adverbs can make writing sound fake or unnatural. A sentence such as "Bilbo quite loudly shouts for greatly needed help" would sound clearer as "Bilbo shouts for help."

 Read the following paragraph. Write down five adjectives or adverbs that should be removed. (Two have been removed.)

1   Bilbo Baggins has never been in such a ~~completely shadowy~~,
2 dark pit. He pulls out his wonderful sword, which glows really
3 bright in the big dark cave. On the floor of the cave, Bilbo sees a
4 shiny, gleaming piece of metal. It is a beautifully lovely ring. Bilbo
5 grabs the ring and quickly and rapidly puts it in his pocket. That's
6 when he hears a scary and frightening sound—the growl of the
7 creature Gollum.

 Remove extra modifiers. Read through your essay and cut any unneeded adjectives and adverbs that you find.

Word Choice
Extra modifiers are removed, and a passive sentence is made active.

>   quiets down.
> Later, the wind ~~gets so very much quieter and~~
> ~~quieter~~. Billie and the boy start to go outside, but
>   they notice that
> ~~the fact that~~ the panther is not budging from the
> cave ~~is noticed by them~~. Billie and the boy decide . . .

LITERATURE

Stress that while adjectives and adverbs can help readers picture what is being described, precise nouns and exact active verbs can create equally strong images. Provide these examples:

- The furry gray animal climbed quickly up the enormously big tree.
- The squirrel scurried up the giant oak tree.

 Answers

Possible choices:
- line 1: completely shadowy
- line 2: wonderful, really
- line 3: bright, big dark
- line 4: shiny, beautifully lovely
- line 5: rapidly
- line 6: scary

If students are not sure whether or not to cut an adjective or an adverb, they should read the sentence without the word in question. If the idea is very clear without that word, they probably should cut it.

English Language Learners

Students may have difficulty judging how many modifiers are "too many" because they may not realize that many of the words mean the same thing.

- Have students read aloud each sentence in the **Try It** activity and identify any adjectives or adverbs, such as *shiny, gleaming*.
- Explain that because both these words mean the same thing, only one is needed; either one could be used in the sentence.
- Guide students in reading aloud each sentence twice, each time using only one of the adjectives or adverbs.

Advanced Learners

Invite students to work with partners and use the rubric at the top of the page to assess word choice in their book reviews. After scoring a partner's essay, each student should give reasons for their rating. As students work on making improvements to their work, remind them to focus on using precise nouns and active verbs. This will help them eliminate extra modifiers.

Revising for Sentence Fluency

Invite a volunteer to read aloud the sample of a rambling sentence, so that students can hear what writing with too many *ands* sounds like. Then ask a volunteer to read the improved sentences. Encourage students to explain why they think these sentences flow better.

Point out to students that they can add variety to their writing by using *and* to connect related ideas in **compound sentences** (*see below*). The problem with rambling sentences is that they try to connect too many ideas at once, and they connect ideas that are not closely related.

✷ For additional information on rambling sentences, see PE page 507.

 Answers

Possible answers:

1. "Lenny's Mountain" is about a teenager named Lenny, who wants to be a mountain climber. The landscape is flat in the Midwest where Lenny lives, so he builds himself a fake mountain.

2. The main character, Lorne, is new in town. He wants to make friends, so he hosts a big party. No one shows up, so Lorne is crushed.

310

Revising for Sentence Fluency

6 My sentences are skillfully written and keep the reader's interest.

5 I avoid rambling sentences and use a variety of sentence beginnings.

4 I avoid rambling sentences, but some subject-verb beginnings need to be changed.

When you revise for *sentence fluency*, you need to check the clarity, flow, and smoothness of your sentences. The rubric above will help you do that.

How many "and's" are too many?

You have used too many *and*'s when they create a rambling sentence. A rambling sentence is a sentence that goes on *and* on *and* on. To fix a rambling sentence, you need to remove an *and* or two and start new sentences.

> **RAMBLING SENTENCE**
>
> *Teen Business* is about a girl who wants to start a baby-sitting service **and** first she asks her friends to help her, but her friends have no experience with kids **and** then she decides to start a business that teaches kids how to be baby-sitters **and** the business is soon very successful.

> **IMPROVED SENTENCES**
>
> *Teen Business* is about a girl who wants to start a baby-sitting service. First, she asks her friends to help her, but her friends have no experience with kids. Then she decides to start a business that teaches kids how to be baby-sitters. The business is soon very successful.

 On your own paper, correct the rambling sentences below by taking out some of the *and*'s. You may also need to change a word or two.

1. "Lenny's Mountain" is about a teenager named Lenny and he wants to be a mountain climber and the landscape is flat in the Midwest where he lives and he builds himself a fake mountain.

2. The main character, Lorne, is new in town and he wants to make friends and he hosts a big party and no one shows up and Lorne is crushed.

Teaching Tip: Compound Sentences

Make sure that students understand the difference between a rambling sentence and a compound sentence.

A compound sentence has the following characteristics:

● It is made up of two or more simple sentences that are combined to form one sentence.

● It usually joins the two sentences together with a coordi-

nating conjunction, such as *and, but,* or *so.*

● It has a comma before the conjunction to separate the ideas.

Each part of a compound sentence expresses a complete thought and can stand alone as an independent sentence.

✷ See PE page 516 for practice with creating and punctuating compound sentences.

evaluate PREVIEW experience
react answer
311
Writing a Book Review

3 I need to fix a few rambling sentences and vary the beginnings. Many sentences begin the same way.

2 I need to fix many rambling sentences and vary the beginnings.

1 My sentences show a number of problems. I need to learn more about sentences.

How do I begin my sentences?

If too many of your sentences begin in the same way, your essay will sound odd. The following paragraph has too many sentences that begin with a subject and verb. (See page 522.)

> Annie Sullivan tries **everything to help Helen.** Annie becomes **frustrated because of Helen's lack of understanding.** Annie **then has Helen fill a pitcher with water.** Annie signs **"water" in the palm of Helen's free hand at the same time.**

The paragraph has been rewritten below. Each sentence after the first one has been changed. Each new sentence begins with either a phrase or a transition word. To add even more variety, the pronoun "she" is used in place of "Annie" in the third sentence.

> **Annie Sullivan tries everything to help Helen. Because Helen lacks understanding, Annie becomes frustrated. Then she has Helen fill a pitcher with water. At the same time, Annie signs "water" in the palm of Helen's free hand.**

 Revise for sentence fluency. Check your writing carefully for rambling sentences. Then check how your sentences begin.

Sentence Fluency
A sentence beginning is changed, and a rambling sentence is fixed.

> *Billie has no way of knowing that a hurricane*
> *   she*
> *is coming soon. Then ~~Billie~~ notices the unusual*
>
> *movement of the animals and ~~she~~ follows them to*
> *   Once again,*
> *higher ground ~~and~~ she ~~once again~~ finds shelter . . .*

LITERATURE

Have students use a **sentence chart** (see below) to identify how each sentence in their essay begins.

✽ See PE page 522 for more instruction on varying sentence beginnings.

Teaching Tip: Sentence Chart

Create a chart to help students keep track of sentence beginnings.

- On a piece of paper, write these column heads: *First Words of Sentence, Phrase, Transition Word,* and *Other.*
- Make a photocopy of the chart for each student.
- Tell students to write the first few words of each sentence in their essay under *First Words of Sentence* and to put an *X* under

the appropriate heading to show how each sentence begins.

When they have checked every sentence, they will be able to see at a glance if they have a variety of sentence beginnings.

Struggling Learners

Assist students as they work on their sentence charts. As students begin to recognize that many of their sentences begin the same way, ask volunteers to share examples that need to be revised. Write each sentence on the board and model how you explore your options for change.

✽ Refer students to PE page 522, so that they can use it independently for ideas.

Revising Using a Checklist

Before students number their papers, make sure they have addressed all the issues and made all the revisions suggested.

- Tell students that they should be as honest as possible as they answer the questions.
- Stress that if they answer "yes" to every question without thinking, their essays will not be as good as they could be.

If students are writing the essay as an in-class assignment, provide time for them to make a clean draft.

- Students can also make a clean copy of their book reviews as a homework assignment.
- Remind them to double-space, so that they will have plenty of room to edit their work.

312

Revising Using a Checklist

 Check your revising. On a piece of paper, write the numbers 1 to 13. If you can answer "yes" to a question, put a check mark after that number. If not, continue to work with that part of your essay.

Ideas

_____ **1.** Have I included my insight in a clear focus statement?
_____ **2.** Have I written informative topic sentences?
_____ **3.** Have I cut unnecessary details?

Organization

_____ **4.** Have I included a beginning, a middle, and an ending?
_____ **5.** Do I use transitions to connect my ideas?
_____ **6.** Do I present my ideas in the best possible order?

Voice

_____ **7.** Do I show interest in—and understanding of—my topic?
_____ **8.** Is my voice knowledgeable and formal?

Word Choice

_____ **9.** Do I use specific nouns and active verbs?
_____ **10.** Have I removed unnecessary modifiers?

Sentence Fluency

_____ **11.** Do I write clear sentences and avoid fragments?
_____ **12.** Have I fixed any rambling sentences?
_____ **13.** Do I use a variety of sentence beginnings and lengths?

 Make a clean copy. When you've finished revising your essay, make a clean copy before you begin to edit.

Advanced Learners

Ask students you consider to be "experts" in revising to become "revision assistants." (Emphasize that they should complete their own revisions first.) Encourage other students in the class to ask for an assistant's expertise as they address all the issues suggested in the checklist. This will enable you to focus attention on students who need the most support.

Before assistants work with classmates, remind them how to give positive feedback and make constructive suggestions.

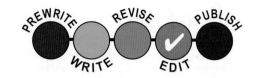

Editing

After you've finished revising your essay, it's time to edit it for your use of conventions: punctuation, capitalization, spelling, and grammar.

Keys to Effective Editing

1. Use a dictionary, a thesaurus, and the "Proofreader's Guide" in the back of this book.

2. Check for any words or phrases that may be confusing to the reader.

3. Check your writing for correctness of punctuation, capitalization, spelling, and grammar.

4. If you are using a computer, edit on a printed computer copy. Then enter your changes on the computer.

5. Use the editing and proofreading marks inside the back cover of this book.

LITERATURE

Editing Keys to Effective Editing

The Keys to Effective Editing lays out the process students will be guided through on pages 314–316.

Remind students that during editing, they have a chance to find and correct mistakes in

- punctuation,
- capitalization,
- spelling, and
- grammar.

This will ensure that their essays are easy to understand and pleasing to read.

Remind students to keep the Keys to Effective Editing on hand as they proceed through the editing stage.

Editing for Conventions

After discussing how to correct **shifts in verb tense** using the samples, provide additional practice (*see below*).

Have students complete the **Try It** activity. Then have them check their own essay for consistent use of verb tense.

- Direct them to circle all present tense verbs in red and all past tense verbs in blue.
- If all verbs are circled in one color only, then students know they've used one verb tense consistently. If not, they can make corrections.

 Answers

1. The story takes a different turn when Mike *asks* Serina for her help.
2. In the middle of the novel, Jason catches the flu, and a doctor *gives* him the wrong medicine.
3. At the end of the story, Sybil clears her throat and *begins* to speak.
4. What happens after Billy *receives* a mysterious e-mail message?
5. At the end of the novel, even though she is still angry, Lila *forgives* her sister.

Editing for Conventions

6 My essay is correct from start to finish.

5 My essay has minor errors that do not interfere with the reader's understanding.

4 I need to correct some errors in punctuation, spelling, or grammar.

When you edit for *conventions*, you need to check your writing for grammar, punctuation, capitalization, and spelling errors. The rubric above will help you edit your essay for this trait.

How do I avoid shifts in verb tense?

When you write, you need to keep all your verbs in the same tense. For example, if you start a sentence in the present tense, you should not, later on, incorrectly switch to the past tense. This would be a shift in verb tense.

> **SHIFT IN VERB TENSE**
>
> Maria, the main character, travels all over the world and never settled down. ("Travels" is in the present tense. "Settled" is in the past tense.)
>
> **CONSISTENT VERB TENSE**
>
> Maria, the main character, travels all over the world and never settles down. (Both verbs are now in the present tense.)

Try It Number your paper from 1 to 5. Correct the shifts in verb tense by rewriting the following sentences in the present tense. (See the examples above.)

1. The story takes a different turn when Mike asked Serina for her help.
2. In the middle of the novel, Jason catches the flu, and a doctor gave him the wrong medicine.
3. At the end of the story, Sybil clears her throat and began to speak.
4. What happens after Billy received a mysterious e-mail message?
5. At the end of the novel, even though she is still angry, Lila forgave her sister.

Teaching Tip: Shifts in Verb Tense

Prepare an overhead transparency or photocopies of at least one paragraph from a book review (or even the entire essay) with unnecessary shifts in verb tense embedded in it.

Have students use the Think/Pair/Share strategy to correct the errors.

- First, have students look for errors and correct them independently.

- Then, students should meet with a partner to compare their editing.
- Finally, lead a group activity in which you invite students to identify and correct shifts in verb tense.

evaluate PREVIEW experience
react answer
315
Writing a Book Review

3 I need to correct errors that may confuse the reader.

2 I need to correct many errors that make my essay confusing and hard to read.

1 I need help making corrections.

Have I checked for commonly misused words?

You need to check your "Proofreader's Guide" if you're not sure which commonly misused word is the one to use. In the paragraphs below, you will find six examples of this problem. The first one is corrected in black.

1   *Hatchet* is a book written by Gary Paulsen. It's a story about a
2 13-year-old named Brian Robeson <u>whose</u> **(who's)** stranded in the
3 Canadian wilderness. When Brian is flying to visit his father, the small
4 plain crashes. Brian is left with the clothes he is wearing and the medal
5 hatchet that his mother gave him before he left on the trip. He must use
6 everything he has ever learned to survive this hole event.
7   During the flight, the pilot teaches Brian how to fly, but not how
8 to land. Than the pilot suddenly dyes of a heart attack. Brian reacts real
9 fast and grabs the controls. As the plane runs out of fuel, Brian must
10 chose where to land. He survives by crashing into a lake.

 On your own paper, write six words that are used incorrectly in the paragraph above. Next to each one, write the correct word.

 Edit for conventions. Pay special attention to any shifts in verb tense. Also correct any misused words.

Conventions
A usage error is corrected, and a tense shift is fixed.

> After her journey, Billie understands that
>   *sees*
> nature speaks to everyone. She ~~seas~~ that the
>   *have*
> animals really ~~had~~ been talking to her all along . . .

LITERATURE

Commonly misused words (for example, *too, to, two; there, their, they're; it's, its*) often become "invisible" after working on a piece of writing for a long time. If there is time, students should put their papers aside for a while before checking for errors. Then they can look for mistakes with a fresh eye.

Remind students who are using a computer to print out a fresh copy of their essay and to edit on paper. Point out that spell-checkers do not usually catch misused words, especially homonyms (such as *who's* instead of *whose*), because the words are not misspelled.

Try IT Answers

- line 2: whose (who's)
- line 4: plain (plane), medal (metal)
- line 6: hole (whole)
- line 8: than (then), dyes (dies), real (really)
- line 10: chose (choose)

Editing Using a Checklist

Give students a few moments to look over the Proofreader's Guide in the back of the pupil edition. Throughout the year, they can refer to the instruction, rules, and examples to clarify any checklist items or to resolve questions about their own writing.

Be sure students have completed several editing passes on their essay before they use the editing checklist. Remind them to pay special attention to the punctuation of titles and to check that they have used present-tense verb forms correctly throughout their essay.

Adding a Title

Students should try all three ideas for adding a title before deciding on one. They can also

- look at their insight statement to see if that suggests an interesting title,
- try out possible titles in a group,
- use or adapt their working title, if they have one.

Discuss the difference between a working title and a final title. Have students validate their working title by sharing it with a partner. Have the partner tell whether they think it can be the final title or whether the writer might think of a more exciting one.

Editing Using a Checklist

 Check your editing. On a piece of paper, write the numbers 1 to 13. If you can answer "yes" to a question, put a check mark after that number. If not, continue to edit for that convention.

Conventions

PUNCTUATION

_____ 1. Did I punctuate titles correctly?

_____ 2. Do I use commas after introductory word groups?

_____ 3. Do I use commas after items in a series?

_____ 4. Do I use commas in all my compound sentences?

_____ 5. Do I use apostrophes to show possession (*boy's bike*)?

_____ 6. Do I use quotation marks around any direct quotations?

CAPITALIZATION

_____ 7. Do I start all my sentences with capital letters?

_____ 8. Have I capitalized all proper nouns?

SPELLING

_____ 9. Have I spelled all my words correctly?

_____ 10. Have I double-checked the words my spell-checker may have missed?

GRAMMAR

_____ 11. Do I use correct forms of verbs (*had gone*, not *had went*)?

_____ 12. Do I keep all my verbs in the same tense?

_____ 13. Have I used the right words (*to, too, two*)?

Adding a Title

- Use the title of the book: ***The Talking Earth***
- Describe the main idea: **Billie Finds Respect**
- Be creative: **Swamp School Lessons**

Publishing Sharing Your Essay

After you have worked so hard to write and improve your essay, you'll want to make a neat-looking copy to share. You may also decide to present your essay in some other form: an illustration, a reading, or an online posting. (See the suggestions in the boxes below.)

 Make a final copy. Follow your teacher's instructions or use the guidelines below to format your paper. (If you are writing with a computer, see page 60.) Write a final copy of your essay and proofread it for errors.

Focus on Presentation

- Use blue or black ink and write neatly.
- Write your name in the upper left corner of page 1.
- Skip a line and center your title; skip another line and start your writing.
- Indent every paragraph and leave a 1-inch margin on all four sides.
- Write your last name and the page number in the upper right corner of every page after the first one.

Illustrate Your Summary
Draw a picture that shows an important event in the story. Post your essay and illustration in your classroom.

Give a Recitation
Read aloud a part of the story in which an important event occurs. Then tell the class how the event helped you find an insight.

Post Online
If you wrote about a book, go to a bookselling Web site and try to post your response. (Be sure to get permission first.)

LITERATURE

Publishing Sharing Your Essay

Allow time for students to suggest additional individual or group publishing ideas. For example,

- a group of students might want to do oral presentations of their reviews as a special program in the library, or
- they might choose to publish their reviews collectively in a booklet and make copies available in the classroom and the school library.

Encourage a variety of presentation forms. Provide time and space for students to present their essays.

Rubric for Response to Literature

A rubric is a chart that helps students evaluate their writing. The rubrics in this book are based on a six-point scale, in which a score of 6 indicates an amazing piece of writing and a score of 1 means the writing is incomplete and not ready to be assessed. The rubric covers the basic traits of writing—ideas, organization, voice, word choice, sentence fluency, and conventions.

Rubrics can guide you as you write because they tell what elements to include in your writing and how to present them.

* Four- and five-point rubrics for response to literature writing can be found on TE pages 771 and 775.

318

Rubric for Response to Literature

Use this rubric for guiding and assessing your writing. Refer to it whenever you want to improve your writing using the six traits.

Ideas

6 The focus statement and related details show real insight into the reading.

5 The response has a clear focus statement and all the necessary details.

4 The response has a clear focus statement. Unnecessary details need to be cut.

Organization

6 The opening, middle, and ending lead the reader smoothly through the response.

5 The organization pattern fits the topic and purpose. All parts of the response are well developed.

4 The organization pattern fits the topic and purpose. A part of the response needs better development.

Voice

6 The writer's voice expresses interest and complete understanding. It engages the reader.

5 The writer's voice expresses interest and understanding.

4 The writer's voice expresses understanding of most of the reading.

Word Choice

6 Clear word choice creates a response that inspires the reader.

5 Specific nouns and active verbs make the response clear and informative.

4 Some nouns and verbs could be more specific.

Sentence Fluency

6 All sentences are skillfully written and keep the reader's interest.

5 No sentence problems exist. Sentence variety is evident.

4 No sentence problems exist. More sentence variety is needed.

Conventions

6 The response is correct from start to finish.

5 The response has minor errors that do not interfere with the reader's understanding.

4 The response has some errors in punctuation, spelling, or grammar.

Advanced Learners

Ask students some "What If" questions, focusing on using the rubrics effectively to assess their progress. For example:

- What if too many general words are used? (possible solution: use more specific nouns and verbs)
- What if the focus statement is too broad? (possible solution: cut unnecessary details)
- What if the response has errors that may confuse the reader?

(possible solution: continue to edit for punctuation, spelling, and grammar)

After locating the problem on the rubric chart, students should decide what a possible solution could be, using the chart and their writing skills. Encourage students to make up additional questions for their peers.

3 The focus statement is too broad. Unnecessary details need to be cut.

2 The focus statement is not developed. Details are needed.

1 The response needs a focus statement and details.

3 The organization fits the response's purpose. All the parts need more development.

2 The organization doesn't fit the purpose.

1 A plan needs to be followed.

3 The writer's voice needs to express a clearer understanding.

2 The writer's voice does not express an understanding.

1 The writer needs to understand how to create voice.

3 Too many general words are used. Specific nouns and verbs are needed.

2 General or overused words make this response hard to understand.

1 The writer needs help finding specific words.

3 Sentence problems are found in a few places.

2 The response has many sentence problems.

1 The writer needs to learn how to construct sentences.

3 The response has errors that may confuse the reader.

2 The number of errors confuses the reader and makes the essay hard to read.

1 Help is needed to make corrections.

LITERATURE

Evaluating a Book Review

Ask students if they agree with the sample self-assessment on PE page 321. Then ask them to suggest improvements for "Zlateh the Goat," based on the comments in the self-assessment.

Ideas **more information**—include details about Aaron's family searching for him

Organization add transitions—Right from the start, Zlateh . . . ; Left with no other choice, Aaron burrows . . .

Voice **more formal**—The short story called "Zlateh and the Goat" is about . . . ; replace *stuff* with *snow*; Aaron, his parents . . . learn that the true value of family is in the love they share.

Word Choice beginnings lack variety—Aaron and Zlateh have trouble . . . They get so tired . . . ; When Aaron tells them . . .

Sentence Fluency rambling sentence—It snows for three days. During that time, Zlateh . . . **combine ideas**—The short story called "Zlateh the Goat" . . . is about . . . ; The father decides that . . . , so he . . .

Conventions misused word—forth (*fourth*); **shift in verb tense**—Zlateh looks at Aaron . . . and follows him

---

320

Evaluating a Book Review

As you read through the following review, focus on the strengths and weaknesses. Then read the student's self-evaluation on page 321. (There will be errors in the book review below.)

"Zlateh the Goat"

I read the short story called "Zlateh the Goat" by Isaac Singer. It's about a village family that doesn't have enough money to celebrate Hanukkah. The father decides that selling Zlateh is the only way that the family can celebrate the holidays. He tells his son Aaron to take the animal to town. The journey to town helps Aaron, his family, and Zlateh realize how much they care for each other.

Zlateh looks at Aaron with trusting eyes and followed him down the long road from their village to town. Suddenly it starts snowing very hard. Aaron and Zlateh have trouble walking as the stuff piles up. Aaron and Zlateh get so tired they can hardly go on. Just when it looks like they will be buried by the blizzard they come to a big haystack.

The boy burrows into the haystack and pulls Zlateh inside his little cave. It snows for three days, and during that time Zlateh eats the hay and Aaron drinks the goat's milk. When the snow stops on the forth day, Aaron digs his way out and leads Zlateh back to his village.

After the storm Aaron's family is glad to see that he is safe. After Aaron tells them how Zlateh kept him warm and gave her milk, the goat is brought home to remain with the family. I think that Aaron, his parents, and his sisters learn that you don't want anyone to get your goat.

Teaching Tip: Understanding Double Meanings

Initiate a discussion about why the sample writer thinks the last line of the review is funny.

- Explain to students that *get your goat* is an idiom, or figure of speech, that has a double meaning.
- Ask students what *get your goat* means literally (take your animal). Ask if anyone knows what it means figuratively (make you mad).

Discuss whether or not the idiom works as the last line.

- Does the figurative meaning make sense here?
- Does the literal meaning make sense here?

Then ask students if they agree that the last line shouldn't be funny and to explain why.

evaluate
react
PREVIEW answer experience
321
Writing a Book Review

Student Self-Assessment

The assessment shown below includes the student writer's comments about her review. In the first comment, she mentions something positive about her writing. In the second comment, she points out something she feels she can improve. (The writer used the rubric and number scale on pages 318-319 to complete this assessment.)

5 Ideas
1. I clearly stated my insight in a focus statement.
2. I could have told about the family's search for Aaron.

5 Organization
1. My writing contains a beginning, a middle, and an ending.
2. I could use transition words between paragraphs.

4 Voice
1. I understand the story, and my voice shows that.
2. My last line is funny, but maybe it shouldn't be.

4 Word Choice
1. I use active verbs.
2. I should have used different sentence beginnings.

4 Sentence Fluency
1. I don't have any rambling sentences.
2. I could have combined some of my sentences.

4 Conventions
1. I didn't make too many errors.
2. I should have fixed a shift in verb tense in my second paragraph.

Use the rubric. Assess your review using the rubric on pages 318–319.

1 On your own paper, list the six traits. Leave room after each trait to write one strength and one weakness.

2 Then choose a number (from 1 to 6) that shows how well you used each trait.

LITERATURE

Student Self-Assessment

If you have time, review students' self-assessments and tell whether you think they provide an accurate evaluation of the strengths and weaknesses of their essays.

■ When offering advice, focus on problems students have had in previous writing assignments.

■ Encourage students to create their own checklists to monitor and eventually eliminate these problem areas in their writing.

To give students additional practice with evaluating a book review, use a reproducible assessment sheet (TE page 799) and one or both of the **benchmark papers** listed in the Benchmark Papers box below. You can use an overhead transparency while students refer to their own copies made from the copy masters. For your benefit, a completed assessment sheet is provided for each benchmark paper.

Struggling Learners

Students may need extra support when completing their self-assessments. In addition to the rubric on PE pages 318–319, the specific information on the revising pages may be helpful.

Work with students to design a class chart that is a clear visual organizer of the information they need in order to assess their work. On chart paper, write the six traits (see PE pages 302–310) as

headings across the top. Have students turn to PE page 302. Together, decide what they should check for when revising for Ideas. List specific guidelines under each heading. For example:

• Focus statement clearly introduces the story and includes your insight

• Include only key details

Continue in this way to fill in the chart.

Benchmark Papers

Caddie Woodlawn (strong)

● TR 7A–7C

● TE pp. 793–795

Gypsy and Woodrow (poor)

● TR 8A–8C

● TE pp. 796–798

Reflecting on Your Writing

In addition to completing the reflection sheet here, have students compare their reflections on their book reviews to previous writing reflections, to determine if they have

- learned anything new about writing in general,
- answered any previous questions about writing that they might have had,
- progressed as a writer.

Reflecting on Your Writing

Now that your book review is finished, you can think about it by completing each starter sentence below. These reflections will help you see how you are growing as a writer.

My Book Review

1. The best part of my book review is . . .

2. The part that most needs change is . . .

3. The main thing I learned about writing a book review is . . .

4. In my next book review, I would like to . . .

5. Here is one question I still have about writing a book review:

6. Right now I would describe my writing ability as . . . (excellent, good, fair, poor)

Response to Literature

Fictionalized Journal Entries

Stories can cast a powerful spell, letting you leap into other worlds. Perhaps you'll land on the deck of a pirate ship—or a galactic cruiser! You might imagine yourself as a warrior in ancient Japan or as a rat on the Zuckerman farm.

One way to imagine yourself into the stories you read is to write fictionalized journal entries. The following pages provide writing samples and guidelines to help you create your own journal entries.

Writing Guidelines

Subject:	A book or short story that you have read and enjoyed
Form:	Fictionalized journal entries
Purpose:	To think and write like someone in the story
Audience:	Classmates

Fictionalized Journal Entry

Objectives
- know what a fictionalized journal entry is
- create, plan, and draft a fictionalized journal entry
- revise, edit, and share a fictionalized journal entry

A **fictionalized journal entry** is a type of reflective writing in which the writer imagines he or she is a character in a book.

Write the word *fictionalized* on the board.

■ Invite a volunteer to circle the word *fiction* within the longer word.
■ Tell students to use what they know about the meaning of *fiction* to figure out the meaning of *fictionalized* (something made up).

Ask students:
If you could be any fictional character you know, which one would you be? Why?

Fictionalized Journal Entries

To prepare students for writing journal entries from the point of view of a character, ask them to discuss the kinds of things they usually write about in their **personal journal** (see below). Explain that out of respect for their privacy, you are not asking for specific details but general kinds of things. For example, students might mention things such as the following:

- things I do with my friends
- my feelings
- what I did during the day
- relationships
- problems I'm having

Before reading and discussing the ideas explored in the sample journal entries for "Charlotte's Web," invite students who have read the book to give a brief summary of the story and the main characters. This will provide helpful background information for students who are not familiar with the book.

324

Fictionalized Journal Entries

Writing fictionalized journal entries is one way to better understand the books you read. In the following student sample, the writer imagines that he is Templeton, the rat in the book *Charlotte's Web*. The side notes will help you understand how to write fictionalized journal entries.

The writer imagines himself as a character in the book.

Each entry is dated.

The character's feelings are included.

Charlotte's Web

<u>Friday, September 20:</u> Wow, I have to admit that old sheep was right when she told me about all the tasty treats I'd find at this fair. I feasted on cheese, sandwiches, candied apples, popcorn, and any other pieces of food I could find.

Before I fell asleep, I told Wilbur that the pig next door had already won the blue ribbon. It's a tough break for Wilbur.

<u>Saturday, September 21:</u> I woke up this morning and had to hold on. The crate was headed on another journey. The truck didn't go far before it stopped. I peeked out and saw hundreds of eyes staring right in my direction. Great, I thought, how can I make my escape?

Wilbur solved that problem. He fainted just as he was about to get a special medal. The Zuckermans panicked. I, once again, came to the rescue. With one mighty bite on Wilbur's tail, I had the little pig back up on his feet. Mission accomplished.

Teaching Tip: Personal Journals

Because journal writing is private and usually is not assessed, students do not feel pressured to write and are more inclined to write freely and openly, which can help them develop and practice a unique style.

✳ See PE pages 432–433 for more on keeping a personal journal.

English Language Learners

Students may not understand some of the idiomatic expressions in this journal entry, particularly if they have not read *Charlotte's Web*. Explain such expressions as the following:

- won the blue ribbon (won first prize in a race or contest)
- It's a tough break (It's a sad situation)
- Mission accomplished (I reached my goal; I was successful)

- I wasn't about to do (I was unwilling to do)
- I couldn't pass up (I couldn't say "no" to)
- He guaranteed me first pickings (He promised that I could have first choice; that I could go first)
- gooey stuff (sticky material)

evaluate *PREVIEW* experience
react *answer*
325

Fictionalized Journal Entries

Each entry reflects on a particular part of the story.

Sunday, September 22: My day began with Wilbur rudely waking me up and tossing me into the air with his pudgy snout. He then loudly ordered me to do just one more favor for him. He kept grunting commands and telling me to hurry up.

I wasn't about to do another favor for him until he made me a promise I couldn't pass up. He guaranteed me first pickings from his trough for every meal of my life!

All I needed to do was climb up and get Charlotte's egg sac. The job sounded easy until I started chewing away at the threads. They were stickier than eating cotton candy and taffy at the same time. It took me forever to get that gooey stuff off my teeth.

Wilbur got so emotional when I gave him the sac. All I wanted to do was take a little nap, so I crawled back inside the crate. I'll be glad to get back to the farm and hear Wilbur tell how I saved Charlotte's family.

Respond to the reading. Answer the following questions about these traits in the sample journal entries.

☐ **Ideas** (1) What main events does the writer talk about?

☐ **Organization** (2) Does the writer use time order, order of importance, or order of location?

☐ **Voice & Word Choice** (3) How does the writer create the character's voice?

LITERATURE

Respond to the reading.

Ask students to provide details and to explain their responses.

Answers

Ideas 1. what happens at the fair; Wilbur faints; Wilbur asks Templeton to get Charlotte's egg sac; Templeton gets the egg sac and gives it to Wilbur, saving Charlotte's family

Organization 2. time order

Voice & Word Choice 3. Exclamation words like *Wow, Great, Mission Accomplished;* descriptive phrases that reveal his love of food and concern for his friends, such as the following:

- tasty treats
- I feasted
- tough break
- with one mighty bite
- first pickings from his trough for every meal of my life
- I'll be glad to get back to the farm

Prewriting Selecting a Novel

For students who are having a difficult time selecting a novel, provide these options:

- Choose a character from the book or story you wrote about in your book review.
- Review the lists of book and story titles you created during prewriting for your paragraph response and book review.
- Skim a recommended book list. (Provide a list, or direct students to an appropriate Web site.)

Prewriting Selecting a Character

Stress how important it is for students to understand the character they select. Point out that although they are writing a fictionalized journal entry, they should not use expressions or describe behavior that would be out of character (not make sense) for the character.

* For more on how to get to know a character, see Writing About a Person on PE page 532.

Encourage students to write thorough answers in their charts.

Prewriting Selecting a Novel

To begin your fictionalized journal entry, choose a book or story you would like to write about. Then think of a character that you would like to become in your writing. This could be a real character from the story or a different character that would fit in the story.

If you have trouble choosing a story, just start listing some that you've read and enjoyed. With a little effort, a favorite book or story will come to mind as you make your list.

List

> The Giver
> Locked in Time
> * Charlotte's Web
> Crispin

 List novels that you have read. Make a list of books or stories that you've enjoyed and would like to write about. Put a star (*) next to the one that you liked the most.

Selecting a Character

Think about the book or story that you have starred. Consider which character is your favorite or which character you could add to the story.

 Select a character and an event. On your own paper, make a chart like the one below. Name the character you will become in your journal and the parts of the story you will focus on. Give reasons for both choices.

> Character: **Templeton**
>
> Explain your selection: **He's most like me.**
>
> Parts of the story you will focus on: **Going to the fair and getting Charlotte's egg sac**
>
> Explain your selection: **These were my favorite parts.**

To help students visualize themselves as story characters, encourage them to choose a story or a novel that has illustrations. Then have them bring the illustrated book to class (or bring in a copy for them) and base their journal entries on what they see in the illustrations.

Below-level and reluctant readers may have difficulty coming up with book titles. Invite them to join you and work as a small group to "jump-start" their thinking. Use the Think/Pair/Share strategy so that each student is responsible for some ideas.

Have students list two or more titles of books they have read or have had read to them. Then have them work in pairs to discuss the titles and the characters from the books. Next, do a whole-group activity. Invite students to share their titles with the rest of the class as you list the books or stories on the board. Then ask the group to name characters from each book or story, and list them next to the appropriate title. Students will now have a long list of book titles and characters from which to choose.

Writing Creating Your First Draft

Remember to write your journal entries as if you were part of the action yourself. Consider the following points as you begin to write.

- **Focus on one event in each journal entry.**
  What does each event mean to the character you are playing?

- **Ask factual questions.**
  What important things happen during this time? Who does what? Who says what?

- **Ask sensory questions.**
  What do the characters see, feel, hear, smell, taste, or touch?

 Read the following part of a story. Imagine being Mario. Then write a short journal entry as if you were Mario and actually had this experience. Afterward, share your results with a classmate.

1 Mario trudged down the sidewalk in the park. Though the
2 night was still, his mind echoed with the shouts of his coach:
3 "If you're going to be on the track team, you've got to run!
4 Run! Run!" The words were almost a bark . . . and then Mario
5 realized it *was* a bark.
6 A big black dog came racing toward him down the
7 sidewalk. It seemed to gather up the shadows of the oak trees,
8 growing until it was the size of a charging rhino.
9 Mario turned and ran. He ran as never before. His coach
10 wouldn't have believed how fast he ran. Ahead stood a tree—
11 a tree Mario had climbed a hundred times. He hurled himself
12 to the lowest branches, caught on, and hauled his feet up.
13 With a monstrous snarl, the dog leaped and snapped at
14 Mario's heels. He scrambled higher, and the beast could not
15 reach him.

 Write your journal entries. After completing an entry from Mario's point of view, write two or three entries for the character that you selected on page 326. Use the three points at the top of this page to guide your writing. (Also review the sample journal entries on pages 324–325.)

LITERATURE

Writing Creating Your First Draft

Provide photocopies of the reproducible sensory chart (TE page 804) for students to use to answer sensory questions about their character.

Some students may find it helpful to also use the 5 W question words to organize notes about the character.

- Provide photocopies of the 5 W's reproducible chart (TE page 803).
- Have students fill in the chart with details about the character and the event they have chosen to write about.

 **Answers**

Wording will vary, but each student should rewrite the journal entry in the first person.

For the **Write your journal entries** activity, tell students to date their entries, and to be sure to use dates that reflect the setting of the book.

Advanced Learners

Challenge students to select a character from another story and try to fit that character into the story they've chosen to write about.

Remind students that they

- are writing from the character's point of view,
- should show the character's feelings,

- should include specific details from the story.

Revising Improving Your Writing

In addition to asking themselves the revising questions, students can exchange papers with a partner. After partners have had a chance to read each other's drafts, writers can ask them the revising questions and then jot down ideas for revising, based on the partner's responses. Ideally, students should be paired with peers who are familiar with the book and character that is the subject of the journal entry.

Editing Checking for Conventions

Since journal entries are written in the first person, students should check carefully to make sure they have consistently used the first-person point of view. They should make sure they have used the personal pronouns *I, me, we,* and *us* and the possessive pronouns *my, mine,* and *ours* correctly.

Publishing Sharing Your Writing

Encourage students to read aloud their journal entries, using gestures and facial expressions that they think the character would use. Some students might like to wear a simple costume or bring in a simple prop for their presentations.

328

Revising Improving Your Writing

After you finish the first draft of your fictionalized journal entries, you need to revise them for the following traits.

- ☐ **Ideas** Does each entry focus on one event or part of the book?
- ☐ **Organization** Have I dated each entry? Is the action in each entry easy to follow?
- ☐ **Voice** Do I sound like a character who actually experienced these things in the story?
- ☐ **Word Choice** Do I use strong nouns and verbs? Do I use words that my character would use?
- ☐ **Sentence Fluency** Are my sentences complete? Do they vary in length and in the way they begin?

 Revise your writing. Ask yourself the questions above as you revise your journal entries.

Editing Checking for Conventions

When you edit your fictionalized journal entries, focus your attention on the *conventions* of writing.

- ☐ **Conventions** Have I checked punctuation and capitalization? Have I checked spelling and grammar?

 Edit your work. Ask yourself the questions above to help you edit your journal entries. Also check the "Proofreader's Guide" (pages 578–749) for additional editing help.

Publishing Sharing Your Writing

Once you've finished your journal entries, it's time to share them with your classmates.

 Write your final copy. Create a final copy of your journal entries. Proofread this copy carefully before sharing it with others.

Response to Literature

Across the Curriculum

In 1977, Earth sent two ambassadors to the stars. *Voyager 1* and *2* each carried a "golden record" that contained sounds from Earth. The records include greetings in 55 languages, whale songs, and animal calls. Any space travelers who find these records could learn about life in 1977 on our planet.

Literature is also a golden record. It tells about events long ago or far away. In social studies, you might read a biography about a person's life in another time and place. In science, you could read articles about distant worlds. Even a poster in your school hallway can open up new horizons for you.

After working with the different forms of response writing in the following pages, you will be able to practice responding to a timed test prompt and analyze what you have learned.

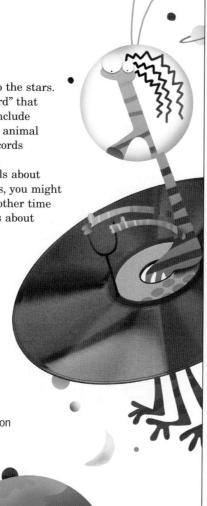

Mini Index

- **Social Studies:** Reviewing a Biography
- **Science:** Summarizing an Article
- **Practical Writing:** Completing an Evaluation
- **Writing for Assessment**

Across the Curriculum

Objectives
- apply what students have learned about responding to literature to other curriculum areas
- practice writing for assessment

The lessons on the following pages provide samples of response writing students might do in different content areas. The particular form used in each content area may also be used in a different content area (for example, students can review a biography for Science just as well as for Social Studies).

Assigning these forms of writing will depend on
- the skill level of your students,
- the subject matter they are studying in different content areas,
- and the writing goals of your school, district, or state.

Social Studies:
Reviewing a Biography

Ask students to recall the insight that they developed for their book review and how their insight guided their writing. Help students recognize that the writer here has used a similar strategy to organize his biography review.

- The first paragraph ends with a statement that expresses an insight about Nelson Mandela's life (. . . nobody should take freedom for granted).
- The writer chooses important events that illustrate and support that insight.
- The last paragraph restates that insight and explains it in different words. It also adds a new insight about a person's ability to change the world.

330

Social Studies:
Reviewing a Biography

Social studies explores the way people have lived in different places and at different times. A good biography can teach you about both.

In his social studies class, Josh read a biography of Nelson Mandela. It told about what life was like for Mandela and other black Africans when South Africa was racially divided.

The **beginning** names the book and author.

The **middle** points out important events in the biography.

The **ending** tells about the importance of the person's life.

Freedom Fighter

Nelson Mandela, A Voice Set Free, by Rebecca Stefoff, tells about a man who fought discrimination in South Africa. The life story of Nelson Mandela shows that nobody should take freedom for granted.

When Nelson Mandela was young, South Africa had a system called "apartheid." It kept black Africans from getting good educations, jobs, or housing. Nelson protested this system by joining the African National Congress (ANC). This group fought for equal rights. Nelson was so successful that the government banned him from ANC activities. He kept working anyway.

In 1956, police arrested Nelson for treason. Four years later, he was found innocent. Police arrested him again in 1962, and this time he was found guilty. Nelson spent 27 years in prison but kept leading the fight for freedom. In 1990, he gained his personal freedom and helped to finally get rid of apartheid. He became South Africa's president in 1994 in the first free elections.

The life of Nelson Mandela shows that freedom is worth fighting for. It also shows that a person who won't give up can change the world.

evaluate *PREVIEW* experience
react answer **331**

Writing in Social Studies

Writing Tips

When you write about a biography, consider these tips.

Before you write . . .

- **Imagine being the person in this biography.**
  Think about what it must have been like to live in another time and place.
- **Think about why this person's life is important.**
  Ask yourself how the person's actions changed society, both in the past and in the present.

During your writing . . .

- **Focus on the person's important experiences.**
  Don't try to include everything.
- **Share interesting details.**
  Select details that show what the person was really like.

After you've written a first draft . . .

- **Revise for ideas, organization, and voice.**
  Make sure the details are well organized and that your voice is formal enough.
- **Double-check important facts.**
  Make sure that the names and dates in your review are correct.
- **Edit and proofread.**
  Check your review for punctuation, capitalization, spelling, and grammar. Then make a final copy of your work and proofread it for errors.

 Search the classroom, the library, or the Internet for a biography that interests you. Then read the biography and write a review of it using the information above as a guide.

LITERATURE

Writing Tips

Help students focus their biographies by suggesting that they concentrate on one facet of a person's life. For example, if they were to choose Theodore Roosevelt, they might focus on his contributions as a conservationist.

Suggest that students use the sample biography on PE page 330 as a model for length and organization as they plan their review for the **Try It** activity.

Provide students with an opportunity for presenting their review in a unique way by holding a **VIP party** (*see below*).

 **Answers**

Reviews will vary but should include

- a beginning paragraph that introduces the book and author and provides an insight about why the person is important,
- middle paragraphs that describe important events and support the insight, and
- an ending that restates why the person is important.

Teaching Tip: VIP Party

Motivate students through the process of reading and writing a book review on a biography by hosting a VIP (Very Important People) party. Invite each student to come dressed as his or her famous person and to take on that persona for the length of the activity.

A twist on this idea is the Living Museum. Students pose as statues in their costumes. When an audi-

ence member strolls by, statues come to life and explain who they are and why they are famous. Dividing up the class into time periods makes this even more fun. Students then read biographies from different historical periods.

Science:
Summarizing an Article

After reading the page, have students find the details in the article that the writer used to write the topic sentence, body, and closing sentence.

Remind students that a summary
- retells only the most important ideas,
- uses the writer's own words,
- is shorter than the original article.

Students may benefit from practice with putting ideas **in their own words** (*see below*) before they write their summary.

332

Science: Summarizing an Article

A summary paragraph captures the main idea of a longer piece of writing. The article on this page describes the possibility of life on one of Jupiter's moons, and the paragraph below it is a student's summary of the article.

Is There Life on Europa?

Scientists are planning to send a probe to one of Jupiter's moons to look for signs of life. The first inkling that the moon Europa might have life came in 1997 when the *Galileo* space probe flew past and photographed its frozen surface. The photographs revealed a possible sea under the ice and showed volcanic activity. Scientists theorize that where there is liquid water and a source of heat, life could exist.

Ironically, the very space probe that discovered the possibility of life on Europa became a threat to further missions. By 2003, the *Galileo* space probe was losing power. If it had accidentally crashed on Europa, it could have spread micro-organisms from Earth on the world. Then, if later probes found life, scientists wouldn't know whether the life originated on Earth. Instead of possibly "contaminating" Europa with terrestrial life forms, NASA scientists decided to steer *Galileo* into Jupiter, where it burned up.

If life does exist on Europa, it may be bacterial, such as life forms found in geothermal pools in Yellowstone. On the other hand, scientists have discovered six-foot-long tube worms living beside volcanic vents at the bottom of Earth's oceans. Perhaps larger life forms such as those could exist on Europa.

A NASA probe could reach Europa as early as 2008. Until then, scientists will have to wait to find out whether the planet contains extraterrestrial life.

Topic sentence

Body

Closing sentence

Extraterrestrial Life?

In 1997, the Galileo space probe discovered that one of Jupiter's moons could have life on it. The moon was Europa, and photos showed that under the moon's frozen surface there may be a sea and volcanoes. Life might exist where there is liquid water and heat. NASA wants to send a probe to find out if Europa has life. They even made Galileo burn up in Jupiter's atmosphere to avoid contaminating Europa with life from Earth. If life does exist there, it might be small like bacteria or big like a tube worm. Scientists won't find out until 2008, when the first NASA probe could reach Europa.

Teaching Tip: In Their Own Words

Students often have difficulty restating in their own words the important information in an article.

Select an article that has three or four paragraphs, so that students won't become overwhelmed by volume. If possible, make an overhead transparency or photocopies to facilitate a large-group lesson.

- Divide students into three or four groups and assign one paragraph of the article to each group.
- After students read the entire article, ask the first group to tell the main idea of the first paragraph in their own words. Suggest that students think about how they would explain the main idea to a younger child. When they do that, they'll be putting the main idea in their own words.
- Have the other groups try this with the other paragraphs.

Writing in Science **333**

Writing Tips

> ### Before you write . . .
>
> - **Read and reread.**
>   Read the article to get an overall sense of it. Then reread the article, focusing on individual details.
> - **Mark up the article and make notes.**
>   Ask yourself, "What is the main idea of this article?" Write it down in a single sentence. Then underline important details that support the main idea.
> - **Plan your paragraph.**
>   Write a topic sentence that sums up the main idea of the article. Consider which facts you will use in the middle. Finally, decide on an interesting closing sentence.
>
> ### During your writing . . .
>
> - **Be brief.**
>   Write a summary that is a third the size of the original—or even smaller. Focus on the main idea of the article and the most important details that support it.
> - **Paraphrase the information.**
>   Put details from the article into your own words. Avoid copying phrases and sentences from the original source.
>
> ### After you've written a first draft . . .
>
> - **Revise your paragraph.**
>   Ask yourself whether you have summed up the main idea and provided the most important details. Revise parts that are incomplete or unclear.
> - **Check your paragraph for correctness.**
>   Make sure there are no mistakes in spelling, punctuation, or other conventions.

 Look for a science-related article in a newspaper or magazine, or use the article that your teacher hands out to you. Follow the tips above as you write a paragraph that summarizes the article.

LITERATURE

Writing Tips

Use any of these strategies as you discuss summarizing.

- Some students may be overwhelmed by having to determine the main idea of an article. Suggest that they ask themselves, *What is this article mostly about?*
- Have students confer in small groups to make sure their topic sentence reflects the main idea of the article they have chosen.
- Once students have identified the main idea of the article, suggest that they write the five most important words from the article. Then have them use these words to organize and plan a summary.
- Provide students with a variety of age-appropriate science magazines to skim through, or copy and distribute a science-related article that you think will interest the majority of students. Ask science teachers for ideas or for suitable articles.

Try It Answers

Summaries will vary but should be shorter than the original article, with a clear topic sentence that states the article's main idea and a brief overview of important supporting details.

English Language Learners

When selecting articles for the **Try It** activity, choose ones with familiar topics and manageable vocabulary. Science or nature magazines written for younger children might be helpful.

Provide support for students as they work through the **Writing Tips.**

- Guide them to tell you or a partner the main idea of the article in their own words by giving them a simple prompt, such as *What does this article tell you?*
- After they respond (*This article tells me . . .*), have students work with a partner to write down the five most important words from the article. They can use these words to organize and plan their summary.

Practical Writing:
Completing an Evaluation

Ask students to explain why they agree or disagree with the student evaluation of the poster.

Point out that in evaluating a poster or other visual display, some of their evaluation will be subjective. In other words, it will depend on their own taste and preferences.

Have students work in pairs to practice evaluating an actual school poster or flyer, using the evaluation form in the sample. Invite students to share and compare their evaluations.

334

Practical Writing:
Completing an Evaluation

Posters use words and graphics to inform, persuade, or entertain. One student filled out the following form to evaluate this poster about "Tutoring."

What's Your Best Subject?
Math? Art? Science?
Reading? Band? Social Studies?
Share What You Know—
TUTOR!

Contact the office for details.

Poster Evaluation: Please complete this form by filling in the subject of the poster, circling its purpose, and rating its parts. Then add your overall comments at the bottom.

Poster Subject: *Tutoring*

Purpose: Inform (Persuade) Entertain

	1	2	3
Information:	(key facts missing)	②(some facts missing)	(no facts missing)
Letter Style:	(too much variety)	②(a few problems)	(just right)
Letter Size:	(too small or too large)	②(a few problems)	(just right)
Colors:	①(too few or too many)	(some don't work)	(great choices)
Design (Words):	(words hard to read)	(some hard to read)	③(easy to read)
Design (Art):	(too empty or crowded)	②(some problems)	(very attractive)

The strong points: *The questions got my attention. The different letter styles make each subject stand out. The poster made me think about becoming a tutor.*

Possible improvements: *The words are crowded at the top of the poster, and the books are just floating there. There should be information about who the reader should contact.*

English Language Learners

Because limited vocabulary leads many students to be visual learners, this might be an activity in which they are particularly proficient. Encourage these students to share their comments about the sample evaluation of the poster. Emphasize that because an evaluation is their opinion, there are no right or wrong answers.

Writing Tips

If you are asked to complete an evaluation form, use the following tips to guide you through the process.

Before you write . . .

● **Study the piece you are evaluating.**
Review the form so that you know what specific things you are to judge.

● **Read the directions on the form.**
Be sure you know how to complete the form.

During your writing . . .

● **Follow all the directions.**
Complete the whole form.

● **Make your comments clear.**
Give all the information that the form requests.

 Review the evaluation form on page 334. Then study the soccer poster below. On your own paper, write at least two "strong points" and two "possible improvements" for the poster. (If your teacher supplies a blank evaluation form, review the tips above before completing the form.)

GET YOUR KICKS!

JOIN NOW!

Informational Meeting
Tuesday at 3:15
See a member for details.

Writing Tips

When creating evaluation forms, be sure to leave room for students to write out comments and recommendations.

If you supply a standard evaluation form for students to use to complete the **Try It** activity, take time now to review the writing tips. After students complete the activity, invite them to share their comments and recommendations.

 Answers

Possible answers:

Strong Points
■ nice use of color
■ good design and use of art

Possible Improvements
■ change headline type to make it easier to read
■ include name of the club, meeting place, and/or a name of a club member

Writing for Assessment

If your students must take school, district, or state assessments this year, focus on the form of writing on which they will be tested.

After reading through the directions for the sample, ask students:

Imagine you are taking this test. Which words and phrases in the directions would you underline or highlight as key words to remember during the test? (Possible choices: 45 minutes; focus on author's message; show your insight; support focus with examples from the text)

Make sure students understand that the marks and notes in blue are the student reader's comments.

Writing for Assessment

On some assessment tests, you may be asked to read a story and write a response to it. The next two pages give you an example of such a test. Read the directions, the story, and the student's comments (in blue). Then read the student's response on pages 338–339.

Response to Literature Prompt

DIRECTIONS:
- Read the following story.
- As you read, make notes. (Your notes will not be graded.)
- After reading the story, write an essay. You have 45 minutes to read, plan, write, and proofread your work.

When you write, focus on the author's message in the story. Show your insight into the characters and ideas. Use clear organization and support your focus with examples from the text.

Amazing

Tomas Mendez smiled as he rounded the turn from Prairie Street to Woodward Avenue. He had run a perfect marathon so far. He'd qualified to start in the top ten, averaged an impressive 5 minutes and 55 seconds per mile, and slowly pulled away from the pack. Now Tomas was alone in front, poised to win his third straight Beloit City Marathon. The homestretch lay ahead, and the crowds on both sides of the street cheered as Tomas came into view. Just 200 more yards . . .   *They both feel happy.*

Tomas's girlfriend, Stacy, stood by the red tape and screamed the loudest. In one hand, she gripped a water bottle, and in the other she waved a sign that said, "Threepeat!"

English Language Learners

Writing prompts, particularly on timed assessment tests, may be extremely challenging for students. Spend as much time as possible analyzing the sample prompt.
- Stress the key words that clarify the goal of the essay (*author's message, your insight, clear organization,* and *support your focus with examples*).

- Then call on volunteers to rephrase the prompt in their own words. Guide students as necessary.
- Write the rephrased prompt on the board, and encourage students to copy it in their learning logs or notebooks. Then, when students work on the practice test on PE page 340, have them refer to the way they rephrased this prompt.

evaluate *PREVIEW* experience
react **answer**
Writing for Assessment **337**

> Seeing Stacy, Tomas kicked into high gear. His legs complained, and his lungs ached, but he wanted to give Stacy and all of them a real show.
>
> The crowd went wild, signs flapping over their heads. One group was <u>chanting something that sounded like "Do it! Do it! Do it!"</u> When Tomas looked to Stacy, though, he saw that her sign hung limp at her side and her eyes were wide with disbelief.
>
> Another runner thundered past Tomas.   *shock*
>
> "What?" he gasped, straining for breath. Shock poured through him as he watched the runner pull away. The back of the guy's sweat-soaked shirt read, "Lewis."
>
> That's what <u>the crowd was shouting—not "Do it!" but "Lewis!"</u>   *Crowd cheers Lewis.*
>
> With a little cry, Tomas clenched his teeth and drove forward, but his legs were wet rags and his gut was a knot. He was still ten feet out when Lewis lunged across the tape and snapped it. Leaving the sidewalk, the crowd flooded into the street to surround the winner.   *No one notices Tomas.*
>
> <u>Unnoticed, Tomas jolted up to cross the line.</u> He grabbed his knees, spat between his feet, and stood there, panting.
>
> Stacy came up to him and patted his shoulder. "Good race."
>
> Tomas shook his head and gasped. "That guy—Lewis—he beat me."   *disappointed*
>
> "Yeah," <u>Stacy said, smiling in admiration at the winner.</u> "Amazing."   *angry*
>
> "Why are you smiling?" Tomas reddened, feeling angry. "What's amazing?"
>
> *hero* ["It's amazing he can run at all. That's the guy who broke his back two years ago. They said he'd never walk again, but he said he'd run a marathon. Not only did he run, but he won. Amazing."
>
> Straightening up and staring through the crowd, <u>Tomas nodded, and he smiled, too.</u> "Amazing."   *They both smile.*

LITERATURE

After students read the story and the comments in blue, ask if there are any additional comments or marks they would have made if they were taking the test.

Advanced Learners

Have students discuss whether or not they think the notes in the student sample are good ones. Then have them reread the story and write their own notes on paper.

- Have students use their notes to make a cluster diagram to show how they would organize their thoughts in order to respond to the prompt on PE page 336.

- Advise students to use the center circle for their insight and the surrounding circles for the examples from the text.
- If time allows and students show interest, they can write a first draft of a response to the story, using their notes and their cluster diagrams.

Review the main traits of a response to literature. Ask students to look for these traits as they read the model:

■ a beginning that introduces the work and includes a focus statement that shows an insight into the work
■ middle paragraphs describing important events from the story that develop the insight
■ an ending that explains a change in the character and that restates the insight
■ clear topic sentences for each paragraph, supported by details
■ transitions that show time order and connect ideas in and between paragraphs
■ use of a knowledgeable, formal voice.

Students may note that the sample shows the insight in the first sentence of the beginning paragraph. Point out that this beginning is fine, especially in a timed writing.

338

Student Response

The following essay shows a student response to the story "Amazing." Note how the student uses details from the story to support the focus.

BEGINNING
The first paragraph shares the focus of the essay.

> The story "Amazing" shows that people can change how they feel about someone. In this story, Tomas and his girlfriend, Stacy, both change their feelings about a man named Lewis.
>
> Tomas is running in a marathon and expects to win for the third time. Stacy is cheering for him. As Tomas rounds the final turn, he is thinking he "had run a perfect marathon." He is feeling great. He sees Stacy at the finish line. They both feel sure he will win.

MIDDLE
The middle paragraphs support the focus with examples from the story.

> Everything changes when a runner shoots past Tomas. Suddenly, he realizes that the crowd was not shouting, "Do it!" for him. They were shouting, "Lewis," the name of the runner who had just passed him.
>
> Then the crowd surrounds the winner. Tomas is exhausted and sees that no one even notices as he crosses the finish line,

Struggling Learners

Students may benefit from a visual reminder of what to look for as they read the student response and also when they write their own responses. As you review the main traits of a response to literature, prepare a graphic organizer.

● On chart paper, write the headings *Beginning, Middle,* and *End.*
● As you review the traits, write notes under each heading that

tell what to look for in that part of the response.
● Post the chart, so that students can refer to it while working.

Respond to the reading.

Answers

second. Of course, he feels disappointed and embarrassed when Stacy says, "Good race." He sees her smiling at the winner and hears her say, "Amazing." That makes him angry. Then Stacy tells Tomas that the winner broke his back two years before.

ENDING

The final paragraph explains the meaning of the story.

Suddenly, Tomas isn't thinking of himself. He and Stacy are thinking about Lewis and his struggle to win a marathon. Tomas still wishes he had won, but in the end, he sees that his opponent really is amazing. The writer is trying to show that thinking about other people is the first step to understanding and respecting them.

Ideas **1.** The story "Amazing" shows that people can change the way they feel about someone.
2. the great feelings Tomas and Stacy have as he appears to be winning, the disappointment and embarrassment he feels when he loses, the anger he feels toward Stacey when she seems to be happy that Lewis won, the understanding they have when they learn what Lewis had to overcome

Organization 3. The notes helped the writer keep track of the changes in Tomas's and Stacey's feelings during and after the race.

Voice **& Word Choice 4.** objective
5. Students should note that the writer achieves an objective voice by not expressing personal feelings or opinions about the book or characters. Possible words:

- The story "Amazing" shows . . .
- Everything changes when . . .
- Suddenly, Tomas isn't thinking of himself.
- The writer is trying to show . . .

Respond to the reading. Answer the following questions about the sample prompt and student response.

☐ Ideas **(1)** What is the focus of the student's response? **(2)** What feelings does this student describe?

☐ Organization **(3)** How did the notes on pages 336–337 help the student organize the response?

☐ Voice & Word Choice **(4)** Is the student's voice objective or personal? **(5)** What words tell you so?

LITERATURE

Practice Writing Prompt

Point out that students must approach writing-on-demand assignments differently from open-ended writing assignments and that timed writing creates pressures for everyone.

To teach students who must take timed assessments how to approach their writing, allow them the same amount of time to write their response essay as they will be allotted on school, district, or state assessments. Break down each part of the process into clear chunks of time. For example, you might give students

- 10 minutes for reading, note-taking and planning,
- 20 minutes for writing,
- 15 minutes for revising, editing, and proofreading.

Tell students when time is up for each section. Start the assignment at the top of the hour or at the half-hour to make it easier for students to keep track of the time.

If your state, district, or school requires students to use and submit a graphic organizer as part of their assessment, provide a copy of one of the reproducible charts (TE pages 800–804) or refer students to PE pages 548–549.

Practice Writing Prompt

 Practice a response to literature. Carefully read the directions to the practice writing prompt on the next two pages. Use 10 minutes at the beginning to read the story, make notes, and plan your writing. Also leave time at the end to proofread your work.

DIRECTIONS:

- Read the following story.
- As you read, make notes on your own paper.
- After reading the story, write an essay. You have 45 minutes to read, plan, write, and proofread your work.

When you write, focus on the author's message in the story. Show your insight into the characters and ideas. Use clear organization and support your focus with examples from the text.

Fishing

"You mean you're spending two whole days with Chad?" I laughed at the look on Jack's face. He had just told me he was going on a weekend fishing trip with none other than Chad Jones, the brainiest kid in class.

"It's not like I want to!" Jack growled. "Our dads are buddies, and they planned this father-son trip. I have to go!"

Chad was always on the edge of our group, eager to be accepted when he just wasn't a part of things. It's not like we were nasty to him. Still, we never went out of our way to include him in things like after-school hoops. He wasn't smelly or weird or anything. He just wasn't—like us.

The whole weekend, every time I thought about Jack and Chad stuck together in a boat, I had to chuckle. I could see Jack, silent and grumpy, while Chad talked his ear off about his dull ideas. I figured Jack would be ready to tip the boat and swim to shore just to get away from Chad.

English Language Learners

Have students refer to the rephrased prompt that they wrote for the sample assessment test on PE page 336.

Struggling Learners

Remind students to refer to the chart on PE page 288 that identifies the information to include in their response. Also encourage students to make their own graphic organizers to put their own ideas in order during the prewriting stage.

Monday, I got to class early so I could kid Jack some more. He was already there, sitting next to Chad. A group of kids were clustered around them, listening. I moved closer to the group and could hear Chad talking about the fishing trip. Jack saw me and signaled me to come over.

"Hey, Max, c'mere!" he yelled. "You gotta hear about this trip. It was amazing! Chad's like the best fly fisherman I've ever seen." Chad blushed—he actually blushed!

"I've been fishing since I was little," he said modestly. "No big deal."

"No big deal?" Jack exploded. "He was amazing! He showed me how to tie flies—look at this one." He held up a delicate little fishing fly that looked enough like a dragonfly to take off around the room. "He made this! And he caught the biggest largemouth bass I have ever seen! Tell 'em about that one, Chad."

Chad started to talk about the fish. As he got more and more into the story, his face and eyes glowed from excitement. He made the fight with the fish sound exciting. I stood there, feeling really left out. Looking up at my reflection in the window, I saw the same look I had seen so often on Chad's face. I suddenly felt ashamed for the way I'd treated him.

"So what do you think of that, Max?" Jack asked.

"I think—" Chad was looking at me shyly, as if what I said really mattered. I smiled. "I think next time I want to go with you guys!" I sat down next to Chad.

"Let's shoot some hoops after school," I said. "You in, Chad?"

LITERATURE

Remind students that the best way to master a skill is to practice it. Since writing is a skill, the more they practice writing, the better writers they will become.

Encourage students to practice writing responses to stories and articles they read in class or on their own. There is a definite side benefit to writing responses for reading assignments in other curriculum areas: They can use the responses to review for tests.

Creative Writing Overview

Writing Standards

The writing standards listed below are based on a blending of state and NCTE standards.

- Freewrite to select a topic for a story.
- Create a plot chart and gather sensory details.
- Revise drafts to sharpen the plot line and reflect personality.
- Gather details and use poetry techniques to write a free-verse poem.
- Revise, edit, and share a poem.

Writing Forms

- short story
- free-verse poem

Focus on the Traits

- **Ideas** Using sensory details
- **Organization** Creating a plot line to organize details
- **Voice** Using a natural voice that reflects the writer's personality
- **Word Choice** Playing with words that make interesting sounds and create strong images
- **Sentence Fluency** Varying sentence length to create a smooth flow
- **Conventions** Checking for errors in punctuation, capitalization, spelling, and grammar

Unit Pacing

Writing Stories: 3.75–6.75 hours

This section asks students to write a **short story**. Use this section if students need to work on crafting a story. Following are some of the topics that are covered.

- Freewriting to select a topic
- Creating a plot chart
- Using a sensory chart to gather details
- Writing a story about a future event

Writing Poems: 3–4.5 hours

This section asks students to write a **free-verse poem**. Use this section if students need to work on crafting a poem. Following are some of the topics that are covered.

- Creating a cluster to choose a topic
- Using special poetry techniques
- Writing other forms of poetry (haiku, limerick, name poem, phrase poem)

Integrated Grammar and Writing Skills

Below are skills lessons from the resources sections of the pupil edition that are suggested at point of use (✳) throughout this unit.

Writing Stories

- ✳ Show, Don't Tell, p. 557
- ✳ Specific Nouns, p. 471
- ✳ Specific Feeling of Verbs, p. 485
- ✳ End Punctuation, pp. 579–580

Writing Poems

- ✳ Sensory Details, p. 489
- ✳ Spelling, pp. 642–651
- ✳ Model Sentences, p. 521
- ✳ Prepositions, pp. 494–495, 742

I stretch,
I stretch,
my ostrich
neck.
Crack!
Crack!
The kinks
are back!

342

Additional Grammar Skills

Below are skills lessons from other components that you can weave into your unit instruction.

Writing Stories

● **SkillsBook**

End Punctuation 1 and 2, p. 3
Punctuation Review 1, 2, and 3,
  p. 33
Specific Nouns, p. 131
Verbs 1 and 2, p. 141

● **Interactive Writing Skills CD-ROM**

Parts of Speech: Nouns 1—Kinds,
  Number, and Gender

● **Daily Language Workout**

Week 31: Another Look at World
  History, pp. 64–65
Week 31: Being in Fashion, p. 108

Writing Poems

● **SkillsBook**

Spelling, p. 51
Prepositional Phrases, p. 71
Prepositional Phrases, p. 171

● **Interactive Writing Skills CD-ROM**

Parts of Speech: Prepositions
Spelling 1, 2
Spelling Review 1

● **Daily Language Workout**

Week 32: The Sixteenth Century,
  pp. 66–67
Week 32: Human Longevity, p. 109

imagine
entertain

Creative Writing

show
create

Creative Writing
Writing Stories

People have always told stories. Early on, they gathered around campfires and spoke of heroes and heroines, kings and queens, beasts and battles. Over time, people began writing their stories down, acting them out, and producing them for the screen. Stories entertain us, and they teach us about life.

Almost all stories use the same simple plan: There are *people* in a *place* doing some *activity,* and a *problem* occurs. Because of the many stories you have heard, read, or written, this simple plan has become part of your own thinking. As a result, writing a story will come naturally to you.

In this chapter, you will read a sample story about the future and then develop a story of your own to share.

Writing Guidelines

Subject:	Future event
Form:	Short story
Purpose:	To entertain
Audience:	Classmates

Writing Stories

Objectives
- understand the content and structure of a short story
- imagine an important event or challenge in the future
- plan, draft, revise, and edit a short story

A **short story** uses characters, actions, and dialogue to engage and entertain the reader.

Ask students to name their favorite stories. Tell them to think about stories that they have
- read,
- heard from friends and family members,
- seen on television or in the movies.

Discuss why students enjoyed these stories. Ask students to share the most memorable aspects of the stories.

Short Story

Have students reflect on any of the stories that the class shared in which the characters faced a problem or challenge. Ask students:

- How did the character face the problem or challenge?
- Did the character change in some way because of that challenge?

Short Story

In many stories, events change the main character in some way. The character may learn something new, gain a friend, achieve a goal, or lose a prized possession. The way a character faces a problem or challenge is what makes a story interesting.

Imagine an important event or challenge that you might face in the future. In the story below, Sarah imagined her journey up the slopes of Mount Everest and the problems she faced. The side notes identify the different parts of the story.

Journey to the Top of the World

BEGINNING

The beginning introduces the main characters and the setting.

I opened my eyes and stared up at the orange roof of my tent. The world was silent. What a wonderful sound! All night, winds had whistled and snow had pounded the tent walls. At last, the storm was over. Today I could head up from Camp 5 to the summit of Mount Everest.

After dressing in my gear and eating an energy bar, I came out of my tent. The sun shone brightly, and wind had carried away much of the snow. Even through the oxygen mask I wore, I could feel the cold, biting air.

"Ready for the climb?" asked Kami, our guide. She stood with the other team members near their tents.

I replied, "I've been ready since fifth grade."

RISING ACTION

The rising action adds a conflict and increases the suspense.

We slid on our backpacks, grabbed our ice axes, and started climbing. My boots bit into the snow, and I paused with each step. Even going slow, I had to fight for breath. I adjusted my oxygen mask and remembered the first time I'd worn one of these.

Just after turning 11, I had my first serious asthma attack. My parents took me to the hospital, and the doctor gave me oxygen and bitter medicine. That night, I saw a National Geographic special about climbing Mount Everest.

English Language Learners

Before reading the story, help students understand the setting.

- Find out what they know about Mt. Everest or another high mountain.
- Sketch a picture of a mountain and point out the summit.
- If possible, show a picture of mountain climbers in their gear, including equipment to help them breathe at high altitudes.

Advanced Learners

There is a whole body of literature on the subject of mountain climbing. Have interested students do the following:

- search to find different sources for mountain climbing literature
- identify several pieces of writing that are appropriate for themselves and classmates

- report back to the class on the different reading options they have found
- read a piece about mountain climbing
- write a review to share with the class

entertain create *imagine* **discover**
show **345**
Writing Stories

CREATIVE

A flashback can tell about earlier events.

The people in the show were short of breath and wore oxygen masks just like me. I decided that someday I would climb Mount Everest. Today that dream would come true.

I looked up the trail. The peak looked so high and black, it made me dizzy. My legs felt like lead. Worst of all, my throat started to tighten up. I stopped walking and dropped to my knees. I couldn't breathe.

"Are you okay?" asked Kami, checking my oxygen mask. "Do you need to go back?"

I shook my head and closed my eyes. Just as I had learned to do in fifth grade, I calmed my heart and relaxed my throat. It took a minute, but I slowly got my throat to open again. "I'll be fine," I gasped.

I stood up and began to walk. My feet soon fell into a regular pace, and my breathing did, too. One step at a time, I would make it to the top.

Just after 1:00 p.m., I stood at the top of the world. The sun couldn't fight off the bitter cold, but my heart burned with joy. The mountains all around me seemed small next to Everest.

Suddenly I knew I could do anything I set my mind to doing. I silently thanked my fifth-grade self for that long-ago decision. That's really when this amazing journey up the mountain began.

HIGH POINT

At the high point in this story, the main character succeeds.

ENDING

The ending tells how the main character has changed.

Respond to the reading. Review the story and answer the following questions about ideas, organization, and voice.

☐ **Ideas** (1) Why is climbing Mount Everest so important to Sarah? (2) What details make her climb believable?

☐ **Organization** (3) Do all the events take place in time order?

☐ **Voice & Word Choice** (4) Does the main character's mood change? What words show this?

Discuss how TV shows and movies treat flashbacks (music, the camera zooming in on a character's face as if it were going inside his or her head). Ask students how writers can indicate a flashback (Use phrases such as "I remembered," "I'll never forget," "that reminded me of").

Respond to the reading.

Answers

Ideas 1. Possible choices:
- Sarah wants to climb Mt. Everest to prove to herself that she has overcome her asthma.
- Sarah wants to realize the dream that she had after her first asthma attack.

Ideas 2. Possible choices:
- My legs felt like lead.
- My throat started to tighten up.
- I couldn't breathe.
- I calmed my heart and relaxed my throat.

Organization 3. No, the writer uses a flashback to explain her motivation.

Voice & Word Choice 4. Yes, her mood changes. The following words show her mood change:
- calmed my heart
- relaxed my throat
- feet soon fell into a regular pace
- heart burned with joy

English Language Learners

Identifying the use of flashback may be challenging for English language learners. After an initial reading, have students

- revisit the story to determine when each part takes place, and
- use sticky notes and the words *now* or *past* to label each paragraph of the story.

Struggling Learners

Help students identify the specific paragraph where the flashback occurs. Together, locate other references to the flashback (I've been ready since fifth grade; Just as I had learned to do in fifth grade, . . . ; I silently thanked my fifth-grade self . . .). Discuss how the story would seem "empty" without this background information.

Prewriting Selecting a Topic

Have students quickly **brainstorm** (*see below*) topic ideas without taking time to evaluate them. Write the ideas on the board or on a transparency.

- Ask students to think of challenges they might face in the future.
- Explain that this is just a time to generate ideas, not elaborate on them. When students stop calling out ideas rapidly, stop the activity.

After the brainstorming is finished, have students freewrite to select their topic.

Focus on the Traits

Organization

Tell students to think of an adventure story that they have read. Have them make a simple outline showing the beginning, the rising action, the high point, and the ending. Remind students that an outline is a skeletal design; it should consist of words and phrases, not full sentences.

Prewriting Selecting a Topic

It's fun to think about the future and imagine the things you might do. Sarah Silverton used freewriting to dream about her future. She kept writing until she found an interesting topic for her story.

> *I'm supposed to think about a future event. Well, if I became a vet, maybe I'd get to work with racehorses. I love horses. Or maybe I could be a forest ranger and help save spotted owls. I hope I'm not allergic to spotted owls. My allergies have been awful since that asthma attack last year. That's when I decided to climb Mount Everest. That might make a cool story. . . .*

 Freewrite to select a topic. Write freely about possible events in your future. Write until you discover a good topic for your story. If you have trouble getting started, follow Sarah's example above and write about careers you would like to try.

Focus on the Traits

Organization

The actions that take place during a story make up the plot line. Each part of the plot plays an important role in the story.

- The **beginning** introduces the characters and setting.
- The **rising action** adds a conflict—a problem for the characters.
- The **high point** is the most exciting part.
- The **ending** tells how the main character has changed.

Teaching Tip: Brainstorming

Brainstorming is a highly creative process, full of energy and action. Students call out ideas as they think of them, and one student's ideas trigger ideas in other students, who in turn call out their ideas. It is an excellent activity to warm up everyone's creativity and interest.

English Language Learners

To avoid distracting students from the creative process, during the freewrite have them concentrate on listing words and phrases or making quick sketches instead of trying to formulate sentences or clauses.

CREATIVE

Creating a Plot

Sarah thought about what it would be like to climb Mount Everest. She used a plot chart to organize the details for her story.

Plot Chart

Beginning	Rising Action	High Point	Ending
The story starts at the camp. I wake up and greet the team.	We start to climb. I remember why I want to do this: the bad asthma attack in fifth grade.	Suddenly I can't breathe! The guide checks my oxygen. I calm myself and keep going.	Victory! I know I can do anything I set my mind to doing.

 Create a plot chart. Make a plot chart like the one above. Imagine what will happen in each part of your story from the beginning to the ending.

Gathering Sensory Details

A well-written story helps readers feel as if they are experiencing the events themselves. To do this, use plenty of sensory details. Sarah created the chart below to gather sensory details for her story.

Sensory Chart

See	Hear	Smell	Taste	Touch/Feel
orange tent, bright sun, tall mountain, rugged rock	whistling wind, snow hitting the tent	fresh air, oxygen mask	bitter medicine, energy bar	cold air, tight throat, spiky shoes, tired legs

 Gather sensory details. Create a sensory chart like the one above. Write down the things you would see, hear, smell, taste, and feel throughout your story. Try to think of at least two details for each sense.

Prewriting Creating a Plot

Remind students that characters experience both inner conflicts and conflicts that arise from external causes. These conflicts may be generated by many sources, including people, natural phenomena (such as changes in the weather), and accidents. Refer students to the terms *conflict* and *plot line* on PE page 351.

Prewriting
Gathering Sensory Details

Explain to students that sensory details help them to show the reader something, rather than just tell the reader. Point out the difference between these two descriptions:

- I woke up. It was quiet, so I knew the storm was over.
- I opened my eyes and stared up at the orange roof of my tent. The world was silent. What a wonderful sound! All night, winds had whistled and snow had pounded the tent walls. At last, the storm was over.

The first paragraph *tells* the reader that the storm is over when Sarah wakes up. The second paragraph *shows* what it is like to wake up in a tent now that the snowstorm is over.

✳ Additional information about Show, Don't Tell can be found on PE page 557.

Advanced Learners

Encourage students to explore the process of creating a plot. Ask students to

- create two or more plot lines for their stories,
- share their ideas with other students, and
- use their classmates' feedback to determine which one to use.

Writing
Developing Your First Draft

Help students develop their first drafts by writing along with them. **Teacher modeling** (*see below*) is an effective way to encourage writers.

Revising **Improving Your Writing**

Explain to students the difference between a specific and a general noun. Use examples like these:

- *General:* building
  Specific: children's hospital
- *General:* shoes
  Specific: sneakers

Ask students which of these sentences gives them the better picture.

- The storm blew over things.
- The blizzard knocked down power lines and uprooted tree limbs.

Point out that specific nouns and verbs help give readers a clear picture of what is happening in stories.

✱ Additional information about specific nouns is on PE page 471 and about verbs is on PE page 485.

348

Writing **Developing Your First Draft**

You now have everything you need to begin writing your story. As you write, keep the following tips in mind.

1 **Begin in the middle of the action.**

Instead of . . . I always wanted to climb Mount Everest.

Write . . . I opened my eyes and stared up at the orange roof of my tent.

2 **Use dialogue to move the story along.**

Instead of . . . I said I would be fine, but it was hard to talk.

Write . . . "I'll be fine," I gasped.

3 **Show what happens instead of just telling about it.**

Instead of . . . I couldn't go on because of an asthma attack.

Write . . . I stopped walking and dropped to my knees. I couldn't breathe.

 Write your first draft. Use your plot chart and sensory chart as you write your first draft. Remember to *show* instead of *tell.* Use dialogue and specific nouns and verbs. Enjoy telling your story!

Revising **Improving Your Writing**

Once you finish your first draft, set it aside for a while. After taking a break, you'll be able to see what changes could make your story better.

- ☐ **Ideas** Do I tell about a future event? Do I use sensory details?
- ☐ **Organization** Have I followed my plot line?
- ☐ **Voice** Does the way I write reflect my personality?
- ☐ **Word Choice** Do I use specific nouns and past tense verbs?
- ☐ **Sentence Fluency** Do my sentences flow smoothly from one to the next? Do I vary the lengths and types of sentences?

 Revise your story. Use the questions above as a guide when you revise your first draft.

Teaching Tip: Teacher Modeling

Modeling is an effective way to motivate writers.

- Display your own first draft on the board or overhead.
- Let students see you as a writer. Students benefit from witnessing your process of trial and error.
- It will also help to have done the prewriting with your students.

Struggling Learners

If students get stuck before they even start, encourage them to make a "fake" beginning that they plan to change later. To their surprise, they may even generate a sentence or two that they want to keep. Explain to students that they can use this technique any time they write.

Advanced Learners

Have students brainstorm vivid synonyms for the word *said,* such as *mumbled, exclaimed, whined,* or *declared.* Then write the following sentence on the board: *He _____, "They're coming on Tuesday evening."* As you fill in the blank with each synonym, have students use different voices to demonstrate how the dialogue would sound if read aloud.

entertain *create* *imagine* **discover** **349**
show
Writing Stories

CREATIVE

Editing Checking for Conventions

Once you have completed your revisions, it is time to edit your story for *conventions*.

☐ **Conventions** Have I corrected any errors in spelling and capitalization? Have I included end punctuation for each sentence? Have I checked easily confused words (*to, too, two; your, you're*)?

Edit your story. Use the questions above to guide your editing. When you finish, use the tips below to write a title. Then write a final copy and proofread it.

Creating a Title

The title of your story should catch the reader's interest. Here are three strategies for writing story titles.

■ Use words from the story: **Journey to the Top of the World**
■ Use colorful words: **A Breathless Victory**
■ Be creative: **Conquering Asthma in the Himalayas**

Publishing Sharing Your Story

Here are three suggestions for sharing your story with others.

● **Hold a storytelling session.** Practice reading your story out loud. Then read it to others. Ask them to read their stories, too.

● **Act out your story.** Choose some friends to act out the story with you. Then present your skit to your class or family.

● **Post your story online.** Search for a Web page that accepts student writing and post your story there. Make sure to get permission from a parent or guardian before doing this.

Present your story. Choose one of the ideas above or make up your own. Then share your story.

Editing
Checking for Conventions

Sometimes sending students to the dictionary for every possible misspelling can discourage them from experimenting with language. Instead, help them to track and learn new words by creating a **Spelling Resource** (*see below*).

Remind students that they put question marks at the end of sentences that ask direct questions, such as "Do you want to shoot some baskets?" They should *not* put a question mark after an indirect question, such as "My brother asked if I wanted to shoot some baskets." (An indirect question tells about a question you or someone else asked.)

✱ Additional information on end punctuation can be found on PE pages 579–580.

Publishing Sharing Your Story

Invite a younger class to listen to the stories your students wrote. If possible, arrange for your students to coach younger students in writing stories about a future challenge (for example, when the younger students reach sixth grade).

Teaching Tip: Spelling Resource

Help students create and use their own personal spelling resources. Have them follow these steps:

● Label index cards or notebook pages—a letter on each card or page.
● Record words they misspell.
● Refer to this resource to find the correct spelling whenever they use one of these words in their writing.

Struggling Learners

To make the editing task more manageable, lead students through the process one step at a time.

● Ask students to check their stories to be sure each sentence has ending punctuation.
● Have them make sure that beginnings of sentences and proper nouns are capitalized.
● Direct students to check two or three more major conventions.

Story Patterns

Have students identify the story pattern that they used to write their stories. Do the following activity with the class.

- Make a chart of the five different story patterns.
- Fill in each category with the student titles that fit.
- Examine the completed chart and see which story pattern is used most often.
- Ask students why they think this is the most common pattern.

 **Answer**

In "Journey to the Top of the World," the writer follows the *rite of passage* pattern. Her ascent of Mount Everest is symbolic of her personal growth from a frightened girl with asthma to a courageous young woman who has overcome her fears.

350

Story Patterns

Here are brief descriptions of five story patterns. These popular patterns may give you ideas for stories of your own.

The Discovery	In a *discovery* story, the main character follows a trail of clues to discover a secret. Mystery and suspense novels use this pattern. **A young man discovers a mountain hideaway.**
The Quest	In a *quest*, the main character goes on a journey into the unknown, overcomes a number of obstacles, and returns either victorious or wiser. Many ancient myths follow this pattern, but so do many modern stories. **A young woman overcomes a severe leg injury so she can walk again.**
The Choice	The *choice* pattern involves the main character making a difficult decision. Suspense builds as the decision draws near. **A middle school student must decide between trying out for softball and helping her grandmother.**
The Rite of Passage	In the *rite of passage* pattern, a difficult experience changes the main character in a major and lasting way. These stories are also called "coming of age" stories. **A young soldier learns about courage while on the battlefield.**
The Reversal	The *reversal* pattern is one in which the main character follows one course of action until something causes him or her to think or act in a different way. **A young man lives for football until his best friend is seriously injured during a game.**

 Look back at the sample short story on pages 344–345. Decide which story pattern it follows. Explain your choice.

Advanced Learners

Students may design additional charts and graphs in order to

- analyze story patterns as they read fictional stories in books and magazines,
- record their findings, and
- share their information with others.

Elements of Fiction

The following list includes many terms used to describe the elements or parts of literature. This information will help you discuss and write about the novels, poetry, essays, and other literary works you read.

Action: Everything that happens in a story

Antagonist: The person or force that works against the hero of the story (See *protagonist.*)

Character: A person or an animal in a story

Characterization: The way in which a writer develops a character, making him or her seem believable
Here are three methods:

- Sharing the character's thoughts, actions, and dialogue
- Describing his or her appearance
- Revealing what others in the story think or say about this character

Conflict: A problem or clash between two forces in a story
There are five basic conflicts:

- **Person Against Person** A problem between characters
- **Person Against Himself or Herself** A problem within a character's own mind
- **Person Against Society** A problem between a character and society, the law, or some tradition
- **Person Against Nature** A problem with some element of nature, such as a blizzard or a hurricane
- **Person Against Destiny** A problem or struggle that appears to be beyond a character's control

Dialogue: The words spoken between two or more characters

Foil: The character who acts as a villain or challenges the main character

Mood: The feeling or emotion a piece of literature or writing creates in a reader

Moral: The lesson a story teaches

Narrator: The person or character who actually tells the story, giving background information and filling in details between portions of dialogue

Plot: The action that makes up the story, following a plan called the plot line

Plot Line: The planned action or series of events in a story (The basic parts of the plot line are the beginning, the rising action, the high point, and the ending.)

PLOT LINE / High Point / Rising Action / Beginning / Ending

- The **beginning** introduces the characters and the setting.
- The **rising action** adds a conflict— a problem for the characters.
- The **high point** is the moment when the conflict is strongest.
- The **ending** tells how the main characters have changed.

CREATIVE

Elements of Fiction

Use PE pages 351–352 as resources.

- Scan these pages with your students so they know what information they can find here.
- When students are prewriting and writing their stories, refer them to the explanations on these resource pages for clarification.
- For example, when students consider conflict and a plot line on PE page 347, they will find detailed information to help them on this page.

Explain to students that the pronouns the narrator uses provide a good clue to a story's point of view.

■ In the first-person point of view, one of the characters tells the story, and uses pronouns such as *I, we, me,* and *us.*

■ In third person, the narrator is outside the story and uses pronouns such as *they, he, she, them, him,* and *her.*

352

Point of View: The angle from which a story is told (The angle depends upon the narrator, or person telling the story.)

● **First-Person Point of View**
This means that one of the characters is telling the story: "We're just friends—that's all—but that means everything to us."

● **Third-Person Point of View**
In third person, someone from outside the story is telling it: "They're just friends—that's all—but that means everything to them." There are three third-person points of view: *omniscient, limited omniscient,* and *camera view.* (See the illustrations on the right.)

Protagonist: The main character or hero in a story (See *antagonist.*)

Setting: The place and the time period in which a story takes place

Theme: The message about life or human nature that is "hidden" in the story that the writer tells

Tone: The writer's attitude toward his or her subject. Tone can be described by words like *angry* and *humorous.*

Total Effect: The overall influence or impact that a story has on a reader

Third-Person Points of View

Omniscient point of view allows the narrator to tell the thoughts and feelings of all the characters.

Limited omniscient point of view allows the narrator to tell the thoughts and feelings of only one character at a time.

Camera view (objective view) allows the story's narrator to record the action from his or her own point of view without telling any of the characters' thoughts or feelings.

 Select one of the five types of conflicts on page 351. In one sentence, describe a conflict from a story you know. In another sentence, describe the setting for this story. Add a sentence that describes the protagonist.

Creative Writing

Writing Poems

Poets love words. They love the way words sound and the way they look on the page. They love the way words create pictures and unlock ideas. Today many poets write free-verse poems, which don't follow a regular pattern. With free-verse, writers can play with the sounds and arrangement of their words, as in the poem to the right.

In the following chapter, you will write a free-verse poem about an animal that you would like to be. You'll also find other types of poetry that you could try. The last pages of the chapter tell about special techniques you can use when writing poetry.

I stretch,
I stretch,
my ostrich
neck.
Crack!
Crack!
The kinks
are back!

Writing Guidelines

Subject:	An animal you would like to be
Form:	Free-verse poem
Purpose:	To entertain
Audience:	Classmates

Writing Poems

Objectives
- understand free-verse poetry
- plan, draft, revise, edit, and publish a free-verse poem

Unlike other forms of poetry, **free-verse** poetry does not have regular patterns. Like other kinds of poems, free-verse poems are filled with sensory details that evoke vivid images. The sounds of the words are as important as the words themselves. Poetry is meant to be read aloud, and so poets pay close attention to each word and its relationship to every other word in the poem.

Display examples of good free-verse poetry. Ask students to bring poems they have written to class, to add to the display. Take turns reading the poems aloud.

Struggling Learners

To encourage students to create their own free-verse poems, follow these steps.

- Bring in old magazines.
- Invite students to cut out words that catch their fancy.
- Tell students to paste their words into a collage.
- Students may add written words if they choose.

Free-Verse Poem

Have students take turns reading "White Flame" aloud. Tell them to listen carefully and think about how the words create vivid images.

Respond to the reading.

Answers

Ideas 1. Possible choices: wailing, roars, crowded, sniff, smoky, blazing, splash, spray, little, gray, salty, sooty

Organization 2. The word *I* is repeated three times. Several sounds are repeated in different lines. The "s" sound is repeated most often. Some reasons the author uses the "s" sound again and again include: it sounds like flames, and water from hoses; its harsh sound creates a tone the dog's presence eases.

Voice 3. The speaker is the dog featured in the picture.

If you choose, turn ahead to PE page 356 and discuss alliteration. Then scan PE pages 360–361 to familiarize students with techniques to use in adding special sounds to their poetry.

354

Free-Verse Poem

Many free-verse poems contain sensory details. Sights, sounds, smells, and other sensations let the reader "experience" the topic of the poem. Caleb Carter wrote the following poem about the life of a firehouse dog.

White Flame

People call me White Flame.
I ride on a wailing fire truck
 as it roars down crowded streets.
I leap off to sniff the smoky air
 and face the blazing flames.
I splash through the hose's spray
 and sit by the little gray girl
 and lick the salty tears
 from her sooty cheeks.

Respond to the reading. On your own paper, reflect on the ideas, organization, and voice of the free-verse poem.

☐ **Ideas** (1) List five details that refer to the senses.

☐ **Organization** (2) What words and letter sounds are repeated in this poem?

☐ **Voice** (3) Who is the speaker in the poem?

Provide an alternative to having students take turns reading the poem aloud.

- Read the poem to students.
- Slowly read it aloud several more times.
- As you continue, invite students to join you in reading out loud.

Encourage students to write poems about other animals' experiences in the same format used by the author of "White Flame":

People call me _____

I _____

I _____

I _____

Invite students to create a poem that repeats a sound throughout. Students might experiment to create a special tone with:

- long vowel sounds (P<u>ea</u>ce fl<u>ow</u>s l<u>i</u>ke <u>a</u> str<u>ea</u>m of l<u>igh</u>t.)
- a consonant, like the "p" sound (Fragile <u>p</u>ink <u>p</u>etunias stand <u>p</u>roudly against the <u>p</u>ounding raindro<u>p</u>s <u>p</u>ouring down u<u>p</u>on them.)

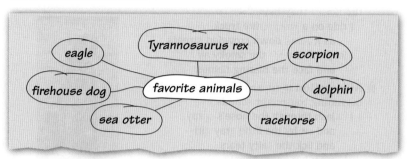

Prewriting Selecting a Topic

Poets are inspired by all sorts of things. You will be writing a poem about an animal you would like to be. Caleb Carter used a cluster to think about his favorite animals.

- eagle
- Tyrannosaurus rex
- scorpion
- firehouse dog
- favorite animals
- dolphin
- sea otter
- racehorse

Create a cluster. Write "favorite animals" in the center of a sheet of paper. Around these words, cluster the types of animals you would like to be. Choose one to write about.

Gathering Details

Poems are full of sensory details. These details help create images in the mind of the reader. Caleb created the following sensory chart to help him think about being a firehouse dog.

See	Hear	Smell	Taste	Touch
black/white	barking	dog breath	biscuit	hot fire
gray	siren wailing	people smells	salty tears	cold water
fire truck	splash	ash		spray
flames	crying	smoke		

Gather sensory details. Create a chart like the one above and list sensory details about your topic. Include details about the animal and about the setting of your poem.

Prewriting Selecting a Topic

Tell students to choose an animal that they know well enough to describe in a poem. Students should be familiar with their animal, either through real-life experience or through previous reading.

Prewriting Gathering Details

To help students gather sensory details, pose the following questions:

- If you had your eyes closed, what clues would let you know that you are close to the animal that you are writing about?
- When you see this animal, do you want to reach out and touch it? Or do you want to keep your distance?
- What is your strongest impression of this animal?

✱ Additional information about sensory details is on PE page 489.

Prewriting
Using Poetry Techniques

Students can have fun with onomatopoeia. Have them go around the room naming examples, such as *clap, buzz, chirp, splash,* and *crash.*

Tell students that as poets, they can make up original words that describe sounds. Challenge them to think of words that embody animal sounds. Examples:

- horse running: *klumpada klumpada klumpada*
- dog snarling: *arragah*
- bird greeting the day: *slee dee dee dee*

List their suggestions of original animal sounds on the board.

Writing
Developing Your First Draft

Remind students to refer to their sensory charts as they write their first drafts. Tell students to feel free to use some details from their charts and to add others as they come to mind.

356

Prewriting Using Poetry Techniques

Poets play with the sounds of words. Two simple techniques will help you create poetic sounds as you write your free-verse poem.

- **Onomatopoeia** (ŏn´ə-măt´ə-pē´ə) is using words that sound like the noises they name.
  > I ride on a wailing fire truck
  >   as it roars down crowded streets.
  > I leap off to sniff the smoky air
  >   and face the blazing flames.
- **Alliteration** (ə-lĭt´ə-rā´shən) is repeating beginning consonant sounds.
  > I splash through the hose's spray
  >   and sit by the little gray girl
  >   and lick the salty tears
  >   from her sooty cheeks.

 Use poetry techniques. Look back at your sensory chart. Circle any words that sound like the noise they name (onomatopoeia). Then underline words that start with the same consonant (alliteration). Add a few more of each kind of word.

Writing Developing Your First Draft

Now that you have gathered sensory details and learned two poetry techniques, you are ready to write the first draft of your poem. Follow these tips.

- **Imagine being the animal.** What things do you sense? What thoughts do you think? How do you feel about your world?
- **Tell your story.** What important things do you do? What will be happening in your poem? (Your animal should be doing something.)
- **Play with words.** What words make the most interesting sounds? What words create the strongest images, or word pictures?

 Write your first draft. Create the first draft of your poem. Write as if you were the animal, telling about something that happens in your life.

English Language Learners

When you introduce the concept of onomatopoeia, encourage students to identify words for sounds that they may know in other languages. Invite them to incorporate some of these into their poetry.

Advanced Learners

To reinforce the concept of alliteration, have students compose tongue twisters using a name and as many words as possible that begin with the same consonant sound. For example: *Sandy saw a sad serpent sitting and sipping a soda.*

Revising Improving Your Poem

Revise your first draft by thinking about these traits of writing.

- ☐ **Ideas** Do I include sensory details? Do I share thoughts and feelings?
- ☐ **Organization** Do I arrange my sentences or ideas in a special way?
- ☐ **Voice** Does my writing voice sound interesting (like the animal)?
- ☐ **Word Choice** Do I use onomatopoeia? Do I use alliteration?
- ☐ **Sentence Fluency** Do my lines flow smoothly? Do they have a pleasant rhythm?

 Revise your writing. Ask yourself the questions above and decide what changes would improve your poem. Continue working with your poem until you like the way it looks and sounds.

Editing Fine-Tuning Your Poem

Focus on the conventions of writing as you edit your poem.

- ☐ **Conventions** Is my work free of spelling errors? Have I used punctuation and capitalization effectively? (In free-verse poetry, you do not have to capitalize the first word in each line.)

 Edit your work. Edit your poem using the questions above as a guide. Make a final copy of your poem and proofread it again for spelling.

Publishing Sharing Your Poem

There are a number of ways you can share your poetry.

- **Perform it.** Read the poem to your classmates or to your family.
- **Post it.** Display your poem where people can read it—on a bulletin board, on a Web site, or on your refrigerator.
- **Send it out.** Submit your work to a local or student newspaper.

 Present your work. Choose one of the presentation suggestions above or come up with one of your own.

Revising Improving Your Poem

Some students embrace revising, while others resist it. The questions listed here will help students improve their poems.

You may want to model improving a poem. Choose a poem you have written, or ask a student to volunteer his or her poem.

Editing Fine-Tuning Your Poem

Good poems should contain complete thoughts, but they don't have to contain complete sentences.

Reinforce rules, such as the one below, to help students improve their spelling.

Write *i* before *e* except after *c*, or when sounded like *a,* as in *neighbor* and *weigh*.

✳ Additional information about spelling is on PE pages 642–651.

Publishing Sharing Your Poem

Read poems at a "coffeehouse."
- Ask students to bring in snacks to share on a chosen day.
- Students take turns sitting on a high stool to read their poems.
- Listeners show appreciation by listening attentively and clapping after each poem.

English Language Learners

If students share their poetry through a coffeehouse or other oral presentation, offer English language learners an alternative, so they do not have to perform under pressure. Have them rehearse their reading thoroughly and record it to play during the coffeehouse. Suggest that they use background music or sound effects on their tapes.

Struggling Learners

To help students organize their poems, ask them to follow these steps:

- Cut the lines of a poem apart.
- Experiment with different arrangements of the lines.
- Choose a line order and make a final copy of the poem.

Advanced Learners

Students who enjoy organizing projects, word processing, or illustrating can work together to create a bound booklet that includes a poem from each member of the class. The booklet can be added to the class library or photocopied so that each contributor has a copy.

Writing Haiku

After volunteers read each haiku aloud, ask listeners to identify the animal being described.

Point out that each haiku poem is really a sentence with sensory details added. The details help create vivid images.

- Plain sentence: Animals lift their heads from the water.
- With sensory details: Huge gray beasts lift their ears and eyes and nostrils from muddy waterways.

Tell students they can model these sentences to make their own sentences more interesting.

✱ Additional information about modeling sentences is on PE page 521.

Ask students to find examples of onomatopoeia and alliteration in the haiku.

Writing Tips

If time permits, have students

- make posters or other artwork to accompany their haiku,
- create a classroom gallery of haiku poetry and artwork, and
- present their poetry and artwork to the rest of the class.

Writing Haiku

Another form of poetry is *haiku*. This type of Japanese poetry presents a picture of nature, so an animal makes a perfect topic. A haiku poem is three lines long. The first line has five syllables, the second has seven, and the third has five. Guess what animal is described in each of the following haiku poems.

> Mud smears on pink skin—
> soft grunts rumble from its snout—
> it loves to wallow.

> Guards all dressed in black,
> patrolling from the treetops,
> nod and caw commands.

> Huge gray beasts lift their
> ears and eyes and nostrils from
> muddy waterways.

> Spreading hood and fangs,
> it slithers from the basket
> to the charmer's tune.

Writing Tips

- **Select a topic.** Think of an interesting animal.
- **Gather details.** List things about the animal that you would see, hear, smell, or feel.
- **Follow the pattern.** Make sure you use five syllables each in the first and last lines and seven in the middle line.

 Create your haiku. Choose an animal and write your haiku poem. Make sure each line has the right number of syllables.

English Language Learners

Trying to concentrate on ideas and syllable counts at the same time may be difficult for students. Have them get their ideas down on paper first. Then they can meet with you or a supportive, positive partner who is proficient in English to work on the syllable requirements.

Struggling Learners

Since some students may have forgotten that the term *syllable* stands for a word unit, model how to isolate the syllables in the sample haikus by counting on your fingers, clapping, or tapping a pencil.

Advanced Learners

Invite students to compose haiku poems about additional nature topics, such as flowers, the sky, or water.

CREATIVE

Writing Other Forms of Poetry

Poems take many forms. Here are three other forms that work well for describing animals.

Limerick

A *limerick* is a humorous poem of five lines. Notice that the first, second, and last lines rhyme with each other, as do the third and fourth. Also notice that the first, second, and last lines have three accented syllables. The third and fourth have two.

A monkey named **Joe** plans to **save**
His **mon**ey to pur**chase** a **shave**.
But **ra**zors can't **hack**
All the **hair** on his **back**,
And **bar**bers in **town** aren't that **brave**.

Name Poem

A *name poem* uses the letters in a name to begin each line.

Feline
Loudly
Utters her
Fierce but
Funny-sounding
Yowl

Phrase Poem

A *phrase poem* states an idea with a list of phrases.

Into the lake
with a swoosh
of flying water
over flapping wings
across bright feathers
with a sparkling splash

Write a poem. Choose one of the forms of poetry on this page and use the example as your model. Try the other forms at another time.

Writing Other Forms of Poetry

Limerick

Bring in some limericks to share with your students. Pass them around and have students read them aloud. Help students to hear the accented syllables and to appreciate the humor!

Name Poem

Have dictionaries available, so students can skim for words if they are stuck on a particular letter.

Phrase Poem

To reinforce this type of poem, have students help you rewrite it as a paragraph. Example:

> The bird flew into the lake with a swoosh. Flying water splashed over its flapping wings and sparkled across its bright feathers.

Point out to students that the prepositional phrases in these sentences (*into* the lake, *with* a swoosh) are pulled out and used to create the poem.

✱ Additional information about prepositions is on PE pages 494–495 and 742.

Tell students that beginning with a short paragraph is one way to create a phrase poem.

English Language Learners

For students who are in the earlier stages of learning English, attempting to write limericks—given their rhyming patterns, rhythm, and their clever use of language—may be frustrating. On the other hand, these students may be very successful in writing name or phrase poems.

Advanced Learners

Have students try an alternative pattern for the name poem, in which the given letter appears first in the top line, second in the next line, and so on. Here is an example using this type of pattern for Carla's name:
Come with me!
H**a**ve you seen them?
Da**r**k funnel clouds are overhead!
Fol**l**ow me down the stairs!
Torn**a**do!

Using Special Poetry Techniques

Encourage students to come up with their own special poetry techniques.

Figures of Speech

Have students work in small groups to brainstorm examples of the figures of speech.

- Simile: My dog's ears feel like sandpaper.
- Metaphor: His tail is a flag of friendliness.
- Personification: His empty food bowl calls his name.
- Hyperbole: My book bag weighs a ton.

Sounds of Poetry

Have students create a "classified ad" for an animal of their choice, using as many sound techniques as possible. Here's an example:

Frightened Cat Fears the City
Please believe me.
Never leave me.
Adopt a pet; treat it right.
Protect a cat from fear and fright.

Use PE pages 360–361 as a resource throughout this unit.

360

Using Special Poetry Techniques

On the next two pages, you will find a number of special techniques that poets use to develop poems.

Figures of Speech

Poets use the following techniques to create strong images in their poems. These techniques are called *figures of speech*.

- A **simile** (*sĭm´ə-lē*) compares two different things using the word *like* or *as*.

  The branch curved like a claw.

- A **metaphor** (*mĕt´ə-fôr*) compares two different things without using the word *like* or *as*.

  Her eyes were flashlights in the dark.

- **Personification** (*pər-sŏn´ə-fĭ-kā´shən*) gives human traits to something that is not human.

  The leaves gossiped among themselves.

- **Hyperbole** (*hī-pûr´bə-lē*) is an exaggeration.

  My heart hit the floor.

Sounds of Poetry

Poets use the following special techniques to add pleasing and interesting sounds to their poems. (Also see page 356.)

- **Alliteration** (*ə-lĭt´ə-rā´shən*) is the repetition of beginning consonant sounds.

  The kids rode a carousel of cartoon characters.

- **Assonance** (*ăs´ə-nəns*) is the repetition of vowel sounds in words.

  A green apple gleams at me from the tree.

- **Consonance** (*kŏn´sə-nəns*) is the repetition of consonant sounds anywhere within words.

  The angry eagle shrieked again.

Struggling Learners

Some students may feel confused by the wide variety of poetry techniques listed on this page and the next. If this happens, divide students into small groups. Have each group become the "expert" on only one figure of speech or sound of poetry and teach it to the rest of the class.

Advanced Learners

Invite students to compose and perform raps about their amazing animals. Discuss the fact that rhythm and end rhyme are already embedded into rap, but other poetry techniques may be used as well.

CREATIVE

Consider using the language experience approach to create a group poem rather than asking individuals to attempt these more sophisticated techniques solo for the first time.

■ **End rhyme** (*ĕnd* \ \ *rīm*) is the use of rhyming words at the ends of two or more lines.

> **My country, 'tis of** thee,
> **sweet land of** liberty . . .

■ **Internal rhyme** (*ĭn-tûr´nəl* \ \ *rīm*) is the use of rhyming words within a line of poetry.

> **The** smoke **could** choke **a chimney.**

■ **Onomatopoeia** (*ŏn´ə-măt´ə-pē´ə*) is the use of words that sound like the noise they name.

> **The** crackling **bag** crumpled **in his fist.**

■ **Repetition** (*rĕp´ĭ-tĭsh´ən*) is the use of the same word, idea, or phrase for rhythm or organization.

> We ran **above.**
> We ran **below.**
> We ran **where no one else would go.**

■ **Rhythm** (*rĭth´əm*) is the way a poem flows from one idea to the next. In free-verse poetry, the rhythm follows the poet's natural voice. In traditional poetry, a regular rhythm is created. Notice how the poet William Blake accented certain syllables to create a regular rhythm.

> **Ti**ger, **Ti**ger, burn**ing** bright
> In **the** for**ests** of **the** night, . . .

Write a poem. In your poem, write about an amazing animal. Include at least one figure of speech and one other special poetry technique.

Teaching Tip: Language Experience

Language experience writing is based on a group or class having a joint experience and then writing about that experience as a group. For example, the group could go on a field trip, invite a speaker to the classroom, or take a walk outside. After the experience, everyone contributes to a piece of writing about the experience. Teachers act as the scribe and write on chart paper or an overhead transparency. Everyone participates in the drafting, revising, and editing: deciding what goes in, what does not, what is added, what is cut, exact wording, and so on.

Research Writing Overview

Writing Standards

The writing standards listed below are based on a blending of state and NCTE standards.

- Apply skills and strategies of the writing process and traits of effective writing in research writing for summary paragraphs and reports.
- Establish a central idea and use reference materials to collect and organize supporting data for a research report.
- Use technology to support aspects of creating, revising, editing, and publishing research writing.

Writing Forms

- summary paragraph
- research report
- multimedia presentation

Focus on the Traits

- **Ideas** Developing a clear thesis statement and topic sentences that include one main idea
- **Organization** Using a sentence outline to determine the best order
- **Voice** Using a formal voice that shows knowledge and interest
- **Word Choice** Defining or explaining unfamiliar words
- **Sentence Fluency** Avoiding rambling sentences and varying sentence lengths
- **Conventions** Checking for errors in punctuation, capitalization, spelling, and grammar

Unit Pacing

Building Research Skills: 45–90 minutes

The section on **building research skills** introduces the unit and lays the groundwork for research writing. Use this section if students need to work on building research skills. Following are some of the topics that are covered.

- Distinguishing between primary and secondary sources
- Locating resources on the Internet and in the library
- Using and evaluating sources and reference materials

Writing a Summary Paragraph: 45–90 minutes

The **summary paragraph** captures the main idea and key supporting facts in an informational article. Use this section if students need to work on crafting a paragraph. Following are some of the topics that are covered.

- Finding the main idea
- Developing a topic sentence
- Including facts to support the main idea

Writing a Research Report: 4.5–9.75 hours

This section asks students to write a **research report** about a natural event or formation that affects people. Use this section if students need to work on using research skills to write a report. Following are some of the topics that are covered.

- Creating a cluster to select a topic
- Using a gathering grid and note cards to organize research
- Paraphrasing and using exact quotations to avoid plagiarism
- Keeping track of sources
- Forming a thesis statement
- Outlining ideas
- Creating a works-cited page

Developing Multimedia Presentations: 2.25 hours

This section provides suggestions for using a computer to create a **multimedia presentation** that incorporates multimedia effects to communicate information. Use this section to focus on developing computer skills. Following are some of the topics that are covered.

- Creating a media grid to gather details
- Making a storyboard
- Developing slides

Integrated Grammar and Writing Skills

Below are skills lessons from the resources sections of the pupil edition that are suggested at point of use (✱) throughout this unit.

Writing a Summary Paragraph, pp. 377–380

- ✱ Topic Sentences, p. 525
- ✱ Types of Sentences, pp. 515–518
- ✱ Paragraph Checklist, p. 541
- ✱ Proofreader's Guide, pp. 578–749

Writing a Research Report, pp. 381–410

- ✱ Essay Plan, p. 540
- ✱ Italics and Underlining, p. 602
- ✱ Organization, p. 551
- ✱ Quotation Marks, pp. 598, 600
- ✱ Graphics, p. 574

Additional Grammar Skills

Below are skills lessons from other components that you can weave into your unit instruction.

Writing a Summary Paragraph

SkillsBook

Commas in Compound Sentences, p. 15
Comma Practice 1, 2, and 3, p. 17
Semicolons and Colons, p. 21
Punctuation Review 1, 2, and 3, p. 33
Kinds of Sentences 1 and 2, p. 97
Types of Sentences, p. 101
Compound Sentences 1 and 2, p. 103
Complex Sentences 1 and 2, p. 107
Sentence Variety Review 1 and 2, p. 117
Coordinating Conjunctions, p. 175
Subordinating Conjunctions, p. 177
Conjunctions Review, p. 179

Interactive Writing Skills CD-ROM

Sentences: Independent and Dependent Clauses
Sentences: Simple and Compound Sentences
Parts of Speech: Conjunctions

Daily Language Workout

Week 33: More History Facts, pp. 68–69
Week 33: The First Step, p. 110

Writing a Research Report

SkillsBook

Quotations Marks and Italics, p. 25
Hyphens and Dashes, p. 31
Mixed Review, p. 39
Capitalization and Abbreviations, p. 45
Numbers, p. 49

Interactive Writing Skills CD-ROM

Mechanics: Abbreviations
Mechanics: Numbers
Punctuation: Punctuating Titles

Daily Language Workout

Week 34: Potpourri, pp. 70–71
Week 34: Snow Joke, p. 111

Developing Multimedia Presentations

Daily Language Workout

Week 35: Who's Counting? pp. 72–73
Week 35: Say the Word, p. 112

362

organize

NOTE

Research Writing

summarize

RESEARCH

Research Writing
Building Skills

Research is a form of exploration. It can take you to remote corners of the world or down to the depths of the ocean. By using the right tools and digging into your subject, you can discover amazing things.

Of course, the tools of your research probably won't include a mini-sub. Instead, you'll use tools such as a computer catalog, *The Readers' Guide to Periodical Literature,* and Internet searches. But once you know how to use these tools of research, you will be ready to explore your world!

Mini Index

- Primary vs. Secondary Sources
- Using the Internet
- Using the Library
- Using Reference Materials
- Evaluating Sources

Research Writing
Building Skills

Objectives

- understand the difference between primary and secondary sources
- learn how to use Internet and library resources
- learn how to evaluate sources
- understand computer and card catalogs, and learn how the Dewey decimal system works
- review parts of a reference book
- learn to use encyclopedias, dictionaries, and periodical guides to magazine articles

Primary vs. Secondary Sources

Write the following descriptions of source information on the board. Ask students to label each as a primary or secondary source. They can write their answers down individually, or work together to compile a class list.

Source Descriptions:
1. An interview with the school principal about the new dress code (primary)
2. A *New York Times* review of a new Broadway show (secondary)
3. A tour of Fenway Park, home of the Boston Red Sox (primary)
4. A letter written by Benjamin Franklin to Thomas Jefferson about the drafting of the Declaration of Independence (primary)
5. A map of Africa showing the countries that existed in 1920 (secondary)

Discuss the answers together.

 Answers

Web-site cookbook review: secondary source

Taste test of vegetarian foods: primary source

364

Primary vs. Secondary Sources

Primary sources of information are original sources. They give you firsthand information. You're working with a primary source when you . . .

- visit a place to learn about your topic,
- ask people questions about your subject, or
- conduct a survey or an experiment.

Secondary sources contain information that has been gathered by someone else. Most nonfiction books, newspapers, magazines, and Web sites are secondary sources of information. You're working with secondary sources when you . . .

- read a magazine article about your subject,
- check out a reference book, or
- visit a Web site.

Primary Sources
1
Visiting a
health-food store
2
Interviewing
a vegetarian
3
Cooking a
vegetarian meal

Secondary Sources
1
Article on
vegetarian diet
2
Encyclopedia entry
about vegetarians
3
TV documentary
about vegetarians

 Decide whether each of the following is a primary or a secondary source of information.

    A Web-site review of a vegetarian cookbook

    A taste test of vegetarian foods

What other resources can you imagine for this topic? Think of one more primary or secondary source about vegetarianism.

Types of Primary Sources

Primary sources of information provide you with firsthand details. Review the following list of primary sources.

Diaries, Journals, and Letters

Reading the diaries, journals, and letters of other people (especially historical figures) is an interesting way to gather information. You can find this sort of information in libraries and museums.

Presentations

Visiting historical sites or museums can provide you with firsthand information about your topic. You can also listen to guest speakers or watch live demonstrations.

Interviews

In an interview, you can talk with someone who is an expert on your subject. You can interview in person, over the phone, by e-mail, or through the mail.

Surveys and Questionnaires

You can also use a survey or questionnaire to gather firsthand information. You can begin by making a list of the questions you would like answered. Then give your questions to people who can answer them. Collect the surveys or questionnaires and study the results.

Observation and Participation

Observing people, places, and things is a common method of gathering information. Taking part in an event also supplies firsthand details. For example, to research ethnic foods, try eating them for a day or two.

 Gather information by observing students in your cafeteria. During lunch, observe what is served and what students select and eat. Also notice what they avoid. Write down what you see. If possible, use this method of research when you do a research report.

REPORT

Types of Primary Sources

Ask students to provide examples of primary sources they have used. The more practice they have in thinking about primary sources, the more likely they will be to use them in their research.

Encourage students to use these research methods whenever possible as they conduct research for their reports.

Try It Answers

Answers will vary.

Students might use a **frequency table** *(see below)*, or tally sheet, to keep track of how many students choose each meal selection.

Teaching Tip: Using a Frequency Table to Conduct a Survey

Students may organize data from surveys, questionnaires, or observations in a frequency table. The table lists the number of times an item or event occurs.

Ask students to create a table showing the number of students who buy each main menu choice during a period of five minutes in the school cafeteria. Have students

- list the menu choices,
- make a tally mark in the correct column as each student chooses a lunch, and
- total the tally marks to get the frequency of each choice (or number of students who chose that lunch).

Compare the results of the surveys.

Advanced Learners

Ask students to develop and administer a questionnaire for friends and family related to space exploration. Begin with these questions:

- Is space exploration worth the billions of dollars it costs?
- Will we find life on another planet?

Ask students how they could report the results.

Using the Internet

Internet tips for teachers:

- Caution students against the www.(insert-a-name-for-my-topic-here).com strategy of Web research. More often than not, this action will not achieve useful results.
- Show students how to use Google, Yahoo!, or another search engine, and explain how it works. Model using a search engine to find information, and show how to filter out junk. Emphasize that the most reliable sites have *.edu, .org,* or *.gov* in the address.
- Teach students to look for dates when finding Web-based research sources. Some information becomes obsolete quickly.
- Remember to discuss bias with students. Often, Web sites don't provide a fair report.
- Require that students get information from many sources—not just the Internet.

366

Using the Internet

The World Wide Web allows people all around the world to publish information, making it a great place to do research. You can find many helpful Web sites, including online encyclopedias, that contain information about your topic. For example, the NASA site offers hundreds of pages about space exploration.

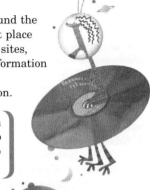

> Since information on the Internet comes from a variety of people and places, you need to evaluate each source carefully. (See page 376 for guidelines.)

Points to Remember

- **Use the Web carefully.** Look for sites that have *.edu, .org,* or *.gov* in the address. These are educational, nonprofit, or government Web sites and will offer the most reliable information. If you are not sure about a site, check with your teacher or librarian.
- **Use a search site.** A search site such as Google.com or yahoo.com is like a computer catalog for the Internet. You can enter keywords to find Web pages about your subject.
- **Look for links.** Often, a Web page includes links to other pages dealing with your topic. Take advantage of these links.
- **Be patient.** The Web is huge and searches can get complicated. New pages are added all the time, and old ones may change addresses or even disappear completely.
- **Know your school's Internet policy.** To avoid trouble, be sure to follow your school's Internet policy. Also follow whatever guidelines your parents may have set up for you.

English Language Learners

To make searches less overwhelming,

- provide students with bookmarked sites, or
- encourage them to use student-friendly search engines.

NOTE RESEARCH
organize summarize *cite*
367
Building Skills

Using the Library

Libraries provide a variety of resources for people seeking information, including books, periodicals, CD's, and much more.

1 **Books** are usually divided into three sections.

- The **fiction** section includes stories and novels. These books are arranged in alphabetical order by the authors' last names.

- The **nonfiction** section contains books that are based on fact. They are arranged according to the Dewey decimal system. (See page **370**.)

- The **reference** section has encyclopedias, atlases, dictionaries, directories, and almanacs.

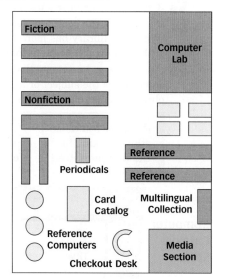

Fiction

Nonfiction

Computer Lab

Periodicals

Reference

Reference

Card Catalog

Multilingual Collection

Reference Computers

Media Section

Checkout Desk

REPORT

2 The periodicals section includes magazines and newspapers.

3 The **computer lab** has computers, often connected to the Internet. You usually sign up to use a computer.

4 The media section includes music CD's, cassettes, DVD's, videotapes, and CD-ROM's. Computer software (encyclopedias, games, and so on) may be found in this section as well.

Try It Visit your school library and look around. Notice where each of the above areas is located. Then draw a map of the library and label each area.

Searching a Computer Catalog

Help your students find sources of information beyond those available in your school.

■ Become familiar with your school's and your public library's computer catalog, so that you can assist your students when they are searching for information.

■ If your public library's catalog is available on the Internet, bookmark the Web site on your classroom computers for easier student access.

 **Answers**

Computer screens will vary. They should include the author, title, publisher, date of publication, subject(s) of the book, status, call number, and location of the book.

368

Searching a Computer Catalog

Every computer catalog is a little different. The first time you use a particular computer catalog, either check the instructions for using it or ask a librarian for help. With a computer catalog, you can find information on the same book in three ways:

1 If you know the book's **title**, enter the title.

2 If you know the book's **author**, enter the author's name. (When the library has more than one book by the same author, there will be more than one entry.)

3 Finally, if you know only the **subject** you want to learn about, enter either the subject or a keyword. (A *keyword* is a word or phrase that is related to the subject.)

If your subject is . . .	your keywords might be . . .
ethnic cooking in the United States,	Mexican meals, southwestern cooking, or Native American recipes.

Computer Catalog Screen

Author: Dent, Huntley
Title: The Feast of Santa Fe: Cooking of the American Southwest
Published: Simon and Schuster, 1985
Subjects: Southwestern Cooking Spanish, Mexican, Anglo, and Native American recipes
STATUS: Available
CALL NUMBER: 641.5979D
LOCATION: General collection

 Create a computer catalog screen like the one above for a book you are reading.

NOTE **RESEARCH** *organize* **summarize** *cite* 369
Building Skills

Searching a Card Catalog

If your library has a card catalog, it will most likely be located in a cabinet of drawers. The drawers contain title, author, and subject cards, which are arranged in alphabetical order.

1 To find a book's **title card**, ignore a beginning *A, An,* or *The* and look under the next word of the title.

2 To find a book's **author card**, look under the author's last name. Then find the author card with the title of the book you want.

3 To find a book's **subject card**, look up an appropriate subject.

All three cards will contain important information about your book—most importantly, its call number. This number will help you find the book on the library's shelves.

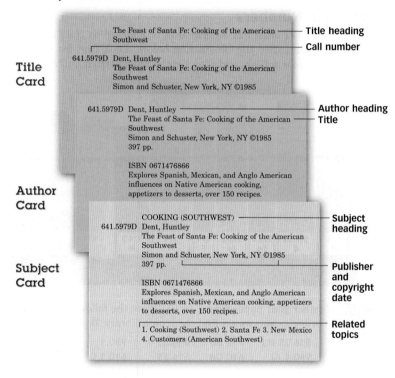

REPORT

Finding Books

Discuss with students proper library etiquette. For example, students should place books on a return cart for the library staff to reshelve rather than trying to reshelve the books themselves.

 Answers

1. 516.35
2. 516.35 Ha
3. 516.35 T
4. 603.99 Se
5. 610 Ce
6. 610.1 C
7. 752 Be
8. 980.1
9. 980.1 Ad
10. 980.1 Al

Finding Books

Each catalog entry for a book includes a **call number**. You can use this number to help you to find the book you are looking for. Most libraries use the Dewey decimal classification system to arrange books. This system divides nonfiction books into 10 subject categories.

000-099	**General Works**	500-599	**Sciences**
100-199	**Philosophy**	600-699	**Technology**
200-299	**Religion**	700-799	**Arts and Recreation**
300-399	**Social Sciences**	800-899	**Literature**
400-499	**Languages**	900-999	**History and Geography**

Using Call Numbers

A call number often has a decimal in it, followed by the first letters of an author's name. (See the illustration below.) Look first for the number when searching for a book, and then for the alphabetized letters.

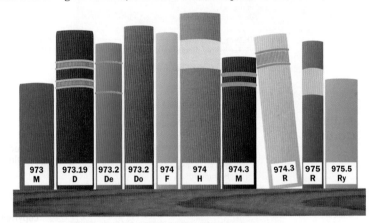

Number your paper from 1 to 10. Place the following call numbers in order as you would find them on a library shelf.

516.35 Ha	752 Be	516.35 T	980.1	603.99 Se
980.1 Al	610 Ce	516.35	610.1 C	980.1 Ad

Some of the vocabulary used as Dewey decimal categories, such as philosophy and social sciences, may be new to students. Explain each term (*philosophy*: the study of knowledge and values; *social sciences*: the study of society and people in society [sociology, psychology, anthropology]) and show examples of books from each category. Have students create a review sheet to help them remember the categories by

- copying the category chart on this page, and
- drawing an icon beside each category to illustrate its meaning.

Ask students to catalog a few nonfiction books in your classroom library.

Students should do the following:

- Work in teams of three.
- Use the call number guidelines on this page to assign some invented call numbers to the classroom books.

Each team member is responsible for the title, author, or subject card.

NOTE *RESEARCH* *organize* summarize *cite*

371

Building Skills

REPORT

Understanding the Parts of a Book

Understanding the parts of a nonfiction book can help you to use that book efficiently.

The title page is usually the first page. It tells the title of the book, the author's name, and the publisher's name and city. (See illustration.)

The copyright page comes next. It tells the year the book was published. This can be important. Some information in an old book may no longer be correct.

An acknowledgement or preface may follow. It may tell what the book is about, why it was written, and how to use it.

Written and Compiled by
Dave Kemper, Patrick Sebranek,
and Verne Meyer

Illustrated by
Chris Krenzke

WRITE SOURCE®

GREAT SOURCE EDUCATION GROUP
a division of Houghton Mifflin Company
Wilmington, Massachusetts

The table of contents shows how the book is organized. It gives the names and page numbers of the sections and chapters.

A cross-reference sends the reader to another page for more information. *Example:* (See page 372.)

An appendix has extra information, such as maps, tables, lists, and so on.

A glossary explains special words used in the book. It's like a mini-dictionary.

A bibliography lists books, articles, and other sources that the author used while writing the book. To learn more about the topic, read the materials listed in the bibliography.

The index is an alphabetical list of all the topics in the book. It gives the page numbers where each topic is covered.

 Find the following information in this book.

1. What year was the book published?

2. Find a cross-reference and tell what is on the page you are referred to.

3. On what page does the index begin?

Understanding the Parts of a Book

For visual and kinesthetic reinforcement, provide students with precut pieces of colored paper. Ask students to follow these steps:

- Choose a nonfiction book.
- On separate pieces of colored paper, write the copyright, acknowledgement and preface information; the page numbers of the table of contents, the glossary, and the bibliography; an example of a cross-reference and the page it occurs on; and a brief list of the contents of the appendix.
- Shuffle the papers and assemble them in the correct order.

Answers

1. 2005
2. Answers will vary. One example of a cross-reference is on PE page 366, in the brackets after the first paragraph. It says, "See page 376 for guidelines." This page has a list of questions to help judge the value of sources.
3. page 751

Using Reference Materials

Using Encyclopedias

Use the index of an encyclopedia borrowed from the school library/media center to reinforce this lesson. Make copies of several index pages.

- Divide students into an even number of small groups.
- Give each group a copy of one index page.
- After examining their page, ask students to write five to ten items of information similar to those in the **Try It** exercises. Have students place responses on a separate sheet of paper.
- Next, have each group exchange its index pages and items (not responses) with another group. After both groups have responded to the items in writing, they should check the response sheets.
- Destroy the copies of the index pages.

 Answers

1. W:651–652
2. B:412
3. B:397

372

Using Reference Materials

The reference section in a library contains materials such as atlases, encyclopedias, and dictionaries.

Using Encyclopedias

An **encyclopedia** is a set of books or a CD with articles on almost every topic you can imagine. The topics are arranged alphabetically. The tips below can guide your use of encyclopedias.

- If the article is long, skim any subheadings to find specific information.
- Encyclopedia articles are written with the most basic information first, followed by more detailed information.
- At the end of an article, you may find a list of related topics. Look them up to learn more about your topic.
- The index lists all the places in the encyclopedia where you will find more information about your topic. (See the sample below.) The index is usually in the back of the last volume of a printed set.

Encyclopedia Index

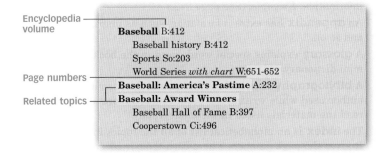

Encyclopedia volume

Page numbers

Related topics

- **Baseball** B:412
    - Baseball history B:412
    - Sports So:203
    - World Series *with chart* W:651-652
- **Baseball: America's Pastime** A:232
- **Baseball: Award Winners**
    - Baseball Hall of Fame B:397
    - Cooperstown Ci:496

 Check the index entries above; then list the volume and page where you might find the following information.

1. A list of teams that have played in the World Series
2. A description of the first baseball game
3. The names of players in the Baseball Hall of Fame

Finding Magazine Articles

Periodical guides are found in the reference section of the library and list magazine articles about many different topics.

- **Locate the right edition** of the *Readers' Guide to Periodical Literature* (or a similar guide). The latest edition will have the newest information, but you may need information from an older edition.
- **Look up your subject.** Subjects are listed alphabetically. If your subject is not listed, try another word related to it.
- **Write down the information** about the article. Include the name of the magazine, the issue date, the name of the article, and its page numbers.
- **Find the magazine.** Ask the librarian for help if necessary.

Readers' Guide Format

BAKE SALES	Subject Entry
Bake sale. S. Gandel. *Money* v32 no10 p32 O 2003.	
Fundraising: It's not just about the money. *Computers in Libraries* v23 no2 p32-35 Fe 2003.	Name, Volume, and Number of Magazine
BAKER, JACK	
Bebe Jodel Arf. *Back Yard Flyer* p60-65 My/Ag 2004.	Author Entry
BAKERY	
Appetite is growing for Parmalat's Archway cookie unit. R. Sidel. *Wall Street Journal* [Eastern] v242 no128 pC1 D 31 2003.	Name of Author
Bread reigns in France, where they say phooey to low-carb fads. *Nation's Restaurant News* v38 no1 Je 5 2004.	
Tainted food. D. Hawaleshka, B. Bethune and S. Ferguson. *Maclean's* v117 no4 p22-27 Je 26 2004.	Title of Article
Valentine's day treats from around the world. *Vanity Fair* no522 p64 Fe 2004.	Page Number/Date
BAKESHOP *See* Bakery	Cross-Reference

Internet-based databases are online subscription services that allow you to search for and read periodicals on the Internet.

 Using the above sample page, write answers to these questions.

1. In which magazine can you learn about the French diet?
2. Who wrote an article on bake sales?
3. On what page can you find out about Valentine's Day foods?

Finding Magazine Articles

Access to many articles listed in the *Readers' Guide* may be limited unless students are able to use the resources of a large public or university library system. Many articles referenced in the *Readers' Guide* are from magazines that are not usually available in school libraries.

The *Readers' Guide* is available online, and therefore many libraries no longer buy the print version. The on-line version only refers to articles published after 1980.

 Answers

1. *Nation's Restaurant News*
2. S. Gandel
3. page 64

REPORT

Checking a Dictionary

To give students practice in decoding dictionary entries, lead them into the dictionary on an "archeological dig."

- Each student works with a partner to dig up a "buried fossil" (an unfamiliar word) and make an entry in the class "field journal" (copy the dictionary entry onto a piece of poster board).
- Next they identify and label each "bone" (or part of the dictionary entry).
- Student partners post their discovery in the classroom above the dictionaries or on a bulletin board.

 Answers

Answers will vary.

374

Checking a Dictionary

A dictionary is the most reliable source for learning the meanings of words. It offers the following aids and information:

- **Guide words** are located at the top of every page. They show the first and last entry words on a page, so you can tell whether the word you're looking up is listed on that page.
- **Entry words** are the words that are defined on the dictionary page. They are listed in alphabetical order for easy searching.
- **Parts of speech** labels tell you the different ways a word can be used. For example, the word *Carboniferous* can be used as a noun or as an adjective.
- **Syllable divisions** show where you can divide a word into syllables.
- **Spelling and capitalization** (if appropriate) are given for every entry word. If an entry is capitalized, capitalize it in your writing, too.
- **Spelling of verb forms** is shown. Watch for irregular forms.
- **Illustrations** are often provided to make a definition clearer.
- **Accent marks** show which syllable or syllables should be stressed when you say a word.
- **Pronunciations** are special spellings of a word to help you say the word correctly.
- **Pronunciation keys** give symbols to help you say or pronounce the entry words correctly.
- **Etymology** gives the history of a word [in brackets]. Knowing a little about a word's history can make it easier to remember.

Remember: Each word may have several definitions. It's important to read all of the meanings and select the one that is best for you.

 Open a dictionary to any page and find the following information.
1. Write down the guide words on that page.
2. Find a multisyllable word and write it out by syllables. Jot down the word's part of speech. (There may be more than one.)
3. Find an entry that includes spelling of verb forms and write them down.

Struggling Learners

Reread and discuss the definitions of *guide words* and *entry words*.

Give students practice in using guide words to locate entry words.

- Write these guide words on the board: bashful   bead
- Then list these entry words:

base	bathroom	basin
basket	badly	batter
beam	beach	beagle

- Ask students to identify which entry words would be found on the dictionary page that has these guide words. (Answer: basket, batter, bathroom, beach, basin)

Remind students that each entry word on the page must fall between the guide words in alphabetical order.

NOTE *RESEARCH* *organize* **summarize** *cite* **375**

Building Skills

Dictionary Page

Guide words ——— **carbon dioxide | carburetor** **150**

Entry word ———

carbon dioxide *n.* A colorless or odorless gas that does not burn, composed of carbon and oxygen in the proportion CO_2 and present in the atmosphere or formed when any fuel containing carbon is burned. It is exhaled from an animal's lungs during respiration and is used by plants in photosynthesis. Carbon dioxide is used in refrigeration, in fire extinguishers, and in carbonated drinks.

Part of speech ———

carbonic acid *n.* A weak acid having the formula H_2CO_3. It exists only in solution and decomposes readily into carbon dioxide and water.

Syllable division ———

car·bon·if·er·ous (kär′bə-nif′ər-əs) *adj.* Producing or containing carbon or coal.

Spelling and capitalization ———

Carboniferous *n.* The geologic time comprising the Mississippian (or Lower Carboniferous) and Pennsylvanian (or Upper Carboniferous) Periods of the Paleozoic Era, from about 360 to 286 million years ago. During the Carboniferous, widespread swamps formed in which plant remains accumulated and later hardened into coal. See table at **geologic time.**—Carboniferous *adj.*

Spelling of verb forms ———

car·bon·ize (kär′bə-nīz′) *tr. v.* car·bon·ized, car·bon·iz·ing, car·bon·iz·es **1.** To change an organic compound into carbon by heating. **2.** To treat, coat, or combine with carbon.—car·bon·i·za·tion (kär′bə-ni-zā′shən) *n.*

Illustration ———

air — air filter
choke valve
gas
gas and air mixture — gas
venturi — float
throttle valve — float chamber
carburetor
cross section of a carburetor

carbon monoxide *n.* A colorless odorless gas that is extremely poisonous and has the formula CO. Carbon monoxide is formed when carbon or a compound that contains carbon burns incompletely. It is present in the exhaust gases of automobile engines.

carbon paper *n.* A paper coated on one side with a dark coloring matter, placed between two sheets of blank paper so that the bottom sheet will receive a copy of what is typed or written on the top sheet.

Accent marks ———

carbon tet·ra·chlor·ide (tĕt′rə-klôr′īd′) *n.* A colorless poisonous liquid that is composed of carbon and chlorine, has the formula CCl_4, and does not burn although it vaporizes easily. It is used in fire extinguishers and as a dry-cleaning fluid.

Pronunciation ———

Car·bo·run·dum (kär′bə-rŭn′dəm) A trademark for an abrasive made of silicon carbide, used to cut, grind, and polish.

Pronunciation key ———

ă	pat	ôr	core
ā	pay	oi	boy
âr	care	ou	out
ä	father	ŏŏ	took
ĕ	pet	ōŏr	lure
ē	be	ōō	boot
ĭ	pit	ŭ	cut
ī	bite	ûr	urge
îr	pier	th	thin
ŏ	pot	*th*	this
ō	toe	zh	vision
ô	paw	ə	about

car·bun·cle (kär′bŭng′kəl) *n.* **1.** A painful inflammation in the tissue under the skin that is somewhat like a boil but releases pus from several openings. **2.** A deep-red garnet.

car·bu·re·tor (kär′bə-rā′tər *or* kär′byə-rā′tər)*n.* A device in a gasoline engine that vaporizes the gasoline with air to form an explosive mixture. [First written down in 1866 in English, from *carburet*, carbide, from Latin *carbō*, carbon.]

Etymology ———

REPORT

Students should sharpen their **alphabetizing** skills *(see below)*. This ability will help them to
- efficiently use a dictionary, an index, or a card catalog, and
- prepare their works-cited page.

Review the Pronunciation key on the dictionary page. Have students apply the key to pronounce several words on the page.

Teaching Tip: Alphabetizing

Use this activity to review alphabetizing words with several beginning letters in common.

- Students number a sheet of paper from 1–11.
- They alphabetize the list of terms on PE page 374 working on their own.
- Work with students to put the list on the board.

1. Accent marks
2. Entry words
3. Etymology
4. Guide words
5. Illustrations
6. Parts of speech
7. Pronunciation keys
8. Pronunciations
9. Spelling and capitalization
10. Spelling of verb forms
11. Syllable divisions

Evaluating Sources

Have students rate sources of information for trustworthiness using their own system.

For example:

- an Encyclopedia Britannica entry on the Second Amendment to the United States Constitution might rate four stars for trustworthiness
- a mission statement from a lobbying group or a television advertisement might rate no stars.

Asking students to create their own rating system will help them to internalize the idea that not all sources are equally fair and unbiased.

Tell students that one way to make sure the information they use is accurate is to find the same information in more than one place. If they find information they want to use in a source that might be biased, encourage them to try to find the same information in other sources.

Evaluating Sources

Before you use any information in your writing, you must decide if it is trustworthy. Ask yourself the following questions to help judge the value of your sources.

Is the source a primary or a secondary source?

Firsthand facts are often more trustworthy than secondhand facts. However, secondary sources can also be trustworthy.

Is the source an expert?

An expert is an authority on a certain subject. You may need to ask a teacher, parent, or librarian for help when deciding how experienced a particular expert is.

Is the information accurate?

Sources that are well respected are more likely to be accurate. For example, a large city newspaper is much more reliable than a supermarket tabloid.

Is the information complete?

If a source of information provides some facts about a subject, but you still have questions, find another source.

Is the information current?

Be sure you have the most up-to-date information on a subject. Check for copyright dates of books and articles and for posting dates of online information.

Is the source biased?

A source is biased when it presents information that is one-sided. Some organizations, for example, have something to gain by using only some of the facts. Avoid such one-sided sources.

Research Writing

Summary Paragraph

How many times have you written a paragraph entitled, "What I Did on My Summer Vacation"? Each time, you condensed three months' worth of activities into a few sentences. You wrote a summary paragraph about your summery days!

Summaries get to the heart of information. They are short and clear. When you write a summary paragraph, you capture the main idea and key supporting facts.

In the next few pages, you'll learn how to read an article and uncover its main idea and most important information. Then you will be shown how to summarize the article. Once you've mastered writing summaries, you'll be ready to use this skill in all of your report writing.

My Summer Vacation

Writing Guidelines

Subject:	A research article
Form:	Summary paragraph
Purpose:	To express the main idea
Audience:	Classmates

Summary Paragraph

Objectives

- apply the steps in the writing process to writing a summary paragraph

Read a short newspaper article with the class and model giving a brief summary by mentioning the main ideas and details.

■ Contrast the summary with a retelling, in which you recount all the details from the article.

■ Discuss the difference between the summary and the retelling as a class.

For additional practice, provide the class with newspapers and magazines. Ask each student to read a short article and write a brief summary.

English Language Learners

Help students differentiate between a summary and a retelling. Have them work together on a group summary paragraph.

- Suggest a recent sports event or school assembly as a topic.
- Emphasize that a retelling is long and includes many details, while a summary is short and contains a main idea and key supporting facts.

Advanced Learners

Ask students to use a Venn diagram (TE page 802) to compare and contrast the similarities and differences between a retelling and a summary. Ask volunteers to share their diagrams with the class.

Summary Paragraph

Use the strategy below (Keep-Delete-Substitute) to help students summarize a short article like "The Giant Awakens." If possible, do this activity on an overhead projector, marking the article as you go.

Keep: Ask students to point out the main idea. (On May 18, 1980, . . . the sleeping giant awoke.) Then ask for three or four important details from the article. Keep this information.

Delete: Next, ask students to find any information that isn't necessary to the main idea and delete it (e.g., Between 1832 and 1857 the volcano had small eruptions).

Substitute: Finally, have students suggest general words to substitute for the descriptive ones in the article (such as *mountain* instead of "the sleeping giant" or *erupted* instead of "awoke").

 Respond to the reading.

Answers

Ideas 1. Mount Saint Helens erupted on May 18, 1980.

Organization 2. in the order in which the events happened

Voice & Word Choice 3. The north face slid off; a huge cloud of ash, rock, and gas shot out; forests were flattened.

378

Summary Paragraph

The following article tells of the eruption of Mount Saint Helens in 1980. The paragraph "Fire Mountain Roars" summarizes the article.

The Giant Awakens

The Native Americans near Mount Saint Helens had always called it "Fire Mountain," and for good reason. Between 1832 and 1857 the volcano had small eruptions. By the time most European settlers arrived, though, the mountain slept, and the stories of eruptions seemed like just legends.

On May 18, 1980, after two months of rumbling, the sleeping giant awoke. An earthquake shook loose the north face of the mountain, which poured down in a gigantic rock slide. The slide released an enormous cloud of rock, ash, and gas. The blast leveled huge trees, laying them like matchsticks, killed thousands of animals, and left 57 people dead. Afterward came a devastating mud slide as the 9,677-foot mountain's ice cap melted and poured down the surrounding valleys.

Mount Saint Helens sleeps now, but it could erupt again. The blast in 1980 was actually small compared to some of the mountain's past eruptions. Three other peaks in the northern Cascades—Mount Rainier, Mount Hood, and Mount Shasta—all have the same explosive potential. Any of them could erupt, threatening communities from Seattle to San Francisco. Perhaps European settlers should have listened to the "Fire Mountain" legends after all.

Topic sentence (main idea)

Body

Closing sentence

Fire Mountain Roars

On May 18, 1980, Mount Saint Helens erupted. Before that, most people near Mount Saint Helens thought that the Native American stories about "Fire Mountain" were just legends. Then, on that day, the volcano's north face slid off, and a huge cloud of ash, rock, and gas shot out. The forests were flattened, and thousands of animals and 57 people died. Mount Saint Helens has been quiet for a while, but it could blow again. Now people near other sleeping volcanoes like Mount Shasta, Mount Hood, and Mount Rainier know the "Fire Mountain" legends are true.

 Respond to the reading. Answer the following questions.

☐ **Ideas** (1) What is the main idea of the summary?

☐ **Organization** (2) How is the paragraph organized?

☐ **Voice & Word Choice** (3) How does the summary writer describe the eruption in his own words?

Struggling Learners

Some students may need practice in writing summary paragraphs. Ask students to follow these steps:

- Think of an interesting or exciting event that occurred in your life.
- Write a topic sentence that presents the main idea (the event and some general information about it).

- In sentence form, list at least three facts related to the event, in the order in which they occurred.
- Write a closing sentence that restates the main idea.

Prewriting Selecting an Article

For this assignment, you must find an article to summarize. Choose one that . . .

- relates to a subject you are studying,
- discusses an interesting topic, and
- is fairly short (between three and six paragraphs).

 Choose an article. Look through magazines and newspapers for an article to summarize. Choose one that has the three features listed above. Ask your teacher if the article will work for your summary paragraph.

Reading the Article

If possible, make a photocopy of your article so that you can underline important facts as you read. Otherwise, take brief notes on the article. The writer of the sample summary underlined the key facts.

> <u>On May 18, 1980,</u> after two months of rumbling, the sleeping giant awoke. <u>An earthquake shook loose the north face of the mountain,</u> which poured down in a gigantic rock slide. <u>The slide released an enormous cloud of rock, ash, and gas.</u> The blast leveled huge . . .

 Read your article. First read through the article. Then reread it and identify the important facts.

Finding the Main Idea

The key to summarizing is finding the main idea of the article. Look over the material you underlined. What main idea do the facts suggest? The writer of the sample summary wrote this main idea: "On May 18, 1980, Mount Saint Helens erupted."

 Write the main idea. Review the facts you identified. What main idea do they suggest? Write the main idea as a single sentence. This sentence (or a version of it) will be the topic sentence for your paragraph.

REPORT

Prewriting Selecting an Article

Ask students to bring in magazines from home to share with the class. If possible, borrow magazines from the school or a public library. You can also have some students look for articles in on-line magazines and print out those that interest them.

Prewriting Reading the Article

Remind students that they can use the Keep-Delete-Substitute strategy to focus on the important information they should include in the summary paragraph.

Prewriting
Finding the Main Idea

A topic sentence in a summary paragraph should state the main idea. To check whether a topic sentence accomplishes this, review the important facts in the article. Ask yourself: Do these key facts relate to and support the topic sentence?

✱ For more information about writing a good topic sentence, see PE page 525.

English Language Learners

Taking their notes on a graphic organizer such as a main idea table may be helpful to some students. Have students draw a horizontal rectangle (the tabletop) with several vertical rectangles under it (table legs). Ask them to write the main idea on the tabletop and indicate supporting ideas on the legs.

Struggling Learners

Stress that the topic sentence in a summary paragraph states the main idea of the article. Ask students to test their topic sentences as follows:

- Read it to a partner.
- Ask your partner to tell you in his or her own words what the main idea is.
- If your partner is not correct, clarify your topic sentence.

Writing
Developing the First Draft

Emphasize that a summary paragraph should include only a few key facts that relate to the main idea.

✸ For a checklist to help students learn the important points in writing effective paragraphs, see PE page 541.

Revising Reviewing Your Writing

Students should review their summary paragraphs by checking the first five writing traits.

✸ For information on how to improve sentence fluency, see PE pages 515–518.

Editing Checking for Conventions

Students must check their writing for errors and verify that the facts they include match those in the article.

✸ Refer students to the Proofreader's Guide, PE pages 578–749, if they have questions about usage or mechanics.

380

Writing Developing the First Draft

A summary paragraph includes a topic sentence, a body, and a closing sentence. As you write each part, follow these tips.

- **Topic sentence:** Introduce the main idea of the article.
- **Body:** Include just enough important facts to support or explain the main idea. As much as possible, use your own words and phrases to share these facts.
- **Closing sentence:** Restate the main idea of the summary in a different way.

 Write the first draft of your summary paragraph. Develop a topic sentence based on the main idea of the article. Add facts that support the main idea. Then end your paragraph with a closing sentence.

Revising Reviewing Your Writing

As you revise, check your first draft for the following traits.

- ☐ **Ideas** Does the topic sentence correctly identify the main idea? Do I include only the most important facts to support it?
- ☐ **Organization** Is all of the information in a logical order?
- ☐ **Voice** Does my voice sound confident and informative?
- ☐ **Word Choice** Do I use my own words? Do I define any difficult terms I use?
- ☐ **Sentence Fluency** Do I use a variety of sentence lengths and types?

 Revise your paragraph. First reread the article and your summary. Then use the questions above as a guide for your revising.

Editing Checking for Conventions

Focus on conventions as you edit your summary.

- ☐ **Conventions** Have I checked the facts against the article? Have I checked for errors in punctuation, spelling, and grammar?

 Edit your work. Use the questions above as your editing guide. Make your corrections, write a neat final copy, and proofread it for errors.

Struggling Learners

To give students support and feedback in revising, ask them to exchange their drafts with a partner.

- Each student checks his or her partner's draft using the revising checklist.
- Partners discuss any items on the checklist for which they answered *no* to the checklist questions.

Research Writing

Research Report

Today, it is easier than ever to find answers to your questions. You might be wondering about new ways to treat some disease. Perhaps you're interested in learning about a strange-looking fish. You can find answers quickly by surfing the Internet. Of course, you can also find answers by talking to people or reading books, magazines, and newspapers. This question-and-answer work is called research.

In this unit, you will write a report about a natural event or formation that affects people. As you develop your report, you will *describe* the formation or event, *explain* some things about it, and *summarize* information from other sources. Then you will organize your ideas and facts into an interesting, informative report.

Writing Guidelines

Subject: A natural event or formation that affects people

Form: Research report

Purpose: To research and share information about nature's effect on people

Audience: Classmates

Research Report

Objectives

- use graphic organizers and questions to choose and refine a research topic
- organize research using a gathering grid and note cards
- learn how to avoid plagiarism by using exact quotes, paraphrasing, and citing sources
- form a thesis statement and outline ideas
- plan, draft, revise, edit, and present a research report
- create a works-cited page and a title page using correct formatting

To help students brainstorm topics on natural events that affect people, offer copies of *National Geographic* or *Smithsonian* magazine in the classroom. Suggest that they think of events that have occurred recently, or formations that exist in their region of the country.

Begin a list of general events such as volcano eruptions, earthquakes, El Niño, mudslides, and hurricanes. Make a list of specific formations including the San Andreas Fault, Mt. Saint Helens, and the Grand Canyon.

Research Report

Examine the Research Paper Checklist on PE page 410 with students. Direct students to refer to the questions in the checklist as they compose their research report.

Suggest that students use the Rubric for Expository Writing on PE pages 194–195 as an additional guide as they write their reports.

382

Research Report

The following research report is about an interesting geological area around the Pacific Ocean. Notice how important information is presented. The side notes point out key features in the report.

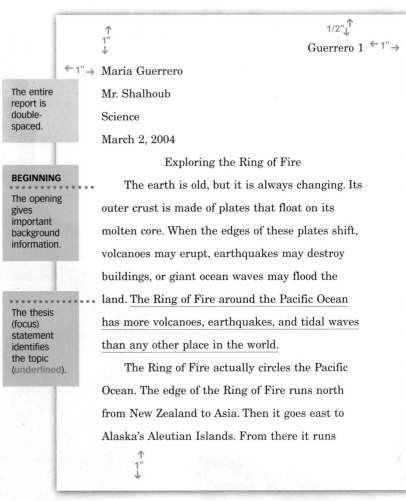

1/2″
Guerrero 1 ←1″→

1″

←1″→ Maria Guerrero

Mr. Shalhoub

Science

March 2, 2004

The entire report is double-spaced.

Exploring the Ring of Fire

BEGINNING

The earth is old, but it is always changing. Its outer crust is made of plates that float on its molten core. When the edges of these plates shift, volcanoes may erupt, earthquakes may destroy buildings, or giant ocean waves may flood the

The opening gives important background information.

land. The Ring of Fire around the Pacific Ocean has more volcanoes, earthquakes, and tidal waves than any other place in the world.

The thesis (focus) statement identifies the topic (underlined).

The Ring of Fire actually circles the Pacific Ocean. The edge of the Ring of Fire runs north from New Zealand to Asia. Then it goes east to Alaska's Aleutian Islands. From there it runs

1″

English Language Learners

Review vocabulary terms that may be unfamiliar to students (*plates, molten, core, erupt, flattened, dense, poisonous, gigantic, disasters*).

Introduce and discuss volcanoes, earthquakes, and tsunamis.

Use a classroom world map to locate the Ring of Fire. Help students find each of the places mentioned in the report (Pacific Ocean; New Zealand; Asia; Alaska; Aleutian Islands; West Coast of North and South America; Mount Saint Helens; state of Washington; San Francisco, California; Anchorage, Alaska; and Hokkaido, Japan). Ask volunteers to read the paragraphs of the report aloud.

NOTE *organize* RESEARCH **summarize** *cite*

Research Report **383**

Ask volunteers to find and read aloud the topic sentence in each of the middle paragraphs. Point out the key facts that support the topic sentence in each paragraph.

Guerrero 2

The writer's last name and page number go on every page.

A source and page number are provided in parentheses.

Only pages are listed in parentheses when the author is mentioned in the text.

MIDDLE
Details are given about the topic, with each paragraph covering one main point.

south along the West Coast of North and South America. More than 75 percent of the world's 1,500 volcanoes exist on this ring (Ado and Dorsey 27).

One of the most famous volcanoes on the Ring of Fire is Mount Saint Helens in the state of Washington.

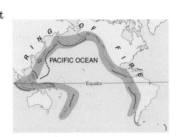

Carleton Ado and Robert Dorsey report that when it erupted on May 18, 1980, the blast was 50 times stronger than an atomic bomb. It flattened the forests in the area and shot out a dense cloud of ash, rock, and poisonous gas. Thousands of animals and 57 people died (31–32).

Earthquakes are also a problem around the Ring of Fire. In 1906, an earthquake destroyed most of San Francisco, California. Another major quake hit Anchorage, Alaska, in 1964. In 2003, a powerful quake beneath the ocean near Hokkaido,

REPORT

Discuss features of the research report that are new to students (thesis statement, citations, headings, works cited).

Point out the way the paragraphs are organized in the report:
- the first paragraph states the topic and thesis statement
- each of the middle paragraphs explains one aspect of the thesis statement
- the final paragraph reviews the main points and emphasizes the topic's importance.

Help students discover how each paragraph transitions to the next. Encourage them to look at the last sentence of a paragraph and the first sentence of the next paragraph. For example, the last sentence in the second paragraph refers to the world's volcanoes, and the first sentence in the third paragraph names a famous volcano on the Ring of Fire.

✽ For further help in organizing paragraphs into a report, see the Essay Plan on PE page 540.

384

Guerrero 3

Japan, caused terrible damage to the city and injured more than 300 people (Juranek 13).

    When an earthquake occurs beneath the ocean, it causes huge waves. Sometimes those waves are big enough to cause destruction when they reach shore. A really gigantic wave is called a tsunami (pronounced tsoo-nä´-mē). A tsunami is so big that as it nears the shore it sucks the water away from the ocean floor. Then all this water crashes onto the land, destroying buildings and flooding whole cities. An average of five tsunamis occur each year in the Ring of Fire (Milburn).

    Scientists study the Ring of Fire to predict when a volcanic eruption, an earthquake, or a tsunami may happen. By understanding these disasters, they hope to warn people ahead of time and save lives. Experts also use this knowledge to build safer buildings. Although people cannot control nature's Ring of Fire, they can study it in order to live more safely with it.

> A difficult word is explained, and its pronunciation is shown.

> **ENDING**
> The writer summarizes and expands upon the main idea.

Struggling Learners

To help make reading the research report on PE pages 382–385 more manageable, create an overhead transparency of the report.

- As you point out and explain features, mark them on the transparency so they will become visible.
- Focus on just a few of the basic features, such as ideas and organization.

Research Report 385

Guerrero 4

Works Cited

Ado, Carleton C., and Robert E. Dorsey. Ring of
Fire: The Edge of the World. Philadelphia:
Countryside Press, 2002.

Juranek, Lucille. "When the Earth Moves."
Discover 16 May 2003: 12–14.

Milburn, Hugh B. "Volcanoes, Earthquakes, and
Tsunamis." Crystalinks.com. 6 June 2003.
Pacific Marine Environmental Laboratory in
Seattle, Washington. 28 March 2004 <http://
crystalinks.com/rof.html>.

The sources used in the report are listed alphabetically.

REPORT

Respond to the reading. After reading the sample research report, answer the following questions about important traits of writing.

☐ **Ideas** (1) What did you learn from reading the report? List at least two things.

☐ **Organization** (2) How are the middle paragraphs arranged? List the main idea for each of these paragraphs.

☐ **Voice & Word Choice** (3) List words and phrases that show the writer's interest in the topic.

Respond to the reading.

Answers

Ideas 1. Possible choices:

- Ring of Fire has the most volcanoes (more than 75%), earthquakes, and tidal waves in the world.
- Earthquakes under the ocean cause giant waves (tsunamis) that can cause great damage.
- Scientists predict natural events to protect people.

Organization 2. Each middle paragraph covers a main point of the report topic. Main ideas: location of the Ring of Fire; volcanoes—Mount Saint Helens eruption; earthquakes cause damage; tsunamis are dangerous waves caused by earthquakes

Voice & Word Choice 3. Possible choices:

- *more . . . than any other place in the world*
- *one of the most famous volcanoes*
- *the blast was 50 times stronger than an atomic bomb. It flattened the forests . . . shot out a dense cloud of ash, rock, and poisonous gas*
- *a powerful quake . . . caused terrible damage*
- *really gigantic wave*

Prewriting
Selecting a Topic

Prewriting for a research report is a difficult task, particularly if this is a student's first experience with a research report. The project may seem so big that students can't see how to break it down. Their prewriting is stressful because their minds are preoccupied with the scope of the job in front of them. Reassure students that the process of writing a research report is broken down in the unit into smaller steps that they can do one at a time and that they will have a lot of time to spend on the report.

To help students determine the suitability of a topic, ask them the following types of questions:

- Which of these topics is the most interesting to you?
- Do you know where to find information about this?
- What do you already know about this topic?
- What would you like to learn?

Prewriting
Selecting a Topic

Before you can begin doing research, you need to choose a topic—either a natural event or a natural formation. One way to do this is to create a cluster around the word "nature," as the writer of the following cluster has done.

Cluster

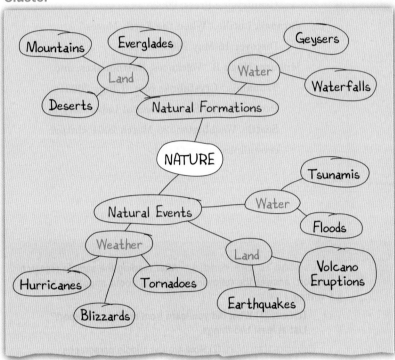

 Create your cluster. Using the example above, create your own cluster. Fill in as many ideas as you can. Look at an atlas, a science book, or a geography book if you need help. Select a topic that interests you—one that you would like to learn more about.

NOTE RESEARCH
organize summarize *cite*   **387**
Research Report

REPORT

Sizing Up Your Topic

Before beginning your research, it's important to have some sort of plan. Otherwise, you may end up with either too little or too much information for an effective report.

Start by writing a list of three to five questions that you want to answer. If you cannot think of at least three questions, you should choose a broader topic. On the other hand, if you have more than five, you should choose a narrower topic.

Lists

Too Narrow	Too Broad
SLEET	**WEATHER**
– What is sleet?	– What causes wind?
– How does it affect people?	– Where is it windiest?
	– What are clouds?
	– How many types of clouds are there?
Well-Focused	– What causes rain?
HURRICANES	– What places get the most rain?
– What are they?	– What places get the least rain?
– What causes them?	– What causes snow?
– How strong are their winds?	– What places get the most snow?
– How often do they occur?	– How is sleet different from rain or snow?
	– How is hail different from sleet?
	– How is an ice storm different from hail or sleet?
	– What causes frost?

Size up your topic. Write a list of questions you want to answer about your topic. Do you have the right number of questions for a report?

Prewriting
Sizing Up Your Topic

Students may need assistance as they fine tune their topics. Some students with good topics won't ask the right questions. Some students with broad topics will ask too few questions.

Use these strategies to assist them.
- Hold student-teacher conferences to help students size up their topics.
- Have students brainstorm in peer groups to generate questions about their topics.

Advanced Learners

Suggest that students choose two topics from their clustering activity on PE page 386.

Ask students to
- list questions for both topics, and then
- determine which of the two has the most potential.

Prewriting Using a Gathering Grid

The gathering grid helps students compare the kinds of information that they collect from each source. By evaluating sources, students can decide where to direct further research.

Prewriting Using Interviews

Practice formulating open-ended questions.

- Encourage *why* and *how* questions.
- Brainstorm a list of key words to use in an interview to get good quality responses (explain, rate, evaluate, compare, describe, etc.)

Have students who are conducting interviews for their report write a list of **questions** (see below) for the interviewee ahead of time. Check their questions to help them; focus on key information.

388

Prewriting Using a Gathering Grid

One way to organize your research is to use a gathering grid. The following grid was created for a research report about hurricanes.

Hurricanes	National Geographic Kids (Internet)	Science World (magazine)	Hurricane Force (book)	World Almanac for Kids (encyclopedia)
What are they?				Largest type of storm
What causes them?		See note card number one. (See page 389.)		
How strong are their winds?		From 74 mph to more than 155 mph!		Up to 250 mph!
How often do they occur?	10 tropical storms each year; 6 become hurricanes		5 reach U.S. shore each year; only 1 is category 3 or higher	

 Create a gathering grid. List the questions you wrote on page 387 down the left-hand margin. Across the top, list sources you will use. Fill in the squares with the answers you find.

Using Interviews

During your research, you may have the chance to interview someone who has experience with your topic. Before your interview, prepare a list of questions. Avoid questions that require only a "yes" or "no" answer. Keep careful notes so that you can accurately quote the person.

Teaching Tip: Questions

Help students develop a set of questions for an interview.

- Select a public figure (athlete, actor, public official) that students would like to interview.
- Use the 5 W and H question words and chart (TE page 803).
- Ask students to suggest questions for the famous person, using the 5 W and H words.

English Language Learners

If students want to conduct an interview but are hesitant to do so, suggest that they tape-record the interview. This will free them from having to speak, listen, and write all at once. You could also suggest that a supportive partner accompany them on interviews to help with any communication challenges.

REPORT

Creating Note Cards

Sometimes the answer to a question won't fit on your gathering grid. Then you can use note cards to keep track of your research.

Number each card and write a question at the top. Underneath the question, write a quotation, a list, or an answer in the form of a paraphrase (see page 390). At the bottom, name the source of the information and the page number. Here are three sample note cards for the report about hurricanes.

Card number ⟶ 1. What causes hurricanes?

Question ⟶

Answer (paraphrase) ⟶ Cool air draws heat and moisture from ocean water, causing winds and thunderstorms. If this continues, it may make a tropical storm. A tropical storm may become a hurricane.

Source ⟶

Science World
pages 4–6

2. How big was hurricane Hugo?

"It was a category 4. If Hugo was a ⟵ **Answer (quotation)**
category 4 storm, I never want to see
a category 5!"

interview with
Uncle Arnie

3. When is hurricane season?

- Starts in June
- Peaks in September
- Ends in November

Answer (list)

www.nationalgeographic.com/
ngkids/0308/hurricane

Create note cards. Use note cards like those above whenever your
answers are too long to appear on your gathering grid.

Prewrite

Prewriting Creating Note Cards

Note cards are one good way to organize all research information, not just answers that are too long for the grid. This will also enable students to easily group and sort their research.

Prewriting Avoiding Plagiarism

Students may need more than one opportunity to practice **paraphrasing** (see below).

- Provide students with a brief passage.
- Ask students to work in pairs to paraphrase it.
- Have volunteers share and discuss their paraphrasing.

Try It Answers

Answers may vary. Possible quotation choice: "A large surge can cause massive damage along shorelines and can flood low-lying escape routes."

Sample paraphrase: Storm surges that arrive before the storm center may cause damage and flooding.

390

Prewriting Avoiding Plagiarism

As you do your research, you will find many interesting ideas, facts, and comments that will help you make your point. You **must not copy** these words and ideas and pretend they are yours. This is called *plagiarism,* and it is a form of stealing. You can avoid plagiarism in one of two ways.

- **Quoting exact words:** If the exact words of a source capture an idea perfectly, you may include them in quotation marks and give credit to the source. (See page 395.)
- **Paraphrasing:** You may also put the ideas from a source into your own words. This is called *paraphrasing.* However, you must still give credit to the original source.

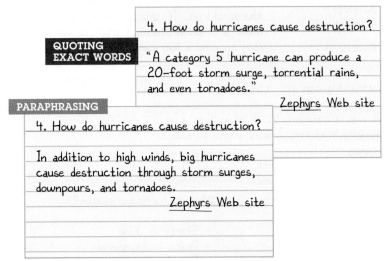

QUOTING EXACT WORDS

4. How do hurricanes cause destruction?

"A category 5 hurricane can produce a 20-foot storm surge, torrential rains, and even tornadoes."

Zephyrs Web site

PARAPHRASING

4. How do hurricanes cause destruction?

In addition to high winds, big hurricanes cause destruction through storm surges, downpours, and tornadoes.

Zephyrs Web site

 Read the following material from the *Zephyrs* Web site. First decide which sentence from this passage would make the best quotation. Then paraphrase the entire passage as you would on a note card.

The storm surge is especially dangerous. It can arrive three to five hours before the center of the storm. A large surge can cause massive damage along shorelines and can flood low-lying escape routes.

Teaching Tip: Paraphrasing vs. Summarizing

Compare and contrast paraphrasing and summarizing.

- You paraphrase when you restate information in your own words. The ideas are those of the writer of the original material, so you must cite the author and his or her work within the text of your report.
- You summarize when you interpret and restate the main idea and a few key points from a large passage. The source of summarized information should be listed in your bibliography but does not need to be cited within the report text.

Keeping Track of Your Sources

Whenever you find a source of information for your report, write down the following information. You'll need it for your works-cited page.

- **Encyclopedia entry:** Author's name (if listed). Entry title. Encyclopedia title. Edition (if given). Publication date.
- **Book:** Author's name. Title. Publisher. City. Copyright date.
- **Magazine:** Author's name. Article title. Title. Date published. Page numbers.
- **Internet:** Author's name (if listed). Page title. Site title. Date posted or copyright (if listed). Date visited. Page address.
- **Interview:** Person's name. Type of interview (personal, telephone, mail, or e-mail). Date.

REPORT

My Source Notes

ENCYCLOPEDIA
"Hurricane." World Almanac for Kids. 2004.

BOOK
Michael C. Miles. Hurricane Force. Countryside Press. Philadelphia. 2002.

MAGAZINE
Libby Tucker. "Now That's Intense!" Science World. Nov. 27, 2003. Pages 4-6.

INTERNET
Renee Skelton. "Flying into the Eye of a Hurricane." National Geographic Kids. Visited March 12, 2004. www.nationalgeographic.com/ngkids/0308/hurricane

INTERVIEW
Arnold Rasmussen. Personal interview. March 13, 2004.

Prewrite **List sources.** List the publication details from each of your sources. Update your list whenever you find new sources.

Prewriting
Keeping Track of Your Sources

Students may get source information from their textbooks and other reading material, such as books, newspapers, and magazines. Textbooks usually have multiple editors and writers, so students will be able to practice gathering some complicated bibliographic information.

Tell students to list the complete source information on the back of each of their note cards as well as on a separate sheet of paper. The information may be repeated several times, but this helps students to remember to find all the needed information.

Point out that the titles of books, magazines, and newspapers must be in *italics* or, in handwritten work, underlined.

✴ For more detailed information on when to use italics and underlining, see PE page 602.

Use a writing handbook, such as those published by the Modern Language Association (MLA) or the University of Chicago, if any citation questions come up that can't be answered with the information on these pages.

Prewriting
Writing Your Thesis Statement

Explain that the thesis statement is similar to the hypothesis that students may have developed for science fair projects and lab assignments. Point out that the root word in *hypothesis* is *thesis*. This may help students to better understand how to frame their thesis statement.

Require students to submit their thesis statement to you on an index card. This will allow you to

- guide and refine the research focus,
- anticipate roadblocks that students may encounter,
- post the thesis statements on a research report bulletin board.

Prewriting Writing Your Thesis Statement

When you finish your research, you must find the best way to state your thesis, or focus. The thesis, which should remain the same throughout your report, is a special part of your topic that you emphasize. Remember this formula to help you write your thesis statement.

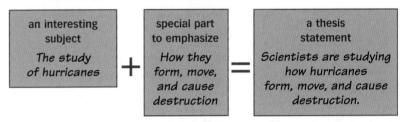

an interesting subject		special part to emphasize		a thesis statement
The study of hurricanes	**+**	How they form, move, and cause destruction	**=**	Scientists are studying how hurricanes form, move, and cause destruction.

Thesis Statements

> *Deserts seem like lifeless stretches of sand* (an interesting subject), *but they are actually home to many plants and animals* (special part to emphasize).

> *The Florida Everglades* (an interesting subject) *is truly one of North America's most unique environments* (special part to emphasize).

Prewrite **Form your thesis statement.** After reviewing your research notes, decide on two main points you could make about your topic. Write a separate thesis statement for each of these ideas, using the formula above. Finally, put a star (✱) next to the statement that says most clearly what you want to share about this topic.

REPORT

Outlining Your Ideas

One way to plan your report is to make an outline. An outline is simply an organized list of ideas. A topic outline lists ideas as words or phrases; a sentence outline lists the ideas as full sentences. (Also see page **550**.)

Sentence Outline

Below is the first part of a sentence outline for the report on pages 406–409. Notice that the outline begins with the thesis statement and then organizes ideas below it. Compare the outline with the opening paragraph and first middle paragraph of the report.

> Thesis statement
>
> I. Topic sentence for first middle paragraph
>
> A. B. C. Supporting ideas
>
> Continue . . .

THESIS STATEMENT: Scientists are studying how hurricanes form, move, and cause destruction.

I. Every hurricane forms because of heat, moisture, and wind.
  A. These combine to make a thunderstorm.
  B. If winds do not blow the storm apart, it grows into a tropical storm.
  C. When winds reach 74 miles per hour, the storm becomes a hurricane.

II. Hurricanes move in a circular motion.
  A. . . .
  B. . . .

> Remember, in an outline, if you have a I, you must have at least a II. If you have an A, you must have at least a B.

Create your outline. Review your research notes and create a sentence outline for your report. Be sure that each topic sentence (I, II, III, . . .) supports your thesis statement and that each detail (A, B, C, . . .) supports the topic sentence above it. Use your outline as a guide when you write the first draft of your report.

Prewriting Outlining Your Ideas

Work with the class to create an outline template. Review **Roman numerals** *(see below)*. Put the template on a chart and post it in the classroom.

To practice the format, outline "Exploring the Ring of Fire" on PE pages 382–384 as a class.

Offer students an alternative form of outlining. Have them choose key words or phrases from their note cards to form the outline, instead of using complete sentences. This will reinforce the paraphrasing of ideas in the draft.

Encourage students to determine the organization of the paper as they create their outline.

- Review the patterns from which students can choose: chronological (time) order, step-by-step, order of location, order of importance, comparison, or logical order.
- Encourage students to think about the best way to organize their information.
- Review their outlines before they begin writing to ensure that they have a well-organized structure.

* For further information about patterns of organization, see PE page 551.

Writing

Starting Your Research Report

Ask students to browse through old newspapers and magazines for articles that have a variety of opening paragraphs.

- Students should work in pairs.
- Invite students to read aloud their favorite paragraphs.
- Discuss how each introduction grabs the reader's attention.
- Ask students to look for a thesis statement in each paragraph.
- Post some of the effective examples in the classroom.

394

Writing

Starting Your Research Report

The opening paragraph of your report should grab your reader's interest, introduce your topic, and share your thesis (focus) statement. Below are two possible ways that you could write the beginning of a hurricane report.

▶ Beginning
Middle
Ending

Beginning Paragraphs

This paragraph begins with interesting details and ends with the thesis (focus) statement.

> *Nature's most powerful storms are hurricanes. These huge, spinning storms build up over the ocean and then move onto land. Hurricanes can cause a lot of damage before they weaken and turn into common thunderstorms. To understand these storms, scientists are studying how hurricanes form, move, and cause destruction.*

This paragraph begins with a question and ends with the thesis statement.

> *Does the thought of a hurricane scare you? It should. Hurricanes cause a lot of damage every year, especially along the southeastern coast of the United States. To understand these storms, scientists are studying how hurricanes form, move, and cause destruction.*

Write your opening paragraph. Use one of the above samples as a guide to write your opening paragraph. Be sure to get your reader's interest, introduce your topic, and make a clear thesis statement.

English Language Learners

As a first step, have students draft a basic, straightforward beginning paragraph. Once they have their ideas in place, have them turn their attention to finding a way to include an attention-grabber.

Struggling Learners

Be sure students understand that the thesis statements are the same in the two sample paragraphs, but the rest of the information differs. Based on this example, ask students to write at least two opening paragraphs for their report. They should

- make both versions exciting and interesting, and
- ask a friend which version works the best, and why.

Citing Sources in Your Report

As you write, remember to give credit to the sources of information that you quote directly or paraphrase.

WHEN YOU HAVE ALL THE INFORMATION

- The most common type of credit (citation) lists the author's last name and the page number in parentheses.

    In 1900, the worst hurricane in United States history hit Galveston, Texas. "A storm surge almost two stories high broke over the city, causing 20-foot (6.1 meter) floods and more than 8,000 deaths" (Skelton 4).

- If you already name the author in your report, just include the page number in parentheses.

    In Hurricane Force, Michael Miles explains that cool air draws heat and moisture from warm bodies of water to form a storm (22).

WHEN SOME INFORMATION IS MISSING

- Some sources do not list an author. In those cases, use the title and page number.

    The winds of a hurricane are most violent around the eye ("Hurricane Season" 7).

- Some sources do not use page numbers. In those cases, list just the author.

    Hurricanes in the Indian Ocean are called cyclones (Nealy).

- If a source does not list the author or page number, use the title.

    In Southeast Asia, they are called typhoons ("Big Wind").

 Rewrite the following sentence giving credit to Libby Tucker's article "Now That's Intense!" from *Science World*, page 6.

Hurricanes in the Pacific Ocean are called typhoons and generally are limited to the coast of Southeast Asia.

REPORT

Remind students to give credit to the sources that they quote or paraphrase. It may feel unnatural to them to include this information in their drafts, but if they wait for the editing and revising stages, they will likely forget to include some of the necessary citations.

Review with students how to correctly punctuate quotes.

＊ For more information about using quotation marks, see PE pages 598 and 600.

Try It Answers

Possible answers:

Libby Tucker says that typhoons are hurricanes that form in the Pacific Ocean. They usually occur only near Southeast Asia.

Typhoons are hurricanes that form in the Pacific Ocean. They usually occur only near Southeast Asia (Tucker 6).

Writing
Developing the Middle Part

Remind students to rely on their outline while writing the middle part of their report. The outline is a valuable tool to help them stay focused on the important points to include. Let students know, however, that it's okay to change an outline after the writing has begun if something isn't working.

Point out the primary source citation in the second paragraph (personal memory).

Writing Developing the Middle Part

Once you have your reader's attention and have stated the thesis of your research report, you can begin writing the middle paragraphs. This part of your report should include facts, details, and examples that support your thesis statement.

Beginning
Middle
Ending

Each middle paragraph should have a topic sentence covering one main idea, and everything you include in the paragraph should support that one idea. Be sure to arrange all your sentences so the reader can easily follow and understand the information. Use your sentence outline as a guide.

Middle Paragraphs

All the details support the topic sentences (underlined).

A personal memory is included.

Every hurricane forms because of heat, moisture, and wind. When cool air lies above a warm ocean, moisture begins to rise, causing a thunderstorm. If the thunderstorm gets strong enough, it is called a tropical storm. If the winds reach at least 74 miles per hour, the storm becomes a hurricane (Tucker 4).

Hurricanes move in a circular motion. The strongest winds of a hurricane are the closest to the center, or "eye." The weather is calm and clear in the eye. My uncle, Arnie Rasmussen, remembers when Hurricane Hugo hit Charleston, South Carolina, in 1989. "When that eye came after all the pounding wind and rain, the quiet was eerie. A high wall of clouds swirled around us. But we knew that when the eye passed, the pounding would begin again."

English Language Learners

If students have used main idea tables to take their notes, they can transform their tabletop notes into topic sentences and their table leg notes into supporting statements.

Struggling Learners

Students can use the following questions to determine if their middle paragraphs are on target.

- Does each paragraph have a topic sentence?
- Does each topic sentence support your thesis?
- Does each detail or example support its topic sentence?
- Do the topic sentences follow in a logical progression?

REPORT

> Hurricanes can destroy buildings, ruin crops, and cause serious injury and even death to people and animals. The sudden flood and high winds do most of the damage. Scientists use a 5-point scale to measure the strength of a hurricane. Category 1 is the weakest, with winds from 74 to 95 miles per hour and waves about 4 to 5 feet above normal tides. The category 5 hurricane is the strongest, with winds of at least 156 miles per hour and waves more than 18 feet above normal (Miles 26). Uncle Arnie said, "If Hugo was a category 4 storm, I never want to see a category 5!"

Hurricane Categories

Category	Wind Speed	Description
1	74 – 95 mph	Weak
2	96 – 110 mph	Moderate
3	111 – 130 mph	Strong
4	131 – 155 mph	Very Strong
5	greater than 155 mph	Devastating

> However, only about five hurricanes form near the United States each year. Just two of those hurricanes reach land, and only one of those is a category 3 or stronger (Miles 30). In 1900, the worst hurricane in United States history hit Galveston, Texas. "A storm surge almost two stories high broke over the city, causing 20-foot floods and more than 8,000 deaths" (Skelton).

Sentences are arranged so that the reader clearly understands the main idea.

A graph makes an idea clearer.

Sources are included in parentheses.

Write your middle paragraphs. At this point, don't worry about getting everything perfect. Just get your main ideas down in writing.

Ask students to find the citations on this page of the report (Miles 26; Miles 30; Skelton).

Pay special attention to the graph. Discuss what information is shown (the five hurricane categories, their wind speed, and descriptions). What is the advantage of placing this data in a table rather than in the report text? (It is easier to understand numerical data when it is set out in a graph rather than in text.)

Writing
Ending Your Research Report

Have students use these strategies for ending their report.

- Write a few different closing paragraphs.
- Get feedback from another student to help you decide which one works best.
- Remember that the final observation should not be an opinion but should be based on the information in the report.

398

Writing   Ending Your Research Report

Your ending paragraph should bring your report to a thoughtful close. Try one or more of the following ideas in your closing paragraph.

- **Remind the reader about the thesis of the report.**
- **Tell one last interesting fact about the topic.**
- **Make a final observation about the topic.**

Ending Paragraph

> **The thesis is restated (underlined).**
>
> **A final observation sums up the report.**
>
> Hurricanes are very dangerous storms. They can cause destruction, injury, and death over a very large area. _It's important to learn how these storms form and move, and that's why scientists spend so much time studying hurricanes._ Hurricanes cannot be stopped, so people must learn how to protect themselves and their belongings when one strikes.

Write your final paragraph. On your paper, write your final paragraph using the strategies above.

Look over your draft. Read your first draft, looking over your notes and outline to see if you included all the necessary details. Make notes about possible changes. You are now ready to begin revising.

English Language Learners

Have students compare the restated thesis on this page with the thesis statement in the first paragraph on PE page 394.

- How are they the same?
- How are they different?

Then have students do the following:

- rewrite their thesis statement in different ways for their ending paragraph
- discuss with a partner which one works best

Struggling Learners

Making a final observation is like drawing a conclusion. Provide this strategy:

- Read your report again.
- Ask yourself, "What was so important about that topic?"
- When you think of the answer, it will be based on what you now know about your topic.
- You have just drawn a conclusion!

Creating Your Works-Cited Page

The first step to creating a works-cited page is to format your sources according to proper style. The two following pages show formats for common types of sources.

BOOKS

Author or editor (last name first). Title (underlined). City where the book was published: Publisher, copyright date.

MAGAZINES

Author (last name first). Article title (in quotation marks). Title of the magazine (underlined) Date (day, month, year): Page numbers of the article.

INTERNET

Author (if available). Page title (if available, in quotation marks). Site title (underlined). Name of sponsor (if available). Date published (if available). Date found <electronic address>.

BOOKS

Miles, Michael C. Hurricane
    Force. Philadelphia: Countryside
    Press, 2002.

MAGAZINES

Tucker, Libby. "Now That's Intense!"
    Science World 17 Nov. 2003: 4-6.

INTERNET

Skelton, Renee. "Flying into the
    Eye of a Hurricane." National
    Geographic Kids. National
    Geographic. 12 Mar. 2004
    <http://www.nationalgeographic.com/
    ngkids/0308/hurricane/>.

REPORT

Writing
Creating Your Works-Cited Page

Students should refer to their note cards (PE page 389) and source notes (PE page 391) to help them create their works-cited page.

Suggest that students check to see if they have included all the sources from which information has been cited.

- Students should be sure that they do not include any sources for material they haven't used in their reports.
- They should be sure this list reflects any information they put in or remove during the revision process.

ENCYCLOPEDIAS

Author (if available). Article title (in quotation marks). Title of the encyclopedia (underlined). Edition (if available). Date published.

INTERVIEWS

Person interviewed (last name first). Type of interview (personal, phone, mail, e-mail). Date.

ENCYCLOPEDIAS

"Hurricane." World Almanac for Kids. 2004.

INTERVIEWS

Rasmussen, Arnold. Personal interview. 13 Mar. 2004.

 Write

Format your sources. Check your report and your list of sources (page 391) to see which sources you actually used. Then follow these directions.

1 Write your sources using the guidelines above and on the previous page. You can write them on a sheet of paper or on note cards.

2 Alphabetize your sources.

3 Create your works-cited page. See the example below.

Works Cited

Miles, Michael C. Hurricane Force. Philadelphia: Countryside Press, 2002.

Rasmussen, Arnold. Personal interview. 13 Mar. 2004.

Skelton, Renee. "Flying into the Eye of a Hurricane." National Geographic Kids. National Geographic. 12 Mar. 2004 <http://www.nationalgeographic.com/ngkids/0308/hurricane/>.

Revising

A solid research report can rarely be written in one draft. Some ideas in the first draft may be incomplete or out of order. The voice may be boring in spots, and the word choice may be weak. Revision can turn your first draft into a clear and informative report.

Keys to Effective Revision

1. Read your entire draft to get an overall sense of your report.

2. Review your thesis statement to be sure that it clearly states your main point about the topic.

3. Make sure your beginning draws readers in. Then check that your ending brings your report to an interesting close.

4. Make sure you sound knowledgeable and interested in the topic.

5. Check for specific, colorful words and complete sentences.

6. Use the editing and proofreading marks inside the back cover of this book.

REPORT

Revising
Keys to Effective Revision

Use this page as a guide for revision. Students should follow each of the steps carefully.

Ask students to write a paragraph assessing the first draft. In the paragraph they should answer the following questions:
- What do I like about the report?
- What can I do to make the report better?
- What areas need more information?
- Is the information well organized?

Remind students to pay attention to sentence structure and word choice as well.
- You've written about a subject that interests you. Will it be interesting to your reader?
- Did you use words that grab your reader's attention?

Have students check the nouns, verbs, and adjectives in their reports. Remind them to refer to a **thesaurus** (*see below*) if they need help with word choice.

Teaching Tip:
When to Use a Thesaurus

Remind students that a thesaurus can be used to replace uninteresting or overused words. Encourage them to look over their drafts for any repeated words that could be replaced.

English Language Learners

Have students undertake this stage of writing with a partner. Be sure to structure peer revision pairs or groups so that these students work with cooperative, helpful students who are proficient English speakers.

Revising Using a Checklist

Emphasize that students must use the checklist as a serious tool—they should not just check the boxes.

Meet with students in one-on-one writing conferences. Discuss the checklist to help each student prepare to revise his or her report.

402

Revising **Using a Checklist**

 Check your revising. On a piece of paper, write the numbers 1 to 12. If you can answer "yes" to a question, put a check mark after that number. If not, continue to work with that part of your report.

Ideas

_____ **1.** Have I written a clear thesis (focus) statement?

_____ **2.** Do I include one main idea in each topic sentence?

_____ **3.** Have I accurately quoted or paraphrased my sources?

Organization

_____ **4.** Do I have an effective beginning, middle, and ending?

_____ **5.** Have I put my middle paragraphs in the best order?

_____ **6.** Do I use transitions?

Voice

_____ **7.** Does my writing show my knowledge and interest?

_____ **8.** Does my voice sound formal?

Word Choice

_____ **9.** Do I define or explain any unfamiliar words?

_____ **10.** Do I use specific nouns and active verbs?

Sentence Fluency

_____ **11.** Do I vary the lengths and beginnings of my sentences?

_____ **12.** Do I avoid rambling sentences?

 Make a clean copy. When you've finished revising your report, make a clean copy for editing.

Editing

After you've finished revising your report, it's time to edit your work for your use of conventions: spelling, punctuation, usage, and grammar.

Keys to Effective Editing

REPORT

1. Use a dictionary, a thesaurus, your computer's spell checker, and the "Proofreader's Guide."

2. Read your essay out loud and listen for words or phrases that may be incorrect.

3. Look for errors in punctuation, capitalization, spelling, and grammar.

4. Check your report for proper formatting. (See pages 382–385 and 406–409 as guides.)

5. Edit on a printed computer copy. Then enter your changes on the computer.

6. Use the editing and proofreading marks on the inside back cover of this book.

Editing Keys to Effective Editing

Have each student share his or her draft with at least one classmate. Remind students to be specific, constructive, and encouraging in their comments.

Editing Using a Checklist

As students do more writing, they will learn which conventions often cause them trouble. Offer these strategies for editing.

- With your guidance, allow students to customize their checklists for the errors they typically make.
- Form editing groups, where each member of the group is responsible for checking a particular convention. Have students change responsibilities for different assignments so they develop an eye for all types of errors.

Caution students against relying too heavily on the spell-check or grammar-check feature on their word-processing software. While these are often handy tools to point out errors, they do not replace the value of careful editing by the writer and his or her peers.

Editing Adding a Title

Suggest that each student create three or four possible titles.

404

Editing Using a Checklist

 Check your editing. On a piece of paper, write the numbers 1 to 12. If you can answer "yes" to a question, put a check mark after that number. If not, continue to edit for that convention.

Conventions

PUNCTUATION

_____ **1.** Do I use end punctuation after all my sentences?
_____ **2.** Have I correctly punctuated all direct quotations?
_____ **3.** Do I use commas in compound sentences?
_____ **4.** Do I use apostrophes to show possession (*boy's bike*)?
_____ **5.** Have I correctly punctuated my works-cited page?

CAPITALIZATION

_____ **6.** Do I start all my sentences with capital letters?
_____ **7.** Do I capitalize proper nouns and titles?

SPELLING

_____ **8.** Do I spell all my words correctly?
_____ **9.** Have I double-checked the spelling of names in my report?

GRAMMAR

_____ **10.** Do I use correct forms of verbs (*had gone,* not *had went*)?
_____ **11.** Do my subjects and verbs agree in number? (Hurricanes *are* dangerous, not Hurricanes *is* dangerous.)
_____ **12.** Do I use the right words (*to, too, two*)?

Adding a Title

- Describe the main idea: **Exploring the Ring of Fire**
- Be creative: **Hurricane Havoc**

Advanced Learners

The title "Hurricane Havoc" is an example of alliteration. Alliteration is repeating beginning consonant sounds. Invite students to make a creative title for their report by using the same technique.

Publishing Sharing Your Report

After you have worked so hard to write and improve your report, you'll want to make a neat-looking final copy to share. You may also decide to prepare your report as an electronic presentation, an online essay, or an illustrated report.

 Make a final copy. Use the following guidelines to format your report. (If you are using a computer, see page 60.) Create a clean final copy and carefully proofread it.

Focus on Presentation

- Use blue or black ink and double-space the entire paper.
- Write your name, your teacher's name, the class, and the date in the upper left corner of page 1.
- Skip a line and center your title; skip another line and start your writing.
- Indent every paragraph and leave a one-inch margin on all four sides.
- Write your last name and the page number in the upper right corner of every page of your report.

Make an Electronic Presentation

Prepare a multimedia presentation of your report. (See "Multimedia Presentations" on pages 411-415 for more information.)

Develop an Illustrated Report

Draw a diagram or prepare a model to illustrate an important part of your topic. (For example, if you wrote about geysers, you might draw a diagram showing how a geyser works.)

Go Online

Look at the Write Source Web site www.thewritesource.com for information on publishing your work online.

REPORT

Publishing Sharing Your Report

Encourage students to keyboard the final copy of their reports and to include a title page (see PE page 409). When keyboarding is not possible, suggest that students place a sheet of unlined white typing or copy paper over a lined sheet of college-ruled paper. They should write on every other line so that their paper looks double-spaced.

Stress that the formatting rules are widely accepted and may be required in many settings.

Encourage students to add graphics to their reports where these will be helpful. Remind students that graphics can add information in a way that the reader will find easy to access and understand.

✱ For more information about the kinds of graphics that may be useful in a research report, see PE pages 574–575.

Final Presentation of a Report

Compare "Hurricane Havoc" to the report "Exploring the Ring of Fire" on PE pages 382–385. What characteristics do they have in common? Discuss how students can model their own reports after these samples.

406

Final Presentation of a Report

The research report begun on page 386 appears on the following pages. Note how careful formatting and helpful graphics give the report a polished look.

Greenberg 1

David Greenberg

Ms. Lin

Science

March 26, 2004

Hurricane Havoc

Does the thought of a hurricane scare you? It should. Hurricanes cause a lot of damage every year, especially along the southeastern coast of the United States. To understand these storms, scientists are studying how hurricanes form, move, and cause destruction.

Every hurricane forms because of heat, moisture, and wind. When cool air lies above a warm ocean, moisture begins to rise, causing a thunderstorm. If the thunderstorm gets strong enough, it is called a tropical storm. If the winds reach at least 74 miles per hour, the storm becomes a hurricane (Tucker 4).

Greenberg 2

Hurricanes move in a circular motion. The strongest winds of a hurricane are closest to the center, or "eye." The weather is calm and clear in the eye. My uncle, Arnie Rasmussen, remembers when Hurricane Hugo hit Charleston, South Carolina, in 1989. "When that eye came after all the pounding wind and rain, the quiet was eerie. A high wall of clouds swirled around us. But we knew that when the eye passed, the pounding would begin again."

Hurricanes can destroy buildings, ruin crops, and cause serious injury and even death to people and animals. The sudden flood and high winds do most of the damage. Scientists use a 5-point scale to measure the strength of a hurricane. Category 1 is the weakest, with winds from 74 to 95 miles per hour and waves about 4 to 5 feet above normal tides. The category 5 hurricane is the strongest, with winds of at least 156 miles per hour and waves more than 18 feet above normal (Miles 26). Uncle Arnie said, "If Hugo was a category 4 storm, I never want to see a category 5!"

REPORT

This report is well written and demonstrates the specific points noted in the questions under each trait in the Research Paper Checklist on PE page 410.
- Have students work in pairs.
- Ask them to identify places in the report that illustrate each feature pointed out by the questions.
- Have a class discussion. Work through the checklist questions. Ask students to share their findings.

For some students, this report will be their first experience with citing sources. Review the specifics of citing sources on PE page 395.

To help them focus on this important feature of research writing, ask them to complete this quick activity.

■ Write the numbers 1 to 6 on a sheet of paper to correspond to the six paragraphs in the report. (The first paragraph is 1; the second is 2, and so on.)

■ Find and list any citations that appear in each paragraph next to the corresponding number of the paragraph. (1. none 2. (Tucker 4) 3. Arnie Rasmussen (attributed before the text quotation, rather than in a formal citation) 4. (Miles 26), a second direct quote attributed in the speaker tag to Arnie Rasmussen 5. (Miles 30), (Skelton) 6. none

Greenberg 3

HURRICANE CATEGORIES

Categories	Wind Speed	Description
1	74 – 95 mph	Weak
2	96 – 110 mph	Moderate
3	111 – 130 mph	Strong
4	131 – 155 mph	Very Strong
5	greater than 155 mph	Devastating

However, only about five hurricanes form near the United States each year. Just two of those hurricanes reach land, and only one of those is a category 3 or stronger (Miles 30). In 1900, the worst hurricane in United States history hit Galveston, Texas. "A storm surge almost two stories high broke over the city, causing 20-foot floods and more than 8,000 deaths" (Skelton).

Hurricanes are very dangerous storms. They can cause destruction, injury, and death over a very large area. It's important to learn how these storms form and move, and that's why scientists spend so much time studying hurricanes. Hurricanes cannot be stopped, so people must learn how to protect themselves and their belongings when one strikes.

Greenberg 4

Works Cited

Miles, Michael C. Hurricane Force. Philadelphia:

Countryside Press, 2002.

Rasmussen, Arnold. Personal interview. 13 Mar. 2004.

Skelton, Renee. "Flying into the Eye of a Hurricane."

National Geographic Kids. National Geographic.

12 Mar. 2004 <http://www.nationalgeographic.com/

ngkids/0308/hurricane/>.

Tucker, Libby. "Now That's Intense!" Science World

17 Nov. 2003: 4–6.

REPORT

Creating a Title Page

If your teacher requires a title page, follow his or her requirements. Usually you center the title one-third of the way down from the top of the page. Then go two-thirds of the way down and center your name, your teacher's name, the class, and the date on separate lines.

Hurricane Havoc

David Greenberg
Ms. Lin
Science
March 26, 2004

Point out that the citations list that students compiled in the activity on TE page 407 contains exactly the sources listed on the Works-Cited page. Suggest that students do a list for their own reports as a check to be sure they have not left out any cited sources.

Research Paper Checklist

Students can use this page as a research report rubric.

Have students complete a reflection of the research process. Ask students to write about the three P's:

- *problems* they encountered when working on this assignment
- *progress* they have made during the course of the assignment
- *possibilities* for improvements or additions they would make to the process next time to make the end result better and easier to achieve

410

Research Paper Checklist

Use the following checklist for your research paper. When you can answer all of the questions with a "yes," your paper is ready to hand in.

Ideas

_____ **1.** Is my research paper interesting and informative?

_____ **2.** Are my sources current and trustworthy?

Organization

_____ **3.** Does my paper have a thesis statement in the opening paragraph and a topic sentence in each middle paragraph?

_____ **4.** Does my ending paragraph bring my paper to a thoughtful close?

Voice

_____ **5.** Do I sound knowledgeable and interested in my topic?

Word Choice

_____ **6.** Have I explained any technical terms or unfamiliar words?

_____ **7.** Do I use quotations and paraphrasing effectively?

Sentence Fluency

_____ **8.** Do my sentences flow smoothly from one to another?

Conventions

_____ **9.** Does my first page include my name, my teacher's name, the class name, the date, and a title? (See page 382.)

_____ **10.** Do I correctly cite my sources? (See pages 383, 395, and 397.)

_____ **11.** Is my works-cited page set up correctly? Are the sources listed in alphabetical order? (See pages 385 and 399–400.)

_____ **12.** If my teacher requires a title page, is mine done correctly? (See page 409.)

Developing
Multimedia Presentations

If you've just written your best report or essay ever, you may want to share it with a larger audience. By creating a multimedia presentation using a computer, you'll be able to reach a larger audience, as well as add special effects to your report.

There are several kinds of software that you can use to produce multimedia presentations. Just add a little imagination, and you'll be connecting with your audience in a new, dynamic way.

Mini Index

- **Creating Multimedia Presentations**
- **Presentation Checklist**

Multimedia Presentations

Objectives

- plan, draft, revise, and edit a multimedia presentation

One strategy for helping those students new to multimedia technology is to pair them with students who are familiar with it. Working in pairs also helps when lab access is limited.

Decide ahead of time whether students will use the presentation as a visual aid for an oral report or as a stand-alone report.

Become familiar with the technology that is available in your school for students.

- Create a short presentation that explains how students can use the software.
- If possible, upload this presentation to a class Web site, so that students can access it whenever they need a refresher.

English Language Learners

Identify students who are proficient in using multimedia software and employ them as class experts. Invite those students to give demonstrations, making sure that if they are uncomfortable with providing commentary, you or a student who is proficient in English can step in.

Creating Multimedia Presentations

Prewriting
Selecting a Topic and Details

Be sure students focus on sharing the important information from their research rather than filling their presentation with graphics, animations, and sounds. Encourage them to write why a picture, animation, or sound will be included in the presentation.

 Answers

Answers will vary. Students should mention why they are including each media component.

412

Creating Multimedia Presentations

With the help of a computer, you can create a multimedia presentation that includes computer-generated slides with graphics and sound effects. These "extras" can make the important points of your presentation clearer and more interesting.

Prewriting Selecting a Topic and Details

For this presentation, you will want to use something you've already written, something that interests both you and your audience. After you've chosen your topic, make a list of the main ideas. Then find or create one or more of the following graphics or sound effects:

- **Pictures** such as photos or "click art"
- **Animations** that show a process or tell a story
- **Videos** of something you've filmed yourself
- **Sounds and music** to use as background or to make a point

 Make a plan and organize your ideas by creating a list or media grid like the one below.

Words on Slides	Pictures or Videos	Animations or Music	Sounds
1. Hurricanes cause a lot of damage each year.	photos	background music	
2. Scientists study the storms to understand them better.		hurricane animation	storm sound effects

 Gather details. Select ideas from your list or media grid for different graphics and sounds to include with each slide. Create them yourself or find them on the Internet. Save these images and sounds on your computer in a special folder created for this assignment.

NOTE organize RESEARCH summarize *cite* **413**
Multimedia Presentations

Writing Preparing the Presentation

Make a *storyboard*. A storyboard is a "map" of the slides you plan to use in your presentation. (See the sample storyboard on the next page.) Use your list or media grid as a guide. Include one box in the storyboard for each main idea.

Use your computer software to design the slides. If you include words, choose a typestyle that is easy to read. Use the graphics and sounds you found earlier. Also consider using bulleted lists and graphs to organize your information. However, don't overdo the graphics.

 Create a storyboard. Refer to your list or media grid to help you map out your storyboard. Include ideas for what your audience will see and hear. This will give you an idea of how the slides should look before you actually make them on the computer.

Revising Improving Your Presentation

Match the spoken parts of your presentation to the slides. To work well, everything in your presentation must be tied together so that it flows smoothly. Practice your presentation with family and friends and listen to any suggestions they may have for making your presentation even better.

 Rehearse your presentation. As you rehearse, you may notice parts that don't work smoothly. Make whatever changes are necessary.

Editing Checking for Conventions

Check the text on each slide for spelling, punctuation, grammar, and capitalization errors. Consider asking an adult or a classmate to check your slides, too.

 Make corrections. After you've made corrections, go through the presentation once more to make sure it works well.

> You can save your presentation on a disk or CD to share with others. Make sure you copy all the necessary files.

REPORT

Writing
Preparing the Presentation

Require students to have a completed storyboard that you can approve before they go to the computer to construct the presentation.

Revising
Improving Your Presentation

Encourage students to use one background for all slides. Using a different one for each slide can cause a visual overload that can detract from the presentation.

Editing
Checking for Conventions

* Refer students to the Proofreader's Guide, PE pages 578–749, if they have questions about the conventions.

Advanced Learners

Encourage students to keep notes on the problems and solutions they encounter while preparing their multimedia presentation. Suggest that when they've completed their project, they can make a "List of Helpful Hints" to share with other students for the next project.

Multimedia Presentation Storyboard

Use the sample storyboard to guide the creation of a storyboard from the research report. Remind students that they must incorporate slide design ideas as well as information.

Multimedia Presentation Storyboard

Here is the storyboard for a multimedia presentation based on the student research report "Hurricane Havoc." (See pages **406–409**.) The author reads the report as the slides are presented.

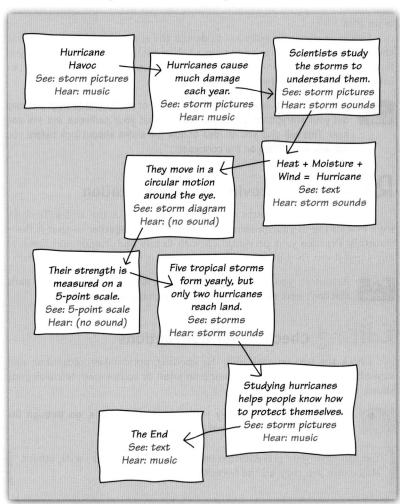

Presentation Checklist

Use the following checklist to make sure your presentation is the best it can be. When you can answer all of the questions with a "yes," you're ready to present!

Ideas

_____ **1.** Did I choose a strong essay or report for my presentation?

_____ **2.** Do my graphics help communicate my ideas clearly?

_____ **3.** Does each slide fit the audience and the purpose of the presentation?

Organization

_____ **4.** Did I introduce my topic clearly in the beginning?

_____ **5.** Did I include the important main points in the middle part?

_____ **6.** Did I end with a summary or wrap-up thought?

Voice

_____ **7.** Did I use an interesting, somewhat formal voice?

_____ **8.** Does my voice fit my audience and topic?

Word and Multimedia Choices

_____ **9.** Are the words on my slides easy to read?

_____ **10.** Did I choose the best pictures and sounds for my ideas?

Presentation Fluency

_____ **11.** Does my presentation flow smoothly from slide to slide?

Conventions

_____ **12.** Is my presentation free of grammar, spelling, and punctuation errors?

REPORT

Presentation Checklist

Suggest that students view their slide presentations several times.

■ They should make changes based on the flow of the presentation.

■ Caution them to be sure the presentation is effective in presenting the intended information. Too many computer-generated visuals and sounds can be confusing and distracting.

Advanced Learners

Have a group of students use the checklist to develop a presentation rubric. When they have finalized it, they should present it to the class to use in assessing the presentations.

Speaking and Writing to Learn Overview

Writing Standards

The writing standards listed below are based on a blending of state and NCTE standards.

- Work effectively in a group.
- Demonstrate strong oral presentation skills by preparing and delivering a demonstration speech.
- Listen carefully to take notes in class.
- Write in a learning log to express thoughts, feelings, and questions about a subject.

Skills

- listening in class
- participating in a group
- speaking in class
- preparing and delivering a demonstration speech

Tools and Techniques

- journals
- learning logs
- writing-to-learn activities
- note taking
- graphic organizers
- writing assignments

Test-Taking

- test preparation
- four basic types of objective tests (true/false, matching, multiple-choice, and fill-in-the-blanks)
- essay tests

Unit Pacing

Listening and Speaking: 45 minutes

This section instructs students on how to become better listeners and speakers, both in groups and in the whole classroom. Following are some of the topics that are covered.

- Understanding your purpose for listening
- Listening for signals
- Learning the rules of respect
- Following guidelines for speaking

Making Oral Presentations: 90 minutes

In this section students are shown how to prepare and present a demonstration speech by adapting a previously written essay. Following are some of the topics that are covered.

- Selecting effective visual aids
- Using note cards
- Understanding and using body language and voice
- Overcoming stage fright

Keeping Journals and Learning Logs: 2.25 hours

This section offers tips on keeping journals and learning logs. Following are some of the topics that are covered.

- Understanding different kinds of journals
- Using graphic organizers and drawings in learning logs
- Learning through writing activities

Taking Notes: 2.25 hours

This section has a dual goal: to help students recognize the value of good note taking and to help them learn how to take good notes. Following are some of the topics that are covered.

- Taking classroom notes
- Setting up and reviewing notes
- Taking reading notes
- Using different graphic organizers (time line, table organizer, Venn diagram) to organize notes

Completing Writing Assignments: 2.25 hours

This section explores the different levels of thinking needed to complete a variety of writing assignments. Following are some of the topics that are covered.

- Understanding the assignment
- Understanding the different levels of thinking (recalling, understanding, applying, analyzing, synthesizing, evaluating)
- Setting up a reasonable schedule for completing an assignment.

Taking Classroom Tests: 2.25 hours

- This section helps students understand the test-taking process. Following are some of the topics that are covered.
- A step-by-step plan for preparing for a test
- Tips to use during a test
- How to take objective tests (true/false, matching, multiple choice, fill-in-the-blanks)
- A four-point strategy for writing effective responses to essay prompts

416

LISTEN
respect
clarify

Speaking and Writing to Learn

revise
speak

Listening and Speaking

No matter where you are in school—in the classroom, in the gym, on the stage—you need to listen carefully. Why? For one thing, you don't want to miss anything. Teachers introduce new ideas, coaches explain new strategies, and directors give stage directions. Listening is one of the most important classroom skills you can master.

Speaking, which goes hand in hand with listening, is another key classroom skill. When you have mastered these two skills, you will be able to work better with others. You will also be more confident in your ability to learn and to succeed.

Mini Index

- Listening in Class
- Participating in a Group
- Speaking in Class

Listening and Speaking

Objectives

- develop good listening habits
- learn skills for working in a group
- understand keys to effective speaking

Share a story (humorous, if possible) of a time when you were distracted and didn't listen closely.

- Describe what happened as a result.
- Then invite students to share similar stories.

Describe the first time you had to speak in front of a classroom.

- Tell how you prepared for that moment and how you felt.
- Point out that many people—including teachers, actors, and politicians—admit that they get nervous speaking in front of an audience. With preparation and experience, however, it does get easier.

Listening in Class

Have on hand a variety of listening scenarios written on slips of paper. Some examples are

- a telephone conversation with a friend,
- a review for a social studies test,
- a funny story,
- directions to a place,
- a critic's review of a new movie,
- instructions for a science project.

Discuss the four tips for becoming a better listener. Then invite volunteers to select a slip of paper (scenario) and describe how they would listen in that situation. They should use the four tips to guide their explanations. Encourage the class to offer suggestions, too.

418

Listening in Class

Listening involves more than just hearing. It means *paying attention, staying focused,* and *thinking about the speaker's ideas.* The following tips will help you become a better listener—in and out of school.

1 **Figure out your purpose for listening.** Is it to learn new information, understand an assignment, review for a test?

2 **Show that you are listening.** Let the speaker know that you are listening by looking at him or her and staying focused. Looking around the room tells the speaker that you don't care very much about what's being said.

3 **Listen carefully.** Hearing is not the same as listening. Hearing involves only your ears; listening involves your ears *and* your mind. To listen, you need to think about what you hear. Taking notes while you listen can help you think about what you hear.

4 **Listen and watch for signals.** Many speakers, especially teachers, will use signals to tell you what is important. Here are some common phrases to listen for.

And don't forget . . .	This all means that . . .
The two main reasons for . . .	The bottom line is . . .

Sometimes speakers use their voice as a signal. Their voice gets higher or lower, louder or softer to help make a point. Speakers also use body language and facial expressions as signals.

 Keep a signal log. Make a chart like the one below for one of your classes. List the specific activities and what signals each teacher uses.

SIGNAL LOG

Class	Date	Activity	Signals
Spanish	Sept. 10	Reviewing for a test	The most important . . . Lo más importante . . .

English Language Learners

Students who are learning another language learn to "read" body language and other signals more quickly than they learn to read words. They can be a great asset when writing signal logs. Provide an opportunity for these students to share their knowledge by having the class work together to create a classroom signal log chart.

Advanced Learners

Instruct students to listen carefully to you or another speaker for fifteen minutes. Have them record the speaker's visual and auditory "signals." Then have students compare their observations.

Possible responses:

- fingers—to stress the first and second points
- arm motions—to reinforce concepts of size or speed
- facial expressions—variations for emotion
- voice—variations in volume, speed, tone, and pitch, for emphasis and emotion

A Closer Look at Listening

419
Listening and Speaking

Good listening is one of the keys to successful learning. As you become a better listener, you will also become a better student. As you practice listening skills, you learn to . . .

- give your full attention to the speaker,
- notice the speaker's body language and tone of voice,
- consider how the speaker's message applies to you, and
- take notes and form questions.

Try It Test your speaking and listening skills by doing the activity below with a classmate.

1. Draw a simple picture using three or four different geometric shapes. (See the *Original* illustration below.)

2. Then have a classmate re-create your picture following your spoken directions. Do **not** let your classmate see the drawing!

3. After you have finished, compare the pictures. (See the *Copy* below.) How close are they? Why do you think they are not exactly alike?

4. Now switch and have your partner draw a picture and give you the directions. What did this activity teach you about speaking and listening?

LEARN

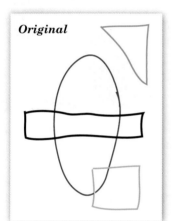

Original

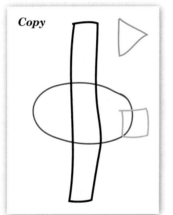

Copy

A Closer Look at Listening

Before assigning the **Try It** activity, model the process. As you give the directions below, draw on a transparency. Keep the overhead projector turned off until the directions are complete. Tell students to follow the directions on their own paper.

1. Draw a diamond in the middle of the paper.
2. Above the diamond, draw three small circles in a row.
3. Draw a square around the diamond.
4. Draw a triangle in each corner of the paper.
5. Turn the paper sideways, and draw a rectangle across the top.

Then turn on the overhead projector and have students compare their versions to your version.

Point out that the illustrations that accompany the **Try It** activity are meant to be examples. They should not be copied.

 **Answers**

Answers will vary but should show an understanding of how speaking and listening can affect learning.

English Language Learners

Students may have difficulty understanding spoken directions and giving directions themselves. Have students practice following spoken step-by-step directions for extremely simple drawings, such as a face or a sun. Then give each student a picture card of a face or a sun to look at as he or she tells a partner how to draw the image, step by step.

Struggling Learners

Modify this activity for students who have difficulty with spatial organization. Have students work in pairs.

- Provide each student with a full-page stick-figure drawing.
- Have one student embellish the stick figure (by adding a hat, cane, jewelry, shoes).
- Then have the partner attempt to re-create the picture by following the first student's spoken directions.
- Then compare drawings.

Participating in a Group

Encourage students to follow the basic rules of respect when working with an individual or a group.

Have students practice group skills by dividing them into small groups.
- Give each group a topic for discussion. Use current events and topics from social studies class.
- Designate one student to be the "observer." During the discussion, the observer should note on paper each time a classmate shows respect according to the rules on this page. Allow time for the observer to give feedback to the group in a respectful way.

For more practice, have students work in small groups to complete the **Try It** activity.

 **Answers**

Possible answers: Situation 1: Sam can say, "I have an idea. Is now a good time to share it?"

Situation 2: Sam should invite the student to share an idea or (if the student is hesitant) to share reactions to the ideas that others have already presented.

420

Participating in a Group

Nearly everything you say and do in a group is a response or reaction to what someone else has said or done. That's why it's important to follow basic rules of respect for yourself and for others.

Respect yourself by . . .
- believing that your own ideas are important.
- sharing your ideas clearly and politely.
- taking responsibility for what you say.

Respect others by . . .
- listening carefully to what others have to say.
- waiting for an opening before speaking, or interrupting politely by raising your hand and saying, "May I add something?"
- complimenting others when you can.
- encouraging everyone to participate.

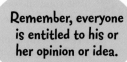

Remember, everyone is entitled to his or her opinion or idea.

 Sam is participating in a classroom group. Read about him below and then write a few sentences telling what you think Sam should do in each situation. Refer to the rules of respect above.

SITUATION 1
Sam has an idea to add, but he's not sure if he should share it immediately. What should Sam do?

SITUATION 2
Sam has been selected group leader. As the group brainstorms for project ideas, Sam notices that one of the students isn't saying anything. What should Sam do?

English Language Learners

Students may have a difficult time presenting ideas in a group discussion. Have them focus on believing that their ideas are important. Point out that they have great ideas to share, and that each time they speak in a discussion, their speaking skills will improve. For extra support, encourage students to draw pictures to help explain their ideas.

Advanced Learners

Advanced learners sometimes have little patience for listening to ideas from others. Belittling body language from such students can devastate an average or struggling learner's confidence. For this reason, it may be beneficial to challenge advanced learners to research accomplishments that stemmed from more than one person's ideas and contributions.

Possible subjects:
- Orville and Wilbur Wright—inventors
- Joanna Cole and Bruce Degen—author/illustrator team
- Rodgers and Hammerstein—composer/lyricist team

Group Skills

You now know why listening and speaking politely are so important to group work. Here are three skills you can use to make working in a group a truly positive experience. All members of a group need to use these skills: *observing, cooperating,* and *clarifying.*

OBSERVE the speaker's . . .
- body language (facial expressions, eye contact, posture).
- tone of voice (for excitement, nervousness, shyness).

COOPERATE by . . .
- staying positive and waiting your turn.
- avoiding put-downs.
- disagreeing in a polite way.

CLARIFY, or make something clearer, by . . .
- asking if there are any questions you can answer.
- restating a speaker's idea if necessary to be sure you understand everything.

Try It Read the statements and questions below about group skills. Then discuss your answers with a classmate.

1. Latifah speaks very softly while looking down at her notes.
What message is Latifah sending with her tone of voice and body language? How could she improve her message?

2. Ivan keeps saying that everything the group is doing is stupid.
What does Ivan need to learn about working in a group?

3. Juan listens to his group, but he doesn't understand what he is supposed to do.
How can Juan make sure that he understands everything?

LEARN

Group Skills

Discuss the difference between **constructive criticism** and **put-downs** *(see below)* before assigning the **Try It** activity.

Try It Answers

1. Latifah is sending the message that she does not believe that her ideas are important. She should look up and speak loudly and clearly.
2. Ivan needs to learn to respect the ideas of others. If he disagrees with an idea, he should present his own ideas politely and clearly, without putting down anyone else's ideas.
3. Juan should not be afraid to point out what he doesn't understand, so that he can get specific instructions.

Teaching Tip: Constructive Criticism vs. Put-Downs

Constructive criticism is advice offered in a polite, respectful way; it is intended to help improve an idea. Constructive criticism may point out why an idea might not work, but it never dismisses the idea without giving an explanation or an alternative suggestion, and it never attacks the person(s) who suggested the idea. Put-downs dismiss an idea without giving any explanation. They often contain insults that attack not only the idea but also the people who suggested it. Examples:

- Proposal: Let's ask for a longer lunch period.
- Constructive criticism: The principal probably won't agree to that, but maybe we can ask for longer breaks between classes.
- Put-down: You're all nuts if you think the principal will extend the lunch period.

Speaking in Class

Students benefit from lots of practice with following the rules for speaking in class.

- Begin each Monday with an opportunity for students to tell one thing about their weekend.
- Suggest that they use the guidelines for speaking to plan what they will say and how they will say it before they speak.
- Give them a time limit—say, thirty seconds—or tell them to condense their thoughts into one sentence.
- Provide an opportunity for students to assess their listening and speaking skills.

Speaking in Class

To speak effectively in class or in small groups, follow the helpful guidelines listed below.

Pay attention. Listen carefully and limit your comments to the topic being discussed.

Think before you speak. Be sure your comments and ideas add to the discussion.

Be respectful. Respond politely to all speakers.

Make eye contact. Respect whomever you are talking to by looking at them. You can also listen more effectively when you watch a speaker's expressions and gestures.

Wait your turn. Show that you care about the opinions and ideas of others by listening until they are finished. Then they will be more willing to listen to you.

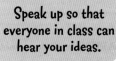
Speak up so that everyone in class can hear your ideas.

Get to the point. Make your point quickly so that others have a chance to respond and join in the discussion.

Follow the rules. On your own paper, write down one of the six speaking rules above that you think is especially important.

1 List all the reasons why you think this is a good rule to follow.

2 Give examples of what might happen if this rule is not followed.

3 Share your responses in small groups.

Struggling Learners

Following the guidelines for waiting their turn and getting to the point is difficult for some students. To help them follow these rules during classroom speaking opportunities, provide a rubber ball or other small object that can be passed from speaker to speaker to indicate who "has the floor" and a timer or a 30-second hourglass to keep track of time.

practice EXPRESS
speak demonstrate
show 423

Making Oral Presentations

You have probably already given lots of oral presentations—from your first show-and-tell in kindergarten to book reports, group projects, and demonstration speeches. Speaking in front of other people is an important lifelong skill, and the more you practice speaking now, the more your skill and confidence will grow.

In this chapter, you will learn how to present a report or an essay you have already written. You will also find some tips on effective speaking and how to apply them to your own presentation. Finally, you'll get some helpful hints on how to relax during your presentation.

Mini Index

Making Oral Presentations

Objectives
- plan, prepare, and present a demonstration speech
- select visual aids to enhance presentation
- use body language and voice to communicate ideas during presentation

Motivate students to make oral presentations. Play this version of the BBC radio game show, "Just a Minute." Here are the rules:

- A speaker speaks for one minute without repetition, hesitation, or deviation from the topic.
- Other players challenge the speaker when they hear a violation. If the challenge is determined to be valid by the teacher, the challenger must try to finish the minute. A player who finishes the minute earns a point.
- Players who finish the minute without being challenged get bonus points.

Ideas for speaking include dinner with the family, family pets, team sports, mall shopping, and so on.

Preparing Your Presentation

A **demonstration speech** is a presentation in which the speaker uses props to *show* as well as *tell*.

First, have students select a previously written essay that can be modified into this type of speech. Remind them to adapt their essays to this format, not simply read them aloud. Next, have them discuss possible essay choices with a partner and select one for an oral presentation. Make sure they know

- how long they will be expected to speak,
- who their audience will be,
- where they will speak,
- what equipment and props they will have available,
- how they will be assessed.

Rewriting in Action

Teacher feedback on the original essay should help students select an appropriate topic and rethink and rewrite their material.

Have each student use the tips at the top of the page to write two or three different beginnings for the oral presentation. Then have partners share their new beginnings to see which one works best.

Preparing Your Presentation

When you are preparing a demonstration speech from an essay you have already written, you know your topic and the details you want to use. Here are some tips to get you started.

Start with an exciting opening to grab the audience.
- Ask a question, tell a surprising fact, or make a strong statement.
- Share an interesting or a surprising story.
- Repeat a famous quotation.

Rewriting in Action

Below is the opening to the written essay "How to Give Your Dog a Bath" (pages 163–164). Notice that the new beginning (on gold paper) is much more interesting for an oral presentation than the original opening.

> If you or any of your friends have a dog, you know how much fun a pet can be. You also know that a dog can be a lot of work, especially if he is very active. It doesn't take long for a high-energy dog to look a mess and smell even worse. When that happens, it's time to gather up the dog shampoo and conditioner and freshen up your dog. If you follow these steps, bathing your dog can be easy and enjoyable.

> *Imagine this:* You're relaxing, playing video games, when suddenly you notice a terrible smell that nearly makes you drop the control. You look down at Rover, who has just plopped down next to you. Shutting off the TV, you sigh, "Sorry, boy, time for you to take a bath!"

 Rethink and rewrite your material. Select and review the essay or report you will use for your presentation. Rewrite parts that sound boring when you read them out loud. Use an exciting or interesting beginning.

English Language Learners

Students may benefit from reading aloud their speeches to you or a trusted partner. Doing so should help them hear passages that need improvement. When necessary, you or the partner can ask leading questions as such as these:

- Do you think your point might be stronger if you turned that sentence into a question?

- What adjectives could you use to show listeners exactly what you mean in that sentence?

Using Visual Aids

Once you have finished writing (or rewriting) your essay or report, you are ready to prepare your presentation. You may want to use visual aids like the ones listed below to make your presentation clear and interesting.

Posters	show words, pictures, or both.
Photographs	help your audience "see" what you are talking about.
Charts	compare ideas or explain main points.
Transparencies	highlight key words, ideas, or graphics.
Maps	show specific places being discussed.
Objects	allow your audience to see the real thing.

Here are some tips for preparing your visual aids.

1 Choose them carefully. Use visual aids that help explain or clarify a main point.

2 Make them big. Be sure your visual aids can be seen from the back of the room.

3 Keep them clear. Choose words and graphics that are to the point and easy to read at a glance.

4 Use a good design. Make visual aids colorful and attractive.

List visual aids. List a number of possible visual aids you could use in your presentation. Then select two that you think will work best.

> List of visual aids
> * washtub and towels
> * shampoo
> * small bucket
> * stuffed dog

Using Visual Aids

In addition to using charts, students may use other **graphics** *(see below)* to enhance their demonstration speeches.

- Remind students that they are going to be speaking at the same time they are trying to manipulate visuals. Caution them against using too many visual aids or unwieldy props, which can distract them and their audience.
- Encourage students to test the effectiveness of their visuals ahead of time. For example, they might stand in the back of the classroom or auditorium to be sure the visual will be clear to the entire audience. Students should also make sure to include their visual aids when they practice their demonstration.

Teaching Tip: Graphics

Students can add information and heighten interest during a presentation by using diagrams, tables, and graphs.

- A diagram is a drawing that shows the parts of something.
- A table shows information or data in rows and columns.
- A graph uses lines or bars to show information.

* See PE pages 574–575 for additional information and examples.

426

Preparing a Demonstration Speech

Explain to students that in speeches, voice refers to not only the ideas and word choice they make in preparing their speeches but also to the tone of voice they use in delivering their speeches.

- Remind students to keep their audience in mind as they prepare their demonstration speeches because they want their voice to be informal and conversational.

- Point out that as students plan what to say and how to say it, they should show respect and consideration for their audience. For example, if their audience will be students from lower grades, they should use words and phrases that young students will understand.

Using Note Cards

As you review the guidelines for writing note cards, model the process using an overhead projector or chart paper. Emphasize that notes on cards should be brief prompts, not a detailed script. Except for the introduction and ending, students should not write what they will say word for word.

Preparing a Demonstration Speech

If you are asked to give a demonstration speech in any of your classes, there are a few things you should know. When you give a demonstration, you don't just *tell* your audience how to do something, you *show* them. Follow these suggestions:

1 Use visual aids, props, and other materials to help your audience *see* what you are explaining.

2 Use an informal or conversational voice during your demonstration.

3 Present your main points and supporting details in an organized, step-by-step way.

Using Note Cards

One way to organize your details is to use note cards. Because you will be showing each step instead of simply reading it, you need to put your information in an easy-to-handle form.

For example, the writer of the how-to essay on pages 163–164, "How to Give Your Dog a Bath," decided to present his essay as a demonstration. He rewrote his main ideas on note cards. Then, as he gave his demonstration, he was able to see his next point by simply glancing at the next card.

> **Note-Card Guidelines**
>
> - Write out your introduction word for word.
> - Number your cards and use a separate card for each main step or idea.
> - Write the main idea at the top of the card. Then add specific details for that idea underneath.
> - At the appropriate points, list your visual aids with instructions for what to do with each one.
> - Write out your ending word for word.

 Create your note cards. Look over the note cards on the next page. Then create a note card for each step in your presentation. Be sure to add notes to yourself about visual aids.

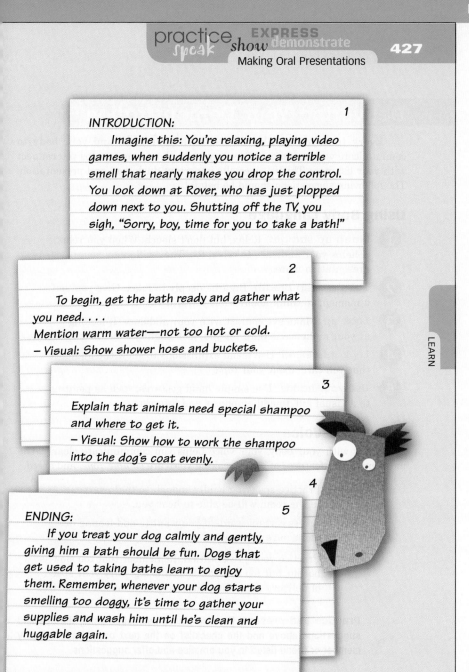

1

INTRODUCTION:

Imagine this: You're relaxing, playing video games, when suddenly you notice a terrible smell that nearly makes you drop the control. You look down at Rover, who has just plopped down next to you. Shutting off the TV, you sigh, "Sorry, boy, time for you to take a bath!"

2

To begin, get the bath ready and gather what you need. . . .
Mention warm water—not too hot or cold.
– Visual: Show shower hose and buckets.

3

Explain that animals need special shampoo and where to get it.
– Visual: Show how to work the shampoo into the dog's coat evenly.

4

5

ENDING:

If you treat your dog calmly and gently, giving him a bath should be fun. Dogs that get used to taking baths learn to enjoy them. Remember, whenever your dog starts smelling too doggy, it's time to gather your supplies and wash him until he's clean and huggable again.

LEARN

Remind students to use a separate note card for each step and to number the cards in order. This will keep their demonstrations moving smoothly from beginning to end, without long, uncomfortable pauses that can ruin a good speech.

Suggest that each student compare the ideas on the note cards to his or her original essay to see if any main points have been omitted.

Students whose verbal skills outshine their writing skills can write less on their note cards. Encourage those students to include only brief phrases as clues or reminders about what they plan to say, even for their introduction and ending. With the pressure of writing removed, these students can focus their preparation time on their speaking strengths.

Delivering Your Demonstration

Ask students why it's important for speakers to connect with listeners (so they keep listening).

Using Body Language

Give a brief speech on a silly topic, like "How to Arrange Canned Goods in Your Kitchen Cabinets."

Use humor and exaggeration to help students recognize the effect of body language and voice on an audience.

- Speak in a monotone, very slowly or very fast.
- Repeat *like* or *uh*.
- Mumble, look down, play with your hair, and sway.

Invite students to point out all the errors and to describe their reactions to them.

Using Your Voice

Students may wish to include guidelines for body language and voice on the note cards they made (PE page 426). As they practice, they can use the note cards and the checklist on PE page 428 to find suggestions for improvement.

Delivering Your Demonstration

Every time you speak, you use both your voice and your body to communicate your message. The way you speak and move helps you connect with your listeners. This is especially important during an oral presentation. The following suggestions should be helpful.

Using Body Language

1 Stand up straight. Relax, but don't slouch. When you relax, it helps your audience to relax, too. They will enjoy your presentation more.

2 Take a deep breath. Breathe deeply to relax. Give yourself a moment to think about what you will say next.

3 Look up. Make eye contact with your audience. If looking at your audience is hard for you, look slightly over their heads.

4 Look interested. Use facial expressions to show the audience that you care about your topic.

5 Use your hands. Use simple hand gestures, such as pointing to a visual aid, to add emphasis and interest.

Using Your Voice

Along with your body, your voice helps you communicate clearly. The most important features of your speaking voice are *volume, tone,* and *speed*.

Volume	Practice speaking loudly enough so that everyone in the room will be able to hear you.
Tone	Stress certain words if you want to add feeling or emphasize an idea.
Speed	Practice your presentation. Remember that too slow is boring, but too fast can be confusing. Vary your speed of delivery depending on what you want to emphasize.

 Practice and present. Practice your presentation using the tips and suggestions above and the checklist on the next page. Have a family member or friend listen to you practice and offer suggestions.

Struggling Learners

Fear of failure can heighten self-consciousness for some students. Videotape or tape-record their presentation before they practice it in front of a family member or classmate. After viewing or listening to their presentation, they can experiment with the delivery. In this way, they can practice without concern about anyone else's opinion.

Overcoming Stage Fright

Most people feel nervous in front of a group. You may feel that way, too. Here are some ways to help you relax and reduce your "stage fright."

1 Practice and be prepared.

Know your presentation. That means you should practice every chance you get. Practice by delivering it in front of a mirror, family, or friends. Also consider videotaping your presentation to evaluate your delivery.

2 Warm up.

Before you begin your presentation, stretch your arms, neck, and shoulders. Breathe deeply.

3 Focus.

Often, nervousness or stage fright comes from losing your focus. When you are making your presentation, concentrate on what you are doing and on what comes next.

Using a Checklist

Whenever you practice your presentation, use the checklist below. If possible, record yourself with a camcorder or have someone else watch your presentation and offer suggestions.

_____ **1.** My posture is relaxed, but I don't slouch.

_____ **2.** I look up from my notes, have some eye contact with my audience, and move naturally.

_____ **3.** I speak clearly and loudly enough to be heard and understood by everyone.

_____ **4.** I look and sound like I'm interested in my topic.

_____ **5.** I control and vary my speed (not too fast, not too slow).

_____ **6.** I avoid unnecessary sounds and words: *um, er, like*.

_____ **7.** My visual aids are clear and large enough for all to see.

_____ **8.** I use my hands to hold my notes and to point out my visual aids.

LEARN

Overcoming Stage Fright

By sixth grade, many students will have had experiences with stage fright. Invite volunteers to share their tricks and tips for overcoming stage fright and relaxing in front of a group.

- Ask students to brainstorm a list of the worst things they can imagine happening in front of an audience. Write ideas on the board. Then have students divide ideas into two groups: things they can control (missing visual aids, out-of-order note cards) and things they can't control (power goes out, principal's announcement over PA system interrupts their speech).

- Encourage students not to worry about things they can't control. Stress that they should focus on things they can address ahead of time to try to prevent problems.

- Encourage students to practice their demonstrations often, in front of a supportive audience (family or friends). This is the greatest way for them to ensure success and overcome stage fright.

English Language Learners

Provide extra support by scheduling guided practice sessions for students who are particularly challenged by stage fright. Build their confidence by having them practice using graphic aids to help express their main ideas. After each student's presentation, lead the class in asking questions that you know the speaker is prepared to answer.

Struggling Learners

Have students practice presenting their demonstrations in small groups. Use the checklist or a rubric like the one below to help observers offer quick and easy-to-comprehend feedback. Sample rubric:

- POSTURE: Relaxed; Some slouching; Too stiff.
- NOTES: Looked up; Read straight from notes.
- SPEECH: Clear and loud; Mumbled.
- INTEREST: Interested in topic; Bored with topic.
- SPEED: Just right; Too fast; Too slow.
- UNNECESSARY SOUNDS: None; Few; Too many *um, er,* or *like* sounds.
- VISUAL AIDS: Clear and colorful; Somewhat helpful; Confusing.
- HANDS: Used well to illustrate points; Distracting.

Demonstration Tips

Encourage students to try to find a new, fresh audience for their final practice.

- Tell students to pay attention to the facial expressions and body language of this audience.
- If listeners appear interested and involved throughout the "dress rehearsal," students are on the right track.
- If listeners fidget or look confused or bored at any point, students should consider making some changes in the presentation.

If possible, videotape student presentations.

- Then provide time for students to watch and assess their own performances.
- Suggest that they use the tips for delivering a demonstration on PE pages 428–430 and the checklist on PE page 429 to guide their assessments.

430

Demonstration Tips

Before your presentation . . .

- **Gather all the materials you will need.**
  Practice your demonstration as much as you can.
- **Time your presentation.**
  If it is too short, add information or personal stories.
- **Be prepared.**
  Put all your main ideas and important details on note cards.

During your presentation . . .

- **Hold up your materials as you explain the process.**
  Be sure that everyone can see what you are doing.
- **Speak up.** Be sure everyone can hear you.
- **Talk slowly.** You want your audience to understand you. Repeat important information if necessary.
- **Keep talking throughout the presentation.**
  If a step takes a little time, fill in with a story or personal experience related to the activity.
- **Show a finished product.**
  If your process takes too long to complete (such as baking a cake), have a finished product to show (a cake).

After your presentation . . .

- **Answer any questions.**
  Ask if anyone has a question about the topic.
- **Then collect your materials** and walk to your seat.

 Practice and present. Have a final practice with a friend or someone at home. Ask for feedback and make changes. Then, after your classroom demonstration, listen to suggestions from your teacher and classmates.

CLUSTER
draw learn record freewrite 431

Keeping Journals and Learning Logs

There are many ways to improve your writing and learning skills. Two of the best ways are writing regularly in a personal journal and keeping a learning log in your classes.

A personal journal is a place for you to record personal thoughts, feelings, and events. When you keep a journal, all your thinking and writing skills come into play, sharpening your mind and making you a better writer. In a learning log, you write about things you are studying. A learning log can help you understand tough subjects and make you a better student.

In the following chapter, you'll learn how to start your own personal journal and learning log.

Mini Index

- Keeping a Personal Journal
- Writing in Other Journals
- Writing in a Learning Log
- Writing-to-Learn Activities

Keeping Journals and Learning Logs

Objectives

- start a personal journal
- understand the reasons for keeping a variety of journals
- learn how to use learning logs for science, math, and social studies
- discover different ways to write in learning logs

Some students may already keep personal journals and learning logs. Invite them to share how they got started keeping their logs and journals and why they keep them.

So as not to burden students with too much journal writing, specify which type of journal or learning log to use, give students a choice, or coordinate with teachers in other curriculum areas. Most of these exercises extend across the curriculum.

Establish classroom routines that will allow you to monitor student use of journals and learning logs.

- For example, announce that you will be collecting and reviewing the logs every Thursday.
- Make sure that students are recording useful data effectively.
- After reviewing the logs, provide constructive feedback.

English Language Learners

Students may be unfamiliar with the term *log,* as used to mean *diary*. Explain that a log is a book in which people record events or information. Point out that ships' captains keep a daily log of their ships' speed, direction, and progress. Later, they can refer back to the log to guide them on future sailings. Point out that in a similar way, students can use a learning log to record what they have learned and then refer back to their log to refresh their memory and review for tests.

Keeping a Personal Journal

To encourage students to write freely about what really matters to them, explain that they will not be required to share their personal journal entries. Point out that, from time to time, you will flip through pages without reading them, just to check that they are writing in the journal regularly. Assure students that if they would like to share an entry with you, you will keep their ideas private.

Getting Started

Set aside at least 5 to 10 minutes each day for students to write in their journals. Have them write without stopping.

- If they can't think of anything to write, suggest that they write about either the most or least interesting thing that happened that day.
- Talk students through the first few writing sessions. Say: *Begin writing now. Write whatever you're thinking, even if it's "I don't know what to write." Just keep your pencil moving. Write whatever comes into your head. You've been writing for one minute. Good job. Keep writing . . .*

432

Keeping a Personal Journal

Keeping a personal journal can be a rewarding and enjoyable activity. You can write about things that happen to you (both good and bad). You can also write stories and poems without worrying about errors in your writing. All of this practice helps you become a better writer.

Getting Started

A personal journal is your own special place to write. Follow these steps to get started.

1 Collect the proper tools.

All you really need is a notebook and a supply of your favorite pens or pencils. Or you can use a computer if you have one available.

2 Choose a time to write.

Write early in the morning, late at night, or anytime in between.

3 Write freely for at least 5 to 10 minutes at a time.

If you regularly write for the same amount of time, count the number of words you get on paper. That number should increase little by little, which means you are learning to write freely and naturally.

4 Write about things that are important to you.

Here are some general subject areas to consider:

- important events,
- subjects you are studying,
- interesting things you see and hear, or
- thoughts and feelings you would like to explore.

5 Keep track of your writing.

Date your journal entries and read through them from time to time. Underline ideas that you would like to write more about in the future.

 Start your journal writing. Write in a personal journal for two weeks for 5 to 10 minutes a day. At the end of the two weeks, put a star next to the entry that you would like to write more about some day. Tell a partner why you chose this entry.

Journal Entry

In the sample journal entry below, the student writes about what she's been doing lately and about her plans for the upcoming week.

May 16

We had our first track meet last night. I ran second in the half-mile relay and was really nervous about the handoffs. I did okay for my first time, and we placed third. All those practices paid off.

Cozzie slept over on Friday night. We played music and watched some TV and talked really late until my mom told us to quiet down. On Saturday morning, we made chocolate chip pancakes for everyone. I really enjoy cooking. Sometimes I even think I'd like to be a chef. Would it be as much fun if I did it every day as a job?

I've got a huge report in science to finish this week. I hope I can use the computer lab and get some help with adding the table to my report. Maybe Mr. Vernor can show me what to do. He helped me with my history report when I needed to create some graphs.

LEARN

Asking questions and wondering are two ways to reflect in journal writing. (*Reflect* means "to think very carefully about something.")

Ask questions. As you write, ask yourself these questions:

> *What did I learn from the experience?*
> *How do I feel about it now?*

Wonder. Consider how the experience may affect your future. Compare your new experiences to others you have had.

Journal Entry

As students read the sample entry, point out how the writer jumps from one topic to another, as people often do when talking to a good friend. Tell students to think of a personal journal as a good friend and an opportunity to share personal thoughts and events in their daily lives.

Writing in Other Journals

When presenting the idea of a **dialogue journal** *(see below),* make sure students understand that they will exchange their journal with another person and take turns writing in it.

Collecting and assessing journals can become an overwhelming task. You may find it easier to divide your students into five groups and assign each one a certain weekday for journal feedback.

Travel journals are a good way to keep students who are on vacation connected to the class.

- Read an excerpt from a published travel journal, such as Thor Heyerdahl's *Kon-Tiki*.
- Encourage students to write in their journals daily, recording details about their adventures, as well as interesting facts and details about the places they visit and people they meet.
- Later, they can share excerpts from their travel journals with the class.

434

Writing in Other Journals

Writing in a personal journal is one way to explore your thoughts and feelings. Here are four other types of journals you can try.

Dialogue Journal

In a dialogue journal, two people (you and a teacher, family member, or friend) talk to each other on paper over a period of time. A dialogue journal can help you and your partner learn more about each other or explore a common interest.

Specialized Journal

When you write in a journal about an ongoing event or experience, you are writing in a specialized journal. You may want to explore your thoughts while at summer camp, while participating in a team sport, while involved in a school play, or while working on a group project.

Travel Journal

One form of specialized journal is a travel journal. It preserves memories of a trip you've taken. You can write while riding on a bus, waiting in lines, or at the beginning or end of each day.

Reader-Response Journal

In a reader-response journal, you react to the books you are reading. Here are some questions that will help you write about literature.

1. What are you feeling after reading the opening chapter? After reading half of the book? After finishing the book?
2. Does the book make you laugh? Cry? Smile? Cheer? Explain.
3. How does the book connect with your life?
4. What about the writing is especially good?
5. Who else should read this book? Why?

 Respond to your reading. For the next short story or novel you read, keep a reader-response journal. Write at least one entry after each chapter. Use the questions above to get started.

Teaching Tip: Dialogue Journals

Dialogue journals can help students reflect on school-related issues. Classmates, students in another class (older or younger), or adult mentors from the community can be partners. Some senior facilities are open to such dialogues, if you can get the journals back and forth. E-mail may also be used for such journals.

English Language Learners

Dialogue journals may be particularly helpful to students whose limited language skills make speaking within a group difficult. Assign a partner, or have each student select one. From time to time, monitor the dialogue journals and compliment each student on his or her growing language skills.

Struggling Learners

Provide students with extra support when assigning reader-response journals. Gather students into a group and have them all read and respond to the same book. Then hold a group discussion in which students work together to answer questions and record responses in a group journal.

CLUSTER record
draw *learn* freewrite **435**
Keeping Journals and Learning Logs

Writing in a Learning Log

A learning log is a place to write down your thoughts, feelings, and questions about the subjects you are studying. Here are some tips to help get you started.

1 Keep a learning log for any subject.
It's especially helpful for the subjects that are hard for you.

2 Keep your learning log well organized.
Use a separate notebook for your learning log, date each entry, and leave space for adding information (in red below).

3 Use graphic organizers and drawings.
Pictures and illustrations can help you remember key ideas.

4 Write freely about any of these ideas:
- what you have learned from an assignment or class presentation,
- questions you have about new material, or
- how new material connects to other things you have learned.

LEARN

Mar. 7

Key words:
heart   oxygen   oxygen = an odorless
pump   blood   gas in the air
life

Without blood pumping through our bodies, we would die. All our organs need whatever is in blood to live. Oxygen, for one thing. Mr. Chavez always calls good citizens the lifeblood of our nation. When I see all those cars going in and out of Chicago, well, they sure do look like blood cells rushing through arteries.

Writing in a Learning Log

Set aside time at the end of each class for students to reflect in their **learning logs** (*see below*).

- Encourage students to keep well-organized and detailed learning logs, which can then be used to review material before unit tests.
- Remind students that they should write about each subject in their own words. Point out that putting ideas in their own words in a learning log is an excellent way for them to identify any ideas that they don't completely grasp. Encourage them to ask for help or clarification in those areas.
- To encourage students to use their learning logs effectively, allow them to refer to their logs while taking tests or quizzes. This is especially beneficial at the beginning of the school year, as you are establishing productive study habits and routines. As skills improve, allow students to use their logs for study only.

Teaching Tip: Learning Logs

With teachers in other subject areas, discuss ways that might be particularly helpful to support students as they create learning logs in various classes. For example, teachers can stress the use of graphic organizers and drawings to help students express and remember key ideas.

Science Log

Before students practice writing entries in their science logs, have them analyze the sample science log using questions like these:

- What key points and ideas does the writer discuss? (mosquitoes and disease; malaria)
- How does the writer highlight key ideas? (calls out key words; draws a mosquito)
- What makes the learning-log entry different from, say, a response to a test question? (the language is conversational; the writer jokes about mosquitoes and history)
- How might the drawing of a mosquito help the writer later? (a test question might ask about parts of a mosquito's body)

Consult with students' science teachers to obtain a list of suitable topics for learning-log entries, or share this activity with the science teacher.

436

Science Log

Learning logs work for any subject. The sample log below was written following a discussion of mosquitoes in a science class. Keep in mind that a learning log works best if you put ideas in your own words.

> Mosquitoes   Feb. 5
>
> Key words: germs
>   malaria
>
> I thought mosquitoes were just summer pests. It turns out that mosquitoes can carry germs that cause serious diseases such as malaria. (Fortunately, mosquitoes in the United States almost never carry malaria.) Doctors think that, in all of history, more people have died of malaria than any other disease. That means that mosquitoes have had a pretty big part in history. It's funny because I don't ever remember reading about mosquitoes in history class!
>
> ← History-making pest!

Log on in science. On your own paper, name the subject of the science unit you are currently studying. Then write a learning-log entry about something in the unit that you find interesting, surprising, or confusing.

Math Log

Many students keep learning logs in math class to help them think about math concepts. One way to set up a math log is to write a question related to the day's lesson and then answer it. Below are two examples.

MATH CLASS   Sept. 13

Question: Why do we need to show our work?
Answer: I know Mr. Manzo wants me to show my work so he knows that I did the problem myself. He can also see how I did it. If I get stuck, he can see how to help me.
    But sometimes it doesn't make sense. I can figure out some problems in my head. Why can't I just write the answer? Why should I write all the stuff about how I got the answer?

                              Sept. 16
Question: What are two meanings of the minus sign?
Answer: The minus sign means "subtraction." Another meaning is "negative number."
    For example, the first minus sign in the equation below means "subtract 7." But the second minus sign on the right side means "negative 4."
    $3 - 7 = -4$

Log on in math. On your own paper, write a learning-log entry for math. First write down a question about a math concept you are studying. Then answer it. (Use the samples above as a guide.)

LEARN

Math Log

Before having students read the sample questions and answers, model on the board how to set up a math log, based on the sample.

- Write the sample questions and have students suggest answers for them.
- Students can then compare their answers to the ones in the sample.
- Students may have a difficult time coming up with math-concept questions on their own. Consult with math teachers for suggestions of appropriate questions for students to explore in learning-log entries.

If students are keeping a daily learning log in math class, math teachers may wish to skim through entries to see which concepts need clarification or reteaching.

Social Studies Log

After students read the sample, help them recognize how the writer connects the concept (of the United States as a melting pot) to her own life and how she explores her feelings and thoughts about it. Students should note that the writer

■ uses the phrase *supposed to be* to show doubt,

■ connects the idea to her city,

■ describes how different ethnic groups live in different sections,

■ does not think America can really call itself a melting pot.

To help students connect social studies concepts to their own lives, have them look through magazines and local newspapers. For example, an article on a water shortage in their community would relate to the study of preserving our natural resources. Students might insert articles and pictures into their learning logs to inspire writing ideas.

438

Social Studies Log

In the following sample, the student writes about a concept introduced in her social studies class. Writing about this idea helps the student explore her thoughts and feelings about it.

> Social Studies   Nov. 17
>
> ### Melting Pot
>
> Today in class we talked about the "melting pot." The United States is supposed to be a place where people from different races and backgrounds blend in or "melt" together. In one way, this idea makes sense because people from all over the world have settled here. And I know some "melting" has gone on, but then I think of this city. There still are definite neighborhoods. Most African Americans live in the central city and on the north side. Most Hispanic Americans live on the south side. Sure, some African Americans live in other places, but it seems to me that we still have a long way to go before we can really call ourselves a melting pot.

Log on in social studies. On your own paper, name the subject of the unit you are now studying in social studies. Then write a learning-log entry about something in the unit that you find interesting, surprising, or confusing.

CLUSTER record *learn* freewrite **439**
draw
Keeping Journals and Learning Logs

Writing-to-Learn Activities

There are many ways to write in a learning log. Three basic ideas are described below, and five additional ideas are listed on the next page.

The Basic Three

Freewriting When you freewrite in a learning log, you write quickly about a subject you are studying. The act of writing freely and rapidly allows you to explore a subject from many different angles. Try to write for at least 5 minutes at a time. Don't stop to judge or correct your writing; just keep writing. (The learning-log entry on page 438 is an example of freewriting.)

Listing Listing is a simple form of freewriting. You make a list of the ideas, feelings, and questions that come to mind as you think about a subject.

Clustering Clustering also works well in a learning log. Place the subject you are studying in the center of the page and circle it. Then write words and phrases about the subject. Circle each one and draw a line connecting it to the closest related word.

LEARN

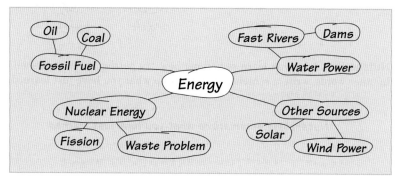

After clustering for 3 or 4 minutes, you may find it helpful to freewrite about the subject using one of the ideas in the cluster as a starting point.

 Make a cluster for a subject you are studying in one of your classes. Remember to write the subject in the middle of your paper. Keep clustering until you run out of ideas.

Writing-to-Learn Activities

Have students flip through their learning logs to see how they explore ideas. Do they use lists, clusters, or any other graphics?

The Basic Three

Before starting a new unit, have students use one of the Basic Three to explore what they already know about a concept or topic.

After completing the unit, have students return to their original freewrite, list, or cluster to add or revise ideas. Have students use a different color pen to make their changes and to see how much they have learned.

Some computer software programs make it easy to create clusters; some programs even enable students to turn a cluster into a writing plan, such as an outline.

Be sure students understand how ideas and details in the sample cluster are connected before they do the **Try It** activity.

Try It Answers

Answers will vary, but clusters should show at least two supporting details for each main idea, as in the model on PE page 439.

English Language Learners

Because clustering may prove to be especially helpful to students with a limited English vocabulary, be sure to provide extra practice. Create a model cluster diagram on the chalkboard or an overhead projector while students make their own clusters on paper. Use familiar subjects such as favorite foods, interesting pets, and team sports.

Struggling Learners

Eliminate the frustration some students experience when frequent erasures cause their paper to become messy or ripped. Instead of having students write clusters on a sheet of paper, provide pre-cut circles (or have students cut circles) on which to write. Students can then easily rearrange the circles as they make their cluster.

Special Writing Activities

As you read aloud about each type of activity, ask students to suggest ideas they might explore or that they actually have explored using that writing activity. If there is time, have volunteers model each activity on the board, using ideas the class suggests.

Invite students to share any learning-log activities they have developed on their own that have consistently worked for them (for example, creating visual icons to highlight key ideas, creating mnemonics or rhymes to make it easier to recall factual information).

 **Answers**

Letters will vary but should explain a concept in the student's own words.

440

Special Writing Activities

Review the five learning-log activities on this page. Each one is quite different from the others and can be used for a special purpose.

First Thoughts When you begin to study something new in one of your classes, write what you think about it. Also write about where this particular subject may take you.

Stop 'n' Write In the middle of learning something new, take a moment to stop and write down what you are thinking. This will help you understand and remember what you are studying.

Picture Outlining A picture can be worth a thousand words. When you see something in class or in a book that will help you remember what you are learning, draw a picture of it and label it. The following picture outline quickly shows the different levels of organization in a person's body.

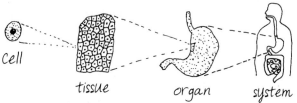

Cell tissue organ system

Nutshelling After you learn something new, try putting it "in a nutshell." In other words, write a sentence that sums up what you have just learned.

Nutshelling summarizes what you have just learned.

Unsent Letters To think deeply about your learning, write a letter about it. You could write to someone real (like the author of a book you like) or to someone imaginary (like a friend in the Andromeda Galaxy). In your letter, describe what you have learned and what it means to you.

 Think about what you have learned so far about writing in a learning log. Then write an unsent letter to someone real or imaginary, explaining what you have learned.

LIST. remember organize
preview listen 441

Taking Notes

To become good at something, you need to roll up your sleeves and get involved. Fortunately, most of you are already involved in your learning. You listen in class and complete reading assignments. You do your homework and review for tests. However, to get totally involved, you must write about the subjects you are studying.

Research has shown that the best way to understand new material is to write about it. The writer of the following proverb appreciates the value of writing in the learning process: "I hear and I forget; I see and I remember; *I write and I understand.*"

Note taking is one of the most valuable writing skills you can develop. The information in this chapter will help you take useful classroom and reading notes.

Mini Index

- **Taking Classroom Notes**
- **Taking Reading Notes**

Taking Notes

Objectives
- understand how taking good classroom notes helps the learning process
- learn guidelines for taking and revising notes
- use graphic organizers to take reading notes

If possible, meet with curriculum or team teachers to agree on a standard approach to note taking and acceptable formats for notes.

After students read the introduction to this section, use the following questions to explore their current note-taking skills:
- What kinds of notes do you usually take in class?
- How do you use the notes you take?
- What would you like to learn about taking notes?
- Why do you think note taking is a valuable writing skill?

Taking Classroom Notes

Invite students to describe a time when writing notes helped them to learn in any of the ways listed at the top of the page.

Guidelines for Note Taking

Conduct a workshop to model the note-taking process.

- Have students read the guidelines. Encourage them to ask for clarification if anything is unclear.
- Invite another teacher or guest to present interesting information.
- During the presentation, model on the board how to take notes. For example, as the topic is introduced, write the topic and date (guideline 1). Next, note the main ideas you should be listening for (guideline 2), key words to remember (guideline 3), and so on.

Stress the importance of listening carefully while taking notes. Read aloud the tip in parentheses at the bottom of the page. Refer students to the listening skills on PE pages 418–419. Ask how these skills can help them take notes.

442

Taking Classroom Notes

Taking notes can help you learn more effectively in class and do well on tests. It helps in three ways:

- Writing notes helps you **pay attention.**
- Reading over notes helps you **understand.**
- Studying notes helps you **remember.**

Guidelines for Note Taking

1 **Write the topic and date at the top of each page.**
You should also number each page of notes. Then, if a page gets out of order, you'll know exactly where it belongs.

2 **Listen carefully when the teacher introduces the topic.**
You may hear important clues. Your teacher may say, "I'm going to explain the three branches of the federal government." Then you can listen for those three branches.

3 **Listen for key words.**
Key words include *first, second, last, most important,* and so on.

4 **Use numbers or symbols to help organize your notes.**
For example, you can identify the steps in a process using 1st, 2nd, 3rd, and so on. A star or an asterisk can mark a key point.

5 **Write down the main ideas using your own words.**
Don't try to write down everything the teacher says.

6 **When you hear a word that is new to you, write it down.**
Don't worry about spelling. Just make your best guess, circle the word, and check a dictionary later.

7 **Copy whatever the teacher writes on the board.**
Usually, this information is important and often ends up on tests.

The real secret to taking good notes is listening. Don't get so involved in taking notes that you forget to listen. If you listen carefully, you will hear details that you can add to your notes later.

 Take class notes. Use the guidelines above and the sample set of notes on the next page to guide you the next time you take notes.

Struggling Learners

Suggest more specific strategies for each guideline. For example, as students *listen for key words,* have them write the words *first, second, last,* and *most important* in the margin beside the corresponding notes. Then have them highlight these words, so they can see at a glance how the information is related.

Setting Up Your Notes

Use a notebook or a three-ring binder for your notes. A three-ring binder allows you to add and remove pages when you need to. The side notes below give additional tips.

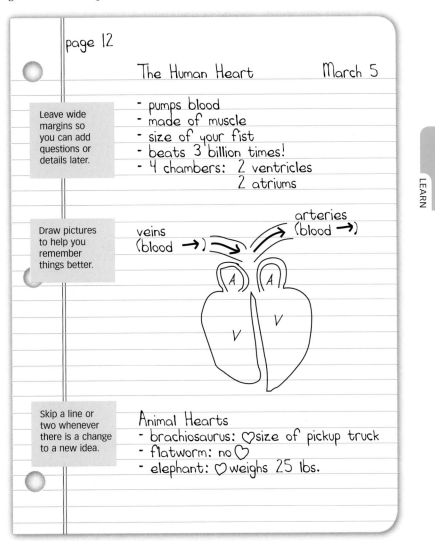

Leave wide margins so you can add questions or details later.

Draw pictures to help you remember things better.

Skip a line or two whenever there is a change to a new idea.

page 12

The Human Heart   March 5

- *pumps blood*
- *made of muscle*
- *size of your fist*
- *beats 3 billion times!*
- *4 chambers: 2 ventricles*
                        2 atriums

veins
(blood →)
arteries
(blood →)

Animal Hearts
- *brachiosaurus: ♡size of pickup truck*
- *flatworm: no ♡*
- *elephant: ♡weighs 25 lbs.*

LEARN

Setting Up Your Notes

Discuss the format of the sample notes and how the writer has applied the tips in the green boxes.

Suggest that students use just one side of the page for notes. This will give them room to add missing information, or to reorganize notes, or to rewrite messy notes.

To encourage students to date and order their notes, hold occasional **notebook checks** (*see below*).

Teaching Tip: Notebook Checks

To check that students are following the guidelines for note taking, give "open notebook" quizzes.

- Select a date and ask students to find that page in their notebooks.
- Then give them a short amount of time to write the topic of that day's notes.

- After selecting a couple of dates, review the topics with the class to see if they have written down similar topics.

Struggling Learners

Emphasize that
- notes need not be written in complete sentences (point out phrases in the sample),
- drawing pictures helps you remember concepts (point out how arrows in the sample drawing show blood flow to and from the heart),
- labeling parts (such as A for *atrium* and V for *ventricle*) eliminates the need for complex descriptions.

Reviewing Your Notes

To encourage students to look at their notes before test time, set aside time for reviewing notes. If it's not possible to do this each day, provide time at least once a week.

- As students review their notes, circulate among them to make suggestions and clarify any points.
- Encourage students to rewrite notes that are messy or visually confusing.
- You may also wish to provide students with sticky notes or tabs to flag questions that you cannot answer on the spot, either because it's not your subject area or because there is not enough time to look up the answer. Later, students can arrange to meet with you, another teacher, or other students to clarify notes.
- Students can also use sticky notes and flags to cross-reference their notes. This will make it even easier for them to find information in their texts and in their notes.

444

Reviewing Your Notes

Read over your notes at the end of each day.

- **Write any questions you have in the margins of your notes.** Talk over your questions with a classmate or your teacher.
- **Circle any words you don't understand.** Look up these words in a dictionary. Add the correct spelling and meaning to your notes.
- **Rewrite your notes if they are sloppy.** It's important to keep your notes organized and easy to read.
- **Cross-reference your notes.** Add the page numbers from your textbook that cover the same material to make reviewing easier.

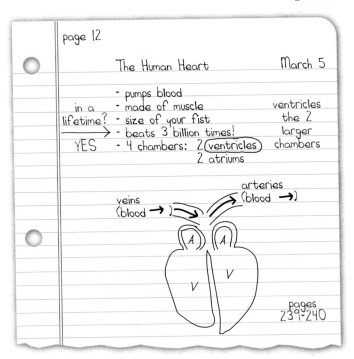

 Review your work. The next time you take notes, check them over using this page as a guide. Did you write any questions in the margins or circle any words?

Advanced Learners

Challenge students to use their notes from a class to write test questions. Screen the questions for duplicates and suitability. Then photocopy the questions and distribute a copy to students of all learning abilities.

- Have students work in small groups to use the questions to check their own notes.
- If possible, include a student from the test-writing group in each group. Direct the writer to read the questions aloud.
- As a question is read, each student should check his or her notes. If someone does not have the information needed to answer the question, encourage other students in the group to share the missing information.

LIST. remember *preview* **listen** organize **445**
Taking Notes

Taking Reading Notes

Taking notes can help you understand what you are reading. As you read, you can stop anytime to write something down. Here are some tips for taking reading notes.

1 Preview the assignment before reading it.

Read the title, introduction, headings, and chapter summaries. Look at any pictures, charts, or other graphics. Each of these can give important information about the reading.

2 Take notes as you read the material.

Read carefully and think about what you are reading. (Use page 443 as a guide to set up your notes.)

- **Write down each heading or subtopic.**
  Then write the most important facts for each heading.
- **Try to write your notes in your own words.**
  Don't just copy from the book.
- **Take notes on any important graphics.** This includes pictures, charts, or maps. Make your own drawings if you wish.
- **Read difficult or important material out loud.**
  This "talking" will help you understand and remember the information better.
- **List each word that is new to you.**
  Look up each word in a glossary or dictionary. Choose the meaning that fits and write that meaning in your notes.
- **Review your notes.** Look over your notes and write down any questions you have for your teacher.

3 Use graphic organizers whenever possible.

Use any of the helpful organizers on the next three pages for taking notes—a time line, a table organizer, and a Venn diagram.

TRYIT List three tips from this page that you could use the next time you take notes on your reading. Why did you choose these three tips?

LEARN

Taking Reading Notes

Underlining, highlighting, and writing comments in margins is the best way for students to interact with texts. However, if this is not possible, they can use sticky notes to flag ideas and write comments. Students can then return to the material to take their notes.

Urge students to use phrases, not complete sentences, as they take notes. This forces them to use their own words and to distill the most important points.

Have students check the **accuracy of their notes** *(see below)* by using them to write a summary.

Review and discuss each of the tips before asking students to complete the **Try It** activity.

 **Answers**

Answers will vary. Students should give thoughtful reasons for their selections.

Using a Time Line

Explain to students that a **time line** (*see below*) shows events in the order in which they happen. As you read aloud the sample time line, point out the title and have students notice that each event is listed in quick note form. Point out that most time lines don't have space for a lot of details.

Have students complete the **Try It** activity alone or with a partner. Provide photocopies of the reproducible time line (TE page 801). Emphasize that students should read through the paragraph at least once to determine how many events they should list. Then they can divide the time line accordingly.

 **Answers**

The Life of Madeleine L'Engle
1918—Born; grew up in New York City
1931—Moved to French Alps; attended boarding school
1945—<u>The Small Rain</u> published
1962—<u>A Wrinkle in Time</u> published
1963—<u>A Wrinkle in Time</u> wins Newbery Award
Present—Continues to write

446

Using a Time Line

Many types of writing are organized by time: first one thing happens and then another. Histories, biographies, and narratives are arranged in this way. When you want to keep track of the events you are reading about, you can use a **time line**.

Read the following short biography. Then look at the time line one student made to remember the details.

Shel Silverstein

The author, artist, and composer Shel Silverstein was born in 1930 in Chicago, Illinois. From an early age, he began to write. His first published work was a cartoon that appeared in 1950 in his college newspaper, *The Torch*. He went on to write classic books such as *The Giving Tree* (1963), *Where the Sidewalk Ends* (1974), *A Light in the Attic* (1982), and *Falling Up* (1996). He died in May of 1999.

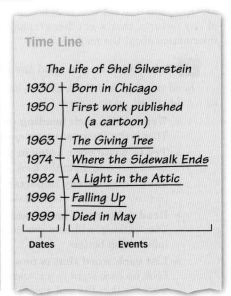

Time Line

The Life of Shel Silverstein
1930 — Born in Chicago
1950 — First work published (a cartoon)
1963 — The Giving Tree
1974 — Where the Sidewalk Ends
1982 — A Light in the Attic
1996 — Falling Up
1999 — Died in May

Dates   Events

 Read the following brief biography. Then create a time line that lists the important events.

1 Madeleine L'Engle was born on November 29, 1918, and
2 grew up in New York City. Her interest in writing began when
3 she was very young. In 1931, she and her parents moved to
4 the French Alps, where she attended a boarding school. She
5 published her first novel, *The Small Rain*, in 1945. Her best-
6 known work, *A Wrinkle in Time*, came out in 1962. It won the
7 Newbery Award in 1963. Madeleine has continued to write. She
8 has written more than 45 books.

Teaching Tip: Time Lines

Most time lines, especially those for histories and biographies, show events and the dates when they occurred, usually from the earliest to the most recent.

Not all time lines use dates, however. Time lines for stories and some other narratives often list events in the order in which they occurred but without dates or times. An example of a story time line is shown on PE page 293.

Some stories are written out of sequence. A time line is a helpful clarifying strategy for stories that have flashbacks. As students build a time line, remind them to leave spaces between events, so they can add any events that are mentioned out of order in the story.

Struggling Learners

To help students develop both the language (sequencing) and spatial organization skills needed to set up a time line, have them write each event on a separate sticky note. Students can then easily rearrange the notes to produce a "rough draft" that can be transposed into a time line.

Using a Table Organizer

Some types of writing are organized around main ideas. Each main idea is supported by details, the way a tabletop is supported by the legs. Essays, articles, feature stories, and textbook chapters are usually organized in this way.

Read the following short article. Then look at the **table organizer** to see how one student took notes on this reading.

Where Did English Come From?

The English language comes from many other languages. Many English words—such as *light, work,* and *good*—come from German. In fact, the word "English" was originally "Anglish," the language spoken by a German tribe called the Angles. Other English words come from French. Words like *courage, petite,* and *elephant* entered English when the French-speaking Normans invaded England. English also contains words from Latin and Greek. *Leopard* and *philosophy* are from these ancient languages.

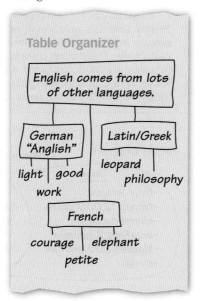

Table Organizer

English comes from lots of other languages.

German "Anglish" — light, good, work

Latin/Greek — leopard, philosophy

French — courage, elephant, petite

LEARN

 Read the following paragraph. Then take notes on it using a table organizer. Put the main idea in the top box (the tabletop). Under it, put supporting details (the table legs).

1 There are three major types of writing. The first type is
2 narrative writing. Narratives tell a story and focus on what happens
3 in a certain place and time. The second type is expository writing.
4 It gives information by presenting main ideas and supporting them
5 with details. The third type is persuasive writing. It presents an
6 opinion and reasons for the opinion. A student who learns all three
7 types will be ready for most writing challenges.

Using a Table Organizer

Read aloud the passage "Where Did English Come From?" Point out that the notes in the table organizer are in the writer's own words and record key ideas from the passage in shortened form. To help students see how the writer took the notes, ask them to match the notes in the table organizer to the actual words in the passage that express these key ideas.

As students do the **Try It** activity, remind them to use their own words and to put key ideas in shortened form. Suggest that students use the sample table as a model for placing the main idea, supporting details, and details that reinforce the supporting details.

 **Answers**

Wording will vary.

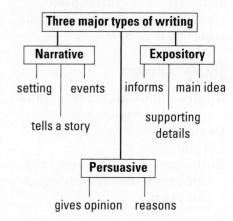

Three major types of writing

Narrative — setting, events, tells a story

Expository — informs, main idea, supporting details

Persuasive — gives opinion, reasons

Struggling Learners

Provide extra support for students who have a hard time understanding how table organizers work.

- Prepare cards with the **Try It** answers on them. Put one answer on each card.
- Then have a volunteer read aloud the paragraph.
- Guide students as they build a table organizer for the paragraph using the cards. Ask which card shows the main idea (the tabletop), which card is a supporting detail (a table leg), which card is a detail that describes or explains that supporting detail, and so on.
- Have students refer to the sample table organizer as a model.

Using a Venn Diagram

Although most students are probably familiar with Venn diagrams, review what the circles represent for those who need a refresher or who have never used or read a Venn diagram. Use the sample Venn diagram for dogs and cats or create your own, using two sports or two familiar games.

Read aloud the sample paragraph and discuss the Venn diagram. Point out the words in the paragraph that signal different categories or relationships *both, but, different*). Explain that writers often use words like these as clues to similarities and differences between topics.

Then have students complete the **Try It** activity independently or in small groups. Remind them to look for words that signal similarities and differences. Provide photocopies of the reproducible Venn diagram (TE page 802).

 Answers

Apples—thin skin, crunchy, white inside, dark brown seeds

Oranges—thick rind, juicy pulp, white seeds

Both—grow on trees, sweet, juice with important vitamins, enjoyable to eat

---

448

Using a Venn Diagram

In some reading assignments, two topics are compared. You can take notes on this type of material by using a **Venn diagram**. A Venn diagram is a pair of overlapping circles that shows similarities and differences between two things.

Dogs and Cats

Dogs and cats are both popular pets in the United States, but they are quite different. Early dogs were actually wolves 12,000 years ago, perhaps tamed as campsite pets. Early cats were wildcats 6,000 years ago, tamed to guard Egyptian grain supplies. Modern dogs come in all shapes and sizes, from a 2-pound Chihuahua to a 200-pound mastiff. Adult house cats weigh between 8 and 20 pounds. Since dogs came from wolves, they are social creatures. Cats came from solitary wildcats, so they are loners. Both creatures make good pets.

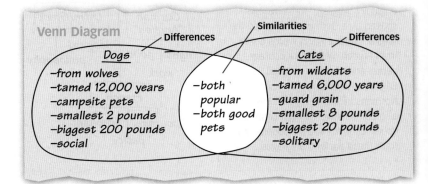

Venn Diagram

Differences — Similarities — Differences

Dogs
- from wolves
- tamed 12,000 years
- campsite pets
- smallest 2 pounds
- biggest 200 pounds
- social

both popular
both good pets

Cats
- from wildcats
- tamed 6,000 years
- guard grain
- smallest 8 pounds
- biggest 20 pounds
- solitary

 Read the following paragraph. Then make a Venn diagram of your own, noting the similarities and differences between apples and oranges.

1   People say you can't compare apples and oranges, but you
2 can. Both fruits grow on trees and are sweet. They both provide
3 juice that has important vitamins in it. But apples have a thin
4 skin, while oranges have a thick rind. Under the skin, an apple is
5 crunchy and white, and its seeds are dark brown. The inside of an
6 orange has juicy pulp with white seeds. So, even though people
7 may say you can't compare apples and oranges, you can—and you
8 can enjoy eating them afterward.

Completing Writing Assignments

Writing is many things. Writing is expressing your feelings, connecting with other people, and telling stories. But more than anything else, writing is thinking on paper. Each time you put pen to paper or fingers to the keyboard, you must think about what you want to say. This is why your teachers give you writing assignments. They want you to *think* about the subjects you are studying.

The first step is to understand your assignment. If you start writing before you know what you are supposed to do, you might as well take a walk and forget the dog! This chapter will help you complete writing assignments by starting you out on the right foot.

Mini Index

- **Understanding the Assignment**
- **Thinking Through Each Assignment**
- **Setting Up an Assignment Schedule**

Completing Writing Assignments

Objectives

- understand different types of writing assignments: open-ended, specific, and in between
- apply different levels of thinking to different writing assignments
- learn how to set up an assignment schedule

To engage students' interest in the topic and, at the same time, reinforce the concept that writing can be fun, have them write a new ending for the sentence in the introduction that begins this way:

If you start writing before you know what you are supposed to do, you might as well . . .

Encourage students to be creative and to have fun as they try to come up with a replacement for the original ending. Provide examples like these:

- . . . put on your coat without getting dressed.
- . . . make a sandwich and forget the bread.

Invite students to share their sentence endings with the class.

Understanding the Assignment

Discuss each type of writing assignment. Then have students complete the **Try It** activity.

 Answers

1. specific
2. open-ended
3. in between

Encourage students to use the checklist for all in-school and at-home writing assignments.

Point out that writing assignments can be presented as statements or as questions. Some students may find it easier to understand a prompt written as a statement by turning it into a question. Then they can answer the question. Have students practice this, using the three **Try It** assignments. (Sample responses: How does photosynthesis work? What is one place you will never forget? How is a cell phone different from other methods of communication?)

Go over the Assignment Checklist to make sure that students understand each step. Emphasize that if anything about an assignment is unclear, they can always ask questions.

Understanding the Assignment

Understanding the Assignment

Writing assignments come in all shapes and sizes, including the three types listed here.

Open-ended: Some writing assignments are open-ended. That means you get to select the topic. (*Recall a memorable experience in your life.*)

Specific: Other writing assignments are specific. They tell you exactly what to write about. (*Prove that the Battle of Gettysburg was a turning point in the Civil War.*)

In between: Still other assignments are somewhere in between. (*Compare Tom Sawyer to someone that you know well.*)

Try It Read the three assignments below. Then decide if each assignment is *open-ended, specific,* or somewhere *in between.*

1. *Explain how photosynthesis works.*
2. *Describe an unforgettable place.*
3. *Contrast the cell phone with another method of communication.*

Assignment Checklist

Before you begin any writing assignment, make sure that you understand everything about it. Use the following checklist as a guide.

_____ 1. **Ask** how your writing will be assessed or graded.

_____ 2. **Find out** how much time you have to finish your work.

_____ 3. **Schedule** a time and place to work on your assignment.

_____ 4. **Read** the directions carefully to make sure you understand them.

_____ 5. **Look for** key words—*recall, prove, compare*—so you know exactly what your writing should do.

English Language Learners

Students may need further help distinguishing among *open-ended, specific,* and *in-between* assignments. Make sure students understand exactly what each assignment asks by providing a few easier examples of each assignment type.

- open-ended: *Describe a friend of yours.*
- specific: *Explain how to sharpen a pencil.*
- in between: *Tell how this story is like another story you have enjoyed reading.*

recall *apply* UNDERSTAND
analyze synthesize evaluate **451**
Completing Writing Assignments

Thinking Through Each Assignment

Your writing assignments require you to think in different ways. These different levels of thinking include *recalling, understanding, applying, analyzing, synthesizing,* and *evaluating.* The chart below introduces the different levels, and the next six pages give you a closer look at each one.

Recalling means remembering information. Use this basic level of thinking when you are asked to . . .
- fill in the blanks
- define terms
- list facts or words
- label parts of something

Understanding means knowing what information means. Use understanding when you are asked to . . .
- explain something
- choose the best answer
- tell if something is true or false
- summarize something

Applying means using information. Use applying when you are asked to . . .
- follow directions
- solve a problem

Analyzing means breaking information down into different parts. Use analyzing when you are asked to . . .
- compare things
- divide things into groups
- give reasons for something
- tell why something is the way it is

Synthesizing means using information to create something new. Use synthesizing when you are asked to . . .
- create something
- add new ideas
- combine things
- predict something

Evaluating means using information to tell the value of something. Use this advanced level of thinking when you are asked to . . .
- assess something
- give your opinion of something

LEARN

Thinking Through Each Assignment

Ask students to give examples of the thinking required to complete current assignments.

- Then ask students which type of assignment they enjoy the most. Which type do they enjoy the least? The students in each class usually represent a range of preferred thinking styles, and they can grow more tolerant and respectful of each other when they realize that others think differently.
- Look for opportunities throughout the day when students can tell you what kind of thinking they are doing.

Recalling

Have students brainstorm a list of words that teachers often use in writing assignments that require recall. (Possible responses: choose, define, describe, discover, how much, locate, match, omit, select, what, when, where, which, who)

Choose a single topic for students to review for the **Try It** activity, to make it easier for classmates to compare and evaluate results. This is also a good opportunity for students to determine if they have been taking complete notes. If they find they have not been taking complete notes, provide them with a **note-taking chart** (*see below*).

 Answers

Answers will vary but should contain enough facts to show that students reviewed the material and understood the directions.

Recalling

When you *recall* information for an assignment, you are remembering what you have learned. To prepare for this type of thinking, listen carefully in class, read your assignments, and take careful notes.

You recall when you . . .

- write down facts, terms, and definitions.
- study the information until you can remember it.

The following test questions ask the student to recall information.

DIRECTIONS: Fill in the blanks below with the correct numbers.

1. Americans throw away __195 million__ tons of trash each year.

2. Almost __55 million__ tons of the total is packaging materials.

DIRECTIONS: Define each term by completing the sentence.

1. A *midden* is __what scientists call a pit where__ __Stone Age people threw their trash__ .

2. The three R's of trash reduction are __reduce__ , __reuse__ , and __recycle__ .

 Carefully review your notes about a topic that you are studying in class. After 10 minutes, put this information away. Then, on a clean sheet of paper, recall as many important facts as you can from your notes. Share your results with a classmate.

Teaching Tip: Note-Taking Chart

In order to take complete notes, some students may need help determining what kinds of information to note. Make a chart (*see below*) on paper positioned horizontally. Photocopy it for students to use the next time they are taking notes.

Note-Taking Chart

Topic: _____

Important Dates	Terms and Definitions	Facts and Numbers	Important People	Names of Places	Steps in a Process	Parts of a Thing

Struggling Learners

Structure the **Try It** activity with prompts based on students' topics. Refer to student notes and ask questions specific to their topics. (Possible prompts: Are there any important dates to remember? Name three facts about _____.)

recall *apply* **UNDERSTAND** synthesize *evaluate*
analyze

453

Completing Writing Assignments

Understanding

When you *understand* information, you know what it means. If you can rewrite information in your own words, then you clearly understand it.

You understand when you . . .

- explain something.
- tell how something works.
- summarize information.

The following question asks the student to show understanding, and the answer does that.

ASSIGNMENT: Explain the three R's of trash reduction.

The three R's of trash reduction are reduce, reuse, and recycle. Reduce means cutting the amount of trash you make. (This is sometimes called precycling.) Reuse means using things again instead of throwing them away. Recycle means using paper, glass, aluminum, and other things to make new products, instead of throwing them away. Using the three R's is a good way to help the environment because all three help reduce the amount of trash we make.

understand

Try It Write a paragraph explaining your understanding of one of the following topics: thunderstorms, tornadoes, or earthquakes.

LEARN

Understanding

Have students brainstorm a list of words that teachers often use in writing assignments that require understanding of an event or an idea. (Possible responses: compare, contrast, explain, interpret, demonstrate, state in your own words, tell what ___ means, give examples of____)

After students read the introductory information, discuss how the sample response shows understanding. Then have students do the **Try It** activity and evaluate each other's understanding of a topic in small groups.

Try It Answers

Paragraphs will vary, but students' explanations should contain enough details to show that they understand how a thunderstorm, a tornado, or an earthquake begins, as well as its force and effects.

English Language Learners

Students may find the writing prompts on PE pages 453–457 difficult. Focus on the concept of reading a prompt and then repeating it in one's own words. Begin by giving a simple prompt: *Describe the appearance of the moon when it is full.* Show students how to rephrase it: *Tell me what a full moon looks like.* Repeat with prompts of increasing difficulty, stressing how to "translate" each

key word: *Describe _____ = What's it like?* Have students create a list of "Meanings for Key Words" in their learning logs. Then, prior to the **Try It** activities on PE pages 453–457, have volunteers read aloud the prompt for each assignment and then rephrase it. *Explain your understanding of tornadoes* might become *What do I know about tornadoes?*

Struggling Learners

Successful completion of the **Try It** activity requires knowledge of the natural phenomena listed. You can provide alternative options by consulting with teachers in other curriculum areas or by asking students to list topics about which they have knowledge.

Applying

Point out that assignments that require this level of thinking often ask students to relate an idea or an event to their own lives. Write the following examples of this kind of prompt on the board, and have students identify the words that suggest applying is involved:

■ Create your version of a food pyramid that busy families can follow.

■ Explain how peer counseling might be put into practice in your school.

Read aloud the directions for the **Try It** activity, and ask students how they can tell this assignment requires applying. (It asks each student to relate the pollution problem to his or her life.)

 Answers

Journal entries will vary but should show how the pollution problem relates to individual students in practical, reasonable ways.

Applying

When you *apply* information, you use it. In order to apply something, you need to understand it completely.

You apply when you . . .

● use information to solve problems.
● follow directions to complete a task.

In this assignment, the writer applies information to her own life.

ASSIGNMENT: Make a trash-reduction plan for your family.

Family Trash-Reduction Plan

We can reduce trash by . . .

– not using paper plates or Styrofoam cups.
– shopping for products that have little or no packaging.

We can reuse by . . .

– taking grocery bags back to the store to use again.
– saving boxes and wrapping paper to use again.

We can recycle by . . .

– taking our newspapers, plastic and glass jars, and soft-drink cans to the recycling center.

apply

 Write a journal entry showing how the problem of pollution relates to some part of your life. Write for at least 5 to 8 minutes.

recall *apply* **UNDERSTAND** synthesize
analyze
455
Completing Writing Assignments

LEARN

Analyzing

When you *analyze* information, you break the information down into parts. There are many different ways to do this.

You analyze when you . . .

- tell how things are alike or different.
- tell which parts are most important.
- divide things into different groups.
- give reasons for something.

In this assignment, the writer analyzes what he knows.

ASSIGNMENT: In a paragraph, tell how a dump and a landfill are different.

A landfill and a dump are quite different. A dump is just a place where trash is put. Garbage is left out in the open, and it attracts animals that may get sick and spread disease. Chemicals in trash (such as paint and insect killer) can leak into the ground and pollute the water. Landfills were invented to prevent these problems. In a landfill, trash is covered with dirt right away to keep animals away. Landfills are also lined with clay and plastic to keep chemicals from leaking into the water supply.

analyze

 Classify (break down into groups) the different types of meals served in your cafeteria or the different types of homework you are assigned. Share the results of your work with a classmate.

Analyzing

Discuss the different ways teachers might word assignments for each of the four ways to analyze. Here are some examples:

- <u>Tell how things are alike or different</u>—compare and contrast . . . , describe similarities and differences between . . .
- <u>Tell which parts are most important</u>—examine the events that led to . . . , what are the three main sections of . . .
- <u>Divide things into different groups</u>—classify according to size and shape, distinguish between fact and opinion
- <u>Give reasons for something</u>— explain why the main character . . . , provide three arguments in favor of . . .

 Answers

Indicate ahead of time if you wish students to write their answers for the **Try It** activity as a list or a paragraph.

Answers (lists or paragraphs) will vary but should indicate that students understand the concept of grouping and why certain things are grouped together.

Synthesizing

Many students may be intimidated by the word *synthesizing*. Explain that, in simple terms, synthesizing means putting ideas together. When students synthesize, they may put together two or more ideas presented by an author; they may put together the ideas of two or more authors; or they may combine someone else's ideas with their own to figure out something or create something new.

Have students work independently or with a partner to complete the **Try It** activity.

 **Answers**

Answers will vary but should contain a mix of factual information and personal opinions and insights.

456

Synthesizing

When you *synthesize*, you create something new using information you have already learned.

You synthesize when you . . .

- add some new ideas to existing information.
- use information to make up a story or some other creative piece of writing.
- predict what may happen in the future because of this information.

In this assignment, the writer synthesizes a report using what she knows.

ASSIGNMENT: Write a title-down report about waste in America. Use the letters in the word "garbage" to begin each sentence.

Garbage is food waste, and trash is all other waste.

Americans make 195 million tons of trash a year.

Reducing, reusing, and recycling can cut down on trash.

Buying products with very little packaging is one good way to reduce trash.

All the packaging we throw away adds up to 55 million tons a year.

Garbage and trash take up a lot of room.

Everything we throw away adds to a mountain of trash somewhere.

synthesize

 Write your own title-down report using the letters from a topic you are studying in one of your classes *(erosion, Brazil, diagonal)*.

recall *apply* **UNDERSTAND**
analyze synthesize evaluate   **457**
Completing Writing Assignments

Evaluating

When you *evaluate*, you tell the value of something (how good or bad it is). Before you can evaluate something, you must know a lot about it.

You evaluate when you . . .

- tell your opinion about something.
- tell the good points and bad points about something.

In this assignment, the writer evaluates something.

ASSIGNMENT: Explain the good points and the bad points about landfills.

Landfills are much better than dumps. Landfills keep chemicals from polluting the water. Also, when a landfill is full, the land can be covered with dirt and reused. Two big airports, JFK in New York and Newark in New Jersey, are built on landfills. But landfills are not perfect. They take up a lot of space that is often needed for homes, schools, and other things. Even though all people need a place to put their trash, none want a landfill in their neighborhood. They don't want the added traffic, noise, or smell. Obviously, landfills are both good and bad at the same time.

evaluate

LEARN

 Write a paragraph that explains the good and the bad points of homework, summer school, or study halls.

Struggling Learners

Break down the **Try It** activity.

- First, have students freewrite about their chosen topics.
- Then have them organize the information on a photocopy of the reproducible T-chart (TE page 800) using the headings *Good Points* and *Bad Points*.

Evaluating

Ask students if they have ever said to someone, "That's a good idea, but . . ." Or, have they ever asked themselves, "Should I do this or shouldn't I?"

- Point out that if they have ever considered two sides of an argument before deciding which side to support, then they have practiced evaluating.
- Evaluating means looking closely at all the information you have about something. Then you may give an opinion.

Before students complete the **Try It** activity, emphasize that they should present both good and bad points.

 **Answers**

Answers will vary but should contain both good and bad points. Some students may include their opinion.

Setting Up an Assignment Schedule

Help students pace themselves for long-term writing assignments.

- When you give the assignment, provide a step-by-step plan for completing that assignment.
- Be sure to include the dates that you want ideas, first drafts, and final copies to be submitted.
- Have students write each of the target dates in their assignment books.

With continued guidance, praise, and support, students will be encouraged to develop good planning habits that will result in the successful completion of tasks.

The sample schedule is broken down into the five stages of the writing process. It also makes references to the six traits of writing and peer reviewing. If necessary, introduce or review these concepts now. (See "Using the Writing Process," which begins on PE page 5.)

458

Setting Up an Assignment Schedule

Your teacher may give you a schedule to follow for completing your writing assignments. If not, you can set up your own. Let's say that you have been asked to write a persuasive essay. You have two weeks to complete your work. Here's a possible schedule that you could follow.

Day	Week One	Day	Week Two
1	**PREWRITING:** • Review the assignment and assessment rubric. • Begin a topic search.	1	**REVISING:** • Revise the completed draft for ideas and organization.
2	**PREWRITING:** • Choose a writing topic. • Start gathering details.	2	**REVISING:** • Revise the draft for voice. • Ask a peer to review it.
3	**PREWRITING:** • Gather and organize details. • Find a focus for the writing.	3	**REVISING:** • Check for word choice and sentence fluency.
4	**WRITING:** • Begin the first draft.	4	**EDITING:** • Check the writing for conventions; then write and proofread the final copy.
5	**WRITING:** • Complete the first draft.	5	**PUBLISHING:** • Share the final copy.

 Change this schedule to fit your assignment. For example, if you have a week to do your work, you could focus on one step in the writing process per day.

Scheduling a Timed Writing

If you must complete a piece of writing in one class period (say 45 minutes), it is very important to plan your work. Try to set aside 5 to 10 minutes at the beginning of the period to plan your writing, 25 to 30 minutes for writing your first draft, and about 10 minutes at the end to make any necessary changes.

review study prepare plan **check** 459

Taking Classroom Tests

Just the mention of the word "test" may cause your palms to sweat and your heart to pound. These are perfectly normal feelings. Taking tests can be very stressful because your performance can mean so much. Tests do, after all, show how well you are learning. Fortunately, you can reduce this stress by preparing properly for each test.

Start by keeping up with your daily work. Pay attention in each class, take good notes, and complete each assignment. It's also important that you understand the test-taking process. You need to know how to study for and how to take different types of classroom tests. This chapter can help you do that.

Mini Index

- **Preparing for a Test**
- **Taking Objective Tests**
- **Taking Essay Tests**

Preparing for a Test

Students will internalize these lessons best if they are preparing for a test as they are studying this material. If you teach on a team, coordinate this lesson with a test that is to be given in another class.

One way for students to review and study for a test is to work with other students to create sample test questions. If a form of the question appears on the test, they will be better prepared to answer it. Tell students to

- use their notes and textbooks to get ideas for questions;
- focus on heads, subheads, and highlighted terms;
- keep in mind the types of questions certain teachers ask;
- write complete answers to the questions using class notes and textbooks.

After reading aloud the **Try It** directions, stress that students should try to answer each question as honestly as possible.

Try It Answers

1.–3. Answers will vary based on each student's honest assessment of test performance and preparation.

460

Preparing for a Test

Use the information that follows to prepare for each test you take.

1 Ask questions.

- Ask what information the test will cover. Will it cover textbook chapters, class notes, experiments, or other material?
- Ask what types of questions will be on the test. Will it include multiple-choice, true/false, fill-in-the-blanks, or essay questions?
- Find out if you can use your textbook or notes for the test. Sometimes essay tests are "open book" tests.

2 Review the material.

- Begin reviewing at least a few days before the test.
- Look over all the test material once. Then make a list of the information that is especially challenging or important. Focus most of your reviewing time on this material.
- Continue reviewing your notes until you feel that you really understand everything.

3 Study carefully.

- Use lists, note cards, or graphic organizers to help you study.
- Say the material out loud. First read from your notes or text. Then explain the information to yourself in your own words.
- Write out the most important information from memory. Afterward, check your notes to see how well you did.
- Picture the information in your mind.
- Study with someone else or explain the material to a friend.

 Write a paragraph about the hardest test you have taken this year or last year.

1. What information did the test cover, and what type of questions were on the test?
2. How did you study for the test, and how well did you do on it?
3. How would you study for this test if you took it again?

Test-Taking Tips

- **Listen carefully.** Listen as your teacher gives directions. Don't try to get a head start while your teacher is talking, or you may miss important comments such as . . .

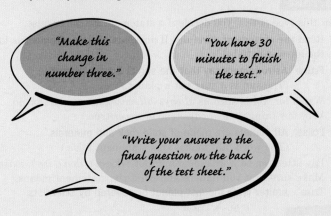

"Make this change in number three."

"You have 30 minutes to finish the test."

"Write your answer to the final question on the back of the test sheet."

- **Put your full name on the test right away.** Then you won't forget!

- **Take a quick look at the entire test.** This will help you decide how much time to spend on each question.

- **Begin the test.** Read the directions carefully before answering each set of questions. Do exactly what they tell you to do.

- **Read each question carefully.** Be sure you understand the question completely before answering it.

- **Answer the questions you are sure of first.** Then go back to the other questions and do your best to answer each one.

- **Check over your answers when you finish the test.** Do whatever double-checking you can in the time you have left.

LEARN

Test-Taking Tips

Encourage students to use the Test-Taking Tips as a checklist whenever they take a test. Provide practice with using the tips.

- Have students participate in a radio talk show, titled "Test-Taking Horrors," in which they share made-up accounts of what might happen when they ignore one of the test-taking tips during a test. Let students take turns being the talk-show host. Encourage them to have fun and, at the same time, help them realize how these tips, along with the guidelines on PE page 460, can help them do their best on a test.

- Use an overhead projector to go over a sample test. Work with students as they use each of the tips. Additionally, use simpler sample tests to provide extra support prior to the exercises on PE pages 462–464, or have students work with trusted partners to complete the exercises together.

Taking Objective Tests

Invite volunteers to make up one true statement and two false ones about a topic they are studying. Tell them to use the true/false statements here as a model. Have volunteers read aloud their statements. Then ask the class to identify the true and false statements.

Point out that in a matching test, words, places, and people are often mixed together. Tell students to be sure that they match the same types of items together.

Clarify any questions students have about these kinds of tests before they do the **Try It** activity.

Try It Answers

1. Sample answer: You have to make sure that no part of the statement is false. You have to watch for words that say something is <u>always</u> or <u>never</u> true. You also have to understand what the statement means.

2. Sample answer: The best way to answer matching questions is to match the items you know for sure first. Cross out each answer as you use it. Then go back and match the rest by a process of elimination.

462

Taking Objective Tests

There are four basic types of questions on objective tests: true/false, matching, multiple-choice, and fill-in-the-blanks.

True/False

For this type of test, you decide if a statement is true or false.

- Read the statement carefully. If any part of the statement is false, the answer is "false."

  False **Astronomers say that the sun is a giant planet.**
  (The sun is a star, not a planet.)

- Watch for words such as *always, all, every, never, none,* or *no.* Very few things are *always* true or *never* true.

  False **All planets are made of solid rock and minerals.**
  (The word "all" makes this statement false.)

- Pay attention to words meaning "not": *doesn't, don't, isn't, wasn't.* Make sure that you understand what the statement means.

  True **Jupiter isn't the last planet discovered by scientists.**

Matching

Matching consists of connecting an item in one list to an item in another.

- Read both lists before beginning. Match the items you are sure of first. Then match the more difficult items using the process of elimination. Cross out each answer after you've used it.

<u>C</u>	1. **A violent windstorm accompanied by a funnel-shaped cloud**	A. **Blizzard**
<u>A</u>	2. **A severe snowstorm with cold winds**	B. **Hurricane**
<u>B</u>	3. **A tropical storm with winds of 74 miles per hour or greater**	C. **Tornado**

- Watch for items in each list that are very close in meaning since they may be the most difficult to match correctly.

Try It On your own paper, answer each of the following questions. Write at least three sentences for each answer.

1. Why can true/false questions be difficult to answer?
2. What is the best way to answer matching questions?

review study prepare plan **check** **463**
Classroom Tests

Multiple-Choice

A multiple-choice question gives you several possible answers to choose from. Follow the tips below.

- Read the directions carefully. There is usually only one correct answer, but sometimes you may have to mark more than one.

  1. Which of the following places are located in the United States?
  - Ⓐ. Utah
  - Ⓒ New Mexico
  - B. Manitoba
  - D. Jamaica

- Look for words like *except, never,* and *unless*.

  2. These forms of government have never been used in the United States except
  - A. a monarchy
  - C. a dictatorship
  - B. a theocracy
  - Ⓓ a democracy

- Questions that include possible answers like "Both A and B" or "None of the above" can be hard to answer, so read carefully.

  3. Which states joined the Union during the 1800s?
  - A. Pennsylvania
  - D. Minnesota
  - B. Nevada
  - Ⓔ Both B and D
  - C. Alaska
  - F. None of the above

(Narrow your choices by eliminating answers you know are incorrect and then focus on the remaining answers.)

Fill-in-the-Blanks

A fill-in-the-blanks test is made up of sentences with some words left out. You have to fill in the missing words.

- Each blank usually stands for one missing word. If there are three blanks, you will have to write in three words.

  1. The three largest wild animals in the United States are ___elk___, ___bison___, **and** ___moose___.

- Look for clues in the sentence. For example, if the word before a blank is *an*, the word you have to fill in will begin with a vowel.

  2. A burrowing mammal with body armor is called an _armadillo_.

 On your paper, explain which type of question you think can be more difficult to answer: multiple-choice or fill-in-the-blank. Why?

LEARN

Stress that the test-taking tips given here are not likely to help students if they have not studied for a test. Sometimes, however, the wording of a question can be confusing, even when students have studied. Then these tips can increase their chances of getting the correct answer.

Read aloud the tip in parentheses in the middle of the page. Explain to students that even if they don't know the correct answer, they can increase their chances of finding it by eliminating the answers they know are not correct.

Explain to students that the blank spaces on a fill-in-the-blanks test are not the same length as the missing word.

Tell students to draw on their own past test-taking experiences to complete the **Try It** activity.

 **Answers**

Possible answers: Some students may say multiple-choice questions are more difficult because of the distractors. Some students may say fill-in-the-blank questions are more difficult because they, the students, have to think up the answer on their own.

Taking Essay Tests

Focus students' attention on the second sentence in the introduction. This explains in a nutshell how to take an essay test.

1 Understand the Question

Before assigning the **Try It** activity, encourage students to become more familiar with the key words and explanations. Tell students to cover the key words with a sticky note or their hand and then try to remember the key word for each explanation. Next, have them cover the explanations and have them give the explanations for each key word.

 Answers

1. *Summarize;* tell the key points about the building of the Central Pacific Railroad
2. *Describe;* use sensory details to tell how a volcanic eruption looks, sounds, and feels
3. *Explain;* show how to find the least common denominator using an example
4. *Prove;* use facts to show that recycling really does make a difference to the environment

---

464

Taking Essay Tests

Answering an essay-test question is like writing an essay. You must understand what you have to do, organize your thoughts, write the essay, and check your work. The biggest difference is that you have a limited amount of time to complete your writing on a test. The information below and on pages 465–467 will help you write effective essay-test answers.

1 Understand the Question

- Read the question very carefully.
- Identify the key word that explains what you have to do. Here are some key words and an explanation of what each asks you to do.

Compare . . .	tell how things are alike.
Contrast . . .	tell how things are different.
Define . . .	give a clear, specific meaning of a term or an object.
Describe . . .	tell how something looks, sounds, and feels.
Diagram . . .	explain using lines, a web, or another graphic organizer.
Evaluate . . .	give your opinion about the value of a topic.
Explain . . .	tell what something means or how something works.
Identify . . .	answer the 5 W's and H about a topic.
Illustrate . . .	show how something works by using examples.
Prove . . .	present facts that show something is true.
Review . . .	give an overall picture of a topic.
Summarize . . .	tell just the key information about a topic.

 For each of the following essay-test questions, write the key word and explain what you need to do for each.

1. Summarize how the Central Pacific Railroad was built.
2. Describe a volcanic eruption.
3. Explain how to find the least common denominator.
4. Prove that recycling plastic and glass really makes a difference.

Advanced Learners

Challenge students to write an example of an essay test question for each key word. (Example for contrast: How does Cinderella differ from her stepsisters?) Then have students create a matching exercise by listing the key words in one column and the examples (out of order) in another.

To reinforce key-word definitions, invite the entire class to complete the matching exercises created by students.

review study prepare plan check **465**
Classroom Tests

2 Plan Your Answer

- Carefully study the question. Make sure that you understand the meaning of the key word.
- Write a topic sentence or a focus statement for your answer.
- Collect important supporting details. (You may be allowed to use your book or class notes.)
- Consider using a list, an outline, or a graphic organizer to organize the details. (See pages 446–448.)
- Double-check to make sure that your ideas answer the question.

Social Studies Test. Chapter 23

Summarize how the Central Pacific Railroad was built.

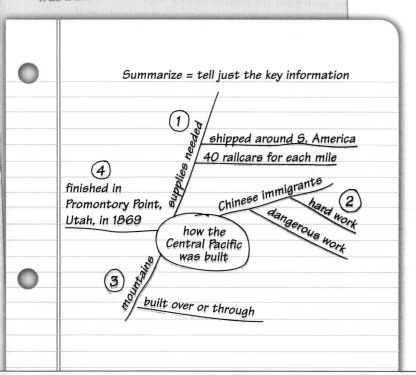

LEARN

2 Plan Your Answer

Students may need help formulating a topic sentence. Remind students that a topic sentence tells the main idea of a paragraph. All the other sentences in the paragraph support the main idea in the topic sentence.

Suggest that students try the following strategies to create a topic sentence for an essay question:

- Underline the important words in the question.
- Turn the question into a topic sentence, being sure to use the underlined words.

Have them practice using this technique to write a topic sentence for the sample. (The Central Pacific Railroad was built in the following way.) Point out that they can always go back later and revise their topic sentence, but this technique will help them get started and stay focused. For additional practice, have students create topic sentences for the other essay questions in the **Try It** activity on the bottom of PE page 464.

✱ For more information about writing topic sentences, see PE pages 552–553.

3. Write a One-Paragraph Answer

Have students read the sample and analyze how the writer incorporated details from the prewriting sample on PE page 465 into the paragraph.

Have students brainstorm a list of stories before having them do the **Try It** activity. Suggest that students use a Venn diagram to explore similarities and differences between themselves and the story character they choose. Provide photocopies of the reproducible Venn diagram (TE page 802). Remind students to use signals words such as *like, similar, different,* and *unlike* in their paragraph to show comparisons.

 Answers

Paragraphs will vary but should show how the writer and the story character are alike and different. Paragraphs should contain a topic sentence with supporting details that have been explored during planning.

466

3. Write a One-Paragraph Answer

In a one-paragraph answer, remember to begin with your topic sentence and follow with the supporting details you have collected. Make sure to use your plan as a general writing guide.

> Social Studies Test. Chapter 23
>
> Summarize how the Central Pacific Railroad was built.
>
> The Central Pacific Railroad was built with a lot of hard work. First, supplies such as timber, metal rails, spikes, and even locomotives had to be sent from the East Coast by ship. The ships had to sail all the way around the southern tip of South America to get to California. That's where the Chinese immigrant workers began the Central Pacific Railroad. The workers used shovels, pickaxes, dynamite, and their bare hands to build the railroad. For each mile of track the workers laid, they used 40 railcars full of supplies. When the workers came to a mountain, they either laid track over it or dug a tunnel through it. Many of the immigrant workers died in explosions or other accidents during this project. The work was finished when the railroad reached Promontory Point, Utah, in 1869.

 Plan and write a one-paragraph answer to the following essay-test question:

> Compare yourself to a main character in a story you have recently read.

English Language Learners

Students may find the one-paragraph answer extremely challenging. Pair them with a trusted, language-proficient partner.

- Have partners work together to analyze the essay prompt, using key words to determine the focus and goal of the paragraph. Encourage students to rephrase the prompt in their own words. *Compare yourself to a main character* might become *How*

am I and a story character the same and how are we different?

- Partners can also work together to brainstorm effective topic sentences.
- Then have partners work independently to flesh out their paragraphs.
- After the activity, review the completed paragraphs and provide one-on-one feedback.

review study prepare plan check

467

Classroom Tests

4 Write an Essay Answer

Sometimes you will need to write an answer in the form of an essay. For example, the question below cannot be answered in one paragraph. You may use a graphic organizer such as a time line, a table organizer, or a Venn diagram to plan your essay answer.

The Union Pacific Railroad had an easier route but still faced many challenges. The company

Social Studies Test. Chapter 23

Summarize how the transcontinental railroad was built by the Central Pacific and Union Pacific Railroad Companies.

The transcontinental railroad was built by two different companies. The Central Pacific Railroad Company worked from Sacramento, California, and went east through the mountains. The Union Pacific Railroad Company went west from Omaha, Nebraska, across the plains. Both companies faced tough challenges along the way.

The Central Pacific Railroad had many challenges. First, supplies such as timber, metal rails, and even locomotives had to be sent from the East Coast by ship. The ships had to sail all the way around South America to get to California. That's where Chinese immigrants began building the Central Pacific Railroad. Using pickaxes, dynamite, and their bare hands, workers built the railroad. For each mile of track laid, they used 40 railcars full of supplies. When the workers came to a mountain, they either laid track over it or dug a tunnel through it.

LEARN

4 Write an Essay Answer

Point out to students that they can conclude their essays with a sentence that summarizes and restates the main idea, which was presented in the topic sentence using key words. Refer students to PE page 39. Then have them work together to create a closing sentence for the sample paragraph on PE page 466 and for the sample essay on this page. (Possible closing for the paragraph: After lots of hard work and many difficulties, the Central Pacific Railroad was finally completed. Possible closing for the essay: Together, and in spite of many challenges, the Central Pacific Railroad Company and the Union Pacific Railroad Company had built the transcontinental railroad.)

Be sure students understand the criteria you and other teachers will use to grade their essay answers. This will help them prepare for future essay tests. The following rubrics can be used:

- Narrative Writing, PE pages 130–131
- Expository Writing, PE pages 194–195
- Persuasive Writing, PE pages 256–257
- Response to Literature, PE pages 318–319

468

agree
vary

The Basic Elements of Writing

CONNECT
organize
model

469

Working with Words

Writing is like cooking. You have eight basic ingredients, called the parts of speech. Take a cupful of specific nouns and add a tablespoon of colorful adjectives. Then blend in a pint of action verbs, seasoned with adverbs. Finally, mix in the pronouns, interjections, prepositions, and conjunctions, and you'll be cooking with words!

Specific *nouns* will help you write clearly, and *pronouns* will help you write smoothly. Action *verbs* will add drama to whatever you are writing, and *conjunctions* will help by connecting the words in your writing.

Besides some basic information about each part of speech, this section answers the question, "How can I use words effectively in my own writing?"

Mini Index

- **Using Nouns**
- **Using Pronouns**
- **Choosing Verbs**
- **Describing with Adjectives**
- **Describing with Adverbs**
- **Connecting with Prepositions**
- **Connecting with Conjunctions**

Using Nouns

A noun is a word that names a person, a place, a thing, or an idea in your writing. (See page 702.)

PERSON	actor, Denzel Washington, students, President Adams
PLACE	state, Arizona, kitchen, San Diego, middle school
THING	bird, Baltimore oriole, books, clock
IDEA	holiday, Veterans Day, courage, thought

 On your own paper, rewrite the sentences below by filling in each blank with the type of noun shown.

1. _____ *(a place)* _____ has spectacular fall colors.
2. The park contains hundreds of _____ *(things)* _____.
3. _____ *(a person)* _____ can spot wildlife throughout the park.
4. The destruction of wilderness areas may lead to the _____ *(an idea)* _____ of certain animals.

Concrete, Abstract, and Collective Nouns

Concrete nouns name things that can be seen or touched.
Abstract nouns name things that you can think about but cannot see or touch.

Concrete	clown	valentine	school	heart
Abstract	happiness	February	education	love

 Write four concrete nouns and four related abstract nouns. For example, a *heart* (concrete) is a symbol of *love* (abstract).

Collective nouns name a collection of persons, animals, or things.

Persons	class	family	jury	audience	committee
Animals	herd	flock	pack	school	pod

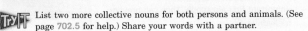 List two more collective nouns for both persons and animals. (See page 702.5 for help.) Share your words with a partner.

Proper and Common Nouns

You can use a **proper noun** in your writing to name a specific person, place, thing, or idea. Proper nouns are always capitalized. A **common noun** is any noun that is not a proper noun.

Common	ranger	park	pet	holiday
Proper	Tom	Yosemite	Fido	Labor Day

Common **The** club visited the national park **last** weekend.

Proper **The** Dyer Biking Club **visited** Yosemite National Park **last** Saturday.

 Make a chart like the one above. Add your own common and proper nouns (four of each). Be sure to capitalize the proper nouns.

General and Specific Nouns

When you use **specific nouns** in your writing, you give the reader a clear picture of people, places, things, and ideas. The following chart shows the difference between **general nouns** and specific nouns.

General	actress	stadium	pants	emotion
Specific	Julia Roberts	Wrigley Field	blue jeans	happiness

 Read each pair of sentences below. Then, on your own paper, copy the sentence from each pair that uses nouns that are more specific.

1. The boy climbed the hill. Jamal climbed Prescot Hill.
2. Climbers like steep rock walls. People like challenges.
3. The girl scraped her leg. Josie scraped her knee and shin.
4. Look at that panorama of the Rocky Mountains. Look at that view.

 Rewrite the following sentences using more specific nouns in place of general nouns.

1. The student biked to a recreational area.
2. The girl painted a piece of art.
3. The storm blew things around the place.
4. The animal lapped up the liquid.

Answers

 Possible answers:
1. Marengo Park
2. ducks
3. A visitor
4. extinction

1. weeping willow, sadness
2. eagle, freedom
3. dove, peace
4. web, mystery

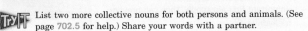
persons   band, crew
animals   pride, litter

Answers

 Possible answers:

common nouns	mother	school	building	nationality
proper nouns	Pauline	Salem School	Fox River Bank	Pakistani

 Answers:
1. Jamal climbed Prescot Hill.
2. Climbers like steep rock walls.
3. Josie scraped her knee and shin.
4. Look at that panorama of the Rocky Mountains.

 Possible answers:
1. Margie biked to Fairy Chasm Park.
2. Annie painted her sculpture.
3. The tornado blew pieces of houses around Centerville.
4. The tomcat lapped up the warm milk.

472–473 The Basic Elements of Writing

472

vary modify *compare* CONNECT
choose
Working with Words **473**

BASIC ELEMENTS

What can I do with nouns in my writing?

Identify People, Places, Things, and Ideas

You use nouns to identify the people, places, things, and ideas you are talking about in your writing. You can add variety to your writing by using these different types of nouns as subjects.

Yosemite National Park **is amazing.** *(a place)*

Ansel Adams **took many photographs in Yosemite.** *(a person)*

His pictures **captured** images **in black and white.** *(things)*

In the park, breathtaking beauty **surrounds you.** *(an idea)*

 Find the subject in each of the following sentences. Is it a person, a place, a thing, or an idea?

    1. In 1890, John Muir helped establish Yosemite National Park.

      1. John Muir, person

    2. Muir wrote many magazine stories about the park's beauty.

    3. The Sierra Club lists Muir as one of its founders.

    4. His love of nature turned into a photography career.

Rename the Subject

A predicate noun follows a "be" verb *(is, are, was, were, will be)* and renames the subject of the sentence. Predicate nouns are useful for making simple, natural comparisons.

My favorite vacation **is a** visit **to the mountains.**

(The predicate noun "visit" renames the subject "vacation.")

 Write a sentence for each of the subjects and predicate nouns below using a "be" verb.

SUBJECT	PREDICATE NOUN
1. mountain hike	experience
1. A mountain hike is an invigorating experience.	
2. walking and climbing	activities
3. fresh air	medicine
4. eagles and deer	companions

Complete the Action of the Verb

Readers may ask questions like *who?* and *what?* after many action verbs. You can use concise nouns to answer these questions and complete the action of the verb.

Campers must plan. (*What* must they plan?)

Yosemite offers an overnight permit. (*Who* gets a permit?)

See how the nouns below—*trips* and *visitors*—answer the questions *what?* or *who?* and complete the action of the verb.

Campers must plan overnight trips. (This answers *what?*)

Yosemite offers overnight visitors **a permit.** (This answers *who?*)

Nouns that answer the question *what?* after a verb are called **direct objects.** Nouns that answer the question *who?* after a verb that has a direct object are called **indirect objects.** (See 692.4–692.5.)

 Number your paper from 1 to 4. Write a noun that answers each *what* and *who* question in the sentences below.

    1. Long-distance hikers need good ___*(what?)*___ for their feet.

    2. The wilderness offers ___*(who?)*___ sightings of rare birds.

    3. Hikers can find ___*(what?)*___ growing along the trail.

    4. Maps give ___*(who?)*___ specific trail information.

Add Specific Information

Prepositional phrases add information to your sentences. Using a specific noun as the **object of a preposition** makes your writing clearer. (See 742.1.) Notice how all of the nouns highlighted below add details to the passage.

A first-aid kit offers hikers medical supplies for minor problems like blisters. A new product, called "second skin," provides moist treatment for blisters and other wounds. Salt packets are also an important first-aid supply. They can prevent dehydration.

SUBJECT	
DIRECT OBJECT	
INDIRECT OBJECT	
PREDICATE NOUN	
OBJECT OF PREPOSITION	

Answers

 Answers:
    2. Muir, person
    3. Sierra Club, thing
    4. love, idea

 Possible answers:
    2. Walking and climbing are healthful activities.
    3. Fresh air is the best medicine.
    4. Eagles and deer are a hiker's companions.

Answers

 Possible answers:
    1. boots
    2. visitors
    3. wildflowers
    4. hikers

Using Pronouns

A pronoun is a word used in place of a noun. The noun replaced, or referred to, by the pronoun is called the pronoun's **antecedent**. The arrows below point to each pronoun's antecedent. (Also see 706.1.)

Edgar Allan Poe rented a home in Philadelphia, and it is now a national historical site.

Amanda read a Poe story before she visited the site.

The personal pronouns listed below are used as subjects and objects. (For a complete list of personal pronouns, see page 710.)

PERSONAL PRONOUNS						
I	you	he	she	it	we	they
me		him	her		us	them

Person and Number of a Pronoun

Pronouns show "person" and "number" in writing. The following chart shows which pronouns are used for the three different persons *(first, second, third)* and the two different numbers *(singular or plural)*. (See 712.1-712.4.)

		Singular	Plural
FIRST PERSON	(The person speaking)	I call.	We call.
SECOND PERSON	(The person spoken to)	You call.	You call.
THIRD PERSON	(The person or thing spoken about)	He calls. It calls.	They call.

 Number your paper from 2 to 5. Write sentences that use the pronouns described below as subjects.

1. first-person singular pronoun
   1. I want to visit the White House.
2. third-person singular pronoun
3. third-person plural pronoun
4. second-person singular pronoun
5. first-person plural pronoun

Indefinite Pronouns

An indefinite pronoun refers to people or things that are not named or known. The chart below lists which indefinite pronouns are singular, which are plural, and which can be singular or plural.

INDEFINITE PRONOUNS				Plural	Singular or Plural
Singular					
another	either	nobody	someone	both	all
anybody	everybody	no one	something	few	any
anyone	everyone	nothing		many	most
anything	everything	one		several	none
each	neither	somebody			

When you use indefinite pronouns as subjects, the verbs and other pronouns used in the sentence must agree with the subject in number.

Singular
Everybody **needs to take** his or her **notebook on the field trip.**

Plural
Several **of the boys took notes on** their **trip to Lincoln's birthplace.**

Singular or Plural
Most **of the information is printed on handouts.** (singular)
Most **of the students are working on** their **research papers.** (plural)

 Number your paper from 1 to 5. Choose the correct pronoun to complete each of the following sentences.

1. Many of the boys will write about *(his, their)* favorite heroes.
2. Everyone posts *(his or her, their)* report on the school Web page.
3. All of the students will send *(his or her, their)* reports to the paper.
4. Someone named Leah sent *(their, her)* comments to the editor.
5. Both of my friends read *(his or her, their)* reports aloud.

If using *his or her* is clumsy, try changing the singular pronoun to a plural pronoun. For example, the first sample sentence above could be rewritten like this: **All** *of the students need to take* **their** *notebooks on the field trip.*

BASIC ELEMENTS

Answers

 Answers to item 2 will use one of the pronouns listed. Possible answers are provided.

2. he, she, it; She ran along the beach.
3. they; They found some seashells.
4. you; Did you find a sand dollar, Holly?
5. We all got thirsty in the hot sun.

Answers

1. their
2. his or her
3. their
4. her
5. their

How can I produce better writing with pronouns?

Avoid Repeating Nouns

You can use pronouns in your writing to avoid repeating the same nouns over and over again. (See pages 706–714.) Read the sample paragraph below. How many times did the writer use "Mary Pickersgill"?

WITHOUT PRONOUNS

> **Mary Pickersgill, a famous flag maker, is the subject of today's lesson. Mary Pickersgill made the flag that inspired "The Star-Spangled Banner." During the War of 1812, Mary Pickersgill made the flag that flew over Fort McHenry. The flag, which Mary Pickersgill's family helped Mary Pickersgill make, measured 30 feet by 42 feet.**

Now read the revised sample below. The writer has replaced some of the nouns with pronouns. Which pronouns refer to Mary Pickersgill?

WITH PRONOUNS

> Mary Pickersgill, a famous flag maker, is the subject of today's lesson. She made the flag that inspired "The Star-Spangled Banner." During the War of 1812, she made the flag that flew over Fort McHenry. The flag, which her family helped her make, measured 30 feet by 42 feet.

 Read the following paragraph. On your own paper, rewrite the paragraph changing some of the underlined nouns to pronouns so that the paragraph reads more smoothly.

(1) Mary Pickersgill learned flag making from **(2)** Mary Pickersgill's mother, Rebecca Flower. **(3)** Mary Pickersgill and Mary Pickersgill's mother worked together to create the huge flag that flew over Fort McHenry during the Battle of Baltimore. This was **(4)** Mary Pickersgill's most famous flag. Francis Scott Key wrote a poem about the flag. **(5)** Francis Scott Key's poem became "The Star-Spangled Banner," the national anthem of the United States.

Improve Sentence Flow

Pronouns can be used to help the reader move easily from one sentence to the next. In the following paragraph, notice how the pronouns (in blue) improve the flow of the sentences. The arrows point to the antecedents (the words the pronouns replace).

Our class went on a field trip. We toured the two-story brick Star-Spangled Banner Flag House in Baltimore, Maryland. It was the home of Mary Pickersgill. In 1807, she moved there with her mother and daughter. Later, they helped Mary sew the 30- by 42-foot flag that inspired "The Star-Spangled Banner." It was Mary's most famous flag. She earned her living making flags to be flown from the masts of ships. Our class wants to visit this site again.

 Number your paper from 2 to 6. Add pronouns from the list below to help improve the sentence flow. (You may use some pronouns more than once.) Then write the antecedent for each pronoun.

it	you	we	them	they	us

1. pronoun: They *antecedent:* landmarks

The students in my class studied national historic landmarks. **(1)** _____ represent the history of the United States in a very important way. **(2)** _____ discovered that landmarks are special buildings, sites, and structures, including Mount Vernon, Pearl Harbor, and Alcatraz. Becoming a national historic landmark is a long process. **(3)** _____ starts with filling out lots of forms and ends when the secretary of the interior gives approval. There are thousands of historic places in America. Only about 2,500 of **(4)** _____ are national historic landmarks. The Flag House in Baltimore, Maryland, is one of **(5)** _____. **(6)** _____ became a national historic landmark in 1969.

Answers

 Possible answers:
1. no change
2. her
3. Mary and her
4. no change
5. His

Answers

 2. We, students
3. It, process
4. them, thousands
5. them, historic landmarks
6. It, Flag House

Working with Words **478–479**

478

479

vary modify CONNECT
choose

Working with Words

BASIC ELEMENTS

How can I use pronouns properly?

Avoid Agreement Problems

You can make your writing clearer by using pronouns properly. You must use pronouns that agree with their antecedents. (An antecedent is the noun or pronoun that a pronoun replaces or refers to. See 474 and 706.1.) Pronouns must agree with their antecedents in number, person, and gender.

The Henry Ford Museum and Greenfield Village are known for their historic importance.

Henry Ford is best known for his automobiles.

Agreement in Number

The **number** of a pronoun is either singular or plural. The pronoun must match the antecedent in number.

■ A singular pronoun refers to a singular antecedent.

Henry Ford invented his own self-propelled vehicle—the quadricycle.

■ A plural pronoun refers to a plural antecedent.

The Ford children grew up on their family's farm in Dearborn, Michigan.

 Number your paper from 2 to 4 and write the correct pronoun for each sentence. Then write the antecedent each pronoun refers to.

1. Henry Ford changed the world when (he, they) built assembly-line automobiles.
   1. he, Henry Ford
2. So that people could learn more about (his or her, their) nation's history, Henry Ford also built a museum.
3. The chair Abraham Lincoln sat in at the time of (their, his) assassination is at the Henry Ford Museum.
4. The bus on which Rosa Parks refused to give up (their, her) seat is also on exhibit.

Agreement in Gender

The **gender** of a pronoun (her, his, its) must be the same as the gender of its antecedent. Singular pronouns can be feminine (female), masculine (male), or neuter (neither male nor female).

The Henry Ford Museum got its name in honor of Henry Ford.

Manuel went to Greenfield Village with his family.

 Number your paper from 1 to 5. Correct each underlined pronoun so that it agrees with its antecedent in gender.

1   Manuel enjoyed her visit to Greenfield Village. He liked
2 his old buildings and the people in historical costumes. Manuel
3 visited Henry Ford's childhood home, and she saw a model of
4 the factory where Mr. Ford made its first automobile. At the
5 end of the tour, she even took a ride in a Model-T car.

Shift in Person

When you use pronouns, you must choose either first-, second-, or third-person pronouns. Using more than one "person" to express an idea, may cause an error called a pronoun shift.

Pronoun shift: If Jerry and I want to see whales, you must be patient.
Correct: If Jerry and I want to see whales, we must be patient.

 In the sentences below, change each underlined pronoun so that it doesn't cause a shift in person. Use all first-person pronouns. (See the chart on page 714.)

1. My friend Jerry and I live near the ocean where you sometimes see whales.
2. When we know whales are migrating, you set up a telescope.
3. We wait and wait, watching through your telescope.
4. When we come home, Dad asks if they have seen any whales.

Answers

2. their, people
3. his, Abraham Lincoln
4. her, Rosa Parks

Answers

1. his
2. its
3. he
4. his
5. he

1. we
2. we
3. our
4. we

Choosing Verbs

Writers must constantly make choices, and one of their most important choices is which verb to use to express their thoughts clearly.

Action Verbs

An **action verb** tells what the subject is doing. Action verbs help bring writing to life. (Also see 718.1.)

During World War II, many women worked in wartime industries.

They built tanks and tested airplanes to help win the war.

Linking Verbs

A **linking verb** connects (links) a subject to a noun or an adjective in the predicate. (Also see 718.2.)

COMMON LINKING VERBS	
Forms of "be"	be, is, are, was, were, am, been, being
Other linking verbs	appear, become, feel, grow, look, remain, seem, smell, sound, taste

Rosie the Riveter was an imaginary character.
(The linking verb "was" connects the subject "Rosie the Riveter" to the noun "character." "Character" is a *predicate noun*.)

She became popular during World War II.
(The linking verb "became" connects the subject "she" to the adjective "popular." "Popular" is a *predicate adjective*.)

 For each sentence below, write the linking verb and the predicate noun or predicate adjective. (One sentence has three predicate nouns.)

1. "Rosie Riveters" were women who got jobs during World War II.
   1. *Linking verb: were predicate noun: women*

2. These women were skilled in a number of ways.

3. They became riveters, welders, and shipbuilders.

4. A park in Richmond, California, is a memorial to these women.

5. Richmond was home to four shipyards where the "Rosies" worked.

Irregular Verbs

Verbs in the English language can be either *regular* or *irregular*.

REGULAR VERBS

Most verbs in the English language are regular. A writer adds *ed* to regular verbs to show a past action. A writer can also use *has, have,* or *had* with the past participle to form other verb tenses. (See the chart below.)

PRESENT	PAST	PAST PARTICIPLE
I watch.	Yesterday I watched.	I had watched.
He watches.	Yesterday he watched.	He had watched.

IRREGULAR VERBS

Irregular verbs do not follow the *ed* rule. Instead of adding *ed* to show a past action, the word might change. (See the two examples below.)

PRESENT	PAST	PAST PARTICIPLE
I speak.	Yesterday I spoke.	I have spoken.
She runs.	Yesterday she ran.	She has run.

Writers use the correct forms of irregular verbs by using them over and over. Since the 10 most common verbs in English are irregular, you should understand them first. The chart below gives the principal parts of these 10 irregular verbs. (See the list of irregular verbs on page 722.)

 Choose three of these verbs and write a short sentence for each principal part (*present, past,* and *past participle*).

PRESENT	PAST	PAST PARTICIPLE
is	was	(has) been
come	came	(has) come
do	did	(has) done
get	got	(has) gotten
go	went	(has) gone
have	had	(has) had
make	made	(has) made
say	said	(has) said
see	saw	(has) seen
take	took	(has) taken

Answers

 2. Linking verb: were
   predicate adjective: skilled
3. Linking verb: became
   predicate nouns: riveters, welders, shipbuilders
4. Linking verb: became
   predicate noun: memorial
5. Linking verb: was
   predicate noun: home

Answers

Possible answers:
1. I make chocolate-chip cookies for my dad.
2. I made two dozen cookies last night.
3. I have made his favorite cookies for years.
4. I take dance lessons.
5. I took guitar lessons last year.
6. I have taken karate lessons a few times.
7. We go to Maine almost every summer.
8. We went to England last year.
9. We have gone to Maine since I was three.

How can I use more effective verbs?

Show Powerful Action

You can use strong action verbs to help show the reader exactly what is happening (or has happened).

> **ORDINARY ACTION VERBS**
>
> **Louis Armstrong** played **a new kind of music—jazz.**
> **He** performed **with many bands.**

> **POWERFUL ACTION VERBS**
>
> **Notes** poured **out of Louis Armstrong's horn.**
> **When jazz became popular, Armstrong** exploded **into fame.**

Try to avoid using linking verbs (*is, are, was, were*) too much. Often, a stronger action verb can be made from another word in the same sentence.

> **Joe "King" Oliver** was **Armstrong's trumpet teacher.** (linking verb)
> **Joe "King" Oliver** taught **Armstrong to play the trumpet.**
> (The action verb "taught" is made from the word "teacher.")

Create Active Voice

A verb is in the active voice if the subject is doing the action. Use active voice more often than passive voice. (See pages 308 and 726.)

> **The trumpet** was played **by Louis Armstrong like no one else.** (passive)
> **Louis Armstrong** played **the trumpet like no one else.** (active)

 Number your paper from 2 to 5. Rewrite each sentence, changing the passive voice verbs to active verbs.

1. Hit songs were recorded by Louis Armstrong for five decades.
   1. Louis Armstrong recorded hit songs for five decades.
2. Many music awards were also won by him.
3. The nickname "Satchmo" was given to Louis Armstrong by a group of musicians.
4. Dozens of famous jazz songs were composed by Mr. Armstrong.
5. His home, a national historic landmark in Queens, New York, can be visited by people.

Show When Something Happens

You can use different verb tenses to "tell time" in sentences. The three simple tenses are *present, past,* and *future*. (Also see page 720.)

THE THREE SIMPLE TENSES OF VERBS		
	Singular	Plural
PRESENT	I dance. You dance. He or she dances.	We dance. You dance. They dance.
PAST	I danced. You danced. He or she danced.	We danced. You danced. They danced.
FUTURE	I will dance. You will dance. He or she will dance.	We will dance. You will dance. They will dance.

 Identify the tense of the underlined verbs in the sentences below.

1. Students enjoy reading books that Laura Ingalls Wilder wrote.
   1. present, past
2. Laura wrote about many "little houses."
3. You will enjoy learning about one of the houses that remains.
4. It is the house where Laura lived in Burr Oak, Iowa.
5. Maybe someday it will become a national historic landmark.

 Find and correct the six incorrect verb tenses used in the following paragraph. (The first verb is correct.)

1 Laura Ingalls' adventures began in Pepin, Wisconsin, in the
2 1870s. Laura and her family are pioneers, and they move often
3 when Laura is a child. Many years later, Laura writes books
4 about her childhood adventures. Today, they were published
5 in America and in many foreign countries. In the future, new
6 "Little House" fans continue to read the stories.

 Choose verbs carefully to tell exactly when the actions in your writing happen.

BASIC ELEMENTS

Answers

 2. He also won many music awards.
3. A group of musicians gave Louis Armstrong the nickname "Satchmo."
4. Mr. Armstrong composed dozens of famous jazz songs.
5. People can visit his home, a national historic landmark, in Queens, New York.

Answers

 2. past
3. future, present
4. present, past
5. future

 line 2 are/were; move/moved
line 3 is/was; writes/wrote
line 4 were/are
line 6 continue/will continue

BASIC ELEMENTS

What else can I do with verbs?

Show Special Types of Action

You need perfect tense verbs to express certain types of actions. (See page 724 in the "Proofreader's Guide.") There are three perfect tenses.

sing, sang, sung	Singular	Plural
Present perfect tense states an action that *began in the past but continues or is completed in the present.*		
Present perfect (use *has* or *have* + past participle)	I have sung. You have sung. He or she has sung.	We have sung. You have sung. They have sung.
Past perfect tense states an action that *began in the past and was completed in the past.*		
Past perfect (use *had* + past participle)	I had sung. You had sung. He or she had sung.	We had sung. You had sung. They had sung.
Future perfect tense states an action that *will begin in the future and will be completed by a specific time in the future.*		
Future perfect (use *will have* + past participle)	I will have sung. You will have sung. He or she will have sung.	We will have sung. You will have sung. They will have sung.

 Identify the tense of each underlined verb in the following paragraph. The first one has been done for you.

(1) present perfect

Probably, you **(1)** <u>have learned</u> of the midnight ride of Paul Revere. Once you read this paragraph, you **(2)** <u>will have learned</u> about Revere's house. His wooden home in Boston's North End **(3)** <u>has stood</u> since about 1680. Paul Revere and his family moved into the house in 1770. They **(4)** <u>had lived</u> there only 10 years when Revere decided to sell the house. By 1902, his great-grandson **(5)** <u>had seen</u> what bad condition the house was in and bought it. Today it is a national historic landmark. Over the years, many people **(6)** <u>have visited</u> Revere's house at 19 North Square, Boston, Massachusetts.

Share the Right Feeling

The verbs that you use should have the right connotation. (*Connotation* means "the feelings suggested by a word.") For example, you could say that a loud noise *alarmed* someone. But that word may not express the right feeling. Perhaps the word *terrified* or *excited* would better share your meaning.

Below are five words similar to *laugh*, but each of these words has a slightly different meaning.

Laugh	Definitions
giggle	to laugh with repeated, brief, soft sounds
snicker	to laugh slyly
chuckle	to laugh quietly to oneself
cackle	to laugh sharply and loudly
guffaw	to burst out in laughter

 Complete a chart like the one above for the word *run, cry,* or *talk.* Use a thesaurus to help you create your list of five similar words. Then define each word with the help of a dictionary.

To get a specific feeling across, writers try to use verbs with the right connotation. In the paragraph below, the underlined verbs create a *rushed* feeling.

Paul Revere <u>devoured</u> his food and <u>gulped</u> from his cup. He then <u>threw</u> his napkin on the table before <u>charging</u> out the door. A sound in the yard caught his attention, and he <u>dashed</u> to the lighthouse. He <u>tore</u> up the stairs and <u>grabbed</u> a lantern.

 Rewrite the paragraph above. Replace the underlined verbs in the paragraph with verbs that create a different feeling—*slow*, rather than *rushed*. Be sure that all your verbs match the new feeling you want to create.

Answers

 2. future perfect
3. present perfect
4. past perfect
5. past perfect
6. present perfect

Answers

 Possible answers:

Talk	Definitions
whisper	to say softly
yell	to cry out loud
mumble	to speak indistinctly
stutter	to speak with an involuntary repetition of sounds
chat	to converse in an easy manner

 devoured/nibbled
gulped/sipped
threw/placed
charging/shuffling
dashed/walked
tore/climbed
grabbed/reached for

Describing with Adjectives

Adjectives are words that describe or modify nouns or pronouns. Sensory adjectives help the reader see, hear, feel, smell, and taste what writers are describing. (Also see pages 732–735.)

WITHOUT ADJECTIVES

> The world is full of landmarks. From the ring of Big Ben in England to the roar of Niagara Falls, landmarks are everywhere.

WITH ADJECTIVES

> The world is full of mysterious and beautiful landmarks. From the deep-sounding ring of Big Ben in England to the thunderous roar of Niagara Falls, landmarks are everywhere.

Adjectives can answer four questions: *What kind? How much? How many? Which one?* Remember that proper adjectives can be made from proper nouns (England, *English;* Italy, *Italian*) and are capitalized.

WHAT KIND?	Chinese **food**	pea **soup**	red **shoes**
HOW MUCH? HOW MANY?	a little **sugar**	two **kittens**	some **bugs**
WHICH ONE?	this **book**	these **students**	those **cars**

 For each blank in the sentences below, write an adjective of the type called for in parentheses.

1. When you visit the historical site of the great Chicago fire, you can almost smell the _(what kind?)_ blaze of 1871.

2. You'll hear _(how many?)_ explosions as work continues on the Crazy Horse Memorial in South Dakota.

3. _(what kind?)_ wildflowers cover _(how many?)_ areas of the park.

4. The circle of stone called the Medicine Wheel, at Lovell, Wyoming, is a/an _(what kind?)_ symbol of native civilization.

5. The Eiffel Tower in Paris is _(how many?)_ landmark known around the world.

6. _(which one?)_ structure is made of iron.

Comparative and Superlative Adjectives

You can use comparative adjectives to compare two things. For most one-syllable adjectives, add er to make the **comparative form**. To compare three or more things, add est to make the **superlative form**. (See 734.3–734.5.)

POSITIVE	COMPARATIVE	SUPERLATIVE
large	larger	largest

Comparative: **The Sears Tower is** taller **than the John Hancock Building.**

Superlative: **The Sears Tower is the** tallest **building in the United States.**

Add er and est to some two-syllable words and use *more* or *most* (or *less* or *least*) with others. Always use *more* or *most* with three-syllable adjectives.

POSITIVE	COMPARATIVE	SUPERLATIVE
joyful	more joyful	most joyful

Comparative: **The Chrysler Building is a** more complex **structure than other skyscrapers.**

Superlative: **The** most complex **structure in my town is a long bridge.**

 Write the comparative and superlative forms of the adjective in each of the following sentences.

1. While Washington, D.C., is an exciting city, New York is a _____ city. Javier thinks Rio de Janeiro is the _____ city in the world.

2. There was a long line to get into the Lincoln Memorial. There was a _____ line than that to get into the Capitol, but the _____ line was at the White House.

3. The Constitution is an important document. Some people think the Declaration of Independence is a _____ document than the Constitution, but I think the Constitution is our country's _____ document.

4. A beautiful park called Lafayette Square overlooks the White House. A _____ park than this one is located nearby in Great Falls, Virginia, and the _____ park I've ever visited is Great Smoky Mountains National Park.

5. The Postal Museum is a small part of the Smithsonian Institution. The American Indian Museum is a bit _____, and the Sackler Gallery is the _____.

BASIC ELEMENTS

Answers

 Possible answers:
1. smoky
2. several
3. Colorful, all
4. amazing
5. one
6. That

Answers

1. more exciting, most exciting
2. longer, longest
3. more important, most important
4. more beautiful, most beautiful
5. smaller, smallest

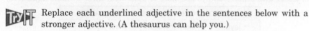
BASIC ELEMENTS

How can I strengthen my writing with adjectives?

Create Stronger Descriptions

Strong adjectives help readers use their senses. For example, "Black Thunder is a cool waterslide" creates a basic picture of the slide, but "Black Thunder is a hair-raising, monster waterslide" creates a sharper picture.

> **Avoid ho-hum adjectives.** Some adjectives really don't provide a clear picture for the reader. Replacing vague words like *nice, good,* and *big* with vivid adjectives will make your writing more effective.

 Replace each underlined adjective in the sentences below with a stronger adjective. (A thesaurus can help you.)

1. Listen to the roar of Niagara Falls, a <u>big</u> waterfall.
2. The Liberty Bell is a <u>good</u> symbol of this country.
3. The <u>strong</u> Colorado River carved the Grand Canyon's <u>tall</u> cliffs.
4. San Francisco's cable cars are <u>different</u> landmarks.

Form "Extra-Strength" Modifiers

Compound adjectives are made of two or more words. Some are spelled as one word; others are hyphenated. (Use a dictionary to check spelling.)

Many natural but little-visited landmarks enjoy worldwide recognition.

 For each of the following sentences, write a compound adjective to fill in the blank. Make your compound adjectives by combining words from the following list.

| earth | first | taking | wind | breath | rate | blown | shaking |

1. There are ＿＿＿＿＿＿ hiking trails in Glacier Park, Montana.
   1. first-rate
2. Chicago could be called a ＿＿＿＿＿＿ city.
3. You get a ＿＿＿＿＿＿ view from the Statue of Liberty.
4. Mauna Loa in Hawaii has ＿＿＿＿＿＿ volcanic eruptions.

Use Sensory Details

Writers often use adjectives to create sensory details. This kind of detail forms pictures in the reader's mind. As you read the paragraph below, think about the pictures formed by the sensory details. Then consider how the underlined adjectives help to create the sensory details.

A <u>thumping</u> "rom-rom-rom" echoes across the <u>muddy</u> Mississippi River. I hurry on. My toes make squishing sounds in the <u>sticky riverbank</u> mud. The smell of <u>rotting</u> leaves and <u>decaying</u> fish doesn't bother me. I see an <u>olive green</u> lump at the edge of the river—a bullfrog! It sits still except for its <u>vibrating yellow</u> throat.

 Draw a chart like the one below and list all the sensory details that are underlined in the paragraph above.

sight	sound	smell	texture (feeling)
olive green lump			

> Try to get into the habit of using sensory details whenever you write. Practice focusing on one sense at a time. See if you can learn to be more aware of what is going on around you.

 List one or two sensory details in response to each of the following statements. (An example is provided for each.)

1. Identify the smells you like.
   Just-baked bread
2. Identify things you like to touch or feel.
   A gentle wind
3. Identify favorite tastes.
   A sour apple
4. Identify sights that you look forward to seeing.
   The fall colors
5. Identify the sounds that you like to hear.
   The 3:00 dismissal bell

Answers

 Possible answers:
1. gigantic
2. wonderful
3. powerful
4. unusual

2. windblown
3. breathtaking
4. earthshaking

Answers

 Answers:

sight	sound	smell	texture (feeling)
muddy olive green vibrating, yellow	thumping vibrating	rotting decaying	sticky riverbank

 Possible answers:
1. roasting hot dogs, freshly mown grass, hot chocolate
2. plush stuffed animal, favorite sweatshirt, snakeskin
3. creamy chocolate, spicy salsa, sour candy
4. blazing sunrise, double rainbow, holiday decorations
5. wind in the pine trees, crashing waves, people laughing

Describing with Adverbs

Adverbs describe or modify verbs, adjectives, or other adverbs. You can use adverbs to answer *how? when? (or how often?) where?* or *how much?* (See pages 736–739.)

How?	slowly	Kiet counts slowly to 20.
When?	yesterday	Tyisha went on a field trip yesterday.
Where?	outside	My classmates are waiting outside.
How much?	barely	Falling debris barely missed the workers.

 For each of the following sentences, write the adverbs you find. (The number of adverbs is shown in parentheses.) Tell what word each adverb describes and what question it answers.

1. Quietly, our class explored the Indian burial grounds. (*1*)
   1. quietly (explored, how)
2. I often go to Mexico City with my father. (*1*)
3. It may be hot outside, but Mammoth Cave is very cool. (*2*)
4. I never knew that Boston had landmarks everywhere. (*2*)
5. My uncle frequently travels to the East Coast. (*1*)
6. Recently we went to San Antonio, Texas, to see the Alamo. (*1*)
7. A famous battle was fought there. (*1*)
8. Our guide turned left and walked quickly away. (*3*)
9. Today I learned that Research Cave has been badly damaged. (*2*)
10. I instantly recognized the White House when I saw it for the first time. (*1*)

Comparative and Superlative Adverbs

You can use adverbs to compare two things. The **comparative form** of an adverb compares two people, places, things, or ideas. The **superlative form** of an adverb compares three or more people, places, things, or ideas.

 For most one-syllable adverbs, add *er* to make the comparative form and *est* to make the superlative form.

POSITIVE	COMPARATIVE	SUPERLATIVE
soon	sooner	soonest

Comparative: I arrived later than Sheila did.
Superlative: Kayla arrived latest of all.

While you add *er* and *est* to some two-syllable adverbs, you need to use *more* or *most* (or *less* or *least*) with others. Always use *more* or *most* with three-syllable adverbs.

POSITIVE	COMPARATIVE	SUPERLATIVE
quickly	more quickly	most quickly

Comparative: Ed has visited the Sears Tower more frequently than I have.
Superlative: Of all of us, Ed visits the Sears Tower most frequently.

 When you use the comparative form, make sure that you state a complete comparison: *I arrived later than Sheila did,* not *I arrived later than Sheila.*

 Write a sentence for each adverb below.

1. later (comparative)
   1. I arrived at Marengo Cave later than the rest of my friends.
2. harder (comparative)
3. slowly (superlative)
4. more effectively (comparative)
5. fastest (superlative)

How can I use adverbs effectively?

Describe Actions

You can make your writing more descriptive by using adverbs. You can add *ly* to some adjectives to create adverbs.

bad badly   **amazing** amazingly   **tight** tightly

The cat was lazy. / The cat stretched out lazily **on the windowsill.**

When you add *ly* to form an adverb, you need to remember these three spelling rules.

- Add *ly* to some words: **neat** neatly
- Drop the *e* and add *ly* to others: **terrible** terribly
- Change the *y* to *i* and add *ly* to still others: **sleepy** sleepily

 Rewrite the following sentences by changing the underlined adjectives to adverbs. (Change other words as needed.)

1. The <u>swift</u> river ran under the bridge in the park.
   1. *The river ran swiftly under the bridge in the park.*
2. I was <u>happy</u> to walk over the bridge.
3. The woman heard a <u>sudden</u> cry.
4. Her <u>gentle</u> voice calmed the child.

Add Emphasis

You can stress the importance of something with adverbs. Generally, use adverbs of degree—those that answer *how much?*—for this job.

San Antonio's Riverwalk is absolutely **beautiful.**

I really **want to explore it.**

 Rewrite the following sentences. Add emphasis by using adverbs to modify the underlined words.

1. I <u>agree</u> with you.
   1. *I completely agree with you!*
2. I <u>suggest</u> that you visit the Riverwalk in the evening.
3. It is <u>scenic</u>.
4. We had an <u>exciting</u> time there last year.

Modify Adjectives

With adverbs, you can describe how often something is a certain way. Adverbs that tell how often include *sometimes, often, usually, occasionally, always,* and so on.

The Badlands are always **spectacular.**

A visit there is rarely **disappointing.**

 Rewrite the following sentences, using a "how often" adverb to modify each underlined adjective.

1. The Badlands' Fossil Exhibit Trail is <u>fascinating</u>.
   1. *The Badlands' Fossil Exhibit Trail is always fascinating.*
2. The yucca plants are <u>interesting</u> to see.
3. Bison are <u>visible</u> on Sage Creek Rim Road.
4. Turkey vultures are <u>overhead</u>.
5. It is <u>rainy</u> in the Badlands.
6. People are <u>amazed</u> at the Badlands formations.

Be Precise

With adverbs, you can tell the reader exactly when *(then, yesterday, now)* or where *(there, nearby, inside)* something happens.

We are going to the Milwaukee Zoo tomorrow.

The buses will pick us up here **at 9:00.**

 Add an adverb that tells "when" or "where" to each one of the following sentences.

1. We need to turn in our permission slips.
   1. *We need to turn in our permission slips today.*
2. I handed mine in.
3. Sheniqua wants to visit the primate house.
4. Carl spotted a bonobo, an African chimpanzee.
5. I will sit on this bench.

BASIC ELEMENTS

Answers

 Answers:
2. I walked happily over the bridge.
3. Suddenly the woman heard a cry.
4. Her voice gently calmed the child.

Possible answers:
2. I definitely suggest you visit the Riverwalk in the evening.
3. It is amazingly scenic.
4. We had a totally exciting time there last year.

Answers

Possible answers:
2. The yucca plants are usually interesting to see.
3. Bison are occasionally visible on Sage Creek Rim Road.
4. Turkey vultures are often overhead.
5. It is seldom rainy in the Badlands.
6. People are endlessly amazed at the Badlands formations.

2. I handed mine in yesterday.
3. Sheniqua wants to visit the primate house first.
4. Carl saw a bonobo, an African chimpanzee, immediately.
5. I will sit here on this bench.

Connecting with Prepositions

A preposition is a word (or words) that shows how one word or idea is related to another. A preposition is the first word of a prepositional phrase like _over the hill_ and _near the river_. (See page 742 for a complete list of prepositions.)

The Gila Cliff Dwellings National Monument is located in New Mexico. (The preposition "in" shows the relationship between the verb "is located" and the object of the preposition "New Mexico." The prepositional phrase acts as an adverb telling "where.")

The monument in the Gila Wilderness **has 50,000 visitors annually.** (The preposition "in" shows the relationship between the noun "monument" and the object of the preposition "Gila Wilderness." The prepositional phrase acts as an adjective telling "which one.")

> **Avoid confusing prepositions and adverbs.** If a word that can also be used as a preposition appears alone in a sentence, it is being used as an adverb.
>
> **Two students lagged** behind the group.
> ("Behind the group" is a prepositional phrase.)
>
> **Two students lagged** behind, **so we waited.**
> ("Behind" is an adverb that modifies the verb "lagged.")

 Identify each prepositional phrase in the sentences below. Then tell whether the phrase acts as an _adverb_ or an _adjective_.

1. Next we went to the visitor center and watched a movie.
   1. to the visitor center, adverb (tells "where")
2. Everyone climbed onto the bus and sat down.
3. "No fooling around during the movie," he warned.
4. "When the movie is over," he said, "meet in the lobby."
5. The movie about the monument was too long.
6. The driver of our bus pulled up immediately.
7. Everyone climbed aboard the bus and sat down.
8. The trip to Gila Wilderness had been fun.
9. As I thought about the trip, I was glad that I had brought my camera along.

What can I do with prepositions?
Add Information

You can use a prepositional phrase as an adjective to describe either a noun or a pronoun. Adjectives answer _what kind? how many?_ or _which one?_

            Which one?   _What kind?_

The Upper Geyser Basin along the Firehole River **is home** to Old Faithful.

 Write a prepositional phrase to describe each of the subjects listed below. Many prepositional phrases that are used as adjectives tell _which one_ or _ones._ (See page 742.)

1. the flowers
   1. the flowers along the trail
2. my cousins
3. the buffalo
4. the river

5. several days
6. the camera
7. the dog
8. a camper

You can also use a prepositional phrase as an adverb to describe a verb, an adjective, or another adverb. Adverbs answer _how? when? where? how long? how often?_ or _how much?_

            Where?   _When?_

You can find Old Faithful in Yellowstone Park. **It erupts** on a regular basis.

 For each sentence below, write the prepositional phrase that is used as an adverb. Tell what question it answers.

1. At Yellowstone National Park, you can see Old Faithful.
   1. At Yellowstone National Park (where)
2. The geyser erupts on a regular schedule.
3. The water underground boils under pressure.
4. It erupts in a blast that sprays hot water and steam.
5. Yellowstone is located in Wyoming, Montana, and Idaho.
6. Old Faithful's eruptions can last for five minutes.

BASIC ELEMENTS

Answers

 2. onto the bus, adverb (where)
    3. during the movie, adverb (when)
    4. in the lobby, adverb (where)
    5. about the monument, adjective (which one)
    6. of our bus, adjective (which one)
    7. aboard the bus, adverb (where)
    8. to Gila wilderness, adjective (which one)
    9. about the trip, adverb (how)

Answers

 Possible answers:

2. my cousins from Montana
3. the buffalo with the young calf
4. the river near the geysers
5. several days after the rainstorm
6. the camera with the zoom lens
7. his dog inside the tent
8. a camper with screen windows

 Answers:

2. on a regular schedule   (when)
3. under pressure   (how)
4. in a blast   (how)
5. in Wyoming, Montana,   (where)
   and Idaho
6. for five minutes   (how long)

Connecting with Conjunctions

Conjunctions connect words, groups of words, and sentences. There are three kinds of conjunctions: *coordinating, subordinating,* and *correlative.* The following sentences show some of the ways to use conjunctions. (See page 744 for a list of common conjunctions.)

COORDINATING CONJUNCTIONS CONNECT WORDS

Artists come to Crazy Horse near Mt. Rushmore in the Black Hills to sketch or paint the memorial.

Skilled crews shape the mountain with explosives and torches.

CONNECT COMPOUND SUBJECTS AND PREDICATES

Today, a museum and a cultural center are part of the memorial.

Visitors view exhibits and meet Native American craftspeople there.

CONNECT SENTENCES

Work on Crazy Horse Memorial began in 1948, yet it is not finished.

The sculptor of Crazy Horse, Korczak Ziolkowski, died in 1982, so his family continues his work.

SUBORDINATING CONJUNCTIONS CONNECT DEPENDENT CLAUSES TO INDEPENDENT CLAUSES

For several years, Ziolkowski worked alone while he sculpted the memorial.

Before he started Crazy Horse, he worked as a sculptor on nearby Mt. Rushmore.

CORRELATIVE CONJUNCTIONS CONNECT NOUN PHRASES AND VERB PHRASES

Both foggy days and moonlit nights make Crazy Horse look mysterious.

People not only watch the work on Crazy Horse from a distance but also ride buses to the base of the huge project.

 Choose three of the sentences above to use as models. Write three sentences of your own imitating the three you've chosen. Underline the conjunctions you use.

What can I do with conjunctions?

Connect a Series of Ideas

You can use conjunctions to connect a series of three or more words or phrases in a row. Place commas between the words or phrases and place a conjunction before the final item.

People hike up the mountain, stand on the statue, and enjoy the view.
(The conjunction connects three verb phrases.)

Wild iris, pine trees, and cone flowers greet the hikers.
(The conjunction connects three noun phrases.)

 Copy the following sentences and place commas where they are needed. Underline the conjunctions.

1. I gaze out over the rocks trees and hills of the Black Hills.
2. I tilt my head back stare up at the face and feel very small.
3. Crazy Horse cared for the children the elderly and the sick.

Expand Sentences (with Coordinating Conjunctions)

You can use **coordinating conjunctions** (*and, but, or, nor, for, so, yet*) to make compound subjects and predicates and to write compound sentences.

Ziolkowski and his sons carved stone for almost 36 years, but they didn't finish the sculpture.
(In this sentence, "and" creates a compound subject, and the conjunction "but" creates a compound sentence.)

For each blank, write a coordinating conjunction. Tell whether it connects a compound subject, a compound predicate, or a compound sentence.

Native Americans have lived in the Black Hills for 12,000 years, **(1)** _____ several tribes consider the area to be sacred land. Its noble history **(2)** _____ spiritual power are valued greatly. It was fitting to honor Crazy Horse with a carving in the Black Hills, **(3)** _____ the chosen sculptor was, surprisingly, not a Native American. Korczak Ziolkowski, a sculptor of Polish descent, worked on the mountain until his death **(4)** _____ did not finish the sculpture. His family continues to work on the monument.

Answers

 Answers:
1. I gaze out over the rocks, trees, <u>and</u> hills of the Black Hills.
2. I tilt my head back, stare up at the face, <u>and</u> feel very small.
3. Crazy Horse cared for the children, the elderly, <u>and</u> the sick.

Possible answers:
1. and (compound sentence)
2. and (compound subject)
3. yet (compound sentence)
4. but (compound predicate)

Expand Sentences (with Subordinating Conjunctions)

You can use a subordinating conjunction to connect a dependent clause to another sentence. A dependent clause (one that *cannot* stand alone as a sentence) must be connected to an independent clause (one that *can* stand alone as a sentence). In the expanded sentences below, the dependent clause is underlined, and the subordinating conjunction is in blue. (See page 517.)

Gutzon Borglum worked on Mt. Rushmore from 1927 until he died in 1941.

When he started his work on the mountain, he planned to include an area to keep historical documents.

 Choose a subordinating conjunction (*before, although, because, while, when*) to complete each sentence in the paragraph below.

Borglum chose Mt. Rushmore **(1)** _____ he knew the granite would last forever. **(2)** _____ any carving was done, workers used dynamite to blast out large chunks of the mountainside. **(3)** _____ the sculptors got to work, they used jackhammers, drills, and chisels on the hard rock. Weather and financial problems halted the work several times **(4)** _____ the sculpture was in progress. **(5)** _____ it took 14 years to finish, sculptors actually worked on the monument for only 6 of those years.

Show a Relationship

You can use correlative conjunctions to show a relationship between two words, phrases, or clauses. Correlative conjunctions are always used in pairs: *both/and, not only/but also, neither/nor, either/or, whether/or.*

Either Gutzon Borglum or his son, Lincoln, supervised the people working on Mount Rushmore.

They weren't sure whether they would find skilled workers in South Dakota or they would have to train workers.

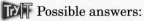 For each of the blanks in the sentences below, write the correlative conjunctions that make the most sense.

1. _____ bad weather _____ a lack of money could stop the work.
2. _____ the hard work _____ the tough conditions scared the workers away.
3. _____ were they paid well _____ they felt pride in their work.

Building Effective Sentences

Imagine eating the same thing every day, at every meal. Eventually, you would dislike even the cheesiest pizza or the most scrumptious cake. People just naturally like variety.

The same is true with writing. A story with one long sentence after another, or one short sentence after another, would soon become boring. Sometimes a short sentence expresses feeling in a way that a long sentence cannot, and a long sentence does a better job of explaining a complicated idea. One key to clear writing is using a variety of sentences.

Mini Index

You will learn about . . .
- writing complete sentences.
- fixing sentence problems.
- adding variety to your sentences.
- combining sentences.
- using different types of sentences.
- expanding and modeling sentences.

Answers

 Answers:
1. because
2. Before
3. When
4. while
5. Although

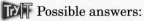 Possible answers:
1. Either . . . or
2. Neither . . . nor
3. Not only . . . but also

Writing Complete Sentences

A sentence is a group of words that forms a complete thought. Writers use complete sentences in order to communicate clearly. Here is a group of words that does not form a complete thought:

The jumble of words above makes no sense. When these same words are rearranged into a sentence, however, they do make sense. They communicate a clear, complete thought:

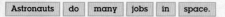

 On your own paper, unscramble the word groups below to create complete sentences. Some sentences can be arranged in more than one way. Remember to capitalize and punctuate each sentence correctly.

1. developed NASA the in 1970s the shuttle space
   1. *NASA developed the space shuttle in the 1970s.*

2. a like shuttle a launches rocket

3. airplane an like lands it

4. used rockets be only can once most

5. be again shuttle can again a used and

6. 1981 first launched shuttle in was the

7. satellites orbit shuttles the to carried first

8. carry and now people shuttles cargo

9. is crew flown a flight by shuttle a

10. do to job member each crew has a special

 Write three or four sentences about space exploration. On another sheet, mix up the words and leave out punctuation and capitalization. Ask a classmate to rearrange the words so they form complete sentences.

Basic Parts of a Sentence

Every sentence has two basic parts: a complete subject—which tells who or what is doing something—and a complete predicate—which tells what the subject is doing. (See 690.3 and 692.3.)

COMPLETE SUBJECT	COMPLETE PREDICATE
Who or what did something?	*What did the subject do?*
Scientists	explored the idea of flight.
George Cayley, an engineer,	studied flight for many years.

 Divide a piece of paper into two columns. For each of the sentences below, write the complete subject in the left column and write the complete predicate in the right column.

> In the following sentences, the words that come before the verb are the *complete subject*. The verb and all the words that follow it are the *complete predicate*.

1. Sir George Cayley *invented* the science of flight.
   1. *Sir George Cayley | invented the science of flight.*

2. Cayley learned from birds soaring long distances.

3. A flying toy top was one of his first inventions.

4. It had a three-bladed propeller.

5. A model of the first glider flew successfully in 1804.

6. A small boy became the first person in history to fly.

7. He made a short flight in Cayley's glider.

8. Cayley prepared the way for other inventors.

 Write three or four sentences about what you think it was like to fly in Cayley's glider. Draw a line between the complete subject and the complete predicate in each of your sentences.

Answers

 2. A shuttle launches like a rocket.

3. It lands like an airplane.

4. Most rockets can be used only once.

5. A shuttle can be used again and again.

6. The first shuttle was launched in 1981.

7. The first shuttles carried satellites to orbit.

8. Now shuttles carry cargo and people.

9. A shuttle is flown by a flight crew.

10. Each crew member has a special job to do.

Answers

 2. Cayley | learned from birds soaring long distances.

3. A flying toy top | was one of his first inventions.

4. It | had a three-bladed propeller.

5. A model of the first glider | flew successfully in 1804.

6. A small boy | became the first person in history to fly.

7. He | made a short flight in Cayley's glider.

8. Cayley | prepared the way for other inventors.

BASIC ELEMENTS

Simple Subjects and Predicates

A simple subject is the subject of a sentence without the words that modify it. A simple predicate is the verb without the words that modify it or complete the thought. In the sentences below, the **simple subjects** are orange and the simple predicates are blue. (See also 690.2 and 692.2.)

COMPLETE SUBJECT	COMPLETE PREDICATE
Governments in many countries	developed airplanes.
Airplanes	changed how people traveled.

 Divide a piece of paper into two columns. For each of the sentences below, write the complete subject in the left column and write the complete predicate in the right column. Then underline the simple subjects and predicates.

1. Leonardo da Vinci drew designs of aircraft in the 1400s.
   1. *Leonardo da Vinci* | *drew designs of aircraft in the 1400s.*
2. He gathered data about birds.
3. His first aircraft moved like a bird's wings.
4. Paul Cornu of France built a man-carrying helicopter in 1907.
5. Charles Lindbergh flew the first solo flight across the Atlantic.
6. Jumbo jets carry almost 500 passengers today.
7. These planes weigh nearly 460 tons!
8. The supersonic *Concorde* began passenger service in 1976.
9. It flew faster than the speed of sound.
10. Some airports need longer runways now.

Write **NOW** Write three sentences about airplanes or airports. Ask a classmate to find and underline the simple subject and simple predicate in each sentence.

Compound Subjects and Predicates

Some sentences have compound subjects or compound predicates, and some have both.

- A **compound subject** includes two or more subjects that share the same predicate (or predicates).
- A compound predicate includes two or more predicates that share the same subject (or subjects).

COMPOUND SUBJECT	COMPOUND PREDICATE
Hospitals and trauma centers	build and maintain heliports.

 Number your paper from 2 to 8. For each sentence below, write any compound subject and any compound predicate.

1. Leonardo da Vinci, Louis Bréguet, and Paul Cornu designed and illustrated early helicopters.
   1. *Leonardo da Vinci, Louis Bréguet, and Paul Cornu designed and illustrated*
2. A huge whirling blade lifts a helicopter and keeps it in the air.
3. Helicopters carry seriously ill people to hospitals and save people from floods.
4. Radio reporters and television newspeople spot and describe traffic delays from helicopters.
5. The coast guard, police departments, and fire departments sometimes use helicopters in emergencies.
6. People explore wilderness areas and search for missing persons from helicopters.
7. Directors and photographers use helicopters for bird's-eye views of movie scenes.
8. A helicopter pilot can even find and track a whale.

Write **NOW** Write one sentence with a compound subject and another one with a compound predicate. Then write a sentence with both a compound subject and a compound predicate.

How can I make sure my sentences are complete?
Check Your Subjects and Predicates

Sentence fragments are incomplete sentences. They may be missing a subject, a predicate, or both. You can learn how to fix sentence fragments by reading the examples below.

FRAGMENT	SENTENCE
Is a place where airplanes take off and land. (*The subject is missing.*)	An airport is a place where airplanes take off and land.
In 2003, Atlanta's Hartsfield Airport, the world's busiest airport. (*The predicate is missing.*)	In 2003, Atlanta's Hartsfield Airport was the world's busiest airport.
At a small airport near Detroit. (*The subject and predicate are missing.*)	My uncle keeps his plane at a small airport near Detroit.

 Number your paper from 2 to 8. For each sentence, write "S" next to the number. For each fragment, write "F." Also tell which part or parts are missing: "subject," "predicate," or "both."

1. Are like small cities.

  1. F – subject

2. Each year, more than 100 million people travel through large airports.

3. Most of the visitors to airports passengers.

4. At areas for ticketing, check-in, and baggage handling.

5. Some concourses hold restaurants and shops.

6. Can eat, shop, and relax.

7. Passengers are only one type of airport customer.

8. Airfreight companies as well.

 Rewrite the fragments above. Add the missing parts so that each fragment is now a complete sentence.

Edit Your Writing Carefully

Sentence fragments may be difficult to spot in your writing. At first glance, a fragment may look like a sentence. It starts with a capital letter, and it ends with a punctuation mark. Reading a sentence out loud can help you figure out if something is missing. (See 690.4 and 692.6.)

In the examples below, the writer found and underlined a number of fragments. Then she turned the fragments into complete sentences, some by combining the fragments with nearby sentences.

FRAGMENT	SENTENCE
An airport is a busy place. <u>On the ground and in the air.</u> An airport doesn't have just planes and jets. <u>Cars, buses, and trains, too.</u>	An airport is a busy place both on the ground and in the air. An airport doesn't have just planes and jets. It has cars, buses, and trains, too.
You might see fire trucks and police cars. <u>Or motorized carts that carry luggage.</u>	You might see fire trucks, police cars, or motorized carts that carry luggage.

 Read the following paragraph and check for fragments. Then on your own paper, tell how many fragments you found. Rewrite the paragraph, correcting each of the fragments.

1   At an airport. You don't see just airplanes. Busy airports
2 also rely on ground vehicles. Like cars and buses. People drive
3 their cars to and from airports. Buses take passengers to local
4 hotels and car-rental offices. Also limousines and taxis. Trains
5 and subways, too. Ground transportation helps passengers get
6 to the airport on time. To catch their flights. It also helps them
7 get back home again.

 Write a short paragraph about an airport, train or bus station, or a busy street in your town. Have a classmate check your writing for fragments.

Answers

 2. S
3. F – predicate
4. F – both
5. S
6. F – subject
7. S
8. F – predicate

Answers

 Five fragments

At an airport, you don't see just airplanes. Busy airports also rely on ground vehicles like cars and buses. People drive their cars to and from airports. Buses, limousines, taxis, trains, and subways take passengers to local hotels and car-rental offices. Ground transportation helps passengers get to the airport on time to catch their flights. It also helps them get back home again.

BASIC ELEMENTS

Fixing Sentence Problems

Check for Run-On Sentences

Sometimes you may accidentally write a **run-on sentence**. A run-on sentence is two or more sentences that run together. Sometimes it is called a *comma splice* because it is connected with a comma instead of a period. Other run-ons may have no punctuation at all.

One way to fix run-on sentences is to divide them into two or more complete sentences. Another way is to add a comma and a conjunction.

RUN-ON SENTENCE	CORRECTED SENTENCES
This year, I learned what flight attendants do I think I might like to be one someday.	This year, I learned what flight attendants do. I think I might like to be one someday. This year, I learned what flight attendants do, and I think I might like to be one someday.

 On your own paper, correct the run-on sentences below by dividing them into two or more shorter sentences.

1. Flight attendants welcome passengers aboard they also help passengers find their seats.

   1. Flight attendants welcome passengers aboard. They also help passengers find their seats.

2. First they check to see that seat belts are fastened then they check to make sure carry-on items are stored safely.

3. Flight attendants are trained for emergencies they know what to do if something unexpected happens.

4. They keep the passengers comfortable they serve food and beverages and supply blankets and pillows.

5. Flight attendants sometimes go to "career days" students can learn a lot by asking flight attendants questions.

Write NOW Choose two of the above run-on sentences and correct them by using a comma and the conjunction "and."

Eliminate Rambling Sentences

A **rambling sentence** happens when you join too many sentences with the word *and,* as in the example below. Notice that there are two ways shown to correct a rambling sentence. (Also see page 310.)

 Of course, some *and*'s are necessary in sentences. See the blue and used in the following rambling sentence.

RAMBLING SENTENCE	CORRECTED SENTENCES
Air traffic controllers work in the control towers at airports and they have very important jobs and they must know where all the planes are, both in the air and on the ground.	Air traffic controllers work in the control towers at airports, and they have very important jobs. They must know where all the planes are, both in the air and on the ground. (Add a comma before the first *and.* Drop the second *and* to make two sentences.) Air traffic controllers work in the control towers at airports. They have very important jobs and must know where all the planes are, both in the air and on the ground. (Drop the first *and* to make two sentences. Drop *they* in the second sentence to make a compound predicate.)

 Correct the following rambling sentences on your own paper. (Watch for three *and*'s that are necessary.)

1. Controllers keep track of planes flying around the airport and they direct planes in and out of the airport and they even guide the planes on the ground.

2. Controllers warn pilots about weather changes and they also report on ground conditions and they tell pilots when and where to land.

3. Miles from the airport, the pilot contacts the tower and a controller in the tower watches the plane on radar and makes sure that the plane lands safely and once the plane lands, a ground controller directs it to its gate.

Write NOW Choose one of the rambling sentences above and correct it by rewriting it in a different way than you did at first.

Answers

 2. First they check to see that seat belts are fastened. Then they check to make sure carry-on items are stored safely.

3. Flight attendants are trained for emergencies. They know what to do if something unexpected happens.

4. They keep passengers comfortable. They serve food and beverages and supply blankets and pillows.

5. Flight attendants sometimes go to "career days." Students can learn a lot by asking flight attendants questions.

Answers

1. Controllers keep track of planes flying around the airport. They direct planes in and out of the airport, and they even guide the planes on the ground.

2. Controllers warn pilots about weather changes, and they also report on ground conditions. They tell pilots when and where to land.

3. Miles from the airport, the pilot contacts the tower. A controller in the tower watches the plane on radar and makes sure that the plane lands safely. Once the plane lands, a ground controller directs it to its gate.

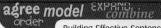

What can I do to write clear sentences?

Make Subjects and Verbs Agree

Writers must be careful to make the subjects and verbs in each of their sentences agree. That means a singular subject needs a singular verb, and a plural subject needs a plural verb. (Also see 728.1.)

SINGULAR OR PLURAL SUBJECTS

A verb must agree with its subject in number.

- If a subject is singular (refers to one person, place, thing, or idea), the verb must be singular, too.

    Luis enjoys airport field trips.

- If a subject is plural (refers to more than one person, place, thing, or idea), the verb must be plural.

    My classmates enjoy airport field trips.

(Don't forget that most nouns ending in *s* or *es* are plural, and most verbs ending in *s* are singular.)

 Number your paper from 2 to 8. For each of these sentences, write the correct verb (or verbs). Make sure each verb agrees with its subject.

1. Each May, the sixth graders goes on a field trip to Atlanta's Hartsfield International Airport.

    1. go

2. A plane arrive there every 40 seconds, 24 hours a day!
3. Almost 150 million passengers passes through the airport yearly.
4. People rides a "people mover" train to get around the airport.
5. The terminal buildings covers about 130 acres.
6. Shops, restaurants, and benches lines the long concourses.
7. Airplanes arrives and leaves from the 176 gates at Hartsfield.
8. People working at the airport helps keep passengers safe.

 Write one sentence using the subject "pilots" and another using the subject "airplane." Make sure your subjects and verbs agree.

COMPOUND SUBJECTS CONNECTED BY "AND"

A compound subject connected by the word *and* needs a plural verb.

    Miss Gonzales and Mr. Peet take us on the field trip.

COMPOUND SUBJECTS CONNECTED BY "OR"

A compound subject connected by the word *or* needs a verb that agrees in number with the subject nearest to it.

    The teachers or the principal organizes the field trip.
    (*Principal*, the subject nearer the verb, is singular, so the singular verb *organizes* is used.)

 Number your paper from 2 to 9. Write the correct verb choice for each of these sentences.

1. Airports and air travel (*is, are*) quite safe.

    1. are

2. Airport rules and airline employees (*help, helps*) passengers stay safe.
3. Each passenger or airline employee (*carry, carries*) personal identification everywhere in the airport.
4. Metal detectors and X-ray scanners (*check, checks*) passengers and luggage.
5. An electronic game or a cell phone (*is, are*) not harmed by X-ray equipment.
6. Passengers or a lost kid (*sets, set*) off security detectors sometimes.
7. Even small scissors and nail files (*cause, causes*) alarms to go off.
8. Security guards or an airport police officer (*question, questions*) passengers who carry metal objects.
9. Checkpoints and security guards (*keep, keeps*) passengers and visitors safe.

 Rewrite sentence 5 above using a plural verb. Rewrite sentence 7 using a singular verb.

Answers

2. arrives
3. pass
4. ride
5. cover
6. line
7. arrive and leave
8. help

Answers

2. help
3. carries
4. check
5. is
6. sets
7. cause
8. questions
9. keep

 Answers
5. Electronic games or cell phones are not harmed by X-ray equipment.
7. Even a small scissors or a nail file causes alarms to go off.

What should I do to avoid nonstandard sentences?

Avoid Double Negatives

A **double negative** happens when two negative words are used together (*don't never, can't hardly*) in the same sentence. Using double negatives is incorrect in both spoken and written language. Your writing will seem careless—or even inaccurate—if you use double negatives.

NEGATIVE WORDS				
nothing	nowhere	neither	never	not
barely	hardly	nobody	none	no
BE CAREFUL: Contractions that end in *n't* are also negative words.				
don't	can't	won't	shouldn't	
wouldn't	couldn't	didn't	hadn't	

 Find the double negatives in the paragraph below. On your own paper, rewrite those sentences correctly. (There is usually more than one way to correct a double negative.)

Example: The family couldn't hardly wait to fly.
Corrected: The family could hardly wait to fly.
Corrected: The family couldn't wait to fly.

1   Almost since the beginning of time, people have wanted
2 to fly like the birds. None of the early inventions were no good.
3 They didn't fly at all. At first, the Wright brothers didn't have no
4 success either. Finally, they found a way to keep their plane in
5 flight. That changed things forever. Other inventors improved
6 on the Wright brothers' idea. Eventually, airplanes were
7 everywhere. Today, there aren't hardly any places that you
8 can't never reach by flying.

 Write a short paragraph about a time when you were frustrated. Use some negative expressions but avoid using any double negatives.

Improving Your Sentence Style

There are a number of ways to add variety to your sentences and improve your writing style. Here are four of the most common ways.

1 **Combine short sentences.**

2 **Use different types of sentences.**

3 **Expand sentences by adding words and phrases.**

4 **Model sentences of other writers.**

What happens when too many sentences in a paragraph are the same length or follow the same pattern? Read the following paragraph to find out.

> LITTLE VARIETY
>
> I visited the Smithsonian's National Air and Space Museum. I saw part of the *Apollo 11* spacecraft. Three astronauts flew in this craft. Astronauts Armstrong, Aldrin, and Collins went to the moon in 1969. They worked, ate, and slept in the command module. They were there for eight days. The command module was very small.

Using a variety of sentences would keep this paragraph from sounding choppy. Read the following version, which has a better variety of sentences.

> GOOD VARIETY
>
> When I visited the Smithsonian's National Air and Space Museum, I saw part of the *Apollo 11* spacecraft. In 1969, astronauts Armstrong, Aldrin, and Collins flew this craft to the moon. The command module was very small, but the astronauts worked, ate, and slept there for eight days.

 Read the paragraph below. Then, on your own paper, change the paragraph by creating more sentence variety.

1   I visited Kitty Hawk last summer. Kitty Hawk is in North
2 Carolina. That is where the Wright brothers first flew their
3 airplane. They flew it in 1903. I liked the museum. I loved walking
4 on the sand and climbing up Kill Devil Hill. I saw the memorial
5 tower up there.

Answers

 Possible answers:
None of the early inventions were good.
At first, the Wright brothers didn't have success either.
Today, there are hardly any places that you can't reach by flying.

Answers

     Last summer, I visited Kitty Hawk, North Carolina, where the Wright brothers first flew their airplane in 1903. I liked the museum, but I loved walking on the sand and climbing up Kill Devil Hill to see the memorial tower.

BASIC ELEMENTS

How can I make my sentences flow more smoothly?

Writers often combine sentences to help their writing flow more smoothly. If you have too many short sentences, your writing will sound choppy. Combining some of the sentences will add variety to your writing and improve your overall writing style.

Combine with Key Words or Phrases

One way to combine sentences is to use key words or phrases.

MOVE A KEY WORD FROM ONE SENTENCE TO ANOTHER	
Short Sentences	*Combined Sentences*
Katherine Stinson was a flier. She was a stunt flier.	**Katherine Stinson was a stunt flier.**

MOVE A KEY PHRASE FROM ONE SENTENCE TO ANOTHER	
Bessie Coleman, the first African American aviator, earned an international pilot's license. She earned it in 1922.	**In 1922, Bessie Coleman, the first African American aviator, earned an international pilot's license.**

 Combine each pair of sentences below by moving a key word or phrase from one sentence to another.

1. Bessie Coleman wanted to open a school for young African Americans. She wanted to open a flight school.

   1. Bessie Coleman wanted to open a flight school for young African Americans.

2. In 1910, Blanche Stuart Scott flew solo in the United States. She became the first woman to do that.

3. Amelia Earhart was the first person to fly alone from Honolulu, Hawaii, to California. She made the flight in 1935.

4. Anne Morrow Lindbergh was a copilot for her husband, Charles Lindbergh. She was also a radio operator for him.

5. Many women are part of aviation history. They were brave.

 Write NOW Write a pair of sentences for a classmate to combine. Make sure your sentences can be combined using a key word or phrase.

Combine with a Series of Words

As you've already seen, sentences can be combined using a key word or phrase. Sentences can also be combined using a series of words or phrases.

COMBINE WITH A SERIES OF WORDS OR PHRASES	
Short Sentences	*Combined Sentences*
Hot-air balloons can be made of nylon. They can be made of acrylic. They can be made of polyester.	**Hot-air balloons can be made of nylon, acrylic, or polyester.**
The hot-air balloon is an aircraft that has an envelope to hold hot air. It has a basket to carry people. It has a heating system to warm the air in the balloon.	**The hot-air balloon is an aircraft that has an envelope to hold hot air, a basket to carry people, and a heating system to warm the air in the balloon.**

> Be sure to use commas between the words or phrases in your series. See 582.1. The items in any series must be alike (or parallel). For example, if the first item is a phrase, all the items must be phrases. The same is true for series containing words or clauses.

 Combine the following groups of sentences with a series of words or phrases. (You may need to change some words to make the sentences work.)

1. The mathematician Archimedes explored the idea of flying in balloons. The English scientist Roger Bacon did, too. So did the German philosopher Albertus Magnus.

2. In 1783, Joseph and Etienne Montgolfier powered the first hot-air balloon by burning straw in a fire pit attached to the bottom of the balloon. They burned wood in the fire pit, too. They also burned other materials in the fire pit.

3. When the brothers tested the balloon, a sheep went up in the balloon basket. A duck was on board. A rooster was also on board.

 Write NOW Write three sentences for a classmate to combine. Make sure that your sentences can be combined using a series of words or phrases.

Answers

 Possible answers:

2. In 1910, Blanche Stuart Scott became the first woman to fly solo in the United States.

3. In 1935, Amelia Earhart was the first person to fly alone from Honolulu, Hawaii, to California.

4. Anne Morrow Lindbergh was a copilot and radio operator for her husband, Charles Lindbergh.

5. Many brave women are part of aviation history.

Answers

1. The mathematician Archimedes, the English scientist Roger Bacon, and the German philosopher Albertus Magnus all explored the idea of flying in balloons.

2. In 1783, Joseph and Etienne Montgolfier powered the first hot-air balloon by burning straw, wood, and other materials in a fire pit attached to the bottom of the balloon.

3. When the brothers tested the balloon, a sheep, a duck, and a rooster went up in the balloon basket.

Combine with Subjects and Predicates

Another way to combine sentences is to move a subject or predicate from one sentence to another. When you do this, you create a compound subject or a compound predicate. (See page 497.)

COMBINE WITH COMPOUND SUBJECTS AND PREDICATES

Short Sentences	Combined with a Compound Subject
Orville Wright was a pilot. Wilbur Wright was a pilot, too.	Orville and Wilbur **Wright were pilots.**

Short Sentences	Combined with a Compound Predicate
The brothers owned a bicycle shop. They explored the idea of flying.	The brothers owned a bicycle shop and explored the idea of flying.

 Combine each set of sentences below by using a compound subject or a compound predicate (change the verb when necessary).

1. Orville Wright was an inventor. So was Wilbur Wright.
   1. Orville and Wilbur Wright were inventors.
2. The brothers built the first airplane. They flew the first airplane.
3. The first flights covered short distances. The first flights lasted less than a minute.
4. Orville made changes to the design. Wilbur made changes to the design.
5. In 1908, the brothers demonstrated the plane. They set several records.
6. Americans were interested in the plane. Europeans were interested, too.
7. The United States government ordered Wright airplanes. Countries in Europe ordered them, too.
8. The Wright brothers formed a company. They built their planes.
9. The brothers earned awards. They received honors.

 Write two related sentences for your classmates to combine. Make sure they can be combined using a compound subject or a compound predicate.

What can I do to add variety to my writing?

Writers use different types of sentences to add variety to their writing and make it sound interesting. The three common types of sentences are **simple**, **compound**, and **complex**. By learning to write these three types of sentences effectively, you can create sentence variety in your writing.

Write Simple Sentences

A **simple sentence** is one independent clause. (An independent clause is a group of words that can stand alone as a sentence.) A simple sentence can, however, have a compound subject, a compound predicate, or both.

SIMPLE SENTENCE = ONE INDEPENDENT CLAUSE

Simple Subject with a Simple Predicate
The early days of aviation had many heroes.

Simple Subject with a Compound Predicate
Pilots faced and overcame dangerous situations.

Compound Subject with a Simple Predicate
Amelia Earhart and Charles Lindbergh flew on heroic flights.

 Find the five simple sentences in the paragraph below and copy them. Underline the subjects once and the predicates twice.

1 Charles Lindbergh was a famous American pilot. Lindbergh
2 flew his airplane nonstop from New York City to Paris. The
3 plane was called the *Spirit of St. Louis*. Lindbergh made the
4 flight because he wanted to win a $25,000 prize. He flew across
5 the Atlantic Ocean and landed in Paris, France. Americans
6 and Europeans cheered for Lindbergh. He had made the first
7 successful transatlantic flight, so people called him a hero.

 Write three simple sentences about someone who is a hero to you.

1 Write one with a simple subject and simple predicate.
2 Write one with a simple subject and compound predicate.
3 Write one with a compound subject and simple predicate.

BASIC ELEMENTS

---

 2. The brothers built and flew the first airplane.
3. The first flights covered short distances and lasted less than a minute.
4. Orville and Wilbur made changes to the design.
5. In 1908, the brothers demonstrated the plane and set several records.
6. Americans and Europeans were interested in the plane.
7. The United States government and countries in Europe ordered Wright airplanes.
8. The Wright brothers formed a company and built their planes.
9. The brothers earned awards and received honors.

 1. Charles Lindbergh <u>was</u> a famous American pilot.
2. <u>Lindbergh</u> <u>flew</u> his airplane nonstop from New York City to Paris.
3. The <u>plane</u> <u>was called</u> the *Spirit of St. Louis*.
4. <u>He</u> <u>flew</u> across the Atlantic Ocean and <u>landed</u> in Paris, France.
5. <u>Americans and Europeans</u> <u>cheered</u> for Lindbergh.

BASIC ELEMENTS

Create Compound Sentences

A **compound sentence** is made up of two or more simple sentences joined together. Often, they are joined with a coordinating conjunction and a comma. (Coordinating conjunctions are words like *and, but,* and *so.*)

COMPOUND SENTENCE = TWO INDEPENDENT CLAUSES

> Yuri Gagarin was a Russian cosmonaut, and he became the first person to orbit Earth. (A comma and the conjunction *and* join the two independent clauses.)
>
> Russia was the first country to enter the "space race," but the United States quickly followed. (A comma and the conjunction *but* join the two independent clauses.)

 On your own paper, combine the pairs of simple sentences below to create compound sentences. Use commas and the coordinating conjunctions *and, but,* or *so.*

1. The United States launched its first manned spacecraft in 1961. Alan Shepard became the first American astronaut in space.

   1. The United States launched its first manned spacecraft in 1961, and Alan Shepard became the first American astronaut in space.

2. The first phase of space travel in this country used *Mercury* spacecraft. The second phase used bigger *Gemini* spacecraft.

3. The *Apollo* spacecraft were the third phase. They were created to explore the moon.

4. In 1969, Neil Armstrong stepped onto the moon. He said, "That's one small step for man, one giant leap for mankind."

5. Five more *Apollo* missions set out for the moon. *Apollo 13* had technical problems and returned to Earth.

6. Later, NASA launched its first space station. Astronauts could live and work in space for several months.

Write NOW Write two compound sentences that tell what you think it would be like to travel in space.

Develop Complex Sentences

A **complex sentence** has both an independent clause and at least one dependent clause. Because a dependent clause cannot stand alone as a sentence, it must be connected to an independent clause.

Complex sentences may contain a subordinating conjunction, such as *after, although, because, before, until, when,* and *while.* (See page 744 for more subordinating conjunctions.) Complex sentences may also contain a relative pronoun such as *that, which,* and *who.* (See page 710 for more.)

COMPLEX SENTENCE =

AN INDEPENDENT CLAUSE	+	A DEPENDENT CLAUSE
Airplanes have instruments		that pilots use in bad weather.

A DEPENDENT CLAUSE	+	AN INDEPENDENT CLAUSE
When pilots fly in a storm,		they have to trust their gauges.

 Number your paper from 2 to 7. Then write the dependent clause found in each sentence below.

1. Since pilots can't always see where they are flying, they use flight instruments to get valuable information.

   1. Since pilots can't always see where they are flying

2. If pilots study their instruments, they will know the plane's altitude, speed, and fuel supply.

3. A compass, which shows the airplane's direction, helps the pilot stay on course.

4. Another gauge measures cabin pressure because planes fly so high.

5. Before they land, pilots get directions from radio air controllers on the ground.

6. Unless planes have altimeters, pilots won't know how high they are above sea level.

7. Some people like to fly planes while others prefer being passengers.

Write NOW Write two complex sentences about an airplane or an airplane flight you've taken or heard about. (Be sure to use commas correctly.)

Answers

2. The first phase of space travel in this country used *Mercury* spacecraft, but the second phase used bigger *Gemini* spacecraft.

3. The *Apollo* spacecraft were the third phase, and they were created to explore the moon.

4. In 1969, Neil Armstrong stepped onto the moon, and he said, "That's one small step for man, one giant leap for mankind."

5. Five more *Apollo* missions set out for the moon, but *Apollo 13* had technical problems and returned to Earth.

6. Later, NASA launched its first space station, so astronauts could live and work in space for several months.

Answers

2. If pilots study their instruments

3. which shows the airplane's direction

4. because planes fly so high

5. Before they land

6. Unless planes have altimeters

7. while others prefer being passengers

Building Effective Sentences **518–519**

518

agree model EXPAND
order *combine* 519
Building Effective Sentences

BASIC ELEMENTS

Use Questions and Commands

Writers use a variety of sentences to make statements, ask questions, give commands, or show strong emotion. See the chart below.

KINDS OF SENTENCES

Declarative .	Makes a statement about a person, a place, a thing, or an idea	Amelia Earhart flew across the Atlantic Ocean alone.	This is the most common kind of sentence.
Interrogative ?	Asks a question	Can you tell me more about Amelia Earhart?	A question gets the reader's attention.
Imperative .	Gives a command	Read about Earhart on the FAA Web site.	Commands often appear in dialogue or directions.
Exclamatory !	Shows strong emotion or feeling	Amelia's plane disappeared!	Use these sentences for occasional emphasis.

 On a piece of paper, write the numbers 1 to 7. Identify each of the sentences shown below by writing "D" for declarative, "INT" for interrogative, "IMP" for imperative, or "EX" for exclamatory.

1. In 1932, Amelia Earhart flew across the Atlantic Ocean in 14 hours and 56 minutes.
2. Amelia Earhart had incredible courage!
3. In 1937, she began a flight around the world with her navigator, Frederick Noonan.
4. "Take a picture of Miss Earhart beside her plane," the editor said.
5. What happened to her and her navigator?
6. When her plane never arrived at Howland Island, southwest of Hawaii, a search found nothing.
7. Can you believe people are still looking for her plane?

 Write four sentences—one of each kind—about someone you feel showed courage.

What can I do to add details to my sentences?

Expand with Prepositional Phrases

Writers use prepositional phrases to add details and information to their sentences. The chart below shows how this is done. Prepositional phrases act like adjectives or adverbs. *Remember:* A prepositional phrase includes a preposition, the object of a preposition, and any words that modify the object. (See page 742 for a list of prepositions.)

PREPOSITIONAL PHRASE	USE IN A SENTENCE
Early biplanes had two pairs *of wings*.	The phrase acts as an **adjective** to describe the noun "pairs."
Pilots took passengers *on short flights*.	The phrase acts as an **adverb** to modify the verb "took."

■ Prepositional phrases that are used as adjectives answer the adjective questions: *How many? Which one? What color? What size?*

■ Prepositional phrases used as adverbs answer the adverb questions: *When? How? How often? How long? Where? How much?*

 Number a piece of paper from 2 to 6. Write the prepositional phrase or phrases that you find in each of these sentences.

1. During the 1920s, the most popular planes were biplanes.
   1. During the 1920s
2. These planes were made of wood and fabric.
3. Supports and wire between the wings gave the biplane strength.
4. Sometimes the front edge of the wooden propeller was covered with metal.
5. There were few airports, so pilots often landed in farm pastures.
6. Pilots called barnstormers flew in air shows across the country.

 Use one or two prepositional phrases to add information to each of the sentences below.

1 Biplanes were popular planes.
2 Pilots wore goggles.
3 The planes had wooden propellers.

Answers

 1. D
2. EX
3. D
4. IMP
5. INT
6. D
7. INT

Answers

 2. of wood and fabric
3. between the wings
4. of the wooden propeller
   with metal
5. in farm pastures
6. in air shows
   across the country

Expand with Appositive Phrases

Writers sometimes make their sentences more interesting by adding appositive phrases. An **appositive phrase** renames the noun or pronoun before it and is set off from the rest of the sentence with commas.

> **APPOSITIVE PHRASES**
>
> **The Tuskegee Airmen,** a group of fighter pilots, **helped win the war.**
> (The appositive "a group of fighter pilots" renames the noun "Tuskegee Airmen.")
>
> **General Daniel "Chappie" James,** a Tuskegee pilot, **became a hero.**
> (The appositive "a Tuskegee pilot" renames the noun "General Daniel 'Chappie' James.")

 On your own paper, make a chart like the one below. Read the paragraph that follows the chart and list the appositive phrases you find. Also list the noun or pronoun each appositive renames. (The first one has been done for you.)

Appositive Phrase	Noun or Pronoun It Renames
a group of fighter pilots	Tuskegee Airmen

1 　The Tuskegee Airmen, a group of fighter pilots, played an
2 important role in World War II. Beginning in 1941, they served
3 with the United States Army Air Force in Tuskegee, Alabama.
4 These men, all highly trained pilots, made up the first African
5 American flying unit in the U.S. military. The first group to train
6 at Tuskegee, the 99th Pursuit Squadron, was led by Lt. Col.
7 Benjamin O. Davis. The 99th was the only escort group not to
8 lose a bomber to enemy planes. The brave Tuskegee pilots, 992
9 men in all, flew 1,578 missions and won more than 850 medals.

Write NOW Write two or three sentences about what you think life would be like as a pilot. Use an appositive in each sentence.

How can I make my sentences more interesting?

Model Sentences

You can learn a great deal about writing by imitating, or modeling, the sentences of other writers. Studying these sentences can teach you how to punctuate and how to put parts together. When you come across sentences that you like, practice writing some of your own that use the same pattern.

PROFESSIONAL MODEL	STUDENT MODELS
The mountains have been my lifelong companions, and I still make my home at their feet.	The gym has been my favorite hangout, but I sometimes ride my unicycle at the playground.
Marisa marveled at the open-air market with stalls of vegetables and cheese, people laughing and chatting, and music blaring. —*National Geographic*	My little sister clapped for the parade of clowns in huge shoes and curly red wigs, horses snorting and prancing, and bands marching.

Guidelines for Modeling

- Find a sentence or a short passage that you like and write it down.
- Follow the pattern of the sentence or passage as you write about your own subject. (You do not have to follow the model exactly.)
- Build each sentence one part at a time and check your work when you are finished. (Take your time.)
- Find other sentences to model and keep practicing. Share your sentences with a classmate.

Write NOW On your own paper, model the following sentences. Remember, you do not have to follow the model sentence exactly.

1 The hill was steep and slick, but I knew there was no turning back.

2 Having completed the work, Joshua carefully packed his toolbox and went home.

Answers

Appositive Phrase	**Noun or Pronoun It Renames**
a group of fighter pilots	Tuskegee Airmen
all highly trained pilots	men
the 99th Pursuit Squadron	group
992 men in all	pilots

Develop a Sentence Style

Modeling sentences can help you make your writing more exciting, lively, and appealing. The following writing techniques will also help you improve your style. (Also see page 43.)

Varying Sentence Beginnings

Do too many of your sentences begin with a subject and a verb? Try beginning with a dependent clause or with a phrase, as in the sentences below. This adds variety to the subject-verb pattern.

When I awoke, **there were snowflakes on my eyes**.
—*True Grit* by Charles Portis

Hobbling on one foot, **Wanda opened the closet door and turned on the light**.
—*Summer of the Swans* by Betsy Byars

From the stable, **the pair of oxen bellowed and rolled their eyes in terror**.
—*The Book of Three* by Lloyd Alexander

Moving Adjectives

Usually, you write adjectives before the nouns they modify. Notice how these writers emphasized the adjectives by placing them after the nouns.

The children, shouting and screaming, **came charging back into their homeroom**.
—*The Friends* by Rosa Guy

Her brown face, upraised, **was stained with tears**.
—*The Red Badge of Courage* by Stephen Crane

Repeating a Word

You can repeat a word to emphasize a particular idea or feeling.

. . . that government of the people, **by** the people, **for** the people **shall not perish from the earth**.
—"Gettysburg Address" by Abraham Lincoln

Life is an exciting **business and most** exciting **when it is lived for others**.
—Interview with Helen Keller

Write NOW On your own paper, model one sentence from each of the three categories listed above.

organize describe explain *tell* share

Constructing Strong Paragraphs

If you can write a paragraph well, you can write anything. Writer Donald Hall calls a paragraph a "maxi-sentence" or a "mini-essay." Think of it as an important building block for all of your writing. If you can create strong, well-organized paragraphs, you can also create effective essays, book reviews, and reports.

A paragraph is made up of a group of sentences focused on one topic. Each sentence should add something to the overall picture. A paragraph can explain a process, share an opinion, describe something, or tell a story.

Mini Index

You will learn about . . .
- the parts of a paragraph.
- types of paragraphs.
- writing effective paragraphs.
- adding details to paragraphs.
- gathering details.
- organizing your details.
- refining your details.
- turning paragraphs into essays.
- using a checklist.

The Parts of a Paragraph

Most paragraphs have three main parts: a topic sentence, a body, and a closing sentence. A paragraph usually begins with a *topic sentence* that tells what the paragraph is about. The sentences in the *body* share details about the topic, and the *closing sentence* brings the paragraph to a close.

Topic sentence
. . . .

Body

Closing sentence
. . . .

> ### Striking It Rich
>
> Blue jeans were invented by a man named Levi Strauss during the California gold rush. In 1850, when so many gold diggers arrived in California, Strauss took bolts of canvas to San Francisco. He planned to make tents to sell to the miners. When that didn't work out, Strauss used the canvas to make pants that miners could wear for their rough work. Miners bought these pants as fast as Strauss could make them. These pants became the very first Levi jeans, and they changed the clothing world forever. Later, Strauss made the pants out of blue denim instead of canvas and added copper rivets. Since that time, blue jeans have become popular throughout the United States and around the world.

 Respond to the reading. What common item of clothing is discussed in this paragraph? Based on the history of Levi jeans, what is the double meaning of the title?

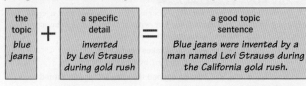

A Closer Look at the Parts

The Topic Sentence

The topic sentence tells the reader what a paragraph is going to be about. A good topic sentence (1) *names the topic* and (2) *states a specific detail or a feeling* about it. Here is a simple formula for writing a topic sentence.

the topic		a specific detail		a good topic sentence
blue jeans	**+**	*invented by Levi Strauss during gold rush*	**=**	**Blue jeans were invented by a man named Levi Strauss during the California gold rush.**

The topic sentence is usually the first sentence in a paragraph, although sometimes it comes later. It guides the direction of the sentences in the rest of the paragraph.

> *Blue jeans were invented by a man named Levi Strauss during the California gold rush.*

The Body

The sentences in the body of the paragraph include the details needed to understand the topic.

- **Use specific details to make your paragraph interesting.** The specific details below are shown in red.

  > *Later, Strauss made the pants out of blue denim instead of canvas and added copper rivets.*

- **Organize your sentences in the best possible order.** Three common ways to organize sentences are chronological (time) order, order of location, and order of importance. (See page 551.)

The Closing Sentence

The closing sentence comes after all the details in the body. It will often restate the topic, give the reader something to think about, or provide a transition to the following paragraph.

> *Since that time, blue jeans have become popular throughout the United States and around the world.*

BASIC ELEMENTS

 Respond to the reading.

Blue jeans

During the gold rush, both the miners and Levi Strauss made a lot of money— the miners from the gold and Levi Strauss from selling his jeans.

How can I vary the types of paragraphs I write?

There are four types of paragraphs: *narrative, descriptive, expository,* and *persuasive.* Each type requires a different way of thinking and planning.

Compose Narrative Paragraphs

In a **narrative paragraph**, you share a personal story or an important experience with the reader. The details in a narrative paragraph should answer the 5 W's *(who? what? when? where? and why?).* A narrative is often organized according to time (what happened *first, next, then, finally*).

Topic sentence

Body

Closing sentence

A Play Day

It was Saturday morning, and I was ready for my first Service Day. Our school requires each student to volunteer for community service once a semester. My friends and I decided to work at Smith House, a place for families who need somewhere to stay. We walked inside the house, and before we could take off our coats, 10 little kids ambushed us and begged, "Please play with us!" We read books, played board games, and even went outside to shoot hoops. When we left at noon, our new playmates hugged us and gave us loads of high fives. My friends and I agreed that a day of playing with young kids was the perfect service project for us.

 Respond to the reading. Find the key word repeated in the topic sentence and the closing sentence. Does this paragraph answer the 5 W's?

 Write your own paragraph. Write a paragraph that tells about an experience you've had recently. Be sure to include the 5 W's and whatever details are needed.

Create Descriptive Paragraphs

When you write a **descriptive paragraph**, you give a detailed picture of a person, a place, an object, or an event. Descriptive paragraphs include many sensory details *(sight, sound, smell, taste, touch).* The following sample describes the sights, sounds, smells, and feelings of a local soup kitchen.

Topic sentence

Body

Closing sentence

Soup's On

One Friday night, my family decided to help at a local soup kitchen. By the time we arrived, the kitchen was filled with noisy people doing all sorts of things. Across the room beside the sink, some of them were washing vegetables, while others were peeling and chopping. Several people gathered around the stove that was in the middle of the kitchen. They added chopped vegetables to the steaming soup pots. Soon the smell of hot vegetable soup filled the room. On the counter between the kitchen and the dining area, another group worked like an assembly line putting together huge stacks of ham and cheese sandwiches. I set the paper plates, salt-and-pepper shakers, and butter plates on the tables. Finally, a stream of hungry people arrived. They seemed to really enjoy the meal and thanked us for everything.

 Respond to the reading. Which of the five senses are covered in the paragraph? Which two or three details are especially descriptive?

 Write your own paragraph. Write a paragraph that describes a place with lots of sights, sounds, and so on.

BASIC ELEMENTS

Answers

 Respond to the reading.

Service

Yes:
Who: narrator and friends
What: volunteered for community
  service
Where: a family shelter
When: Saturday morning
Why: school requirement

Answers

 Respond to the reading.

sights: people beside the sink; washing, peeling, and chopping vegetables; people gathered around the stove; steaming soup pots; assembly line; stacks of ham and cheese sandwiches; stream of hungry people
sounds: noisy people, chopping vegetables
smells: hot vegetable soup
feelings: enjoyed the meal and thanked us

528–529 The Basic Elements of Writing

528

529

organize *share* explain *tell*
describe

Constructing Strong Paragraphs

BASIC ELEMENTS

Write Expository Paragraphs

In an **expository paragraph**, you share information. You can explain a subject, give directions, or show how to do something. Transition words like *first, next, then,* and *finally* are often used in expository writing.

Topic sentence
....

Body

Closing sentence
....

How to Start a Pet Pantry

A pet pantry is a place for citizens with low incomes to get free food and supplies for their pets. To create a pet pantry in your neighborhood, first meet with the people at your local humane society. See if they will help you find a place for the pantry and a way to distribute food and supplies. Then talk with grocery-store managers and local veterinarians. Ask if you may set up donation containers in their stores and clinics. Next, contact local newspapers and television stations to get the word out. Also make posters and flyers to make sure that people know about the pet pantry. Finally, ask your parents to help you collect the pet food and supplies and take them to the pantry. A well-run pet pantry can help keep people and their pets together.

 Respond to the reading. List the transitions used between sentences in the paragraph above. How many transitions did the writer use? (See pages 572–573 for a list of transitions.)

 Write an expository paragraph. Write a paragraph that explains how to do something—like play a game, make a snack, or plant a garden. Be sure to use transitions to connect your ideas.

Develop Persuasive Paragraphs

In a **persuasive paragraph**, you give your opinion (or strong feeling) about a topic. To be persuasive, you must include plenty of reasons, facts, and details to support your opinion. Persuasive writing is usually organized by order of importance or by logical order (as in the paragraph below).

Topic sentence
....

Body

Closing sentence
....

Get Involved in a Trash Bash

Participating in a trash bash or neighborhood cleanup is a great way to improve your community. First of all, you will help the city's trash collectors get rid of some of the garbage in places where it is hard to pick up. This will save the city time and money. In addition, if you help clean up piles of trash, you will make your neighborhood a better place to live and play. Most importantly, if you clean up the garbage, your neighborhood will be a safer place. Piles of garbage can contain things like broken glass and dangerous chemicals. Germs produced by piles of garbage can make people sick. There are many good reasons to clean up your environment, and a trash bash can help you do it.

 Respond to the reading. What is the writer's opinion in the paragraph? What reasons does she give to support her opinion? When is the most important reason given?

 Give your opinion. Write an opinion about an environmental topic. Then list three strong reasons to support your opinion.

Answers

 Respond to the reading.

first meet with the people . . .
Then talk with grocery-store . . .
Next, contact . . .
Also make . . .
Finally, ask . . .

Answers

 Respond to the reading.

Participating in a trash bash or neighborhood cleanup is a great way to improve your community.
1. You will help get rid of garbage in places where it is hard to pick up.
2. You will save the city time and money.
3. You will make your neighborhood a better place to live and play.
4. Your neighborhood will be safer.
The most important reason is given last.

Writing Effective Paragraphs

Whenever you write paragraphs, use the following general guidelines.

Prewriting **Selecting a Topic and Details**

- Select a specific topic.
- Collect facts, examples, and details about your topic.
- Write a topic sentence that states what your paragraph is going to be about. (See page **525** for help.)
- Decide on the best way to arrange your details.

Writing **Creating the First Draft**

- Start your paragraph with the topic sentence.
- Write sentences in the body that support your topic. Use the details you collected as a guide.
- Connect your sentences with transitions. (See pages **572–573**.)
- End with a sentence that restates your topic, leaves the reader with a final thought, or leads into the next paragraph.

Revising **Improving Your Writing**

- Add information if you need to say more about your topic.
- Move sentences that aren't in the correct order.
- Cut sentences that do not support the topic.
- Rewrite any sentences that are not clear.

Editing **Checking for Conventions**

- Check the revised version of your writing for capitalization, punctuation, grammar, and spelling errors.
- Then write a neat final copy and proofread it.

 When you write a paragraph, remember that readers want . . .
- original ideas. *(They want something new and interesting.)*
- personality. *(They want to hear the writer's voice.)*

How can I find interesting details?

No paragraph is complete without good supporting details. Here are some types of details you can use in expository and persuasive paragraphs: facts, explanations, definitions, reasons, examples, and comparisons. You might get these details from personal knowledge and memories or from other sources of information.

Use Personal Details

For narrative and descriptive writing, personal details can add interest. Personal details can include sensory, memory, and reflective details.

- **Sensory details** are things that you see, hear, smell, taste, and touch. (These details are important in descriptive paragraphs.)

    Soon the smell of hot vegetable soup filled the room.

- **Memory details** are things you remember from experience. (These details are important in narrative paragraphs.)

    When we left at noon, our new playmates hugged us and gave us loads of high fives.

- **Reflective details** are things you think about or hope for. (These details are often used in narrative and descriptive paragraphs.)

    I felt good about helping at the soup kitchen, and I hope my family decides to do it again soon.

Use Other Sources of Details

To collect details from other sources, use the following tips.

1. **Talk with someone you know.** Parents, neighbors, friends, or teachers may know a lot about your topic.

2. **Write for information.** If you think a museum, a business, or a government office has information you need, send for it.

3. **Read about your topic.** Gather details from books, magazines, and newspapers.

4. **Use the Internet.** The quickest source of information is the Internet. Remember to check Web sites carefully for reliability. (See page **376**.)

BASIC ELEMENTS

532-533   The Basic Elements of Writing

532

organize *share* **explain** *tell*
describe

Constructing Strong Paragraphs

533

BASIC ELEMENTS

How do I know what kinds of details to gather?

Here are tips that will help you collect the right kinds of details when you write paragraphs about people, places, objects, and events—and also when you write definitions.

Writing About a Person

When writing about or describing a person, make sure you collect plenty of information. The following guidelines will help.

Observe ■ If possible, carefully watch the person. Maybe the person laughs in a special way or wears a certain type of clothing.

Interview ■ Talk with your subject. Write down words and phrases that the person uses.

Research ■ Use whatever sources are necessary—books, articles, the Internet—to find out more about this person.

Compare ■ Could your subject be compared to some other person?

Writing About a Place

When describing or writing about a place, use details that help the reader understand why the place is important to you.

Observe ■ Study the place you plan to write about. Use photos, postcards, or videos if you can't observe the place in person.

Remember ■ Think of a story (or an anecdote) about this place.

Describe ■ Include the sights, sounds, and smells of the place.

Compare ■ Compare your place to other places.

Writing About an Object

When writing about an object, tell your reader what kind of object it is, what it looks like, how it is used, and why this object is important to you.

Observe ■ Think about these questions: How is the object used? Who uses it? How does it work? What does it look like?

Research ■ Learn about the object. Try to find out when it was first made and used. Ask other people about it.

Define ■ What class or category does this object fit into? (See "Writing a Definition" on page 533.)

Writing About an Event

When writing about or describing an event, focus on the important actions or on one interesting part. Also include sensory details and answer the 5 W's. The following guidelines will help.

Observe ■ Study the event carefully. What sights, sounds, tastes, and smells come to mind? Listen to what people around you are saying.

Remember ■ When you write about something that happened to you, recall as many details connected with the event as you can.

List ■ Answer the *who? what? when? where?* and *why?* questions for facts about the event.

Writing a Definition

When you write a definition, you need to think about three things.

● First put the **term** you are defining *(coyote)* into a **class** or category of similar things *(wild member of the dog family)*.

● Then list special **characteristics** that make this individual different from others in that class *(like a wolf, only smaller)*.

Term—*A coyote*

Class—*is a wild member of the dog family*

Characteristic—*that is like a wolf, only smaller.*

What can I do to organize my details effectively?

After you've gathered your details, you need to organize them in the best possible way. You can organize a paragraph by *time, location, importance,* or *comparison*. Graphic organizers can help you keep your details in order.

Use Chronological Order

Chronological means "according to time." Transition words and phrases that tell days, months, and years are often used in chronological paragraphs. So are words like *first, second, then,* and *finally*. A time line can help you organize your details.

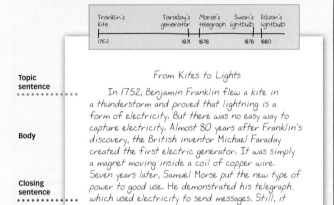

Topic sentence

Body

Closing sentence

From Kites to Lights

In 1752, Benjamin Franklin flew a kite in a thunderstorm and proved that lightning is a form of electricity. But there was no easy way to capture electricity. Almost 80 years after Franklin's discovery, the British inventor Michael Faraday created the first electric generator. It was simply a magnet moving inside a coil of copper wire. Seven years later, Samuel Morse put the new type of power to good use. He demonstrated his telegraph, which used electricity to send messages. Still, it took another 40 years before Sir Joseph Swan (in England) and Thomas Edison (in America) created the most famous electrical invention, the lightbulb.

 Respond to the reading. How are dates given in the time line? How are they given in the paragraph?

Use Order of Location

Often, you can organize descriptive details by order of location. For example, a description may move from left to right, from top to bottom, or from one direction (north) to another (south). Words or phrases like *next to, before, above, below, east, west, north,* and *south* are used to show location. A drawing or map can help you organize your details.

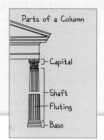

Parts of a Column

Topic sentence

Body

Closing sentence

Parts of a Corinthian Column

A Corinthian column has three main parts: a base, a shaft, and a capital. The base is a large disk of stone that looks like rings stacked up. It has to be very strong to hold the weight of everything above it. The shaft stands on top of the base. This long cylinder is built from shorter sections of stone. Grooves called "flutes" run up and down its sides. On top of the column is the capital. It's shaped like an upside-down bell. Stone carvings of leaves surround the capital. All these parts come together to form a column that is both strong and beautiful.

 Respond to the reading. On the drawing, why is the column shown in two sections? In the paragraph, with what part of the column does the description begin? Where does it end?

BASIC ELEMENTS

Answers

 Respond to the reading.

In the time line the dates are given as years.
In the paragraph the first date is given as a year, but the remaining dates are given in terms of time spans: 80 years after, seven years later, another 40 years.

Answers

 Respond to the reading.

The shaft is shown in two sections because it is built from shorter sections of stone.
The description begins with the base and ends with the capital.

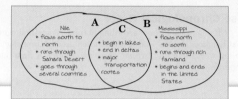

Use Order of Importance

Persuasive and expository paragraphs are often organized by order of importance—from *most* to *least* important, or from *least* to *most* important.

Most important		Least important
1. _____		3 _____
2. _____	**or**	2. _____
3. _____		1. _____
Least important		Most important

Topic sentence

Body

Closing sentence

The Aztecs

    Aztec civilization clearly was the most advanced culture in the Americas at one time. The Aztecs were the first people to make hot cocoa and other chocolate treats. They also wrote books and made colorful paintings. Aztec miners found gold, silver, and turquoise that artists used for jewelry and carvings. Engineers built a city named Tenochtitlan that had palaces, temples, and the world's largest pyramid. Astronomers watched the movements of the sun, the moon, and the stars to create calendars. If you still aren't sure that the Aztecs were the most advanced people of their time, here is one last fact: They could even predict the coming of comets!

 Respond to the reading. How are the details organized in this paragraph? On your own paper, list them in reverse order (most to least, least to most). Which order works better?

Use Comparison-Contrast Order

    When you write a comparison-contrast paragraph, you want to show how two subjects are both alike and different. A Venn diagram can be used to show differences (**A** and **B**) and similarities (**C**).

Topic sentence

Body

Closing sentence

Two Mighty Rivers

    The Nile and the Mississippi Rivers are alike in many ways, but they are also very different. Each of these long rivers begins in a lake and ends in a delta, but they flow in different directions. The Mississippi flows from north to south, while the Nile flows from south to north. These rivers run through very different types of land. The Mississippi travels through rich farmland, while the Nile flows through the Sahara Desert. Both rivers are major transportation routes for business and wildlife. These two great rivers are truly wonders of nature.

 Respond to the reading. Find two body sentences that include contrasting details about the two rivers. What two words are used to show the contrast?

 Write a paragraph. Choose two rivers, lakes, or oceans to compare. Use a Venn diagram to list the details. Then write your paragraph.

BASIC ELEMENTS

 Respond to the reading.

The details are organized from least to most important.

1. The Aztecs could predict the coming of comets.
2. Astronomers watched the movements of the sun, the moon, and the stars to create calendars.
3. Engineers built a city named Tenochtitlán that had palaces, temples, and the world's largest pyramid.
4. Artists made jewelry and carvings.
5. Aztec miners found gold, silver, and turquoise.
6. They wrote books and made colorful paintings.
7. Aztecs were the first people to make hot cocoa and other chocolate treats.

Organizing the details from least to most important feels more powerful.

 Respond to the reading.

Each of these long rivers begins in a lake and ends in a delta, but they flow in different directions.

The Mississippi travels through rich farmland, while the Nile flows through the Sahara Desert.

but, while

Constructing Strong Paragraphs **538-539**

538

539

organize share explain tell
describe

Constructing Strong Paragraphs

How can I be sure all my details work well?

Create Unity in Your Writing

In a well-written paragraph, each detail tells something about the topic. If a detail does not tell something about the topic, it breaks the *unity* of a paragraph and should probably be cut.

The detail (sentence) shown in blue in the following passage does not fit in with the rest of the paragraph. It disrupts the unity and should be cut.

> Many young boys served in both armies during the Civil War. Some fought alongside the men and did everything soldiers normally do. One thing these soldiers didn't do was shave regularly. Most boys, however, were either drummers or flag bearers.

 In the paragraph below, find three details (sentences) that do not support the topic sentence. Then read the paragraph aloud without those sentences. Did the unity of the paragraph improve?

1   Did you know that many famous writers played roles in the
2 Civil War? Probably other creative people also took part in the
3 war. Harriet Beecher Stowe wrote a novel called *Uncle Tom's*
4 *Cabin* that showed how slavery was wrong. My grandma has a
5 copy of that book. Louisa May Alcott, who wrote *Little Women,*
6 was a wartime nurse in an army hospital. Her novel was made
7 into a movie. Walt Whitman was a wartime nurse, too. After the
8 war, he wrote a poem about President Lincoln's death called
9 "O Captain! My Captain!" The poet Julia Ward Howe edited a
10 magazine that was against slavery. Each of these writers did
11 what they could to help with the war.

 Look at your paragraph. Study the comparison-contrast paragraph you wrote on page 537. Do all your details support your topic? Would the unity of your paragraph be improved if you cut a detail or two?

Develop Coherence from Start to Finish

An effective paragraph reads smoothly and clearly. When all the details in a paragraph are tied together well, the paragraph has *coherence* and is easy for the reader to follow. One way to make your writing smooth and coherent is to use transitions.

 Number your paper 1 to 7. Use the transitions listed below to help tie the essay together. (Use each transition only once.) When you finish, read the paragraph. Does it read smoothly? If not, switch some transitions.

first	in addition	besides	although
then	also	second	

A well-trained dog has many career opportunities. _____ (1) , there are jobs herding cattle and sheep. _____ (2) , there are jobs in law enforcement. _____ (3) tracking down criminals, dogs can keep the suspects under control once they're caught.

_____ (4) there are opportunities for dogs in the social services. Of course, dogs can be trained to guide people who are blind. They can _____ (5) pick up objects for people in wheelchairs or cheer up people in nursing homes. _____ (6) , dogs are natural athletes and entertainers. The TV and movie industries are always looking for a few good dogs. _____ (7) dogs have so many career opportunities, most dog owners are happy that their dogs are content to be pets.

 Read your paragraph. Read your comparison-contrast paragraph from page 537. Underline any parts that don't flow smoothly. Then use transitions to make the writing smoother. (See pages 572–573.)

BASIC ELEMENTS

Answers

 Probably other creative people also took part in the war.
My grandma has a copy of that book.
Her novel was made into a movie.

Answers

 1. First
2. Second
3. Besides
4. Then
5. also
6. In addition
7. Although

How can I turn my paragraphs into essays?

Use an Essay Plan

Turning a group of paragraphs into an essay is not simply a matter of placing one after another. To begin with, each paragraph needs to be well written and well organized. Here are some additional tips to follow.

1 Plan the organization.

Organize your essay in a way that fits your topic—time order, order of importance, order of location, and so on.

2 State the topic and focus in the first paragraph.

Use an interesting fact, example, or story to catch the reader's interest. Then tell what your essay is about in a focus statement, which includes the topic and a main idea or feeling about it.

3 Develop your writing idea in the middle paragraphs.

Use each paragraph in the body of your essay to explain and support one part of your focus statement. Each paragraph must have a topic sentence that deals with one part of the focus, followed with supporting details.

4 End with a concluding paragraph.

The final paragraph is usually a review of the main points in the essay. Your ending may emphasize the importance of the topic, or it may leave the reader with something to think about.

5 Use transition words or phrases to connect paragraphs.

In the topic sentences below, the transitions are shown in red. For a complete list of transitions, see pages 572–573.

> **In addition to** jeans, athletic shoes and sports jerseys are worn in nearly every nation in the world.
> ....
> **For many reasons,** clothing trends have begun in the United States.

How do I know if I have a strong paragraph?

You'll know that you have a strong paragraph if it gives the reader complete information on a specific topic. The first sentence should identify the topic and the other sentences should support it. Use the checklist below to help you plan and write effective paragraphs.

Ideas

_____ **1.** Do I focus on an interesting idea?

_____ **2.** Do I use enough specific details?

Organization

_____ **3.** Is my topic sentence clear?

_____ **4.** Have I organized the details in the best order?

Voice

_____ **5.** Do I show interest in—and knowledge of—my topic?

_____ **6.** Does my voice fit my audience? My purpose? My topic?

Word Choice

_____ **7.** Do I use specific nouns and active verbs?

_____ **8.** Do I use colorful adjectives and adverbs?

Sentence Fluency

_____ **9.** Have I written clear and complete sentences?

_____ **10.** Do I use a variety of sentence beginnings and lengths?

Conventions

_____ **11.** Do I use correct punctuation and capitalization?

_____ **12.** Do I use correct spelling and grammar?

improve
support

A Writer's Resource

organize
REFERENCE
select

A Writer's Resource

If you're like most students, you often have questions when you are in the middle of a writing assignment. If a question pops up when you're in class, you can ask your teacher or a classmate. If, however, a question pops up when you're not in class, you need another source to ask or check. This "Writer's Resource" chapter can be a great source of information for answering many of your questions, like "How can I find the best topics to write about?" or "How can I make my voice more colorful?" or "What can I do to make my final copy look better?"

Mini Index

You will learn how to . . .

- find topics and get started.
- collect and organize details.
- write terrific topic sentences.
- improve your writing style.
- use new forms and techniques.
- increase your vocabulary.
- improve your final copy.

How can I find the best topics to write about?

Try a Topic-Selecting Strategy

A distinguished writer once said, "There are few experiences quite so satisfactory as getting a good writing idea. You're pleased with it, and feel good about it." Many writing assignments are related to a general subject area you are studying. Let's say, for example, you are asked to write a report about a current health issue as part of a science unit. Your job would be to select a certain part of that subject—a specific topic—to write about.

> **General Subject Area:** Current health and medicine
> **Specific Writing Topic:** Exercising to improve strength

The following strategies will help you select effective, specific topics that you can feel good about.

Journal Writing Write on a regular basis in a personal journal, recording your thoughts and experiences. Review your entries from time to time and underline ideas that you would like to write more about later. (See pages 431–434.)

Clustering Begin a cluster (also called a web) with a key word. Select a general term or idea that is related to your writing assignment. Then cluster related words around the key word, as in the model below.

Listing Freely list ideas as they come to mind when you think about your assignment. Keep your list going as long as you can. Then look for words in your list that you feel would make good writing topics.

Freewriting Write nonstop for 5 to 10 minutes to discover possible writing ideas. Begin writing with a particular idea in mind (one related to your writing assignment). Underline ideas that might work as topics for your assignment.

Sentence Completion Complete an open-ended sentence in as many ways as you can. Try to word your sentence so that it leads you to a topic you can use for a particular writing assignment.

I wonder how . . .	I hope our school . . .	Television is . . .
Too many people . . .	I just learned . . .	Cars can be . . .
The good thing about . . .	One place I enjoy . . .	Grades are . . .

Review the "Basics of Life" List

The words listed below name many of the categories or groups of things that people need in order to live a full life. The list provides an endless variety of possibilities for topics. Consider the first category, *clothing*. You could write about . . .

- the wardrobe of a friend or a family member,
- your all-time favorite piece of clothing, or
- clothing as a statement (the "we are what we wear" idea).

clothing	machines	rules/laws
housing	intelligence	tools/utensils
food	history/records	heat/fuel
communication	agriculture	natural resources
exercise	land/property	personality/identity
education	work/occupation	recreation/hobby
family	community	trade/money
friends	science	literature/books
purpose/goals	plants/vegetation	health/medicine
love	freedom/rights	art/music
senses	energy	faith/religion

RESOURCE

What can I do to get started?

Use a List of Writing Topics

The writing prompts listed below and the sample topics listed on the next page provide plenty of starting points for writing assignments.

Writing Prompts

Every day is full of experiences that make you think. You do things that you feel good about. You hear things that make you mad. You wonder how different things work. You're reminded of a past experience. These common, everyday thoughts can make excellent prompts for writing.

How-To
Skateboard, snowboard, surf
Do a headstand, a flip, or a swan dive
Saddle a horse, show a dog, lift weights
Recognize constellations
Do origami, build a radio
Be patient, kind, brave, or helpful
Make or bake a favorite food
Get from one place to another

Describe
A bull moose, a fawn, a camel
A parrot, a guinea pig, a ferret
Newborn lambs, calves, chickens
Stalking cats, galloping horses
Pioneer days, wagon-train life
Life in ancient Egypt, Greece, or Rome
Solar or lunar eclipses, rainbows
Meteor showers, hailstorms, sun dogs

Tell Your Story
Meeting an unusual person
Learning something amazing, surprising
Visiting a special place
Overcoming a challenge
A sudden or a big change
Learning a lesson
Another person's triumph or determination

Parts of the Whole
Types of workouts
Kinds of clouds, weather
Different games
Personality types
Variety of musical styles
Clothing styles

Promote
Individual sports in school
An environment-friendly idea
Ways to help your community
Supporting a worthwhile cause
Ideas for avoiding boredom
Putting an end to something unfair
More field trips for students

Respond to . . .
A book that changed your thinking
A poem that helped explain something
A character that you identify with
The biography of someone you admire

Research
Aquifers, oil wells, salt mines
Hot springs, mud slides, droughts
Importance of natural forest fires
Deserts, tide pools, glaciers

Sample Topics

You come across many people, places, experiences, and things every day that could be topics for writing. A number of possible topics are listed below for descriptive, narrative, expository, and persuasive writing.

Descriptive
People: teacher, relative, classmate, coach, neighbor, bus driver, hero, someone you spend time with, someone you admire, brothers and sisters, someone with a special talent, someone from history

Places: hangout, garage, room, rooftop, historical place, zoo, park, hallway, barn, bayou, lake, cupboard, yard, empty lot, alley, valley, campsite, river, city street

Things: billboard, poster, video game, cell phone, bus, frostbite, boat, gift, drawing, rainbow, doll, junk drawer, flood, mascot, movie

Animals: dolphin, elephants, snake, armadillo, eagle, deer, toad, spoonbill, squirrel, pigeon, pet, coyote, catfish, octopus, beaver, turtle

Narrative
just last week, a big mistake, a reunion, a surprise, getting hurt, learning to _____, getting wet, getting caught, cleaning up, being a friend, a scary time, solving a problem, an important lesson, making a decision

Expository
How to . . . make a taco, improve your memory, care for a pet, entertain a child, impress your teacher, earn extra money, get in shape, overcome fear, get organized, plan a party

The causes of . . . sunburn, acne, hiccups, tornadoes, dropouts, rust, computer viruses, arguments, success, failure

Kinds of . . . crowds, friends, commercials, dreams, neighbors, pain, clouds, joy, stereos, heroes, chores, homework, frustration

Definition of . . . a good time, a conservative, "soul," a grandmother, loyalty, one type of music, advice, courage, hope, strength, fun, freedom, pride

Persuasive
dieting, homework, testing, air bags, teen centers, something that needs improving, something that deserves support, something that's unfair, something that everyone should see, need for more or less of something, healthful habits, dangerous situations, education issues, protecting the environment, preserving historical places, preventing accidents

organize
select support
REFERENCE
improve
549
A Writer's Resource

RESOURCE

How can I collect details for my writing?

Try Graphic Organizers

Graphic organizers can help you gather and organize your details for writing. Clustering is one method. (See page 544.) These two pages list other useful organizers.

Cause-Effect Organizer

Use to collect and organize details for cause-effect essays.

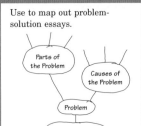

Subject: _____

Causes	Effects
•	•
•	•
•	•
•	•
•	•

Problem-Solution Web

Use to map out problem-solution essays.

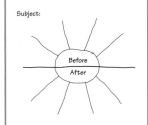

Time Line

Use to collect details for personal narratives and how-to essays.

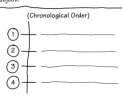

Subject: _____

(Chronological Order)
1
2
3
4

Before-After

Use to collect details for a before-after essay.

Subject: _____

Before
After

Venn Diagram

Use to collect details to compare and contrast two subjects.

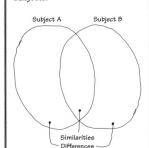

Subject A   Subject B

Similarities
Differences

5 W's Chart

Use to collect the *Who? What? When? Where?* and W*hy?* details for personal narratives and news stories.

Subject: _____

Who?	What?	When?	Where?	Why?

Sensory Chart

Use to collect details for descriptive essays and observation reports.

Subject: _____

Sights	Sounds	Smells	Tastes	Feelings

Process (Cycle)

Use to collect details for science-related writing, such as how a process or cycle works.

Subject: _____

(Chronological Order)

Step 1
↓
Step 2
↓
Step 3

What can I do to organize my details better?

Make Lists and Outlines

List Your Details

You can use a variety of ways to organize details as you prepare to write an essay or a report. For most writing, you can make a simple list.

Manatees
— eat 80 to 120 lbs. of water plants a day
— grow to 10 feet in length and live for 60 years
— are fun to watch in tropical areas
— can get caught in locks and dams
— are endangered—about 3,000 in U.S.
People hurt manatees
— drive boats that hit, injure, and kill manatees
— destroy manatee habitat
People help manatees
— enforce slow boat speeds in manatee areas
— install safety devices on locks and dams
— pass laws to protect manatee habitat

Outline Your Information

After gathering facts and details, select two or three main points that best support your focus. Write an outline to organize your information.

I. Manatees worth saving
  A. Keep rivers clear of plants
  B. Fun for people to watch these gentle giants
  C. Save an endangered animal
II. People harming manatees
  A. Injuring and killing in boating collisions
  B. Trapping in locks and dams
  C. Destroying habitat
III. People rescuing manatees
  A. Enforcing boat speed laws
  B. Installing lock and dam safety devices
  C. Protecting habitat

Use Patterns of Organization

■ **Chronological (Time) Order** or **Step-by-Step** You can arrange your details in the order in which they happen (*first, then, next,* and so on). Use these patterns for narratives, history reports, directions, how-to essays, and explaining a process. (See pages 38 and 534.)

> You can make a delicious omelet even if you've never cooked before. First, break the eggs into a bowl and add the milk. Second, mix everything with the beater until it is foamy. Next, heat . . .

■ **Order of Location** You can arrange details in the order in which they are located (*above, below, beside,* and so on). Use order of location for descriptions, explanations, and directions. (See pages 38 and 535.)

> From my mom's office window, I can see the west and south sides of the city. The town hall with its square clock tower is directly in front of me. To my left I see the top of the oldest church in town . . .

■ **Order of Importance** You can arrange details in your writing from the most important to the least—or from the least important to the most. Persuasive and expository essays are often organized this way. (See pages 38 and 536.)

> Participating in a neighborhood cleanup is a great way to improve your community. First of all, you will help the city get rid of some of the garbage. In addition, if you help clean up piles of trash, you will make your neighborhood cleaner. Most importantly, if you . . .

■ **Comparison-Contrast** You can write about two or more subjects by showing how they are alike and how they are different. Compare subjects by talking about each separately or by talking about both, point by point, as in the following example. (See page 537.)

> The Nile and the Mississippi Rivers are alike in many ways, but they are also very different. Each of these long rivers begins with a lake and ends in a delta, but they flow in different directions. The Mississippi flows from north to south, while the Nile flows from . . .

■ **Logical Order** Use this pattern to organize information in a way that makes sense. Begin with a main idea followed by details, or lead up to a main point. (See page 38.)

> Hurricanes are very dangerous storms. They can cause destruction, injury, and death over a very large area. It's important to learn how these storms form and move. That's why scientists spend so much time studying hurricanes. . . .

RESOURCE

How can I write terrific topic sentences?

Try Eight Special Strategies

Writing a good topic sentence is a key to writing a great paragraph. A good topic sentence names the topic and states a specific feeling about it. Use the following strategies the next time you need to write a terrific topic sentence. (Also see page 525.)

Use a Number

Topic sentences can use number words to tell what the paragraph will be about.

NUMBER WORDS		
two	couple	a pair
few	three	a number
several	four	many
a variety	five	a list

Each cell has three main parts.

Ms. Chen should change the menu for several reasons.

Create a List

A topic sentence can list the things the paragraph will talk about.

Egyptians built step pyramids, bent pyramids, and straight pyramids.

To stay healthy and alert, get eight hours of sleep, eat a good breakfast, and walk a mile every day.

Start with *To* and a Verb

A topic sentence that starts with "to" and a verb helps the reader know why the information in the paragraph is important.

To learn a one-and-a-half flip, divers first need to learn a single flip.

To understand rock and roll, people should first learn about the blues.

Use Word Pairs

Conjunctions that come in pairs can help organize a topic sentence.

WORD PAIRS
if . . . then
either . . . or
not only . . . but also
both . . . and
whether . . . or
as . . . so

Connelly Middle School needs not only a new track but also new bleachers.

Some scientists debate whether T. rex was a hunter or a scavenger.

Join Two Ideas

A topic sentence can state two equal ideas. You can do this by writing a compound sentence. (See page 516.)

A tree fort is easy to build, and even beginning carpenters can lend a hand.

The principal wants to ban hats in school, but some students don't think that's a good idea.

Use a "Why-What" Word

A "why-what" word is a subordinating conjunction that shows how ideas are connected.

"WHY-WHAT" WORDS	
So that	Once
Before	Since
Until	Whenever
Because	While
If	As long as
As	After
In order that	When

So that everyone can hear the candidates' ideas, the student council should hold a debate.

Because you want a smooth texture, use a mixer or blender.

Use a "Yes, But" Word

A "yes, but" word is a subordinating conjunction that tells how two ideas are different.

"YES, BUT" WORDS
However
Instead of
Although
Even though
Even if
Unless
Whether
Whereas

Instead of just complaining about it, students should help clean up roadside litter.

Even though the writers' group is small, the members have written lots of material.

Quote an Expert

Sometimes the best way to start a paragraph is to quote someone who knows about your topic.

Michael Jordan once said, "You have to expect things of yourself before you can do them."

Amelia Earhart put it best: "It is far easier to start something than to finish it."

A Writer's Resource **554–555**

554

organize
select *support* *improve*
555
A Writer's Resource
RESOURCE

What other forms can I use for my writing?

Try These Forms of Writing

Finding the right *form* for your writing is just as important as finding the right topic. When you are selecting a form, be sure to ask yourself who you're writing for (your audience) and why you're writing (your purpose).

Anecdote	A brief story that makes a point
Autobiography	A writer's story of his or her own life
Biography	A writer's story of some other person's life
Book review	A brief essay giving a response or an opinion about a book (See pages 287–322.)
Character sketch	Writing that describes a specific character in a story
Composition	A longer piece of writing, such as a story or an essay
Descriptive writing	Writing that uses details to help the reader clearly imagine a certain person, place, thing, or idea (See pages 71–91.)
Editorial	Newspaper letters or articles giving an opinion
Essay	A piece of writing in which ideas are presented, explained, argued, or described in an interesting way
Expository writing	Writing that explains by presenting the steps, the causes, or the kinds of something (See pages 157–217.)
Fable	A short story that often uses talking animals as the main characters and teaches a lesson or moral
Fantasy	A story set in an imaginary world in which the characters usually have supernatural powers or abilities
Freewriting	Writing whatever comes to mind about any topic
Historical fiction	A made-up story based on something real in history in which fact is mixed with fiction
Myth	A traditional story intended to explain a mystery of nature, religion, or culture
Narrative	Writing that tells about an event, an experience, or a story (See pages 93–155.)

Novel	A book-length story with several characters and a well-developed plot
Personal narrative	Writing that shares an event or experience in the writer's personal life (See pages 97–134.)
Persuasive writing	Writing that is meant to persuade the reader to agree with the writer about someone or something (See pages 219–281.)
Play	A form that uses dialogue to tell a story and is meant to be performed in front of an audience
Poem	Writing that uses rhythm, rhyme, and imagery (See pages 353–361.)
Proposal	Writing that includes specific information about an idea or a project that is being considered for approval
Research report	An essay that shares information on a topic that has been researched well and organized carefully
Response to Literature	Writing that is a summary or a reaction to something the writer has read (novel, short story, poem, article, and so on)
Science fiction	Writing based on real or imaginary science and often set in the future
Short story	A short piece of literature with only a few characters and one problem or conflict (See pages 343–349.)
Summary	Writing that presents only the most important ideas from a longer piece of writing (See pages 377–380.)
Tall tale	A humorous, exaggerated story (often based on the life of a real person) about a character who does impossible things
Tragedy	Literature in which the hero is destroyed because of some serious flaw or defect in his or her character

RESOURCE

How can I make my voice more colorful?

You can make your writing voice more colorful by using strong dialogue and by "showing" instead of "telling."

Include Strong Dialogue

Each person you write about has a unique way of saying things, and well-written dialogue lets the reader *hear* the speaker's personality and thoughts. For example, notice how the following message can be spoken in several different ways.

Message: Your new car is impressive.

Speaker 1: **"Whoa, Dad! Cool new wheels!"**

Speaker 2: **"Nice coupe, Bill. I've always been a sedan man myself."**

Speaker 3: **"Such a fancy car, Son! Hope you didn't spend too much."**

Each of these speakers delivers the same message in a unique way. The dialogue tells as much about the speaker as it does about the topic.

One way to improve your dialogue is to think about the speaker and his or her personality. Look at the three personality webs below and try to decide which one is *Speaker 1, Speaker 2,* or *Speaker 3* from above. How does the dialogue show their personalities?

humble   worrying

Sylvia

helpful   old-fashioned

young   Geoff   friendly

wild

professional

Anthony

middle-aged   knows cars

Tips for Punctuating Dialogue

- Indent every time a different person speaks.
- Put the exact words of a speaker in quotation marks.
- Set off the quoted words from the rest of the sentence by using a comma.
- At the end of quoted words, put a period or comma inside the quotation marks.

For more information and examples on how to punctuate dialogue, see 588.1, 598.1, and 600.1 in the "Proofreader's Guide."

Show, Don't Tell

The old saying "Seeing is believing" is especially true in writing. Writing that tells the reader is not as strong as writing that shows the reader something, allowing him or her to decide how to feel about it. Notice the difference between the two paragraphs below.

Telling: **I rode on the roller coaster. It was frightening but fun.**

Showing: As the roller coaster topped the first big hill, I could see my mom down below. She looked so small. Then the coaster began to surge down the hill. My hands went up, my heart jumped into my throat, and I let out a sound that was half laugh and half scream.

The first paragraph *tells* the reader that the roller coaster ride was "frightening but fun." The second paragraph *shows* just how "frightening but fun" it really was.

Key Strategies for Showing

Next time you realize your writing is telling rather than showing, try one of these strategies.

- **Add sensory details.** Include sights, sounds, smells, tastes, and touch sensations. That way, the reader can "experience" the event.

  Telling: **The ice cream was delicious.**

  Showing: The creamy vanilla ice cream and gooey caramel hid chunks of sweet chocolate.

- **Explain body language.** Write about facial expressions and the way people stand, gesture, and move.

  Telling: **Sharissa was upset with me.**

  Showing: Sharissa glared at me, tapped her foot, pursed her lips, and snorted.

- **Use dialogue.** Let the people in your writing speak for themselves.

  Telling: **Sharon Whitecloud wanted to go to the Art Institute.**

  Showing: Sharon Whitecloud piped up, "You're not going to the Art Institute without me!"

A Writer's Resource **558-559**

558

organize
select support improve
A Writer's Resource

559

RESOURCE

What can I do to improve my writing style?

Learn Some Writing Techniques

Writers put special effects in their stories and essays in different ways. Look over the following writing techniques and then experiment with some of them in your own writing.

Analogy	A comparison of similar objects to help clarify one of the objects **Personal journals are like photograph albums. They both share personal details and tell a story.**
Anecdote	A brief story used to illustrate or make a point **Abe Lincoln walked two miles to return several pennies he had overcharged a customer.** (This anecdote shows Lincoln's honesty.)
Exaggeration	An overstatement or a stretching of the truth used to make a point or paint a clearer picture (See *overstatement*.) **After getting home from summer camp, I slept for a month.**
Foreshadowing	Hints or clues that a writer uses to suggest what will happen next in a story **Halfway home, Sarah wondered whether she had locked her locker.**
Irony	A technique that uses a word or phrase to mean the opposite of its normal meaning **Marshall just loves cleaning his room.**
Local color	The use of details that are common in a certain place or local area (A story taking place on a seacoast would contain details about the water and the life and people near it.) **Everybody wore flannel shirts to the Friday fish fry.**
Metaphor	A figure of speech that compares two things without using the word *like* or *as* (See page 360.) **In our community, high school football is king.**
Overstatement	An exaggeration or a stretching of the truth (See *exaggeration*.) **When he saw my grades, my dad hit the roof.**

Parallelism	Repeating similar words, phrases, or sentences to give writing rhythm (See page 522.) **We will swim in the ocean, lie on the beach, and sleep under the stars.**
Personification	A figure of speech in which a nonhuman thing (an idea, object, or animal) is given human characteristics (See page 360.) **Rosie's old car coughs and wheezes on cold days.**
Pun	A phrase that uses words in a way that gives them a humorous effect **The lumberjack logged on to the site to order new boots.**
Sarcasm	The use of praise to make fun of or "put down" someone or something (The expression is not sincere and is actually intended to mean the opposite thing.) **Micah's a real gourmet; he loves peanut butter and jelly sandwiches.** (A *gourmet* is a "lover of fine foods.")
Sensory details	Specific details that help the reader see, feel, smell, taste, and/or hear what is being described (See page 489.) **As Lamont took his driver's test, his heart thumped, his hands went cold, and his face began to sweat.**
Simile	A figure of speech that compares two things using the word *like* or *as* (See page 360.) **Faye's little brother darts around like a water bug.** **Yesterday the lake was as smooth as glass.**
Slang	Informal words or phrases used by particular groups of people when they talk to each other **chill out hang loose totally awesome**
Symbol	An object that is used to stand for an idea **The American flag is a symbol of the United States. The stars stand for the 50 states, and the stripes stand for the 13 original U.S. colonies.**
Understatement	Very calm language (the opposite of exaggeration) used to bring special attention to an object or an idea **These hot red peppers may make your mouth tingle a bit.**

How can I expand my writing vocabulary?

Study Writing Terms

This glossary includes terms used to describe the parts of the writing process. It also includes terms that explain special ways of stating an idea.

Antonym	A word that means the opposite of another word: *happy* and *sad; large* and *small* (See page 563.)
Audience	The people who read or hear what has been written
Body	The main or middle part in a piece of writing that comes between the *beginning* and the *ending* and includes the main points
Brainstorming	Collecting ideas by thinking freely about all the possibilities
Closing	The ending or final part in a piece of writing (In a paragraph, the closing is the last sentence. In an essay or a report, the closing is the final paragraph.)
Coherence	Tying ideas together in your writing (See page 539.)
Connotation	The "feeling" a word suggests (See page 485.)
Denotation	The dictionary meaning of a word
Dialogue	Written conversation between two or more people
Figurative language	Special comparisons, often called figures of speech, that make your writing more creative (See page 360.)
Focus statement	The statement that tells what specific part of a topic is written about in an essay (See *thesis statement* and page 35.)
Form	A type of writing or the way a piece of writing is put together (See pages 554–555.)
Grammar	The structure of language; the rules and guidelines that you follow in order to speak and write acceptably
Jargon	The special language of a certain group, occupation, or field **Computer jargon: byte digital upload**
Journal	A notebook for writing down thoughts, experiences, ideas, and information (See pages 431–434.)

Limiting the subject	Taking a general subject and narrowing it down to a specific topic General subject Specific topic **sports → golf → golf skills → putting**
Modifiers	Words, phrases, or clauses that describe another word Our black **cat** slowly **stretched and** then **leaped** onto the wicker chair. (Without the blue modifiers, all we know is that a "cat stretched and leaped.")
Point of view	The angle from which a story is told (See page 352.)
Purpose	The specific reason that a person has for writing **to describe to narrate to persuade to explain**
Style	How an author writes (choice of words and sentences)
Supporting details	Facts or ideas used to tell a story, explain a topic, describe something, or prove a point
Synonym	A word that means the same thing as another word (*dog* and *canine*) (See page 563.)
Theme	The main point, message, or lesson in a piece of writing
Thesis statement	A statement that gives the main idea of an essay (See *focus statement.*)
Tone	A writer's attitude toward his or her subject **serious humorous sarcastic**
Topic	The specific subject of a piece of writing
Topic sentence	The sentence that contains the main idea of a paragraph (See page 525.) **Blue jeans are a popular piece of American clothing.**
Transition	A word or phrase that connects or ties two ideas together smoothly (See pages 572–573.) **also however lastly later next**
Usage	The way in which people use language (*Standard usage* generally follows the rules of good grammar. Most of the writing you do in school will require standard usage.)
Voice	A writer's unique, personal tone or feeling that comes across in a piece of writing (See page 40.)

What can I do to increase my vocabulary skills?

Try Vocabulary-Building Techniques

Technique	Description	Why It Works
Learn common roots, prefixes, and suffixes.	If you know common word parts, you will be able to figure out many new words.	Tens of thousands of English words come from Greek and Latin word parts. (See pages 564–569.)
Use context.	Look at the passage surrounding the word you don't know. (See page 563.)	Words and ideas around a word often give hints as to what the word means.
Look up words in the dictionary.	Read the dictionary meaning. Also read the history of the word. (See pages 374–375.)	Sometimes the word history helps you connect the new word with one you already know.
Keep a vocabulary notebook.	Write down words you don't know. Include the pronunciation and meaning. Use each word in a sentence.	Writing reinforces your learning. The notebook is also a handy study guide.
Say your new words out loud.	Read your new words out loud and look for places in your writing where you can use them effectively.	Saying new words out loud means you hear them. Using that extra sense helps you remember.
Use your new words often.	Concentrate on using new words whenever possible in your writing.	Research shows that you need to use a new word to make it your own.

Use Context

When you come across a word you don't know, you can often figure out its meaning from the other words in the sentence. The other words form a familiar context, or setting, for the unfamiliar word. Looking closely at these surrounding words will give you clues to the meaning of the new word.

When you come to a word you don't know . . .

- Look for a synonym—a word or words that have the same meaning as the unknown word.

  Sara had an ominous feeling when she woke up, but the feeling was less threatening when she saw she was in her own room. (An *ominous* feeling is a threatening one.)

- Look for an antonym—a word that has the opposite meaning as the unknown word.

  Boniface had always been quite heavy, but he looked gaunt when he returned from the hospital.
  (*Gaunt* is the opposite of *heavy*.)

- Look for a comparison or contrast.

  Riding a mountain bike in a remote area is my idea of a great day. I wonder why some people like to ride motorcycles on busy six-lane highways.
  (A *remote* area is out of the way, in contrast to a *busy* area.)

- Look for a definition or description.

  Manatees, large aquatic mammals (sometimes called sea cows), can be found in the warm coastal waters of Florida.
  (An *aquatic* mammal is one that lives in the water.)

- Look for words that appear in a series.

  The campers spotted sparrows, chickadees, and indigo buntings on Saturday morning.
  (An *indigo bunting*, like a *sparrow* or *chickadee*, is a bird.)

- Look for a cause and effect relationship.

  The amount of traffic at 6th and Main doubled last year, so crossing lights were placed at that corner to avert an accident.
  (*Avert* means "to prevent.")

How can I build my vocabulary across the curriculum?

On the next several pages, you will find many of the most common prefixes, suffixes, and roots in the English language. Learning these word parts can help you increase your writing vocabulary.

Learn About Prefixes

A **prefix** is a word part that is added before a word to change the meaning of the word. For example, when the prefix *un* is added to the word *fair* (*unfair*), it changes the word's meaning from "fair" to "not fair."

ambi *[both]*
ambidextrous (skilled with both hands)

anti *[against]*
antifreeze (a liquid that works against freezing)
antiwar (against wars and fighting)

astro *[star]*
astronaut (person who travels among the stars)
astronomy (study of the stars)

auto *[self]*
autobiography (writing that is about yourself)

bi *[two]*
bilingual (using or speaking two languages)
biped (having two feet)

circum *[in a circle, around]*
circumference (the line or distance around a circle)
circumnavigate (to sail around)

co *[together, with]*
cooperate (to work together)
coordinate (to put things together)

ex *[out]*
exhale (to breathe out)
exit (the act of going out)

fore *[before, in front of]*
foremost (in the first place, before everyone or everything else)
foretell (to tell or show beforehand)

hemi *[half]*
hemisphere (half of a sphere or globe)

hyper *[over]*
hyperactive (overactive)

im *[not, opposite of]*
impatient (not patient)
impossible (not possible)

in *[not, opposite of]*
inactive (not active)
incomplete (not complete)

inter *[between, among]*
international (between or among nations)
interplanetary (between the planets)

macro *[large]*
macrocosm (the entire universe)

mal *[bad, poor]*
malnutrition (poor nutrition)

micro *[small]*
microscope (an instrument used to see very small things)

mono *[one]*
monolingual (using or speaking only one language)

non *[not, opposite of]*
nonfat (without the normal fat content)
nonfiction (based on facts; not made-up)

over *[too much, extra]*
overeat (to eat too much)
overtime (extra time; time beyond regular hours)

poly *[many]*
polygon (a figure or shape with three or more sides)
polysyllable (a word with more than three syllables)

post *[after]*
postscript (a note added at the end of a letter, after the signature)
postwar (after a war)

pre *[before]*
pregame (activities that occur before a game)
preheat (to heat before using)

re *[again, back]*
repay (to pay back)
rewrite (to write again or revise)

semi *[half, partly]*
semicircle (half a circle)
semiconscious (half conscious; not fully conscious)

sub *[under, below]*
submarine (a boat that can operate underwater)
submerge (to put underwater)

trans *[across, over; change]*
transcontinental (across a continent)
transform (to change from one form to another)

tri *[three]*
triangle (a figure that has three sides and three angles)
tricycle (a three-wheeled vehicle)

un *[not]*
uncomfortable (not comfortable)
unhappy (not happy; sad)

under *[below, beneath]*
underage (below or less than the usual or required age)
undersea (beneath the surface of the sea)

uni *[one]*
unicycle (a one-wheeled vehicle)
unisex (a single style that is worn by both males and females)

Numerical Prefixes

deci *[tenth part]*
decimal system (a number system based on units of 10)

centi *[hundredth part]*
centimeter (a unit of length equal to 1/100 meter)

milli *[thousandth part]*
millimeter (a unit of length equal to 1/1000 meter)

micro *[millionth part]*
micrometer (one-millionth of a meter)

deca or **dec** *[ten]*
decade (a period of 10 years)
decathlon (a contest with 10 events)

hecto or **hect** *[one hundred]*
hectare (a metric unit of land equal to 100 ares)

kilo *[one thousand]*
kilogram (a unit of mass equal to 1,000 grams)

mega *[one million]*
megabit (one million bits)

A Writer's Resource   **566–567**

566

organize
select support improve   **567**
A Writer's Resource

RESOURCE

Study Suffixes

A **suffix** is a word part that is added after a word. Sometimes a suffix will tell you what part of speech a word is. For example, many adverbs end in the suffix *ly*.

able *[able, can do]*
agreeable (able or willing to agree)
doable (can be done)

al *[of, like]*
magical (like magic)
optical (of the eye)

ed *[past tense]*
called (past tense of *call*)
learned (past tense of *learn*)

ess *[female]*
lioness (a female lion)

ful *[full of]*
helpful (giving help; full of help)

ic *[like, having to do with]*
symbolic (having to do with symbols)

ily *[in some manner]*
happily (in a happy manner)

ish *[somewhat like or near]*
childish (somewhat like a child)

ism *[characteristic of]*
heroism (characteristic of a hero)

less *[without]*
careless (without care)

ly *[in some manner]*
calmly (in a calm manner)

ology *[study, science]*
biology (the study of living things)

s *[more than one; plural noun]*
books (more than one book)

ward *[in the direction of]*
westward (in the direction of west)

y *[containing, full of]*
salty (containing salt)

Comparative Suffixes

er *[comparing two things]*
faster, later, neater, stronger

est *[comparing more than two]*
fastest, latest, neatest, strongest

Noun-Forming Suffixes

er *[one who]*
painter (one who paints)

ing *[the result of]*
painting (the result of a painter's work)

ion *[act of, state of]*
perfection (the state of being perfect)

ist *[one who]*
violinist (one who plays the violin)

ment *[act of, result of]*
amendment (the result of amending, or changing)
improvement (the result of improving)

ness *[state of]*
goodness (the state of being good)

or *[one who]*
actor (one who acts)

Understand Roots

A **root** is a word or word base from which other words are made by adding a prefix or a suffix. Knowing the common roots can help you figure out the meaning of difficult words.

aster *[star]*
aster (star flower)
asterisk (starlike symbol [*])

aud *[hear, listen]*
audible (can be heard)
auditorium (a place to listen to speeches and performances)

bibl *[book]*
Bible (sacred book of Christianity)
bibliography (list of books)

bio *[life]*
biography (book about a person's life)
biology (the study of life)

chrome *[color]*
monochrome (having one color)
polychrome (having many colors)

chron *[time]*
chronological (in time order)
synchronize (to make happen at the same time)

cide *[the killing of; killer]*
homicide (the killing of one person by another person)
pesticide (pest [bug] killer)

cise *[cut]*
incision (a thin, clean cut)
incisors (the teeth that cut or tear food)
precise (cut exactly right)

cord, cor *[heart]*
cordial (heartfelt)
coronary (relating to the heart)

corp *[body]*
corporation (a legal body; business)
corpse (a dead human body)

cycl, cyclo *[wheel, circular]*
bicycle (a vehicle with two wheels)
cyclone (a very strong circular wind)

dem *[people]*
democracy (ruled by the people)
epidemic (affecting many people at the same time)

dent, dont *[tooth]*
dentures (false teeth)
orthodontist (dentist who straightens teeth)

derm *[skin]*
dermatology (the study of skin)
epidermis (outer layer of skin)

fac, fact *[do, make]*
factory (a place where people make things)
manufacture (to make by hand or machine)

fin *[end]*
final (the last of something)
infinite (having no end)

flex *[bend]*
flexible (able to bend)
reflex (bending or springing back)

flu *[flowing]*
fluent (flowing smoothly or easily)
fluid (waterlike, flowing substance)

forc, fort *[strong]*
force (strength or power)
fortify (to make strong)

fract, frag *[break]*
fracture (to break)
fragment (a piece broken from the whole)

568–569   A Writer's Resource

568

organize
select support improve
A Writer's Resource
569

Learn More Roots

gen *[birth, produce]*
congenital (existing at birth)
genetics (the study of inborn traits)

geo *[of the earth]*
geography (the study of places on the earth)
geology (the study of the earth's physical features)

graph *[write]*
autograph (writing one's name)
graphology (the study of handwriting)

homo *[same]*
homogeneous (of the same birth or kind)
homogenize (to blend into a uniform mixture)

hydr *[water]*
dehydrate (to take the water out of)
hydrophobia (the fear of water)

ject *[throw]*
eject (to throw out)
project (to throw forward)

log, logo *[word, thought, speech]*
dialogue (speech between two people)
logic (thinking or reasoning)

luc, lum *[light]*
illuminate (to light up)
translucent (letting light come through)

magn *[great]*
magnificent (great)
magnify (to make bigger or greater)

man *[hand]*
manicure (to fix the hands)
manual (done by hand)

mania *[insanity]*
kleptomania (abnormal desire to steal)
maniac (an insane person)

mar *[sea, pool]*
marine (of or found in the sea)
mariner (sailor)

mega *[large]*
megalith (large stone)
megaphone (large horn used to make voices louder)

meter *[measure]*
meter (unit of measure)
voltmeter (device to measure volts)

mit, miss *[send]*
emit (to send out; give off)
transmission (sending over)

multi *[many, much]*
multicultural (of or including many cultures)
multiped (an animal with many feet)

numer *[number]*
innumerable (too many to count)
numerous (large in number)

omni *[all, completely]*
omnipresent (present everywhere at the same time)
omnivorous (eating all kinds of food)

onym *[name]*
anonymous (without a name)
pseudonym (false name)

ped *[foot]*
pedal (lever worked by the foot)
pedestrian (one who travels by foot)

phil *[love]*
Philadelphia (city of brotherly love)
philosophy (the love of wisdom)

phobia *[fear]*
acrophobia (a fear of high places)
agoraphobia (a fear of public, open places)

phon *[sound]*
phonics (related to sounds)
symphony (sounds made together)

photo *[light]*
photo-essay (a story told mainly with photographs)
photograph (picture made using light rays)

pop *[people]*
population (number of people in an area)
populous (full of people)

port *[carry]*
export (to carry out)
portable (able to be carried)

psych *[mind, soul]*
psychiatry (the study of the mind)
psychology (science of mind and behavior)

sci *[know]*
conscious (being aware)
omniscient (knowing everything)

scope *[instrument for viewing]*
kaleidoscope (instrument for viewing patterns and shapes)
periscope (instrument used to see above the water)

scrib, script *[write]*
manuscript (something written by hand)
scribble (to write quickly)

spec *[look]*
inspect (to look at carefully)
specimen (an example to look at)

spir *[breath]*
expire (to breathe out; die)
inspire (to breathe into; give life to)

tele *[over a long distance; far]*
telephone (machine used to speak to people over a distance)
telescope (machine used to see things that are very far away)

tempo *[time]*
contemporary (from the current time period)
temporary (lasting for a short time)

tend, tens *[stretch, strain]*
extend (to stretch and make longer)
tension (stretching something tight)

terra *[earth]*
terrain (the earth or ground)
terrestrial (relating to the earth)

therm *[heat]*
thermal (related to heat)
thermostat (a device for controlling heat)

tom *[cut]*
anatomy (the science of cutting apart plants and animals for study)
atom (a particle that cannot be cut or divided)

tract *[draw, pull]*
traction (the act of pulling)
tractor (a machine for pulling)

typ *[print]*
prototype (the first printing or model)
typo (a printing error)

vac *[empty]*
vacant (empty)
vacuum (an empty space)

vid, vis *[see]*
supervise (to oversee or watch over)
videotape (record on tape for viewing)

vor *[eat]*
carnivorous (flesh-eating)
herbivorous (plant-eating)

zoo *[animal or animals]*
zoo (a place where animals are kept)
zoology (the study of animal life)

RESOURCE

A Writer's Resource 570-571

570

organize
select support improve
571
A Writer's Resource

RESOURCE

What can I do to write more effective sentences?

Study Sentence Patterns

Sentences in the English language follow the basic patterns below. Use a variety of patterns to add interest to your writing. (Also see page 571.)

1 Subject + Action Verb

    S   AV
Gus giggles. (Some action verbs, like *giggles*, are intransitive. This means that they *do not need* a direct object to express a complete thought. See 728.3.)

2 Subject + Action Verb + Direct Object

    S   AV   DO
Jesse tells ghost stories at camp. (Some action verbs, like *tells*, are transitive. This means that they *need* a direct object to express a complete thought. See 728.2.)

3 Subject + Action Verb + Indirect Object + Direct Object

    S AV IO   DO
Mom gave me this book.

4 Subject + Action Verb + Direct Object + Object Complement

    S AV   DO   OC
We named Jamaal the best storyteller.

5 Subject + Linking Verb + Predicate Noun

    S   LV   PN
Christina is a beautiful singer.

6 Subject + Linking Verb + Predicate Adjective

    S   LV PA
My teacher was terrific.

In the patterns above, the subject comes before the verb. In the patterns below, the subject (called a *delayed subject*) comes after the verb.

    LV S   PN
7 Is Larisa a poet? (A question)

         LV   S
8 There was a meeting. (A sentence beginning with *there* or *here*)

Practice Sentence Diagramming

Diagramming sentences can help you understand how the parts of a sentence fit together. Here are the most common diagrams. (See page 570.)

1   S   AV
Gus giggles.

Gus | giggles

2   S AV   DO
Jesse tells ghost stories at camp.

Note: Place a preposition on a diagonal line under the word it modifies, with its object on an attached line (*at camp*).

Jesse | tells | stories / ghost \ at / camp

3   S AV IO   DO
Mom gave me this book.

Mom | gave | book \ this / me

4   S AV   DO   OC
We named Jamaal the best storyteller.

We | named | Jamaal \ storyteller / the \ best

5   S LV   PN
Christina is a beautiful singer.

Christina | is \ singer / a \ beautiful

Note: Place an adjective or adverb on a diagonal line under the word it modifies.

6   S LV PA
My teacher was terrific.

teacher | was \ terrific / my

How can I connect my sentences and paragraphs?

Use Transitions

Transitions can be used to connect one sentence to another sentence or one paragraph to another within a longer essay or report. The lists below show a number of transitions and how they are used.

Note: The **colored lists** are groups of transitions that could work well together in a piece of writing.

Words that can be used to show location

above	around	between	inside	outside
across	behind	by	into	over
against	below	down	near	throughout
along	beneath	in back of	next to	to the right
among	beside	in front of	on top of	under

Above	In front of	On top of
Below	Beside	Next to
To the left	In back of	Beneath
To the right		

Words that can be used to show time

about	during	yesterday	until	finally
after	first	meanwhile	next	then
at	second	today	soon	as soon as
before	to begin	tomorrow	later	in the end

First	To begin	Now	First	Before
Second	To continue	Soon	Then	During
Third	To conclude	Later	Next	After
Finally			In the end	

Words that can be used to compare two things

likewise	as	in the same way	one way
like	also	similarly	both

In the same way	One way
Also	Another way
Similarly	Both

Words that can be used to contrast things (show differences)

but	still	although	on the other hand
however	yet	otherwise	even though

On the other hand	Although
Even though	Yet
Still	Nevertheless

Words that can be used to emphasize a point

again	truly	especially	for this reason
to repeat	in fact	to emphasize	

For this reason	Truly
Especially	To emphasize
In fact	To repeat

Words that can be used to conclude or summarize

finally	as a result	to sum up	in conclusion
lastly	therefore	all in all	because

Therefore	As a result	To sum it up
Because	All in all	Because
In conclusion	Finally	Finally

Words that can be used to add information

again	another	for instance	for example
also	and	moreover	additionally
as well	besides	along with	other
next	finally	in addition	

For example	For instance	Next	Another
Additionally	Besides	Moreover	Along with
Finally	Next	Also	As well

Words that can be used to clarify

that is	for instance	in other words

For instance	For example
In other words	Equally important

What can I do to make my final copy look better?

Add Graphics to Your Writing

You can add information and interest to essays and reports by using diagrams, tables, and graphs.

Diagrams are drawings that show the parts of something. A diagram may leave out some parts to show only the parts you need to learn.

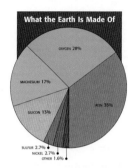

crust
mantle
outer core
inner core

Picture diagrams show how something is put together.

The Structure of the Earth

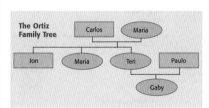

The Ortiz Family Tree

Carlos — Maria

Jon | Maria | Teri | Paulo

Gaby

Line diagrams also show how something is put together, but they show something you can't really see. Instead of objects, line diagrams show ideas and relationships.

Tables have two parts: rows and columns. Rows go across and show one kind of information or data. Columns go up and down and show a different kind of data.

To read a table, find where a row and a column meet. In the table to the right, if the wind speed is 15 and the air temperature is 20, the windchill factor is -5.

The Windchill Factor

Wind speed (mph)	Thermometer reading (degrees Fahrenheit)										
	35	30	25	20	15	10	5	0	-5	-10	-15
5	33	27	21	19	12	7	0	-5	-10	-15	-21
10	22	16	10	3	-3	-9	-15	-22	-27	-34	-40
15	16	9	2	-5	-11	-18	-25	-31	-38	-45	-51
20	12	4	-3	-10	-17	-24	-31	-39	-46	-53	-60
25	8	1	-7	-15	-22	-29	-36	-44	-51	-59	-66
30	6	-2	-10	-18	-25	-33	-41	-49	-56	-64	-71

NOTE: This chart gives equivalent temperatures for combinations of wind speed and temperatures. For example, the combination of a temperature of 10° Fahrenheit and a wind blowing at 10 mph has a cooling power equal to -9° F. Wind speeds of higher than 45 mph have little additional cooling effect.

Graphs are pictures of information. **Bar graphs** show how things compare to one another. The bars on a bar graph may be vertical or horizontal. (*Vertical* means "up and down." *Horizontal* means "from side to side.") Sometimes the bars on graphs are called *columns*. The part that shows numbers is called the *scale*.

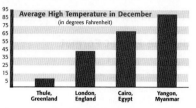

Average High Temperature in December
(in degrees Fahrenheit)

Thule, Greenland | London, England | Cairo, Egypt | Yangon, Myanmar

What the Earth Is Made Of

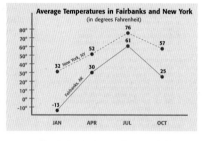

OXYGEN 28%
MAGNESIUM 17%
IRON 35%
SILICON 13%
SULFUR 2.7%
NICKEL 2.7%
OTHER 1.6%

Pie graphs show how all the parts of something add up to make the whole. A pie graph often shows percentages. (A percentage is the part of a whole stated in hundredths: 35% = 35/100.) It's called a pie graph because it is usually in the shape of a pie or circle.

Line graphs show how something changes as time goes by. A line graph always begins with an L-shaped grid. One line of the grid shows passing time; the other line shows numbers.

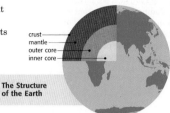

Average Temperatures in Fairbanks and New York
(in degrees Fahrenheit)

76
52
61
57
32
New York, NY
30
25
-13
Fairbanks, AK

JAN | APR | JUL | OCT

RESOURCE

organize
select support
REFERENCE
improve
A Writer's Resource
577

How should I set up my practical writing?

Use the Proper Format

Memos

A memo is a brief written message that you can share with a teacher, a coach, or a principal. Memos create a flow of information—asking and answering questions, giving instructions, describing work to be done, or reminding people about meetings.

Date: March 14, 2005

To: Mr. Ortega

From: Rebecca Ehly

Subject: Mid-Project Report on Training Rats

The goal of my science fair project is to train my rat Carmel to play basketball. I want to teach him to do four things:

1. Go to the rubber ball (about 1" in diameter).
2. Push the ball with his nose across the basketball court that I made in his cage.
3. Pick up the ball with his forepaws.
4. Put the ball through the hoop (about 2" above the floor of the cage).

Carmel has learned two steps: (1) go to the ball, and (2) push it. I taught him how to do these things by luring him with pieces of cheddar cheese (extra sharp).

Unfortunately, I haven't been able to get Carmel to do [num]ers 3 and 4. He won't lift the ball. I'm not sure what [ ] next. Do you have any suggestions?

Date: January 18, 2005
To: Mr. William Pasma
From: Brian Krygsman
Subject: Castle Construction for History Project

Project Description: For my history project on medieval life, I plan to build a scale model (2′ x 2′ x 2′) of an English castle and write an essay on the construction of castles for protection.

Materials Needed:

1. Books on medieval life and on castles
2. 3′ x 3′ plywood board (for base)
3. Clay (for walls)
4. Toilet paper rolls (for frame of towers)
5. Toothpicks and glue (for ladders, gates)
6. Popsicle sticks and string (for drawbridge)
7. Cloth (for banners and tapestries)

Deadlines and Procedure:

1. Jan. 25   Research medieval castles
2. Feb. 1   Choose a castle to build
3. Feb. 3   Design my model on paper as a blueprint
4. Feb. 10   Construct a scale model of castle
5. Feb. 16   Plan and write first draft of paper
6. Feb. 22   Complete paper and present project to class

Outcome: My project will help the class understand how a castle was built and how it was used.

Proposals

A proposal is a detailed plan for doing a project, solving a problem, or meeting a need.

Follow Guidelines

Letters

A letter is a written message sent through the mail. Letters follow a set format, including important contact information, a salutation or greeting, a body, and a closing signature. (See pages 276–277 for more information.)

1414 Johnson Street
Walvan, WI 53000
April 20, 2004

Mayor Phillip Smith
Walvan City Hall
111 Main Street
Walvan, WI 53000

Dear Mayor Smith:

I am a student at Parker Lane Middle School. At a city council meeting last October, I asked the council to put up a stoplight at the intersection of 34th Avenue and Cottage Street. Six months later, cars are still going by too fast on 34th Avenue.

I am not the only one who thinks this corner is dangerous. I passed around a petition asking for the stoplight, and more than 400 students, teachers, parents, and neighbors signed it. I have enclosed my petition. Mayor Smith, please vote for putting a traffic light at 34th Avenue and Cottage Street.

Sincerely,

Ruby Keast

Ruby Keast

Envelope Addresses

Place the return address in the upper left corner, the destination address in the center, and the correct postage in the upper right corner.

RUBY KEAST
1414 JOHNSON ST
WALVAN WI 53000

MAYOR PHILLIP SMITH
WALVAN CITY HALL
111 MAIN ST
WALVAN WI 53000

U.S. Postal Service Guidelines

1. Capitalize everything and leave out ALL punctuation.
2. Use the list of common abbreviations found on 634.1. Use numerals rather than words for numbered streets and avenues (9TH AVE NE, 3RD ST SW).
3. If you know the ZIP + 4 code, use it.

capitalize
SPELL
punctuate

Proofreader's Guide

revise
edit

PUNCTUATION

Marking Punctuation

Periods

Use a **period** to end a sentence. Also use a period after initials, after abbreviations, and as a decimal point.

579.1

At the End of Sentences

Use a period to end a sentence that makes a statement or a request. Also use a period for a mild command, one that does not need an exclamation point. (See page 518.)

> The Southern Ocean surrounds Antarctica. (statement)
> Please point out the world's largest ocean on a map. (request)
> Do not use a laser pointer. (mild command)

NOTE It is not necessary to place a period after a statement that has parentheses around it if it is part of another sentence.

> The Southern Ocean is the fourth-largest ocean (it is larger than the Atlantic).

579.2

After Initials

Place a period after an initial.

> J. K. Rowling (author)
> Colin L. Powell (politician)

579.3

After Abbreviations

Place a period after each part of an abbreviation. Do not use periods with acronyms or initialisms. (See page 636.)

> Abbreviations: Mr. Mrs. Ms. Dr. B.C.E. C.E.
> Acronyms: AIDS NASA
> Initialisms: NBC FBI

NOTE When an abbreviation is the last word in a sentence, use only one period at the end of the sentence.

> My grandfather's full name is William Ryan James Koenig, Jr.

579.4

As Decimal Points

Use a period to separate dollars and cents and as a decimal point.

> The price of a loaf of bread was $1.54 in 1992.
> That price was only 35 cents, or 77.3 percent less, in 1972.

Question Marks

A **question mark** is used after an interrogative sentence and also to show doubt about the correctness of a fact or figure. (See page 518.)

580.1
At the End of Direct Questions

Use a question mark at the end of a direct question (an interrogative sentence).

Is a vegan a person who eats only vegetables?

580.2
At the End of Indirect Questions

No question mark is used after an indirect question. (An indirect question tells about a question you or someone else asked.)

Because I do not eat meat, I'm often asked if I am a vegetarian.
I asked the doctor if going meatless is harmful to my health.

580.3
To Show Doubt

Place a question mark within parentheses to show that you are unsure that a fact or figure is correct.

By the year 2020 (?) the number of vegetarians in the United States may approach 15 percent of the population.

Exclamation Points

An **exclamation point** may be placed after a word, a phrase, or a sentence to show emotion. (The exclamation point should not be overused.)

580.4
To Express Strong Feelings

Use an exclamation point to show excitement or strong feeling.

Yeah! Wow! Oh my!
Surprise! You've won the million-dollar sweepstakes!

Caution: Never use more than one exclamation point in writing assignments.

Incorrect: **Don't ever do that to me again!!!**
Correct: **Don't ever do that to me again!**

End Punctuation

 On your own paper, write whether each of the following sentences needs a period, a question mark, or an exclamation point at the end.

1. Wow, listen to that alarm ringing
   exclamation point

2. Uh-oh, it's a fire drill

3. How many fire drills do you have at your school

4. Drills are held to make sure everyone knows how to get out of the building in an emergency

5. What can you do to make sure you will safely get out of a burning building

6. Should you take all of your books and belongings with you

7. You should simply get up and quickly walk out without taking anything with you

8. To prevent confusion and panic, everyone needs to exit calmly

9. Absolutely no pushing is allowed

10. Make sure those with a disability are assisted to the exit

11. Close the door on your way out to prevent a fire from spreading

12. Would you know another way out if the first exit was blocked

13. Meet at a chosen place to make sure everyone got out

14. Firefighter Jim asked us if we should go back into a burning building for any reason

15. The answer was a loud no

Next Step: Write about a fire drill you remember. End at least one sentence with a period, one with a question mark, and one with an exclamation point.

Answers

2. exclamation point
3. question mark
4. period
5. question mark
6. question mark
7. period
8. period
9. period or exclamation point
10. period
11. period
12. question mark
13. period
14. period
15. exclamation point

Commas

Use a **comma** to indicate a pause or a change in thought. This helps to keep words and ideas from running together so that the writing is easier to read. For a writer, no other form of punctuation is more important to understand than the comma.

582.1
Between Items in a Series

Use commas between words, phrases, or clauses in a series. (A series contains at least three items.) (See page 513.)

> **Chinese, English, and Hindi** are the three most widely used languages in the world. (words)

> **Being comfortable with technology, working well with others, and knowing another language** are important skills for today's workers. (phrases)

> **My dad works in a factory, my mom works in an office, and I work in school.** (clauses)

582.2
To Keep Numbers Clear

Use commas to separate the digits in a number in order to distinguish hundreds, thousands, millions, and so on.

> More than **104,000** people live in Kingston, the capital of Jamaica.

> The population of the entire country of Liechtenstein is only **29,000**.

NOTE Commas are not used in years.

> The world population was 6.1 billion by 2003.

582.3
In Dates and Addresses

Use commas to set off items in an address and items in a date.

> On August **28, 1963**, Martin Luther King, Jr., gave his famous "I Have a Dream" speech.

> The address of the King Center is 449 Auburn Avenue NE, Atlanta, Georgia 30312.

NOTE No comma is placed between the state and ZIP code. Also, when only the month and year are given, no comma is needed.

> In January 2029 we will celebrate the 100th anniversary of Reverend King's birth.

Commas 1

- Between Items in a Series
- To Keep Numbers Clear
- In Dates and Addresses

 For each sentence below, write the series, date, address, or number that should include a comma. Add the comma.

1. A democracy, as Abraham Lincoln said, is a government of the people by the people and for the people.
   of the people, by the people, and for the people

2. The first democracy was created in ancient Greece over 2000 years ago.

3. When colonial Americans declared independence from England on July 4 1776, they created a democracy.

4. Benjamin Franklin Thomas Jefferson and George Washington were men who worked to create an independent country.

5. Jefferson wrote the Declaration of Independence Franklin edited it and they both signed it.

6. The reasons for declaring independence included complaints about the king of England a wish to give power to the people and the desire for individual freedoms.

7. The people wanted the right to "life liberty and the pursuit of happiness."

8. The Declaration was signed on August 2 1776 in Philadelphia, which had a population at the time of about 25000.

9. The original document is kept in the National Archives Building 700 Pennsylvania Avenue Washington DC 20408.

Next Step: Write a sentence telling what you think your world would be like if the Declaration of Independence had not been adopted. Include commas between items in a series.

Answers

2. 2,000
3. July 4, 1776
4. Benjamin Franklin, Thomas Jefferson, and George Washington
5. Jefferson wrote the Declaration of Independence, Franklin edited it, and they both signed it.
6. complaints about the king of England, a wish to give power to the people, and the desire for individual freedoms
7. "life, liberty, and the pursuit of happiness"
8. August 2, 1776, 25,000
9. National Archives Building, 700 Pennsylvania Avenue, Washington, DC 20408

Commas . . .

584.1
To Set Off Nonrestrictive Phrases and Clauses

Use commas to set off nonrestrictive phrases and clauses—those not necessary to the basic meaning of the sentence.

> **People get drinking water from surface water or groundwater, which makes up only 1 percent of the earth's water supply.**

(The clause *which makes up only 1 percent of the earth's water supply* is additional information; it is nonrestrictive—not required. If the clause were left out, the meaning of the sentence would remain clear.)

Restrictive phrases or clauses—those that are needed in the sentence—restrict or limit the meaning of the sentence; they are not set off with commas.

> **Groundwater that is free from harmful pollutants is rare.**

(The clause *that is free from harmful pollutants* is restrictive; it is needed to complete the meaning of the basic sentence and is not set off with commas.)

584.2
To Set Off Titles or Initials

Use commas to set off a title, a name, or initials that follow a person's last name. (Use only one period if an initial comes at the end of a sentence.)

> **Melanie Prokat, M.D., is our family's doctor. However, she is listed in the phone book only as Prokat, M.**

NOTE Although commas are not necessary to set off "Jr." and "Sr." after a name, they may be used as long as a comma is used both before and after the abbreviation.

584.3
To Set Off Interruptions

Use commas to set off a word, phrase, or clause that interrupts the main thought of a sentence. These interruptions usually can be identified through the following tests:

1. You can leave them out of a sentence without changing its meaning.

2. You can place them other places in the sentence without changing its meaning.

> **Our school, as we all know, is becoming overcrowded again.**
> (clause)
> **The gym, not the cafeteria, was expanded a while ago.** (phrase)
> **My history class, for example, has 42 students in it.** (phrase)
> **There are, indeed, about 1,000 people in my school.** (word)
> **The building, however, has room for only 850 students.** (word)

Commas 2

- To Set Off Nonrestrictive Phrases and Clauses
- To Set Off Titles or Initials
- To Set Off Interruptions

Rewrite each of the following sentences, placing commas where they are needed.

1. Dr. Martin Luther King Jr. was originally named Michael.
   Dr. Martin Luther King, Jr., was originally named Michael.

2. His parents Alberta and Martin Luther King Sr. renamed their son Martin when he was about six years old.

3. Benjamin Mays Ph.D. convinced Martin to begin a religious career when he finished college in 1948.

4. Reverend King became a very important leader as you may already know in the civil rights movement.

5. He believed that all people no matter what race or gender should be able to live and work together.

6. His nonviolent efforts toward peace which won him the Nobel Peace Prize in 1964 made him unpopular with some people.

7. His home for instance was bombed, and he was arrested several times.

8. King's assassination in 1968 however did not end his work.

9. His birthday in fact is a national holiday that is celebrated on the third Monday of January.

10. George Washington and Abraham Lincoln whose birthdays are also celebrated as national holidays are two other Americans who are honored in this way.

Next Step: Write a short paragraph describing what your school does for Presidents' Day or Martin Luther King, Jr., Day. Use sentences with commas that set off nonrestrictive phrases or clauses, titles or initials, and interruptions.

Answers

2. His parents, Alberta and Martin Luther King, Sr., renamed their son Martin when he was about six years old.

3. Benjamin Mays, Ph.D., convinced Martin to begin a religious career when he finished college in 1948.

4. Reverend King became a very important leader, as you may already know, in the civil rights movement.

5. He believed that all people, no matter what race or gender, should be able to live and work together.

6. His nonviolent efforts toward peace, which won him the Nobel Peace Prize in 1964, made him unpopular with some people.

7. His home, for instance, was bombed, and he was arrested several times.

8. King's assassination in 1968, however, did not end his work.

9. His birthday, in fact, is a national holiday that is celebrated on the third Monday of January.

10. George Washington and Abraham Lincoln, whose birthdays are also celebrated as national holidays, are two other Americans who are honored in this way.

586

Commas . . .

586.1
To Set Off Appositives

Commas set off an appositive from the rest of the sentence. An appositive is a word or phrase that identifies or renames a noun or pronoun. (See page 520.)

> The capital of Cyprus **,** Nicosia **,** has a population of almost 643,000. (*Nicosia* renames *capital of Cyprus*, so the word is set off with commas.)

> Cyprus **,** an island in the Mediterranean Sea **,** is about half the size of Connecticut. (*An island in the Mediterranean Sea* identifies *Cyprus*, so the phrase is set off with commas.)

Do not use commas with appositives that are necessary to the basic meaning of the sentence.

> The Mediterranean island Cyprus is about half the size of Connecticut. (*Cyprus* is not set off because it is needed to make the sentence clear.)

586.2
To Separate Equal Adjectives

Use commas to separate two or more adjectives that equally modify the same noun.

> Comfortable **,** efficient cars are becoming more important to drivers. (*Comfortable* and *efficient* are separated by a comma because they modify *cars* equally.)

> Some automobiles run on clean **,** renewable sources of energy. (*Clean* and *renewable* are separated by a comma because they modify *sources* equally.)

> Conventional gasoline engines emit a lot of pollution. (*Conventional* and *gasoline* do not modify *engines* equally; therefore, no comma separates the two.)

Use these tests to help you decide if adjectives modify equally:

1. Switch the order of the adjectives; if the sentence is clear, the adjectives modify equally.

   Yes: Efficient **,** comfortable cars are becoming more important to drivers.

   No: Gasoline conventional engines emit a lot of pollution.

2. Put the word *and* between the adjectives; if the sentence is clear, use a comma when *and* is taken out.

   Yes: Comfortable and efficient cars are becoming more important to drivers.

   No: Conventional and gasoline engines emit a lot of pollution.

Commas 3

To Set Off Appositives

For each sentence below, write the appositive phrase and the noun it renames. Set off the appositive with commas.

1. "Mexamerica" the region between Houston and Los Angeles is the location of choice for many people.

   "Mexamerica," the region between Houston and Los Angeles,

2. San Diego California's second-largest city boasts some of the best weather in the country.

3. Austin the capital of Texas has a strong Tejano music scene.

4. San Antonio another Texas city hosts the annual Fiesta San Antonio to remember its war heroes.

5. Las Cruces, New Mexico, was ranked by *Forbes* a financial newsmagazine as the best small city to live and work in.

To Separate Equal Adjectives

For each numbered sentence below, write the adjectives that need commas between them. Add the commas.

> *Example:* Los Angeles is located along the rugged sandy coast of southern California.
>
> *Answer:* **rugged, sandy**

(6) Considered the "capital" of Mexamerica by some, Los Angeles is an exciting spread-out city. **(7)** It is full of lively unique neighborhoods. **(8)** Although many people live an enjoyable rewarding life in Los Angeles, the city also has its problems. **(9)** Everyone seems to know about the slow-moving congested traffic and the very high cost of living. **(10)** Despite the city's troubles, many people still like living in golden sunny Los Angeles.

Commas . . .

588.1
To Set Off Dialogue

Use commas to set off the exact words of a speaker from the rest of the sentence. (Also see page 556.)

> The firefighter said, "When we cannot successfully put out a fire, we try to keep it from spreading."

> "When we cannot successfully put out a fire, we try to keep it from spreading," the firefighter said.

NOTE Do not use a comma or quotation marks for indirect quotations. The words *if* and *that* often signal dialogue that is being reported rather than quoted.

> The firefighter said that when they cannot successfully put out a fire, they try to keep it from spreading. (These are not the speaker's exact words.)

588.2
In Direct Address

Use commas to separate a noun of direct address from the rest of the sentence. (A noun of direct address is a noun that names a person spoken to in the sentence.)

> Hanae, did you know that an interior decorator can change wallpaper and fabrics on a computer screen?

> Sure, Jack, and an architect can use a computer to see how light will fall in different parts of a building.

588.3
To Set Off Interjections

Use commas to separate an interjection or a weak exclamation from the rest of the sentence.

> No kidding, you mean that one teacher has to manage a class of 42 pupils? (weak exclamation)

> Uh-huh, and that teacher has other classes that size. (interjection)

588.4
To Set Off Explanatory Phrases

Use commas to separate an explanatory phrase from the rest of the sentence.

> English, the language computers speak worldwide, is also the most widely used language in science and medicine.

> More than 750 million people, about an eighth of the world's population, speak English as a foreign language.

Commas 4

- To Set Off Dialogue
- In Direct Address
- To Set Off Interjections
- To Set Off Explanatory Phrases

Rewrite each of the following sentences, placing commas where they are needed.

1. Whales are warm-blooded mammals breathing air through their blowholes and are found in all oceans.
   Whales are warm-blooded mammals, breathing air through their blowholes, and are found in all oceans.

2. While most whales swim in groups, others like fin whales swim alone or in pairs.

3. Ms. Smith asked "Laticia did you know the longest dive by a sperm whale lasted more than an hour?"

4. Laticia replied "Uh-uh but I know sperm whales can dive to depths of more than a mile."

5. Jeremy said "Well that's hard to believe. Ms. Smith how do they do that?"

6. "Fish swim by moving their tails from side to side, but whales swim by pumping their tails up and down" she said.

7. Some of the sea creatures we know as dolphins are actually whales such as the killer whale and the pilot whale.

8. Humpback whales named for the hump behind the dorsal fin are an endangered species.

9. Laticia said "Other whales including the right and blue whales are also endangered."

Next Step: Write a brief, imagined conversation between whales. Use commas correctly to set off dialogue and nouns of direct address.

Answers

2. While most whales swim in groups, others, like fin whales, swim alone or in pairs.

3. Ms. Smith asked, "Laticia, did you know the longest dive by a sperm whale lasted more than an hour?"

4. Laticia replied, "Uh-uh, but I know sperm whales can dive to depths of more than a mile."

5. Jeremy said, "Well, that's hard to believe. Ms. Smith, how do they do that?"

6. "Fish swim by moving their tails from side to side, but whales swim by pumping their tails up and down," she said.

7. Some of the sea creatures we know as dolphins are actually whales, such as the killer whale and the pilot whale.

8. Humpback whales, named for the hump behind the dorsal fin, are an endangered species.

9. Laticia said, "Other whales, including the right and blue whales, are also endangered."

Commas . . .

590.1
To Separate Introductory Clauses and Phrases

Use a comma to separate an adverb clause or a long phrase from the independent clause that follows it.

> If every automobile in the country were a light shade of red, we'd live in a pink-car nation. (adverb clause)

> According to some experts, solar-powered cars will soon be common. (long modifying phrase)

590.2
In Compound Sentences

Use a comma between two independent clauses that are joined by a coordinating conjunction (such as *and, but, or, nor, for, so,* and *yet*), forming a compound sentence. An independent clause expresses a complete thought and can stand alone as a sentence. (Also see page 516.)

> Many students enjoy working on computers, so teachers are finding new ways to use them in the classroom.

> Computers can be valuable in education, but many schools cannot afford enough of them.

Avoid Comma Splices: A comma splice results when two independent clauses are "spliced" together with only a comma—and no conjunction. (See page 506.)

SCHOOL DAZE

Ann, we've completed two-thirds of the quarter, and you haven't turned in one assignment. What do you have to say for yourself?

Ah . . . is there anything I can do for extra credit?

---

 punctuate *edit* capitalize
improve SPELL **591**
Marking Punctuation

PUNCTUATION

Commas 5

■ To Separate Introductory Clauses and Phrases
■ In Compound Sentences

 For each sentence below, write the word or words that should be followed by a comma. Add the comma.

1. I sat down to eat lunch and I began to slurp my soup.
lunch,

2. Aunt Marianna wanted me to improve my table manners so she enrolled me in a class.

3. After the teacher, Ms. Wyatt, introduced herself she said, "The main thing to remember is to be polite."

4. If you are a guest at someone else's house don't sit down at the table or begin eating before the host does.

5. Along with Ms. Wyatt we sat at a beautifully set table.

6. Ramón wanted to sip some of his water but he didn't know which glass was his.

7. Your glass is always placed to the right of your plate and your bread plate goes on the left.

8. Before doing anything else put your napkin on your lap.

9. When you want to butter your bread put some butter on your bread plate first.

10. Since there was more than one fork at each place setting Ms. Wyatt said that we should use the utensils from the outside in.

11. Then she said, "While you're eating take your time yet try to keep pace with the other guests."

Next Step: Write two sentences telling how your table manners could be improved. Include an introductory phrase or clause in one sentence; the other should be a compound sentence. Use commas correctly.

Answers

2. manners,
3. herself,
4. house,
5. Wyatt,
6. water,
7. plate,
8. else,
9. bread,
10. setting,
11. eating, time,

PUNCTUATION

Test Prep

Number your paper from 1 to 12. For each underlined part of the paragraphs below, write the letter (from the next page) of the best way to punctuate it.

Our science <u>teacher Ms. Hewlitt</u> told us that the word *robot* comes
₁
from a Czech word that means "forced labor" or "slave." What is a <u>robot</u>
₂
It is a machine that works for people.

There are almost a million robots in the world <u>today and</u> 90 percent
₃
of them work in factories. Every day, these robots do the same thing over
and over again. In other <u>words they</u> do boring tasks. Robots also do work
₄
that is <u>too faraway too dangerous or even impossible</u> for people to
₅
perform.

In the late 1950s, one of the first modern <u>robots the Unimate</u> was
₆
set up at a factory. In the '80s, better computers made more powerful
robots <u>possible</u> At the same <u>time, the</u> automotive industry started using
₇ ₈
robots on its assembly lines. <u>Today in fact</u> robots can make cars faster
₉
than people ever could. As a result, all that's left for people to do is
<u>supervise maintain and repair</u> the machines.
₁₀

In the future, robots may be programmed to do more complex tasks.
Robots will probably always be part of our <u>world but</u> it is unlikely that
₁₁
they'll ever take over. <u>Whew</u>
₁₂

1. **A** teacher Ms. Hewlitt,
   B teacher, Ms. Hewlitt,
   C teacher, Ms. Hewlitt
   D correct as is

2. **A** robot?
   B robot.
   C robot!
   D correct as is

3. **A** today and,
   B today, and
   C today, and,
   D correct as is

4. **A** words they,
   B words, they
   C words, they,
   D correct as is

5. **A** too faraway, too
   dangerous, or even
   impossible
   B too faraway, too
   dangerous or even
   impossible
   C too faraway too
   dangerous, or even
   impossible
   D correct as is

6. **A** robots, the Unimate,
   B robots the Unimate,
   C robots, the Unimate
   D correct as is

7. **A** possible?
   B possible.
   C possible!
   D correct as is

8. **A** time the
   B time. The
   C time the,
   D correct as is

9. **A** Today in fact,
   B Today, in fact,
   C Today, in fact
   D correct as is

10. **A** supervise, maintain,
    and repair
    B supervise, maintain,
    and repair,
    C supervise, maintain and
    repair
    D correct as is

11. **A** world, but
    B world but,
    C world, but,
    D correct as is

12. **A** Whew.
    B Whew!
    C Whew?
    D correct as is

Answers

1. B
2. A
3. B
4. B
5. A
6. A
7. B
8. D
9. B
10. A
11. A
12. B

Semicolons

Use a **semicolon** to suggest a stronger pause than a comma indicates. A semicolon may also serve in place of a period.

594.1
To Join Two Independent Clauses

In a compound sentence, use a semicolon to join two independent clauses that are not connected with a coordinating conjunction. (See **744.1**.)

> The United States has more computers than any other country**;** its residents own more than 164 million of them.

594.2
With Conjunctive Adverbs

A semicolon is also used to join two independent clauses when the clauses are connected by a conjunctive adverb (such as *as a result, for example, however, therefore,* and *instead*). (See **738.1**.)

> Japan is next on that list**;** however, the Japanese have only 50 million computers.

> You might think that the billion people of China own a lot of computers**;** instead, the smaller country of Germany has twice as many computers as China.

594.3
To Separate Groups That Contain Commas

Use a semicolon between groups of words in a series when one or more of the groups already contain commas.

> Many of our community's residents separate their garbage into bins for newspapers, cardboard, and junk mail**;** glass, metal, and plastic**;** and nonrecyclable trash.

SCHOOL DAZE

> It's true that I have only a few minutes to finish this**;** however, I am not worried.

> Well, that makes one of us.

Semicolons

 For each of the following sentences, write the word or words that should be followed by a semicolon. Add the semicolon.

1. Go to the library first then do your homework.
   first;

2. Mom said I could go to Jean's house however, I have to do the dishes before I go.

3. Cam must be an artist this drawing is fantastic!

4. Sanjay is sick therefore, he can't go to Manny's party.

5. I have already read this book it's about a two-headed monster.

 The following directions will help you create a sentence that uses semicolons. The semicolons will separate groups of words that already contain commas.

6. Think of three toys that involve imagination and write down their names.

7. Next write a list of three games.

8. Finally, write three toys a child would use outside.

9. Now copy and complete the following sentence. Fill in the blanks with your own toy lists. Make sure to include both the commas and the semicolons to separate your lists.

   My little sister Keisha's favorite toys are her _____, _____, and _____ ; her _____ game, _____ game, and _____ game; and her _____, _____, and _____.

Next Step: Write a sentence about your favorite foods. Think of plenty of choices. Use semicolons between groups of words in a series, as in the sentence above.

Answers

 2. house;
3. artist;
4. sick;
5. book;

 6–9. (Answers will vary.)

Example of answers:
My little sister Keisha's favorite toys are her dolls, paints, and puppets; her card game, computer game, and board game; and her bicycle, stilts, and skateboard.

Colons

A **colon** may be used to introduce a list or an important point. Colons are also used in business letters and between the numbers in time.

596.1
To Introduce Lists

Use a colon to introduce a list. The colon usually comes after words describing the subject of the list (as in the first example below) or after summary words, such as *the following* or *these things*. Do not use a colon after a verb or preposition.

Certain items are still difficult to recycle: foam cups, car tires, and toxic chemicals.

To conserve water, you should do the following three things: fix drippy faucets, install a low-flow showerhead, and turn the water off while brushing your teeth.

Incorrect: To conserve water, you should: install a low-flow showerhead, turn the water off while brushing your teeth, and fix drippy faucets.

596.2
To Introduce Sentences

A colon may be used to introduce a sentence, a question, or a quotation.

This is why air pollution is bad: We are sacrificing our health and the health of all other life on the planet.

Answer this question for me: Why aren't more people concerned about global warming?

Joaquin shared this with us: "Iceland is the world's leader in the use of renewable energy."

596.3
After Salutations

A colon may be used after the salutation of a business letter.

Dear Ms. Manners: Dear Dr. Warmle: Dear Professor Potter:

Dear Captain Elliot: Dear Senator:

596.4
For Emphasis

Use a colon to emphasize a word or phrase.

The newest alternative energy is also the most common element on earth: hydrogen.

Here's one thing that can help save energy: a programmable thermostat.

596.5
Between Numbers in Time

Use a colon between the parts of a number that indicate time.

My thermostat automatically sets my heat to 60 degrees between 11:00 p.m. and 6:00 a.m.

Colons

The following letter needs colons placed correctly. Write the words or numbers that need colons. Then add them.

Example: These are a few reasons to go to the dentist to have your teeth cleaned, to relieve a toothache, and to get a cavity filled.

Answer: dentist:

1 Dear Dr. Meyer

2   It was 330 p.m. last Thursday, almost time to have my cavity

3 filled. I was a bit nervous. As I was gnawing on my fingernails, I

4 thought of a question What are these things made of, anyway?

5   I remember hearing that fingernails are made of the same stuff

6 as these other things horses' hooves, birds' feathers, and bulls' horns.

7 They're also made of the same substance as another thing hair.

8   One great thing about nails and hair is that it doesn't hurt to

9 cut into them. By 400, as the drill was making the hole in my tooth

10 even bigger, I had this thought It would be fantastic to have teeth

11 like nails and hair, too! Just think, Dr. Meyer—without using any

12 anesthetic, you could do any of these procedures fill a cavity, fix a

13 broken tooth, or file a chipped tooth.

14   Well, Dr. Meyer, it doesn't hurt to dream! Thanks for helping

15 me take care of something very important to me my teeth.

16 Sincerely,

17 James Ormon

Next Step: Write a sentence containing a colon; after the colon, list all the different ways a colon can be used.

Answers

line 1   Meyer:
line 2   3:30
line 4   question:
line 6   things:
line 7   thing:
line 9   4:00
line 10   thought:
line 12   procedures:
line 15   me:

Quotation Marks

Quotation marks are used in a number of ways:

- to set off the exact words of a speaker,
- to punctuate material quoted from another source,
- to punctuate words used in a special way, and
- to punctuate certain titles.

598.1 **To Set Off a Speaker's Exact Words**	Place quotation marks before and after a speaker's words in dialogue. Only the exact words of the speaker are placed within quotation marks. **Marla said, "I've decided to become a firefighter."** **"A firefighter," said Juan, "can help people in many ways."**
598.2 **For Quotations Within Quotations**	Use single quotation marks to punctuate a quotation within a quotation. **Sung Kim asked, "Did Marla just say, 'I've decided to become a firefighter'?"** When titles occur within a quotation, use single quotation marks to punctuate those that require quotation marks. **Juan said, "Springsteen's song 'The Rising' really inspired her."**
598.3 **To Set Off Quoted Material**	When quoting material from another source, place quotation marks before and after the source's exact words. **In her book _Living the Life You Deserve_, Tess Spyeder explains, "Choose a job you'll enjoy doing day after day over one that will fatten your bank account."**
598.4 **To Set Off Long Quoted Material**	If more than one paragraph is quoted from a single source, quotation marks are placed before each paragraph and at the end of the last paragraph. Quotations that are more than four lines are usually set off from the rest of the paper by indenting each line 10 spaces from the left. Quotations that are set off in this way require no quotation marks either before or after the quoted material.

Quotation Marks 1

- To Set Off a Speaker's Exact Words
- For Quotations Within Quotations

 Rewrite the following conversation, using quotation marks correctly.

Example: Ms. Green said, Don't forget that your book reports are due next week.

Answer: Ms. Green said, *"Don't forget that your book reports are due next week."*

1 Renée asked, What book will you use for your book report?

2 Fadi said, I've always liked the first Harry Potter book, so I'll

3 probably use that.

4 I just read a new book called *Hoot*, Renée said. That's what I'm

5 going to report on.

6 I haven't heard of that book. What's it about? asked Fadi.

7 It's about three kids who help save some endangered miniature

8 owls. See, this big company wants to build a pancake house where

9 the owls' nest is, she said.

10 When you say, build a pancake house, do you mean they want

11 to build a house out of pancakes? Fadi asked.

12 Very funny, said Renée. I think you know what I mean. It's a

13 restaurant that sells pancakes.

14 And so the kids stop this restaurant from being built? Fadi

15 asked.

16 I'm not going to tell you, Renée said. You'll have to read the

17 book yourself if you want to find out!

Next Step: Imagine a conversation you have with a friend about a book you've read recently. Write a few lines of this dialogue. Make sure you use quotation marks correctly.

Answers

line 1	Renée asked, "What book will you use for your book report?"
line 2–3	Fadi said, "I've always liked the first Harry Potter book, so I'll probably use that."
line 4–5	"I just read a new book called *Hoot*," Renée said. "That's what I'm going to report on."
line 6	"I haven't heard of that book. What's it about?" asked Fadi.
line 7–9	"It's about three kids who help save some endangered miniature owls. See, this big company wants to build a pancake house where the owls' nest is," she said.
line 10–11	"When you say, 'build a pancake house,' do you mean they want to build a house out of pancakes?" Fadi asked.
line 12–13	"Very funny," said Renée. "I think you know what I mean. It's a restaurant that sells pancakes."
line 14	"And so the kids stop this restaurant from being built?" Fadi asked.
line 16–17	"I'm not going to tell you," Renée said. "You'll have to read the book yourself if you want to find out!"

PUNCTUATION

Quotation Marks . . .

600.1
Placement of Punctuation

Always place periods and commas inside quotation marks.

> "I don't know**,**" said Lac.
> Lac said, "I don't know**.**"

Place an exclamation point or a question mark inside the quotation marks when it punctuates the quotation.

> Ms. Wiley asked, "Can you actually tour the Smithsonian on the Internet?"

Place it outside when it punctuates the main sentence.

> Did I hear you say, "Now we can tour the Smithsonian on the Internet"?

Place semicolons or colons outside quotation marks.

> First, I will read the article "Sonny's Blues"**;** then I will read "The Star Café" in my favorite music magazine.

600.2
For Special Words

Quotation marks also may be used (1) to set apart a word that is being discussed, (2) to indicate that a word is slang, or (3) to point out that a word or phrase is being used in a special way.

1. Renny uses the word **"**like**"** entirely too much.
2. Man, your car is really **"**phat.**"**
3. Aunt Lulu, an editor at a weekly magazine, says she has **"**issues.**"**

600.3
To Punctuate Titles

Use quotation marks to punctuate titles of songs, poems, short stories, lectures, episodes of radio or television programs, chapters of books, and articles found in magazines, newspapers, or encyclopedias. (Also see **602.3**.)

"21 Questions" (song)
"The Reed Flute's Song" (poem)
"Old Man at the Bridge" (short story)
"Birthday Boys" (a television episode)
"The Foolish and the Weak" (a chapter in a book)
"Science Careers Today" (lecture)
"Teen Rescues Stranded Dolphin" (newspaper article)

NOTE When you punctuate a title, capitalize the first word, last word, and every word in between—except for articles (*a, an, the*), short prepositions (*at, to, with,* and so on), and coordinating conjunctions (*and, but, or*). (See **624.2**.)

Quotation Marks 2

■ **Placement of Punctuation**

 Rewrite the following sentences, placing commas and end punctuation where needed.

1. "We're learning some new songs in chorus" said Ryan.
   "We're learning some new songs in chorus," said Ryan.

2. "I hear that's a fun class" said Elisa.

3. "Who is the new teacher" she asked.

4. Ryan said, "Mr. Pescados"

5. "Did you say 'Mr. Pescados' If you did, that's funny" Elisa said.

6. She continued, "*Pescados* means 'fish' in Spanish"

■ **To Punctuate Titles**

 For each of the following sentences, write the title that needs quotation marks. (Be careful to place commas or periods correctly.)

7. The article Remember When talks about pleasant childhood memories.
   "Remember When"

8. When I was little, I've Been Workin' on the Railroad was my favorite song.

9. I also remember learning the poem One, Two, Buckle My Shoe.

10. Mom read short bedtime stories from *Grimms' Fairy Tales,* and I never got tired of listening to Rapunzel.

11. I must have watched Day of the Dumpster, the pilot episode of *Mighty Morphin' Power Rangers,* a dozen times!

12. The recent *Time for Kids* magazine article Having a Blast in the Past made me think of all these memories.

Answers

2. "I hear that's a fun class**,**" said Elisa.
3. "Who is the new teacher**?**" she asked.
4. Ryan said, "Mr. Pescados**.**"
5. "Did you say 'Mr. Pescados'**?** If you did, that's funny**,**" Elisa said.
6. She continued, "*Pescados* means 'fish' in Spanish**.**"

8. "I've Been Workin' on the Railroad"
9. "One, Two, Buckle My Shoe."
10. "Rapunzel."
11. "Day of the Dumpster,"
12. "Having a Blast in the Past"

Italics and Underlining

Italics is slightly slanted type. In this sentence, the word *happiness* is typed in italics. In handwritten material, each word or letter that should be in italics is **underlined**. (See an example on page **400**.)

602.1
In Printed Material

Print words in italics when you are using a computer.

In *Tuck Everlasting*, the author explores what it would be like to live forever.

602.2
In Handwritten Material

Underline words that should be italicized when you are writing by hand.

In <u>Tuck Everlasting</u>, the author explores what it would be like to live forever.

602.3
In Titles

Italicize (or underline) the titles of books, plays, book-length poems, magazines, newspapers, radio and television programs, movies, videos, cassettes, CD's, and the names of aircraft and ships.

Walk Two Moons (book)	*Teen People* (magazine)
Fairies and Dragons (movie)	*Everwood* (TV program)
The Young and the Hopeless (CD)	*U.S.S. Arizona* (ship)
Columbia (space shuttle)	*Daily Herald* (newspaper)

Exception: Do not italicize or put quotation marks around your own title at the top of your written work.

A Day Without Water (personal writing: do not italicize)

602.4
For Scientific and Foreign Words

Italicize (or underline) scientific and foreign words that are not commonly used in everyday English.

Spinacia oleracea is the scientific term for spinach.

Many store owners who can help Spanish-speaking customers display an *Hablamos Español* sign in their windows.

602.5
For Special Uses

Italicize (or underline) a number, letter, or word that is being discussed or used in a special way. (Sometimes quotation marks are used for this same reason.)

Matt's hat has a bright red *A* on it.

Italics and Underlining

 Write the word or words that should be italicized in each sentence. Underline the words.

1. I just finished reading an article in Teen People.
   Teen People

2. In the article, it says that one of the singers in Coldplay has 007 on his license plate.

3. Yes, he's a James Bond fan—his favorite movie is Thunderball.

4. You might say some of the characters in this movie, featuring some amazing underwater action, are benthic (they're bottom-dwellers).

5. James Bond, introduced in Ian Fleming's novel Casino Royale, first appeared on film in the television series Climax! in 1954.

6. Bond works for the British Secret Service; an actual British navy ship, the Devonshire, was used in the Bond movie Tomorrow Never Dies.

7. Two of Bond's associates have the letters M and Q for their names.

8. His boss used the word prism in telegrams as a sign of approval.

9. Did Bond's enemies ever say non, merci (no, thanks) to him?

10. A French media company publishes James Bond Magazine, and 007 Magazine is available to members of the James Bond International Fan Club.

11. Almost all the Bond movies have a soundtrack available on CD, and my favorite is The World Is Not Enough.

Next Step: Write some sentences that include the names of your favorite CD, movie, and book or magazine. Use italics (underlining) correctly.

Answers

2. <u>007</u>
3. <u>Thunderball</u>
4. <u>benthic</u>
5. <u>Casino Royale</u>, <u>Climax!</u>
6. <u>Devonshire</u>, <u>Tomorrow Never Dies</u>
7. <u>M</u>, <u>Q</u>
8. <u>prism</u>
9. <u>non, merci</u>
10. <u>James Bond Magazine</u>, <u>007 Magazine</u>
11. <u>The World Is Not Enough</u>

Apostrophes

Use **apostrophes** to form contractions, to form certain plurals, or to show possession.

604.1
In Contractions

Use an apostrophe to form a contraction, showing that one or more letters have been left out of a word.

Common Contractions

can**'**t (cannot)	couldn**'**t (could not)	didn**'**t (did not)
doesn**'**t (does not)	don**'**t (do not)	hasn**'**t (has not)
haven**'**t (have not)	isn**'**t (is not)	I**'**ll (I will)
I**'**d (I would)	I**'**m (I am)	I**'**ve (I have)
they**'**ll (they will)	they**'**d (they would)	they**'**ve (they have)
they**'**re (they are)	you**'**re (you are)	wouldn**'**t (would not)
you**'**ll (you will)	you**'**d (you would)	you**'**ve (you have)

604.2
In Place of Omitted Letters or Numbers

Use an apostrophe to show that one or more digits have been left out of a number, or that one or more letters have been left out of a word to show a special pronunciation.

class of **'**99 (*19* is left out)

g**'**bye (the letters *ood* are left out of *good-bye*)

NOTE Letters and numbers should not be omitted in most writing assignments; however, they may be omitted in dialogue to make it sound like real people are talking.

604.3
To Form Some Plurals

Use an apostrophe and *s* to form the plural of a letter, a sign, a number, or a word being discussed as a word.

A**'**s   +**'**s   8**'**s   *to***'**s

Don't use too many *and* **'**s in your writing.

604.4
To Form Singular Possessives

To form the possessive of a singular noun, add an apostrophe and *s*.

the game**'**s directions	Dr. Mill**'**s theory
Ross**'**s bike	Roz**'**s hair

NOTE When a singular noun with more than one syllable ends with an *s* or *z* sound, the possessive may be formed by adding just an apostrophe.

Texas**'** oil (or) Texas**'**s oil   Carlos**'** mother (or) Carlos**'**s mother

Apostrophes 1

■ In Contractions
■ In Place of Omitted Letters or Numbers

 In the following sentences, apostrophes are missing from numbers or words. Write the words or numbers with their apostrophes.

1. Comets arent solid rock, but when Grandpa was in school (the class of 55), people thought they were.
   aren't   '55

2. Jermaine enjoys reading his science book, published in 98.

3. The book says that space travelers wouldnt be able to take enough food and fuel for a trip to the stars.

4. Theyd run out of supplies long before they reached Pluto.

5. Back in 79, astronomers saw Pluto cross Neptune's orbit.

6. For the next 20 years, Pluto wasnt the most distant planet in our solar system—Neptune was.

■ To Form Some Plurals
■ To Form Singular Possessives

 In the following sentences, apostrophes are missing from some words. Write the words with their apostrophes.

7. A rocket must travel 25,000 miles per hour to escape Earths gravity.
   Earth's

8. How many 0s are needed to show the distance already covered by the space probe *Voyager 2*?

9. *Voyagers* cameras took pictures around Jupiter and Neptune.

10. In 1977, an astronomers powerful telescope helped him see rings around Uranus.

11. Today, the worlds most powerful telescopes allow us to see galaxies that are 13 billion light-years away.

Answers

2. '98
3. wouldn't
4. They'd
5. '79
6. wasn't

8. O's
9. *Voyager's*
10. astronomer's
11. world's

Apostrophes . . .

606.1
To Form Plural Possessives

The possessive form of plural nouns ending in *s* is usually made by adding just an apostrophe.

 students' homework teachers' lounge

For plural nouns not ending in *s*, an apostrophe and *s* must be added.

 children's book people's opinions

Remember: The word immediately before the apostrophe is the owner.

 student's project (*student* is the owner)
 students' project (*students* are the owners)

606.2
To Show Shared Possession

When possession is shared by more than one noun, add an apostrophe and *s* to the last noun in the series.

 Uncle Reggie, Aunt Rosie, and my mom's garden
 (All three own the garden.)

 Uncle Reggie's, Aunt Rosie's, and my mom's gardens
 (Each person owns a garden.)

606.3
To Form Possessives with Compound Nouns

The possessive of a compound noun is formed by placing the possessive ending after the last word.

 her sister-in-law's hip-hop music (singular)
 her sisters-in-law's tastes in music (plural)
 the secretary of state's husband (singular)
 the secretaries of state's husbands (plural)

606.4
To Form Possessives with Indefinite Pronouns

The possessive of an indefinite pronoun is formed by adding an apostrophe and *s*.

 no one's anyone's somebody's

NOTE In pronouns that use *else*, add an apostrophe and *s* to the second word.

 somebody else's anyone else's

606.5
To Express Time or Amount

Use an apostrophe with an adjective that is part of an expression indicating time (month, day, hour) or amount.

 In today's Spanish class, we talked about going to Spain.
 My father lost more than an hour's work when that thunderstorm knocked out our power.
 I bought a couple dollars' worth of grapes at the roadside stand.

Apostrophes 2

- To Form Plural Possessives
- To Show Shared Possession
- To Form Possessives with Compound Nouns
- To Form Possessives with Indefinite Pronouns
- To Express Time or Amount

 In each of the following sentences, one or more words are missing an apostrophe. Write the words with the apostrophes placed correctly.

1. James Madison and Alexander Hamiltons report called for revising the Articles of Confederation.
 Hamilton's

2. More than four years work was needed to create the new Constitution of the United States.

3. Our forefathers first ideas for a United States government were written in 1781 as the Articles of Confederation.

4. George Washington had accepted the commander in chiefs role in the Continental Army.

5. By 1787, however, he was not sure that the Articles truly represented everyones best interests.

6. Twelve of the original thirteen states delegates met to discuss the country's future, and Washington was named president of this Constitutional Convention.

7. It was an opportunity for everybodys ideas to be heard.

8. The delegates new document, called the Constitution of the United States, was the product of the convention.

9. George Washingtons, Benjamin Franklins, and Alexander Hamiltons signatures all appeared on that document.

10. The summers efforts had been successful.

11. In 1788, two final states votes for the Constitution meant that nine states had ratified it, and it became law.

Answers

2. years'
3. forefathers'
4. commander in chief's
5. everyone's
6. states'
7. everybody's
8. delegates'
9. Washington's, Franklin's, Hamilton's
10. summer's
11. states'

608–609 Proofreader's Guide

608

punctuate *edit* capitalize
improve SPELL 609
Marking Punctuation

PUNCTUATION

Hyphens

Use a **hyphen** to divide words at the end of a line and to form compound words. Also use a hyphen between the numbers in a fraction and to join numbers that indicate the life span of an individual, the scores of a game, and so on.

608.1
To Divide Words

Use a hyphen to divide a word when you run out of room at the end of a line. A word may be divided only between syllables. Here are some additional guidelines:

- Never divide a one-syllable word: *raised, through.*
- Avoid dividing a word of five letters or fewer: *paper, study.*
- Never divide a one-letter syllable from the rest of the word: *omit-ted,* **not** *o-mitted.*
- Never divide abbreviations or contractions: *NASA, wouldn't.*
- Never divide the last word in more than two lines in a row or the last word in a paragraph.
- When a vowel is a syllable by itself, divide the word after the vowel: *epi-sode,* **not** *ep-isode.*

NOTE Refer to a dictionary if you're not sure how to divide a word.

608.2
In Compound Words

A hyphen is used in some compound words, including numbers from twenty-one to ninety-nine.

about-face	warm-up	time-out
down-to-earth	ice-skating	high-rise
thirty-three	seventy-five	

608.3
To Create New Words

A hyphen is often used to form new words beginning with the prefixes *self, ex, all,* and *great.* A hyphen is also used with suffixes such as *elect* and *free.*

self-cleaning	ex-friend	all-natural	mayor-elect
self-esteem	ex-president	great-aunt	germ-free

608.4
Between Numbers in a Fraction

Use a hyphen between the numbers in a fraction. Do not, however, use a hyphen between the numerator and denominator when one or both are already hyphenated.

four-tenths	five-sixteenths	seven thirty-seconds (7/32)

Hyphens 1

■ To Divide Words
■ In Compound Words

 If the underlined words are presented correctly, write "correct." If not, write the correct form. Check a dictionary if you are not sure.

1. <u>Twenty-one</u> gym students went outside just as a <u>po-werful</u> storm soaked the playing field.
   correct, power-ful or pow-erful

2. <u>Fifty five</u> minutes of exercise is required each week, and that doesn't include a <u>warm-up</u>.

3. A <u>top-notch</u> physical education teacher instructs students <u>a-bout</u> the value of regular exercise.

4. We'd rather play a game than do calisthenics, but that <u>would-n't</u> make us sweat enough, I guess.

5. Still, playing <u>volleyball</u> is more fun than doing <u>pushups</u>.

■ To Create New Words
■ Between Numbers in a Fraction

 For each of the following sentences, write the correct form of the underlined words.

6. The coach was surprised that <u>three fourths</u> of his students were very fast runners.
   three-fourths

7. Jamal saw that <u>two thirds</u> of his class ran faster than he could.

8. Since the coach was an <u>exrunner</u>, he knew that Jamal might be a better sprinter.

9. Jamal ran the 50-yard dash and beat <u>ninetenths</u> of the class.

10. Now Jamal is <u>self motivated</u> to improve his running skills.

11. He told his <u>greatgrandmother</u> about his new goal.

 2. Fifty-five, correct
3. correct, about
4. wouldn't
5. correct, push-ups

 7. two-thirds
8. ex-runner
9. nine-tenths
10. self-motivated
11. great-grandmother

610

PUNCTUATION

Hyphens . . .

**610.1
To Form
Adjectives**

Use a hyphen to join two or more words that work together to form a single-thought adjective before a noun. Generally, hyphenate any compound adjective that might be misread if it is not hyphenated—use common sense. (See page 488.)

    smiley-face sticker   dress-up clothes   fresh-breeze scent

Use the tests below to determine if a hyphen is needed.

1. When a compound adjective is made of a noun plus an adjective, it should be hyphenated.

    microwave-safe cookware   book-smart student

2. When a compound adjective is made of a noun plus a participle (*ing* or *ed* form of a verb), it should be hyphenated.

    bone-chilling story   vitamin-enriched cereal

3. Hyphenate a compound adjective that is a phrase (includes conjunctions or prepositions).

    heat-and-serve meals   refrigerator-to-oven dishes

Do *not* hyphenate compound adjectives in these instances:

1. When words forming the adjective come after the noun, do not hyphenate.

    This cookware is microwave safe.
    The cereal was vitamin enriched.

2. If the first of the two words ends in *ly,* do not hyphenate.

    newly designed computer   rarely seen species

3. Do not use a hyphen when a number or letter is the final part of a one-thought adjective.

    grade A milk   level 6 textbook

**610.2
To Join Letters
to Words**

Use a hyphen to join a capital letter to a noun or participle.

    U-turn   Y-axis   T-bar   A-frame
    PG-rated movie   X-ray

**610.3
To Avoid
Confusion**

Use a hyphen with prefixes or suffixes to avoid confusion or awkward spelling.

    Re-collect (not recollect) **the reports we handed back last week.**
    It has a shell-like (not shelllike) **texture.**

Hyphens 2

■ To Form Adjectives
■ To Join Letters to Words

 For each of the following sentences, write the word or words that should be joined by a hyphen.

1. Truc found his T shirt rolled up in a ball under his bed.
    T-shirt

2. The tie dyed shirt was all wrinkled, but he didn't have time to iron it.

3. Truc put the shirt on and looked for his acid washed jeans.

4. He raced from his fifth floor apartment to the sidewalk in front of the building.

5. It was early October, and he could smell a burning leaves odor in the air.

6. He ran back up to the apartment and grabbed his V neck sweater.

7. He decided to take his fleece lined jacket, too, just in case it got colder.

8. Truc was meeting Matt, and they were going to see a G rated, animated movie at the new theater in town.

9. Matt said it looked like a color blind designer had painted the lobby of the theater.

10. Truc and Matt sat in the top row seats of the balcony and settled in to watch the movie.

Next Step: Write two sentences about the movie Truc and Matt saw. Include a hyphenated adjective in each sentence.

Answers

2. tie-dyed
3. acid-washed
4. fifth-floor
5. burning-leaves
6. V-neck
7. fleece-lined
8. G-rated
9. color-blind
10. top-row

Dashes

The **dash** can be used to show a sudden break in a sentence, to emphasize a word or clause, and to show that someone's speech is being interrupted.

612.1
To Indicate a Sudden Break

A dash can be used to show a sudden break in a sentence.

The three of us came down with colds, lost our voices, and missed the football game—all because we had practiced in the rain.

612.2
For Emphasis

A dash may be used to emphasize or explain a word, a series of words, a phrase, or a clause.

Vitamins and minerals—important dietary supplements—can improve your diet.

The benefits of vitamin A—better vision and a stronger immune system—are well known.

612.3
To Indicate Interrupted Speech

Use a dash to show that someone's speech is being interrupted by another person.

Well—yes, I understand—no, I remember—oh—okay, thank you.

NOTE A dash is indicated by two hyphens--without spacing before or after the hyphens--in all typed material.

Parentheses

Parentheses are used around words that are included in a sentence to add information or to help make an idea clearer.

612.4
To Add Information

Use parentheses when adding information or clarifying an idea.

Cures for diseases (from arthritis to AIDS) may be found in plants in the rain forest.

Only about 10 percent (27,000) of the plant species in the world have been studied.

Dashes

 The following sentences use dashes in different ways. Using each as a model, write your own sentence.

1. Yes, Dara, I know that green is your favorite color—it's mine, too!
   Why, Evan, I thought that green was a natural color—it's organic, man!

2. Dara, you really should—wait, listen—what?—never mind.

3. Yellow—the color of happiness—is often used for decorations at celebrations.

4. A person who feels blue—as in sad—would probably not wear bright red.

5. Hey, Maurice, how did—no, I didn't know—okay, no shorts.

6. She wants to paint her room—why, I'll never understand—purple and red.

7. Maybe she thinks purple and red will make her feel "royal"—like a queen.

Parentheses

 Write the "added information" in the following sentences, enclosing it in parentheses.

1. Ancient people Egyptians, Chinese, and Greeks believed in healing with colors.
   (Egyptians, Chinese, and Greeks)

2. Warm colors red, yellow, and orange remind people of excitement and activity, while cool colors blue, green, and violet are calming.

3. Our reactions to color are based on our experiences both cultural and emotional.

Answers

 (Answers will vary.)

 2. (red, yellow, and orange), (blue, green, and violet)
3. (both cultural and emotional)

Ellipses

Use an **ellipsis** (three periods) to show a pause in dialogue or to show that words or sentences have been left out. Leave one space before, after, and between each period.

614.1
To Show Pauses

Use an ellipsis to show a pause in dialogue.

"My report," said Reggie, "is on . . . ah . . . cars of the future. One place that I . . . uh . . . checked on the Internet said that cars would someday run on sunshine."

614.2
To Show Omitted Words

Use an ellipsis to show that one or more words have been left out of a quotation. Read this statement about hibernation.

Some animals, such as the chipmunk and the woodchuck, hibernate in winter. During this time, the animal's heart beats very slowly—only a few times per minute. Its body cools down so much that it nearly freezes, and this is called going into torpor.

Here's how you would type part of the above quotation, leaving some of the words out. If the words left out are at the end of a sentence, use a period followed by three dots.

Some animals . . . hibernate in winter. During this time, the animal's heart beats very slowly . . . and this is called going into torpor.

SCHOOL DAZE

Max, where is your project? Today is the last day to turn it in!

Well . . . ah . . . can I fax it to you before midnight?

Ellipses

 To Show Pauses

 Rewrite the following brief conversation, inserting ellipses where appropriate to show a pause in dialogue.

Example: "Please open your books to um page 23."

Answer: *"Please open your books to . . . um . . . page 23."*

"Mr. O'Dell, why is it like so *important* to learn about civil rights?"

"Hmm well, we need to know how unfair life was how hard it was for people who were denied their civil rights, so we can make sure that it doesn't happen again."

"I see. That uh makes sense."

 To Show Omitted Words

Rewrite the following paragraph, leaving out words in three places. Use ellipses to show where you have left out words.

Some civil rights, such as freedom of speech, freedom of the press, the right to vote, and the right to equality, can be taken for granted. It is important for these rights to be spelled out in our laws so that our nation can avoid discrimination. The United States Constitution, with a number of amendments, makes sure that people's rights are protected. Under the Civil Rights Act of 1964, discrimination based on race, color, or religion against any person in a public place is illegal.

Next Step: Write two sentences about why freedom of speech is important. Trade papers with a classmate and rewrite each other's sentences, omitting words and using ellipses in two places.

Answers

 "Mr. O'Dell, why is it . . . like . . . so *important* to learn about civil rights?"

"Hmm . . . well, we need to know how unfair life was . . . how hard it was for people who were denied their civil rights, so we can make sure that it doesn't happen again."

"I see. That . . . uh . . . makes sense."

(Answers may vary)

Some civil rights, such as freedom of speech . . . and the right to equality, can be taken for granted. It is important for these rights to be spelled out in our laws . . . The United States Constitution, with a number of amendments, makes sure that people's rights are protected. Under the Civil Rights Act of 1964, discrimination based on race, color, or religion . . . is illegal.

616–617 Proofreader's Guide

616

punctuate *edit* capitalize
improve SPELL **617**

Marking Punctuation

PUNCTUATION

Test Prep

For each sentence below, write the letter of the line that contains a mistake. If there is no mistake, choose "D."

1. **A** Art asked, "Why can't
  B we go see the new Harry
  C Potter movie today"?
  D correct as is

2. **A** Franco's new book,
  B "Portable Poetry," was a
  C gift from his grandma.
  D correct as is

3. **A** Mr. Roire isn't very
  B happy about the class's
  C English test scores.
  D correct as is

4. **A** Three fourths of
  B my friends have read the
  C poem "September."
  D correct as is

5. **A** The three boy's dogs
  B don't have tags on
  C their collars.
  D correct as is

6. **A** Mom wrote an article
  B called *Finding Treasures*
  C for *Antiques* magazine.
  D correct as is

7. **A** Seth says two-thirds
  B of his dads' garage is
  C full of car parts.
  D correct as is

8. **A** Did you just say,
  B "I won't be at band
  C practice today?"
  D correct as is

9. **A** The song *Mandy*
  B was actually about the
  C writer's dog.
  D correct as is

10. **A** Deshawn said, "You
  B should'nt be watching
  C television right now."
  D correct as is

11. **A** It's a sad fact that
  B four fifths of teen girls
  C get too little calcium.
  D correct as is

12. **A** Ms. Gray's niece got
  B a part in the play
  C "Hansel and Gretel."
  D correct as is

For each line, write the letter of the correct way (see choices below) to write the underlined part.

13. According to the magazine "Telephone Users Monthly,"

14. a full seven eighths of phone users prefer cordless phones.

15. In an article titled "Cordless Rules," writer Maggie Pie

16. says, "People don't want to be tied to a twisted, tangled

17. phone cord any longer". She continues, "Research shows

18. that most phone user's choices are based on experience."

13. **A** "Telephone Users Monthly",
  B *Telephone Users Monthly,*
  C telephone users monthly
  D correct as is

14. **A** seven-eighths
  B 7 eighths
  C seven 8ths
  D correct as is

15. **A** "Cordless Rules",
  B *Cordless Rules,*
  C Cordless rules
  D correct as is

16. **A** dont want
  B dont' want
  C do'nt want
  D correct as is

17. **A** any longer."
  B any longer.".
  C any longer"
  D correct as is

18. **A** users choices
  B users' choices
  C user's choice's
  D correct as is

Answers

1. C   **7.** B
2. B   **8.** C
3. A   **9.** A
4. A   **10.** B
5. A   **11.** B
6. B   **12.** C

Answers

13. B   **16.** D
14. A   **17.** A
15. D   **18.** B

618

Editing for Mechanics
Capitalization

618.1
Proper Nouns and Adjectives

Capitalize all proper nouns and all proper adjectives. A proper noun is the name of a particular person, place, thing, or idea. A proper adjective is an adjective formed from a proper noun.

Common Noun: country, president, continent
Proper Noun: Canada, Andrew Jackson, Asia
Proper Adjective: Canadian, Jacksonian, Asian

618.2
Names of People

Capitalize the names of people and also the initials or abbreviations that stand for those names.

Samuel L. Jackson   Aung San Suu Kyi
Mary Sanchez-Gomez

618.3
Titles Used with Names

Capitalize titles used with names of persons; also capitalize abbreviations standing for those titles.

President Mohammed Hosni Mubarak   Dr. Linda Trout
Governor Michael Easley   Rev. Jim Zavaski
Senator John McCain

618.4
Words Used as Names

Capitalize words such as *mother, father, aunt,* and *uncle* when these words are used as names.

Uncle Marius **started to sit on the couch.** (*Uncle* is a name; the speaker calls this person "Uncle Marius.")

Then Uncle **stopped in midair.** (*Uncle* is used as a name.)

"So, Mom, **what are you doing here?" I asked.** (*Mom* is used as a name.)

Words such as *aunt, uncle, mom, dad, grandma,* and *grandpa* are usually not capitalized if they come after a possessive pronoun *(my, his, our).*

My aunt **had just called him.** (The word *aunt* describes this person but is not used as a name.)

Then my dad **and** mom **walked into the room.** (The words *dad* and *mom* are not used as names in this sentence.)

Capitalization 1

- Proper Nouns and Adjectives
- Names of People
- Titles Used with Names
- Words Used as Names

 Number your paper from 2 to 11. In one column, capitalize the words in each sentence that should be capitalized. In the other column, change the words that are incorrectly capitalized.

1. Edgar R. burroughs wrote science Fiction Books.
Burroughs   fiction, books

2. Jules verne began writing science fiction in 1851.

3. Science fiction is a mix of Reality and the imagination.

4. H. G. wells became a famous science-fiction writer in 1898 when he published *War of the Worlds.*

5. In 1938, orson welles broadcast *War of the Worlds* on the Radio.

6. Because mr. Welles used a real american town in New jersey as the setting for the broadcast, it caused people to panic.

7. Douglas Adams, Author of *The Hitchhiker's Guide to the Galaxy,* wrote science fiction in a humorous way.

8. *Jurassic Park* by michael crichton was published in 1990 and released as a Movie in 1993.

9. In the science-fiction Movie *The Empire Strikes Back,* the villain Darth vader told commander Luke Skywalker, "I am your Father."

10. As his Dad lay hurt, Luke said, "I won't leave you here, father."

11. *The Matrix* introduced the villain agent smith to the world.

Next Step: Think about a science-fiction book you have read or a science-fiction movie you have seen. List three proper nouns, three proper adjectives, and a title used with a name from the work you have chosen.

Answers

	Column 1	Column 2
2.	Verne	
3.		reality
4.	Wells	
5.	Orson Welles	radio
6.	Mr., American, Jersey	
7.		author
8.	Michael Crichton	movie
9.	Vader, Commander	movie, father
10.	Father	dad
11.	Agent Smith	

620

punctuate *edit* capitalize
SPELL
improve
Editing for Mechanics

621

MECHANICS

Capitalization . . .

620.1
School Subjects

Capitalize the name of a specific educational course, but not the name of a general subject. (Exception—the names of all languages are proper nouns and are always capitalized: *French, English, Hindi, German, Latin.*)

Roberto is studying accounting **at the technical college.** (Because *accounting* is a general subject, it is not capitalized.)

He likes the professor who teaches Accounting Principles. (The specific course name is capitalized.)

620.2
Official Names

Capitalize the names of businesses and the official names of their products. (These are called trade names.) Do not, however, capitalize a general word like "toothpaste" when it follows the trade name.

Old Navy	Best Buy	Microsoft	Kodak
Sony Playstation	Tombstone pizza	Mudd jeans	

620.3
**Races,
Languages,
Nationalities,
Religions**

Capitalize the names of languages, races, nationalities, and religions, as well as the proper adjectives formed from them.

Arab	Spanish	Judaism	Catholicism
African art	Irish linen	Swedish meatballs	

620.4
**Days, Months,
Holidays**

Capitalize the names of days of the week, months of the year, and special holidays.

Thursday	Friday	Saturday
July	August	September
Arbor Day	Independence Day	

Do not capitalize the names of seasons.

winter, spring, summer, fall (autumn)

620.5
**Historical
Events**

Capitalize the names of historical events, documents, and periods of time.

World War II	the Bill of Rights	the Magna Carta
the Middle Ages	the Paleozoic Era	

Capitalization 2

◼ School Subjects
◼ Days, Months, Holidays
◼ Historical Events

 For each numbered sentence below, write the word or words that should be capitalized.

Example: What is armistice day?
Answer: Armistice Day

(1) Last friday Mr. Allis, who teaches biology II, told us that veterans day was celebrated on the fourth monday of october between 1968 and 1978. **(2)** In world history, we learned that veterans day was originally called armistice day. **(3)** The holiday was a remembrance of the day in 1918 when world war I ended. **(4)** That day, in the eleventh hour of the eleventh day of the eleventh month (november), a truce was signed to end the fighting. **(5)** Now we remember veterans of all wars, including world war II, the vietnam war, and the gulf war, on november 11 every year.

◼ Official Names
◼ Races, Languages, Nationalities, Religions

 Write the word or words that should be capitalized in each sentence.

6. Textiles are an important part of Pakistan's economy; proline footbags are made there, as are nizam tents.

7. A pakistani company supplies jeans to american companies such as wal-mart and the gap.

8. Pakistan was established in 1947 by indian muslims.

9. Only 3 percent of pakistanis are christian or hindu.

10. Only 8 percent of the population speaks urdu, the official language, but 48 percent speak punjabi.

Answers

1. Friday, Biology, Veteran's Day, Monday, October

2. World History, Veteran's Day, Armistice Day

3. World War

4. November

5. World War, Vietnam War, Gulf War, November

6. Proline, Nizam

7. Pakistani, American, Wal-Mart, Gap

8. Indian Muslims

9. Pakistanis, Christian, Hindu

10. Urdu, Punjabi

Capitalization . . .

622.1
Geographic Names

Capitalize the following geographic names.

Planets and heavenly bodies . . . . **Venus, Jupiter, Milky Way**

Lowercase the word "earth" except when used as the proper name of our planet, especially when mentioned with other planet names.

What on earth are you doing here?

Sam has traveled across the face of the earth several times.

Jupiter's diameter is 11 times larger than Earth's.

The four inner planets are Mercury, Venus, Earth, and Mars.

Continents . . . . **Europe, Asia, South America, Australia, Africa**
Countries . . . **Morocco, Haiti, Greece, Chile, United Arab Emirates**
States . . . . . **New Mexico, Alabama, West Virginia, Delaware, Iowa**
Provinces . . . . **Alberta, British Columbia, Quebec, Ontario**
Counties . . . . **Sioux County, Kandiyohi County, Wade County**
Cities . . . . **Montreal, Baton Rouge, Albuquerque, Portland**
Bodies of water . . . . **Delaware Bay, Chickamunga Lake, Indian Ocean, Gulf of Mexico, Skunk Creek**
Landforms . . . . **Appalachian Mountains, Bitterroot Range**
Public areas . . . . **Tiananmen Square, Sequoia National Forest, Mount Rushmore, Open Space Park, Vietnam Memorial**
Roads and highways . . . . **New Jersey Turnpike, Interstate 80, Central Avenue, Chisholm Trail, Mutt's Road**
Buildings . . . **Pentagon, Paske High School, Empire StateBuilding,**
Monuments . . . . **Eiffel Tower, Statue of Liberty**

622.2
Particular Sections of the Country

Capitalize words that indicate particular sections of the country. Also capitalize proper adjectives formed from names of specific sections of a country.

Having grown up on the hectic East Coast, I find life in the South to be refreshing.

Here in Georgia, Southern hospitality is a way of life.

Words that simply indicate a direction are not capitalized; nor are adjectives that are formed from words that simply indicate direction.

The town where I live, located east of Memphis, is typical of others found in western Tennessee.

MECHANICS

Capitalization 3

■ Geographic Names
■ Particular Sections of the Country

 Write the word or words that should be capitalized in each sentence.

1. The united states, canada, and mexico have many national parks.
   United States, Canada, Mexico

2. One of the most famous parks is yellowstone national park, located in wyoming, idaho, and montana.

3. Just south of yellowstone, on rockefeller parkway, is grand teton national park.

4. The park's string lake is reserved for nonmotorized boats.

5. There are many national parks in the west, but the midwest has some interesting parks, too.

6. Sleeping bear dunes national lakeshore is located on the eastern shore of lake michigan.

7. The appalachian national scenic trail runs from katahdin, maine, to springer mountain in the northern part of georgia.

8. You might see polar bears at wapusk national park in manitoba, canada.

9. Some islands in a national park located on the saint lawrence river in ontario, canada, can be reached only by boat.

10. El chico was the first national park in mexico.

11. Copper canyon in chihuahua, mexico, is deeper than the grand canyon.

Next Step: Use complete sentences to answer the following questions. Be sure to use proper capitalization.

- In what section of the country is your state found?
- What large city is closest to your home?

Capitalization . . .

624.1
First Words

Capitalize the first word of every sentence and the first word in a direct quotation.

> In many families, pets are treated like people, according to an article in the *Kansas City Star*. (sentence)

> Marty Becker, coauthor of *Chicken Soup for the Pet Lover's Soul*, reports, "Seven out of ten people let their pets sleep on the bed." (direct quotation)

> "I get my 15 minutes of fame," he says, "every time I come home." (Notice that *every* is not capitalized because it does not begin a new sentence.)

> "It's like being treated like a rock star," says Becker. "I have to tell you that feels pretty good." (The pronoun *I* is always capitalized, but in this case it also begins a new sentence.)

Do not capitalize the first word in an indirect quotation.

> Becker says that in the last 10 years, pets have moved out of kennels and basements and into living rooms and bedrooms. (indirect quotation)

624.2
Titles

Capitalize the first word of a title, the last word, and every word in between except articles (*a, an, the*), short prepositions, and coordinating conjunctions. Follow this rule for titles of books, newspapers, magazines, poems, plays, songs, articles, movies, works of art, pictures, stories, and essays. (See **600.3**.)

> *Locked in Time* (book)
> *Boston Globe* (newspaper)
> *Dog Fancy* (magazine)
> "Roses Are Red" (poem)
> *The Phantom of the Opera* (play)
> *Daddy Day Care* (movie)
> "Intuition" (song)
> *Mona Lisa* (work of art)

Capitalization 4

- First Words
- Titles

Number your paper from 1 to 3. As you read the following paragraphs, write the words that should be capitalized in each.

Example: The Natural History book of dinosaurs says the Tyrannosaurus rex died out 65 million years ago.

Answer: Book   Dinosaurs

1. Because dinosaurs lived long before people, no one really knows how they behaved. for example, scientists have long thought that *Tyrannosaurus rex* was a fierce, meat-eating predator. In the movie *jurassic park*, the *T. rex* chases other dinosaurs and people.

2. Recently, however, Dr. Jack Horner determined that *T. rex* was actually a scavenger. In an article in *national geographic* magazine, Dr. Horner compared the teeth of *T. rex* with those of other hunters. He also studied the dinosaur's leg bones and compared them with those of modern predators. he thinks that *T. rex* could not move fast enough to be a predator. in addition, he points to its tiny arms, which could not hold a struggling animal.

3. Another expert, Dr. Angela Milner, says that more information is needed to be sure that *T. rex* was only a scavenger. here is what we do know: a *T. rex* could grow to be over 40 feet long, stand 15 feet tall, and weigh about 6 tons. would *the mysterious Tyrannosaurus rex* make a good title for a book on this subject?

Next Step: Write a short paragraph about a book, movie, or poem you like. Exchange papers with a classmate. Are first words and titles capitalized correctly?

1. For, *Jurassic Park*
2. *National Geographic*, He, In
3. Here, A, Would, *The Mysterious*, Rex

626

Capitalization . . .

626.1
Abbreviations

Capitalize abbreviations of titles and organizations.

Dr. (Doctor)   **M.D.** (Doctor of Medicine)

Mr. (Mister)   **UPS** (United Parcel Service)

SADD (Students Against Destructive Decisions)

626.2
Organizations

Capitalize the name of an organization, an association, or a team.

New York State Historical Society	the Red Cross
General Motors Corporation	the Miami Dolphins
Republicans	the Democratic Party

626.3
Letters

Capitalize the letters used to indicate form or shape.

T-shirt   **U-turn**   **A-frame**

Capitalize	Do Not Capitalize
American	un-American
January, February	winter, spring
Missouri and Ohio Rivers	the rivers Missouri and Ohio
The South is humid in summer.	Turn south at the stop sign.
Duluth Middle School	a Duluth middle school
Governor Bob Taft	Bob Taft, our governor
President Luiz Lula Da Silva	Luiz Lula Da Silva, Brazil's president
Nissan Altima	a Nissan automobile
The planet Earth is egg shaped.	The earth on Grandpa's farm is rich.
I'm taking World Cultures.	I'm taking social studies.

Capitalization 5

■ Abbreviations
■ Organizations
■ Letters

 Write the words or abbreviations that should be capitalized in each sentence below.

1. Dad took me to see dr. Zani Patell.
   Dr.

2. The two major political parties in this country are the democrats and the republicans.

3. One of the most successful professional football teams in the country is the Dallas cowboys.

4. When a tornado hits a community, the red Cross sends help.

5. Our new social studies teacher is ms. Kenal.

6. An organization of mothers who try to prevent people from driving after drinking alcohol is called madd.

7. The b-pillar on a car is located right behind the front door.

8. America's space program is run by nasa.

9. The city building code says steel i-beams must be used in new skyscrapers.

10. Some of the biggest companies in the world include GE, ibm, AT&T, and gm.

11. The washing machine repairman replaced an o-ring.

Next Step: Write a sentence about a teacher you have now. Use an abbreviated title (such as *Ms., Dr.,* and so on) for this person in your sentence. Check your capitalization.

MECHANICS

Answers

2. Democrats, Republicans
3. Cowboys
4. Red
5. Ms.
6. MADD
7. B-pillar
8. NASA
9. I-beams
10. IBM, GM
11. O-ring

MECHANICS

Test Prep

For each underlined part of the paragraphs below, choose the letter (on the next page) that shows the correct capitalization. If the underlined part is correct, choose "D."

Paragraph I

My dad is a mechanic at the local <u>toyota dealer. of course</u>, he
1
says <u>the japanese cars</u> are superior. <u>but mrs. Weiler</u>, who has had
2 3
her car repaired there many times, might disagree.

Paragraph II

Today in one of my classes (<u>Cultures in everyday life</u>), we had a
4
surprise visitor: <u>governor Consuela Jones. She</u> told us that when her
5
family first lived in <u>the United States</u>, they spoke <u>only spanish (no</u>
6 7
<u>English)</u>.

Paragraph III

My new friend <u>Aziza is egyptian</u>. She and her family practice
8
<u>islam, so</u> they needed to find a mosque where they could worship. They
9
found that, compared to <u>the Eastern states</u>, there aren't many <u>mosques</u>
10 11
<u>in the Southwest</u>.

Paragraph IV

Grandma was a member of the <u>Women's Army Corps, or wac</u>,
12
during <u>world war II. Lately</u> she's been reading <u>*Battle Of The WAC*</u>,
13 14
the story of one woman's experience in the army.

1. **A** Toyota Dealer. of course
   B Toyota dealer. Of course
   C Toyota Dealer. Of course
   D correct as is

2. **A** The Japanese cars
   B The Japanese Cars
   C the Japanese cars
   D correct as is

3. **A** but Mrs. Weiler
   B But Mrs. Weiler
   C But mrs. Weiler
   D correct as is

4. **A** Cultures In everyday Life
   B Cultures in everyday Life
   C Cultures in Everyday Life
   D correct as is

5. **A** Governor Consuela Jones. She
   B governor Consuela Jones. she
   C governor consuela Jones. She
   D correct as is

6. **A** the united States
   B The united States
   C The United States
   D correct as is

7. **A** only spanish (no english)
   B only Spanish (no english)
   C only Spanish (no English)
   D correct as is

8. **A** Aziza Is Egyptian
   B aziza is Egyptian
   C Aziza is Egyptian
   D correct as is

9. **A** islam, So
   B Islam, so
   C Islam, So
   D correct as is

10. **A** the eastern states
    B The Eastern States
    C the Eastern States
    D correct as is

11. **A** mosques in the southwest
    B Mosques in the southwest
    C mosques in The Southwest
    D correct as is

12. **A** Women's Army Corps, or WAC
    B women's army corps, or WAC
    C women's Army corps, or wac
    D correct as is

13. **A** world war II. lately
    B World war II. Lately
    C World War II. Lately
    D correct as is

14. **A** *Battle of The WAC*
    B *Battle of the WAC*
    C *Battle of the wac*
    D correct as is

Answers

1. B
2. C
3. B
4. C
5. A
6. D
7. C

8. C
9. B
10. A
11. D
12. A
13. C
14. B

630

Plurals

630.1
Most Nouns

The **plurals** of most nouns are formed by adding *s* to the singular.

    cheerleader — **cheerleaders**   wheel — **wheels**
    bubble — **bubbles**

630.2
Nouns Ending in *ch, sh, s, x,* and *z*

The plural form of nouns ending in *ch, sh, s, x,* and *z* is made by adding *es* to the singular.

    lunch — **lunches**   dish — **dishes**   mess — **messes**
    buzz — **buzzes**   fox — **foxes**

630.3
Nouns Ending in *o*

The plurals of nouns ending in *o* with a vowel just before the *o* are formed by adding *s*.

    radio — **radios**   studio — **studios**   rodeo — **rodeos**

The plurals of most nouns ending in *o* with a consonant just before the *o* are formed by adding *es*.

    echo — **echoes**   hero — **heroes**   tomato — **tomatoes**

Exceptions: Musical terms and words of Spanish origin always form plurals by adding *s*.

    alto — **altos**   banjo — **banjos**   taco — **tacos**
    solo — **solos**   piano — **pianos**   burro — **burros**

630.4
Nouns Ending in *ful*

The plurals of nouns that end with *ful* are formed by adding an *s* at the end of the word.

    three **platefuls**   six **tankfuls**   four **cupfuls**   five **pailfuls**

630.5
Nouns Ending in *f* or *fe*

The plurals of nouns that end in *f* or *fe* are formed in one of two ways: If the final *f* sound is still heard in the plural form of the word, simply add *s*; if the final sound is a *v* sound, change the *f* to *ve* and add *s*.

    roof — **roofs**   chief — **chiefs**   belief — **beliefs**
    (plural ends with *f* sound)
    wife — **wives**   loaf — **loaves**   leaf — **leaves**
    (plural ends with *v* sound)

Plurals 1

- Nouns Ending in *ch, sh, s, x,* and *z*
- Nouns Ending in *o*
- Nouns Ending in *ful*
- Nouns Ending in *f* or *fe*

 For each of the following sentences, write the plural form of the word or words in parentheses.

1. Tawon and Richard grabbed (*handful*) of popcorn.
handfuls

2. Every fall, as the (*leaf*) change colors, football season begins.

3. People can see the games on their (*television*) or at (*stadium*), or they can listen to the games on their (*radio*).

4. At high school and college football games, marching (*band*) play during halftime.

5. At one game, a trumpet player in the band played two (*solo*).

6. That made him so thirsty that he drank two (*glassful*) of water.

7. A few football (*stadium*), called domes, have (*roof*).

8. Some professional football (*player*) are like (*hero*) to their fans.

9. Even when these guys end up with (*helmetful*) of mud and grass, (*echo*) of adoration from their fans can be heard on the field.

10. For many of the (*player*), their professional (*life*) are rather short—many end up playing for only a few (*year*).

11. I wonder what some of these men think when they look back on their short (*career*).

Next Step: Write two sentences about an outdoor activity. Use plurals in your sentences. Then double-check to make sure all the plural words are correct.

Answers

2. leaves
3. televisions, stadiums, radios
4. bands
5. solos
6. glassfuls
7. stadiums, roofs
8. players, heroes
9. helmetfuls, echoes
10. players, lives, years
11. careers

Plurals . . .

632.1
Nouns Ending in *y*

The plurals of common nouns that end in *y* with a consonant letter just before the *y* are formed by changing the *y* to *i* and adding *es*.

> fly — **flies**　　baby — **babies**　　　cavity — **cavities**

The plurals of common nouns that end in *y* with a vowel before the *y* are formed by adding only *s*.

> key — **keys**　　holiday — **holidays**　　attorney — **attorneys**

The plurals of proper nouns ending in *y* are formed by adding *s*.

> **There are three Circuit Citys in our metro area.**

632.2
Compound Nouns

The plurals of some compound nouns are formed by adding *s* or *es* to the main word in the compound.

> **brothers-in-law**　　**maids of honor**　　**secretaries of state**

632.3
Plurals That Do Not Change

The plurals of some words are the same in singular and plural form.

> **deer**　　**sheep**　　**trout**　　**aircraft**

632.4
Irregular Spelling

Some words (including many foreign words) form a plural by taking on an irregular spelling; others are now acceptable with the commonly used *s* or *es* ending.

> child — **children**　　woman — **women**　　man — **men**
>
> goose — **geese**　　mouse — **mice**　　ox — **oxen**
>
> tooth — **teeth**　　octopus — **octopuses** or **octopi**
>
> index — **indexes** or **indices**

632.5
Adding an *'s*

The plurals of letters, figures, symbols, and words discussed as words are formed by adding an apostrophe and an *s*.

> **Dr. Walters has two Ph.D.'s.**
>
> **My dad's license plate has three 2's between two B's.**
>
> **You've got too many *but*'s and *so*'s in that sentence.**

For information on forming plural possessives, see 606.1.

MECHANICS

Plurals 2

- Nouns Ending in *y*
- Compound Nouns
- Plurals That Do Not Change
- Irregular Spelling
- Adding an *'s*

For each of the following sentences, write the plural form of the word or words in parentheses. You may need to use a dictionary.

1. There are about a dozen (*fish*) in Ashlee's tank.
   fish

2. Have you heard the story of Santa and his eight tiny (*reindeer*)?

3. I got one A, three (*B*), and two (*C*) on my report card.

4. The (*monkey*) escaped from the lab and ran down the (*hallway*).

5. I have many (*ability*), but writing (*essay*) is one skill that I definitely need to work on.

6. Nishan broke one of his (*foot*) and chipped two (*tooth*).

7. A few (*Kennedy*) have held political office.

8. We're not supposed to use any (*&*) or (*#*) in our final papers.

9. Fresh foods do not have (*bar code*) printed on them.

10. Aunt Patti's job is to take customer satisfaction (*survey*) for different (*company*).

11. Many (*African American*) become (*attorney-at-law*).

12. It's not uncommon to see (*moose*) in northern Maine.

Next Step: Write sentences using the plurals of the following words: *chin-up, toy, child,* and *city*.

Answers

2. reindeer
3. *B*'s, *C*'s
4. monkeys, hallways
5. abilities, essays
6. feet, teeth
7. Kennedys
8. &'s, #'s
9. bar codes
10. surveys, companies
11. African Americans, attorneys-at-law
12. moose

Abbreviations

634.1
Abbreviations

An **abbreviation** is the shortened form of a word or phrase. The following abbreviations are always acceptable in any kind of writing:

Mr.	Mrs.	Ms.	Dr.	a.m., p.m. (A.M., P.M.)	

B.C.E. (before the Common Era)   C.E. (Common Era)

B.A.   M.A.   Ph.D.   M.D.   Sr.   Jr.

Caution: Do not abbreviate the names of states, countries, months, days, or units of measure in formal writing. Also, do not use signs or symbols (%, &) in place of words.

Common Abbreviations

AC	alternating current	**kg**	kilogram	**pd.**	paid
a.m.	ante meridiem	**km**	kilometer	**pg.**	(or p.) page
ASAP	as soon as possible	**kW**	kilowatt	**p.m.**	post meridiem
COD	cash on delivery	**l**	liter	**ppd.**	postpaid, prepaid
DA	district attorney	**lb.**	pound	**qt.**	quart
DC	direct current	**m**	meter	**R.S.V.P.**	please reply
etc.	and so forth	**M.D.**	doctor of medicine	**tbs., tbsp.**	tablespoon
F	Fahrenheit	**mfg.**	manufacturing	**tsp.**	teaspoon
FM	frequency modulation	**mpg**	miles per gallon	**vol.**	volume
GNP	gross national product	**mph**	miles per hour	**vs.**	versus
i.e.	that is (Latin *id est*)	**oz.**	ounce	**yd.**	yard

Address Abbreviations

	Standard	Postal		Standard	Postal		Standard	Postal
Avenue	Ave.	AVE	Lake	L.	LK	Rural	R.	R
Boulevard	Blvd.	BLVD	Lane	Ln.	LN	South	S.	S
Court	Ct.	CT	North	N.	N	Square	Sq.	SQ
Drive	Dr.	DR	Park	Pk.	PK	Station	Sta.	STA
East	E.	E	Parkway	Pky.	PKY	Street	St.	ST
Expressway	Expy.	EXPY	Place	Pl.	PL	Terrace	Ter.	TER
Heights	Hts.	HTS	Plaza	Plaza	PLZ	Turnpike	Tpke.	TPKE
Highway	Hwy.	HWY	Road	Rd.	RD	West	W.	W

MECHANICS

Abbreviations 1

For each of the following sentences, write the correct abbreviation for the underlined word or words.

1. Last week I talked to <u>Doctor</u> Wesley Brown.
   Dr.

2. He earned his <u>doctor of medicine</u> degree from Franklin University.

3. The electric appliances in most homes and apartments use <u>alternating current</u> electricity.

4. Flashlights and other battery-operated items use <u>direct current</u> electricity.

5. This fan will use about one <u>kilowatt</u> of electricity every day.

6. Next week the city will elect a new <u>district attorney</u>.

7. <u>Mister</u> Hawthorn expects his science students to do their best.

8. He asked me to bring in my extra-credit project <u>as soon as possible</u>.

9. Our assignment was to convert 15 degrees <u>Fahrenheit</u> to its metric equivalent.

10. The <u>gross national product</u> of the United States in 2000 was $10.5 trillion.

11. My mom's car is supposed to get 30 <u>miles per gallon</u>.

12. The top speed for an electric car is 80 <u>miles per hour</u>.

13. Some fast-food places offer 32-<u>ounce</u> soft drinks.

14. The recipe includes a cup of flour, a <u>tablespoon</u> of cinnamon, and a <u>teaspoon</u> of salt.

Next Step: Write the words for these postal abbreviations: AVE, CT, EXPY, and RD. Now write the postal abbreviations for your own state or province and one near it.

Answers

2. M.D.
3. AC
4. DC
5. kW
6. DA
7. Mr.
8. ASAP
9. F
10. GNP
11. mpg
12. mph
13. oz.
14. tbs., tsp.

636

MECHANICS

Abbreviations . . .

636.1
Acronyms

An **acronym** is an abbreviation that can be pronounced as a word. It does not require periods.

WHO — World Health Organization   **ROM** — read-only memory

FAQ — frequently asked question

636.2
Initialisms

An **initialism** is similar to an acronym except that it cannot be pronounced as a word; the initials are pronounced individually.

PBS — Public Broadcasting Service

BLM — Bureau of Land Management

WNBA — Women's National Basketball Association

Common Acronyms and Initialisms

AIDS	acquired immune deficiency syndrome	**ORV**	off-road vehicle
CETA	Comprehensive Employment and Training Act	**OSHA**	Occupational Safety and Health Administration
CIA	Central Intelligence Agency	**PAC**	political action committee
FAA	Federal Aviation Administration	**PIN**	personal identification number
FBI	Federal Bureau of Investigation	**PSA**	public service announcement
FCC	Federal Communications Commission	**ROTC**	Reserve Officers' Training Corps
FDA	Food and Drug Administration	**SADD**	Students Against Destructive Decisions
FDIC	Federal Deposit Insurance Corporation	**SSA**	Social Security Administration
FHA	Federal Housing Administration	**SUV**	sport-utility vehicle
FTC	Federal Trade Commission	**SWAT**	special weapons and tactics
HTML	Hypertext Markup Language	**TDD**	telecommunications device for the deaf
IRS	Internal Revenue Service	**TMJ**	temporomandibular joint
MADD	Mothers Against Drunk Driving	**TVA**	Tennessee Valley Authority
NAFTA	North American Free Trade Agreement	**VA**	Veterans Administration
NASA	National Aeronautics and Space Administration	**VISTA**	Volunteers in Service to America
		WAC	Women's Army Corps
NATO	North Atlantic Treaty Organization	**WAVES**	Women Accepted for Volunteer Emergency Service
OEO	Office of Economic Opportunity		
OEP	Office of Emergency Preparedness		

Abbreviations 2

■ Acronyms
■ Initialisms

Number your paper from 1 to 15. For each name or phrase on the left, write the letter of the abbreviation on the right that matches it.

1. all-terrain vehicle
2. telecommunications device for the deaf
3. magnetic resonance imaging
4. special weapons and tactics
5. Federal Bureau of Investigation
6. computer-aided design
7. World Health Organization
8. parental guidance
9. North Atlantic Treaty Organization
10. light amplification by stimulated emission of radiation
11. Organization of Petroleum Exporting Countries
12. personal identification number
13. master of business administration
14. attention deficit disorder
15. certified public accountant

A. ADD
B. ATV
C. CAD
D. CPA
E. FBI
F. LASER
G. MBA
H. MRI
I. NATO
J. OPEC
K. PG
L. PIN
M. SWAT
N. TDD
O. WHO

Next Step: Make up an organization name that can be abbreviated as an acronym. Share your new abbreviation—and what it stands for—with the class.

Answers

1. B
2. N
3. H
4. M
5. E
6. C
7. O
8. K
9. I
10. F
11. J
12. L
13. G
14. A
15. D

MECHANICS

Numbers

638.1
Numbers Under 10

Numbers from one to nine are usually written as words; all numbers 10 and over are usually written as numerals.

two   seven   nine   10   25   106

638.2
Numerals Only

Use numerals to express any of the following forms:

money **$2.39**
decimals **26.2**
percentages . . . . **8 percent**
chapters . . . . **chapter 7**
pages . . . . **pages 287–289**
time (with "a.m." or "p.m.") . . . . **4:30 p.m.**
telephone numbers **1-800-555-1212**
dates . . . . **44 B.C.E.; July 6, 1942**
identification numbers . . . . **Highway 36**
addresses . . . . **2125 Cairn Road**
ZIP codes **60004**
statistics . . . . **a vote of 23 to 4**

When abbreviations and symbols are used (for instance, in science or math), always use numerals with them.

12° C   7%   33 kg   9 cm   55 mph

638.3
Very Large Numbers

You may use a combination of numerals and words for very large numbers.

Of the 17 million **residents of the three Midwestern states, only** 1.3 million **are blondes.**

You may spell out a large number that can be written as two words. If more than two words are needed, use the numeral.

More than nine thousand **people attended the concert.**

About 3,500 **people missed the opening act.**

Numbers 1

▨ Numbers Under 10
▨ Numerals Only
▨ Very Large Numbers

 Each sentence below has a choice of how a number should be written. Write the answers that make the sentences correct.

1. There are (*nine, 9*) planets in our solar system.
nine

2. The sun is one of more than (*100 billion, 100,000,000,000*) stars in our galaxy.

3. The sun's diameter is (*one million three hundred ninety thousand, 1.39 million*) kilometers.

4. The sun contains more than (*99 percent, ninety-nine percent*) of the total mass of the solar system.

5. Is Earth about (*4 billion, 4,000,000,000*) years old?

6. While Mars has (*two, 2*) moons, Earth has only (*one, 1*).

7. On July (*twentieth, 20*), 1969, the first humans landed on the moon.

8. Just six hours after *Apollo 11* landed at (*4:17, four-seventeen*) p.m. eastern daylight time, the astronauts stepped onto the moon's surface.

9. That summer, you could buy a model of *Apollo 11* for only $(*2.50, two-fifty*).

10. The last astronauts to land on the moon were those in *Apollo 17* in December (*nineteen seventy-two, 1972*).

Next Step: Use complete sentences to answer the following questions. Be sure to use numbers correctly.

● On what day and in what year were you born?
● What time is it right now?

Answers

2. 100 billion
3. 1.39 million
4. 99 percent
5. 4 billion
6. two, one
7. 20
8. 4:17
9. 2.50
10. 1972

640

Numbers . . .

640.1
Comparing Numbers

If you are comparing two or more numbers in a sentence, write all of them the same way: as numerals or as words.

Students from 9 to 14 years old are invited.

Students from nine to fourteen years old are invited.

640.2
Numbers in Compound Modifiers

A compound modifier may include a numeral.

The floorboards come in 10-foot lengths.

When a number comes before a compound modifier that includes a numeral, use words instead of numerals.

We need eleven 10-foot lengths to finish the floor.

Ms. Brown must grade twenty 12-page reports.

640.3
Sentence Beginnings

Use words, not numerals, to begin a sentence.

Nine students had turned in their homework. Fourteen students said they were unable to finish the assignment.

640.4
Time and Money

When time or money is expressed with an abbreviation, use numerals. When either is expressed with words, spell out the number.

6:00 a.m. or six o'clock

$25 or twenty-five dollars

SCHOOL DAZE

Jerry, haven't you finished your paper yet?

No, it's not due until **three o'clock**, and Mrs. Wright told me to add a few new twists and wrinkles.

MECHANICS

Numbers 2

■ Comparing Numbers

Rewrite the underlined parts of the following sentences so that they are correct.

1. Depending on which staircase I use, I have to climb <u>eight or 11</u> stairs on my way to our apartment.
   8 or 11 (or) eight or eleven

2. The renters of the top-floor apartment sometimes have <u>five to 15</u> guests at once.

3. The children in that apartment are from <u>nine to 18</u> years old.

4. Apartments may have from <u>two to 10</u> windows.

5. They usually have <u>nine to 20</u> electrical outlets.

6. Our building has <u>seven</u> furnished <u>and 11</u> unfurnished units.

■ Sentence Beginnings
■ Time and Money

Rewrite the following sentences so that the numbers are correct.

7. 9 apartments will be rented for 825 dollars per month.
   Nine apartments will be rented for $825 per month.

8. The manager has agreed to show the apartment at eight p.m. tonight.

9. 60 people have already called about the new apartment complex.

10. Some people are interested in the smaller units renting for $6 hundred a month.

11. Three apartments were rented by 9 o'clock this morning.

12. 20 units remain available for rent.

Answers

2. 5 to 15 or five to fifteen
3. 9 to 18 or nine to eighteen
4. 2 to 10 or two to ten
5. 9 to 20 or nine to twenty
6. 7, and 11 or seven, and eleven

8. The manager has agreed to show the apartment at 8:00 p.m. (or) eight o'clock tonight.

9. Sixty people have already called about the new apartment complex.

10. Some people are interested in the smaller units renting for $600 (or) six hundred dollars a month.

11. Three apartments were rented by 9:00 a.m. (or) nine o'clock this morning.

12. Twenty units remain available for rent.

Improving Spelling **642-643**

642

punctuate *edit* capitalize
improve **SPELL**
Improving Spelling

643

Improving Spelling

642.1
i before e

Write *i* before *e* except after *c*, or when sounded like *a* as in *neighbor* and *weigh*.

Some Exceptions to the Rule: *counterfeit, either, financier, foreign, height, heir, leisure, neither, science, seize, sheik, species, their, weird.*

642.2
Silent e

If a word ends with a silent *e*, drop the *e* before adding a suffix that begins with a vowel.

state stating statement	use using useful
like liking likeness	nine ninety nineteen

NOTE You do not drop the *e* when the suffix begins with a consonant. Exceptions include *truly, argument,* and *ninth.*

642.3
Words Ending in y

When *y* is the last letter in a word and the *y* comes just after a consonant, change the *y* to *i* before adding any suffix except those beginning with *i*.

fry fries frying	happy happiness
hurry hurried hurrying	beauty beautiful
lady ladies	

When forming the plural of a word that ends with a *y* that comes just after a vowel, add *s*.

toy toys	play plays	monkey monkeys

642.4
Consonant Endings

When a one-syllable word ends in a consonant (*bat*) preceded by one vowel (*bat*), double the final consonant before adding a suffix that begins with a vowel (*batting*).

sum summary   god goddess

When a multisyllable word ends in a consonant preceded by one vowel (*control*), the accent is on the last syllable (*contról*), and the suffix begins with a vowel (*ing*)—the same rule holds true: double the final consonant (*controlling*).

prefer preferred   begin beginning

Spelling 1

■ *i before e*
■ Silent *e*

 If the underlined word is spelled correctly, write "correct." If it is spelled incorrectly, spell the word the right way.

1. Jorge's family enjoys <u>dineing</u> out now and then.
   dining
2. Jorge can't hide his <u>excitment</u> at seeing flan on the menu.
3. He likes <u>useing</u> lots of chocolate sauce on his dessert.
4. Jorge says he could eat <u>nineteen</u> scoops of chocolate.
5. We don't <u>beleive</u> that's possible.
6. But Jorge's best <u>friend</u> saw him eat that much once.
7. We're surprised he doesn't gain a lot of <u>wieght</u>!

■ Words Ending in *y*
■ Consonant Endings

 If the underlined word is spelled correctly, write "correct." If it is spelled incorrectly, spell the word the right way.

8. Buses are an important means of transportation in many <u>cityes</u>.
   cities
9. Although buses must stop often, they always seem to be <u>hurrying</u> along city streets.
10. During the evening, some routes are <u>omited</u> from the schedule.
11. On most <u>holidaies</u>, buses run on a reduced schedule.
12. One passenger was <u>carriing</u> four bags of <u>groceries</u> on a bus.
13. When he asked if he was on the right bus, the driver <u>refered</u> him to another bus route.

Answers

2. excitement
3. using
4. correct
5. believe
6. correct
7. weight

9. correct
10. omitted
11. holidays
12. carrying, correct
13. referred

Spelling 2

- ▥ *i* before *e*
- ▥ Silent *e*

Find the misspelled word or words in each sentence and write the words the right way.

1. The largeest state in the union is Alaska.

   largest

2. Hawaii recieves the most rainfall of all the states, so umbrellas are quite usful for its residents.

3. Niether Connecticut nor Delaware is the smallest state.

4. In Wyoming, Yellowstone Park is part of an anceint volcano.

5. Ohio and New York are loseing many older people who prefer liveing in warmer states like Florida or Arizona.

- ▥ Words Ending in *y*
- ▥ Consonant Endings

If the underlined word is spelled correctly, write "correct." If it is spelled incorrectly, spell the word the right way.

6. The mountains and valleies in the Smoky Mountains of Tennessee attract tourists.

   valleys

7. A volcanic explosion, which occured a long time ago, formed Crater Lake in Oregon.

8. Squirrels burying nuts are a common sight in the Midwestern states of Iowa and Missouri.

9. In North Dakota, you can see jackrabbits hoping across the fields.

10. The new governor of California is planing next year's budget.

11. Do people in Mississippi eat lots of fryed chicken?

Yellow Pages Guide to Improved Spelling

Be patient. Becoming a good speller takes time.

Check your spelling by using a dictionary or list of commonly misspelled words (like the list that follows). And, remember, don't rely too much on computer spell-checkers.

Learn the correct pronunciation of each word you are trying to spell. Knowing the correct pronunciation of a word will help you remember how it's spelled.

Look up the meaning of each word as you are checking the dictionary for pronunciation. (Knowing how to spell a word is of little use if you don't know what it means.)

Practice spelling the word before you close the dictionary. Look away from the page and try to see the word in your mind's eye. Write the word on a piece of paper. Check the spelling in the dictionary and repeat the process until you are able to spell the word correctly.

Keep a list of the words that you misspell.

Write often. As noted educator Frank Smith said, "There is little point in learning to spell if you have little intention of writing."

A			
	account	after	almost
	accurate	afternoon	already
	accustom (ed)	afterward	although
abbreviate	ache	again	altogether
aboard	achieve (ment)	against	aluminum
about	acre	agreeable	always
above	across	agree (ment)	amateur
absence	actual	ah	ambulance
absent	adapt	aid	amendment
absolute (ly)	addition (al)	airy	among
abundance	address	aisle	amount
accelerate	adequate	alarm	analyze
accident	adjust (ment)	alcohol	ancient
accidental (ly)	admire	alike	angel
accompany	adventure	alive	anger
accomplice	advertise (ment)	alley	angle
accomplish	advertising	allowance	angry
according	afraid	all right	animal

Answers

2. receives, useful
3. Neither
4. ancient
5. losing, living

7. occurred
8. correct
9. hopping
10. planning
11. fried

SPELLING

anniversary
announce
annoyance
annual
anonymous
another
answer
Antarctic
anticipate
anxiety
anxious
anybody
anyhow
anyone
anything
anyway
anywhere
apartment
apiece
apologize
apparent (ly)
appeal
appearance
appetite
appliance
application
appointment
appreciate
approach
appropriate
approval
approximate
architect
Arctic
aren't
argument
arithmetic
around
arouse
arrange (ment)
arrival
article
artificial

asleep
assassin
assign (ment)
assistance
associate
association
assume
athlete
athletic
attach
attack (ed)
attempt
attendance
attention
attitude
attorney
attractive
audience
August
author
authority
automobile
autumn
available
avenue
average
awful (ly)
awkward

B

baggage
baking
balance
balloon
ballot
banana
bandage
bankrupt
barber
bargain
barrel

basement
basis
basket
battery
beautiful
beauty
because
become
becoming
before
began
beggar
beginning
behave
behavior
being
belief
believe
belong
beneath
benefit (ed)
between
bicycle
biscuit
blackboard
blanket
blizzard
bother
bottle
bottom
bough
bought
bounce
boundary
breakfast
breast
breath (n.)
breathe (v.)
breeze
bridge
brief
bright
brilliant

brother
brought
bruise
bubble
bucket
buckle
budget
building
bulletin
buoyant
bureau
burglar
bury
business
busy
button

C

cabbage
cafeteria
calendar
campaign
canal
cancel (ed)
candidate
candle
canister
cannon
cannot
canoe
can't
canyon
capacity
captain
carburetor
cardboard
career
careful
careless
carpenter
carriage

carrot
cashier
casserole
casualty
catalog
catastrophe
catcher
caterpillar
catsup
ceiling
celebration
cemetery
census
century
certain (ly)
certificate
challenge
champion
changeable
character (istic)
chief
children
chimney
chocolate
choice
chorus
circumstance
citizen
civilization
classmates
classroom
climate
climb
closet
clothing
coach
cocoa
cocoon
coffee
collar
college
colonel
color

colossal
column
comedy
coming
commercial
commission
commit
commitment
committed
committee
communicate
community
company
comparison
competition
competitive (ly)
complain
complete (ly)
complexion
compromise
conceive
concerning
concert
concession
concrete
condemn
condition
conductor
conference
confidence
congratulate
connect
conscience
conscious
conservative
constitution
continue
continuous
control
controversy
convenience
convince
coolly

cooperate
corporation
correspond
cough
couldn't
counter
counterfeit
country
county
courage
courageous
court
courteous
courtesy
cousin
coverage
cozy
cracker
cranky
crawl
creditor
cried
criticize
cruel
crumb
crumble
cupboard
curiosity
curious
current
custom
customer
cylinder

D

daily
dairy
damage
danger (ous)
daughter
dealt

deceive
decided
decision
declaration
decorate
defense
definite (ly)
definition
delicious
dependent
depot
describe
description
desert
deserve
design
desirable
despair
dessert
deteriorate
determine
develop (ment)
device (n.)
devise (v.)
diamond
diaphragm
diary
dictionary
difference
different
difficulty
dining
diploma
director
disagreeable
disappear
disappoint
disapprove
disastrous
discipline
discover
discuss
discussion

SPELLING

disease
dissatisfied
distinguish
distribute
divide
divine
divisible
division
doctor
doesn't
dollar
dormitory
doubt
dough
dual
duplicate

E

eager (ly)
economy
edge
edition
efficiency
eight
eighth
either
elaborate
electricity
elephant
eligible
ellipse
embarrass
emergency
emphasize
employee
employment
enclose
encourage
engineer
enormous
enough

entertain
enthusiastic
entirely
entrance
envelop (v.)
envelope (n.)
environment
equipment
equipped
equivalent
escape
especially
essential
establish
every
evidence
exaggerate
exceed
excellent
except
exceptional (ly)
excite
exercise
exhaust (ed)
exhibition
existence
expect
expensive
experience
explain
explanation
expression
extension
extinct
extraordinary
extreme (ly)

F

facilities
familiar
family

famous
fascinate
fashion
fatigue (d)
faucet
favorite
feature
February
federal
fertile
field
fierce
fiery
fifty
finally
financial (ly)
foliage
forcible
foreign
forfeit
formal (ly)
former (ly)
forth
fortunate
forty
forward
fountain
fourth
fragile
freight
friend (ly)
frighten
fulfill
fundamental
further
furthermore

G

gadget
gauge
generally

generous
genius
gentle
genuine
geography
ghetto
ghost
gnaw
government
governor
graduation
grammar
grateful
grease
grief
grocery
grudge
gruesome
guarantee
guard
guardian
guess
guidance
guide
guilty
gymnasium

H

hammer
handkerchief
handle (d)
handsome
haphazard
happen
happiness
harass
hastily
having
hazardous
headache
height

hemorrhage
hesitate
history
hoarse
holiday
honor
hoping
hopping
horrible
hospital
humorous
hurriedly
hydraulic
hygiene
hymn

I

icicle
identical
illegible
illiterate
illustrate
imaginary
imaginative
imagine
imitation
immediate (ly)
immense
immigrant
immortal
impatient
importance
impossible
improvement
inconvenience
incredible
indefinitely
independence
independent
individual
industrial

inferior
infinite
inflammable
influential
initial
initiation
innocence
innocent
installation
instance
instead
insurance
intelligence
intention
interested
interesting
interfere
interpret
interrupt
interview
investigate
invitation
irrigate
island
issue

J

jealous (y)
jewelry
journal
journey
judgment
juicy

K

kitchen
knew
knife
knives

knock
knowledge
knuckles

L

label
laboratory
ladies
language
laugh
laundry
lawyer
league
lecture
legal
legible
legislature
leisure
length
liable
library
license
lieutenant
lightning
likable
likely
liquid
listen
literature
living
loaves
loneliness
loose
lose
loser
losing
lovable
lovely

M

machinery
magazine
magnificent
maintain
majority
making
manual
manufacture
marriage
material
mathematics
maximum
mayor
meant
measure
medicine
medium
message
mileage
miniature
minimum
minute
mirror
miscellaneous
mischievous
miserable
missile
misspell
moisture
molecule
monotonous
monument
mortgage
mountain
muscle
musician
mysterious

SPELLING

N

naive
natural (ly)
necessary
negotiate
neighbor (hood)
neither
nickel
niece
nineteen
nineteenth
ninety
ninth
noisy
noticeable
nuclear
nuisance

O

obedience
obey
obstacle
occasion
occasional (ly)
occur
occurred
offense
official
often
omission
omitted
operate
opinion
opponent
opportunity
opposite
ordinarily
original
outrageous

P

package
paid
pamphlet
paradise
paragraph
parallel
paralyze
parentheses
partial
participant
participate
particular (ly)
pasture
patience
peculiar
people
perhaps
permanent
perpendicular
persistent
personal (ly)
personnel
perspiration
persuade
phase
physician
piece
pitcher
planned
plateau
playwright
pleasant
pleasure
pneumonia
politician
possess
possible
practical (ly)
prairie
precede
precious

precise (ly)
precision
preferable
preferred
prejudice
preparation
presence
previous
primitive
principal
principle
prisoner
privilege
probably
procedure
proceed
professor
prominent
pronounce
pronunciation
protein
psychology
pumpkin
pure

Q

quarter
questionnaire
quiet
quite
quotient

R

raise
realize
really
receipt
receive
received

recipe
recognize
recommend
reign
relieve
religious
remember
repetition
representative
reservoir
resistance
respectfully
responsibility
restaurant
review
rhyme
rhythm
ridiculous
route

S

safety
salad
salary
sandwich
satisfactory
Saturday
scene
scenery
schedule
science
scissors
scream
screen
season
secretary
seize
sensible
sentence
separate
several

sheriff
shining
similar
since
sincere (ly)
skiing
sleigh
soldier
souvenir
spaghetti
specific
sphere
sprinkle
squeeze
squirrel
statue
stature
statute
stomach
stopped
straight
strength
stretched
studying
subtle
succeed
success
sufficient
summarize
supplement
suppose
surely
surprise
syllable
sympathy
symptom

T

tariff
technique
temperature
temporary
terrible
territory
thankful
theater
their
there
therefore
thief
thorough (ly)
though
throughout
tired
tobacco
together
tomorrow
tongue
touch
tournament
toward
tragedy
treasurer
tried
tries
trouble
truly
Tuesday
typical

U

unconscious
unfortunate (ly)
unique
university
unnecessary
until
usable
useful
using
usual (ly)
utensil

V

vacation
vacuum
valuable
variety
various
vegetable
vehicle
very
vicinity
view
villain
violence
visible
visitor
voice
volume
voluntary
volunteer

W

wander
wasn't
weather
Wednesday
weigh
weird
welcome
welfare
whale
where
whether
which
whole
wholly
whose
width
women
worthwhile
wouldn't
wreckage
writing
written

Y

yellow
yesterday
yield

Using the Right Word

652.1
a, an

A is used before words that begin with a consonant sound; *an* is used before words that begin with any vowel sound except long "u."

> a heap, a cat, an idol, an elephant, an honor, a historian, an umbrella, a unicorn

652.2
accept, except

The verb *accept* means "to receive"; the preposition *except* means "other than."

> Melissa graciously accepted defeat. (verb)

> All the boys except Zach were here. (preposition)

652.3
affect, effect

Affect is almost always a verb; it means "to influence." *Effect* can be a verb, but it is most often used as a noun that means "the result."

> How does population growth affect us?

> What are the effects of population growth?

652.4
allowed, aloud

The verb *allowed* means "permitted" or "let happen"; *aloud* is an adverb that means "in a normal voice."

> We aren't allowed to read aloud in the library.

652.5
allusion, illusion

An *allusion* is a brief reference to or hint of something (person, place, thing, or idea). An *illusion* is a false impression or idea.

> The Great Dontini, a magician, made an allusion to Houdini as he created the illusion of sawing his assistant in half.

652.6
a lot

A lot is not one word, but two; it is a general descriptive phrase meaning "plenty." (It should be avoided in formal writing.)

652.7
all right

All right is not one word, but two; it is a phrase meaning "satisfactory" or "okay." (Please note, the following *are* spelled correctly: *always, altogether, already, almost.*)

RIGHT WORD

Using the Right Word 1

■ a, an; accept, except; affect, effect; allowed, aloud

 For each of the following sentences, write a word from the list above to fill in the blank.

1. Louis Braille had _____ accident that left him blind when he was three years old.
   an

2. At the school he attended, everyone _____ Louis Braille could see.

3. Not being able to read can _____ anyone's life dramatically.

4. Louis Braille was _____ to become a teacher in 1926, when he was only 15 years old.

5. He created _____ alphabet of raised dots to make teaching easier.

6. It was _____ marvelous invention.

7. These dots _____ a blind person to read and write.

8. The Braille alphabet had quite an _____ on the blind population.

9. Most sight-impaired students _____ the challenge of learning the Braille system.

10. Today, people can also hear many books read _____ on cassettes or CD's.

11. This has had an _____ on my mom (who is not blind) because now she can "read" while driving her car!

Next Step: Write a brief paragraph about learning a new skill. Use the words *a lot* and *all right* correctly.

Answers

2. except
3. affect
4. allowed
5. an
6. a
7. allowed
8. effect
9. accept
10. aloud
11. effect

Using the Right Word **654–655**

654

punctuate *edit* capitalize
improve SPELL

655

Using the Right Word

654.1 already, all ready	*Already* is an adverb that tells when. *All ready* is a phrase meaning "completely ready." We have already eaten breakfast; now we are all ready for school.
654.2 altogether, all together	*Altogether* is always an adverb meaning "completely." *All together* is used to describe people or things that are gathered in one place at one time. Ms. Monces held her baton in the air and said, "Okay, class, all together now: sing!" Unfortunately, there was altogether too much street noise for us to hear her.
654.3 among, between	*Among* is used when speaking of more than two persons or things. *Between* is used when speaking of only two. The three friends talked among themselves as they tried to choose between trumpet or trombone lessons.
654.4 amount, number	*Amount* is used to describe things that you cannot count. *Number* is used when you can actually count the persons or things. The amount of interest in playing the tuba is shown by the number of kids learning to play the instrument.
654.5 annual, biannual, semiannual, biennial, perennial	An *annual* event happens once every year. A *biannual* (or *semiannual*) event happens twice a year. A *biennial* event happens once every two years. A *perennial* event happens year after year. The annual PTA rummage sale is so successful that it will now be a semiannual event. The neighbor has some wonderful perennial flowers.
654.6 ant, aunt	An *ant* is an insect. An *aunt* is a female relative (the sister of a person's mother or father). My aunt is an entomologist, a scientist who studies ants and other insects.
654.7 ascent, assent	*Ascent* is the act of rising or climbing; *assent* is agreement. After the group's ascent of five flights of stairs to the meeting room, plans for elevator repairs met with quick assent.

Using the Right Word 2

■ already, all ready; **altogether, all together;** among, between; amount, number; ant, aunt

 For each of the following sentences, write the correct choice from each set of words in parentheses.

1. We (*already, all ready*) have plans for the holiday.
   already

2. Every Memorial Day my family meets at my (*ant's, aunt's*) house for a family picnic.

3. Many members of the family (*all ready, already*) live in the same town she lives in.

4. When the out-of-town people arrive, there are 53 of us (*all together, altogether*).

5. Last year, as we were (*all ready, already*) to start eating our food, a large (*amount, number*) of (*ants, aunts*) invaded the picnic area.

6. The family was (*all together, altogether*) disappointed in that year's picnic.

7. As the adults talked (*among, between*) themselves, I heard them say we should get together more often.

8. All my cousins expressed a strong (*amount, number*) of interest when they heard this idea.

9. Maybe we can squeeze in another family gathering sometime (*among, between*) Independence Day and Labor Day.

Next Step: Write three sentences that show your understanding of these words: *amount, among,* and *between*.

RIGHT WORD

656.1 **bare, bear**	The adjective *bare* means "naked." A *bear* is a large, heavy animal with shaggy hair. **Despite his bare feet, the man chased the polar bear across the snow.** The verb *bear* means "to put up with" or "to carry." **Dwayne could not bear another of his older brother's lectures.**
656.2 **base, bass**	*Base* is the foundation or the lower part of something. *Bass* (pronounced like "base") is a deep sound or tone. **The stereo speakers are on a base so solid that even the loudest bass tones don't rattle it.** *Bass* (rhymes with "mass") is a fish. **Jim hooked a record-setting bass, but it got away . . . so he says.**
656.3 **beat, beet**	The verb *beat* means "to strike, to defeat," and the noun *beat* is a musical term for rhythm or tempo. A *beet* is a carrot-like vegetable (often red). **The beat of the drum in the marching band encouraged the fans to cheer on the team. After they beat West High's team four games to one, many team members were as red as a beet.**
656.4 **berth, birth**	*Berth* is a space or compartment. *Birth* is the process of being born. **We pulled aside the curtain in our train berth to view the birth of a new day outside our window.**
656.5 **beside, besides**	*Beside* means "by the side of." *Besides* means "in addition to." **Besides a flashlight, Kedar likes to keep his pet boa beside his bed at night.**
656.6 **billed, build**	*Billed* means either "to be given a bill" or "to have a beak." The verb *build* means "to construct." **We asked the carpenter to build us a birdhouse. She billed us for time and materials.**
656.7 **blew, blue**	*Blew* is the past tense of "blow." *Blue* is a color and is also used to mean "feeling low in spirits." **As the wind blew out the candles in the dark blue room, I felt more blue than ever.**

Using the Right Word 3

■ bare, bear; base, bass; beat, beet; billed, build; blew, blue

 For each pair of words in parentheses below, write the line number and the correct choice.

Example: 1 The city decided to (*billed*, *build*) a skateboard
2 park near the baseball diamond.
Answer: 1 *build*

1   In 1958, ocean surfers became frustrated by small waves
2 and bad weather. They couldn't (*bare*, *bear*) being off their boards
3 for long, so they took to the streets with skateboards. Soon
4 skateboarding became a craze on the West Coast.
5   The first contest to see who could (*beat*, *beet*) all the other
6 competitors was held in Hermosa, California, in 1963. Some guided
7 their skateboards with their (*bare*, *bear*) feet, but most wore gym
8 shoes. However, it would be almost 10 years before boarders could
9 (*billed*, *build*) up the sport's popularity nationwide. By this time,
10 better wheels and trucks (the metal parts that hold the wheels to
11 the board) made jumps and other tricks possible. Skateboarders
12 now seemed to sail right into the (*blew*, *blue*) sky as their boards
13 climbed up specially built, steep walls.
14   A strong (*base*, *bass*) of support among the real competitors
15 kept the sport going. In 2003, skateboarding (*blew*, *blue*) past
16 artificial wall climbing and paintball to become the fastest growing
17 extreme sport in the country.

Next Step: Write three sentences that show your understanding of these words: *bare*, *billed*, and *bass*.

line 2	bear
line 5	beat
line 7	bare
line 8	build
line 12	blue
line 14	base
line 15	blew

658.1
board, bored

A *board* is a piece of wood. *Board* also means "a group or council that helps run an organization."

> The school board approved the purchase of 50 pine boards for the woodworking classes.

Bored means "to become weary or tired of something." It can also mean "made a hole by drilling."

> Dulé bored a hole in the ice and dropped in a fishing line. Waiting and waiting for a bite bored him.

658.2
borrow, lend

Borrow means "to *receive* for temporary use." *Lend* means "to *give* for temporary use."

> I asked Mom, "May I borrow $15 for a CD?"
> She said, "I can lend you $15 until next Friday."

658.3
brake, break

A *brake* is a device used to stop a vehicle. The verb *break* means "to split, crack, or destroy"; as a noun, *break* means "gap or interruption."

> After the brake on my bike failed, I took a break to fix it so I wouldn't break a bone.

658.4
bring, take

Use *bring* when the action is moving toward the speaker; use *take* when the action is moving away from the speaker.

> Grandpa asked me to take the garbage out and bring him today's paper.

658.5
by, buy, bye

By is a preposition meaning "near" or "not later than." *Buy* is a verb meaning "to purchase."

> By tomorrow I hope to buy tickets for the final match of the tournament.

Bye is the position of being automatically advanced to the next tournament round without playing.

> Our soccer team received a bye because of our winning record.

658.6
can, may

Can means "able to," while *may* means "permitted to."

> "Can I go to the library?"
> (This actually means "Are my mind and body strong enough to get me there?")
> "May I go?"
> (This means "Do I have your permission to go?")

Using the Right Word 4

■ board, bored; brake, break; bring, take; **by, buy**; can, may

 For each numbered sentence below, write the word "correct" if the underlined word is used correctly. If it is incorrect, write the right word.

> *Example:* A tornado can drive a <u>bored</u> into a tree.
> *Answer:* board

(1) A tornado is a powerful, twisting windstorm that <u>can</u> destroy just about anything in its path. **(2)** A tornado will easily <u>brake</u> a wooden house into many pieces. **(3)** A tornado <u>takes</u> destruction wherever it touches down.

(4) <u>Buy</u> the time a storm has passed, relief workers are on their way to the scene. **(5)** Usually, only residents or relief workers <u>may</u> enter an area damaged by a tornado.

 For each of the following sentences, write the correct choice from each set of words in parentheses.

6. An elevator has a special (*break, brake*) to prevent accidents.
brake

7. Would you please (*bring, take*) that garbage out to the dumpster?

8. Dad, (*can, may*) I use your set of wrenches?

9. Leander plans to (*by, buy*) a new CD next week.

10. Someone bumped the table, causing the glass to (*brake, break*).

11. Pablo has to walk (*by, buy*) an abandoned building every day.

12. Mrs. Serbins said we (*can, may*) stay inside for recess today.

13. Johar is always complaining that he is (*board, bored*) and has nothing to do.

14. Felipe said, "Please (*bring, take*) me a glass of water."

RIGHT WORD

Answers

1. correct
2. break
3. brings
4. By
5. correct

7. take
8. may
9. buy
10. break
11. by
12. may
13. bored
14. bring

660

660.1
canvas, canvass

Canvas is a heavy cloth; *canvass* means "ask people for votes or opinions."

> Our old canvas tent leaks.

> Someone with a clipboard is canvassing the neighborhood.

660.2
capital, capitol

Capital can be either a noun, referring to a city or to money, or an adjective, meaning "major or important." *Capitol* is used only when talking about a building.

> The capitol building is in the capital city for a capital (major) reason: The city government contributed the capital (money) for the building project.

660.3
cell, sell

Cell means "a small room" or "a small unit of life basic to all plants and animals." *Sell* is a verb meaning "to give up for a price."

> Today we looked at a human skin cell under a microscope.

> Let's sell those old bicycles at the rummage sale.

660.4
cent, sent, scent

Cent (1/100 of a dollar) is a coin; *sent* is the past tense of the verb "send"; *scent* is an odor or a smell.

> After our car hit a skunk, we sent our friends a postcard that said, "One cent doesn't go far, but skunk scent seems to last forever."

660.5
chord, cord

Chord may mean "an emotion or a feeling," but it is more often used to mean "the sound of three or more musical tones played at the same time." A *cord* is a string or rope.

> The band struck a chord at the exact moment the mayor pulled the cord on the drape covering the new statue.

660.6
chose, choose

Chose (chōz) is the past tense of the verb *choose* (chōōz).

> This afternoon Mom chose tacos and hot sauce; this evening she will choose an antacid.

660.7
coarse, course

Coarse means "rough or crude." *Course* means "a path" or "a class or series of studies."

> In our cooking course, we learned to use coarse salt and freshly ground pepper in salads.

Using the Right Word 5

 capital, capitol; cell, sell; sent, scent; chose, choose; coarse, course

 For each of the following sentences, write the correct choice from each set of words in parentheses.

1. Carlos's Coffee Shops (*sell, cell*) the world's best breakfast burritos.

   sell

2. If I had lots of (*capital, capitol*) to spend, I'd buy a big-screen TV.

3. Is your state's (*capital, capitol*) building located on the highest ground in your (*capital, capitol*) city?

4. Johnson City's old jailhouse, which had only three (*cells, sells*), is now a small restaurant.

5. Rigid walls surround the (*cells, sells*) of most plants, bacteria, fungi, and algae.

6. Reggie's older sister is taking a creative writing (*course, coarse*) at the community center.

7. We often smell the (*sent, scent*) from Pizza Heaven drifting up to our second-floor apartment.

8. I even (*sent, scent*) my cousin Cade an e-mail to tell him how good it smells!

9. On Monday, Rhea (*chose, choose*) to color her hair pink, but tomorrow she may (*chose, choose*) to make it bright green.

10. Did Leroy and Tamra use fine or (*course, coarse*) sandpaper to make the sand dunes for their geography project?

Next Step: Write four sentences that show your understanding of the following words: *choose, scent, capitol,* and *sell.*

RIGHT WORD

Answers

2. capital
3. capitol, capital
4. cells
5. cells
6. course
7. scent
8. sent
9. chose, choose
10. coarse

662.1 complement, compliment	*Complement* means "to complete or go with." *Compliment* is an expression of admiration or praise. **Aunt Athena said, "Your cheese sauce really complements this cauliflower!"** **"Thank you for the compliment," I replied.**
662.2 continual, continuous	*Continual* refers to something that happens again and again; *continuous* refers to something that doesn't stop happening. **Sunlight hits Peoria, Iowa, on a continual basis; but sunlight hits the earth continuously.**
662.3 counsel, council	When used as a noun, *counsel* means "advice"; when used as a verb, *counsel* means "to advise." *Council* refers to a group that advises. **The student council asked for counsel from its trusted adviser.**
662.4 creak, creek	A *creak* is a squeaking sound; a *creek* is a stream. **I heard a creak from the old dock under my feet as I fished in the creek.**
662.5 cymbal, symbol	A *cymbal* is a metal instrument shaped like a plate. A *symbol* is something (usually visible) that stands for or represents another thing or idea (usually invisible). **The damaged cymbal lying on the stage was a symbol of the band's final concert.**
662.6 dear, deer	*Dear* means "loved or valued"; *deer* are animals. **My dear, old great-grandmother leaves corn and salt licks in her yard to attract deer.**
662.7 desert, dessert	A *desert* is a barren wilderness. *Dessert* is a food served at the end of a meal. **In the desert, cold water is more inviting than even the richest dessert.** The verb *desert* means "to abandon"; the noun *desert* (pronounced like the verb) means "deserving reward or punishment." **A spy who deserts his country will receive his just deserts if he is caught.**

Using the Right Word 6

■ counsel, council; creak, creek; cymbal, symbol; dear, deer; desert, dessert

 For each of the following sentences, write the correct choice from each set of words in parentheses.

1. My dad's shed door (*creaks, creeks*) every time it opens.
   creaks

2. I heard a fish splash in the (*creek, creak*).

3. Sometimes we see (*deer, dear*) drinking water from a nearby pond.

4. Last year when we were in the (*dessert, desert*), we saw vultures flying overhead.

5. The bald eagle is our country's (*cymbal, symbol*) of freedom.

6. Our family dinners at Grandma's are always followed by (*dessert, desert*).

7. After such a big meal, Grandpa's old wooden chair begins to (*creek, creak*).

8. The leader of the band (*councils, counsels*) students to store their instruments properly.

9. After the school concert, Janelle put her (*cymbal, symbol*) away.

10. Her (*deer, dear*) grandfather was so proud of her performance.

11. The student (*counsel, council*) decided that another concert should be scheduled.

12. If the floodwaters continue to rise, we will be forced to (*dessert, desert*) our house.

Next Step: Write three sentences that show your understanding of these words: *symbol, dessert,* and *deer.*

RIGHT WORD

664.1
die, dye

Die (dying) means "to stop living." *Dye* (dyeing) is used to change the color of something.

> The young girl hoped that her sick goldfish wouldn't die.
> My sister dyes her hair with coloring that washes out.

664.2
faint, feign, feint

Faint means "to be feeble, without strength." *Feign* is a verb that means "to pretend or make up." *Feint* is a noun that means "a move or an activity that is pretended in order to divert attention."

> The actors feigned a sword duel. One man staggered and fell in a feint. The audience gave faint applause.

664.3
farther, further

Farther is used when you are writing about a physical distance. *Further* means "additional."

> Alaska reaches farther north than Iceland. For further information, check your local library.

664.4
fewer, less

Fewer refers to the number of separate units; *less* refers to bulk quantity.

> I may have less money than you have, but I have fewer worries.

664.5
fir, fur

Fir refers to a type of evergreen tree; *fur* is animal hair.

> The Douglas fir tree is named after a Scottish botanist.
> An arctic fox has white fur in the winter.

664.6
flair, flare

Flair means "a natural talent"; *flare* means "to light up quickly" or "burst out."

> Jenrette has a flair for remaining calm when other people's tempers flare.

664.7
for, four

The preposition *for* means "because of" or "directed to"; *four* is the number 4.

> Mary had grilled steaks and chicken for the party, but the dog had stolen one of the four steaks.

Using the Right Word 7

 die, dye; farther, further; fewer, less; fir, fur; for, four

For each of the following sentences, write the correct choice from each set of words in parentheses.

1. Yesterday I spent (*fewer, less*) money at the mall than I did last time I was there.
   less

2. An elephant separates itself from the rest of the herd when it is about to (*dye, die*).

3. Leona walks six blocks (*further, farther*) to school than Tomei does.

4. I spend (*less, fewer*) time studying than my brother does, so I have (*less, fewer*) A's on my report card than he does.

5. Sometimes, when cattle and horses rub against (*fur, fir*) trees, bits of their (*fur, fir*) get stuck in the rough bark.

6. Do you want to (*dye, die*) your shoes orange or chartreuse for "Crazy Shoe Day"?

7. Sloan wants to trade her lunch (*four, for*) yours.

8. Sloan's lunch is a day-old sandwich, soggy potato chips, and (*four, for*) rock-hard chocolate chip cookies.

9. Ramón is helping his dad plant some Douglas (*furs, firs*) in their yard.

10. Does Seattle, Washington, or Portland, Oregon, have (*less, fewer*) sunny days?

11. If you need (*further, farther*) help with the assignment, call me after dinner.

Next Step: Show your understanding of the words *dye*, *further*, and *fewer* by using each of them correctly in a sentence.

RIGHT WORD

Answers

2. die
3. farther
4. less, fewer
5. fir, fur
6. dye
7. for
8. four
9. firs
10. fewer
11. further

666.1
good, well

Good is an adjective; *well* is nearly always an adverb.

The strange flying machines flew well. (The adverb *well* modifies *flew*.)

They looked good as they flew overhead. (The adjective *good* modifies *they*.)

When used in writing about health, *well* is an adjective.

The pilots did not feel well, however, after the long, hard race.

666.2
hare, hair

A *hare* is an animal similar to a rabbit; *hair* refers to the growth covering the head and body of mammals and human beings.

When a hare darted out in front of our car, the hair on my head stood up.

666.3
heal, heel

Heal means "to mend or restore to health." *Heel* is the back part of a human foot.

I got a blister on my heel from wearing my new shoes. It won't heal unless I wear my old ones.

666.4
hear, here

You *hear* sounds with your ears. *Here* is the opposite of *there* and means "nearby."

666.5
heard, herd

Heard is the past tense of the verb "to hear"; *herd* is a group of animals.

The herd of grazing sheep raised their heads when they heard the collie barking in the distance.

666.6
heir, air

An *heir* is a person who inherits something; *air* is what we breathe.

Will the next generation be heir to terminally polluted air?

666.7
hole, whole

A *hole* is a cavity or hollow place. *Whole* means "entire or complete."

The hole in the ozone layer is a serious problem requiring the attention of the whole world.

666.8
immigrate, emigrate

Immigrate means "to come into a new country or area." *Emigrate* means "to go out of one country to live in another."

Martin Ulferts immigrated to this country in 1882. He was only three years old when he emigrated from Germany.

Using the Right Word 8

■ good, well; hare, hair; hear, here; heard, herd; heir, air; hole, whole

 For each of the following sentences, write the correct choice from each set of words in parentheses.

1. Mammals are animals covered with (*hare, hair*).
   hair

2. A wood duck looks for a (*hole, whole*) in a tree to build a nest.

3. Although you can't see turtles' ears, they can (*hear, here*) very (*good, well*).

4. The peregrine falcon can dive through the (*heir, air*) at 200 miles per hour.

5. I'd say that's a pretty (*good, well*) speed!

6. Caribou always travel in a large (*heard, herd*).

7. The sounds a whale makes underwater can be (*heard, herd*) for miles.

8. A (*hare, hair*) has long ears and very long hind legs.

9. The sailfish can swim from (*hear, here*) to there faster than any other fish.

10. While humans grow (*hare, hair*) in just a few places, most mammals are covered with it.

11. As an (*heir, air*) of his uncle, Rashid was given the scarlet macaw.

12. Listen! The (*hole, whole*) forest is filled with singing birds.

13. They sound (*good, well*), don't they?

Next Step: Write three sentences about animals. Show your understanding of these words: *herd, whole,* and *hair.*

RIGHT WORD

668

668.1 imply, infer	*Imply* means "to suggest indirectly"; *infer* means "to draw a conclusion from facts." "Since you have to work, may I infer that you won't come to my party?" Guy asked. "No, I only meant to imply that I would be late," Rochelle responded.
668.2 it's, its	*It's* is the contraction of "it is." *Its* is the possessive form of "it." It's a fact that a minnow's teeth are in its throat.
668.3 knew, new	*Knew* is the past tense of the verb "know." *New* means "recent or modern." If I knew how to fix it, I would not need a new one!
668.4 know, no	*Know* means "to recognize or understand." *No* means "the opposite of yes." Phil, do you know Cheri? No, I've never met her.
668.5 later, latter	*Later* means "after a period of time." *Latter* refers to the second of two things mentioned. The band arrived later and set up the speakers and the lights. The latter made the stage look like a carnival ride.
668.6 lay, lie	*Lay* means "to place." (*Lay* is a transitive verb; that means it needs a word to complete the meaning.) *Lie* means "to recline." (*Lie* is an intransitive verb.) Lay your sleeping bag on the floor before you lie down on it. (*Lay* needs the word *bag* to complete its meaning.)
668.7 lead, led	*Lead* (lēd) is a present tense verb meaning "to guide." The past tense of the verb is *led* (lĕd). The noun *lead* (lĕd) is the metal. Guides planned to lead the settlers to safe quarters. Instead, they led them into a winter storm. Peeling paint in old houses may contain lead.
668.8 learn, teach	*Learn* means "to get information"; *teach* means "to give information." I want to learn how to sew. Will you teach me?

RIGHT WORD

Using the Right Word 9

◼ it's, its; knew, new; know, no; lay, lie; lead, led; learn, teach

 For each numbered sentence below, write the correct choice from each set of words in parentheses.

Example: Ancient stone carvings show that the Egyptians (*new, knew*) about swimming 5,000 years ago.

Answer: knew

(1) Doctors (*no, know*) that swimming is good exercise. **(2)** All children should (*learn, teach*) how to swim, but parents need to make sure they (*lie, lay*) down the ground rules about water safety.

Some kids take swimming lessons. **(3)** After a short talk, the swimming instructor will (*led, lead*) students to the pool and (*learn, teach*) them basic strokes. The most common stroke is called the front crawl. **(4)** (*Its, It's*) how most people swim. **(5)** Some people like to (*lie, lay*) on their backs when they swim—this is called the backstroke. **(6)** Some Olympic swimmers have (*lead, led*) the race doing the butterfly stroke. **(7)** A (*new, knew*) swimmer might think that this stroke is too difficult to do, but (*no, know*) stroke is impossible to learn.

(8) Many people have tried to swim the English Channel; (*it's, its*) water is very cold. **(9)** Although the swimmers (*new, knew*) what a difficult task it would be, I'm sure they looked forward to going home to (*lie, lay*) down in a nice, warm bed!

Next Step: *Lay* and *lie* are challenging words to use correctly. Write two or more sentences that show you know the meanings of those words.

Answers

1. know
2. learn, lay
3. lead, teach
4. It's
5. lie
6. led
7. new, no
8. its
9. knew, lie

670.1
leave, let

Leave means "fail to take along." *Let* means "allow."

Rozi wanted to leave her boots at home, but Jorge wouldn't let her.

670.2
like, as

Like is a preposition meaning "similar to"; *as* is a conjunction meaning "to the same degree" or "while." *Like* usually introduces a phrase; *as* usually introduces a clause.

The glider floated like a bird. The glider floated as the pilot had hoped it would.

As we circled the airfield, we saw maintenance carts moving like ants below us.

670.3
loose, lose, loss

Loose (lüs) means "free or untied"; *lose* (lo͞oz) means "to misplace or fail to win"; *loss* (lôs) means "something lost."

These jeans are too loose in the waist since my recent weight loss. I still want to lose a few more pounds.

670.4
made, maid

Made is the past tense of "make," which means to "create," "prepare," or "put in order." A *maid* is a female servant; *maid* is also used to describe an unmarried girl or young woman.

The hotel maid asked if our beds needed to be made.

Grandma made a chocolate cake for dessert.

A maid strolled in the garden before the concert.

670.5
mail, male

Mail refers to letters or packages handled by the postal service. *Male* refers to the masculine sex.

My little brother likes getting junk mail.

The male sea horse, not the female, takes care of the fertilized eggs.

670.6
main, mane

Main refers to the most important part. *Mane* is the long hair growing from the top or sides of the neck of certain animals, such as the horse, lion, and so on.

The main thing we noticed about the magician's tamed lion was its luxurious mane.

670.7
meat, meet

Meat is food or flesh; *meet* means "to come upon or encounter."

I'd like you to meet the butcher who sells the leanest meat in town.

Using the Right Word 10

leave, let; like, as; loose, lose, loss; main, mane; meat, meet

For each of the following sentences, write the correct choice from each set of words in parentheses.

1. Emme and James swim (*as, like*) fish.
   like
2. They glide across the surface (*as, like*) water bugs (*as, like*) we sit and watch.
3. Your tomcat's (*mane, main*) makes him look like a miniature lion.
4. Don't (*leave, let*) the dog eat cake anymore.
5. The straps on Brad's backpack are very (*loose, lose*).
6. If he's not careful, he may (*loose, lose*) it.
7. The (*lose, loss*) of his valuable art supplies would be a disaster!
8. Mom wouldn't (*leave, let*) me go to Jule's party until 6:30.
9. At this weekend's (*main, mane*) event, Vegan Fest, no one will be eating any (*meat, meet*).
10. At the stable, a woman was braiding her horse's (*main, mane*).
11. (*As, Like*) a ballerina, Marta pranced across her room, twirling and hopping.
12. I don't want to (*lose, loss*) my ring while I'm swimming, so I'll (*leave, let*) it at home.
13. "I'm happy to finally (*meat, meet*) you," said Rocco's pen pal.
14. "You look (*as, like*) your picture," he said.

Next Step: Write two sentences that show your understanding of the words *leave* and *let*.

RIGHT WORD

Answers

2. like, as
3. mane
4. let
5. loose
6. lose
7. loss
8. let
9. main, meat
10. mane
11. Like
12. lose, leave
13. meet
14. like

672.1
medal, metal, meddle, mettle

A *medal* is an award. *Metal* is an element like iron or gold. *Meddle* means "to interfere." *Mettle*, a noun, refers to quality of character.

> Grandpa's friend received a medal for showing his mettle in battle. Grandma, who loves to meddle in others' business, asked if the award was a precious metal.

672.2
miner, minor

A *miner* digs in the ground for valuable ore. A *minor* is a person who is not legally an adult. *Minor* means "of no great importance" when used as an adjective.

> The use of minors as miners is no minor problem.

672.3
moral, morale

Moral relates to what is right or wrong or to the lesson to be drawn from a story. *Morale* refers to a person's attitude or mental condition.

> The moral of this story is "Everybody loves a winner."

> After the unexpected win at football, morale was high throughout the town.

672.4
morning, mourning

Morning refers to the first part of the day (before noon); *mourning* means "showing sorrow."

> Abby was mourning her test grades all morning.

672.5
oar, or, ore

An *oar* is a paddle used in rowing or steering a boat. *Or* is a conjunction indicating choice. *Ore* refers to a mineral made up of several different kinds of material, as in iron ore.

> Either use one oar to push us away from the dock, or start the boat's motor.

> Silver-copper ore is smelted and refined to extract each metal.

672.6
pain, pane

Pain is the feeling of being hurt. A *pane* is a section or part of something.

> Dad looked like he was in pain when he found out we broke a pane of glass in the neighbor's front door.

672.7
pair, pare, pear

A *pair* is a couple (two); *pare* is a verb meaning "to peel"; *pear* is the fruit.

> A pair of doves nested in the pear tree.

> Please pare the apples for the pie.

Using the Right Word 11

■ medal, metal; miner, minor; oar, ore, or; pain, pane; pair, pare, pear

For each of the following sentences, write the correct choice from each set of words in parentheses.

1. (*Miners, Minors*) work underground to find (*oar, ore*) used in manufacturing.
   Miners, ore

2. Should I use my (*oar, or*) on the left side of the canoe (*ore, or*) on the right side?

3. We are required to wear a (*pare, pair*) of blue socks with our uniforms.

4. A first-place winner in the Olympic Games receives a (*metal, medal*) made of a precious (*metal, medal*)—gold.

5. Do you know that some states still call people between the ages of 18 and 21 (*minors, miners*)?

6. When Abe stumbled and fell, he felt a sharp (*pane, pain*) as his arm went through a (*pane, pain*) of glass in the patio door.

7. Juan received our school's (*metal, medal*) of excellence during the graduation ceremony.

8. If you are going to put that (*pare, pear*) in the fruit salad, you don't have to (*pare, pear*) it first.

9. Huge barges carry iron (*oar, ore*) to steel mills along the Mississippi River.

10. Most fine jewelry is made of (*metal, medal*).

11. A (*pare, pair*) of red-handled scissors and a (*pare, pear*)-shaped pincushion are on Grandma Delora's sewing table.

Next Step: Write a short paragraph in which you correctly use four of the italicized words above.

Answers

2. oar, or
3. pair
4. medal, metal
5. minors
6. pain, pane
7. medal
8. pear, pare
9. ore
10. metal
11. pair, pear

674.1
past, passed

Passed is always a verb; it is the past tense of *pass*. *Past* can be used as a noun, as an adjective, or as a preposition.

A motorcycle passed my dad's 'Vette. (verb)

The old man won't forget the past. (noun)

I'm sorry, but I'd rather not talk about my past life. (adjective)

Old Blue walked right past the cat and never saw it. (preposition)

674.2
peace, piece

Peace means "harmony, or freedom from war." A *piece* is a part or fragment of something.

In order to keep peace among the triplets, each one had to have an identical piece of cake.

674.3
peak, peek, pique

A *peak* is a "high point" or a "pointed end." *Peek* means "brief look." *Pique*, as a verb, means "to excite by challenging"; as a noun, it means "a feeling of resentment."

Just a peek at Pike's Peak in the Rocky Mountains can pique a mountain climber's curiosity.

In a pique, she marched away from her giggling sisters.

674.4
personal, personnel

Personal means "private." *Personnel* are people working at a job.

Some thoughts are too personal to share.

The personnel manager will be hiring more workers.

674.5
plain, plane

A *plain* is an area of land that is flat or level; it also means "clearly seen or clearly understood" and "ordinary."

It's plain to see why the early settlers had trouble crossing the Great Plains.

Plane means "a flat, level surface" (as in geometry); it is also a tool used to smooth the surface of wood.

When I saw that the door wasn't a perfect plane, I used a plane to make it smooth.

674.6
pore, pour, poor

A *pore* is an opening in the skin. *Pour* means "to cause a flow or stream." *Poor* means "needy."

People perspire through the pores in their skin. Pour yourself a glass of water. Your poor body needs it!

Using the Right Word 12

past, passed; **peace, piece;** peak, peek; **personal, personnel;** plain, plane

 For each of the following sentences, write the correct choice from each set of words in parentheses.

1. Imaginative wrapping on a gift box can make it more (*personal, personnel*).

    personal

2. Uleasha's mom said to her friends, "I like the (*personal, personnel*) gifts Uleasha gives me."

3. She can make even a simple (*peace, piece*) of (*plain, plane*) paper into a work of art.

4. As Janet (*past, passed*) the group of women, she stopped to listen.

5. Janet took a (*peak, peek*) at one of Uleasha's origami cranes.

6. She could see how it would give Uleasha's mom a feeling of (*peace, piece*).

7. In the (*past, passed*), origami was practiced only in the Far East.

8. Still a Japanese tradition, origami is now created everywhere—from the Great (*Plains, Planes*) to Greenland.

9. At the scene of the accident, the driver said he hadn't had a ticket in the (*past, passed*) 10 years.

10. Then the driver admitted he had been looking at a nearby mountain (*peak, peek*).

11. "We'll need more (*personal, personnel*) to get this mess cleaned up," said the officer.

Next Step: Write three sentences in which you use the word *past* in these different ways: as an adjective, as a noun, and as a preposition.

RIGHT WORD

Answers

2. personal
3. piece, plain
4. passed
5. peek
6. peace
7. past
8. Plains
9. past
10. peak
11. personnel

676

676.1
**principal,
principle**

As an adjective, *principal* means "primary." As a noun, it can mean "a school administrator" or "a sum of money." *Principle* means "idea or doctrine."

My mom's principal goal is to save money so she can pay off the principal balance on her loan from the bank.

Hey, Charlie, I hear the principal gave you a detention.

The principle of freedom is based on the principle of self-discipline.

676.2
quiet, quit, quite

Quiet is the opposite of "noisy." *Quit* means "to stop." *Quite* means "completely or entirely."

I quit mowing even though I wasn't quite finished.
The neighborhood was quiet again.

676.3
raise, rays, raze

Raise is a verb meaning "to lift or elevate." *Rays* are thin lines or beams. *Raze* is a verb that means "to tear down completely."

When I raise this shade, bright rays of sunlight stream into the room.

Construction workers will raze the old theater to make room for a parking lot.

676.4
real, very, really

Do not use the adjective *real* in place of the adverbs *very* or *really*.

The plants scattered throughout the restaurant are not real.
Hiccups are very embarrassing.
Her nose is really small.

676.5
red, read

Red is a color; *read*, pronounced the same way, is the past tense of the verb meaning "to understand the meaning of written words and symbols."

"I've read five books in two days," said the little boy.
The librarian gave him a red ribbon.

---

improve *edit* capitalize
SPELL **677**
Using the Right Word

Using the Right Word 13

■ quiet, quit, quite; raise, rays, raze; real, very, really; red, read

 For each of the following sentences, write the correct choice from each set of words in parentheses.

1. It's (*quiet, quite*) nice to read a good book on a (*really, real*) rainy afternoon.
   quite, really

2. Max's sister has beautiful (*read, red*) hair.

3. Have you ever seen the colors and patterns formed when (*raze, rays*) of sunlight pass through a prism?

4. Mom pleaded, "(*Quit, Quiet*) playing that CD so loudly and be (*quite, quiet*) for a while."

5. "That would make me (*quiet, quite*) happy!" she added.

6. The city will (*rays, raze*) the old water tower a week before the new one goes up.

7. A huge crane will (*raise, raze*) the new water tank to the top of the new tower.

8. I (*read, red*) an article about miniature horses.

9. It's (*real, really*) hard to believe that they are horses since they are not (*very, real*) tall.

10. I saw one in a parade once, and it definitely was a (*real, really*) horse.

11. I think it would be an interesting hobby to (*raise, rays*) these animals.

Next Step: Write a few sentences about a hobby that you find interesting. Use at least four of the italicized words above in your sentences. Then exchange papers with a classmate and read about each other's hobby.

RIGHT WORD

Answers

2. red
3. rays
4. Quit, quiet
5. quite
6. raze
7. raise
8. read
9. really, very
10. real
11. raise

678.1
right, write, rite

Right means "correct or proper"; *right* is the opposite of "left"; it also refers to anything that a person has a legal claim to, as in "copyright." *Write* means "to record in print." *Rite* is a ritual or ceremonial act.

> We have to **write** an essay about how our **rights** are protected by the Constitution.
>
> Turn **right** at the next corner.
>
> A **rite** of passage is a ceremony that celebrates becoming an adult.

678.2
scene, seen

Scene refers to the setting or location where something happens; it also means "sight or spectacle." *Seen* is a form of the verb "see."

> The **scene** of the crime was roped off. We hadn't **seen** anyone go in or out of the building.

678.3
seam, seem

A *seam* is a line formed by connecting two pieces of material. *Seem* means "appear to exist."

> Every Thanksgiving, it **seems**, I stuff myself so much that my shirt **seams** threaten to burst.

678.4
sew, so, sow

Sew is a verb meaning "to stitch"; *so* is a conjunction meaning "in order that." The verb *sow* means "to plant."

> In Colonial times, the wife would **sew** the family clothes, and the husband would **sow** the family garden so the children could eat.

678.5
sight, cite, site

Sight means "the act of seeing" or "something that is seen." *Cite* means "to quote or refer to." A *site* is a location or position (including a Web site on the Internet).

> The Alamo at night was a **sight** worth the trip. I was also able to **cite** my visit to this historical **site** in my history paper.

678.6
sit, set

Sit means "to put the body in a seated position." *Set* means "to place." (*Set* is a transitive verb; that means it needs a direct object to complete its meaning.)

> How can you just **sit** there and watch as I **set** up all these chairs?

Using the Right Word 14

■ right, write, rite; scene, seen; sight, cite, site; sit, set

 For each numbered sentence below, write the correct choice from each set of words in parentheses.

> *Example:* A student needs to (*sight, cite*) sources used for a research report.
> *Answer:* cite

(1) Mali will (*rite, write*) about the history of bicycles. **(2)** Several Web (*sites, cites*) about it can be found on the Internet. According to one Web page, Baron von Drais invented the first bike, a wooden one without pedals, in 1817. **(3)** He would (*sit, set*) on the bike and use his feet on the ground to make the bike move. **(4)** Men riding these bikes were quite a (*sight, site*) to see! **(5)** For a long time, women were only (*scene, seen*) riding tricycles. **(6)** It was not considered (*right, rite*) for a woman to ride a bicycle. **(7)** If a woman rode a bike, she'd cause a (*scene, seen*)! **(8)** Now people see learning to ride a bike as a (*write, rite*) of growing up.

 For each of the following sentences, write the correct choice from each set of words in parentheses.

9. Is it (*write, right*) that I always have to take the garbage out? right

10. Maybe you'd prefer to (*sit, set*) the table for dinner every evening.

11. Allow me to (*site, cite*) my mother: "Life is not fair."

12. James said he had already (*scene, seen*) that movie.

13. Just the (*sight, site*) of a skunk makes its enemies run.

14. Please (*write, rite*) a thank-you note to Grandma.

Answers

1. write
2. sites
3. sit
4. sight
5. seen
6. right
7. scene
8. rite

10. set
11. cite
12. seen
13. sight
14. write

680.1
sole, soul

Sole means "single, only one"; *sole* also refers to the bottom surface of a foot or shoe. *Soul* refers to the spiritual part of a person.

Maggie got a job for the sole purpose of saving for a car.

The soles of these shoes are very thick.

"Who told you dogs don't have souls?" asked the kind veterinarian.

680.2
some, sum

Some means "an unknown number or part." *Sum* means "the whole amount."

The sum in the cash register was stolen by some thieves.

680.3
sore, soar

Sore means "painful"; to *soar* means "to rise or fly high into the air."

Craning to watch the eagle soar overhead, we soon had sore necks.

680.4
stationary, stationery

Stationary means "not movable"; *stationery* is the paper and envelopes used to write letters.

Grandpa designed and printed his own stationery.

All of the built-in furniture is stationary, of course.

680.5
steal, steel

Steal means "to take something without permission"; *steel* is a metal.

Early ironmakers had to steal recipes for producing steel.

680.6
than, then

Than is used in a comparison; *then* tells when.

Since tomorrow's weather is supposed to be nicer than today's, we'll go to the zoo then.

680.7
their, there, they're

Their is a possessive pronoun, one that shows ownership. (See 714.2.) *There* is an adverb that tells where. *They're* is the contraction for "they are."

They're upset because their dog got into the garbage over there.

680.8
threw, through

Threw is the past tense of "throw." *Through* means "passing from one side to the other" or "by means of."

Through sheer talent and long practice, Nolan Ryan threw baseballs through the strike zone at more than 100 miles per hour.

Using the Right Word 15

 some, sum; sore, soar; steal, steel; their, there, they're

 For each of the following sentences, write the correct choice from each set of words in parentheses.

1. Hearing such beautiful music makes my spirits (*sore, soar*).
   soar

2. The rummage sale earned us the (*sum, some*) of $62.45.

3. There's a little (*sore, soar*) on my dog's paw.

4. Little League coaches spend hours teaching baseball players how to (*steal, steel*) a base.

5. Only (*sum, some*) of my teammates were able to save enough money for baseball camp.

6. (*Their, They're*) parents are helping them out.

7. Watching a kite (*sore, soar*) in the afternoon sky, Rubi felt peaceful.

8. Blueprints often call for (*steel, steal*) I-beams to support large buildings.

9. Linc's legs grew (*sore, soar*) as he struggled to finish the marathon.

10. Ms. Ramsay pointed to room 102 and whispered, "Shhh! (*Their, They're*) taking a test in (*they're, there*)."

11. (*They're, Their*) jackets, books, and papers were scattered here, (*their, there*), and everywhere.

12. Robin Hood would (*steel, steal*) from the rich and give to the poor.

Next Step: See if you can, in one sentence, use the words *their, there,* and *they're* correctly.

Answers

2. sum
3. sore
4. steal
5. some
6. Their
7. soar
8. steel
9. sore
10. They're, there
11. Their, there
12. steal

RIGHT WORD

682.1
to, too, two

To is the preposition that can mean "in the direction of." (*To* also is used to form an infinitive. See 730.4.) *Too* is an adverb meaning "very or excessive." *Too* is often used to mean "also." *Two* is the number 2.

Only two of Columbus's first three ships returned to Spain from the New World.

Columbus was too restless to stay in Spain for long.

682.2
vain, vane, vein

Vain means "worthless." It may also mean "thinking too highly of one's self; stuck-up." *Vane* is a flat piece of material set up to show which way the wind blows. *Vein* refers to a blood vessel or a mineral deposit.

The weather vane indicates the direction of wind.

A blood vein determines the direction of flowing blood.

The vain mind moves in no particular direction and thinks only about itself.

682.3
vary, very

Vary is a verb that means "to change." *Very* can be an adjective meaning "in the fullest sense" or "complete"; it can also be an adverb meaning "extremely."

Garon's version of the event would vary from day to day. His very interesting story was the very opposite of the truth.

682.4
waist, waste

Waist is the part of the body just above the hips. The verb *waste* means "to wear away" or "to use carelessly"; the noun *waste* refers to material that is unused or useless.

Don't waste your money on fast-food meals. What a waste to throw away all this food because you're concerned about the size of your waist!

682.5
wait, weight

Wait means "to stay somewhere expecting something." *Weight* is the measure of heaviness.

When I have to wait for the bus, the weight of my backpack seems to keep increasing.

682.6
ware, wear, where

Ware means "a product to be sold"; *wear* means "to have on or to carry on one's body"; *where* asks the question "in what place or in what situation?"

Where can you buy the best cookware to take on a campout— and the best rain gear to wear if it rains?

Using the Right Word 16

■ to, too, two; **waist, waste**; wait, weight; **wear, where**

 For each of the following sentences, write the correct choice from each set of words in parentheses.

1. I am not sure what costume I will (*wear, where*) to Alberto's Halloween party.
   wear

2. I thought about being a knight, but then I'd have the (*wait, weight*) of all that armor.

3. Perhaps if I just wrap a grass skirt around my (*waist, waste*), I'll look like a hula dancer.

4. I do have a wig that I can (*wear, where*).

5. I got it last year, but I didn't use it—what a (*waist, waste*)!

6. I will (*wait, weight*) until this weekend (*to, too, two*) make my costume.

7. I hope making it won't be (*to, too, two*) much work.

8. I'll have (*to, too, two*) days to work on it, but I can't (*waist, waste*) any time because the party is on Monday.

9. Mom and Dad will drive me (*to, too, two*) the party, but they don't want me out (*to, too, two*) late on a school night.

10. I must look at a map to see (*wear, where*) Alberto's house is.

11. He said it's close to the public library; in fact, it's just (*to, too, two*) houses away.

12. It sounds like so much fun—I can't (*wait, weight*)!

Next Step: Write three sentences that show your understanding of the words *where, waste,* and *weight*.

RIGHT WORD

Answers

2. weight
3. waist
4. wear
5. waste
6. wait, to
7. too
8. two, waste
9. to, too
10. where
11. two
12. wait

684

685

684.1
way, weigh

Way means "path or route" or "a series of actions." *Weigh* means "to measure weight."

What is the correct way to weigh **liquid medicines?**

684.2
weather,
whether

Weather refers to the condition of the atmosphere. *Whether* refers to a possibility.

The weather **will determine** whether **I go fishing.**

684.3
week, weak

A *week* is a period of seven days; *weak* means "not strong."

Last week **when I had the flu, I felt light-headed and** weak.

684.4
wet, whet

Wet means "soaked with liquid." *Whet* is a verb that means "to sharpen."

Of course, going swimming means I'll get wet, **but all that exercise really** whets **my appetite.**

684.5
which, witch

Which is a pronoun used to ask "what one or ones?" out of a group. A *witch* is a woman believed to have supernatural powers.

Which of the women in Salem in the 1600s were accused of being witches?

684.6
who, which,
that

When introducing a clause, *who* is used to refer to people; *which* refers to animals and nonliving beings but never to people (it introduces a nonrestrictive, or unnecessary, clause); *that* usually refers to animals or things but can refer to people (it introduces a restrictive, or necessary, clause).

The idea that **pizza is junk food is crazy.**

Pizza, which **is quite nutritious, can be included in a healthy diet.**

My mom, who **is a dietician, said so.**

684.7
who, whom

Who is used as the subject in a sentence; *whom* is used as the object of a preposition or as a direct object.

Who asked you to play tennis?

You beat whom **at tennis? You played tennis with** whom?

NOTE To test for who/whom, arrange the parts of the clause in a subject–verb–direct-object order. *Who* works as the subject, *whom* as the object. (See page 570.)

Using the Right Word 17

 way, weigh; **weather, whether;** week, weak; **which, witch;** who, which, that

For each of the following sentences, write the correct choice from each set of words in parentheses.

1. Ms. Sebastian asked, "(*Which, witch*) one of you can watch the news tonight?"
Which

2. "We need to know what the (*weather, whether*) is going to be like for our field trip to the zoo on Friday," she said.

3. Rain will determine (*weather, whether*) we go or not.

4. Quentin, (*who, which, that*) had already watched the news, said it might rain for the rest of the (*week, weak*).

5. I hoped that (*weather, whether*) forecast, (*who, which, that*) was on channel 13, was wrong.

6. I think the weather forecast (*who, which, that*) is on channel 29 is the best.

7. Once the weather reporter there dressed as a (*which, witch*) on Halloween.

8. I like the (*way, weigh*) she explains things.

9. So I watched her report, and she said there was only a (*week, weak*) chance of rain on Friday.

10. When I (*way, weigh*) the facts, I trust her report the most.

11. So it looks like our field trip, (*who, which, that*) we planned months ago, will happen after all!

Next Step: Write two sentences using the words *which* and *that* correctly. *Hint:* If the clause you're introducing is not required to understand the meaning of the sentence, use *which* and set the clause off with commas. Otherwise, use *that*—without commas—to introduce the clause.

RIGHT WORD

Answers

2. weather
3. whether
4. who, week
5. weather, which
6. that
7. witch
8. way
9. weak
10. weigh
11. which

686.1
who's, whose

Who's is the contraction for "who is." *Whose* is a possessive pronoun, one that shows ownership.

> **Who's the most popular writer today?**
>
> **Whose bike is this?**

686.2
wood, would

Wood is the material that comes from trees; *would* is a form of the verb "will."

> **Sequoia trees live practically forever, but would you believe that the wood from these giants is practically useless?**

686.3
your, you're

Your is a possessive pronoun, one that shows ownership. *You're* is the contraction for "you are."

> **You're the most important person in your parents' lives.**

SCHOOL DAZE

> David, you know **you're** supposed to be doing **your** homework.

> I am, Mom. I'm doing firsthand research on energy conservation.

RIGHT WORD

Using the Right Word 18

■ who's, whose; **wood, would**; your, you're

 For each of the following sentences, write the correct choice from each set of words in parentheses.

1. Dentists say you should floss (*your, you're*) teeth every day.
your

2. (*Whose, Who's*) going to the dentist next month?

3. (*Whose, Who's*) dentist is the friendliest?

4. George Washington's false teeth were not really made of (*wood, would*).

5. It's important to take care of (*your, you're*) teeth if (*your, you're*) going to keep them.

6. (*Wood, Would*) you be willing to brush twice a day?

Using the Right Word Review

 For each of the following sentences, write the correct choice from each set of words in parentheses.

1. The teacher (*accepted, excepted*) (*a, an*) award from the school (*board, bored*).

2. Nadia's (*coarse, course*) hair frizzes when it's humid.

3. Death Valley is a vast (*desert, dessert*).

4. Randall managed to run (*among, between*) the (*to, two*) fences.

5. After some (*miner, minor*) surgery, Will's foot looks (*good, well*).

6. I'd like a (*peace, piece*) of the cake (*which, that*) Dad made.

7. A semi (*can, may*) carry a huge (*amount, number*) of grain.

8. I (*heard, herd*) Mom say, "Please don't (*brake, break*) that vase."

9. Did you (*know, no*) that (*it's, its*) my birthday today?

Answers

 2. Who's
3. Whose
4. wood
5. your, you're
6. Would

 1. accepted, an, board
2. coarse
3. desert
4. between, two
5. minor, good
6. piece, that
7. can, amount
8. heard, break
9. know, it's

Test Prep

For each sentence below, write the letter of the line in which the underlined word or words are used incorrectly. If there is no mistake, choose "D."

1. **A** The prices at two stores
B will determine whether
C we by a new oven.
D correct as is

2. **A** I sent a letter to my
B dear great-grandmother,
C who's 100 years old.
D correct as is

3. **A** When Mom was billed
B for the lawyer's council,
C I heard her gasp.
D correct as is

4. **A** The whole school was
B not allowed to tour the
C capital building at once.
D correct as is

5. **A** Terry, is this the right
B weigh to make tonight's
C ice-cream cake dessert?
D correct as is

6. **A** With a pare of binoculars,
B Grandpa can see farther
C than anyone I know.
D correct as is

7. **A** Iron ore is turned
B into steel in a
C real complicated process.
D correct as is

8. **A** Maria failed to break in
B time, and she passed right
C by her aunt.
D correct as is

9. **A** We are all ready to
B taste a piece of that
C barbequed meet.
D correct as is

10. **A** Do you know which
B bear—grizzly or panda—
C has white and black fur?
D correct as is

11. **A** I just can't except the idea
B that you would choose a
C plain donut over an eclair!
D correct as is

12. **A** Twice a week, Dad does
B weight-bearing exercises
C to tone his waste.
D correct as is

13. **A** In order to give you're
B hair a new look, use
C some temporary dye.
D correct as is

14. **A** A cymbal makes such a
B loud noise because it's
C made of medal.
D correct as is

15. **A** I have scene that even
B minor pain has a big effect
C on people's personal lives.
D correct as is

16. **A** That mountain peak looks
B as a big red triangle
C between two gray ones.
D correct as is

17. **A** The twins will put four
B of they're paintings
C here and two over there.
D correct as is

18. **A** Marcus, please set the
B bass level on the stereo
C to a lower number.
D correct as is

19. **A** Uncle Ted won't let her
B out of his site, so Angie
C says that she's bored.
D correct as is

20. **A** If you bring balloons to
B my party, I'll have fewer
C work to do this week.
D correct as is

RIGHT WORD

Answers

1. C
2. D
3. B
4. C
5. B
6. A

7. C
8. A
9. C
10. D
11. A
12. C

Answers

13. A
14. C
15. A
16. B

17. B
18. D
19. B
20. B

Understanding Sentences

Sentences

A **sentence** is a group of words that expresses a complete thought. A sentence must have both a subject and a predicate. A sentence begins with a capital letter; it ends with a period, a question mark, or an exclamation point.

> I like my teacher this year.
> Will we go on a field trip?
> We get to go to the water park!

Parts of a Sentence

690.1 Subjects	A subject is the part of a sentence that does something or is talked about. **The kids on my block play basketball at the local park.** **We meet after school almost every day.**	
690.2 Simple Subjects	The simple subject is the subject without the words that describe or modify it. (Also see page 502.) **My friend Chester plays basketball on the school team.**	
690.3 Complete Subjects	The complete subject is the simple subject and all the words that modify it. (Also see page 501.) **My friend Chester plays basketball on the school team.**	
690.4 Compound Subjects	A compound subject has two or more simple subjects. (See page 503.) **Chester, Malik, and Meshelle play on our pickup team.** **Lou and I are the best shooters.**	

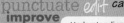

Parts of a Sentence 1

- Simple Subjects
- Complete Subjects

 For each sentence below, write the complete subject. Circle the simple subject.

1. A group of people in one neighborhood wanted to make a difference in society.
   A (group) of people in one neighborhood

2. A special week for doing good things was announced.

3. The positive actions of some kids were reported in the paper.

4. One boy in the neighborhood carried groceries for someone in a wheelchair.

5. Two strong, young men cleaned the hallway in their apartment building.

6. A teenage girl cleaned the kitchen in her home for her mother.

7. Kindness can be something easy to do.

8. Many people doing good things will change the world.

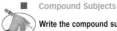 Compound Subjects

 Write the compound subject in each of the following sentences.

9. My cousin and his friends went to the movies.
   cousin, friends

10. The big black box and the gray snake belong to me.

11. Did Bill or Sophia buy balloons for the party?

12. Students, teachers, and school staff enjoy good school assemblies.

13. Simone, Alister, Ramona, Shaleen, and Leia donated canned goods for the hunger drive.

14. Hoping to catch the bus, Raul and Malcolm raced across the lawn.

Answers

2. A special (week) for doing good things

3. The positive (actions) of some kids

4. One (boy) in the neighborhood

5. Two strong, young (men)

6. A teenage (girl)

7. (Kindness)

8. Many (people) doing good things

10. box, snake
11. Bill, Sophia
12. Students, teachers, staff
13. Simone, Alister, Ramona, Shaleen, Leia
14. Raul, Malcolm

Parts of a Sentence . . .

692.1 Predicates

The predicate, which contains the verb, is the part of the sentence that shows action or says something about the subject.

Hunting has reduced the tiger population in India.

692.2 Simple Predicates

The simple predicate is the predicate (verb) without the words that describe or modify it. (See page 502.)

In the past, poachers killed too many African elephants. Poaching is illegal.

692.3 Complete Predicates

The complete predicate is the simple predicate with all the words that modify or describe it. (See page 501.)

In the past, poachers killed too many African elephants. Poaching is illegal.

692.4 Direct Objects

The complete predicate often includes a direct object. The direct object is the noun or pronoun that receives the action of the simple predicate—directly. The direct object answers the question *what* or *whom*. (See page 570.)

Many smaller animals need friends who will speak up for them.

The direct object may be compound.

We all need animals, plants, wetlands, deserts, and forests.

692.5 Indirect Objects

If a sentence has a direct object, it may also have an indirect object. An indirect object is the noun or pronoun that receives the action of the simple predicate—indirectly. An indirect object names the person *to whom* or *for whom* something is done. (See page 570.)

I showed the class my multimedia report on endangered species. (*Class* is the indirect object because it says *to whom* the report was shown.)

Remember, in order for a sentence to have an indirect object, it must first have a direct object.

692.6 Compound Predicates

A compound predicate is composed of two or more simple predicates. (See page 503.)

In 1990 the countries of the world met and banned the sale of ivory.

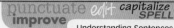

Parts of a Sentence 2

- Simple Predicates
- Compound Predicates

 For each numbered sentence below, write the simple or compound predicate.

Example: Henry "Hank" Aaron hit 755 home runs during his career.

Answer: hit

(1) Henry Aaron was born in Mobile, Alabama, on February 5, 1934, and became a great baseball player. **(2)** For a long time, segregation kept him from the major leagues. **(3)** Finally, he joined the Milwaukee Braves baseball team. **(4)** Hank was one of the most dependable and valuable players on the team. **(5)** He played 3,298 games and batted in 2,297 runs.

- Complete Predicates
- Direct and Indirect Objects

 For each numbered sentence below, write the complete predicate. Underline the direct object once. If there's an indirect object, underline it twice.

Example: Hank Aaron's career spanned 23 years.

Answer: spanned 23 <u>years</u>

(6) Hank won the Most Valuable Player award for 1957. **(7)** He gave baseball a very memorable moment in 1974. **(8)** "Hammerin' Hank" hit his 715th home run in the fourth inning. **(9)** That hit broke Babe Ruth's record. **(10)** Hank Aaron showed the world his determination during his successful career.

SENTENCES

Answers

1. was, became
2. kept
3. joined
4. was
5. played, batted

6. won the Most Valuable Player <u>award</u> for 1957
7. gave <u>baseball</u> a very memorable <u>moment</u> in 1974
8. hit his 715th <u>home run</u>
9. broke Babe Ruth's <u>record</u>
10. showed the <u>world</u> his <u>determination</u> during his successful career

Parts of a Sentence . . .

694.1
Understood Subjects and Predicates

Either the subject or the predicate (or both) may not be stated in a sentence, but both must be clearly understood.

[You] Get involved! (*You* is the understood subject.)

Who needs your help? Animals [do]. (*Do* is the understood predicate.)

What do many animals face? [They face] Extinction. (*They* is the understood subject, and *face* is the understood predicate.)

694.2
Delayed Subjects

In sentences that begin with *there* followed by a form of the "be" verb, the subject usually follows the verb. (See page 570.)

There are laws that protect endangered species. (The subject is *laws*; *are* is the verb.)

The subject is also delayed in questions.

How can we preserve the natural habitat? (*We* is the subject.)

SCHOOL DAZE

John, I've got all the projects. Now which one is yours?

I'm not sure. See if there's one with a missing piece.

694.3
Modifiers

A modifier is a word (adjective, adverb) or a group of words (phrase, clause) that changes or adds to the meaning of another word. (See pages 486–493.)

Many North American zoos and aquariums voluntarily participate in breeding programs that help prevent extinction.

The modifiers in this sentence include the following: *many, North American* (adjectives), *voluntarily* (adverb), *in breeding programs* (phrase), *that help prevent extinction* (clause).

Parts of a Sentence 3

- Understood Subjects and Predicates
- Delayed Subjects

 For each of the sentences below, write down the part or parts named in parentheses.

1. Study for the math test. (*understood subject*)
   You

2. When will we have the test? (*delayed subject*)

3. Tomorrow. (*understood subject and predicate*)

4. Get some help with your homework. (*understood subject*)

5. What is the lesson on page 244? (*delayed subject*)

6. Long division. (*understood predicate*)

7. Be sure to read it carefully. (*understood subject*)

- Modifiers

 Rewrite the following simple sentences, adding modifiers to expand them.

8. Lalita talks.
   Lalita talks endlessly on her cordless phone.

9. Dominic runs.

10. She read a book.

11. Brigitte plays basketball.

12. Theo listened.

13. Habib writes.

14. I will walk.

15. Prem asked a question.

16. Shaquana paints.

SENTENCES

Answers

2. we
3. we will have the test
4. You
5. lesson
6. is the lesson on page 244
7. You

9–16. (Answers will vary.)

Test Prep

Number your paper from 1 to 14. For each underlined part in the following paragraphs, choose the letter or letters from the list below that best describe it.

A. simple subject   **D.** simple predicate

B. complete subject   **E.** complete predicate

C. compound subject   **F.** compound predicate

Today, <u>one in eight people in the United States</u> is Hispanic.
1
Grocery <u>stores</u> now offer more Hispanic foods than ever before.
2
This <u>is changing</u> the buying habits of the rest of the U.S.
3
population. Americans <u>are exploring foods from other cultures,</u>
4
and Hispanic foods top the list of favorites.

Not long ago, <u>tomatillos, serrano peppers, and other</u>
5
<u>Hispanic items</u> were not easy to find. Then, in the early 1990s,
more people were trying Latino cooking. They <u>enjoyed</u>
<u>traditional Latin food such as black beans and rice, mangoes,</u>
6
<u>and avocados.</u> Now most of these ingredients can be found in
just about any grocery store.

Much Hispanic food is spicy. <u>Hundreds of kinds of chile</u>
7
peppers add a kick to plain food. <u>Americans</u> like hot foods. In
8
fact, people across the country now <u>buy and eat</u> more salsa
9
than ketchup.

The <u>avocado and the plantain,</u> a couple of other traditional
10
Hispanic foods, are also becoming more popular. Plantains <u>look</u>
11
like bananas. They <u>can be boiled, baked, or fried, and served</u> as
12
a vegetable or as a sweet dessert. Avocados are the main
ingredient in guacamole. Lately, they are also showing up in
salads and on sandwiches.

The <u>largest Hispanic food company in the U.S., Goya</u>
13
<u>Foods,</u> employs 2,500 people in seven states, Puerto Rico,
Spain, and the Dominican Republic. Many other food
companies are also beginning to supply Hispanic products.
With so many fans, Hispanic <u>food</u> is surely here to stay.
14

SENTENCES

Answers

1. B

2. A

3. D

4. E

5. B and C

6. E

7. B

8. A and B

9. F

Answers

10. C

11. D

12. F

13. B

14. A

Parts of a Sentence . . .

698.1
Clauses

A clause is a group of related words that has both a subject and a verb. (Also see pages 515–517.)

> **a whole chain of plants and animals is affected**
> (*Chain* is the subject, and *is affected* is the verb.)

> **when one species dies out completely**
> (*Species* is the subject; *dies out* is the verb.)

698.2
Independent Clauses

An independent clause presents a complete thought and can stand alone as a sentence.

> **This ancient oak tree may be cut down.**
> **This act could affect more than 200 different species of animals!**
> **Why would anyone want that to happen?**

698.3
Dependent Clauses

A dependent clause does not present a complete thought and cannot stand as a sentence. A dependent clause *depends* on being connected to an independent clause to make sense. Dependent clauses begin with either a subordinating conjunction (*after, although, because, before, if*) or a relative pronoun (*who, whose, which, that*). (See pages 710 and 744 for complete lists.)

> **If this ancient oak tree is cut down, it could affect more than 200 different species of animals!**
> **The tree, which experts think could be 400 years old, provides a home to many different kinds of birds and insects.**

SCHOOL DAZE

Boy, are you in for a real blockbuster next hour!

Yeah . . . Mr. Runge is showing a movie called *A Day in the Life of a Dependent Clause.*

Parts of a Sentence 4

 ▨ Clauses

Write the dependent clause in each numbered sentence below. If the sentence does not contain a dependent clause, write "none."

Example: Spiral notebooks, which are held together with strong wire, can be dangerous in the wrong hands.

Answer: **which are held together with strong wire**

(1) One day in eighth grade, I learned to be more careful around my spiral notebooks. **(2)** During science class, an end of the wire that was sticking out managed to corkscrew its way into my thumb. **(3)** Because I couldn't get it out, Mr. Gibson, my teacher, saw what had happened. **(4)** He clipped the wire from the notebook and tried unsuccessfully to pull the other part out of my thumb. **(5)** Then Mr. Zold, who was the gym teacher, had a go at it. **(6)** Since he couldn't get it out either, I went to the office. **(7)** As the secretary looked at my thumb, she decided right then to call my mother. **(8)** When my mother picked me up, she rushed me to the emergency room at St. Luke's Hospital. **(9)** I didn't have much pain through all of this, but the wire, which was still sticking out of my thumb, sure made me feel foolish. **(10)** After the doctor examined my injury, she froze my thumb and twisted the wire out with some kind of medical pliers. **(11)** From that day on, I always covered the spiral part of my notebooks with tape.

Next Step: Read the dependent clauses that you wrote. Circle the clauses that begin with a subordinating conjunction and underline those beginning with a relative pronoun.

SENTENCES

Answers

1. none
2. <u>that was sticking out</u>
3. ⟨Because I couldn't get it out⟩
4. none
5. <u>who was the gym teacher</u>
6. ⟨Since he couldn't get it out either⟩
7. ⟨As the secretary looked at my thumb⟩
8. ⟨When my mother picked me up⟩
9. <u>which was still sticking out of my thumb</u>
10. ⟨After the doctor examined my injury⟩
11. none

700

Parts of a Sentence . . .

700.1
Phrases

A phrase is a group of related words that lacks either a subject or a predicate (or both). (See pages 519–520.)

guards the house (The predicate lacks a subject.)

the ancient oak tree (The subject lacks a predicate.)

with crooked old limbs (The phrase lacks both a subject and a predicate.)

The ancient oak tree with crooked old limbs guards the house. (Together, the three phrases form a complete thought.)

700.2
Types of Phrases

Phrases usually take their names from the main words that introduce them (prepositional phrase, verb phrase, and so on). They are also named for the function they serve in a sentence (adverb phrase, adjective phrase).

The ancient oak tree (noun phrase)

with crooked old limbs (prepositional phrase)

has stood its guard, (verb phrase)

very stubbornly, (adverb phrase)

protecting the little house. (verbal phrase)

For more information on verbal phrases, see page 730.

SCHOOL DAZE

Give me an example of a **verbal phrase** used as a subject.

Hanging upside down refreshes my brain.

Parts of a Sentence 5

■ Phrases

Write whether each of the following phrases is missing a subject, a predicate, or both. Then use the phrase in a sentence.

1. won a prize
   missing a subject
   My brother won a prize at the school science fair.

2. in Kansas

3. her parents

4. ran her first race

5. was the librarian

6. at a summer festival

7. other kids in the class

8. is not feeling well

9. writes letters to his grandchildren

10. Zack's blond hair

11. between the fence and the oak tree

12. lived in Chicago

Next Step: Go back to the phrases above and identify each as a noun phrase, a verb phrase, or a prepositional phrase.

SENTENCES

Answers

2. missing both; prepositional phrase
3. missing a predicate; noun phrase
4. missing a subject; verb phrase
5. missing a subject; verb phrase
6. missing both; prepositional phrase
7. missing a predicate; noun phrase with an embedded prepositional phrase
8. missing a subject; verb phrase
9. missing a subject; verb phrase with an embedded prepositional phrase
10. missing a predicate; noun phrase
11. missing both; prepositional phrase
12. missing a subject; verb phrase with an embedded prepositional phrase

Using the Parts of Speech

Nouns

A **noun** is a word that names a person, a place, a thing, or an idea.

Person: **John Ulferts** (uncle) Thing: **"Yankee Doodle"** (song)

Place: **Mississippi** (state) Idea: **Labor Day** (holiday)

Kinds of Nouns

Common Nouns	A common noun is any noun that does not name a specific person, place, thing, or idea. These nouns are not capitalized. **woman museum book weekend**
Proper Nouns	A proper noun is the name of a specific person, place, thing, or idea. Proper nouns are capitalized. **Hillary Clinton Central Park *Maniac McGee* Sunday**
Concrete Nouns	A concrete noun names a thing that is physical (can be touched or seen). Concrete nouns can be either proper or common. **space station pencil Statue of Liberty**
Abstract Nouns	An abstract noun names something you can think about but cannot see or touch. Abstract nouns can be either common or proper. **Judaism poverty satisfaction illness**
Collective Nouns	A collective noun names a group or collection of persons, animals, places, or things. Persons: **tribe, congregation, family, class, team** Animals: **flock, herd, gaggle, clutch, litter** Things: **batch, cluster, bunch**
Compound Nouns	A compound noun is made up of two or more words. **football** (written as one word) **high school** (written as two words) **brother-in-law** (written as a hyphenated word)

punctuate *edit* capitalize
improve   SPELL   703
Using the Parts of Speech

Nouns 1

Common and Proper Nouns

 For each line of the following paragraph, write the nouns and label them either "C" for common or "P" for proper.

Example: In Iraq, date-palm trees are a source of wealth.

Answer: *Iraq – P, trees – C, source – C, wealth – C*

1 The trees are passed down from one generation to the next. In
2 Europe, families often pass down jewelry or art. In America, families
3 may save fine furniture or dishes for future generations. Wherever
4 families live, most people are interested in giving their children
5 keepsakes from their past.

Concrete and Abstract Nouns

 For each line of the following paragraph, write the underlined nouns and label them either "C" for concrete or "A" for abstract.

Example: Grandpa said he doesn't know his true age.

Answer: *Grandpa – C, age – A*

6 Research shows that the life span of people is increasing in
7 most countries of the world. Georgia, a country that used to be part
8 of the Soviet Union, has many people who are more than 110 years
9 old. When one old man was asked for the secret to his long life, he
10 replied, "I sleep with my hat on."

Next Step: Write two sentences about your family. Use an abstract noun in one sentence and a proper noun in the other.

PARTS OF SPEECH

Answers

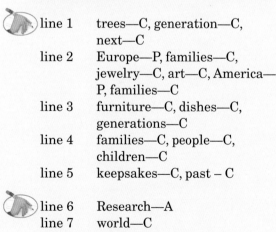

line 1   trees—C, generation—C, next—C

line 2   Europe—P, families—C, jewelry—C, art—C, America—P, families—C

line 3   furniture—C, dishes—C, generations—C

line 4   families—C, people—C, children—C

line 5   keepsakes—C, past – C

line 6   Research—A
line 7   world—C
line 8   people—C, years—A
line 9   man—C, secret—A, life—A
line 10 hat—C

Nouns . . .

Number of Nouns

The number of a noun is either singular or plural.

Singular Nouns

A singular noun names one person, place, thing, or idea.

boy   group   audience   stage   concert   hope

Plural Nouns

A plural noun names more than one person, place, thing, or idea.

boys   groups   audiences   stages   concerts   hopes

Gender of Nouns

Noun Gender

Nouns are grouped according to gender: *feminine, masculine, neuter,* and *indefinite.*

Feminine (female): mother, sister, women, cow, hen
Masculine (male): father, brother, men, bull, rooster
Neuter (neither male nor female): tree, cobweb, closet
Indefinite (male or female): president, duckling, doctor

Uses of Nouns

Subject Nouns

A noun that is the subject of a sentence does something or is talked about in the sentence.

The roots of rap can be traced back to West Africa and Jamaica.

Predicate Nouns

A predicate noun follows a form of the *be* verb (*am, is, are, was, were, being, been*) and renames the subject.

In the 1970s, rap was a street art.

Possessive Nouns

A possessive noun shows possession or ownership.

Early rap had a drummer's beat but no music.
The rapper's words are set to music.

Object Nouns

A noun is an object noun when it is used as the direct object, the indirect object, or the object of the preposition.

Some rappers tell people their story about life in the city.
(indirect object: *people*; direct object: *story*)
Rap is now a common music choice in this country. (object of the preposition: *country*)

punctuate *edit* capitalize
improve SPELL **705**
Using the Parts of Speech

Nouns 2

 Number and Gender of Nouns

For each of the following sentences, write the correct singular or plural noun from the choices in parentheses. Then write whether it is masculine, feminine, neuter, or indefinite.

1. Hanukkah is a happy Jewish (*holiday, holidays*).
   holiday (neuter)
2. It usually falls during the (*month, months*) of December.
3. The holiday includes eight (*day, days*) of celebration.
4. All the (*member, members*) of the family take part.
5. My (*aunt, aunts*) makes a huge dinner.
6. My (*brother, brothers*) like to light the candles on the menorah.

 Subject, Predicate, Possessive, and Object Nouns

Identify each underlined noun in the sentences below as a subject noun, a predicate noun, a possessive noun, or an object noun.

7. One of Hanukkah's symbols is a dreidel.
   possessive noun, predicate noun
8. The dreidel is a square-shaped top with letters on each side.
9. The letters on the dreidel stand for the words "A Great Miracle Happened There."
10. In ancient times, the study of the Jewish holy books was forbidden in some countries.
11. Soldiers checking Jewish homes would find people playing with the dreidel.
12. The dreidel's meaning is that freedom is a miracle.

Answers

2. month (neuter)
3. days (neuter)
4. members (indefinite)
5. aunt (feminine)
6. brothers (masculine)

8. subject noun
9. subject noun, object noun
10. object noun, subject noun
11. subject noun, object noun
12. possessive noun, subject noun

Pronouns

A **pronoun** is a word used in place of a noun. Some examples are *I, you, he, she, it, we, they, his, hers, her, its, me, myself, us, yours,* and so on.

Without pronouns: Kevin said Kevin would be going to Kevin's grandmother's house this weekend.

With pronouns: Kevin said he would be going to his grandmother's house this weekend.

706.1 Antecedents

An antecedent is the noun that the pronoun refers to or replaces. All pronouns (except interrogative and indefinite pronouns) have antecedents. (See page 474.)

Jamal and Rick tried out for the team, and they both made it. (*They* refers to *Jamal* and *Rick*; *it* refers to *team*.)

NOTE Pronouns must agree with their antecedents in number, person, and gender.

Types of Pronouns

There are several types of pronouns. The most common type is the personal pronoun. (See the chart on page 710.)

706.2 Personal Pronouns

A personal pronoun takes the place of a specific person (or thing) in a sentence. Some common personal pronouns are *I, you, he, she, it, we,* and *they*.

Suriana would not like to live in Buffalo, New York, because she does not like snow.

706.3 Relative Pronouns

A relative pronoun is both a pronoun and a connecting word. It connects a dependent clause to an independent clause in a complex sentence. Relative pronouns include *who, whose, which,* and *that*. (See 684.6.)

Buffalo, which often gets more than eight feet of snow in a year, is on the northeast shore of Lake Erie.

The United States city that gets the most snow is Valdez, Alaska.

706.4 Interrogative Pronouns

An interrogative pronoun helps ask a question.

Who wants to go to Alaska?

Which of the cities would you visit?

Whom would you like to travel with?

What did you say?

---

punctuate *edit* capitalize
improve SPELL **707**
Using the Parts of Speech

Pronouns 1

■ Antecedents and Personal, Relative, and Interrogative Pronouns

The type of pronoun that's missing is indicated at the end of each sentence. First write the antecedent of the missing pronoun and then write a pronoun that agrees with it. (See the chart on page 710.)

NOTE An interrogative pronoun doesn't have an antecedent, so write "none" in place of the antecedent.

1. Kathryn says _____ favorite holiday is Labor Day. (*personal*)
Kathryn – her

2. Holidays have been celebrated for a long time, and _____ were originally known as "holy days." (*personal*)

3. Because many people traveled during the holy days, tradesmen along the way were there to meet _____. (*personal*)

4. Fairs and bazaars, _____ became part of many holiday celebrations, encouraged spending. (*relative*)

5. Now that spending is a big part of these holidays, many products are associated with _____. (*personal*)

6. _____ can guess what my favorite holiday is? (*interrogative*)

7. It is a holiday _____ is celebrated each January. (*relative*)

8. Sunee, if _____ guessed New Year's Day, _____ are correct. (*personal, personal*)

9. Aunt Fabiola wishes New Year's Day were celebrated in March; _____ thinks that's when the earth is new again. (*personal*)

10. _____ of the holidays is your favorite? (*interrogative*)

Next Step: Write two sentences about a holiday. Use pronouns in both sentences. Exchange papers with a classmate and circle the antecedents in each other's sentences.

PARTS OF SPEECH

Answers

2. Holidays—they
3. people—them
4. Fairs, bazaars—which
5. holidays—them
6. none—Who
7. holiday—that
8. Sunee—you, Sunee—you
9. Aunt Fabiola—she
10. none—Which

Pronouns . . .

Types of Pronouns

708.1
Demonstrative Pronouns

A demonstrative pronoun points out or identifies a noun without naming the noun. When used together in a sentence, *this* and *that* distinguish one item from another, and *these* and *those* distinguish one group from another. (See page 710.)

> **This is a great idea; that was a nightmare.**

> **These are my favorite foods, and those are definitely not.**

NOTE When these words are used before a noun, they are *not* pronouns; rather, they are demonstrative adjectives.

> **Coming to this picnic was fun—and those ants think so, too.**

708.2
Intensive Pronouns

An intensive pronoun emphasizes, or *intensifies*, the noun or pronoun it refers to. Common intensive pronouns include *itself, myself, himself, herself,* and *yourself.*

> **Though the chameleon's quick-change act protects it from predators, the lizard itself can catch insects 10 inches away with its long, sticky tongue.**

> **When a chameleon changes its skin color—seemingly matching the background—the background colors themselves do not affect the chameleon's color changes.**

NOTE These sentences would be complete without the intensive pronoun. The pronoun simply emphasizes a particular noun.

708.3
Reflexive Pronouns

A reflexive pronoun refers back to the subject of a sentence, and it is always an object (never a subject) in a sentence. Reflexive pronouns are the same as the intensive pronouns—*itself, myself, himself, herself, yourself,* and so on.

> **A chameleon protects itself from danger by changing colors.**
> (direct object)

> **A chameleon can give itself tasty meals of unsuspecting insects.**
> (indirect object)

> **I wish I could claim some of its amazing powers for myself.**
> (object of the preposition)

NOTE Unlike sentences with intensive pronouns, these sentences would *not* be complete without the reflexive pronouns.

Pronouns 2

■ Demonstrative Pronouns

Write whether the underlined word is a demonstrative adjective or a demonstrative pronoun. *Extra challenge:* Rewrite any sentence that contains a demonstrative adjective so that the word is used as a pronoun instead.

1. <u>This</u> pie is good!
   demonstrative adjective   This is good pie!

2. Is <u>that</u> ring valuable?

3. <u>Those</u> cars are the finest available.

4. <u>That</u> was useful two years ago, but not now.

5. <u>These</u> apples are expensive.

■ Intensive Pronouns
■ Reflexive Pronouns

For each sentence below, write whether the underlined pronoun is intensive or reflexive.

6. Although Elijah McCoy <u>himself</u> was not a slave, he was the son of former slaves.
   intensive

7. In 1858, Elijah McCoy traveled from Canada to Scotland to better <u>himself</u> with a college education.

8. McCoy earned a degree in engineering and then moved to Michigan, where he went into business for <u>himself</u>.

9. Elijah believed that he <u>himself</u> could invent products that would save companies both time and money.

10. He invented a tool that allowed a machine to oil <u>itself</u>.

11. Over time, the oiling tool <u>itself</u> became so popular that people would ask whether it was the "real McCoy."

Answers

2. demonstrative adjective
   Is that a valuable ring?

3. demonstrative adjective
   Those are the finest cars available.

4. demonstrative pronoun

5. demonstrative adjective
   These are expensive apples.

7. reflexive
8. reflexive
9. intensive
10. reflexive
11. intensive

Pronouns . . .
Types of Pronouns

An indefinite pronoun is a pronoun that does not have a specific antecedent (the noun or pronoun it replaces). (See page 475.)

Everything about the chameleon is fascinating.

Someone donated a chameleon to our class.

Anyone who brings in a live insect can feed our chameleon.

Types of Pronouns

Personal Pronouns

I, me, mine, my, we, us, our, ours, you, your, yours, they, them, their, theirs, he, him, his, she, her, hers, it, its

Relative Pronouns

who, whose, whom, which, what, that, whoever, whomever, whichever, whatever

Interrogative Pronouns

who, whose, whom, which, what

Demonstrative Pronouns

this, that, these, those

Intensive and Reflexive Pronouns

myself, himself, herself, itself, yourself, yourselves, themselves, ourselves

Indefinite Pronouns

all	both	everything	nobody	several
another	each	few	none	some
any	each one	many	no one	somebody
anybody	either	most	nothing	someone
anyone	everybody	much	one	something
anything	everyone	neither	other	such

punctuate *edit* capitalize
improve SPELL
Using the Parts of Speech 711

Pronouns 3

■ Indefinite Pronouns

 Write the indefinite pronoun in each of the following sentences.

1. Rodeo events offer entertainment for everybody.
  everybody

2. Most are designed to showcase a person's skill and strength.

3. Calf roping is enjoyed by many.

4. Nothing harmful is done to the animals.

5. Each must be lassoed, thrown down, and tied.

6. None are hurt, and riders earn points for speed.

7. No one can deny that bull riding is an exciting event.

Pronoun Review

 For each numbered sentence below, identify the underlined pronoun as "personal," "relative," or "indefinite."

Example: In a rodeo, even the clowns have their own event.
Answer: personal

(1) Rodeo events can be dangerous, and sometimes someone gets hurt. **(2)** Bull riding, which is the most dangerous event, is very exciting. **(3)** The rider must stay on a bucking bull for eight seconds, holding on to a rope that is tied around the bull's middle.

Women riders enjoy the rodeo as well. **(4)** They have their own events, including barrel racing. **(5)** The contestants ride around a series of three barrels as fast as possible without knocking any over.

Those are just a couple of the many events at a rodeo. **(6)** Anyone may take part, but he or she had better know how to ride!

Answers

2. Most
3. many
4. Nothing
5. Each
6. None
7. No one

1. indefinite
2. relative
3. relative
4. personal
5. indefinite
6. personal

Pronouns . . .

punctuate *edit* capitalize
improve   SPELL   713
Using the Parts of Speech

712.1
Singular and Plural Pronouns

Number of a Pronoun

Pronouns can be either singular or plural in number.

Singular: I, you, he, she, it   Plural: we, you, they

NOTE The pronouns *you, your,* and *yours* may be singular or plural.

Person of a Pronoun

The person of a pronoun tells whether the pronoun is speaking, being spoken to, or being spoken about. (See page 474.)

712.2
First Person Pronouns

A first-person pronoun is used in place of the name of the speaker or speakers.

I am speaking.   We are speaking.

712.3
Second Person Pronouns

A second-person pronoun is used to name the person or thing spoken to.

Eliza, will you please take out the garbage?

You better stop grumbling!

712.4
Third Person Pronouns

A third-person pronoun is used to name the person or thing spoken about.

Bill should listen if he wants to learn the words to this song.

Charisse said that she already knows them.

They will perform the song in the talent show.

Uses of Pronouns

A pronoun can be used as a subject, as an object, or to show possession. (See the chart on page 714.)

712.5
Subject Pronouns

A subject pronoun is used as the subject of a sentence (*I, you, he, she, it, we, they*).

I like to surf the Net.

A subject pronoun is also used after a form of the *be* verb (*am, is, are, was, were, being, been*) if it repeats the subject. (See "Predicate Nouns," 704.5.)

"This is she," Mom replied into the telephone.

"Yes, it was I," admitted the child who had eaten the cookies.

Pronouns 4

■ Number of a Pronoun
■ Person of a Pronoun

For each of the following sentences, write the pronouns and identify them as first, second, or third person. (See the chart on page 714.)

1. We studied the Civil War in my history class.
   We (first person), my (first person)

2. Abraham Lincoln was elected president of the United States in 1860; he was the sixteenth president.

3. In January of 1861, South Carolina decided it would leave the United States of America.

4. In class, we learned that 11 states decided to leave the United States, and they created the Confederate States of America.

5. In February of 1861, the Confederate States elected Jefferson Davis as their new president.

6. He became the first—and last—president of the Confederacy.

7. Our teacher said, "I will test you on the Civil War next week."

8. I said, "José, I am sure you can pass the test easily."

9. "Your study habits are better than mine."

10. The night before the test, we reviewed the study sheets together.

11. Dad brought us some brownies and chocolate milk.

12. José told me, "You could try rereading each chapter carefully, Joanne."

13. He was right; it helped me get a passing grade.

Next Step: Look at your answers for the exercise above. Underline the pronouns that are singular and circle those that are plural.

PARTS OF SPEECH

Answers

2. he (third person)

3. it (third person)

4. we (first person)
   they (third person)

5. their (third person)

6. He (third person)

7. Our (first person), I (first person), you (second person)

8. I (first person), I (first person), you (second person)

9. Your (second person), mine (first person)

10. we (first person)

11. us (first person)

12. me (first person), You (second person)

13. He (third person), it (third person), me (first person)

714

Pronouns . . .
Uses of Pronouns

714.1
Object Pronouns

An object pronoun (*me, you, him, her, it, us, them*) can be used as the object of a verb or preposition. (See 692.4, 692.5, and 742.1.)

> I'll call her as soon as I can. (direct object)
> Hand me the phone book, please. (indirect object)
> She thinks these flowers are from you. (object of the preposition)

714.2
Possessive Pronouns

A possessive pronoun shows possession or ownership. These possessive pronouns function as adjectives before nouns: *my, our, his, her, their, its,* and *your*.

> School workers are painting our classroom this summer. Its walls will look much better.

These possessive pronouns can be used after verbs: *mine, ours, hers, his, theirs,* and *yours*.

> I'm pretty sure this backpack is mine and that one is his.

NOTE An apostrophe is not needed with a possessive pronoun to show possession.

Uses of Personal Pronouns

	Singular Pronouns			Plural Pronouns		
	Subject Pronouns	Possessive Pronouns	Object Pronouns	Subject Pronouns	Possessive Pronouns	Object Pronouns
First Person	I	my, mine	me	we	our, ours	us
Second Person	you	your, yours	you	you	your, yours	you
Third Person	he	his	him	they	their, theirs	them
	she	her, hers	her			
	it	its	it			

---

punctuate *edit* capitalize
improve   SPELL   **715**
Using the Parts of Speech

Pronouns 5
■ Subject, Object, and Possessive Pronouns

 For each numbered sentence in the paragraphs below, identify the underlined pronoun as a subject, an object, or a possessive pronoun.

> *Example:* Roberto Clemente liked many sports, but his favorite sport was baseball.
> *Answer:* **possessive pronoun**

(1) Roberto Clemente was born in Puerto Rico in 1934; he was the youngest of four children. **(2)** As a young boy, Roberto discovered sports were easy for him. **(3)** He played baseball for several teams, but his big break came when he signed with the Brooklyn Dodgers. **(4)** At first, they sent Roberto to play on a minor-league team. **(5)** In 1954, the Pittsburgh Pirates drafted him, and he spent 17 years with them. **(6)** Roberto was named the most valuable player in a World Series, and it was a great honor for him.

(7) For many years, Clemente helped those in need. **(8)** When a devastating earthquake hit Nicaragua in 1972, Clemente helped arrange relief for Nicaragua and its people. **(9)** Determined to see that food and other supplies got to the people, he chartered a plane and accompanied four others on the flight. **(10)** Before the flight, Roberto's wife said she was worried about his safety. **(11)** On December 31, 1972, the plane flew into storm winds that caused it to crash, leaving no survivors. **(12)** Today, many people remember Roberto Clemente not only for his baseball skills but also for his desire to help others.

Next Step: Go back to the "Colons" exercise on page 597. Identify the pronouns in the last paragraph of the letter as subject, object, or possessive pronouns.

PARTS OF SPEECH

Answers

1. subject pronoun
2. object pronoun
3. possessive pronoun
4. subject pronoun
5. object pronoun
6. subject pronoun
7. object pronoun
8. possessive pronoun
9. subject pronoun
10. subject pronoun
11. object pronoun
12. possessive pronoun

punctuate *edit* capitalize SPELL
improve
Using the Parts of Speech   717

Test Prep

Number your paper from 1 to 18. For each underlined word in the paragraphs below, write the letter of the best description from the following list.

A. subject noun
B. object noun
C. predicate noun
D. subject pronoun
E. object pronoun
F. possessive pronoun

My <u>aunt</u> is a <u>nurse</u>. <u>She</u> works in a doctor's office. Aunt
1 2 3
Margy made a <u>decision</u> a few years ago to finish college and get
4
<u>her</u> nursing degree. I really admire <u>her</u> for that because she is
5 6 7
a busy <u>wife</u> and mother who took the time to improve herself.
8
<u>Aunt Margy</u> knew that she would need her family's
9
support while she was in school. She asked <u>Uncle Tim</u>, her
10
husband, to spend a little more time with the kids. <u>They</u> all
11
agreed to help out more around the <u>house</u>.
12
<u>My</u> aunt went to school part-time for her degree, and she
13
worked hard for <u>it</u>. She studied her <u>books</u> and practiced her
14 15
skills. <u>Uncle Tim</u> helped her review for tests. The whole <u>family</u>
16 17
went to the graduation ceremony, where Aunt Margy saw <u>our</u>
18
great pride in her achievement.

 Write the letter of the answer that correctly completes each of the following sentences.

19. Mari and _____ went to the movies yesterday.
    A. me   **B.** I   **C.** her

20. On the way, Mari lost _____ new wallet.
    A. hers   **B.** she   **C.** her

21. Luckily, Mom gave _____ some extra money.
    A. me   **B.** I   **C.** he

22. It was enough for both of _____.
    A. we   **B.** us   **C.** ours

23. _____ passed the park on the way back home.
    A. We   **B.** Us   **C.** Ours

24. A woman said that _____ had found a wallet.
    A. us   **B.** her   **C.** she

25. The woman asked Mari if it was _____.
    A. hers   **B.** her   **C.** they

26. Mari excitedly said, "Yes, it is _____!"
    A. it   **B.** me   **C.** mine

27. Mari asked the woman, "May I offer _____ a reward?"
    A. you   **B.** yours   **C.** she

28. It was such a relief for both Mari and _____.
    A. me   **B.** I   **C.** we

Answers

1. A
2. C
3. D
4. B
5. F
6. D
7. E
8. C
9. A
10. B
11. D
12. B
13. F
14. E
15. B
16. A
17. A
18. F

Answers

19. B
20. C
21. A
22. B
23. A
24. C
25. A
26. C
27. A
28. A

718

Verbs

A **verb** is a word that shows action or links a subject to another word in a sentence.

> Tornadoes cause tremendous damage. (action verb)
> The weather is often calm before a storm. (linking verb)

Types of Verbs

718.1
Action Verbs

An action verb tells what the subject is doing. (See page 480.)

> Natural disasters hit the globe nearly every day.

718.2
Linking Verbs

A linking verb connects—or links—a subject to a noun or an adjective in the predicate. The most common linking verbs are forms of the verb *be* (*is, are, was, were, being, been, am*). Verbs such as *smell, look, taste, feel, remain, turn, appear, become, sound, seem, grow,* and *stay* can also be linking verbs. (See page 480.)

> The San Andreas Fault is an earthquake zone in California. (The linking verb *is* connects the subject to the predicate noun *zone.*)
> Earthquakes there are fairly common. (The linking verb *are* connects the subject to the predicate adjective *common.*)

718.3
Helping Verbs

A helping verb (also called an auxiliary verb) helps the main verb express tense and voice. The most common helping verbs are *shall, will, should, would, could, must, might, can, may, have, had, has, do, did,* and the forms of the verb *be—is, are, was, were, am, being, been.* (See pages 482–484.)

> It has been estimated that 500,000 earthquakes occur around the world every year. (These helping verbs indicate that the tense is present perfect and the voice is passive.)
> Fortunately, only about 100 of those will cause damage. (*Will* helps express the future tense of the verb.)

---

punctuate edit capitalize improve SPELL
Using the Parts of Speech
719

Verbs 1 ■ Action Verbs, Linking Verbs, and Helping Verbs

Number your paper from 1 to 10. Then identify the underlined verbs as action, linking, or helping verbs.

> *Example:* The Baldwin Locomotive Works <u>built</u> 75,000 locomotives.
> *Answer: action*

1. Matthias Baldwin <u>founded</u> the Baldwin Locomotive Works in
2. 1831. His company <u>built</u> train locomotives to fit the needs of his
3. customers. Baldwin technicians <u>designed</u> powerful steam engines,
4. and buyers <u>were</u> pleased. The company <u>grew</u> bigger.
5. Steam engines eventually <u>were</u> <u>challenged</u> by diesel engines.
6. One steam locomotive <u>was</u> more powerful than one diesel
7. locomotive, but the train engineers <u>used</u> several diesel engines
8. hooked together to pull more freight. The Age of Steam <u>was</u> <u>coming</u>
9. to an end. After more than 120 years, Baldwin Works <u>closed</u> its
10. doors in 1954.

Write the linking verb in each of the following sentences. Then write the word it links the subject to and tell whether it is a noun or an adjective.

11. Railroads were the fastest transportation in the 1800s.
were, transportation (noun)
12. The South Carolina Railroad was the first company to have a passenger train.
13. In 1852, the Pacific Railroad of Missouri became the first railroad in the West.
14. To some people, trains seemed scary.
15. Today, automobiles are the most common form of passenger travel.
16. However, many people remain fans of train travel.

Answers

line 1   action
line 2   action
line 3   action
line 4   linking, action
line 5   helping, action
line 6   linking
line 7   action
line 8   helping, action
line 9   action

12. was, company (noun)
13. became, railroad (noun)
14. seemed, scary (adjective)
15. are, form (noun)
16. remain, fans (noun)

punctuate *edit* capitalize
improve   SPELL   **721**
Using the Parts of Speech

Verbs . . .

Tenses of Verbs

A verb has three principal parts: *present, past,* and *past participle.* (The part used with the helping verbs *has, have,* or *had* is called the past participle.)

All six of the tenses are formed from these principal parts. The past and past participle of regular verbs are formed by adding *ed* to the present tense. The past and past participle of irregular verbs are formed with different spellings. (See the chart on page 722.)

720.1
Present Tense Verbs

The present tense of a verb expresses action (or a state of being) that is happening now or that happens continually or regularly. (See page 483.)

The universe is gigantic. It takes my breath away.

720.2
Past Tense Verbs

The past tense of a verb expresses action (or a state of being) that was completed in the past. (See page 483.)

To most people many years ago, the universe was the earth, the sun, and some stars. The universe reached only as far as the eye could see.

720.3
Future Tense Verbs

The future tense of a verb expresses action that *will* take place. (See page 483.)

Maybe I will visit another galaxy in my lifetime.
Somebody will find a way to do it.

SCHOOL DAZE

I **know** the answer!

Okay, but I **said** you **will have** to sing the answer . . . go ahead!

Verbs 2

■ Present Tense Verbs
■ Past Tense Verbs
■ Future Tense Verbs

 For each of the following sentences, write the verb or verbs and identify them as "present tense," "past tense," or "future tense."

1. The "Great War" started in Europe more than 90 years ago.
   started (past tense)

2. Now we call that war World War I.

3. The conflict began in the summer of 1914.

4. The Central Powers (Germany and Austria-Hungary) fought against the Allies.

5. England and France, two countries on the Allied side, sent more than 2 million soldiers to the battlefields.

6. England and France are still allies (friends) to this day.

7. Both countries also maintain a friendly relationship with the United States.

8. These three nations probably will remain allies for years to come.

9. Leaders of these countries meet together often.

10. These nations depend on one another economically.

11. They will support each other during times of crisis.

12. It is good to have political friends!

Next Step: Whom do you depend on? Write three sentences about this person. Write one sentence for each of the verb tenses: *past, present,* and *future.*

PARTS OF SPEECH

Answers

2. call (present tense)
3. began (past tense)
4. fought (past tense)
5. sent (past tense)
6. are (present tense)
7. maintain (present tense)
8. will remain (future tense)
9. meet (present tense)
10. depend (present tense)
11. will support (future tense)
12. is (present tense)

Common Irregular Verbs and Their Principal Parts

The principal parts of the common irregular verbs are listed below. The part used with the helping verbs *has, have,* or *had* is called the **past participle**. (Also see page 481.)

Present Tense: I write.   She hides.
Past Tense: Earlier I wrote.   Earlier she hid.
Past Participle: I have written.   She has hidden.

Present Tense	Past Tense	Past Participle	Present Tense	Past Tense	Past Participle
am, is, are	was, were	been	lead	led	led
begin	began	begun	lie (recline)	lay	lain
bid (offer)	bid	bid	lie (deceive)	lied	lied
bid (order)	bade	bidden	make	made	made
bite	bit	bitten	ride	rode	ridden
blow	blew	blown	ring	rang	rung
break	broke	broken	rise	rose	risen
bring	brought	brought	run	ran	run
burst	burst	burst	see	saw	seen
buy	bought	bought	set	set	set
catch	caught	caught	shake	shook	shaken
come	came	come	shine (polish)	shined	shined
dive	dived, dove	dived	shine (light)	shone	shone
do	did	done	shrink	shrank	shrunk
draw	drew	drawn	sing	sang, sung	sung
drink	drank	drunk	sink	sank, sunk	sunk
drive	drove	driven	sit	sat	sat
eat	ate	eaten	sleep	slept	slept
fall	fell	fallen	speak	spoke	spoken
fight	fought	fought	spring	sprang, sprung	sprung
flee	fled	fled	steal	stole	stolen
fly	flew	flown	strive	strove	striven
forsake	forsook	forsaken	swear	swore	sworn
freeze	froze	frozen	swim	swam	swum
get	got	gotten, got	swing	swung	swung
give	gave	given	take	took	taken
go	went	gone	tear	tore	torn
grow	grew	grown	throw	threw	thrown
hang (execute)	hanged	hanged	wake	woke, waked	woken, waked
hang (dangle)	hung	hung	wear	wore	worn
hide	hid	hidden, hid	weave	wove	woven
know	knew	known	wring	wrung	wrung
lay (place)	laid	laid	write	wrote	written

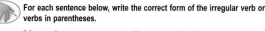
Verbs 3

- Present Tense Verbs
- Past Tense Verbs
- Past Participle Verbs

 For each sentence below, write the correct form of the irregular verb or verbs in parentheses.

1. I have always _____ a roller-coaster fan. (*am*)
   been

2. Mom _____ us to the amusement park last Saturday. (*take*)

3. Alberto and Jim _____ along. (*come*)

4. They had _____ at my house the night before, and we nearly _____ with excitement. (*sleep, burst*)

5. On Saturday morning, Mom _____ us up at 7:00, and we _____ a light breakfast. (*wake, eat*)

6. As soon as we arrived at the park, we _____ in line for the super roller coaster. (*get*)

7. If we had _____ that we would wait more than an hour, we wouldn't have _____ in line. (*know, get*)

8. After we _____ the roller coaster, we _____ from the water fountain. (*ride, drink*)

9. Dad had _____ me money to purchase a souvenir. (*give*)

10. Just as I _____ my money on the counter, a gust of wind _____ it away. (*lay, blow*)

11. I _____ after it, and, luckily, I _____ it. (*run, catch*)

12. You have never _____ someone so relieved! (*see*)

13. I _____ a cap with the park's name on the front. (*buy*)

Next Step: Write three sentences using the present tense, past tense, and past participle of the word *begin*.

Answers

2. took
3. came
4. slept, burst
5. woke, ate
6. got
7. known, gotten
8. rode, drank
9. given
10. laid, blew
11. ran, caught
12. seen
13. bought

Verbs . . .

Tenses of Verbs

724.1
Present Perfect Tense Verbs

The present perfect tense verb expresses action that began in the past but continues or is completed in the present. The present perfect tense is formed by adding *has* or *have* to the past participle. (Also see page 484.)

> **I have wondered** for some time how the stars got their names.
>
> A visible star **has emitted** light for thousands of years.

724.2
Past Perfect Tense Verbs

The past perfect tense verb expresses action that began in the past and was completed in the past. This tense is formed by adding *had* to the past participle. (Also see page 484.)

> **I had hoped** to see a shooting star on our camping trip.

724.3
Future Perfect Tense Verbs

A future perfect tense verb expresses action that will begin in the future and will be completed by a specific time in the future. The future perfect tense is formed by adding *will have* to the past participle. (Also see page 484.)

> By the middle of this century, we probably **will have discovered** many more stars, planets, and galaxies.

724.4
Present Continuous Tense Verbs

A present continuous tense verb expresses action that is not completed at the time of stating it. The present continuous tense is formed by adding *am, is,* or *are* to the *ing* form of the main verb.

> Scientists **are learning** a great deal from their study of the sky.

724.5
Past Continuous Tense Verbs

A past continuous tense verb expresses action that was happening at a certain time in the past. This tense is formed by adding *was* or *were* to the *ing* form of the main verb.

> Astronomers **were beginning** their quest for knowledge hundreds of years ago.

724.6
Future Continuous Tense Verbs

A future continuous tense verb expresses action that will take place at a certain time in the future. This tense is formed by adding *will be* to the *ing* form of the main verb.

> Someday astronauts **will be going** to Mars.

This tense can also be formed by adding a phrase noting the future (*are going to*) plus *be* to the *ing* form of the main verb.

> They **are going to be performing** many experiments.

punctuate *edit* capitalize
improve SPELL
Using the Parts of Speech
725

Verbs 4

- ■ Present Perfect Tense Verbs
- ■ Past Perfect Tense Verbs
- ■ Future Perfect Tense Verbs

 For each of the sentences below, write the verb and identify the tense as "present perfect," "past perfect," or "future perfect."

1. Students in the ecology club had thought quite a bit about the environment.

had thought (past perfect)

2. Progress has caused some negative effects on our world.

3. As early as the 1970s, research scientists in Antarctica had noticed the growth of a hole in our atmosphere's ozone layer.

4. The hole has grown due to pollution.

5. The ozone layer has protected us from the sun's dangerous radiation since the beginning of time.

6. Scientists have attempted new and better ways to stop pollution.

7. By 2010, manufacturers will have removed many forms of air pollution.

8. Perhaps by the middle of the century, our planet will have begun to heal.

9. The ecology club students had wanted to help in some way.

10. They have worked to spread the word about saving the ozone.

11. They will have made 100 posters by the end of the week.

12. The club members have promised to put the posters up this weekend.

Next Step: Write two sentences about what your community is doing to reduce pollution. Use a perfect tense verb in each sentence.

PARTS OF SPEECH

Answers

2. has caused (present perfect)
3. had noticed (past perfect)
4. has grown (present perfect)
5. has protected (present perfect)
6. have attempted (present perfect)
7. will have removed (future perfect)
8. will have begun (future perfect)
9. had wanted (past perfect)
10. have worked (present perfect)
11. will have made (future perfect)
12. have promised (present perfect)

Verbs . . .
Forms of Verbs

726.1
Active or Passive Voice

The voice of a verb tells you whether the subject is doing the action or is receiving the action. A verb is in the active voice (in any tense) if the subject is doing the action in a sentence. (See page 482.)

> I dream of going to galaxies light-years from Earth.

> I will travel in an ultrafast spaceship.

A verb is in the passive voice if the subject is not doing the action. The action is done *by* someone or something else. The passive voice is always indicated with a helping verb plus a past participle or a past tense verb.

> My daydreams often are shattered by reality. (The subject *daydreams* is not doing the action.)

> Of course, reality can be seen differently by different people. (The subject *reality* is not doing the action.)

Tense	Active Voice		Passive Voice	
	Singular	**Plural**	**Singular**	**Plural**
Present Tense	I find	we find	I am found	we are found
	you find	you find	you are found	you are found
	he/she/it finds	they find	he/she/it is found	they are found
Past Tense	I found	we found	I was found	we were found
	you found	you found	you were found	you were found
	he found	they found	he/she/it was found	they were found
Future Tense	I will find	we will find	I will be found	we will be found
	you will find	you will find	you will be found	you will be found
	he will find	they will find	he/she/it will be found	they will be found
Present Perfect	I have found	we have found	I have been found	we have been found
	you have found	you have found	you have been found	you have been found
	he has found	they have found	he/she/it has been found	they have been found
Past Perfect	I had found	we had found	I had been found	we had been found
	you had found	you had found	you had been found	you had been found
	he had found	they had found	he/she/it had been found	they had been found
Future Perfect	I will have found	we will have found	I will have been found	we will have been found
	you will have found	you will have found	you will have been found	you will have been found
	he will have found	they will have found	he/she/it will have been found	they will have been found

punctuate *edit* capitalize
improve SPELL
Using the Parts of Speech

Verbs 5
■ Active or Passive Voice

 For each sentence below, write the verb and tell whether it is active (doing the action) or passive (receiving the action).

1. William Shakespeare has been called the greatest writer of the English language.
   has been called (passive)

2. People feel his influence in many ways.

3. Many words and phrases were invented by Shakespeare.

4. He created the words "moonbeam," "elbow," and "buzzer."

5. Most people know Shakespeare best for his plays.

6. He wrote 37 plays in his lifetime.

7. Additional plays might have been written by Shakespeare and another writer.

8. Shakespeare also created beautiful poems, including many sonnets.

 Rewrite each of the following sentences in the active voice. Add or delete words as necessary.

9. Shakespeare's plays have been enjoyed by millions of people.
   Millions of people have enjoyed Shakespeare's plays.

10. His plays have been explained in different ways by different audiences.

11. The play *The Taming of the Shrew* was made by Gil Junger into the movie *10 Things I Hate About You.*

12. The part of the "shrew" was played by Julia Stiles.

13. Whatever you think about the play, it will be enjoyed by you.

14. Shakespeare's plays are loved by people who have read them.

Answers

2. feel (active)
3. were invented (passive)
4. created (active)
5. know (active)
6. wrote (active)
7. might have been written (passive)
8. created (active)

(Answers will vary.)

10. Different audiences have explained his plays in different ways.
11. Gil Junger made the play *The Taming of the Shrew* into the movie *10 Things I Hate About You.*
12. Julia Stiles played the part of the "shrew."
13. Whatever you think about the play, you will enjoy it.
14. People who have read Shakespeare's plays love them.

punctuate *edit* capitalize
SPELL
improve
Using the Parts of Speech
729

Verbs . . .

Forms of Verbs

728.1
Singular and Plural Verbs

A singular subject needs a singular verb. A plural subject needs a plural verb. For action verbs, only the third-person singular verb form is different: *I wonder, we wonder, you wonder, she wonders, they wonder*. Some linking verbs, however, have several different forms.

First Person	**Singular:** I am (or was) **a good student.**
	Plural: We are (or were) **good students.**
Second Person	**Singular:** You are (or were) **a cheerleader.**
	Plural: You are (or were) **cheerleaders.**
Third Person	**Singular:** He is (or was) **on the wrestling team.**
	Plural: They are (or were) **also on the team.**

728.2
Transitive Verbs

A transitive verb is a verb that transfers its action to a direct object. The object makes the meaning of the verb complete. A transitive verb is always an action verb (never a linking verb). (See page 570.)

An earthquake shook San Francisco in 1906. (*Shook* transfers its action to the direct object *San Francisco*. Without *San Francisco* the meaning of the verb *shook* is incomplete.)

The city's people spent many years rebuilding. (Without the direct object *years*, the verb's meaning is incomplete.)

A transitive verb transfers the action directly to a direct object and indirectly to an indirect object.

Fires destroyed the city. (direct object: *city*)

Our teacher gave us the details. (indirect object: *us*; direct object: *details*)

See 692.4 and 692.5 for more on direct and indirect objects.

728.3
Intransitive Verbs

An intransitive verb does not need an object to complete its meaning. (See page 570.)

Abigail was shopping. (The verb's meaning is complete.)

Her stomach felt queasy. (*Queasy* is a predicate adjective describing *stomach*; there is no direct object.)

She lay down on the bench. (Again, there is no direct object. *Down* is an adverb modifying *lay*.)

Verbs 6

■ **Singular and Plural Verbs**

 For each sentence below, write the correct choice from the verb forms in parentheses and identify it as "singular" or "plural."

1. She (*was, were*) the perfect actress for the role.
   was—singular

2. I (*am, are*) going to try out for the next play.

3. We (*am, are*) fine actors.

4. We (*was, were*) in the last play.

5. She (*love, loves*) to be the star.

6. They (*are, is*) in the chorus.

7. You must (*shine, shines*) the spotlights on Kim.

■ **Transitive Verbs**
■ **Intransitive Verbs**

 For each of the following sentences, write whether the underlined verb is transitive or intransitive.

8. Nigel threw a forward pass to Manuel.
   transitive

9. Manuel turned sideways to catch it.

10. Suddenly, Roger ran up to Manuel and grabbed the football.

11. Roger carried it all the way down the field for a touchdown.

12. He spiked the ball onto the artificial turf.

13. Then he danced around the end zone.

14. Unfortunately, the referee had blown his whistle.

15. Roger looked surprised that he hadn't scored the touchdown.

16. The team gloomily walked back up the field.

Answers

2. am
3. are
4. were
5. loves
6. are
7. shine

9. intransitive
10. transitive
11. transitive
12. transitive
13. intransitive
14. transitive
15. intransitive
16. intransitive

Verbs . . .

Forms of Verbs

730.1
Transitive or Intransitive Verbs

Some verbs can be either transitive or intransitive.

Transitive: She reads my note.   Albert ate an apple.

Intransitive: She reads aloud.   Albert ate already.

Verbals

A **verbal** is a word that is made from a verb but acts as another part of speech. Gerunds, participles, and infinitives are verbals.

730.2
Gerunds

A gerund is a verb form that ends in *ing* and is used as a *noun*. A gerund often begins a gerund phrase.

Worrying is useless. (The gerund is the subject noun.)

You should stop worrying about so many things. (The gerund phrase is the direct object.)

730.3
Participles

A participle is a verb form ending in *ing* or *ed*. A participle is used as an *adjective* and often begins a participial phrase.

The idea of the earth shaking and splitting both fascinates and frightens me. (The participles modify *earth*.)

Rattling in the cabinets, the dishes were about to crash to the floor. (The participial phrase modifies *dishes*.)

Why doesn't this tired earth just stand still? (The participle modifies *earth*.)

730.4
Infinitives

An infinitive is a verb form introduced by *to*. It may be used as a *noun*, an *adjective*, or an *adverb*. It often begins an infinitive phrase.

My need to whisper is due to this secret. (The infinitive is an adjective modifying *need*.)

I am afraid to swim. (The infinitive is an adverb modifying the predicate adjective *afraid*.)

To overcome this fear is my goal. (The infinitive phrase is used as a noun and is the subject of this sentence.)

punctuate edit capitalize SPELL
improve
Using the Parts of Speech   731

Verbs 7

■ Gerunds, Participles, and Infinitives

 In each numbered sentence below, identify the underlined verb form as a gerund, a participle, or an infinitive.

Example: A Michigan man, J. Sterling Morton, worked to improve agricultural practices in Nebraska.

Answer: infinitive

(1) Arbor Day began in 1872 when Morton decided to settle in Nebraska. **(2)** He came up with a plan to get more trees growing in his adopted state. **(3)** Working as a newspaper editor, he wrote articles that encouraged people to plant more trees. **(4)** He said the trees would be good for blocking the winds, preventing soil erosion, and making the prairie lands more beautiful. **(5)** Morton proposed that people observe a special day dedicated to tree planting, and in 1885, Arbor Day was named a legal holiday in Nebraska. **(6)** In the beginning, April 22 (Morton's birthday) was the selected date. **(7)** Today, the date for Arbor Day varies by state, depending on the best time for planting trees locally. **(8)** Improving the look of a community is a great result of Arbor Day. **(9)** The success of the holiday in the United States has caused the idea to spread to other countries, as well.

 For each of the following sentences, write the infinitive phrase and label how it is used: noun, adjective, or adverb.

10. To improve the natural environment is the ecology club's cause. *To improve the natural environment (noun)*

11. Our efforts to plant trees will result in a more scenic landscape.

12. A local business offered to supply seedlings.

13. We are eager to make a difference in our community.

14. Would you be willing to help us?

Answers

1. infinitive
2. participle
3. infinitive
4. gerund
5. participle
6. participle
7. gerund
8. gerund
9. infinitive

11. to plant trees (adjective)
12. to supply seedlings (noun)
13. to make a difference in our community (adverb)
14. to help us (adverb)

Adjectives

An **adjective** is a word used to describe a noun or a pronoun. Adjectives tell *what kind, how many,* or *which one.* They usually come before the word they describe. (See pages 486–489.)

ancient dinosaurs   800 species   that triceratops

Adjectives are the same whether the word they describe is singular or plural.

small **brain**—or—small **brains**   large **tooth**—or—large **teeth**

732.1
Articles

The articles *a, an,* and *the* are adjectives.

A brontosaurus was **an** animal about 70 feet long.

The huge dinosaur lived on land and ate plants.

732.2
Proper Adjectives

A proper adjective is formed from a proper noun, and it is always capitalized. (See 618.1.)

A **Chicago** museum is home to the skeleton of one of these beasts. (*Chicago* functions as a proper adjective describing the noun *museum.*)

732.3
Common Adjectives

A common adjective is any adjective that is not proper. It is not capitalized (unless it is the first word in a sentence).

Ancient mammoths were **huge, woolly** creatures.

They lived in the **ice** fields of Siberia.

Special Kinds of Adjectives

732.4
Demonstrative Adjectives

A demonstrative adjective points out a particular noun. *This* and *these* point out something nearby; *that* and *those* point out something at a distance.

This mammoth is huge, but **that** mammoth is even bigger.

NOTE When a noun does not follow *this, these, that,* or *those,* these words are pronouns, not adjectives. (See 708.1.)

732.5
Compound Adjectives

A compound adjective is made up of two or more words. (Sometimes it is hyphenated.)

Dinosaurs were **egg-laying** animals.

The **North American Allosaurus** had sharp teeth and powerful jaws.

---

punctuate *edit* capitalize
improve SPELL **733**
Using the Parts of Speech

Adjectives 1

- Articles
- Proper Adjectives
- Common Adjectives

 Label the underlined adjectives in the following sentences by writing "article," "proper," or "common."

1. In 1957, Althea Gibson was *the* first *African American* *tennis* player to win at Wimbledon.

   article, proper, common

2. As a *young* woman, Althea set out to be *the* best woman tennis player of all time.

3. This goal motivated her to win *a* girls' *singles* championship in New York in 1942 when she was 15 years old.

4. Ms. Gibson was the *first* African American to enter the *American Lawn Tennis Association* championships in 1950.

5. After college, she entered a *French* competition in 1956, and that tournament became her *first* *major* victory.

6. Althea also won *the* singles competition of the U.S. Open *two* years in a row.

7. Trophies from these championships lined a *broad* glass shelf.

8. After retiring from tennis, she toured America with the *Harlem Globetrotters* basketball team.

9. Later, Althea tried *professional* golf, and she became *an* athletic advisor for the state of New Jersey.

10. Ms. Gibson enjoyed those duties for *several* years.

11. Althea Gibson died on September 28, 2003, in a *New Jersey* hospital.

Next Step: Read the sentences above again, this time looking for demonstrative adjectives (not underlined). Write them down as you find them. (There are four.)

Answers

2. common, article
3. article, common
4. common, proper
5. proper, common
6. article, common
7. common
8. proper
9. common, article
10. common
11. proper

Next Step: This, that, these, those

Using the Parts of Speech **734-735**

734

punctuate *edit* capitalize
improve SPELL 735
Using the Parts of Speech

Adjectives . . .

Special Kinds of Adjectives

734.1
Indefinite Adjectives

An indefinite adjective gives approximate, or indefinite, information (*any, few, many, most,* and so on). It does not tell exactly how many or how much.

Some **mammoths** were heavier than today's elephants.

734.2
Predicate Adjectives

A predicate adjective follows a linking verb and describes the subject.

Mammoths were once **abundant,** but now they are **extinct.**

Forms of Adjectives

734.3
Positive Adjectives

The positive form describes a noun or pronoun without comparing it to anyone or anything else.

The Eurostar is a **fast** train that runs between London, Paris, and Brussels.

It is an **impressive** train.

734.4
Comparative Adjectives

The comparative form of an adjective (*er*) compares two persons, places, things, or ideas. (See page 487.)

The Eurostar is **faster** than the Orient Express.

Some adjectives that have more than one syllable show comparisons by their *er* suffix, but many of them use the modifiers *more* or *less.*

It is a **speedier** commuter train than the Tobu Railway trains in Japan.

This train is **more impressive** than my commuter train.

734.5
Superlative Adjectives

The superlative form (*est* or *most* or *least*) compares three or more persons, places, things, or ideas. (See page 487.)

In fact, the Eurostar is the **fastest** train in Europe.

It is the **most impressive** commuter train in the world.

734.6
Irregular Forms

Some adjectives use completely different words to express comparison.

good, better, best   bad, worse, worst
many, more, most   little, less, least

Adjectives 2

■ Indefinite Adjectives
■ Predicate Adjectives

 For each of the following sentences, identify and label the indefinite adjectives and the predicate adjectives.

1. Many homes were destroyed during the great Chicago fire of 1871.
   many (indefinite)

2. Before the fire, most buildings were wooden.

3. Few buildings escaped the fire.

4. Wooden sidewalks were flammable and added fuel to the fire.

5. Almost 100,000 city residents became homeless due to the fire.

6. Some residents rebuilt their homes after the fire.

■ Positive, Comparative, and Superlative Adjectives

 Write the correct form of the underlined adjectives in the following sentences.

7. The Panama Canal was one of the <u>expensive</u> projects ever to be built.
   most expensive

8. The <u>bad</u> problem affecting the construction workers was disease caused by mosquito bites.

9. The engineers had to make the canal 100 feet <u>wide</u> than they originally planned in order to let large ships through.

10. The *Jahre Viking,* currently the <u>large</u> ship in the world, is too wide to pass through the canal.

11. The first toll (in 1914) of 90 cents per ton was <u>cheap</u> than today's rate, which is almost three dollars per ton.

12. The <u>quick</u> travel time through the canal is eight hours.

Answers

2. most (indefinite), wooden (predicatc)
3. Few (indefinite)
4. flammable (predicate)
5. Almost (indefinite), homeless (predicate)
6. Some (indefinitc)

8. worst
9. wider
10. largest
11. cheaper
12. quickest

736

Adverbs

An **adverb** is a word used to modify a verb, an adjective, or another adverb. It tells *how, when, where, how often,* or *how much.* Adverbs can come before or after the words they modify. (See pages 490–492.)

> **Dad snores loudly.** (*Loudly* modifies the verb *snores.*)
>
> **His snores are really explosive.** (*Really* modifies the adjective *explosive.*)
>
> **Dad snores very loudly.** (*Very* modifies the adverb *loudly.*)

Types of Adverbs

There are four basic types of adverbs: *time, place, manner,* and *degree.*

736.1
Adverbs of Time

Adverbs of time tell *when, how often,* and *how long.*

> tomorrow   often   never   always
>
> Jen **rarely** has time to go swimming.

736.2
Adverbs of Place

Adverbs of place tell *where, to where,* or *from where.*

> there   backward   outside
>
> We'll set up our tent **here.**

736.3
Adverbs of Manner

Adverbs of manner often end in *ly* and tell *how* something is done.

> unkindly   gently   well
>
> Ahmed **boldly** entered the dark cave.

Some words used as adverbs can be written with or without the *ly* ending. When in doubt, use the *ly* form.

> slow, slowly   deep, deeply

NOTE Not all words ending in *ly* are adverbs. *Lovely,* for example, is an adjective.

736.4
Adverbs of Degree

Adverbs of degree tell *how much* or *how little.*

> scarcely   entirely   generally   very   really
>
> Jess is **usually** the leader in these situations.

---

punctuate edit capitalize
SPELL
improve
737
Using the Parts of Speech

Adverbs 1

- Adverbs of Time
- Adverbs of Place
- Adverbs of Manner
- Adverbs of Degree

 The number of adverbs in each sentence below is indicated in parentheses at the end of the sentence. Write the adverbs and identify them as adverbs of "time," "place," "manner," or "degree."

1. We are going to see a Chicago Cubs game tomorrow. (*1*)
   tomorrow (time)

2. The Chicago Cubs always play home games at Wrigley Field, generally during the day. (*2*)

3. Cubs fans really like to watch games there. (*2*)

4. People even stand outside of the stadium, waiting patiently for home runs that completely clear the fence. (*4*)

5. The last time the Cubs were world champions was 1908; now the Cubs rarely make it to the play-offs. (*2*)

6. Their fans often say, "Wait till next year," and they faithfully attend as many games as they can. (*2*)

7. Some of them openly complain that the Cubs will never win a World Series again. (*3*)

8. Although the Cubs may be a very poor team in some critics' opinions, their fans love them deeply. (*2*)

9. The fans eagerly purchase Cubs T-shirts and caps. (*1*)

10. They support their team enthusiastically. (*1*)

11. Occasionally, their faith is rewarded, as it was when the Cubs actually made it to the 2003 play-offs. (*2*)

Next Step: Write a short paragraph about a favorite sport or team. Include one of each type of adverb in the paragraph.

Answers

2. always (time), generally (degree)
3. really (degree), there (place)
4. even (degree), outside (place), patiently (manner), completely (degree)
5. now (time), rarely (degree)
6. often (time), faithfully (manner)
7. openly (manner), never (time), again (time)
8. very (degree), deeply (manner)
9. eagerly (manner)
10. enthusiastically (manner)
11. Occasionally (time), actually (degree)

Using the Parts of Speech **738-739**

738

improve *edit* capitalize
punctuate SPELL 739
Using the Parts of Speech

Adverbs . . .
Special Kinds of Adverbs

738.1
Conjunctive Adverbs

A conjunctive adverb can be used as a conjunction and shows a connection or a transition between two independent clauses. Most often, a conjunctive adverb follows a semicolon in a compound sentence; however, it can also appear at the beginning or end of a sentence. (Note that the previous sentence has an example of a conjunctive adverb.)

also	besides	however	instead
meanwhile	nevertheless	therefore	

Forms of Adverbs

Many adverbs—especially adverbs of manner—have three forms: *positive, comparative,* and *superlative.*

738.2
Positive Adverbs

The positive form describes but does not make a comparison.

Juan woke up late.

He quickly ate some breakfast.

738.3
Comparative Adverbs

The comparative form of an adverb (*er*) compares two things.

Juan woke up later than he usually did. (See page 491.)

Some adverbs that have more than one syllable show comparisons by their *er* suffix, but many of them use the modifiers *more* or *less.*

He ate his breakfast more quickly than usual.

738.4
Superlative Adverbs

The superlative form (*est* or *most* or *least*) compares three or more things. (See page 491.)

Of the past three days, Juan woke up latest on Saturday.

Of the past three days, he ate his breakfast least quickly on Saturday.

738.5
Irregular Forms

Some adverbs use completely different words to express comparison.

Positive	Comparative	Superlative
well	better	best
badly	worse	worst

Adverbs 2

 ■ Conjunctive Adverbs

Number your paper from 1 to 3 and write the three conjunctive adverbs that appear in the following paragraph.

> *Example:* When money was invented, it made buying and selling easier. Thus, one coin could replace a basketful of vegetables.
>
> *Answer:* Thus

Many people like to pay with cash; others, however, prefer to barter for goods. Buying from these people may be more difficult. A lot of shoppers today prefer to buy what they want at a mall instead. Meanwhile, the computer age and its electronic money are steering us toward a cashless economy. Electronic credit may eventually be all that people use to buy and sell.

 ■ Comparative Adverbs

For each sentence below, write the correct comparative form of the underlined adverb.

4. A computer can solve a difficult arithmetic problem <u>fast</u> than a human can.

   faster

5. Some students think the computer in Ms. Stowe's room works <u>well</u> than the one in the library.

6. The new word processor program actually runs <u>slowly</u> than the old one.

7. This green mouse moves <u>smoothly</u> than that red one.

8. The keys on Kayla's keyboard stick <u>badly</u> than mine do.

PARTS OF SPEECH

Answers

1. however
2. instead
3. Meanwhile

5. better
6. more slowly
7. more (or) less smoothly
8. worse

punctuate edit capitalize
improve SPELL **741**
Using the Parts of Speech

Test Prep

Number your paper from 1 to 12. For each underlined part of the paragraphs below, write the letter (from the next page) of the best choice.

Have you <u>seed</u> any news about the future of dentistry?
<u>   **1**</u>
Cavities and gum disease won't be problems. Tiny robots in your

mouth <u>will brush and flossed</u> your teeth for you. Artificial
<u> **2**</u>

materials <u>maked</u> of teeth and bone cells will rebuild the teeth,
<u> **3**</u>

gum tissue, and jawbone. People will have <u>fewer</u> worries about
<u> **4**</u>

losing their teeth than they do now.

Actually, humans <u>had began</u> to work at keeping their teeth
<u> **5**</u>
clean a <u>long</u> time ago than you might think. The ancient Egyptians
<u> **6**</u>
<u>chew</u> twigs so the ends would fray, and—presto!—they had a
<u>**7**</u>
toothbrush. Europeans rubbed their teeth with cloth after they

<u>eated</u>. Sometime during the 1700s, man-made toothbrushes
<u> **8**</u>
<u>will be invented</u>; the brush part was created from hog bristles.
<u> **9**</u>

Today, dental products can keep teeth <u>healthy and white</u> than
<u> **10**</u>
in the past. To make sure your teeth are <u>taken</u> care of, brush twice
<u> **11**</u>
a day, floss daily, eat a balanced diet, and see a dentist regularly.

Technology has not <u>bringed</u> us carefree dentistry yet!
<u> **12**</u>

1. **A** saw
   B seen
   C sawed
   D correct as is

2. **A** will brush and floss
   B will brushed and flossed
   C will brushed and floss
   D correct as is

3. **A** make
   B made
   C maded
   D correct as is

4. **A** few
   B fewest
   C the fewest
   D correct as is

5. **A** began
   B beginned
   C begun
   D correct as is

6. **A** longest
   B more longer
   C longer
   D correct as is

7. **A** chewing
   B will chew
   C chewed
   D correct as is

8. **A** eaten
   B ate
   C had ate
   D correct as is

9. **A** were invented
   B are invented
   C was invented
   D correct as is

10. **A** healthier and white
    B healthier and whiter
    C healthiest and whiter
    D correct as is

11. **A** took
    B taked
    C takened
    D correct as is

12. **A** bring
    B brought
    C broughted
    D correct as is

PARTS OF SPEECH

Answers

1. B	**7.** C
2. A	**8.** B
3. B	**9.** A
4. D	**10.** B
5. A	**11.** D
6. C	**12.** B

Prepositions

Prepositions are words that show position, direction, or how two words or ideas are related to each other. Specifically, a preposition shows the relationship between its object and some other word in the sentence.

> **Raul hid under the stairs.** (*Under* shows the relationship between *hid* and *stairs*.)

742.1
Prepositional Phrases

A preposition never appears alone; it is always part of a prepositional phrase. A prepositional phrase includes the preposition, the object of the preposition, and the modifiers of the object. (See pages 494–495.)

> **Raul's friends looked in the clothes hamper.** (preposition: *in*; object: *hamper*; modifiers: *the, clothes*)

A prepositional phrase functions as an adjective or as an adverb.

> **They checked the closet with all the winter coats.** (*With all the winter coats* functions as an adjective modifying *closet*.)

> **They wandered around the house looking for him.** (*Around the house* functions as an adverb modifying *wandered*.)

NOTE If a word found in the list of prepositions has no object, it is not a preposition. It is probably an adverb.

> **Raul had never won at hide 'n' seek before.** (*Before* is an adverb that modifies *had won*.)

Prepositions

aboard	apart from	beyond	from	like	outside	under
about	around	but	from among	near	outside of	underneath
above	aside from	by	from between	near to	over	until
according to	at	by means of	from under	next	over to	unto
across	away from	concerning	in	of	owing to	up
across from	back of	considering	in addition to	off	past	up to
after	because of	despite	in front of	on	prior to	upon
against	before	down	in place of	on account of	regarding	with
along	behind	down from	in regard to	on behalf of	since	within
along with	below	during	in spite of	on top of	through	without
alongside	beneath	except	inside	onto	throughout	
alongside of	beside	except for	inside of	opposite	to	
amid	besides	excepting	instead of	out	together with	
among	between	for	into	out of	toward	

---

punctuate *edit* capitalize
improve SPELL
Using the Parts of Speech **743**

Prepositions

 For each sentence below, write the prepositional phrase or phrases. (The number of phrases in each sentence is in parentheses.) Circle the prepositions.

1. The first issue of the *Cherokee Phoenix* newspaper was printed in English and in Cherokee. *(3)*
   ⟨of⟩ the Cherokee Phoenix newspaper, ⟨in⟩ English, ⟨in⟩ Cherokee

2. For many years, Cherokee history was told from memory. *(2)*

3. No written form of their language existed at the time. *(2)*

4. A Native American named Sequoya was a silversmith and a trader in Georgia. *(1)*

5. His name was given to him by missionaries. *(2)*

6. Until his creation of a symbol for each sound in Cherokee, none of the Cherokee could read or write. *(5)*

7. Sequoya wrote a story in Cherokee on some paper, and his daughter read it. *(2)*

8. He traveled throughout Arkansas so he could teach other Cherokee. *(1)*

9. Then he moved with the whole tribe to Oklahoma. *(2)*

10. Without his assistance, the Cherokee might not have become such a strong, united people. *(1)*

11. On account of Sequoya's achievement, the Cherokee people became leaders among Native Americans. *(2)*

12. The giant California trees called *sequoias* are named after him. *(1)*

13. He is remembered, along with other great Americans, for his contributions. *(2)*

Next Step: Pick five prepositions from the list on the facing page. Write several sentences using those prepositions correctly. Exchange papers with a classmate and circle each other's prepositional phrases.

Answers

(Answers may vary.)

2. ⟨For⟩ many years, ⟨from⟩ memory

3. ⟨of⟩ their language, ⟨at⟩ the time

4. ⟨in⟩ Georgia

5. ⟨to⟩ him, ⟨by⟩ missionaries

6. ⟨Until⟩ his creation, ⟨of⟩ a symbol, ⟨for⟩ each sound, ⟨in⟩ Cherokee, ⟨of⟩ the Cherokee

7. ⟨in⟩ Cherokee, ⟨on⟩ some paper

8. ⟨throughout⟩ Arkansas

9. ⟨with⟩ the whole tribe, ⟨to⟩ Oklahoma

10. ⟨Without⟩ his assistance

11. ⟨On account of⟩ Sequoya's achievement, ⟨among⟩ Native Americans

12. ⟨after⟩ him

13. ⟨along with⟩ other great Americans, ⟨for⟩ his contributions

punctuate edit capitalize
improve SPELL 745
Using the Parts of Speech

Conjunctions

A **conjunction** connects individual words or groups of words. There are three kinds of conjunctions: *coordinating, correlative,* and *subordinating.* (See pages 496–498.)

744.1
Coordinating Conjunctions

A coordinating conjunction connects a word to a word, a phrase to a phrase, or a clause to a clause. The words, phrases, or clauses joined by a coordinating conjunction must be equal, or of the same type.

> **Polluted rivers and streams can be cleaned up.** (Two nouns are connected by *and.*)

> **Ride a bike or plant a tree to reduce pollution.** (Two verb phrases are connected by *or.*)

> **Maybe you can't invent a pollution-free engine, but you can cut down on the amount of energy you use.** (Two equal independent clauses are connected by *but.*)

NOTE When a coordinating conjunction is used to make a compound sentence, a comma always comes before it.

744.2
Correlative Conjunctions

Correlative conjunctions are conjunctions used in pairs.

> **We must reduce not only pollution but also excess energy use.**

> **Either you're part of the problem, or you're part of the solution.**

Conjunctions

Coordinating Conjunctions
and, but, or, nor, for, so, yet

Correlative Conjunctions
either, or   neither, nor   not only, but also   both, and   whether, or   as, so

Subordinating Conjunctions
after, although, as, as if, as long as, as though, because, before, if, in order that, provided that, since, so, so that, that, though, till, unless, until, when, where, whereas, while

Conjunctions

■ **Coordinating Conjunctions**

 Combine the following pairs of sentences by using a coordinating conjunction to connect the sentence parts given in parentheses.

1. Every country has a flag. Each flag is different. (*clauses*)
   Every country has a flag, but each flag is different.

2. Sonja likes the Canadian flag. Sanjeev likes the Canadian flag. (*words*)

3. Displaying a flag can be patriotic. Carrying a flag can be patriotic. (*words*)

4. You can buy a cotton flag. You can buy a nylon flag. (*phrases*)

5. The school flag got very wet. The janitor dried it. (*clauses*)

6. Does this flag belong to Sweden? Does this flag belong to Denmark? (*words*)

7. Citizens honor their flag. A flag represents the country. (*clauses*)

■ **Correlative Conjunctions**

 Use a different set of correlative conjunctions to combine each sentence pair below. Underline the conjunctions.

8. Jaguars live in rain forests. Tapirs live in rain forests.
   Both jaguars and tapirs live in rain forests.

9. Elephants do not live in South America. Tigers do not live in South America.

10. In a rain forest, people walk. They also ride in boats.

11. The Amazon is one of the longest rivers in the world. It flows through one of the largest rain forests in the world.

12. If we want to use rain-forest plants for medicines, we must save the rain forests. If we want to use rain-forest plants for food, we must save the rain forests.

Answers

 (Some answers may vary.)
2. Sonja and Sanjeev like the Canadian flag.
3. Displaying or carrying a flag can be patriotic.
4. You can buy a cotton flag or a nylon flag.
5. The school flag got very wet, so the janitor dried it.
6. Does this flag belong to Sweden or Denmark?
7. Citizens honor their flag, for a flag represents the country.

9. <u>Neither</u> elephants <u>nor</u> tigers live in South America.
10. In the rain forest, people <u>either</u> walk <u>or</u> ride in boats.
11. <u>Not only</u> is the Amazon one of the longest rivers in the world, <u>but</u> it <u>also</u> flows through one of the largest rain forests in the world.
12. <u>Whether</u> we want to use rain forest plants for medicines <u>or</u> for food, we must save the rain forests.

746

Conjunctions . . .

746.1
Subordinating Conjunctions

A subordinating conjunction is a word or group of words that connects two clauses that are not equally important. A subordinating conjunction begins a dependent clause and connects it to an independent clause to make a complex sentence. (See page 517 and the chart on page 744.)

> Fuel-cell engines are unusual because they don't have moving parts.

> Since fuel-cell cars run on hydrogen, the only waste products are water and heat.

As you can see in the sentences above, a comma sets off the dependent clause only when it begins the sentence. A comma is usually not used when the dependent clause follows the independent clause.

NOTE Relative pronouns and conjunctive adverbs can also connect clauses. (See 706.3 and 738.1.)

Interjections

An **interjection** is a word or phrase used to express strong emotion or surprise. Punctuation (a comma or an exclamation point) is used to separate an interjection from the rest of the sentence.

> Wow, would you look at that!   Oh no! He's falling!

SCHOOL DAZE

Forget it! We aren't using activity money for that.

Yikes, I've told everyone that we could buy a plasma-screen TV for our classroom!

---

punctuate edit capitalize
improve SPELL **747**
Using the Parts of Speech

Conjunctions and Interjections

- Subordinating Conjunctions
- Interjections

 Write the subordinating conjunction that connects the clauses in each of the sentences below. (The chart on page 744 will help.)

1. The buffalo has become a symbol of the Native Americans because it was vital to their survival.
   because

2. After the Native Americans killed the huge animals they needed, they used every part of the buffalo, from horns to tail hairs. Wow!

3. Before the settlers moved into Native American areas, millions of buffalo roamed through the prairies.

4. Because buffalo herds were overhunted during the 1800s, the herds have declined in the United States.

5. Oh dear, the buffalo was almost extinct when President Ulysses S. Grant created Yellowstone National Park.

6. Although the buffalo no longer rules the prairies, many tribes of Native Americans are working to increase the herd numbers.

7. Gee, more than 40 tribes have joined together to help restore the buffalo herds since the Intertribal Bison Cooperative was formed in 1991.

8. While Native Americans no longer need food from the buffalo to survive, selling buffalo meat has become a huge industry.

9. Whereas the buffalo once meant food and clothing to the Native Americans, today the meat can be sold to help support the tribes.

10. Well, the Native Americans can still make use of the majestic animal as long as the buffalo herds continue to grow.

Next Step: Find the interjections in the sentences above and write them on your paper. You should find four of them.

PARTS OF SPEECH

Answers

2. After
3. Before
4. Because
5. when
6. Although
7. since
8. While
9. Whereas
10. as long as

Next Step: Wow, Oh dear, Gee, Well

Quick Guide: Parts of Speech

In the English language, there are eight parts of speech. Understanding them will help you improve your writing skills. Every word you write is a part of speech—a noun, a verb, an adjective, and so on. The chart below lists the eight parts of speech.

Noun	A word that names a person, a place, a thing, or an idea **Alex Moya Belize ladder courage**
Pronoun	A word used in place of a noun **I he it they you anybody some**
Verb	A word that shows action or links a subject to another word in the sentence **sing shake catch is are**
Adjective	A word that describes a noun or a pronoun **stormy red rough seven grand**
Adverb	A word that describes a verb, an adjective, or another adverb **quickly today now bravely softer**
Preposition	A word that shows position or direction and introduces a prepositional phrase **around up under over between to**
Conjunction	A word that connects other words or groups of words **and but or so because when**
Interjection	A word (set off by commas or an exclamation point) that shows strong emotion **Stop! Hey, how are you?**

 punctuate *edit* capitalize SPELL
improve
Using the Parts of Speech   **749**

Parts of Speech Review

 For each numbered sentence below, write whether the underlined word is a noun, a pronoun, a verb, an adjective, an adverb, a preposition, a conjunction, or an interjection.

Example: <u>Wow</u>, it took months for an immigrant to travel across the ocean in the 1800s.

Answer: interjection

(1) Ellis Island was the first <u>stop</u> for many immigrants seeking a better life in the United States. **(2)** Between 1892 and 1954, the island was the country's <u>main</u> immigration center. **(3)** More than 12 million immigrants <u>passed</u> through its gates during that time.

(4) In its first year of operation, nearly 450,000 people stepped <u>on</u> American soil for the first time at Ellis Island. **(5)** <u>It</u> welcomed 11,747 immigrants, the most in a single day, on April 17, 1907. **(6)** About 40 percent of all Americans have an ancestor who arrived at Ellis Island, <u>but</u> it accepted its last immigrant in November 1954.

(7) After the center closed, the great limestone walls of the Main Arrival Building <u>slowly</u> began to crumble. **(8)** Then, in 1965, Ellis Island <u>became</u> part of the Statue of Liberty National Monument. **(9)** Through <u>generous</u> private donations, the building was restored to its original state. **(10)** The <u>cost</u> was more than $156 million. **(11)** <u>Wow!</u> **(12)** In 1990, the doors of the old building, now a museum, <u>finally</u> reopened.

(13) Today, museum visitors research <u>their</u> ancestors. **(14)** Exhibits <u>and</u> hundreds of photographs honor this country's immigrant heritage. **(15)** Every U.S. citizen should make a trip <u>to</u> Ellis Island.

Next Step: Write a two-word sentence (noun and verb). Exchange papers with a classmate and keep adding words to each other's sentences until they have all eight parts of speech.

Answers

1. noun
2. adjective
3. verb
4. preposition
5. pronoun
6. conjunction
7. adverb
8. verb
9. adjective
10. noun
11. interjection
12. adverb
13. pronoun
14. conjunction
15. preposition

Introducing the Traits

Write Source offers a way of teaching writing that helps students understand what good writing is and how to achieve it. The program provides instruction in the six traits of effective writing. The term *trait,* as it is used here, refers to a characteristic or quality that defines writing.

The six-trait model of writing instruction and assessment was developed in 1984 by teachers in the Beaverton, Oregon, School District. Because it has been so widely embraced by teachers at all grade levels, kindergarten through college, the model has since spread throughout the country—and much of the world. Traits themselves, of course, have been around as long as writing; writers have always needed intriguing ideas, good organization, a powerful voice, and so on. What is *new* is using consistent language with students to define writing at various levels of performance.

The six traits of writing are the following:

Ideas

> **Excellent writing has a clear message, purpose, or focus. The writing contains plenty of specific ideas and details.**

Organization

> **Effective writing has a clear beginning, middle, and ending. The overall writing is well organized and easy to follow.**

Voice

> **The best writing reveals the writer's voice—his or her special way of saying things.**

Word Choice

> **Good writing contains strong words, including specific nouns and verbs. The words fit the audience and deliver a clear message.**

Sentence Fluency

> **Effective writing flows smoothly from one sentence to the next. Sentences vary in length and begin in a variety of ways.**

Conventions

> **Good writing is carefully edited to make sure it is easy to understand. The writing follows the rules for punctuation, grammar, and spelling.**

Students learn to use the six traits of effective writing as a guide while they write and as a tool to assess their writing when they revise. A rubric based on the six traits is at the center of the instruction in each major genre lesson in *Write Source.* Using the traits and rubrics based on the traits, students learn to recognize a strong piece of writing and to pinpoint aspects of writing that may need improvement.

Teaching the Traits of Good Writing

Six-trait writing is based on the premise that students who become strong self-assessors become better writers and revisers. No matter where student writers are now, working with the traits will improve their skills and will also give them the confidence that comes from knowing writer's language and having options for revision.

Use the following definitions and examples from trade books to introduce the traits to students. (See *Books, Lessons, Ideas for Teaching the Six Traits* by Vicki Spandel, Great Source Education Group, 2001.) As students become comfortable with the traits, encourage them to assess many pieces of writing, including other students' work, professional writing, and your own writing.

Ideas

The first trait provides an understanding of what constitutes good, strong ideas in a piece of writing and encourages students to work with ideas to shape and improve them.

Ideas are all about information. In a strong creative piece, ideas paint a picture in the reader's mind. In an informational piece, strong ideas make difficult or complex information easy to understand. Three things make ideas work well, and they should be the focus of your instruction: a *main idea* that is easy to identify and narrow enough to be manageable, *interesting details* that bring the main idea to life, and *clarity,* which is achieved in part through the careful selection and presentation of important details. Finally, good writing always includes details about those beyond-the-obvious bits of information that thoughtful, observant writers notice.

Organization

The second trait focuses on putting information in an order that makes sense and that both entertains and enlightens a reader.

Organization is about the logical and effective presentation of key ideas and details. Good organization holds a piece of writing together and makes it easy to follow—like good instructions or a clear road map. Several things make organization work well: an organizational pattern that makes sense and matches the purpose for the writing, strong transitions that link the writer's ideas together, a compelling lead that pulls the reader in, and an appropriate conclusion that effectively wraps things up.

Voice

The third trait focuses on the skillful blending of detail, enthusiasm, topic knowledge, audience awareness, and a writer's personality.

As one teacher put it, your ideas are what you have to say; **your voice is how you say it.** Students and teachers often worry that voice cannot be taught because it is too closely linked to personality. Voice is much more than personality, however. It is the skillful use of detail that helps readers make personal connections. It is the writer's concern for the audience; voice changes as audience changes so that the voice in a business letter is not the voice in an impassioned personal narrative. Voice is also a reflection of the confidence gained from knowing a topic well.

Word Choice

The fourth trait teaches students to use sensory language to make readers part of the writer's experience, revise writing to take it from flat to lively, and cut excess language to make writing concise and readable.

Word choice is the selection of appropriate words to fit audience, topic, and purpose. Good word choice results in clear, colorful, and precise writing, and helps readers see, hear, and feel the world of the writer. The secrets to successful word choice include simplicity, sensory detail, use of powerful verbs, and, of course, variety—all of which come from an expanded vocabulary. In a business letter, writing must be brisk, clear, and to the point. A technical or research report calls for knowledge of content expressed through the skillful use of a specialized vocabulary. A poem or personal narrative allows the writer more freedom to use words in unexpected ways.

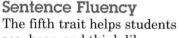

Sentence Fluency

The fifth trait helps students see, hear, and think like readers as they create text that is readable. Writers who look and listen for the flow in a piece of writing usually come up with something smooth and pleasurable to read silently or aloud.

Sentence fluency is the rhythm and flow of language. It is more than how words look on the page; it is also how they play to the ear. Reading aloud is a good way to test fluency, since fluent writing invites strong, expressive reading. Sentences that vary in both structure and length contribute significantly to fluency by snapping the reader to attention—much the way a shift in musical rhythm helps wake up a sleepy listener. In general, a strong writer avoids repetition or run-ons, although either may be used sparingly by a skilled writer for stylistic effect. The fluent writer also recognizes the difference between complete sentences and fragments but may slip in a fragment to lend punch to the writing now and then. Good dialogue is also a component of fluency.

Conventions

The sixth trait provides students with skills and tools for editing their writing. Editors' tools include not only such basics as a sharp pencil, a good dictionary, and a handbook but more personal things as well. For example, a good editor needs to develop an editor's eye and an editor's ear in order to weed out every mistake hiding within the text. Editors also need a code—a set of symbols with which to mark the text for editing—and a personal checklist to keep track of hard-to-remember conventional rules.

The trait of conventions includes anything a copy editor would deal with: spelling, punctuation, usage and grammar, capitalization, and indentation (or other indicators of paragraphing, such as spacing). Editing for the conventions shows respect for the writer, the writing, and the reader. Writers want to be recognized as skilled and considerate creators, not as people who care little about their profession and who are disinterested or lazy. By presenting error-free pieces, writers demonstrate self-respect. In addition, writers who have respect for their writing want nothing to interfere with their ability to convey their message. They want to honor their ideas by presenting them as cleanly and clearly as possible. If they don't show respect for their writing, they cannot expect their audience to respect it either. Finally, writers who attend to the conventions respect their readers. Errors in grammar, usage, and spelling put up barriers to comprehension and force readers to work harder than necessary to discern the meaning the author is trying to convey. Sloppy editing interrupts the flow of the reading and causes readers to stumble through a piece of writing.

Presentation

This characteristic is sometimes described as a separate trait, but *Write Source* addresses it as part of the publishing stage of the writing process. Presentation describes the qualities and features writers should attend to when presenting their work.

Presentation includes anything that affects how the written piece looks: general layout, headings and subheadings, citations, use of white space, formatting, use of fonts for stylistic effect, and incorporation of charts, graphs, illustrations.

The material on the six traits of effective writing was taken from *Write Traits Classroom Kits* by Vicki Spandel and Jeff Hicks (Great Source Education Group, 2002).

Using the Traits in *Write Source*

Instruction in *Write Source* integrates the six traits of effective writing into the writing process. Three traits relate to the development of the content and the form of writing. In the instruction, these traits provide a focus during the prewriting, drafting, and revising stages.

- Ideas
- **Organization**
- Voice

The other three traits relate more to form. In the instruction, checking them is part of the revising and editing process.

- **Word Choice**
- Sentence Fluency
- Conventions

In addition to being a vital part of the writing process, the traits also form the backbone of the evaluation process in *Write Source*. Students use rubrics based on the six traits to evaluate not only their own writing but also models and benchmark papers provided throughout the program. Discussing as a group students' evaluations of various pieces of writing allows them to gain a solid understanding of the rubric and a sense of its scale. Finally, the six traits are at the core of the Six-Trait Checklist (see TE page 767), which teachers can use as a generic evaluation form or an assessment guide.

Students develop their understanding of the traits over time. It is best to focus on one or two traits at first and help students to understand those traits thoroughly before expanding the focus to include other traits. For a more in-depth approach to the traits, we recommend *Creating Writers Through 6-Trait Writing Assessment and Instruction,* 3rd ed., by Vicki Spandel (Addison Wesley Longman, 2001) and the *Write Traits Classroom Kits* by Vicki Spandel and Jeff Hicks (Great Source Education Group, 2002).

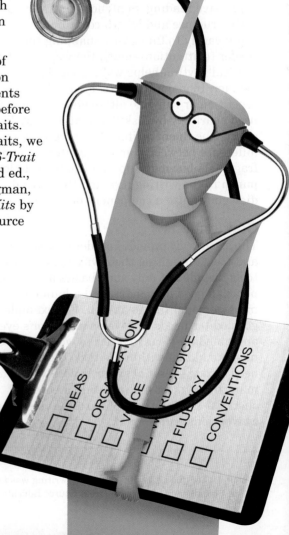

The Writing Process and the Six Traits

In the four core units of *Write Source*—Narrative Writing, Expository Writing, Persuasive Writing, and Response to Literature—students are taught how to develop each kind of writing using the traits that are specific to the genre *at the appropriate stages* of the writing process. The following chart shows which traits are the focus during different stages of the writing process and provides some of the questions writers can ask themselves as they develop their writing.

Prewriting

Ideas,
Voice

Writer's Questions:
- Who is my audience?
- What do they know now?
- What do they need or want to know?
- What information is new and interesting?
- How well do I know this topic?

Drafting

Ideas,
Organization

Writer's Questions:
- Do I have enough information to answer readers' questions?
- Do I have so much information it's overwhelming?
- What is an organizational pattern that makes sense?
- Where do I begin?
- Where do I go next?
- How do I know when I've covered everything?
- How do I know when to stop?

Revision

Ideas,
Organization,
Voice,
Word Choice,
Sentences

Writer's Questions:
- What are the unanswered questions?
- Does the organizational pattern work?
- Did I waste time telling readers things they know already?
- Is my opening a grabber?
- What is my MAIN message? Is it clear?
- Did I end in a good spot? Did I end with a thought, surprise, or question that will make my readers think?
- Is this the right tone and voice for this audience and topic and format?
- Does the language communicate with this audience?
- Is it formal or informal enough?
- Do the sentences show enough variety to keep a reader interested?
- Are sentences in informational or business writing concise and to the point?

Editing

Conventions,
Presentation

Writer's Questions:
- Is this text as error-free as I can make it?
- Is it readable? Can I breeze right through it?
- Did I read it both silently and aloud?
- Did I use page layout in a way that will attract the reader's eye and make main points easy to find?

Writing Across the Curriculum

What is writing across the curriculum?

Writing across the curriculum (WAC) is an instructional approach that recognizes the importance of writing as a teaching and learning tool in all curriculum areas. Research shows that writing can help students synthesize, analyze, and apply course content. Teachers who participate in WAC choose appropriate writing activities on the basis of the course content and their learning goals for students.

What types of WAC activities work best?

Two approaches that work well are writing to learn and writing in the disciplines. Writing to learn makes use of journals, logs, short essays, and other informal writing assignments. Students who use these tools to write personal reactions to information received in class or from reading often comprehend and retain the information better. Frequent writing also helps students improve and maintain their writing skills. In "Keeping Journals and Learning Logs" on PE pages 431–440, there is a discussion of specific writing to learn activities.

Writing in the disciplines makes use of reports, article reviews, research papers, and other formal writing assignments. This approach takes into consideration the terminology and conventions unique to science, geography, mathematics, and other disciplines. Students who write for a particular discipline learn to use the appropriate terms and apply logical thinking. In "Completing Writing Assignments" on PE pages 449–458, you see basic thinking and writing skills that support writing in the disciplines.

The *Write Source 6, 7,* and *8* pupil editions each contain twenty WAC activities, several summary paragraphs, and a unit on developing a research paper, in addition to extensive lessons with step-by-step analyses of essays that are useful across the curriculum.

Why should students write in all courses?

WAC activities help students to

- think through and find meaning in their learning,
- retain what they learn, and
- develop their writing skills.

WAC gives students practice in such writing skills as gathering and organizing information, evaluating arguments, and supporting ideas. In addition, writing helps students construct meaning in a course, make connections between ideas in various courses across the curriculum, and connect learning to their daily lives.

How does writing enhance learning?

Whether a WAC activity is a 10-minute freewriting or a research paper, writing helps students learn by enabling them to

- develop and record their thoughts,
- connect and analyze their ideas,
- receive input from classmates and teachers,
- refine specific points or arguments,
- take ownership for what they say and how they say it.

Setting Up Writing Across the Curriculum (WAC)

Without being aware of it, many content area teachers already do things that support a writing curriculum. However, when faced with a formal WAC program, their first questions are often about how they can make writing across the curriculum work. With the knowledge you already have about writing, and with *Write Source* at your fingertips, you can help your colleagues work successfully with WAC. Following are some questions content area teachers ask when they are first asked to participate in a WAC program.

How will I make WAC work? For me? For my students?

When you and your colleagues begin a WAC program, the *Write Source* materials can play a critical role. The information is reassuring and the teaching methods are helpful. *Write Source* provides a wide variety of WAC activities and assignments. This teacher's edition provides information to help you help your colleagues adopt teaching strategies that will support WAC.

Why am I expected to teach writing?

When adopting WAC, writing is not added to the content, but the content is entered and learned through writing. Students will still acquire the skills and knowledge of the course's content as set forth in the course objectives. The success of WAC will depend on the professional commitment of all teachers to active learning, not on their ability to teach writing.

Am I expected to check grammar, spelling, verb agreement, and so on?

Content area teachers will correct the formal WAC activities such as research papers and essay tests as they have in the past. The informal activities such as keeping learning logs and journals are not checked for grammar. Content area teachers will use WAC to become aware of the progress each student is making in developing the following skills:

- Thinking clearly
- Expressing thoughts precisely
- Asking worthwhile questions
- Understanding and using facts and opinions appropriately
- Developing support for an argument
- Thinking beyond first impressions
- Dealing with difficult problems and concepts

How does WAC promote learning?

There are several reasons students write in the content areas. Teachers need to decide what the goal is for students before assigning writing. Once they understand the purpose they want to achieve, they can choose an appropriate activity. On the next three pages are several of the reasons for using WAC, along with suggested activities from *Write Source* that teachers can fit into the curriculum.

Writing to Show Learning

The most common reason content-area teachers have students write is to show learning. The following forms of writing are commonly used for this purpose. The numbers in parentheses below indicate page numbers in *Write Source* where guidelines and models are found.

- The (Writing) Process in Action (8–9)
- Descriptive Paragraph (71–74, 527)
  - Writing About a Person (532)
  - Writing About a Place (532)
  - Writing About an Object (532)
  - Writing About an Event (533)
- Descriptive Essay (75–82)

- Narrative Paragraph (93–96, 526)
- Personal Narrative (97–112)
- Biographical Narrative (135–142)

- Expository Paragraph (157–160, 528)
- Expository Essay (161–176)
- Classification Essay (199–204)

- Persuasive Paragraph (219–222, 529)
- Persuasive Essay (223–238)
- Pet-Peeve Essay (261–266)

- Paragraph Response (283–286)
- Book Review (287–300)
- Fictionalized Journal Entry (323–328)

- Classroom Report (332–333)
- Summary Paragraph (378–380)
- Research Report (381–410)
- Paraphrasing (390)

- Learning Logs (435–438)
- Freewriting, Listing, Clustering (439–440)
- Taking Classroom Tests (460–467)
- Writing a Definition (523)
- Writing Effective Paragraphs (530–531)

Writing to Share Learning

Having students share their writing lets them interact with an audience and builds a healthy learning community. Writing that will be shared is revised and edited for that purpose, and the means of presenting is often graded. The numbers in parentheses below indicate page numbers in *Write Source* where guidelines and models are found.

- Listening and Speaking (417–422)
- Making Oral Presentations (423–430)
- Book Review (287–300)
- Editorial (554)
- Multimedia Presentation (411–415)
- Publishing Ideas (57–64, 129, 193, 255, 317, 349, 357, 405)

Writing to Learn New Concepts and Ideas

Popular writing-to-learn activities are unrehearsed and ungraded activities like those listed below. The purpose is not to produce a finished piece of writing but rather to record one's thoughts on paper in order to organize, explore, and understand them.

- **Taking Notes** (441–448)
- **Using Graphic Organizers** (548–549)
- **Question-of-the-Day**

    Students respond to a "What if?" or "Why?" question that is important to a clear understanding of the lesson. These responses may be read in class to promote discussion.

- **Warm-Ups**

    Students write for the first 5 or 10 minutes of class. The writing can be a question of-the-day, a freewriting, a focused writing, or any other writing-to-learn activity that is appropriate. Warm-ups not only help students focus on the lesson at hand but also provide students with material to use for reviewing. Students find warm-ups are an opportunity to rehearse answers, opinions, and perspectives for discussion.

Writing to Reflect on Learning

Exploring personal thoughts and feelings helps students to extend a line of thought beyond the range of first impressions, to actively look for connections among subjects, and to enlarge their global perspective.

- **Keeping Journals and Writing Logs** (431–440)
- **First Thoughts**

    Students write or list their immediate impressions or what they already know about a topic they are preparing to study. The writing helps students focus on the topic, and it serves as a reference point for measuring learning.

- **K-W-L**

    Students use a three-column graphic organizer to list what they know (the *K* column), what they want to learn (the *W* column), and after the lesson is completed what they learned (the *L* column). K-W-L helps students connect with prior learning, find gaps in what they know, and measure their learning.

Writing to Plan and Complete Classroom Tasks

Writing to plan is a beneficial lifelong skill. When assigning writing for this purpose, teachers often choose forms of workplace writing. Workplace writing helps students (1) organize materials, develop plans, and budget time; (2) correspond with others regarding progress on course work; and (3) learn how to use writing to do work in the marketplace.

- **Completing Writing Assignments** (449–458)
    - Recalling (452)
    - Applying (454)
    - Synthesizing (456)
    - Understanding (453)
    - Analyzing (455)
    - Evaluating (457)

■ **Proposals**

Students write detailed plans for a project, research, solving a problem, and other activities. Proposals should include the date, teacher's name, student's name, subject, project description, materials needed, deadlines, procedure, and expected outcome. (555, 576)

■ **Class Minutes**

Students may take turns recording what happens in class. Minutes remind students and teachers about important information. Minutes also help absent students know what happened in class. Some teachers send these to parents. (150–151)

Specific WAC Activities for Content Areas

Social Studies

- Describing a Scene in a Different Time (84–85)
- Writing Classroom Journals (144–145)
- Creating a Survey (206–207)
- Creating an Editorial Cartoon (268–269)
- Reviewing a Biography (330–331)
- Social Studies Log (438)

Math

- Describing Geometric Terms (86–87)
- Writing Story Problems (146–147)
- Explaining a Concept (208–209)
- Presenting a Proof (270–271)
- Math Log (437)

Science

- Describing a Natural Event (88–89)
- Writing an Anecdote (148–149)
- Writing an Explanation (210–211)
- Supporting a Theory (272–273)
- Summarizing an Article (332–333)
- Science Log (436)

Practical Writing

- Creating a Thank-You Note (90–91)
- Recording Class Minutes (150–151)
- Drafting Directions (212–213)
- Drafting a Persuasive Letter (274–277)
- Completing an Evaluation (334–335)

Editing and Proofreading Strategies

Editing and proofreading are difficult tasks for most students. To help them be successful, you may want to use a variety of techniques. The goal is not only to help students correct errors but also to give them opportunities to grow more independent when editing. The following techniques help meet both these goals. They employ a variety of learning styles and offer ample teaching opportunities.

Published Checklists

Editing checklists are a part of each writing unit in the pupil edition. These checklists remind students what to look for when editing and proofreading. They work well for students who understand the concepts and rules being checked. For students who need more help with grammar, usage, and mechanics, however, the checklists may need to be worked with over time, covering one rule at a time. After each skill on the checklist is taught, students can be held responsible for corrections. You can use mini-lessons for small groups and modeling on overhead transparencies to teach the rules that students don't know.

Personal Checklists

Students make personal checklists by keeping a list of errors that they frequently make in their writing. They use this list to edit their writing for all classes, and it can be shared with parents. The lists are maintained by the student. Teachers may ask students to use a listed rule correctly three to four times in their writing before students can cross it off the list.

Personal Spelling Book

A personal spelling book is a list of words that students frequently misspell. Students can use either a notebook or index cards to compile their spelling list and can refer to it when editing. When time permits, learning partners can help each other learn to spell their words correctly. This list can be shared with parents.

Buddy System

When editing and proofreading, two heads are definitely better than one! Having students look for errors in each other's writing is always a good idea because first-time readers find errors more easily. Students may edit each other's papers and then meet to compare their findings and fix the errors. The checklists at the end of each unit can help students edit one another's papers.

Brackets

Students come to class with brackets around the places in their writing where they have doubts about their correct use of conventions. Students are then given class time (10–15 minutes) to find the information they need in a resource and, if necessary, make a correction. The Proofreader's Guide (the yellow pages at the back of the pupil edition, PE pages 578–749) is most useful.

Using resources such as the Proofreader's Guide is a lifetime skill that students need to be practice. In real life, students will often need to depend on a resource to answer their editing questions. While students look for the rules they need, the teacher can help them by suggesting where to look. In this way, students learn terminology that is needed in order to look up and understand grammar rules.

Classroom Editors

Students serve as editors for specific problems. A person who knows the most about capitalization becomes the "Capital Editor." Another who knows about end punctuation becomes the editor who helps classmates with end punctuation. Being able to teach a rule to another not only helps the recipient, but it also helps the "editor" clarify and understand the rules. Sometimes the last 10 minutes of a class period is a good time to have classroom editors open for business. Other times classroom editors may hang a sign on their desk announcing they can help classmates at this time.

Ask a Question

When using this technique, a teacher sets aside a period of time—10 to 15 minutes—for students to ask questions. Students should locate and fix as many errors as possible on their own, saving their questions for something they don't understand or something that seems to conflict with a rule or concept. Teachers often request that students ask specific questions, and when first using this technique, you may want to model how to ask specific questions. For example, "Do I need a comma here because this is an introductory word group?" Ask a Question can be done as a whole group or individually. This is an excellent technique to use several times just before a paper is due.

Target List

A Target List is a checklist written by the teacher for a particular writing unit. The list contains the grammar rules and concepts that will be assessed in the unit and is given to students at the beginning of the unit. Mini-lessons, desk-side conferences, and worksheets are used throughout the unit to teach each rule on the list. Using this method provides for instruction before assessment, and it limits the types of errors that will be assessed. Students who have a lot of trouble with grammar can often gain self-confidence and score well.

Modeling the Use of Resources

The teacher becomes the editor-with-a-resource, looking up the answer to a question using any resource available. Modeling the use of a resource sets a good example for students. The teacher talks out loud while using the resource. Usually this is done as a whole class so that all students hear the questions and the answers. Students learn to ask specific questions that reveal how much the student knows. For example, "Do I capitalize *mom* in this sentence, 'Today Mom starts a new job'?" indicates the student is aware that sometimes *mom* is capitalized and other times it is not.

In this case, the teacher could say, "I'm going to look under capitalization in the yellow pages of your book. Once I find that section, I'll read the headings to find the rule. Here it is. Look on page 618 at number 4."

Teacher Editing and Proofreading

When using this technique, the teacher places brackets around the errors in a student's writing. The teacher will add a number from the Proofreader's Guide to which students can go to find the information they need to make a correction. This technique can precede the use of the technique called "Brackets." It is also an excellent technique to use for ESL students and other students who need extra support.

Practice Sentences

The teacher prints a number of incorrect sentences on a piece of paper or an overhead transparency (or the teacher can use *Daily Language Workout*). As a group, the class works to make these sentences correct. After the teacher models this technique several times, students themselves may take the place of the teacher. If a student has a particular sentence that he or she would like help correcting, the student can copy the sentence onto a transparency and present it to the class. This technique can be used with small groups or the class as a whole on a weekly basis or shortly before an assignment is due.

When students need or want a piece of information, both their attention span and their commitment to the task increase. These NOW (Needed Or Wanted) moments are teaching opportunities. Many variations of this technique are used. Sometimes students are given a number of sentences to correct on their own. The activity is often graded. Sometimes a corner of the blackboard is reserved where students can write sentences they need help with. Classmates copy these sentences, correct them, and turn them in for credit before giving them to their classmate.

Assessment and Instruction

In past decades, writing assessment was generally held to be the province of the teacher. Students turned in work—then waited to see what grades they would receive. Now it is widely recognized that learning to be a good assessor is one of the best ways to become a strong writer. In order to assess well, students must learn to recognize good writing. They must know and be able to describe the difference between writing that works and writing that does not work. Students learn to assess, generally, by going through three key steps:

- Learning about the traits of writing by which their work—and that of others— will be assessed
- Applying the traits to a wide variety of written texts
- Applying the traits to their own work—first assessing it for strengths and weaknesses, then revising it as needed

Why should students be assessors?

Students who learn to be assessors also

- learn to think like professional writers,
- take responsibility for their own revising, and
- make meaningful changes in their writing—instead of simply recopying a draft to make it look neater.

Role of Teachers and Students

Here is a quick summary of the kinds of activities teachers and students usually engage in while acting as assessors in the classroom.

Teachers

As assessors, teachers often engage in the following activities:

- roving conferences: roaming the classroom, observing students' work, and offering comments or questions that will help take students to the next step
- one-on-one conferences, in which students are asked to come prepared with a question they need answered
- informal comments—written or oral—in which the teacher offers a personal response or poses a reader's question
- reading student work, using a checklist such as the one in this teacher's edition (TE page 767)
- tracking scores over time to calculate a final grade for a grading period

Students

As assessors, students often engage in the following activities:

- using the rubrics in the student text
- using an *assessment sheet* such as the one on page 55 in the pupil edition and page 799 in the teacher's edition
- assessing and discussing written work that the teacher shares with the class
- assessing their own work, using a rubric
- compiling a portfolio and reflecting on the written work included

Effective Assessment in the Classroom

Good assessment gives students a sense of how they are growing as writers. It indicates to teachers which students are finding success, as well as the specific kinds of help other students may need. To ensure that assessment is working in your classrooms, here are some things you can do.

■ Make sure ALL students know the criteria you will use to assess their writing. If you are going to use a rating sheet or rubric, provide them with copies.

■ Give copies of rubrics or checklists to parents, too, so they can help their children know what is expected of them.

■ Make sure your instruction and assessment match.

■ Involve students regularly in assessing
  ▪ published work from a variety of sources,
  ▪ your work (share your writing—even if it's in unfinished draft form), and
  ▪ their own work.

■ Don't grade *everything* students write. Instead, encourage students to write *often*; then choose or have students choose a few pieces to grade.

■ Respond to the content *first*. Then look at the conventions. Correctness is important, but if you comment on spelling and mechanics before content, the message to students is, "I don't care so much about what you say as I do about whether you spell everything correctly."

■ Encourage students to save rough drafts and to collect pieces of work regularly in a portfolio. This type of collection gives students a broad picture of how they are progressing as writers.

■ Ask students if they mind having comments written directly on their work. For some students, comments on sticky notes may seem less obtrusive.

Conducting Conferences

Conduct conferences to maintain an open line of communication with student writers at all points during the development of a piece of writing. Here are three common practices that you can employ to communicate with student writers during a writing project:

■ **Desk-Side Conferences** occur when you stop at a student's desk to ask questions and make responses. Questions should be open-ended. This gives the writers "space" to talk and clarify his or her own thinking about the writing.

■ **Scheduled Conferences** give you and a student a chance to meet in a more structured setting. In such a conference, a student may have a specific problem or need to discuss or simply want you to assess his or her progress on a particular piece of writing.

  Note: A typical conference should last from 3 to 5 minutes. Always try to praise one thing, ask an appropriate question, and offer one or two suggestions.

■ **Small-Group Conferences** give three to five students who are at the same stage of the writing process or are experiencing the same problem a chance to meet with you. The goal of such conferences is twofold: first, to help students improve their writing, and, second, to help them develop as evaluators of writing.

Formative vs. Summative Assessment

Formative assessment is ongoing and is often not linked to a letter grade or score. It may be as simple as a brief one-on-one conference or an informal review of the beginning of a student's draft to suggest possible next steps. **Summative assessment**, on the other hand, is a summing up of a student's performance and is generally reflected in a grade. Formative assessments usually occur in the form of a comment—oral or written. Summative assessments take the form of

- a letter grade,
- total points earned,
- a percentage score, or
- some combination of these.

Responding to Nongraded Writing (Formative)

- React noncritically with positive, supportive language.
- Use marginal dialogue. Resist writing on or over the student's writing.
- Respond whenever possible in the form of questions. Nurture curiosity.
- Encourage risk taking.

Evaluating Graded Writing (Summative)

- Ask students to submit prewriting and rough drafts with their final drafts.
- Scan final drafts once, focusing on the writing as a whole.
- Reread them, evaluating their adherence to previously established criteria.
- Make marginal notations as you read the drafts a second time.
- Scan the writing a third and final time. Note the feedback you have given.
- Complete your rating sheet or rubric, and write a summary comment.

Approaches for Assessing Writing (Summative)

The most common forms of direct writing assessment are listed below.

Analytical assessment identifies the features, or traits, that characterize effective writing, and defines them along a continuum of performance from *incomplete* (the first or lowest level) through *fair* (the middle level) to *excellent* (the highest level). Many analytical scales run from a low of 1 point to a high of 5 or 6 points. This form of assessment tells students exactly where their strengths and weaknesses lie: "Your writing has strong ideas but needs work on voice," or "Your writing has powerful voice but lacks accuracy."

Holistic assessment focuses on a piece of writing as a whole. In this sense, it is like letter grading. Holistic assessors often use a checklist of traits to identify the kinds of characteristics they're looking for; this is called focused holistic assessment. The assessors do not, however, score traits separately, so student writers do not know where they were most or least successful in their work.

Mode-specific assessment is similar to analytic assessment except that the rating scales or scoring guides (rubrics) are designed specifically for particular modes of writing, such as narrative, expository, persuasive, and so on. This kind of assessment works best in a structured curriculum where students will be assigned particular forms and subjects for writing.

Portfolio assessment gives students a chance to showcase their best writing or to document their growth as writers over time. In assembling a portfolio, students generally choose which pieces of writing they will complete and which ones they will include in their portfolios. (See pages 65–69 in the pupil edition.)

Assessment in *Write Source*

Using Rubrics Assessment of writing in *Write Source* is based on mode-specific rubrics. In each core unit—narrative, expository, persuasive, and response to literature—genre-specific rubrics guide both the development of written work and the evaluation of the work. The rubrics are organized around the six traits of effective writing: ideas, organization, voice, word choice, sentence fluency, and conventions. Each trait is evaluated individually as part of a total assessment. When you first start using rubrics in the classroom, either with students' own work or with published writing, it may be more manageable to have students focus on one specific trait (such as organization). Gradually, you can add other traits until you ask them to evaluate a piece of writing for all of the traits.

Benchmark Papers In addition to assessing their own writing, in each core unit of the pupil edition—narrative, expository, persuasive, and response to literature—students (and teachers) have the opportunity to evaluate a student paper and review the student's self-assessment of that paper. This evaluation follows in-depth instruction on the genre. Furthermore, for each of these units there are two additional writing samples, or benchmark papers, representing different levels of expertise that teachers can use with students for further assessment practice. The writing samples are provided in transparency form so that you can discuss them together as a group, and in copy master form so that students can have a version in front of them. A blank assessment sheet, based on the traits of writing, allows students and you to rate the writing samples. Finally, a completed assessment sheet is provided for each benchmark paper to guide teachers through the assessment. Following are the benchmark papers and their level of competence.

Benchmark Papers

Narrative Writing
Suzie (strong)
A Knotty Problem (good)
A January Surprise (poor)

Expository Writing
Malcolm X and Eleanor Roosevelt (strong)
Making Amazing Maps (good)
Yo-Yos Flood Del Mar Hills School (poor)

Persuasive Writing
Zoos (strong)
Get Moving (good)
Letter to the Editor (poor)

Response to Literature
Caddie Woodlawn (strong)
Zlateh the Goat (good)
Gypsy and Woodrow (poor)

Assessment Book In addition to rubrics-based assessment of students' writing, teachers can assess students' writing skills through the four tests in the *Assessment Book*. These 3-part tests are designed to be taken throughout the year, with a pretest at the beginning of the year, two progress tests during the year, and a post-test at the end of the year. The first two parts of each test are aligned with two reference sections in the back of the pupil edition, the Basic Elements of Writing and the Proofreader's Guide. The third part is a writing prompt. These tests are available in the Teacher's Resource Pack.

Six-Trait Checklist

Ideas

- ☐ focuses on a specific topic
- ☐ has a clear focus statement
- ☐ contains specific details

Organization

- ☐ has a beginning, middle, and ending
- ☐ has a topic sentence for each paragraph
- ☐ has enough details to develop each topic sentence
- ☐ uses transitions to connect paragraphs

Voice

- ☐ speaks in an engaging way that keeps readers wanting to hear more
- ☐ shows that the writer really cares about the subject

Word Choice

- ☐ contains specific nouns and action verbs
- ☐ presents an appropriate level of language (not too formal or too informal)

Sentence Fluency

- ☐ flows smoothly from sentence to sentence
- ☐ shows variety in sentence beginnings and lengths
- ☐ uses transitions to connect sentences

Conventions

- ☐ follows the basic rules of grammar, spelling, capitalization, and punctuation.

4-Point

Rubric for Narrative Writing

Use this rubric for guiding and assessing your narrative writing. Refer to it whenever you want to improve your writing using the six traits.

Ideas

4 The narrative tells about an unforgettable experience. The details make the story truly memorable.

3 The writer tells about an interesting experience. More details are needed.

2 The writer needs to focus on one experience. Some details do not relate to the story.

1 The writer needs to tell about an experience and use details.

Organization

4 The narrative is well organized, with a clear beginning, middle, and ending, making it enjoyable and easy to read.

3 The narrative is well organized. Transitions are used well.

2 The order of events needs to be corrected. More transitions need to be used. One part of the narrative is weak.

1 The beginning, middle, and ending all run together. The order is unclear.

Voice

4 The writer's voice sounds natural and creates interest in the story. Dialogue is used.

3 The writer's voice creates interest in the story. More dialogue is needed.

2 A voice can usually be heard. More dialogue is needed.

1 The voice is weak. Dialogue is needed.

Word Choice

4 Strong nouns and verbs and well-chosen modifiers create vivid, clear pictures.

3 Modifiers are used. Strong nouns and active verbs would improve sensory images.

2 Strong nouns, verbs, and modifiers are needed to create sensory images.

1 General and overused words do not create sensory images.

Sentence Fluency

4 The sentences are skillfully written and original. They keep the reader's interest.

3 The sentences show variety. Most are easy to read and understand, but some should flow more smoothly.

2 A better variety of sentences is needed. Sentences do not read smoothly.

1 Incomplete and/or short sentences make the writing choppy.

Conventions

4 The narrative is error free.

3 The narrative has several errors in punctuation, spelling, or grammar.

2 Many errors make the narrative confusing and hard to read.

1 Help is needed to make corrections.

4-Point

Rubric for Expository Writing

Use this rubric for guiding and assessing your expository writing. Refer to it to help you improve your writing using the six traits.

Ideas

4 The essay is informative with a clear focus and specific details.

3 The focus of the essay needs to be clearer, and more specific details are needed.

2 The topic needs to be narrowed or expanded. Many more specific details are needed.

1 A new topic needs to be selected.

Organization

4 The beginning interests the reader. The middle supports the focus. The ending works well. Transitions are used.

3 The beginning or ending is weak. The middle needs a paragraph for each main point. More transitions are needed.

2 The beginning, middle, and ending all run together. Paragraphs and transitions are needed.

1 The essay should be reorganized.

Voice

4 The writer's voice sounds confident, knowledgeable, and enthusiastic.

3 The writer's voice sounds well-informed most of the time, but the voice needs to fit the audience better.

2 The writer sounds unsure. The voice needs to fit the audience.

1 The writer needs to learn about voice.

Word Choice

4 Specific nouns and action verbs make the essay clear, informative, and fun to read.

3 Some nouns and verbs could be more specific.

2 Too many general words are used. Specific nouns and verbs are needed.

1 General or missing words make this essay hard to understand.

Sentence Fluency

4 The sentences flow smoothly, and people will enjoy reading them.

3 Most of the sentences read smoothly, but some are short and choppy.

2 Many short, choppy sentences need to be rewritten to make the essay read smoothly.

1 Most sentences are choppy or incomplete and need to be rewritten.

Conventions

4 The essay is error free.

3 The essay has several errors in punctuation, spelling, or grammar.

2 Many errors make the essay confusing and hard to read.

1 Help is needed to make corrections.

4-Point

Rubric for Persuasive Writing

Use the following rubric for guiding and assessing your persuasive writing. Refer to it whenever you want to improve your writing using the six traits.

Ideas

4 The essay has a clear opinion statement. Logical reasons support the writer's opinion.

3 The opinion statement is clear. Reasons and details are not as complete as they need to be.

2 The opinion statement is unclear. Reasons and details are needed.

1 An opinion statement, reasons, and details are needed.

Organization

4 The opening contains the opinion statement. The middle provides clear support. The transitions build strong connections.

3 The opening contains the opinion statement. The middle provides support. Some transitions do not work.

2 The beginning, middle, and ending exist. Transitions are needed.

1 The organization is unclear. The reader is easily lost.

Voice

4 The writer's voice is confident and helps persuade the reader.

3 The writer's voice is confident. It needs to persuade the reader.

2 The writer's voice needs to be more confident and persuade the reader.

1 The writer's voice can't be heard.

Word Choice

4 Strong, engaging, positive words contribute to the main message. Every word counts.

3 Strong, positive words are used, but some overused words need synonyms.

2 Many words need to be stronger and more positive.

1 The same weak words are used throughout the essay.

Sentence Fluency

4 The sentences flow smoothly, and people will enjoy reading the variety of sentences.

3 Varied sentence beginnings are used. Sentence variety would make the essay more interesting to read.

2 Most sentences begin the same way. Most of the sentences are simple. Compound and complex sentences are needed.

1 Sentence fluency has not been established. Ideas do not flow smoothly.

Conventions

4 The essay is free of errors.

3 Grammar and punctuation errors are seen in a few sentences. They distract the reader in those areas.

2 Frequent errors make the essay difficult to read.

1 Nearly every sentence contains errors.

4-Point
Rubric for Response to Literature

Use this rubric for guiding and assessing your writing. Refer to it whenever you want to improve your writing using the six traits.

Ideas

4 The focus statement and related details show real insight into the reading.
3 The response has a clear focus statement. Unnecessary details need to be cut.
2 The focus statement is too broad. Unnecessary details need to be cut.
1 The focus statement is not developed. Details are needed.

Organization

4 The organization pattern fits the topic and purpose. All parts of the response are well developed.
3 The organization pattern fits the topic and purpose. A part of the response needs better development.
2 The organization fits the response's purpose. All the parts need more development.
1 The organization doesn't fit the purpose.

Voice

4 The writer's voice express interest and complete understanding. It engages the reader.
3 The writer's voice expresses interest and understanding of most of the reading.
2 The writer's voice does not express an understanding.
1 The writer needs to understand how to create voice.

Word Choice

4 Specific nouns and action verbs make the response clear and informative.
3 Too many general words are used. Specific nouns and verbs are needed.
2 General or overused words make this response hard to understand.
1 The writer needs help finding specific words.

Sentence Fluency

4 All sentences are skillfully written and keep the reader's interest.
3 No sentence problems exist. More sentence variety is needed.
2 The response has many sentence problems.
1 The writer needs to learn how to construct sentences.

Conventions

4 The response is correct from start to finish.
3 The response has some errors in punctuation, spelling, or grammar.
2 The number of errors confuses the reader and makes the essay hard to read.
1 Help is needed to make corrections.

5-Point

Rubric for Narrative Writing

Use this rubric for guiding and assessing your narrative writing. Refer to it whenever you want to improve your writing using the six traits.

Ideas

5 The narrative tells about an unforgettable experience. The details make the story truly memorable.

4 The writer tells about an interesting experience. More details are needed.

3 The writer needs to focus on one experience. Some details do not relate to the story.

2 The writer needs to focus on one experience. Details are needed.

1 The writer needs to tell about an experience and use details.

Organization

5 The narrative is well organized, with a clear beginning, middle, and ending, making it enjoyable and easy to read.

4 The narrative is well organized. Transitions are used well.

3 The order of events needs to be corrected. More transitions need to be used. One part of the narrative is weak.

2 The beginning, middle, and ending all run together. The order is unclear.

1 The narrative needs to be organized.

Voice

5 The writer's voice sounds natural and creates interest in the story. Dialogue is used.

4 The writer's voice creates interest in the story. More dialogue is needed.

3 A voice can usually be heard. More dialogue is needed.

2 The voice is weak. Dialogue is needed.

1 The writer has not gotten involved in the story. Dialogue is needed.

Word Choice

5 Strong nouns and verbs and well-chosen modifiers create vivid, clear pictures.

4 Modifiers are used. Strong nouns and active verbs would improve sensory images.

3 Strong nouns, verbs, and modifiers are needed to create sensory images.

2 General and overused words do not create sensory images.

1 The writer has not yet considered word choice.

Sentence Fluency

5 The sentences are skillfully written and original. They keep the reader's interest.

4 The sentences show variety. Most are easy to read and understand, but some should flow more smoothly.

3 A better variety of sentences is needed. Sentences do not read smoothly.

2 Incomplete and/or short sentences make the writing choppy.

1 Few sentences are written well. Help is needed.

Conventions

5 The narrative is error free.

4 The narrative has several errors in punctuation, spelling, or grammar.

3 Some errors confuse the reader.

2 Many errors make the narrative confusing and hard to read.

1 Help is needed to make corrections.

5-Point

Rubric for Expository Writing

Use this rubric for guiding and assessing your expository writing. Refer to it to help you improve your writing using the six traits.

Ideas

5 The essay is informative with a clear focus and specific details.
4 The essay is informative with a clear focus. More specific details are needed.
3 The focus of the essay needs to be clearer, and more specific details are needed.
2 The topic needs to be narrowed or expanded. Many more specific details are needed.
1 A new topic needs to be selected.

Organization

5 The beginning interests the reader. The middle supports the focus. The ending works well. Transitions are used.
4 The essay is divided into a beginning, a middle, and an ending. Some transitions are used.
3 The beginning or ending is weak. The middle needs a paragraph for each main point. More transitions are needed.
2 The beginning, middle, and ending all run together. Paragraphs and transitions are needed.
1 The essay should be reorganized.

Voice

5 The writer's voice sounds confident, knowledgeable, and enthusiastic.
4 The writer's voice sounds well-informed most of the time and fits the audience.
3 The writer sometimes sounds unsure, and the voice needs to fit the audience better.
2 The writer sounds unsure. The voice needs to fit the audience.
1 The writer needs to learn about voice.

Word Choice

5 Specific nouns and action verbs make the essay clear, informative, and fun to read.
4 Some nouns and verbs could be more specific.
3 Too many general words are used. Specific nouns and verbs are needed.
2 General or missing words make this essay hard to understand.
1 The writer needs help finding specific words.

Sentence Fluency

5 The sentences flow smoothly, and people will enjoy reading them.
4 Most of the sentences read smoothly, but some are short and choppy.
3 Many short, choppy sentences need to be rewritten to make the essay read smoothly.
2 Many sentences are choppy or incomplete and need to be rewritten.
1 Most sentences need to be rewritten.

Conventions

5 The essay is error free.
4 The essay has several errors in punctuation, spelling, or grammar.
3 Some errors confuse the reader.
2 Many errors make the essay confusing and hard to read.
1 Help is needed to make corrections.

5-Point

Rubric for Persuasive Writing

Use the following rubric for guiding and assessing your persuasive writing. Refer to it whenever you want to improve your writing using the six traits.

Ideas

5 The essay has a clear opinion statement. Logical reasons support the writer's opinion.

4 The opinion statement is clear, and most reasons support the writer's opinion.

3 The opinion statement is clear. Reasons and details are not as complete as they need to be.

2 The opinion statement is unclear. Reasons and details are needed.

1 An opinion statement, reasons, and details are needed.

Organization

5 The opening contains the opinion statement. The middle provides clear support. The transitions build strong connections.

4 The opening contains the opinion statement. The middle provides support. Some transitions do not work.

3 The beginning, middle, and ending exist. Transitions are needed.

2 The beginning, middle, and ending run together.

1 The organization is unclear. The reader is easily lost.

Voice

5 The writer's voice is confident and helps persuade the reader.

4 The writer's voice is confident. It needs to persuade the reader.

3 The writer's voice needs to be more confident and persuade the reader.

2 The writer's voice sounds bored.

1 The writer's voice can't be heard.

Word Choice

5 Strong, engaging, positive words contribute to the main message. Every word counts.

4 Strong, positive words are used, but some overused words need synonyms.

3 Many words need to be stronger and more positive.

2 The same weak words are used throughout the essay.

1 Word choice has not been considered.

Sentence Fluency

5 The sentences flow smoothly, and people will enjoy reading the variety of sentences.

4 Varied sentence beginnings are used. Sentence variety would make the essay more interesting to read.

3 Varied sentence beginnings are needed. Sentence variety would make the essay more interesting.

2 Most sentences begin the same way. Most of the sentences are simple. Compound and complex sentences are needed.

1 Sentence fluency has not been established. Ideas do not flow smoothly.

Conventions

5 The essay is free of errors.

4 Grammar and punctuation errors are seen in a few sentences. They distract the reader in those areas.

3 There are a number of errors that may confuse the reader.

2 Frequent errors make the essay difficult to read.

1 Nearly every sentence contains errors.

5-Point
Rubric for Response to Literature

Use this rubric for guiding and assessing your writing. Refer to it whenever you want to improve your writing using the six traits.

Ideas
5 The focus statement and related details show real insight into the reading.
4 The response has a clear focus statement. Unnecessary details need to be cut.
3 The focus statement is too broad. Unnecessary details need to be cut.
2 The focus statement is not developed. Details are needed.
1 The response needs a focus statement and details.

Organization
5 The organization pattern fits the topic and purpose. All parts of the response are well developed.
4 The organization pattern fits the topic and purpose. A part of the response needs better development.
3 The organization fits the response's purpose. All the parts need more development.
2 The organization doesn't fit the purpose.
1 A plan needs to be followed.

Voice
5 The writer's voice expresses interest and complete understanding. It engages the reader.
4 The writer's voice expresses interest and understanding of most of the reading.
3 The writer's voice needs to express a clearer understanding.
2 The writer's voice does not express an understanding.
1 The writer needs to understand how to create voice.

Word Choice
5 Specific nouns and action verbs make the response clear and informative.
4 Some nouns and verbs could be more specific.
3 Too many general words are used. Specific nouns and verbs are needed.
2 General or overused words make this response hard to understand.
1 The writer needs help finding specific words.

Sentence Fluency
5 All sentences are skillfully written and keep the reader's interest.
4 No sentence problems exist. More sentence variety is needed.
3 Sentence problems are found in a few places.
2 The response has many sentence problems.
1 The writer needs to learn how to construct sentences.

Conventions
5 The response is correct from start to finish.
4 The response has some errors in punctuation, spelling, or grammar.
3 The response has errors that may confuse the reader.
2 The number of errors confuses the reader and makes the essay hard to read.
1 Help is needed to make corrections.

Narrative Writing

Suzie

1   It was a hot summer day. My dad and I were getting ready to go
2   out for a ride on the boat with my friend Katie and our dog. That's
3   when the phone call came, the call that made that bright, beautiful
4   day a cold, dark, gloomy one.

5   I had just put on my suit, shorts, and tank top, and packed my
6   bag with sunscreen and everything else I would need for the day. I
7   ran into my parents' room to find Dad. When I saw him on the phone,
8   he was crying. I'd never seen my dad cry before. My heart sank. What
9   possibly could have happened?

10   "Max, I'm so sorry," I heard him say. That's when it hit me. I knew
11   that Suzie had died.

12   Max has been my dad's best friend for years. Suzie, his daughter,
13   had a rare disease that mainly affected her body. Her brain was okay.
14   She knew what was going on; she knew that she had problems and
15   was different from other kids. Once she told her dad that she wished
16   she could die and be born in a different body. Although she couldn't
17   live a normal life, she was still happy.

18   When Suzie and I were little, we spent quite a bit of time
19   together. As we grew up, we grew apart. She lived in New York, and I
20   lived in the Midwest. When Suzie was ten, she had to live in a hospital

21 in Virginia. About eight months before she died, Max gave us her

22 telephone number at the hospital and we talked at least twice a week

23 until the end. Suzie was always so excited to talk to us and wanted to

24 know every detail about my life. She wanted to know everything I did

25 and everything I ate. In a way, she lived through me.

26   After we found out about her death, we made our plans to go to

27 New York for the funeral. When she was alive, I sent her a teddy bear

28 and she sent one back to me. I had bought her another one but never

29 had the chance to send it to her, so I took it with me to give to her

30 parents.

Assessment Sheet

Title _Suzie_

_5_ Ideas

- The details you have included show readers this is a very moving narrative about a difficult experience.

- Details such as knowing what Suzie's illness was and having her described more would help readers know her better and feel your loss more strongly.

_6_ Organization

- Your excellent organization using time order shows your writing skill.

- Using a flashback (see lines 12–25) helps you give readers background information after you chose to start in the middle of the action.

_4_ Voice

- Your personal voice adds feeling.

- Showing instead of telling helps create a strong voice. Including a conversation that you had with Suzie could show she "wanted to know everything. . . . "

_5_ Word Choice

- You use an appropriate level of language for this serious and moving experience.

- Words like "beautiful" (see line 3) and "happy" (see line 17) are common words. You could find other words (synonyms) that help readers create clear pictures.

_6_ Sentence Fluency

- The variety of sentence beginnings as well as a variety of sentence structures—simple, compound, and complex—show writing skill.

- Your use of short, simple sentences for the most critical events works well: "My heart sank" and "I knew Suzie had died."

_6_ Conventions

- You obviously edited and proofread very well.

- There are no errors even when you use dialogue and beginning word groups.

Narrative Writing

A January Surprise

1   I had always wondered what it was like to have surgery. My

2   questions were answered on a morning last January. I woke up with

3   stomach pains.

4   "Mom my stomach really hurts."

5   "You probably have the flu."

6   "I don't think so. The pains are . . ."

7   Dad interrupted "It's probably just something you ate."

8   "I think I'm really sick I'm scared."

9   Dad turned the bedside lamp on and looked at me "I think we'll

10   go to the hospital" he said as he swung his legs onto the floor.

11   I didn't want to go to the hospital. It was 3 a.m. Dad got dressed.

12   By that time I was so sick he carried me to the car. At the emergency

13   room the doctors and nurses took tests. They gave me shots. My

14   stomach hurt so much that I didn't mind the shots. I heard a nurse

15   tell my Dad that she thought it was my appendix. I was getting

16   worried!

17   They took me upstairs on a gurney a rolling bed. It was kind

18   of fun being wheeled around. When I got upstairs they gave me a

19   hospital gown. It didn't have a back. It was embarrassing. The doctor

20   came to my room. He examine me. He said he thought it was my

21 appendix. It would have to come out. Another doctor came to my room.

22 He told me they were going to operate at 9 a.m. They were afraid my

23 appendix would burst. I don't remember much after that. They took

24 me up to the surgery floor. They put a mask on me and I fell asleep.

25 I woke up in the recovery room with a new mask on I kept trying to

26 take it off. A nurse yelled at me a couple of times I was really annoyed

27 but I kept it on after that.

28   The worst thing about surgery was that I was so thirsty. I was

29 mad I yelled at everybody. A nurse finally gave me some ice chips

30 to suck on. I fell asleep. I didn't see any visitors that day. The best

31 part about surgery was that all my friends gave me gifts. I got game

32 puzzles magazines and balloons. The balloons were the best because

33 they made my sister jealous.

34   I spent three days in the hospital. After three days I was ready

35 to go home because of the four-year-old in the next bed who just had

36 his tonsils out. His mom and dad watch M*A*S*H all night while I

37 was trying to sleep. Getting my appendix out was one of the strangest

38 times of my life. Now that I know what surgery is like I don't think I

39 want to go through it again.

Assessment Sheet

Title *A January Surprise*

_4_ Ideas

- *You keep your focus on one event very well.*
- *More specific details—especially when you first knew that you were ill and when you woke up from the operation—would keep your reader's interest.*

_4_ Organization

- *You have used a time line to organize your paper well.*
- *Transitions between paragraphs would connect one event to the other. It was hard to figure out that you went to your parents' room when you woke up sick.*

_2_ Voice

- *Your voice sounds honest because you report everything that happened.*
- *Because this was an important and frightening experience, you could use a stronger voice. For example, "I think I'm really sick" could become "I'm in pain." Your word choice helps build your writing voice.*

_3_ Word Choice

- *Your title grabs the reader's attention.*
- *Stronger verbs would add action and more adjectives would help readers create images.*

_2_ Sentence Fluency

- *Some of the short sentences you have used work well because they add to the nervous tension that you want your readers to know you were feeling.*
- *Combine other shorter sentences to avoid choppiness (see line 11).*

_2_ Conventions

- *You have spelled difficult words correctly: embarrassing, appendix, whiny.*
- *Find two verbs that should be in the past tense ("examined" [see line 20], "watched" [see line 36]) and add missing commas and periods.*

Expository Writing

Malcolm X and Eleanor Roosevelt

1   Malcolm X and Eleanor Roosevelt were two people with entirely
2 different backgrounds. Malcolm X was a controversial black civil
3 rights leader and a convicted felon. Eleanor Roosevelt was the wife of
4 one of our most loved presidents, Franklin Delano Roosevelt. She was
5 also an avid women's rights leader. Although on the surface it might
6 seem that the two are very different, in reality they actually had
7 much in common.

8   I believe that one reason these two are viewed so differently is
9 because of how they were raised. Malcolm X was raised in a chaotic
10 family and began dealing drugs at an early age. Eleanor Roosevelt
11 started her life as a shy, smart little girl, totally lacking in self-
12 confidance. Although Malcolm X was a criminal early in his life, as
13 an adult he became one of the most articulate speakers our world
14 has ever known. The same can be said for Eleanor Roosevelt. She
15 overcame her shyness and became a great public speaker.

16   Both of these great leaders experienced early struggles and
17 hardships. Malcolm X was convicted and sent to jail. He had a difficult
18 time in jail because he could not properly write what he wanted to
19 say in his letters. Yet he turned his life around by learning to read
20 well and to write eloquently. He taught himself by copying an entire

21   dictionary. Eleanor Roosevelt had low self-esteem because she always

22   thought she was an ugly ducking. This lack of confidance prevented

23   her from properly expressing herself. Eleanor got over her low self-

24   esteem and went on to become one of the most powerful women in our

25   history by fighting for women's rights.

26   These historical figures also have great accomplishments in

27   common. Eleanor was a vocal supporter of equal rights for women,

28   who at that time faced significant discrimination. Malcolm X also

29   fought for equal rights, only he fought for blacks during a time when

30   racism was rampunt in our society. Today both women and African

31   Americans enjoy more equal rights partially because of the work of

32   these two people.

Assessment Sheet

Title *Malcolm X and Eleanor Roosevelt*

_5_ Ideas

- *The comparison of these two people is an unusual and interesting idea!*
- *You repeat your main points. It would be good to know other details about the people.*

_6_ Organization

- *You made your point-by-point comparison work very well.*
- *All the topic sentences support the focus statement.*

_4_ Voice

- *Your voice is appropriate for a formal essay.*
- *Quoting these two people would show us their voices, increase interest, and make the voice in this piece stronger.*

_5_ Word Choice

- *Precise adjectives like "controversial" (see line 2), "avid" (see line 5), and "chaotic" (see line 9) help your readers create images.*
- *Saying both "in reality" and "actually" in paragraph 1 is redundant. Using "got over" (see line 23) is too informal.*

_6_ Sentence Fluency

- *You used a variety of sentences, including complex sentences (see lines 5–9). This shows good fluency.*
- *Varied sentence beginnings and lengths of sentences make reading them enjoyable.*

_5_ Conventions

- *Punctuation and grammar are correct.*
- *A few spelling errors tell readers that you need to edit and proofread more carefully.*

Expository Writing

Yo-Yos Flood Del Mar Hills School

1   Why did the chicken cross the road? To get to Del Mar Hills

2   School and see all the yo-yos. You don't walk out of your classroom

3   without seeing at least eight yo-yoers throwing those yo-yos. A lot of

4   people claim they started this fad. Most of the yo-yo population at Del

5   Mar Hills is fourth, fifth, and sixth graders. Some people don't see

6   what's so special about yo-yos.

7   Do teachers dislike this yo-yo craze. No they don't mind. As long

8   as the kids don't do it in the classroom. There are pretty much two

9   rules for yo-yos at school; no hitting people and no playing whit the

10   yo-yos near other kids.

11   Yo-yos come in different sizes, shapes, quality, and physical

12   features. Some yo-yos you might see are the Brain, Fireball, tornado,

13   Tiger shark, Turbo Bumble Bee, Viper, and Silver Bullet. The Brain

14   has a special physical feeture that allows it to come up automatically

15   after it sleeps. The Viper is a very large yo-yo. The Bumble Bee and

16   Silver Bullet are said to sleep for along time. If you owned a yo-yo,

17   some common questions you could be asked might be "what kind of

18   yo-yo is that?" or "can you do a rock-the-baby"?

19   If you have a yo-yo stashed away somewhere, go find it. Play with

20   it for awhile. If you don't like it, stash it away again. Who knows, you

21   might like it someday.

Assessment Sheet

Title   _Yos-Yos Flood Del Mar Hills School_

_3_ Ideas

- You stayed on topic in the essay.
- You need to focus your idea in the first paragraph. Do you want to write about how popular yo-yos are or that some people like them and others don't?

_2_ Organization

- In the future, be sure to focus your writing. Then you can plan an organization.
- Neither the riddle at the beginning nor the ending works well.

_4_ Voice

- The friendly, enthusiastic voice that you use fits the topic well.
- Using "you" to connect with your readers helps create a friendly voice.
- A different voice at the beginning and end would improve this essay.

_3_ Word Choice

- Using the names of yo-yos and the throwing techniques adds interest. It also makes you sound knowledgeable.
- You could describe "rock-the-baby" and "sleep" since many readers will not understand these terms.

_3_ Sentence Fluency

- You could learn how to start sentences in a variety of ways.
- Check for sentence fragments (paragraph 2).

_2_ Conventions

- Carefully check spelling, punctuation, grammar, and usage before turning in a piece of writing.

Persuasive Writing

Zoos

1   "Look, Mom," the little girl says, tugging on her mothers hand.

2 Its a baby elephant!" I watch her eyes light up as she stares at the live

3 Elephant.cam. Like her, I enjoy watching the mother elephant care

4 for her baby. It had been born several months ago. The hidden camera

5 makes it possible to view them, yet no crowds upset them. Zoos, one of

6 my favorite places to visit, are an important part of American society

7 and should receive more funding.

8   Zoos have many different species of animals from aardvarks to

9 zebras. Of the eighteen giant pandas that live outside of China, 10 of

10 them are in American zoos. A giant panda was born at the San Diego

11 Zoo in 1999. Colo, the first western lowland gorilla born in captivity

12 will celebrate her 47th birthday this year. I would probably have

13 never seen a giant panda or a gorilla if they were not in zoos.

14   Zoos help save and protect endangered species. In zoos

15 endangered species are mated with subspecies so that they can be

16 returned to the wild and removed from the endangered list. This has

17 saved the european bison, the Hawaiian goose, and Przhevalski's

18 horse from disappearing from Earth forever. The Manatee Rescue

19 and Rehabilitation Program is an example of how zoos help protect

20 endangered species. This program cares for injured, sick, or orphaned

21   manatees at different zoos and aquariums. If possible, manatees are

22   released back to the wild.

23   Zoos give scientists a chance to study animals. Scientists have

24   already learned much about animal habits, diseases, and the structure

25   and function of animal bodies. With this knowledge, scientists can

26   better understand and work on saving more endangered species. For

27   example, there are major cheetah projects at many zoos because the

28   population of wild cheetahs continues to decrease. The cheetah in

29   India is already extinct. About 250 cheetahs live in North American

30   zoos.

31   Zoos provide education for the public. Interactive educational

32   exhibits focus on saving animal habitats and educating visitors

33   about the ways humans and wildlife can live together. Schools and

34   individuals often take part in "adoption" programs. In Columbus,

35   teachers and students donated time and money to help mountain

36   gorillas in Rwanda and Congo. Education helps children appreciate

37   animals and be sensitive to the rights of animals on our planet.

38   If you feel the way I do about zoos, take action now. Zoos need

39   more funding so that people and scientists can enjoy viewing animals

40   and helping endangered species survive. With the help of concerned

41   citizens and animal lovers, we will be able to view and admire

42   magnificent animals for years to come.

Assessment Sheet

Title _Zoos_

_6_ Ideas
- *The topic, focus, and details make this essay a great piece of writing.*
- *Using an anecdote at the beginning adds interest.*

_6_ Organization
- *A well-planned organization makes it easy to understand the essay.*
- *All the topic sentences support the opinion statement.*

_5_ Voice
- *Your voice sounds like you know a lot about your topic. It is informative and confident.*
- *I would like to hear your personal voice, too. You could write about some of your visits to zoos, especially where and when you saw a giant panda.*

_5_ Word Choice
- *I liked the way each of your middle paragraphs started with the word "zoos." This helped me realize that the focus of your essay was always zoos.*
- *You explain Elephant.cam through context clues, but it would help to move the explanation closer to the term. You could explain Przhevalski's horse.*

_5_ Sentence Fluency
- *You write clear and complete sentences.*
- *A greater variety of sentence beginnings could be used. Most of the sentences begin with a subject followed by a predicate.*

_4_ Conventions
- *You have correctly spelled every word!*
- *Be sure to proofread. Pay attention to punctuation (apostrophes, quotation marks, commas), capitalization, and other conventions (numbers).*

Persuasive Writing

1   San Diego Union-Tribune

2   Letter to the Editor

3   Dear Editor:

4   I am a sixth grader. Some things that the government do bother

5   me. The thing that bothers me is the port of entry at San Ysidro

6   California. People have to open these gates. They should open with a

7   pulley or open electricly.

8   Someone I know was seriously hurt opening one of those big

9   heavy gates. Each lane has a heavy gate at the port of entry. She has

10   been out of work a long time. Worse than that, she is in alot of pain.

11   People should not get hurt on the job.

12   There are alot of different agencys at the Port of Entry. One of

13   them could look at this problem. There is the INS (Immigration and

14   Naturalization Service). There is Customs. There is the Border Patrol.

15   There is the GSA (General Services Administration). All these agencys

16   are busy spending money on computer systems. They forgot about

17   some of the simple things like gates. I'm going to tell you that one

18   more time. All these agencys are busy spending money on computer

19   systems. They forget about simple things like gates. Then, they pay

20   alot of money to the people who is hurt and can't work.

21   The solution is simple. All the agencys could band together and

22   worry about simple things, like opening and closing a gate, which

23   must be done alot every day. They could do that instead of worrying

24   about computer systems.

25   Sincerely,

Assessment Sheet

Title *Letter to the Editor*

_3_ Ideas
- *It is clear you feel strongly about this issue.*
- *Write a clear opinion statement. Do you want these gates to open easily, or do you want government agencies to take action?*
- *You say the same thing again and again, but readers need more details (facts and examples) to be persuaded.*

_3_ Organization
- *Your first paragraph is organized well. You introduce yourself. Then you describe a problem, and finally, you offer a solution.*
- *Transitions would help connect your paragraphs.*

_4_ Voice
- *You use a very sincere, confident voice.*
- *Ask yourself if your voice would be more persuasive if it didn't sound bitter in some sentences.*

_4_ Word Choice
- *You did a great job of listing the agencies (see lines 13–15).*
- *Always try to find a specific word to use in place of "thing."*

_2_ Sentence Fluency
- *You write complete sentences.*
- *Combining many of your short sentences would make your writing read smoothly. Using a lot of short sentences makes the writing sound choppy.*

_3_ Conventions
- *Learn to spell "a lot" and "agencies."*
- *In your future writing, pay attention to subject-predicate agreement. For example, write "government does" (see line 1) and "people who are hurt" (see line 20).*
- *Your paper also has several comma errors.*

Response to Literature

Caddie Woodlawn

1   *Caddie Woodlawn*, a book by Carol Ryrie Brink, is a true story

2 about a real person. It tells about a girl who grew up in Wisconsin

3 in the 1860s. That girl was the author's grandmother. Caddie, an 11-

4 year-old tomboy with red hair, lives on a farm with her two sisters and

5 three brothers. Caddie and her brothers get into all sorts of mischief.

6 Caddie's mother wishes she could make her daughter into a lady.

7 Caddie's father wants her to grow up as free as the new land. Caddie

8 Woodlawn shows us what it is like to be a young American pioneer.

9   Caddie and her brothers learn many skills to survive in the wild

10 land. When Caddie falls through the ice while skating, her brothers

11 have to figure out how to save her. Another time, the children help put

12 out a prairie fire that threatens them and their school. They also learn

13 to carefully watch for rattlesnakes.

14   Caddie and her family find ways to have fun yet still live with

15 dangers. Caddie and her brothers make up games and stories while

16 they are working. They play pranks and get in trouble. Although they

17 manage to have fun, they never forget that there are many dangers.

18 Caddie and her family have to worry about surviving Indian attacks,

19 wild animals, and awful weather.

20   They do survive and they grow strong. After a while, Mr.

21 Woodlawn has to decide whether to return to an easier life in
22 England. Caddie and her family vote to stay in the wilderness. At the
23 end of the book, Caddie realizes how much she has changed in the
24 year that just happened. She is growing into a lady. But she will be a
25 pioneer lady—strong, proud, independent, and ready to face whatever
26 comes her way.

Assessment Sheet

Title *Caddie Woodlawn*

_5_ Ideas

- *The essay has a clear focus statement in the last sentence of the first paragraph.*
- *Using more specific details would make the essay more interesting to readers. For example, you could tell about one of the pranks or the games.*

_5_ Organization

- *All your paragraphs help develop the focus statement.*
- *Transitions help connect sentences.*

_4_ Voice

- *Your formal voice is appropriate for an essay about a book.*
- *Think about how you could make your voice more enthusiastic.*

_5_ Word Choice

- *The phrase "as free as the new land" and the description of Caddie as a pioneer lady in the last paragraph are good, strong images.*
- *You use strong nouns and active verbs.*

_6_ Sentence Fluency

- *None of your sentences contain a problem.*
- *Good sentence variety creates an essay that flows smoothly.*

_6_ Conventions

- *Your paper shows you know and use the rules of grammar.*
- *Your spelling and punctuation are very good.*

Response to Literature

Gypsy and Woodrow

1 *Belle Prater's Boy* by Ruth White is a story about two cusins.
2 Gypsy and Woodrow. They live in a mining town called Coal Station,
3 Virginia. Woodrow is poor and Gypsy lives in a nice house. Woodrow's
4 mother, Belle, disappeared one morning without a trace. Gypsy's
5 father died when she was little.

6 Gypsy tells the story. Everything about her life is pretty. She has
7 long, golden hair, her mother, named Love, is beautiful, she lives in a
8 beautiful house and has beautiful clothes. She still has bad dreams.
9 Woodrow is cross-eyed and wears thick glasses and he always talks
10 about how he wants to get an operation to fix them.

11 When Woodrow's mother disappears he come to live next door
12 to his cusin Gypsy, with their grandparents. We also meet Porter's
13 brother Doc and his family, and they are all like one big family. Even
14 the people in town are like family, like Clint the barber and Blind
15 Benny the local bum. Belle was Gypsy's mother's sister, but she wasn't
16 beautiful. She ran off one day and married Woodrow's father, and they
17 were dirt poor.

18 The cusins become best friends and have many adventures,
19 sometimes sneaking out at night to sit in their tree house, or hanging
20 out with Blind Benny and they also tell jokes a lot. Woodrow makes

21 up stories about where his mother went, saying she was invizible and

22 things like that. He has a copy of a poem that she loved. Woodrow

23 beats up a boy who makes fun of Gypsy's father. At the end, both

24 children have changed. They both understand life a little better.

25   *Belle Prater's Boy* is a good book. It is funny and exciting, and I

26 really liked everyone in the story. Except maybe Buzz. It makes you

27 see that even pretty people have problems. I recomend it to anyone.

Assessment Sheet

Title _Gypsy and Woodrow_

_3_ Ideas

- _You need to include a focus statement._
- _The specific details you use in paragraph 4 help build interest._
- _Always identify all people. Who is "Porter" (see line 12)?_

_2_ Organization

- _Some of the events are out of order, so the essay is difficult to follow._
- _Transitions are needed._

_4_ Voice

- _The voice helps readers feel that you enjoyed this book._
- _You switch to first-person point of view ("I") in the ending. This does add interest, and you can do this when writing about literature, but it may not be acceptable for other essays._

_4_ Word Choice

- _The repetition of "beautiful" (see lines 7 and 8) works well as emphasis._
- _The words you use to describe Woodrow clearly show the difference between him and Gypsy. Well done!_
- _Word groups like "without a trace," "like one big family," and "dirt poor" have been used a lot. Think about words that you could use to replace these._

_3_ Sentence Fluency

- _You need to avoid sentence fragments and run-on sentences._
- _Some sentences read smoothly. Other sentences sound choppy._
- _Be certain your subjects and predicates agree._

_3_ Conventions

- _Always check your spelling._
- _Proofread more carefully. Sometimes you use commas and other times—in the same kind of situation—you leave them out._

Assessment Sheet

Directions Use one of the rubrics listed below to rate a piece of writing. Circle the rubric your teacher tells you to use. If you need information about assessing with a rubric, see pages 52 and 55 in your *Write Source* book.

Narrative Rubric (pages 130–131)   Expository Rubric (pages 194–195)
Persuasive Rubric (pages 256–257)   Response to Literature (pages 318–319)

Title _____

____ **Ideas**

____ **Organization**

____ **Voice**

____ **Word Choice**

____ **Sentence Fluency**

____ **Conventions**

Evaluator _____

T-Chart

Subject:

Time Line

Subject:

(Chronological Order)

1. _____

2. _____

3. _____

4. _____

5. _____

6. _____

7. _____

8. _____

Venn Diagram

Subject A

Differences

Subject B

Similarities

5 W's Chart

Subject:

Who?	What?	When?	Where?	Why?

Sensory Chart

Subject: _____

Sights	Sounds	Smells	Tastes	Feelings

Scavenger Hunt 1: Find the Threes

❰ Directions ❱ Find the following "threes" in your book by turning to the pages listed in parentheses.

1. **Three** parts of a descriptive paragraph (page 72)

_____

2. **Three** ways to start a personal narrative (page 109)

_____

_____

3. **Three** transitions that could work well when comparing two things (page 572)

_____

4. **Three** methods you could use to develop a character (page 351)

_____

_____

_____

5. **Three** strategies that will help you "show" instead of "tell" (page 557)

_____

6. **Three** collective nouns (page 702)

_____

7. **Three** types of titles that need to be italicized (underlined) (page 602)

_____

_____

8. **Three** acronyms (page 636)

_____

Scavenger Hunt 2: What Is It?

> **Directions** Find the answers to the following questions using the index in the back of the book. The underlined words below tell you where to look in the index.

1. What are the five <u>patterns of organization</u>?

_____

_____

2. What is the <u>"Basics of Life"</u> list?

_____

_____

3. What is a <u>first draft</u>?

_____

4. What is a <u>gathering grid</u>?

_____

5. What is an <u>electronic portfolio</u>?

_____

6. What are the <u>Five W's</u>?

_____

7. What is a <u>classification essay</u>?

_____

_____

8. What is <u>brainstorming</u>?

_____

Getting to Know *Write Source*

Directions Locate the pages in *Write Source* where answers to the following learning tasks can be found. Both the index and the table of contents can help you.

_____ 1. You are doing research for a report and you come across the acronym "NATO." You need to know what the acronym stands for.

_____ 2. You have been asked to contribute a poem to a school anthology. You need to know how to write a free-verse poem.

_____ 3. Your social studies teacher has asked you to write a short essay about your state's interest in young people. You are to use the "first-person point of view." You need to know what that means.

_____ 4. You have joined the school newspaper staff, and the editor asks you to create an editorial cartoon about student behavior at sporting events. You need to know how to create an editorial cartoon.

_____ 5. You want to use a Venn diagram to compare two wars. You need to know how to use a Venn diagram.

_____ 6. Your teacher asks you to make a poster of common contractions for the classroom. You need to know what contractions to include.

_____ 7. Your teacher asks you to use a cause/effect organizer to show what happens when rainwater floods the sewer system in your city. You need to find a cause/effect organizer.

_____ 8. You want to make your sentences more interesting, so your teacher tells you to model sentences. You need to know how to model sentences.

_____ 9. Everybody who has read it says it is the best "rite of passage" story they have ever read. You need to know what they mean.

_____ 10. You have been asked to take class minutes for the week. You need some guidelines.

Unit Planning

Writing Form

PARAGRAPH

___ days

- **FOCUS**

- **SKILLS**

ESSAY 1

___ days

Prewriting

- **FOCUS**

- **SKILLS**

Writing

___ days

- **FOCUS**

- **SKILLS**

Revising

___ days

- **IDEAS**

- **ORGANIZATION**

- **VOICE**

- **WORD CHOICE**

- **SENTENCE FLUENCY**

See Lesson Planning Guidelines on pp. xxvii–xviii.

Unit Planning (continued)

Editing ___ days

- **PUNCTUATION**

- **CAPITALIZATION**

- **SPELLING**

- **GRAMMAR**

Publishing ___ days

- **OPTIONS**

Evaluating ___ days

- **SELF-ASSESSMENT**

- **BENCHMARK PAPERS**

ESSAY 2 ___ days

- **FOCUS**

- **SKILLS**

ACROSS THE CURRICULUM ___ days

- **SOCIAL STUDIES**

- **SCIENCE**

- **MATH**

- **PRACTICAL**

Index

Credits

Pupil Edition

Photos:

comstock.com: pages vi, ix, xi, xii, 1, 5, 9, 29, 32, 57, 60, 93, 96, 97, 101, 107, 113, 125, 129, 135, 140, 143, 157, 161, 165, 171, 174, 177, 186, 189, 193, 198, 199, 223, 227, 233, 235, 239, 251, 255, 261, 264, 266, 274, 283, 291, 295, 301, 313, 323, 329, 363, 365, 366, 381, 401, 403, 405, 411, 417, 420, 423, 430, 441, 449, 464, 469, 499, 521, 523, 533, 750

Getty Images: pages iii, v, x, xi, xviii, 10, 11, 33, 44, 45, 60, 65, 68, 75, 82, 83, 97, 105, 129, 143, 157, 161, 169, 193, 205, 219, 261, 266, 267, 276, 287, 317, 321, 343, 349, 363, 368, 376, 377, 381, 398, 405, 411, 459, 466, 523, 547, 555

Hemera: page 71

Ulead Systems: pages 300, 353, 354, 356, 359, 431

www.jupiterimages.com: page 361

Teacher Edition

Photos:

comstock.com: pages iv, ix, xiv, xvi, xliv, 4B, 92B, 282B, 416B, 759, 762
Getty Images: pages x, xiii, 70B, 156B, 218B, 362B, 753, 754, 757
Ulead Systems: page 342B

Credits:

Page 375: Copyright © 2003 by Houghton Mifflin Company, Adapted by permission from *The American Heritage Student Dictionary.*

Acknowledgements

We're grateful to many people who helped bring *Write Source* to life. First we must thank all the teachers and students from across the country who contributed writing models and ideas.

In addition, we want to thank our Write Source/Great Source team for all their help:

Steven J. Augustyn, Laura Bachman, Ron Bachman, William Baughn, Colleen Belmont, Lisa Bingen, Evelyn Curley, Sandra Easton, Chris Erickson, Jean Fischer, Sherry Gordon, Mariellen Hanrahan, Kathy Henning, Mary Anne Hoff, Kathy Kahnle, Rob King, Lois Krenzke, Joyce Becker Lee, Ellen Leitheusser, Douglas Niles, Sue Paro, Pat Reigel, Jason C. Reynolds, Susan Rogalski, Janae Sebranek, Lester Smith, Richard Spencer, Julie Spicuzza, Thomas Spicuzza, Jean Varley, Sandy Wagner, and Claire Ziffer.